INSIDE MACINTOSH

QuickTime Components

Addison-Wesley Publishing Company

Reading, Massachusetts   Menlo Park, California   New York
Don Mills, Ontario   Wokingham, England   Amsterdam   Bonn
Sydney   Singapore   Tokyo   Madrid   San Juan
Paris   Seoul   Milan   Mexico City   Taipei

Apple Computer, Inc.
© 1993, Apple Computer, Inc.
All rights reserved.

No part of this publication may be reproduced, stored in a retrieval system, or transmitted, in any form or by any means, mechanical, electronic, photocopying, recording, or otherwise, without prior written permission of Apple Computer, Inc. Printed in the United States of America.

No licenses, express or implied, are granted with respect to any of the technology described in this book. Apple retains all intellectual property rights associated with the technology described in this book. This book is intended to assist application developers to develop applications only for Apple Macintosh computers.

Apple Computer, Inc.
20525 Mariani Avenue
Cupertino, CA 95014
408-996-1010

Apple, the Apple logo, APDA, AppleLink, LaserWriter, Macintosh, MPW, and MultiFinder are trademarks of Apple Computer, Inc., registered in the United States and other countries.

Balloon Help, QuickDraw, QuickTime, and System 7 are trademarks of Apple Computer, Inc.

Adobe Illustrator and PostScript are trademarks of Adobe Systems Incorporated, which may be registered in certain jurisdictions.

AGFA is a trademark of Agfa-Gevaert.

America Online is a service mark of Quantum Computer Services, Inc.

Classic is a registered trademark licensed to Apple Computer, Inc.

CompuServe is a registered service mark of CompuServe, Inc.

FrameMaker is a registered trademark of Frame Technology Corporation.

Helvetica and Palatino are registered trademarks of Linotype Company.

Internet is a trademark of Digital Equipment Corporation.

ITC Zapf Dingbats is a registered trademark of International Typeface Corporation.

Windows is a registered trademark of Microsoft.

Simultaneously published in the United States and Canada.

LIMITED WARRANTY ON MEDIA AND REPLACEMENT

ALL IMPLIED WARRANTIES ON THIS MANUAL, INCLUDING IMPLIED WARRANTIES OF MERCHANTABILITY AND FITNESS FOR A PARTICULAR PURPOSE, ARE LIMITED IN DURATION TO NINETY (90) DAYS FROM THE DATE OF THE ORIGINAL RETAIL PURCHASE OF THIS PRODUCT.

Even though Apple has reviewed this manual, APPLE MAKES NO WARRANTY OR REPRESENTATION, EITHER EXPRESS OR IMPLIED, WITH RESPECT TO THIS MANUAL, ITS QUALITY, ACCURACY, MERCHANTABILITY, OR FITNESS FOR A PARTICULAR PURPOSE. AS A RESULT, THIS MANUAL IS SOLD "AS IS," AND YOU, THE PURCHASER, ARE ASSUMING THE ENTIRE RISK AS TO ITS QUALITY AND ACCURACY.

IN NO EVENT WILL APPLE BE LIABLE FOR DIRECT, INDIRECT, SPECIAL, INCIDENTAL, OR CONSEQUENTIAL DAMAGES RESULTING FROM ANY DEFECT OR INACCURACY IN THIS MANUAL, even if advised of the possibility of such damages.

THE WARRANTY AND REMEDIES SET FORTH ABOVE ARE EXCLUSIVE AND IN LIEU OF ALL OTHERS, ORAL OR WRITTEN, EXPRESS OR IMPLIED. No Apple dealer, agent, or employee is authorized to make any modification, extension, or addition to this warranty.

Some states do not allow the exclusion or limitation of implied warranties or liability for incidental or consequential damages, so the above limitation or exclusion may not apply to you. This warranty gives you specific legal rights, and you may also have other rights which vary from state to state.

ISBN 0-201-62202-5
1 2 3 4 5 6 7 8 9-MU-9796959493
First Printing, May 1993

The paper used in this book meets the EPA standards for recycled fiber.

Contents

Figures and Listings   xiii

Preface **About This Book**   xvii

Format of a Typical Chapter   xviii
Conventions Used in This Book   xix
  Special Fonts   xix
  Types of Notes   xix
Development Environment   xx
For More Information   xx

Chapter 1 **Overview**   1-1

Providing Movie Playback   1-3
Capturing Sequences of Images   1-6
Compressing and Decompressing Still Images   1-8
Converting Data for Use in QuickTime Movies   1-11
Creating Previews of QuickTime Movies   1-11

Chapter 2 **Movie Controller Components**   2-1

About Movie Controller Components   2-4
  The Elements of a Movie Controller   2-4
  Badges   2-6
Spatial Properties   2-6
Using Movie Controller Components   2-10
  Playing Movies   2-10
  Customizing Movie Controllers   2-13
Movie Controller Components Reference   2-14
  Movie Controller Actions   2-15
  Movie Controller Functions   2-28
    Associating Movies With Controllers   2-28
    Managing Controller Attributes   2-33
    Handling Movie Events   2-44
    Editing Movies   2-50
    Getting and Setting Movie Controller Time   2-56
    Customizing Event Processing   2-58
  Application-Defined Function   2-61

Summary of Movie Controller Components 2-63
  C Summary 2-63
    Constants 2-63
    Data Types 2-66
    Movie Controller Functions 2-67
    Application-Defined Function 2-69
  Pascal Summary 2-69
    Constants 2-69
    Data Types 2-73
    Movie Controller Routines 2-73
    Application-Defined Routine 2-75
  Result Codes 2-75

Chapter 3 Standard Image-Compression Dialog Components 3-1

About Standard Image-Compression Dialog Components 3-4
Using Standard Image-Compression Dialog Components 3-6
  Opening a Connection to a Standard Image-Compression Dialog Component 3-8
  Displaying the Dialog Box to the User 3-8
    Setting Default Parameters 3-8
    Designating a Test Image 3-9
    Displaying the Dialog Box and Retrieving Parameters 3-10
  Extending the Basic Dialog Box 3-11
Creating a Standard Image-Compression Dialog Component 3-14
Standard Image-Compression Dialog Components Reference 3-15
  Request Types 3-15
    The Spatial Settings Request Type 3-15
    The Temporal Settings Request Type 3-17
    The Data-Rate Settings Request Type 3-19
    The Color Table Settings Request Type 3-20
    The Progress Function Request Type 3-20
    The Extended Functions Request Type 3-21
    The Preference Flags Request Type 3-22
    The Settings State Request Type 3-24
    The Sequence ID Request Type 3-24
    The Window Position Request Type 3-25
    The Control Flags Request Type 3-25
  Standard Image-Compression Dialog Component Functions 3-25
    Getting Default Settings for an Image or a Sequence 3-26
    Displaying the Standard Image-Compression Dialog Box 3-28
    Compressing Still Images 3-29
    Compressing Image Sequences 3-31
    Working With Image or Sequence Settings 3-34
    Specifying a Test Image 3-37

Positioning Dialog Boxes and Rectangles   3-42
Utility Function   3-44
Application-Defined Function   3-45
Summary of Standard Image-Compression Dialog Components   3-47
C Summary   3-47
Constants   3-47
Data Types   3-49
Standard Image-Compression Dialog Component Functions   3-50
Application-Defined Function   3-52
Pascal Summary   3-52
Constants   3-52
Data Types   3-54
Standard Image-Compression Dialog Component Routines   3-55
Application-Defined Routine   3-57
Result Codes   3-57

Chapter 4 Image Compressor Components   4-1

About Image Compressor Components   4-3
Banding and Extending Images   4-4
Spooling of Compressed Data   4-6
Data Loading   4-6
Data Unloading   4-7
Compressing or Decompressing Images Asynchronously   4-8
Progress Functions   4-9
Using Image Compressor Components   4-10
Performing Image Compression   4-10
Choosing a Compressor   4-10
Compressing a Horizontal Band of an Image   4-13
Decompressing an Image   4-16
Choosing a Decompressor   4-17
Decompressing a Horizontal Band of an Image   4-21
Image Compressor Components Reference   4-26
Constants   4-26
Image Compressor Component Capabilities   4-26
Format of Compressed Data and Files   4-32
Data Types   4-35
The Compressor Capability Structure   4-35
The Compression Parameters Structure   4-40
The Decompression Parameters Structure   4-46
Functions   4-53
Direct Functions   4-54
Indirect Functions   4-62
Image Compression Manager Utility Functions   4-65

Summary of Image Compressor Components 4-69
  C Summary 4-69
    Constants 4-69
    Data Types 4-72
    Functions 4-76
      Image Compression Manager Utility Functions 4-77
  Pascal Summary 4-77
    Constants 4-77
    Data Types 4-80
    Routines 4-83
      Image Compression Manager Utility Functions 4-84
  Result Codes 4-84

Chapter 5 Sequence Grabber Components 5-1

About Sequence Grabber Components 5-3
Using Sequence Grabber Components 5-5
  Previewing and Recording Captured Data 5-9
    Previewing 5-9
    Recording 5-10
  Playing Captured Data and Saving It in a QuickTime Movie 5-11
    Initializing a Sequence Grabber Component 5-11
    Creating a Sound Channel and a Video Channel 5-12
    Previewing Sound and Video Sequences in a Window 5-14
    Capturing Sound and Video Data 5-18
    Setting Up the Video Bottleneck Functions 5-19
    Drawing Information Over Video Frames During Capture 5-20
Sequence Grabber Components Reference 5-22
  Data Types 5-22
    The Compression Information Structure 5-22
    The Frame Information Structure 5-23
  Sequence Grabber Component Functions 5-24
    Configuring Sequence Grabber Components 5-24
    Controlling Sequence Grabber Components 5-36
    Working With Sequence Grabber Settings 5-47
    Working With Sequence Grabber Characteristics 5-53
    Working With Channel Characteristics 5-58
    Working With Channel Devices 5-72
    Working With Video Channels 5-77
    Working With Sound Channels 5-92
    Video Channel Callback Functions 5-99
    Utility Functions for Video Channel Callback Functions 5-102
  Application-Defined Functions 5-111
Summary of Sequence Grabber Components 5-123
  C Summary 5-123
    Constants 5-123

Data Types   5-127
Sequence Grabber Component Functions   5-129
Application-Defined Functions   5-135
Pascal Summary   5-136
Constants   5-136
Data Types   5-140
Sequence Grabber Component Routines   5-141
Application-Defined Routines   5-148
Result Codes   5-149

Chapter 6   Sequence Grabber Channel Components   6-1

About Sequence Grabber Channel Components   6-3
Creating Sequence Grabber Channel Components   6-5
  Component Type and Subtype Values   6-6
  Required Functions   6-6
  Component Manager Request Codes   6-7
  A Sample Sequence Grabber Channel Component   6-10
    Implementing the Required Component Functions   6-10
    Initializing the Sequence Grabber Channel Component   6-15
    Setting and Retrieving the Channel State   6-16
    Managing Spatial Properties   6-17
    Controlling Previewing and Recording Operations   6-20
    Managing Channel Devices   6-24
    Utility Functions for Recording Image Data   6-24
    Providing Media-Specific Functions   6-28
    Managing the Settings Dialog Box   6-29
    Displaying Channel Information in the Settings Dialog Box   6-31
Using Sequence Grabber Channel Components   6-33
  Previewing   6-33
  Recording   6-34
  Working With Callback Functions   6-35
    Using Callback Functions for Video Channel Components   6-35
    Using Utility Functions for Video Channel Component Callback Functions   6-36
Sequence Grabber Channel Components Reference   6-37
  Functions   6-37
    Configuring Sequence Grabber Channel Components   6-38
    Controlling Sequence Grabber Channel Components   6-39
    Configuration Functions for All Channel Components   6-46
    Working With Channel Devices   6-58
    Configuration Functions for Video Channel Components   6-61
    Configuration Functions for Sound Channel Components   6-77
    Utility Functions for Sequence Grabber Channel Components   6-84

Summary of Sequence Grabber Channel Components 6-91
  C Summary   6-91
    Constants   6-91
    Data Types   6-94
    Functions   6-94
  Pascal Summary   6-99
    Constants   6-99
    Data Types   6-101
    Routines   6-102
  Result Codes   6-107

Chapter 7 Sequence Grabber Panel Components   7-1

About Sequence Grabber Panel Components   7-4
Creating Sequence Grabber Panel Components   7-7
  Implementing the Required Component Functions   7-9
  Managing the Dialog Box   7-11
  Managing Your Panel's Settings   7-13
Sequence Grabber Panel Components Reference   7-14
  Component Flags for Sequence Grabber Panel Components   7-15
  Functions   7-15
    Managing Your Panel Component   7-15
    Processing Your Panel's Events   7-21
    Managing Your Panel's Settings   7-24
Summary of Sequence Grabber Panel Components   7-27
  C Summary   7-27
    Constants   7-27
    Functions   7-28
  Pascal Summary   7-29
    Constants   7-29
    Routines   7-29
  Result Codes   7-30

Chapter 8 Video Digitizer Components   8-1

About Video Digitizer Components   8-3
  Types of Video Digitizer Components   8-5
  Source Coordinate Systems   8-6
Using Video Digitizer Components   8-7
  Specifying Destinations   8-7
  Starting and Stopping the Digitizer   8-7
  Multiple Buffering   8-8

Obtaining an Accurate Time of Frame Capture　　8-8
Creating Video Digitizer Components　　8-8
　　Component Type and Subtype Values　　8-11
　　Required Functions　　8-11
　　Optional Functions　　8-12
　　　Frame Grabbers Without Playthrough　　8-12
　　　Frame Grabbers With Hardware Playthrough　　8-12
　　　Key Color and Alpha Channel Devices　　8-13
　　　Compressed Source Devices　　8-13
Video Digitizer Components Reference　　8-14
　　Constants　　8-14
　　　Capability Flags　　8-14
　　　Current Flags　　8-19
　　Data Types　　8-20
　　　The Digitizer Information Structure　　8-20
　　　The Buffer List Structure　　8-22
　　　The Buffer Structure　　8-23
　　Video Digitizer Component Functions　　8-23
　　　Getting Information About Video Digitizer Components　　8-24
　　　Setting Source Characteristics　　8-26
　　　Selecting an Input Source　　8-30
　　　Setting Video Destinations　　8-34
　　　Controlling Compressed Source Devices　　8-42
　　　Controlling Digitization　　8-52
　　　Controlling Color　　8-60
　　　Controlling Analog Video　　8-65
　　　Selectively Displaying Video　　8-81
　　　Clipping　　8-89
　　　Utility Functions　　8-92
　　Application-Defined Function　　8-98
Summary of Video Digitizer Components　　8-99
　　C Summary　　8-99
　　　Constants　　8-99
　　　Data Types　　8-104
　　　Video Digitizer Component Functions　　8-105
　　　Application-Defined Function　　8-111
　　Pascal Summary　　8-111
　　　Constants　　8-111
　　　Data Types　　8-116
　　　Video Digitizer Component Routines　　8-117
　　　Application-Defined Routine　　8-123
　　Result Codes　　8-124

| Chapter 9 | **Movie Data Exchange Components** 9-1 |

About Movie Data Exchange Components   9-3
Using Movie Data Exchange Components   9-5
  Importing and Exporting Movie Data   9-6
  Configuring a Movie Data Exchange Component   9-6
  Finding a Specific Movie Data Exchange Component   9-6
Creating a Movie Data Exchange Component   9-8
  A Sample Movie Import Component   9-9
    Implementing the Required Import Component Functions   9-10
    Importing a Scrapbook File   9-12
  A Sample Movie Export Component   9-15
    Implementing the Required Export Component Functions   9-16
    Exporting Data to a PICS File   9-18
Movie Data Exchange Components Reference   9-20
  Importing Movie Data   9-20
  Configuring Movie Data Import Components   9-26
  Exporting Movie Data   9-34
  Configuring Movie Data Export Components   9-37
Summary of Movie Data Exchange Components   9-41
  C Summary   9-41
    Constants   9-41
    Data Type   9-42
    Functions   9-42
  Pascal Summary   9-44
    Constants   9-44
    Data Type   9-45
    Routines   9-45
  Result Codes   9-47

| Chapter 10 | **Derived Media Handler Components** 10-1 |

About Derived Media Handler Components   10-4
  Media Handler Components   10-4
  Derived Media Handler Components   10-6
Creating a Derived Media Handler Component   10-7
  Component Flags for Derived Media Handlers   10-8
  Request Processing   10-8
  A Sample Derived Media Handler Component   10-9
    Implementing the Required Component Functions   10-9
    Initializing a Derived Media Handler Component   10-12
    Drawing the Media Sample   10-13
Derived Media Handler Components Reference   10-15
  Data Type   10-15

Functions   10-18
    Managing Your Media Handler Component   10-18
    General Data Management   10-23
    Graphics Data Management   10-31
    Sound Data Management   10-37
    Base Media Handler Utility Function   10-38
Summary of Derived Media Handler Components   10-41
    C Summary   10-41
        Constants   10-41
        Data Type   10-43
        Functions   10-43
    Pascal Summary   10-45
        Constants   10-45
        Data Type   10-46
        Routines   10-47

Chapter 11   Clock Components   11-1

About Clock Components   11-3
Clock Components Reference   11-5
    Component Capability Flags for Clocks   11-5
    Component Types for Clocks   11-6
    Data Type   11-6
    Clock Component Functions   11-7
        Getting the Current Time   11-9
        Using the Callback Functions   11-9
        Managing the Time   11-15
    Movie Toolbox Clock Support Functions   11-18
Summary of Clock Components   11-22
    C Summary   11-22
        Constants   11-22
        Data Type   11-24
        Clock Component Functions   11-24
        Movie Toolbox Clock Support Functions   11-25
    Pascal Summary   11-25
        Constants   11-25
        Data Type   11-27
        Clock Component Routines   11-27
        Movie Toolbox Clock Support Routines   11-28

| Chapter 12 | Preview Components 12-1 |

About Preview Components 12-3
  Obtaining Preview Data 12-3
  Storing Preview Data in Files 12-5
  Using the Preview Data 12-5
Creating Preview Components 12-6
  Implementing Required Component Functions 12-7
  Displaying Image Data as a Preview 12-8
Preview Components Reference 12-10
  Functions 12-10
    Displaying Previews 12-10
    Handling Events 12-11
    Creating Previews 12-11
  Resources 12-13
    The Preview Resource 12-14
    The Preview Resource Item Structure 12-15
Summary of Preview Components 12-16
  C Summary 12-16
    Constants 12-16
    Data Types 12-16
    Functions 12-17
  Pascal Summary 12-17
    Constants 12-17
    Data Types 12-18
    Routines 12-19

| Glossary GL-1 |

| Index IN-1 |

Figures and Listings

Chapter 1　Overview　1-1

Figure 1-1	QuickTime components for movie playback	1-5
Figure 1-2	QuickTime components for image capture	1-7
Figure 1-3	QuickTime components for compressing still images	1-9
Figure 1-4	QuickTime components for decompressing still images	1-10

Chapter 2　Movie Controller Components　2-1

Figure 2-1	The standard movie controller	2-5
Figure 2-2	A movie with a badge	2-6
Figure 2-3	Movie controller spatial elements for attached controllers	2-7
Figure 2-4	Movie controller spatial elements for detached controllers	2-8
Figure 2-5	Clipping the controller window region with the controller clipping region	2-9
Listing 2-1	Playing a movie with a movie controller component	2-10
Listing 2-2	Using a movie controller filter function	2-13

Chapter 3　Standard Image-Compression Dialog Components　3-1

Figure 3-1	Dialog box for single-frame compression	3-4
Figure 3-2	Dialog box for image-sequence compression	3-5
Figure 3-3	Elements of the standard image-compression dialog box	3-7
Listing 3-1	Specifying a test image	3-9
Listing 3-2	Displaying the dialog box to the user and compressing an image	3-11
Listing 3-3	Defining a custom button in the dialog box	3-12
Listing 3-4	A sample hook function	3-12
Listing 3-5	Positioning related dialog boxes	3-13

Chapter 4　Image Compressor Components　4-1

Figure 4-1	Image bands and their measurements	4-7
Listing 4-1	Preparing for simple compression operations	4-12
Listing 4-2	Performing simple compression on a horizontal band of an image	4-13
Listing 4-3	Preparing for simple decompression	4-20
Listing 4-4	Performing a decompression operation	4-21

Chapter 5	Sequence Grabber Components 5-1	
Figure 5-1	Relationships among your application, a sequence grabber component, and channel components	5-4
Figure 5-2	The effect of the SGSetCompressBuffer function	5-88
Listing 5-1	Initializing a sequence grabber component	5-11
Listing 5-2	Creating a sound channel and a video channel	5-12
Listing 5-3	Previewing sound and video sequences in a window	5-14
Listing 5-4	Capturing sound and video	5-18
Listing 5-5	Setting up the video bottleneck functions	5-19
Listing 5-6	Drawing information over video frames during capture	5-20

Chapter 6	Sequence Grabber Channel Components 6-1	
Figure 6-1	Relationships of an application, a sequence grabber component, and channel components	6-4
Listing 6-1	Setting up global variables and implementing required functions	6-10
Listing 6-2	Initializing the sequence grabber channel component	6-15
Listing 6-3	Determining usage parameters and getting usage data	6-16
Listing 6-4	Managing spatial characteristics	6-17
Listing 6-5	Controlling previewing and recording operations	6-20
Listing 6-6	Coordinating devices for the channel component	6-24
Listing 6-7	Recording image data	6-25
Listing 6-8	Showing the tick count	6-28
Listing 6-9	Including a tick count checkbox in a dialog box in the panel component	6-29
Listing 6-10	Displaying channel settings	6-31

Chapter 7	Sequence Grabber Panel Components 7-1	
Figure 7-1	Sequence grabbers, channel components, and panel components	7-5
Figure 7-2	A sample sequence grabber settings dialog box	7-6
Listing 7-1	Implementing the required functions	7-9
Listing 7-2	Managing the settings dialog box	7-12
Listing 7-3	Managing the settings for a panel component	7-13

Chapter 8	Video Digitizer Components 8-1	
Figure 8-1	Basic tasks of a video digitizer	8-4
Figure 8-2	Video digitizer rectangles	8-6

Chapter 9	Movie Data Exchange Components 9-1	
	Figure 9-1	The Movie Toolbox, movie data import components, and your application 9-4
	Figure 9-2	The Movie Toolbox, movie data export components, and your application 9-5
	Listing 9-1	Implementing the required import functions 9-10
	Listing 9-2	Importing a Scrapbook file 9-12
	Listing 9-3	Implementing the required export functions 9-16
	Listing 9-4	Exporting a frame of movie data to a PICS file 9-18
Chapter 10	Derived Media Handler Components 10-1	
	Figure 10-1	Logical relationships between the Movie Toolbox and media handlers 10-5
	Figure 10-2	Relationship between the base media handler component and derived media handlers 10-6
	Listing 10-1	Implementing the required functions 10-9
	Listing 10-2	Initializing a derived media handler 10-13
	Listing 10-3	Drawing the media sample 10-13
Chapter 11	Clock Components 11-1	
	Figure 11-1	Relationships of an application, the movie controller component, the Movie Toolbox, and a clock component 11-4
Chapter 12	Preview Components 12-1	
	Figure 12-1	Relationships of a preview component, the Image Compression Manager, and an application 12-5
	Listing 12-1	Implementing the required Component Manager functions 12-7
	Listing 12-2	Converting data into a form that can be displayed as a preview 12-9
	Listing 12-3	The preview resource 12-14
	Listing 12-4	The preview resource item structure 12-15

PREFACE

About This Book

This book describes the components supplied by Apple Computer, Inc., with QuickTime. A **component** is a code resource that is registered by the Component Manager. To understand components fully, you should be familiar with the material in the chapter "Component Manager" in *Inside Macintosh: More Macintosh Toolbox*, which describes how to build a component.

This book provides a complete technical reference to movie controller components, standard image-compression dialog components, image compressor components, sequence grabber components, sequence grabber channel components, sequence grabber panel components, video digitizer components, movie data exchange components, derived media handler components, clock components, and preview components.

You should read this book if you are developing an application that uses QuickTime components, or if you are developing a component that will be managed by the Component Manager. Whether you are developing a component or an application that uses components, you need to know how to call component functions. See the chapter "Component Manager" in *Inside Macintosh: More Macintosh Toolbox* for information on using components. If you are developing a component, you should also read the material in that chapter that describes how to build a component.

Each of these chapters discusses the features provided by a component type as well as the interface supported by components of that type. The interfaces are formatted for use by application developers. If you are developing a component, you must design and implement your component in a way that satisfies this interface.

If you are developing an application that can play movies, you should consider using movie controller components to manage your movie user interface. To learn about the capabilities of movie controllers, read the chapter "Movie Controller Components." If you are developing a movie controller component, the chapter also describes the interfaces that your component must support.

If you want to use a standard image-compression dialog component in your application, you should read the chapter "Standard Image-Compression Dialog Components." If you want to create your own standard image-compression dialog component, you should be familiar with all of the information in that chapter.

If you are developing an image compressor component, you should read all the material in the chapter "Image Compressor Components."

If you are writing an application that needs to acquire data from sources external to the Macintosh computer, or if you are developing a sequence grabber channel component, you should read the chapter "Sequence Grabber Components."

If you are developing a sequence grabber channel component, you should also read the chapter "Sequence Grabber Channel Components."

If you plan to create a sequence grabber panel component, you should read the chapter "Sequence Grabber Panel Components."

If you want to develop or use a video digitizer component, you should read the chapter "Video Digitizer Components."

If you plan to create either movie data import or movie data export components, or if you are writing an application that uses components of this type, you should read the chapter "Movie Data Exchange Components."

If you plan to develop a derived media handler component, you should read the chapter "Derived Media Handler Components."

If you want to develop your own clock component for use by the Movie Toolbox, you should read the chapter "Clock Components," which describes what you must do to create a clock component.

If you want to develop your own preview component, you should read the chapter "Preview Components," which tells what to do to create a preview component.

If you are going to play movies or compress images, you should be familiar with QuickDraw and Color QuickDraw, described in *Inside Macintosh: Imaging*. If you are going to create QuickTime movies, you should be familiar with the Sound Manager, described in *Inside Macintosh: More Macintosh Toolbox*, and with the human interface guidelines, described in *Macintosh Human Interface Guidelines*.

The companion to this book, *Inside Macintosh: QuickTime*, describes QuickTime, an extension of the Macintosh system software that enables you to integrate time-based data into mainstream Macintosh applications. That book also provides a complete technical reference to the Movie Toolbox, the Image Compression Manager, and the movie resource formats.

Format of a Typical Chapter

Almost all chapters in this book follow a standard structure. For example, the chapter "Movie Controller Components" contains these sections:

- "About Movie Controller Components." This section provides an overview of the features provided by movie controller components.

- "Using Movie Controller Components." This section describes the tasks you can accomplish using movie controller components. It describes how to use the most common functions, gives related user interface information, provides code samples, and supplies additional information.

PREFACE

- "Movie Controller Components Reference." This section provides a complete reference to movie controller components by describing the constants, data structures, and functions that they use. Each function description also follows a standard format, which gives the function declaration and description of every parameter of the function. Some function descriptions also give additional descriptive information, such as result codes.
- "Summary of Movie Controller Components." This section provides the C interface, as well as the Pascal interface, for the constants, data structures, functions, and result codes associated with movie controller components.

Conventions Used in This Book

Inside Macintosh uses various conventions to present information. Words that require special treatment appear in specific fonts or font styles. Certain information, such as parameter blocks, uses special formats so that you can scan it quickly.

Special Fonts

All code listings, reserved words, and the names of actual data structures, constants, fields, parameters, and functions are shown in Courier (`this is Courier`).

Words that appear in **boldface** are key terms or concepts and are defined in the glossary.

Types of Notes

There are several types of notes used in this book.

Note
A note like this contains information that is interesting but possibly not essential to an understanding of the main text. (An example appears on page 2-24.) ◆

IMPORTANT
A note like this contains information that is essential for an understanding of the main text. (An example appears on page 5-87.) ▲

▲ **WARNING**
Warnings like this indicate potential problems that you should be aware of as you design your application. Failure to heed these warnings could result in system crashes or loss of data. (An example appears on page 5-39.) ▲

Development Environment

The system software functions described in this book are available using C, Pascal, or assembly-language interfaces. How you access these functions depends on the development environment you are using. This book shows system software functions in their C interface using the Macintosh Programmer's Workshop (MPW) version 3.2.

All code listings in this book are shown in C. They show methods of using various functions and illustrate techniques for accomplishing particular tasks. All code listings have been compiled and, in most cases, tested. However, Apple does not intend that you use these code samples in your application.

For More Information

APDA is Apple's worldwide source for over three hundred development tools, technical resources, training products, and information for anyone interested in developing applications on Apple platforms. Customers receive the quarterly *APDA Tools Catalog* featuring all current versions of Apple development tools and the most popular third-party development tools. Ordering is easy; there are no membership fees, and application forms are not required for most of our products. APDA offers convenient payment and shipping options, including site licensing.

To order products or to request a complimentary copy of the *APDA Tools Catalog*, contact

APDA
Apple Computer, Inc.
P.O. Box 319
Buffalo, NY 14207-0319

Telephone	800-282-2732 (United States)
	800-637-0029 (Canada)
	716-871-6555 (International)
Fax	716-871-6511
AppleLink	APDA
America Online	APDA
CompuServe	76666,2405
Internet	APDA@applelink.apple.com

If you provide commercial products and services, call 408-974-4897 for information on the developer support programs available from Apple.

For information on registering signatures, file types, Apple events, and other technical information, contact

Macintosh Developer Technical Support

Apple Computer, Inc.

20525 Mariani Avenue, M/S 75-3T

Cupertino, CA 95014-6299

CHAPTER 1

Overview

Contents

Providing Movie Playback   1-3
Capturing Sequences of Images   1-6
Compressing and Decompressing Still Images   1-8
Converting Data for Use in QuickTime Movies   1-11
Creating Previews of QuickTime Movies   1-11

CHAPTER 1

Overview

Each QuickTime component provides an interface to a general class of features associated with the manipulation of time-based data. QuickTime provides components so that developers may use a component—for example, one that provides image compression services—without extensive knowledge of all the possible services that that component might provide. Developers are therefore isolated from the details of implementing and managing a given technology.

Since each QuickTime component is registered by the Component Manager, the component's code can be available systemwide or in a resource that is local to a particular application.

QuickTime components supply these services:

- movie playback (including the provision of basic time information and the interpretation of the data to be played)
- image capture
- compression and decompression of still images
- exchange of movie data
- creation and display of movie previews

This book addresses two audiences—developers who communicate directly with existing components and developers who want to create their own components.

Providing Movie Playback

Figure 1-1 shows the QuickTime components that allow your application to provide movie playback.

- Your application calls the movie controller component in order to play movies. **Movie controller components** implement movie controllers, which present a user interface for playing and editing movies. For details on the features of movie controller components and the interfaces they must support, see the chapter "Movie Controller Components" in this book.

- The movie controller component communicates with the Movie Toolbox's functions in order to obtain and receive time-based information from the clock component. **Clock components** supply basic time information to their clients. For details, see the chapter "Clock Components" in this book.

Overview

- The Movie Toolbox passes control to media handler components, which actually interpret the data that will be played. **Media handlers** allow the Movie Toolbox to access the data in a media. They isolate the Movie Toolbox from the details of how or where a particular media is stored. This makes QuickTime extensible to new data formats and storage devices. If you want to develop a media handler component, read the chapter "Derived Media Handler Components" in this book.

- The media handler component passes control to the Image Compression Manager's decompression functions, which send the movie data to a decompressor component. A decompressor component is one kind of **image compressor component,** a code resource that may provide either compression or decompression services. For details on decompressor components, see the chapter "Image Compressor Components" in this book.

- The decompressor component actually decompresses the movie data so that it can be played on the screen of the Macintosh computer.

CHAPTER 1

Overview

Figure 1-1 QuickTime components for movie playback

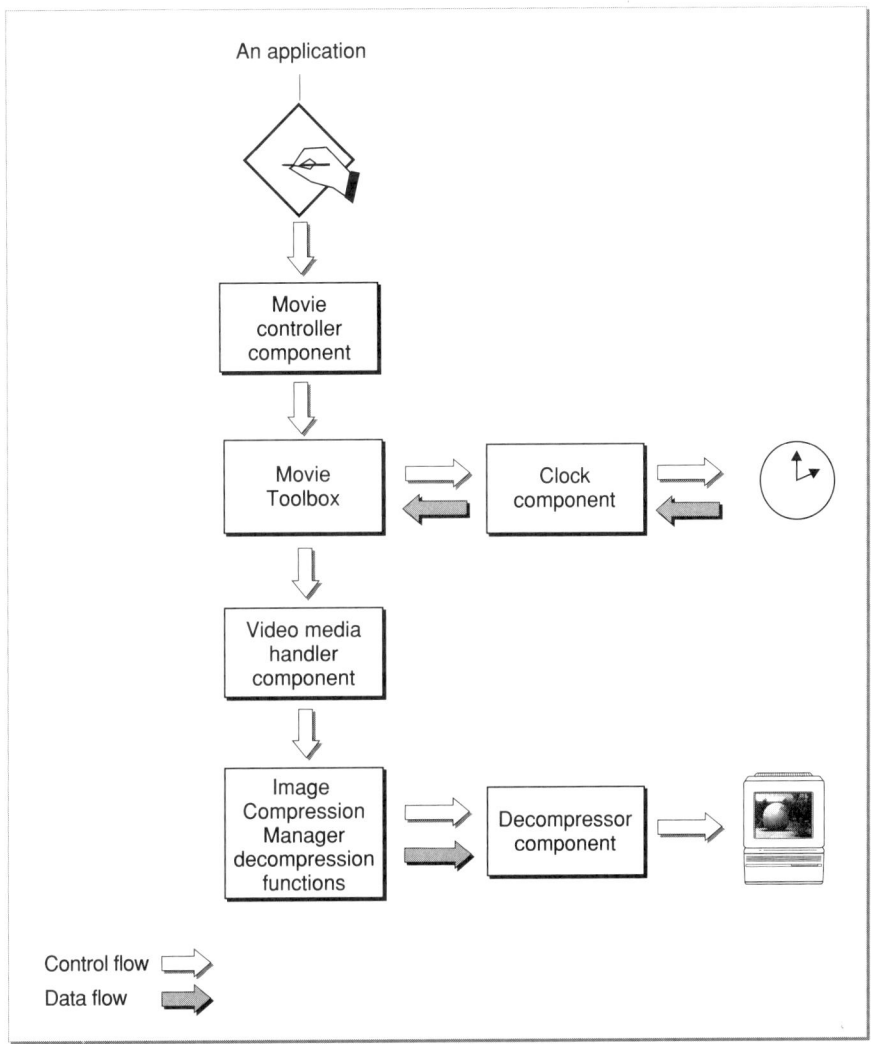

Capturing Sequences of Images

Figure 1-2 shows the QuickTime components that allow your application to capture image data for storage or for further processing by video equipment.

- Your application calls the sequence grabber component to digitize data. **Sequence grabber components** allow applications to obtain digitized data from sources that are external to a Macintosh computer. For more information on how to use these components to acquire images, read the chapter "Sequence Grabber Components" in this book.

- The sequence grabber component uses both sequence grabber panel components and sequence grabber channel components.
    - The **sequence grabber panel component** obtains configuration information before it calls the sequence grabber channel component to manipulate the captured data. For details on creating sequence grabber panel components, see the chapter "Sequence Grabber Panel Components" in this book.
    - The **sequence grabber channel component** manipulates the captured data. For details on sequence grabber channel components, see the chapter "Sequence Grabber Channel Components" in this book.
    - Image compressor components are used by the sequence grabber channel component, if necessary.

- The sequence grabber channel component calls either a video digitizer component or the Image Compression Manager.
    - The **video digitizer component** obtains the digitized data from an analog video source. To understand how to use or create a video digitizer component, see the chapter "Video Digitizer Components" in this book.
    - The Image Compression Manager's compression functions store the image in a storage media—for example, in a data pack.

CHAPTER 1

Overview

Figure 1-2 QuickTime components for image capture

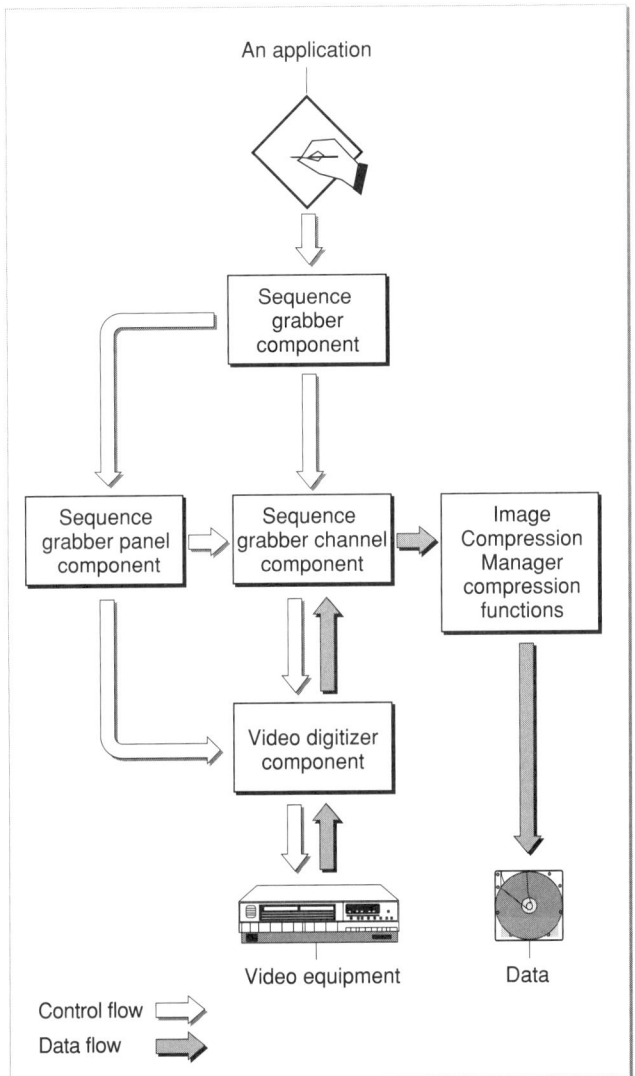

Compressing and Decompressing Still Images

QuickTime components allow your application to compress and decompress still images.

Figure 1-3 provides an overview of QuickTime components for the compression and decompression of still images.

- Your application calls the standard image-compression dialog component to select parameters for governing the compression of an image and for managing the compression operation.
- The standard image-compression dialog component calls the Image Compression Manager.
- The Image Compression Manager may commence the compression operation in one of two ways:
    - It may send the image directly to an image compressor component and then to a storage media, such as a data pack.
    - It may send the image to the Apple-supplied decompressor, the `'raw '` decompressor, and then through a band buffer (for conversion to the image depth required by the compressor component) before sending it to the image compressor component.
- The compressor component compresses the image and sends it to the storage media.

CHAPTER 1

Overview

Figure 1-3 QuickTime components for compressing still images

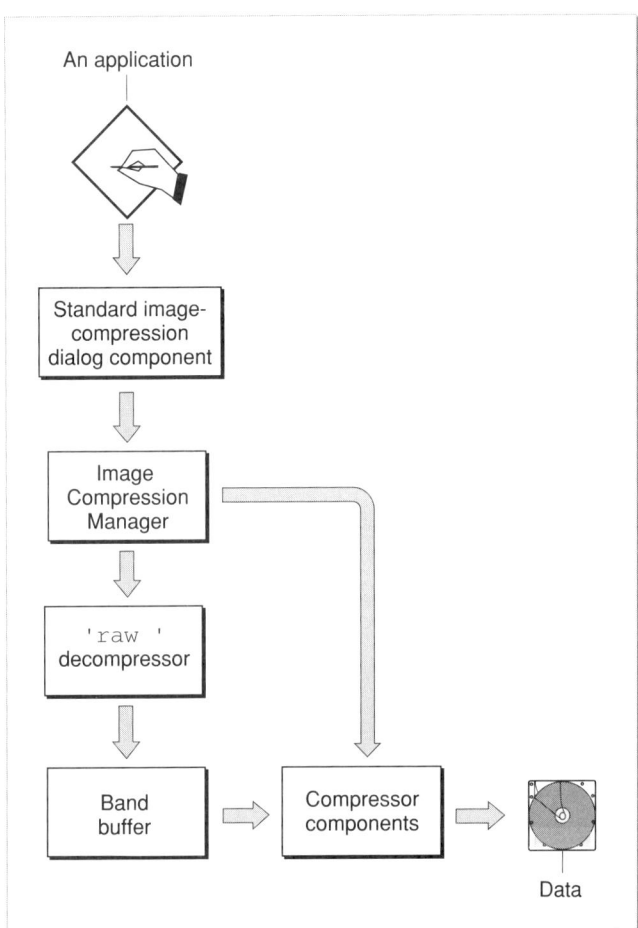

Overview

Figure 1-4 shows the relationships of the components that allow your application to take an image from a storage media and decompress it so that it may be displayed on the Macintosh screen.

- Your application calls the QuickDraw `DrawPicture` routine, which the Image Compression Manager intercepts. The Image Compressor decompresses the image. Alternatively, your application may communicate directly with the Image Compression Manager, which sends the compressed image to the decompressor component.

- The decompressor component sends the image directly to the Macintosh screen or to a band buffer that meets the requirements of the decompressor (in features such as pixel depth and dimension). The contents of the band buffer are then copied to the screen by the `'raw '` decompressor, which performs any necessary conversion.

Figure 1-4 QuickTime components for decompressing still images

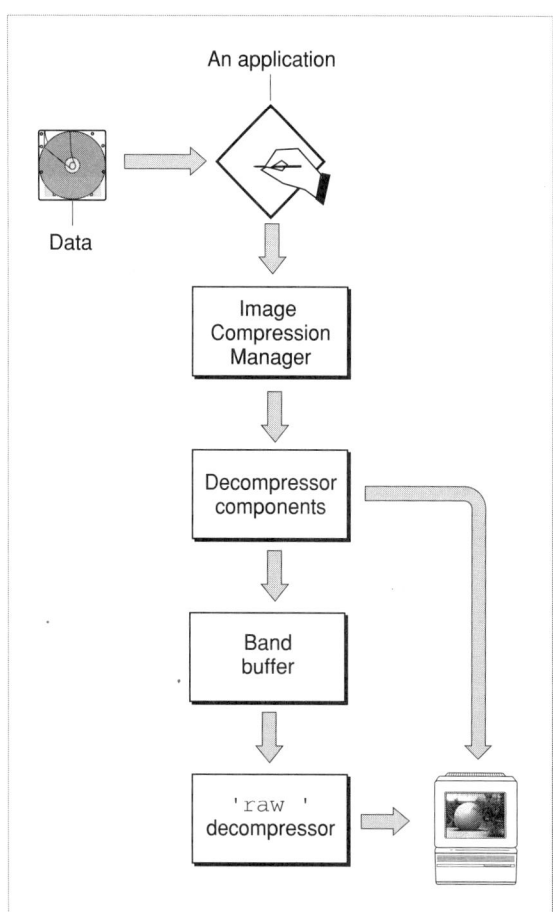

Converting Data for Use in QuickTime Movies

Movie data exchange components allow your application to convert data in various formats so that it can be imported to or exported from a QuickTime movie. For information on using or creating these components, see the chapter "Movie Data Exchange Components" in this book.

Creating Previews of QuickTime Movies

Preview components let your application create and display previews of QuickTime movies. The Image Compression Manager is the primary client of movie preview components. For details on developing preview components, see the chapter "Preview Components" in this book.

CHAPTER 2

Movie Controller Components

Contents

About Movie Controller Components   2-4
    The Elements of a Movie Controller   2-4
    Badges   2-6
Spatial Properties   2-6
Using Movie Controller Components   2-10
    Playing Movies   2-10
    Customizing Movie Controllers   2-13
Movie Controller Components Reference   2-14
    Movie Controller Actions   2-15
    Movie Controller Functions   2-28
       Associating Movies With Controllers   2-28
       Managing Controller Attributes   2-33
       Handling Movie Events   2-44
       Editing Movies   2-50
       Getting and Setting Movie Controller Time   2-56
       Customizing Event Processing   2-58
    Application-Defined Function   2-61
Summary of Movie Controller Components   2-63
    C Summary   2-63
       Constants   2-63
       Data Types   2-66
       Movie Controller Functions   2-67
       Application-Defined Function   2-69
    Pascal Summary   2-69
       Constants   2-69
       Data Types   2-73

Movie Controller Routines   2-73
Application-Defined Routine   2-75
Result Codes   2-75

Movie Controller Components

This chapter describes movie controller components. Movie controller components provide a high-level interface that allows your application to present movies to users quickly and easily. **Movie controllers,** the controls managed by movie controller components, present a user interface for playing and editing movies. Movie controller components eliminate much of the complexity of working with movies by assuming primary responsibility for the movie, freeing your application to focus on the unique services it offers to users.

This chapter has been divided into the following sections:

- "About Movie Controller Components" describes the capabilities of movie controller components in general and discusses the movie controller component supplied by Apple.
- "Spatial Properties" discusses the display regions that are supported by movie controller components—your application can manipulate these regions to control how the controller is displayed.
- "Using Movie Controller Components" provides sample code that shows you how to play, edit, and customize movies with movie controller components.
- "Movie Controller Components Reference" describes the functions provided to your application by movie controller components.
- "Summary of Movie Controller Components" provides a condensed listing of the constants, data structures, and functions supported by these components.

If you are developing an application that can play movies, you should consider using movie controller components to manage your movie user interface. They provide a consistent user interface that shields you from the details of using the Movie Toolbox. To learn about the capabilities of movie controllers, read "About Movie Controller Components." If your application allows the user to play movies, read "Spatial Properties." If you anticipate doing event management, read "Customizing Movie Controllers" beginning on page 2-13 and "Application-Defined Function" beginning on page 2-61 as well. All movie controller functions are described in "Movie Controller Components Reference"—you should read the portions that are relevant to your application.

If you are developing a movie controller component, the information in this chapter describes the interface that your component must support. In addition, you should be familiar with the material in the chapter "Component Manager" in *Inside Macintosh: More Macintosh Toolbox*, which describes how to build a component.

About Movie Controller Components

Movie controller components provide movie playback and editing capabilities to applications. In so doing, movie controller components remove from your application much of the burden of presenting an interface for movie playback and editing. It is possible to have the controller do nearly all the work involved with playing movies, including updating and idling. Alternatively, your application can take care of some or all of these tasks.

You can think of movie controller components in terms of more familiar Macintosh controls. Movie controller components, in addition to handling update, activate, and mouse-down events, also know how to interact with the data that they control. Consequently, the movie controller components can actually perform the commands requested by users (the controls handled by the Control Manager merely report user actions to your application). In this way, your application is relieved of much of the work of controlling movies. Furthermore, movie controller components can be updated to provide improved functionality with no impact on your application.

Movie controller components have a component type value of `'play'`. You can use the following constant to specify this value.

```
#define MovieControllerComponentType 'play'
```

Apple has defined the functional interface that is supported by movie controller components so that you can create a wide variety of movie controls. For example, you could create a control that is separate from the movie image. Consequently, the interface is a bit more complex than might seem necessary for simple controls that support only playback. For details on the functions that your component must support, see "Movie Controller Components Reference," which begins on page 2-14.

The Elements of a Movie Controller

The movie controller component provided with QuickTime by Apple provides control elements for regulating sound, starting, stopping, pausing, single-stepping (forward and backward), and moving to a specified time. Figure 2-1 shows the controls supported by Apple's movie controller component. If the user resizes the controller so that there is not enough space to display all the individual control elements, the movie controller component eliminates elements from the display. Note that this controller allows the user to start and stop the movie by clicking the movie image itself. This is an important feature, because it allows the user to control the movie even in circumstances where no control elements are visible.

CHAPTER 2

Movie Controller Components

Figure 2-1 The standard movie controller

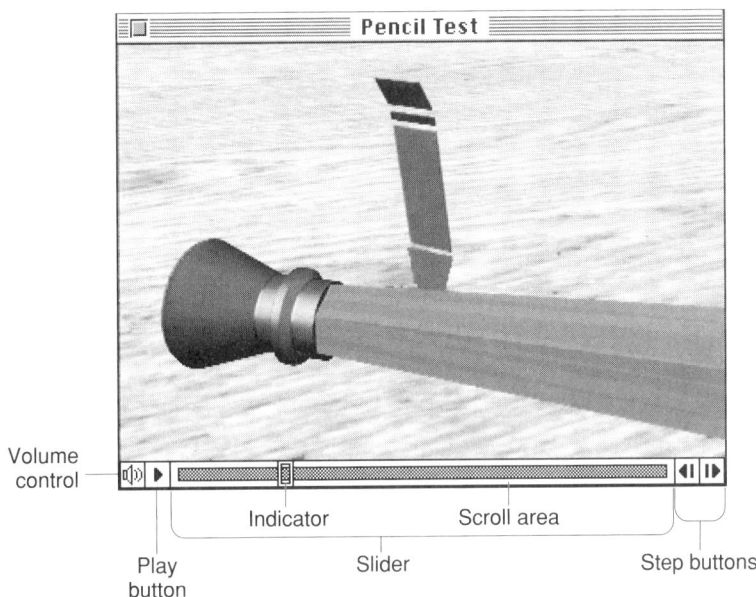

The movie controller presented by Apple's movie controller component contains a number of individual controls, as shown in Figure 2-1. These controls include:

- **A volume control.** This control allows the user to adjust the sound volume—holding down the mouse button while the cursor is on this control causes the controller to display a slider that allows the user to change the sound volume while the movie is playing (if a movie does not have any sound, the movie controller component disables the volume control).

- **A play button.** This control allows the user to start and stop the movie. Clicking the play button causes the movie to start playing; in addition, the movie controller component changes the play button into a pause button. Clicking the pause button causes the movie to stop playing. If the user starts the movie and does not stop it, the movie controller plays the movie once and then stops the movie.

- **A slider.** This control allows the user to quickly navigate through a movie's contents. Dragging the indicator within the slider displays a single frame of the movie that corresponds to the position of the indicator. Clicking within the slider causes the indicator to jump to the location of the mouse click and causes the movie controller component to display the corresponding movie data.

- **Step buttons.** These controls allow the user to move through the movie frame by frame, either forward or backward. Holding the mouse button down while the cursor is on a step button causes the movie controller to step through the movie, frame by frame, in the appropriate direction.

Badges

The movie controller component supplied by Apple allows your application to distinguish movies from static graphics in documents by the use of a badge. A **badge** is a visual element that the movie controller can display as part of a movie when the other controls are not visible and the movie is not playing. Figure 2-2 shows a movie with a badge.

Figure 2-2   A movie with a badge

Movie badge

The badge lets the user know that the image represents a movie rather than a static image. A badge appears under the following conditions:

- the movie is in badge mode—that is, the `mcActionSetUseBadge` movie controller action was called with a value of `true`
- the movie is not playing
- the movie controller is hidden

When the user double-clicks the movie, the movie starts playing and the badge disappears; a single click stops the movie, and the badge reappears. When the user clicks the badge itself, the movie controller component displays the controls, as shown in Figure 2-1.

Your application can control whether the movie controller component displays a badge with a movie. Use the `NewMovieController` function (described on page 2-29) to create a new controller.

Spatial Properties

Movie controller components define several display regions that govern how a controller and its movie are displayed. In addition, movie controller components support a number

Movie Controller Components

of functions that allow your application to manipulate these regions and thereby control the display of a controller and its associated movie. This section discusses each of these regions and the movie controller component functions that your application can use to work with these regions.

The displayed representation of a movie controller consists of two parts: the movie and the controller itself. The movie consists of the QuickTime movie image. The controller consists of the visual elements that allow the user to control the movie. Figure 2-1 on page 2-5 shows a sample controller. In this figure, note that the movie is attached to the controller—that is, the movie and the controller are contiguous. Movie controller components also allow you to create controllers that are separate from, or detached from, their associated movies. You use the `MCSetControllerAttached` function (described on page 2-35) to control this attribute. This gives you the freedom to position the movie and the controller.

Movie controller components define several spatial elements that allow your application to control the display of a movie and its controller. Figure 2-3 shows the relationships between these spatial elements for **attached controllers,** whereas Figure 2-4 shows the relationships between these spatial elements for **detached controllers.**

Figure 2-3 Movie controller spatial elements for attached controllers

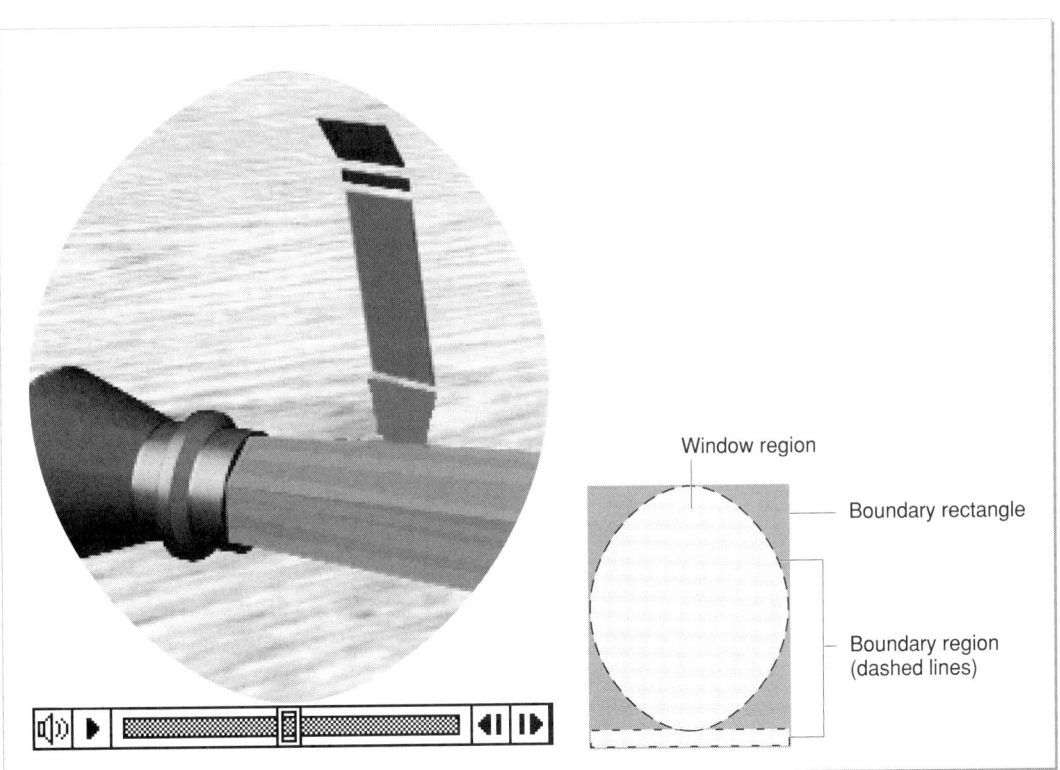

CHAPTER 2

Movie Controller Components

The **controller boundary rectangle** is a rectangle that completely encloses the controller. If the controller is attached to its movie, the controller boundary rectangle also encloses the movie. The width of this rectangle corresponds to the widest part of the displayed representation of the controller (and its attached movie). Similarly, its height is derived from the highest part of the controller (and its attached movie). You can use the `MCSetControllerBoundsRect` function to modify the controller boundary rectangle to define display transformations to be applied to a controller and its movie. You can retrieve a controller's boundary rectangle by calling the `MCGetControllerBoundsRect` function (described on page 2-39).

The **controller boundary region** defines the region occupied by the controller. If the movie is attached to the controller, the controller boundary region also includes the movie. The controller boundary region corresponds exactly to the display footprint of the controller (and its attached movie). You can retrieve the boundary region of a controller by calling the `MCGetControllerBoundsRgn` function (described on page 2-40).

Figure 2-4 Movie controller spatial elements for detached controllers

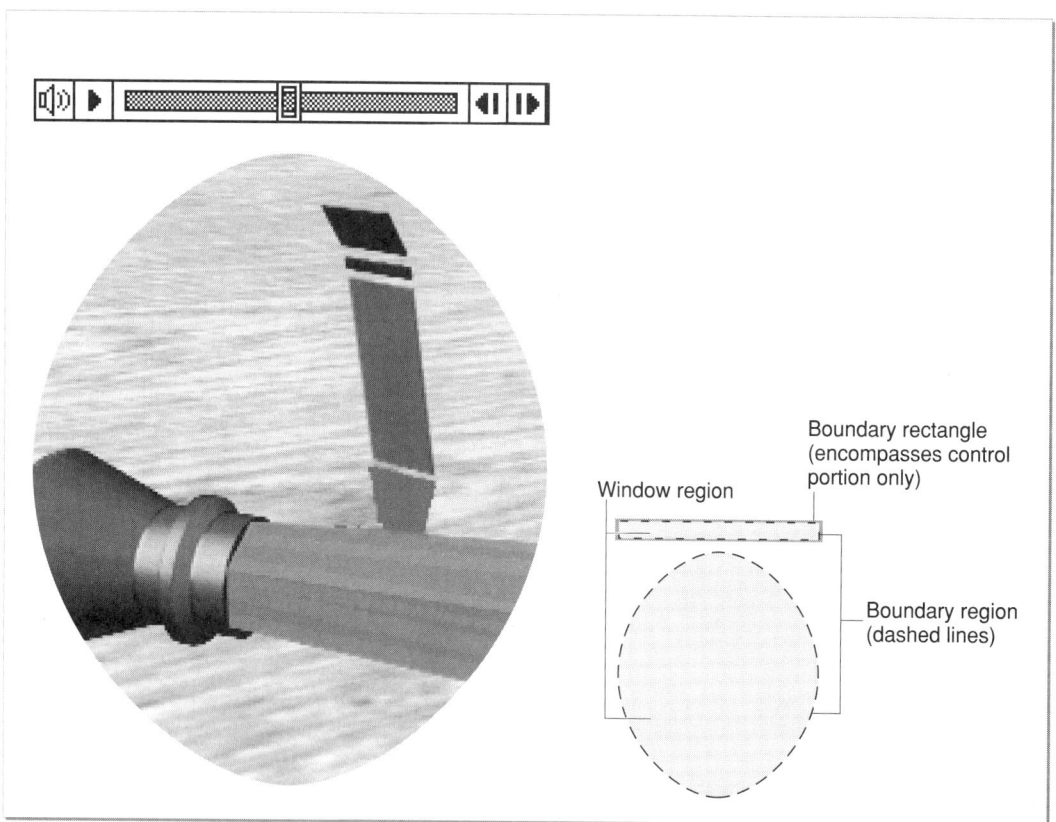

Movie Controller Components

The controller boundary rectangle and controller boundary region both work with the unclipped display representation of the controller and its movie. The **controller window region** represents the portion of the controller and its movie that is actually displayed on the computer screen, after clipping by the **controller clipping region.** The controller window region always includes both the controller and its movie, whether the controller is attached or detached. You can retrieve a controller's window region by calling the `MCGetWindowRgn` function (described on page 2-41). You can manipulate a controller's clipping region by calling the `MCSetClip` and `MCGetClip` functions (described on page 2-42 and page 2-43, respectively). Figure 2-5 shows how the controller clipping region affects the controller window region.

Figure 2-5 Clipping the controller window region with the controller clipping region

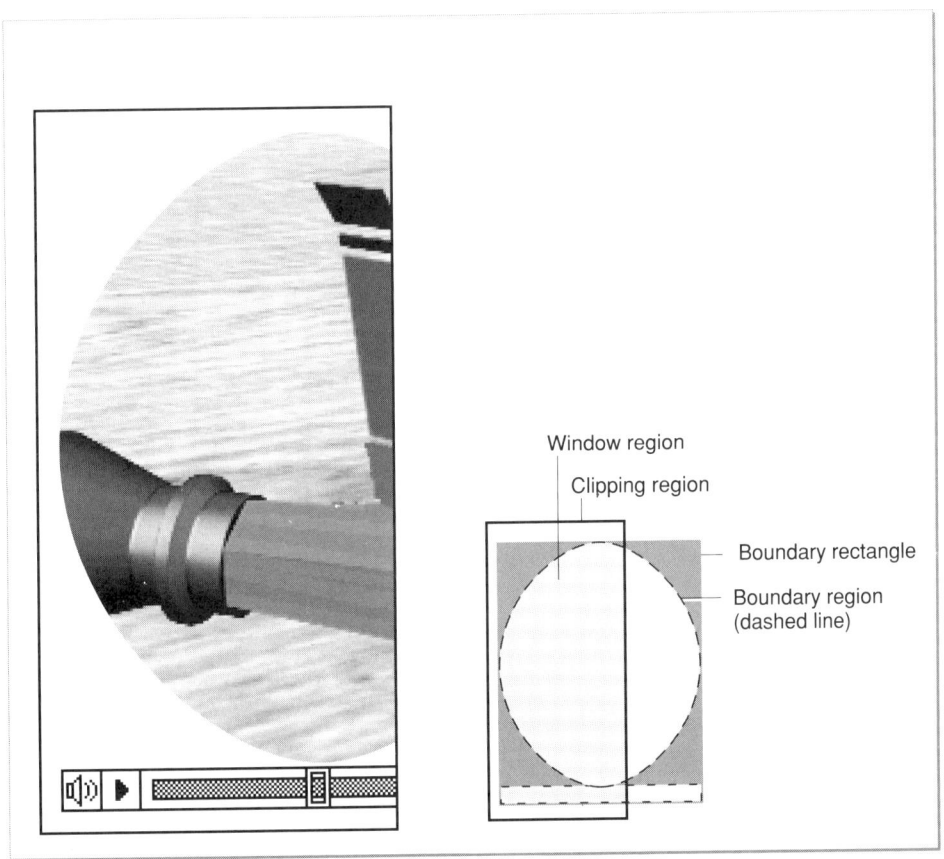

Spatial Properties

Using Movie Controller Components

This section supplies examples of how to use the standard movie controller to play movies. It also provides sample code for customizing movie controller components.

Playing Movies

The following sample code demonstrates how to use the standard movie controller component to play a movie. The `GetMovie` function prompts the user to select a movie file and then get a movie out of it. It then opens the movie and allows the user to play it.

Listing 2-1 Playing a movie with a movie controller component

```
MovieController    gController;
WindowPtr          gWindow;
Rect               windowRect;
Movie              gMovie;
Boolean            gDone;
OSErr              gErr;
ComponentResult    gCErr;
Boolean            gResult;
EventRecord        gTheEvent;
WindowPtr          whichWindow;
short              part;

pascal Movie    GetMovie(void);
pascal Movie    GetMovie(void)
{
    OSErr              err;
    SFTypeList         typeList;
    StandardFileReply  reply;
    Movie              aMovie;
    short              movieResFile;
    short              movieResID;
    Str255             movieName;
    Boolean            wasChanged;

    aMovie = nil;
    typeList[0] = MovieFileType;
    StandardGetFilePreview ( (FileFilterProcPtr)nil, 1,
                            typeList, &reply);
```

CHAPTER 2

Movie Controller Components

```
    if (reply.sfGood) {
       err = OpenMovieFile (&reply.sfFile, &movieResFile,
                       fsRdPerm);
       if (err == noErr) {
          movieResID = 0;
          err = NewMovieFromFile (&aMovie, movieResFile,
                             &movieResID,
                             movieName,
                             newMovieActive,
                             &wasChanged);
          err = CloseMovieFile (movieResFile);
       }
    }
    return aMovie;
}
void main(void);
void main(void)

{
    InitGraf(&qd.thePort);
    InitFonts();
    InitWindows();
    InitMenus();
    TEInit();
    InitDialogs(nil);
    gErr = EnterMovies();

    SetRect (&windowRect, 100, 100, 200, 200);
    gWindow = NewCWindow (nil,
             &windowRect,
             "\pMovie",
             false,
             noGrowDocProc,
             (WindowPtr)-1,
             true,
             0);
    SetPort (gWindow);
    gMovie = GetMovie();
    if (gMovie != nil) {
       SetRect(&windowRect, 0, 0, 100, 100);
       gController = NewMovieController (gMovie, &windowRect,
                                    mcTopLeftMovie);
```

Using Movie Controller Components

CHAPTER 2

Movie Controller Components

```
        if (gController != nil) {
           gCErr = MCGetControllerBoundsRect (gController,
                                              &windowRect);
           SizeWindow (gWindow, windowRect.right, windowRect.bottom,
                    true);
           ShowWindow (gWindow);
           gCErr = MCDoAction (gController, mcActionSetKeysEnabled,
                            (Ptr)true);
           gDone = false;

           while (! gDone) {
              gResult = GetNextEvent (everyEvent, &gTheEvent);
              if (MCIsPlayerEvent (gController, &gTheEvent) == 0) {
                 switch (gTheEvent.what) {
                    case updateEvt:
                       whichWindow = (WindowPtr)gTheEvent.message;
                       BeginUpdate (whichWindow);
                       EraseRect (&(*whichWindow).portRect);
                       EndUpdate (whichWindow);
                       break;
                    case mouseDown:
                       part = FindWindow (gTheEvent.where,
                                       &whichWindow);
                       if (whichWindow == gWindow) {
                          switch (part) {
                             case inGoAway:
                                gDone = TrackGoAway (whichWindow,
                                           gTheEvent.where);
                                break;

                             case inDrag:
                                DragWindow (whichWindow,
                                        gTheEvent.where,
                                        &(qd.screenBits.bounds) );
                                break;
                          }
                       }
                 }
              }
           }
           DisposeMovieController(gController);
        }
        DisposeMovie(gMovie);
```

Customizing Movie Controllers

Movie controller components allow you to create an action filter function in your application. The component calls your action filter function whenever an action occurs in the control. (An **action** is an integer constant used by the movie controller component.) You can then customize the behavior of the control or simply monitor user actions. You establish an action filter function by calling the `MCSetActionFilterWithRefCon` function, which is described on page 2-47.

The sample code in Listing 2-2 demonstrates the use of an action filter function. This filter function resizes the window whenever the user hides the controller. Therefore, this sample function handles the `mcActionControllerSizeChanged` action. Your application should include a similar action filter function so that you can determine when the user resizes the controller. This function supports only attached controllers.

Listing 2-2 Using a movie controller filter function

```
pascal Boolean myMCActionFilter ( MovieController mc,
                                   short* Action, long* params);

{
   RgnHandle   controllerRgn;
   Rect        controllerBox;
   WindowPtr   movieWindow;
   switch (*Action) {
      case mcActionControllerSizeChanged:
         /* size of controller/movie has changed */
         movieWindow = (WindowPtr)MCGetControllerPort(mc);
         controllerRgn = MCGetWindowRgn(mc, movieWindow);
         if (controllerRgn != nil) {
            controllerBox = (**controllerRgn).rgnBBox;
            DisposeRgn (controllerRgn);
            SizeWindow (movieWindow, controllerBox.right,
                     controllerBox.bottom, true);
         }
      break;
   }
   return false;
}
```

Movie Controller Components Reference

This section describes some of the constants and functions associated with movie controller components.

You can use the following constants to refer to the request codes for each of the functions that your movie controller component must support.

```
enum {
    kMCSetMovieSelect                   = 2,   /* MCSetMovie */
    kMCRemoveMovieSelect                = 3,   /* MCRemoveMovie */
    kMCIsPlayerEventSelect              = 7,   /* MCIsPlayerEvent */
    kMCSetActionFilterSelect            = 8,   /* MCSetActionFilter */
    kMCDoActionSelect                   = 9,   /* MCDoAction */
    kMCSetControllerAttachedSelect      = 10,
                                               /* MCSetControllerAttached */
    kMCIsControllerAttachedSelect       = 11,
                                               /* MCIsControllerAttached */
    kMCSetControllerPortSelect          = 12,  /* MCSetControllerPort */
    kMCGetControllerPortSelect          = 13,  /* MCGetControllerPort */
    kMCGetVisibleSelect                 = 14,  /* MCGetVisible */
    kMCSetVisibleSelect                 = 15,  /* MCSetVisible */
    kMCGetControllerBoundsRectSelect
                                        = 16,
                                               /* MCGetControllerBoundsRect */
    kMCSetControllerBoundsRectSelect
                                        = 17,
                                               /* MCSetControllerBoundsRect */
    kMCGetControllerBoundsRgnSelect     = 18,
                                               /* MCGetControllerBoundsRgn */
    kMCGetWindowRgnSelect               = 19,  /* MCGetWindowRgn */
    kMCMovieChangedSelect               = 20,  /* MCMovieChanged */
    kMCSetDurationSelect                = 21,  /* MCSetDuration*/
    kMCGetCurrentTimeSelect             = 22,  /* MCGetCurrentTime */
    kMCNewAttachedControllerSelect      = 23,
                                               /* MCNewAttachedController */
    kMCDrawSelect                       = 24,  /* MCDraw */
    kMCActivateSelect                   = 25,  /* MCActivate */
    kMCIdleSelect                       = 26,  /* MCIdle */
    kMCKeySelect                        = 27,  /* MCKey */
    kMCClickSelect                      = 28,  /* MCClick */
    kMCEnableEditingSelect              = 29,  /* MCEnableEditing */
```

CHAPTER 2

Movie Controller Components

```
    kMCIsEditingEnabledSelect          = 30, /* MCIsEditingEnabled */
    kMCCopySelect                      = 31, /* MCCopy */
    kMCCutSelect                       = 32, /* MCCut */
    kMCPasteSelect                     = 33, /* MCPaste */
    kMCClearSelect                     = 34, /* MCClear */
    kMCUndoSelect                      = 35, /* MCUndo */
    kMCPositionControllerSelect        = 36,
                                       /* MCPositionController */
    kMCGetControllerInfoSelect         = 37,
                                       /* MCGetControllerInfo */
    kMCSetClipSelect                   = 40, /* MCSetClip */
    kMCGetClipSelect                   = 41, /* MCGetClip */
    kMCDrawBadgeSelect                 = 42  /* MCDrawBadge */
    kMCSetUpEditMenuSelect             = 43, /* MCSetUpEditMenu */,
    kMCGetMenuStringSelect             = 44, /* MCGetMenuString */
    kMCSetActionFilterWithRefConSelect = 45
                                       /* MCSetActionFilterWithRefCon */
};
```

Movie Controller Actions

This section discusses actions, which are integer constants (defined by the `mcAction` data type) used by movie controller components. Applications that use movie controller components can invoke these actions by calling the `MCDoAction` function, which is described on page 2-46. If your application includes an action filter function, that function may receive any of these actions (see the discussion of the `MCSetActionFilterWithRefCon` function on page 2-47 for more information about action filter functions).

Your action filter function should refer any actions that you do not want to handle back to the calling movie controller component. Your function refers actions back to the movie controller component by returning a value of `false`. If your function returns a value of `true`, the movie controller component performs no further processing for the action.

If you use any Movie Toolbox functions that modify the movie in your action filter function, be sure to call the `MCMovieChanged` function (described on page 2-49).

```
enum {
    mcActionIdle              = 1,  /* give event-processing time to
                                       movie controller */
    mcActionDraw              = 2,  /* send update event to movie
                                       controller */
    mcActionActivate          = 3,  /* activate movie controller */
    mcActionDeactivate        = 4,  /* deactivate controller */
    mcActionMouseDown         = 5,  /* pass mouse-down event */
```

CHAPTER 2

Movie Controller Components

```
mcActionKey                   = 6,  /* pass key-down or auto-key event */
mcActionPlay                  = 8,  /* start playing movie */
mcActionGoToTime              = 12, /* move to specific time in a movie */
mcActionSetVolume             = 14, /* set a movie's volume */
mcActionGetVolume             = 15, /* retrieve a movie's volume */
mcActionStep                  = 18, /* play a movie a specified number
                                        of frames at a time */
mcActionSetLooping            = 21, /* enable or disable looping */
mcActionGetLooping            = 22, /* find out if movie is looping */
mcActionSetLoopIsPalindrome   = 23, /* enable palindrome looping */
mcActionGetLoopIsPalindrome   = 24, /* find out if palindrome looping
                                        is on */
mcActionSetGrowBoxBounds      = 25, /* set limits for resizing a movie */
mcActionControllerSizeChanged = 26, /* user has resized movie
                                        controller */
mcActionSetSelectionBegin     = 29, /* start time of movie's current
                                        selection */
mcActionSetSelectionDuration  = 30, /* set duration of movie's current
                                        selection */
mcActionSetKeysEnabled        = 32, /* enable or disable keystrokes for
                                        movie */
mcActionGetKeysEnabled        = 33, /* find out if keystrokes are
                                        enabled */
mcActionSetPlaySelection      = 34, /* constrain playing to the current
                                        selection */
mcActionGetPlaySelection      = 35, /* find out if movie is constrained to
                                        playing within selection */
mcActionSetUseBadge           = 36, /* enable or disable movie's
                                        playback badge */
mcActionGetUseBadge           = 37, /* find out if movie controller is
                                        using playback badge */
mcActionSetFlags              = 38, /* set movie's control flags */
mcActionGetFlags              = 39, /* retrieve movie's control flags */
mcActionSetPlayEveryFrame     = 40, /* instruct controller to play all
                                        frames in movie */
mcActionGetPlayEveryFrame     = 41, /* find out if controller is playing
                                        every frame in movie */
mcActionGetPlayRate           = 42, /* determine playback rate */
mcActionShowBalloon           = 43, /* find out if controller wants to
                                        display Balloon Help */
```

CHAPTER 2

Movie Controller Components

```
        mcActionBadgeClick          = 44, /* user clicked movie's badge */
        mcActionMovieClick          = 45, /* user clicked in movie *
        mcActionSuspend             = 46, /* suspend event received */
        mcActionResume              = 47  /* resume event received */
typedef short mcAction;
};
```

The action descriptions that follow are divided into those used by your application and those received by your action filter.

Actions for Use by Applications

`mcActionIdle`

> Your application can use this action to grant event-processing time to a movie controller.
>
> There are no parameters for this action.

`mcActionDraw`

> Your application can use this action to send an update event to a movie controller.
>
> The parameter for this action is a pointer to a window.

`mcActionActivate`

> Your application can use this action to activate a movie controller.
>
> There are no parameters for this action.

`mcActionDeactivate`

> Your application can use this action to deactivate a movie controller.
>
> There are no parameters for this action.

`mcActionMouseDown`

> Your application can use this action to pass a mouse-down event to a movie controller.
>
> The parameter data must contain a pointer to an event structure—the `message` field in the event structure must specify the window in which the user clicked.

`mcActionKey`

> Your application can use this action to pass a key-down or auto-key event to a movie controller.
>
> The parameter data must contain a pointer to an event structure that describes the key event.
>
> Your action filter function receives this action when the movie controller has received a key-down or auto-key event.

`mcActionPlay`

> Your application can use this action to start or stop playing a movie.
>
> The parameter data must contain a fixed value that indicates the rate of play. Values greater than 0 correspond to forward rates; values less than 0 play the movie backward. A value of 0 stops the movie.

Movie Controller Components Reference

`mcActionGotoTime`
: Your application can use this action to move to a specific time in a movie.

    The parameter data must contain a pointer to a time structure that specifies the target position in the movie.

`mcActionSetVolume`
: Your application can use this action to set a movie's volume.

    The parameter data must contain a pointer to a 16-bit, fixed-point number that indicates the relative volume of the movie. Volume values range from –1.0 to 1.0. Negative values play no sound but preserve the absolute value of the volume setting.

`mcActionGetVolume`
: Your application can use this action to determine a movie's volume.

    The parameter data must contain a pointer to a 16-bit, fixed-point number that indicates the relative volume of the movie. Volume values range from –1.0 to 1.0. Negative values play no sound but preserve the absolute value of the volume setting.

`mcActionStep`
: Your application can use this action to play a movie while skipping a specified number of frames at a time.

    The parameter data must contain a long integer value that specifies the number of steps (that is, the frames and the play direction). Positive values step the movie forward the specified number of frames; negative values step the movie backward. A value of 0 steps the movie forward one frame.

`mcActionSetLooping`
: Your application can use this action to enable or disable looping for a movie.

    The parameter data must contain a Boolean value—a value of `true` indicates that looping is to be enabled.

`mcActionGetLooping`
: Your application can use this action to determine whether a movie is looping.

    The parameter data must contain a pointer to a Boolean value. The movie controller sets this value to `true` if looping is enabled for the movie that is assigned to this controller. Otherwise, it sets the value to `false`.

`mcActionSetLoopIsPalindrome`
: Your application can use this action to enable palindrome looping. **Palindrome looping** causes a movie to play alternately forward and backward. Looping must also be enabled for palindrome looping to take effect.

    The parameter data must contain a Boolean value—a value of `true` indicates that palindrome looping is to be enabled.

`mcActionGetLoopIsPalindrome`
: Your application can use this action to determine whether palindrome looping is enabled for a movie. Looping must also be enabled for palindrome looping to take effect.

CHAPTER 2

Movie Controller Components

The parameter data must contain a pointer to a Boolean value. The movie controller sets this value to `true` if palindrome looping is enabled for the movie that is assigned to this controller. Otherwise, it sets the value to `false`.

`mcActionSetGrowBoxBounds`

Your application can use this action to set the limits for resizing a movie.

The parameter data consists of a `rect` structure.

`mcActionSetSelectionBegin`

Your application can use this action to set the start time of a movie's current selection. After using this action, you must use the `mcActionSetSelectionDuration` action to set the duration of the selection.

The parameter data must contain a pointer to a time structure specifying the starting time of the movie's current selection.

`mcActionSetSelectionDuration`

Your application can use this action to set the duration of a movie's current selection. You can only use this action immediately after the `mcActionSetSelectionBegin` action.

The parameter data must contain a pointer to a time structure specifying the ending time of the movie's current selection.

Your action filter function receives this action when the movie controller has received a request to set the movie's current selection duration.

`mcActionSetKeysEnabled`

Your application can use this action to enable or disable keystrokes for a movie.

The parameter data must contain a Boolean value—a value of `true` indicates that keystrokes are to be enabled. By default, this value is set to `false`.

`mcActionGetKeysEnabled`

Your application can use this action to determine whether keystrokes are enabled for a movie controller.

The parameter data must contain a pointer to a Boolean value. The movie controller sets this value to `true` if keystrokes are enabled for the movie that is assigned to this controller. Otherwise, it sets the value to `false`.

`mcActionSetPlaySelection`

Your application can use this action to constrain playing to the current selection.

The parameter data must contain a Boolean value—a value of `true` indicates that playing within the current selection is to be enabled.

`mcActionGetPlaySelection`

Your application can use this action to determine whether a movie has been constrained to playing within its selection.

The parameter data must contain a pointer to a Boolean value. The movie controller sets this value to `true` if playing is constrained to the current selection. Otherwise, it sets the value to `false`.

mcActionSetUseBadge

Your application can use this action to enable or disable a movie's playback badge. If a controller's badge is enabled, then the badge is displayed whenever the controller is not visible. When the controller is visible, the badge is not displayed. If the badge is disabled, the badge is never displayed.

The parameter data must contain a Boolean value—a value of `true` indicates that the playback badge is to be enabled.

mcActionGetUseBadge

Your application can use this action to determine whether a controller is using a badge. If a controller's badge is enabled, then the badge is displayed whenever the controller is not visible. When the controller is visible, the badge is not displayed. If the badge is disabled, the badge is never displayed.

The parameter data must contain a pointer to a Boolean value. The movie controller sets this value to `true` if the controller is using a badge. Otherwise, it sets the value to `false`.

mcActionSetFlags

Your application can use this action to set a movie's control flags.

The parameter data must contain a long integer that contains the new control flag values. The following flags are defined:

mcFlagSuppressMovieFrame

Controls whether the controller displays a frame around the movie. If this flag is set to 1, the controller does not display a frame around the movie. By default, this flag is set to 0.

mcFlagSuppressStepButtons

Controls whether the controller displays the step buttons. The step buttons allow the user to step the movie forward or backward a frame at a time. If this flag is set to 1, the controller does not display the step buttons. By default, this flag is set to 0.

mcFlagSuppressSpeakerButton

Controls whether the controller displays the speaker button. The speaker button allows the user to control the movie's sound. If this flag is set to 1, the controller does not display the speaker button. By default, this flag is set to 0.

mcActionGetFlags

Your application can use this action to retrieve a movie's control flags.

The parameter data must contain a pointer to a long integer. The movie controller places the movie's control flags into that long integer. The following movie control flags are defined:

mcFlagSuppressMovieFrame

Controls whether the controller displays a frame around the movie. If this flag is set to 1, the controller does not display a frame around the movie. By default, this flag is set to 0.

`mcFlagSuppressStepButtons`
: Controls whether the controller displays the step buttons. The step buttons allow the user to step the movie forward or backward a frame at a time. If this flag is set to 1, the movie controller does not display the step buttons. By default, this flag is set to 0.

`mcFlagSuppressSpeakerButton`
: Controls whether the controller displays the speaker button. The speaker button allows the user to control the movie's sound. If this flag is set to 1, the movie controller does not display the speaker button. By default, this flag is set to 0.

`mcFlagsUseWindowPalette`
: Controls whether the controller manages the palette for the window containing the movie. This ensures that a movie's colors are reproduced as accurately as possible. This flag is particularly useful for movies with custom color tables. If this flag is set to 1, the movie controller does not manage the window palette. By default, this flag is set to 0.

`mcActionSetPlayEveryFrame`
: Your application can use this action to instruct the movie controller to play every frame in a movie. In this case, the movie controller may play the movie at a slower rate than you specify with the `mcActionPlay` action. However, the controller does not play the movie faster than the movie rate. In addition, the controller does not play the movie's sound tracks.

   The parameter data must contain a Boolean value—a value of `true` instructs the controller to play every frame in the movie, even if that means playing the movie at a slower rate than you previously specified.

`mcActionGetPlayEveryFrame`
: Your application can use this action to determine whether the movie controller has been instructed to play every frame in a movie. You tell the controller to play every frame by using the `mcActionSetPlayEveryFrame` action, which is described earlier in this section.

   The parameter data must contain a pointer to a Boolean value—the movie controller sets this value to `true` if the controller has been instructed to play every frame in the movie, even if that means playing the movie at a slower rate than you previously specified. Otherwise, the controller sets the value to `false`.

Movie Controller Components

`mcActionSetGrowBoundsBox`

> The parameter data must contain a pointer to a rectangle—set the rectangle to the boundary coordinates for the movie. If you want to prevent the movie from being resized, supply an empty rectangle (note that enabling or disabling the size box may change the appearance of some movie controllers). By default, movie controllers do not have size boxes. You must use this action to establish a size box for a movie controller.
>
> If the movie controller's boundary rectangle intersects the lower-right corner of your window, your window cannot have a size box.

`mcActionGetPlayRate`

> Your application can use this action to determine a movie's playback rate. You set the playback rate when you start a movie playing by using the `mcActionPlay` action.
>
> The parameter data must contain a pointer to a fixed value. The movie controller returns the movie's playback rate in that fixed value. Values greater than 0 correspond to forward rates; values less than 0 play the movie backward. A value of 0 indicates that the movie is stopped.

`mcActionBadgeClick`

> Indicates that the badge was clicked. The parameter is a pointer to a Boolean value. On entry, the Boolean is set to `true`. Set the Boolean to `false` if you want the controller to ignore the click in the badge.

`mcActionMovieClick`

> Indicates that the movie was clicked. The parameter is a pointer to an event structure containing the mouse-down event. If you want the controller to ignore the mouse-down event, change the `what` field of the event structure to a null event.

`mcActionSuspend`

> Indicates that a suspend event has been received. There is no parameter.

`mcActionResume`

> Indicates that a resume event has been received. There is no parameter.

Actions for Use by Action-Filter Functions

`mcActionIdle`

> Your action filter function receives this action when the application has granted null event-processing time to the movie controller.
>
> There are no parameters for this action.

`mcActionDraw`

> Your filter function receives this action when the controller has received an update event.
>
> The parameter for this action is a pointer to a window.

`mcActionActivate`

> Your filter function receives this action when the controller has received an activate or resume event.
>
> There are no parameters for this action.

Movie Controller Components

`mcActionDeactivate`
: Your filter function receives this action when the controller has received a deactivate or suspend event.

  There are no parameters for this action.

`mcActionMouseDown`
: Your action filter function receives this action when the movie controller has received a mouse-down event.

  The parameter data must contain a pointer to an event structure—the `message` field in the event structure must specify the window in which the user clicked.

`mcActionKey`
: Your action filter function receives this action when the movie controller has received a key-down or auto-key event.

  The parameter data must contain a pointer to an event structure that describes the key event.

`mcActionPlay`
: Your action filter receives this action when the movie controller has received a request to start or stop playing a movie.

  The parameter data must contain a fixed value that indicates the rate of play. Values greater than 0 correspond to forward rates; values less than 0 play the movie backward. A value of 0 stops the movie.

`mcActionGotoTime`
: Your action filter function receives this action when the movie controller has received a request to go to a specified time in the movie.

  The parameter data must contain a pointer to a time structure that specifies the target position in the movie.

`mcActionSetVolume`
: Your action filter function receives this action when the movie controller has received a request to set the movie's volume.

  The parameter data must contain a pointer to a 16-bit, fixed-point number that indicates the relative volume of the movie. Volume values range from –1.0 to 1.0. Negative values play no sound but preserve the absolute value of the volume setting.

`mcActionGetVolume`
: Your action filter function receives this action when the movie controller has received a request to retrieve the movie's volume.

  The parameter data must contain a pointer to a 16-bit, fixed-point number that indicates the relative volume of the movie. Volume values range from –1.0 to 1.0. Negative values play no sound but preserve the absolute value of the volume setting.

Movie Controller Components Reference

`mcActionStep`
: Your action filter function receives this action when the movie controller has received a request to play a movie while advancing a specified number of frames at a time.

    The parameter data must contain a long integer value that specifies the number of steps (that is, the frames and the play direction). Positive values step the movie forward the specified number of frames; negative values step the movie backward. A value of 0 steps the movie forward one frame.

`mcActionSetLooping`
: Your action filter function receives this action when the movie controller has received a request to turn looping on or off.

    The parameter data must contain a Boolean value—a value of `true` indicates that looping is to be enabled.

`mcActionGetLooping`
: Your action filter function receives this action when the controller has received a request to indicate whether looping is enabled for its movie.

    The parameter data must contain a pointer to a Boolean value. The movie controller sets this value to `true` if looping is enabled for the movie that is assigned to this controller. Otherwise, it sets the value to `false`.

`mcActionSetLoopIsPalindrome`
: Your action filter function receives this action when the movie controller has received a request to turn palindrome looping on or off. Palindrome looping causes a movie to play alternately forward and backward. Looping must also be enabled for palindrome looping to take effect.

    The parameter data must contain a Boolean value—a value of `true` indicates that palindrome looping is to be enabled.

`mcActionGetLoopIsPalindrome`
: Your action filter function receives this action when the controller has received a request to indicate whether palindrome looping is enabled for its movie.

    The parameter data must contain a pointer to a Boolean value. The movie controller sets this value to `true` if palindrome looping is enabled for the movie that is assigned to this controller. Otherwise, it sets the value to `false`.

`mcActionControllerSizeChanged`
: Your filter function receives this action when the user has resized the movie controller—the controller component issues this action before it updates the screen, allowing your application to change the controller's location or appearance before the user sees the resized controller.

    There are no parameters for this action.

    Note
    Your application should never use this action. ◆

Movie Controller Components

`mcActionSetSelectionBegin`

Your action filter function receives this action when the movie controller has received a request to set the movie's current selection start time.

The parameter data must contain a pointer to a time structure specifying the starting time of the movie's current selection.

`mcActionSetSelectionDuration`

Your action filter function receives this action when the movie controller has received a request to set the movie's current selection duration.

The parameter data must contain a pointer to a time structure specifying the ending time of the movie's current selection.

`mcActionSetKeysEnabled`

Your action filter function receives this action when the movie controller has received a request to enable or disable keystrokes.

The parameter data must contain a Boolean value—a value of `true` indicates that keystrokes are to be enabled. By default, this value is set to `false`.

`mcActionGetKeysEnabled`

Your filter function receives this action when the controller has received a request to indicate whether keystrokes are enabled for its movie.

The parameter data must contain a pointer to a Boolean value. The movie controller sets this value to `true` if keystrokes are enabled for the movie that is assigned to this controller. Otherwise, it sets the value to `false`.

`mcActionSetPlaySelection`

Your action filter function receives this action when the movie controller has received a request to constrain playing to the current selection.

The parameter data must contain a Boolean value—a value of `true` indicates that playing within the current selection is to be enabled.

`mcActionGetPlaySelection`

Your action filter function receives this action when the movie controller has received a request to indicate whether playing is constrained to the current selection.

The parameter data must contain a pointer to a Boolean value. The movie controller sets this value to `true` if playing is constrained to the current selection. Otherwise, it sets the value to `false`.

`mcActionSetUseBadge`

Your action filter function receives this action when the movie controller has received a request to turn the playback badge on or off.

The parameter data must contain a Boolean value—a value of `true` indicates that the playback badge is to be enabled.

`mcActionGetUseBadge`

Your action filter function receives this action when the controller has received a request to indicate whether it is using a badge during playback.

The parameter data must contain a pointer to a Boolean value. The movie controller sets this value to `true` if the controller is using a badge. Otherwise, it sets the value to `false`.

CHAPTER 2

Movie Controller Components

`mcActionSetFlags`
: Your action filter function receives this action when the movie controller has received a request to set the movie's control flags.

  The parameter data must contain a long integer that contains the new control flag values. The following flags are defined:

  `mcFlagSuppressMovieFrame`
  : Controls whether the controller displays a frame around the movie. If this flag is set to 1, the controller does not display a frame around the movie. By default, this flag is set to 0.

  `mcFlagSuppressStepButtons`
  : Controls whether the controller displays the step buttons. The step buttons allow the user to step the movie forward or backward a frame at a time. If this flag is set to 1, the controller does not display the step buttons. By default, this flag is set to 0.

  `mcFlagSuppressSpeakerButton`
  : Controls whether the controller displays the speaker button. The speaker button allows the user to control the movie's sound. If this flag is set to 1, the controller does not display the speaker button. By default, this flag is set to 0.

`mcActionGetFlags`
: Your action filter function receives this action when the movie controller has received a request to retrieve the movie's control flags.

  The parameter data must contain a pointer to a long integer. The movie controller places the movie's control flags into that long integer. The following movie control flags are defined:

  `mcFlagSuppressMovieFrame`
  : Controls whether the controller displays a frame around the movie. If this flag is set to 1, the controller does not display a frame around the movie. By default, this flag is set to 0.

  `mcFlagSuppressStepButtons`
  : Controls whether the controller displays the step buttons. The step buttons allow the user to step the movie forward or backward a frame at a time. If this flag is set to 1, the movie controller does not display the step buttons. By default, this flag is set to 0.

  `mcFlagSuppressSpeakerButton`
  : Controls whether the controller displays the speaker button. The speaker button allows the user to control the movie's sound. If this flag is set to 1, the movie controller does not display the speaker button. By default, this flag is set to 0.

Movie Controller Components

`mcFlagsUseWindowPalette`
Controls whether the controller manages the palette for the window containing the movie. This ensures that a movie's colors are reproduced as accurately as possible. This flag is particularly useful for movies with custom color tables. If this flag is set to 1, the movie controller does not manage the window palette. By default, this flag is set to 0.

`mcActionSetPlayEveryFrame`

Your action filter function receives this action when the movie controller has received a request to play every frame in a movie.

The parameter data must contain a Boolean value—a value of `true` instructs the controller to play every frame in the movie, even if that means playing the movie at a slower rate than you previously specified.

`mcActionGetPlayEveryFrame`

Your action filter function receives this action when the movie controller has received a request to indicate whether it has been instructed to play every frame in a movie.

The parameter data must contain a pointer to a Boolean value—the movie controller sets this value to `true` if the controller has been instructed to play every frame in the movie, even if that means playing the movie at a slower rate than you previously specified. Otherwise, the controller sets the value to `false`.

`mcActionSetGrowBoundsBox`

Your action filter function receives this action when the movie controller has received a request to set the limits for resizing the movie.

The parameter data contains a pointer to a rectangle—the rectangle defines the boundary coordinates for the movie. If the rectangle is empty, the application wants to disable the size box. You may change the appearance of your controller in response to such a request.

`mcActionShowBalloon`

Your action filter function receives this action when the controller wants to display Balloon Help. Your filter function instructs the controller whether to display the Balloon Help. This action allows you to override the movie controller's default Balloon Help behavior.

The parameter data contains a pointer to a Boolean value. Set the value to `true` to display the appropriate Balloon Help. Otherwise, set the value to `false`.

Note
Your application should never use this action. ◆

Movie Controller Functions

This section describes the functions that are supported by movie controller components. It is divided into the following topics:

- "Associating Movies With Controllers," which describes the movie controller component functions that allow applications to assign movies to controllers
- "Managing Controller Attributes," which discusses the movie controller component functions that allow applications to alter the display characteristics of the controller
- "Handling Movie Events," which discusses the movie controller component functions that applications use to handle movie actions
- "Editing Movies," which describes the movie controller component functions that help applications edit movies
- "Getting and Setting Movie Controller Time," which discusses the movie component controller functions that allow applications to get and set movie controller time information
- "Customizing Event Processing," which describes movie controller component functions that allow applications to perform customized event processing

These functions are discussed from the perspective of the developer of an application that uses movie controllers. If you are developing a movie controller component, your component must behave as described here.

Associating Movies With Controllers

Once your application has established a connection to a movie controller component, you may associate one movie with a movie controller. By default, the new controller has editing and keystroke processing turned off.

You create a new movie controller and assign it to a movie by calling the `NewMovieController` function. This is the easiest way to use a movie controller component.

If you want to exert more control over the assignment of movies to controllers, you can use other movie controller functions. If you want to assign a movie to an existing controller, you can use the `MCNewAttachedController` function. Use the `MCSetMovie` function to assign a movie to or remove a movie from a controller. You can use the `MCGetMovie` function to retrieve a reference to the movie that is assigned to a controller.

When you are done with a controller, use the `DisposeMovieController` function to dispose of the controller.

CHAPTER 2

Movie Controller Components

NewMovieController

The `NewMovieController` function locates a movie controller component for you and assigns a movie to that controller. This function always creates a controller that is attached to a movie.

This function is actually implemented by the Movie Toolbox, not by movie controller components. If you are creating your own movie controller component, you do not need to support this function.

```
pascal MovieController NewMovieController (Movie theMovie,
                                    const Rect *movieRect,
                                    long someFlags);
```

theMovie　　Identifies the movie to be associated with the movie controller.

movieRect　　Points to the display rectangle that is to contain the movie and its controller.

someFlags　　Contains flags that control the operation. If you set these flags to 0, the movie controller component centers the movie in the rectangle specified by the `movieRect` parameter and scales the movie to fit in that rectangle. The control portion of the controller is also placed within that rectangle. You may control how the movie and the control are drawn by setting one or more of the following flags to 1:

　　mcTopLeftMovie

　　　　If this flag is set to 1, the movie controller component places the movie into the upper-left corner of the display rectangle specified by the `movieRect` parameter. The component scales the movie to fit into the rectangle. Note that the control portion of the controller may fall outside of the rectangle, depending upon the results of the scaling operation.

　　mcScaleMovieToFit

　　　　If this flag is set to 1, the movie controller component resizes the movie to fit into the display rectangle specified by the `movieRect` parameter after it places the control portion of the controller into the rectangle.

　　　　If you set this flag and the `mcScaleMovieToFit` flag to 1, the movie controller component resizes the movie to fit into the specified rectangle and places the control portion of the controller outside of the rectangle.

　　mcWithBadge

　　　　Controls whether the movie controller uses a badge (see "Badges," which begins on page 2-6, for more information about movie badges). If you set this flag to 1, the movie controller component displays the movie with a badge whenever the controller portion is not displayed. If you set this flag to 0, the movie controller component does not use a badge.

CHAPTER 2

Movie Controller Components

mcNotVisible
: Controls whether the controller portion is visible. If you set this flag to 0, the movie controller component displays the controller along with the movie. If you set this flag to 1, the component does not display the controller. If you have set the mcWithBadge flag to 1, specifying that the component uses a badge, the component displays a badge whenever the controller is not visible.

mcWithFrame
: Specifies whether the component displays a frame around the movie as part of the controller. If you set this flag to 1, the component displays a frame around the movie, including the movie's name. If you set this flag to 0, the component does not display a frame as part of the controller.

DESCRIPTION

The `NewMovieController` function returns a movie controller identifier value. This value identifies a connection to a movie controller component, and it is a component instance.

MCNewAttachedController

The `MCNewAttachedController` function associates a specified movie with a movie controller.

```
pascal ComponentResult MCNewAttachedController (MovieController
                                                    mc, Movie theMovie,
                                                    WindowPtr w,
                                                    Point where);
```

mc
: Specifies the movie controller for the operation. You obtain this identifier from the Component Manager's `OpenComponent` or `OpenDefaultComponent` function.

theMovie
: Identifies the movie to be associated with the movie controller.

w
: Identifies the window in which the movie is to be displayed. The movie controller component sets the movie's graphics world to match this window. If you set the w parameter to `nil`, the component uses the current window.

where
: Specifies the upper-left corner of the movie within the window specified by the w parameter. The movie controller component uses the movie's boundary rectangle to determine the size of the movie (the Movie Toolbox's `GetMovieBox` function returns this rectangle).

CHAPTER 2

Movie Controller Components

DESCRIPTION

The `MCNewAttachedController` function forces the controller to be attached to the movie and sets the controller to be visible.

MCSetMovie

The `MCSetMovie` function associates a movie with a specified movie controller.

```
pascal ComponentResult MCSetMovie (MovieController mc,
                                    Movie theMovie,
                                    WindowPtr movieWindow,
                                    Point where);
```

mc
: Specifies the movie controller for the operation. You obtain this identifier from the Component Manager's `OpenComponent` or `OpenDefaultComponent` function, or from the `NewMovieController` function (described on page 2-29).

theMovie
: Identifies the movie to be associated with the movie controller. Set this value to `nil` to remove the movie from the controller.

movieWindow
: Identifies the window in which the movie is to be displayed. The movie controller component sets the movie's graphics world to match this window. If you set the w parameter to `nil`, the component uses the current window.

where
: Specifies the upper-left corner of the movie within the window specified by the `movieWindow` parameter. The movie controller component uses the movie's boundary rectangle to determine the size of the movie (the Movie Toolbox's `GetMovieBox` function returns this rectangle).

DESCRIPTION

You can also use the `MCSetMovie` function to remove a movie from its controller.

SEE ALSO

If you want to scale the movie, call the Movie Toolbox's `SetMovieBox` function (described in *Inside Macintosh: QuickTime*) before calling `MCSetMovie`.

CHAPTER 2

Movie Controller Components

MCGetMovie

The `MCGetMovie` function allows your application to retrieve the movie reference for a movie that is associated with a movie controller. The movie controller component returns the movie's identifier value.

```
pascal Movie MCGetMovie (MovieController mc);
```

mc   Specifies the movie controller for the operation. You obtain this identifier from the Component Manager's `OpenComponent` or `OpenDefaultComponent` function, or from the `NewMovieController` function (described on page 2-29).

DESCRIPTION

The `MCGetMovie` function returns the movie identifier for the movie that is assigned to the specified controller. If there is no movie assigned to the controller, the returned movie identifier is set to `nil`.

DisposeMovieController

The `DisposeMovieController` function disposes of a movie controller. Your application is responsible for disposing of the movie that is associated with the movie controller. Do not dispose of the movie before disposing of the controller.

```
pascal void DisposeMovieController (MovieController mc);
```

mc   Specifies the movie controller for the operation. You obtain this identifier from the Component Manager's `OpenComponent` or `OpenDefaultComponent` function, or from the `NewMovieController` function (described on page 2-29).

DESCRIPTION

The `DisposeMovieController` function is implemented by the Movie Toolbox, not by movie controller components. If you are creating your own movie controller component, you do not have to support this function.

CHAPTER 2

Movie Controller Components

Managing Controller Attributes

Movie controller components provide a number of functions that allow your application to control the display attributes of a movie controller. For example, you can detach the controller from its movie, so that the controller and movie can be managed as separate graphics entities. In addition, movie controller components provide a number of functions that allow you to work with a controller's boundary rectangles and regions. For a complete discussion of these rectangles and regions, see "Spatial Properties," which begins on page 2-6.

The `MCSetControllerAttached` function lets you control whether the movie controller is attached to its movie. The `MCIsControllerAttached` function allows you to determine if a controller is attached to its movie.

You can use the `MCSetControllerPort` and `MCGetControllerPort` functions to work a movie controller's graphics port.

The `MCSetVisible` and `MCGetVisible` functions enable you to control the visibility of the movie controller.

The `MCSetControllerBoundsRect` and `MCGetControllerBoundsRect` functions help you work with a movie controller's boundary rectangle. You can use the `MCGetControllerBoundsRgn` and `MCGetControllerWindowRgn` functions if the controller is not rectangular. You can position a controller and its movie separately by calling the `MCPositionController` function.

MCPositionController

The `MCPositionController` function allows you to control the position of a movie and its controller on the computer display.

```
pascal ComponentResult MCPositionController (MovieController mc,
                                    const Rect *movieRect,
                                    const Rect *controllerRect,
                                    long someFlags);
```

mc   Specifies the movie controller for the operation. You obtain this
            identifier from the Component Manager's `OpenComponent` or
            `OpenDefaultComponent` function, or from the `NewMovieController`
            function (described on page 2-29).

movieRect   Points to a `Rect` structure that specifies the coordinates of the movie's
            boundary rectangle. (For details on the `Rect` structure, see the chapter
            "Basic QuickDraw" in *Inside Macintosh: Imaging*.)

CHAPTER 2

Movie Controller Components

`controllerRect`
: Points to a `Rect` structure that specifies the coordinates of the controller's boundary rectangle. The movie controller component always centers the control portion of the controller inside this rectangle. The movie controller component only uses this parameter when the control portion of the controller is detached from the movie. If you are working with an attached controller, you can set this parameter to `nil`.

`someFlags`
: If you set these flags to 0, the movie controller component centers the movie in the rectangle specified by `movieRect` and scales the movie to fit in that rectangle. You may control how the movie is drawn by setting one or more of the following flags to 1:

    `mcTopLeftMovie`
    : If this flag is set to 1, the movie controller component places the movie into the upper-left corner of the display rectangle specified by the `movieRect` parameter. The component scales the movie to fit into the rectangle. Note that the control portion of the controller may fall outside of the rectangle, depending upon the results of the scaling operation.

    `mcScaleMovieToFit`
    : If this flag is set to 1, the movie controller component resizes the movie to fit into the display rectangle specified by the `movieRect` parameter after it places the control portion of the controller into the rectangle.

        If you set this flag and the `mcTopLeftMovie` flag to 1, the movie controller component resizes the movie to fit into the specified rectangle and places the control portion of the controller outside of the rectangle.

    `mcPositionDontInvalidate`
    : If this flag is set to 1, the movie controller component is requested not to invalidate areas of the window that are changed as a result of repositioning the movie or the controller. This flag is useful for applications that use the movie controller as part of a larger document. In particular, if the document is scrolled using QuickDraw's `ScrollRect` routine, optimal redrawing occurs (that is, scrolled areas are not redrawn) if this flag is set. For details on `ScrollRect`, see the chapter "Basic QuickDraw" in *Inside Macintosh: Imaging*.

DESCRIPTION

The `MCPositionController` function works with controllers that are attached to movies and controllers that are not attached to movies.

CHAPTER 2

Movie Controller Components

MCSetControllerAttached

The `MCSetControllerAttached` function allows your application to control whether a movie controller is attached to its movie or detached from it. "About Movie Controller Components," which begins on page 2-4, discusses the differences between attached and detached movie controllers.

```
pascal ComponentResult MCSetControllerAttached
                                (MovieController mc,
                                 Boolean attach);
```

mc Specifies the movie controller for the operation. You obtain this identifier from the Component Manager's `OpenComponent` or `OpenDefaultComponent` function, or from the `NewMovieController` function (described on page 2-29).

attach Specifies the action for this function. Set the `attach` parameter to `true` to cause the controller to be attached to its movie. Set this parameter to `false` to detach the controller from its movie.

DESCRIPTION

By default, a new movie controller is attached to its movie.

SPECIAL CONSIDERATIONS

Your application should not make any assumptions about the location of an attached movie controller with respect to its movie. The controller may be above, below, or surrounding the movie image.

SEE ALSO

If you need to know the location of the controller, you can use the `MCGetControllerBoundsRect` function, described on page 2-39, to obtain its boundary rectangle.

MCIsControllerAttached

The `MCIsControllerAttached` function returns a value that indicates whether a movie controller is attached to its movie.

```
pascal ComponentResult MCIsControllerAttached
                                (MovieController mc);
```

Movie Controller Components Reference

CHAPTER 2

Movie Controller Components

mc Specifies the movie controller for the operation. You obtain this identifier from the Component Manager's `OpenComponent` or `OpenDefaultComponent` function, or from the `NewMovieController` function (described on page 2-29).

DESCRIPTION

The `MCIsControllerAttached` function returns a `ComponentResult` value that indicates whether a movie controller is attached to its movie. If the controller is attached, the returned value is set to 1. If the controller is not attached, the returned value is set to 0.

SEE ALSO

You can use the `MCSetControllerAttached` function, described in the previous section, to attach or detach a movie controller.

MCSetVisible

The `MCSetVisible` function allows your application to control the visibility of a movie controller.

```
pascal ComponentResult MCSetVisible (MovieController mc,
                                      Boolean visible);
```

mc Specifies the movie controller for the operation. You obtain this identifier from the Component Manager's `OpenComponent` or `OpenDefaultComponent` function, or from the `NewMovieController` function (described on page 2-29).

visible Specifies the action for this function. Set the `visible` parameter to `true` to cause the controller to be visible. Set this parameter to `false` to make the controller invisible.

DESCRIPTION

Movie controller components support badges, which allow you to create a visual cue that helps the user distinguish between static images and images that represent movies. The movie controller component displays a badge in the movie image whenever the movie is visible but the control portion of the controller is not visible. To work with movie controller badges, you must use the `mcActionSetUseBadge` action, which is described in "Movie Controller Actions" beginning on page 2-15.

CHAPTER 2

Movie Controller Components

SPECIAL CONSIDERATIONS

By default, a new controller is hidden so that your application can freely set the display attributes before showing the controller to the user. You should note, however, that the `MCNewAttachedController` function (described on page 2-30) automatically sets the movie controller to be visible. Your application must make the controller visible before the user can work with its associated movie.

SEE ALSO

You can use the `MCGetVisible` function, described in the next section, to determine the visibility of a movie controller.

MCGetVisible

The `MCGetVisible` function returns a value that indicates whether a movie controller is visible.

```
pascal ComponentResult MCGetVisible (MovieController mc);
```

mc   Specifies the movie controller for the operation. You obtain this identifier from the Component Manager's `OpenComponent` or `OpenDefaultComponent` function, or from the `NewMovieController` function (described on page 2-29).

DESCRIPTION

The `MCGetVisible` function returns a `ComponentResult` value that indicates whether a movie controller is visible. If the controller is visible, the returned value is set to 1. If the controller is not showing, the returned value is set to 0.

SEE ALSO

Use the `MCSetVisible` function, described in the previous section, to change the visibility of a movie controller.

CHAPTER 2

Movie Controller Components

MCDrawBadge

The `MCDrawBadge` function allows you to display a controller's badge. This function places the badge in an appropriate location based on the location of the controller's movie.

```
pascal ComponentResult MCDrawBadge (MovieController mc,
                                    RgnHandle movieRgn,
                                    RgnHandle *badgeRgn);
```

mc
: Specifies the movie controller for the operation. You obtain this identifier from the Component Manager's `OpenComponent` or `OpenDefaultComponent` function, or from the `NewMovieController` function (described on page 2-29).

movieRgn
: Specifies the boundary region of the controller's movie.

badgeRgn
: Points to a region that is to receive information about the location of the badge—your application must dispose of this handle. The movie controller returns the region where the badge is displayed. If you are not interested in this information, you may set this parameter to `nil`.

DESCRIPTION

The `MCDrawBadge` function can be useful in circumstances where you are using a movie controller component but do not want to incur the overhead of having the QuickTime movie in memory all the time. This function allows you to display the badge without having to display the movie. In addition, you can use the badge region to perform mouse-down event testing.

MCSetControllerBoundsRect

The `MCSetControllerBoundsRect` function lets you change the position and size of a movie controller. A controller's boundary rectangle encloses the control portion of the controller. In addition, in cases where the movie is attached to the controller, the boundary rectangle also encloses the movie. Note that changing the size of the boundary rectangle may result in the movie being resized as well, if the movie is attached to the controller.

```
pascal ComponentResult MCSetControllerBoundsRect
                                    (MovieController mc,
                                     const Rect *bounds);
```

mc
: Specifies the movie controller for the operation. You obtain this identifier from the Component Manager's `OpenComponent` or `OpenDefaultComponent` function, or from the `NewMovieController` function (described on page 2-29).

CHAPTER 2

Movie Controller Components

bounds   Points to a rectangle structure that contains the new boundary rectangle for the movie controller.

DESCRIPTION

Movie controller components can reject your request for a number of reasons. For example, some movie controller components may support only fixed-size controllers or controllers whose size is fixed in one dimension. Also, note that your application cannot change the location of an attached controller.

The movie controller component returns a value of `controllerBoundsNotExact` if the boundary rectangle has been changed but does not correspond to the rectangle you specified. In this case, the new boundary rectangle is always smaller than the requested rectangle.

RESULT CODES

`controllerBoundsNotExact`	–9996	Controller has altered the bounds you supplied
`controllerHasFixedHeight`	–9998	You cannot change the height of this controller
`cannotMoveAttachedController`	–9999	You cannot move an attached controller

SEE ALSO

To find the dimensions of the new boundary rectangle, call the `MCGetControllerBoundsRect` function, described in the next section.

MCGetControllerBoundsRect

The `MCGetControllerBoundsRect` function returns a movie controller's boundary rectangle. This rectangle reflects the size and location of the controller even if the controller is currently hidden. If the controller is detached from its movie, the rectangle encompasses only the controller, not the movie. If the controller is attached to its movie, the rectangle encompasses both the controller and the movie.

```
pascal ComponentResult MCGetControllerBoundsRect
                                    (MovieController mc,
                                     Rect *bounds);
```

mc   Specifies the movie controller for the operation. You obtain this identifier from the Component Manager's `OpenComponent` or `OpenDefaultComponent` function, or from the `NewMovieController` function (described on page 2-29).

Movie Controller Components

bounds Contains a pointer to a rect structure that is to receive the coordinates of the movie controller's boundary rectangle. If there is insufficient screen space to display the controller, the function may return an empty rectangle.

DESCRIPTION

The returned rectangle is the boundary rectangle for the region occupied by the controller and its movie (if the movie is attached to the controller), even if the controller is not rectangular.

SPECIAL CONSIDERATIONS

Note that if the controller cannot obtain enough screen space, the movie controller component may return an empty rectangle.

SEE ALSO

You can use the MCGetControllerBoundsRgn function, described in the next section, to obtain the boundary region for a controller. You can use the MCGetWindowRgn function, described on page 2-41, to determine the portion of the window that is currently in use by the controller.

MCGetControllerBoundsRgn

Some movie controllers may not be rectangular in shape. The MCGetControllerBoundsRgn function returns the actual region occupied by the controller and its movie, if the movie is attached to the controller. If the movie is not attached to its controller, the boundary region encloses only the control portion of the controller. The rectangle returned by the MCGetControllerBoundsRect function (described in the previous section) bounds the region returned by MCGetControllerBoundsRgn.

```
pascal RgnHandle MCGetControllerBoundsRgn (MovieController mc);
```

mc Specifies the movie controller for the operation. You obtain this identifier from the Component Manager's OpenComponent or OpenDefaultComponent function, or from the NewMovieController function.

CHAPTER 2

Movie Controller Components

DESCRIPTION

As with the `MCGetControllerBoundsRect` function, the `MCGetControllerBoundsRgn` function returns a region that reflects the size, shape, and location of the controller, even if the controller is hidden. Your application must dispose of the returned region.

The `MCGetControllerBoundsRgn` function returns a handle to the boundary region. Your application must dispose of this region.

RESULT CODES

Memory Manager errors

SEE ALSO

You can use the `MCGetWindowRgn` function, described in the next section, to determine the portion of the window that is currently in use by the controller.

MCGetWindowRgn

The `MCGetWindowRgn` function allows your application to determine the window region that is actually in use by a controller and its movie. The region returned by this function contains only the visible portions of the controller and its movie.

```
pascal RgnHandle MCGetWindowRgn (MovieController mc, WindowPtr w);
```

mc   Specifies the movie controller for the operation. You obtain this identifier from the Component Manager's `OpenComponent` or `OpenDefaultComponent` function, or from the `NewMovieController` function (described on page 2-29).

w   Identifies the window in which the movie controller and its movie are displayed, if the control portion of the controller is attached to the movie. If the controller is detached and in a separate window from the movie, specify one of the windows.

DESCRIPTION

The returned region may consist of several discontiguous areas. For example, if a controller is detached from its movie, the window region may define separate areas for the movie and the controller. If you want to consider just the controller, you must subtract the movie from the returned region.

Your application must dispose of the returned region.

The `MCGetWindowRgn` function returns a handle to the window region. Your application must dispose of this region.

CHAPTER 2

Movie Controller Components

RESULT CODES

Memory Manager errors

SEE ALSO

You can control the clipping region that is applied to the controller by calling the `MCSetClip` function, which is described in the next section.

MCSetClip

The `MCSetClip` function allows you to set a movie controller's clipping region. This clipping region is equivalent to the movie display clipping region supported by the Movie Toolbox.

```
pascal ComponentResult MCSetClip (MovieController mc,
                                  RgnHandle theClip,
                                  RgnHandle movieClip);
```

mc
: Specifies the movie controller for the operation. You obtain this identifier from the Component Manager's `OpenComponent` or `OpenDefaultComponent` function, or from the `NewMovieController` function (described on page 2-29).

theClip
: Contains a handle to a region that defines the controller's clipping region. This clipping region affects the entire movie controller and its movie, including the controller's badge and associated controls. Set this parameter to `nil` to clear the controller's clipping region.

movieClip
: Contains a handle to a region that defines the clipping region of the controller's movie. This clipping region affects only the movie and the badge, not the movie controller. Set this parameter to `nil` to clear the movie clipping region.

DESCRIPTION

Your application must dispose of the regions you supply to the `MCSetClip` function.

SPECIAL CONSIDERATIONS

Do not use the Movie Toolbox's `SetMovieDisplayClipRgn` function to modify movies that are associated with movie controllers.

RESULT CODES

Memory Manager errors

CHAPTER 2

Movie Controller Components

SEE ALSO

You can retrieve information about a controller's clipping information by calling the `MCGetClip` function, which is described in the next section.

MCGetClip

The `MCGetClip` function allows you to obtain information describing a movie controller's clipping regions.

```
pascal ComponentResult MCGetClip (MovieController mc,
                                  RgnHandle *theClip,
                                  RgnHandle *movieClip);
```

mc
: Specifies the movie controller for the operation. You obtain this identifier from the Component Manager's `OpenComponent` or `OpenDefaultComponent` function, or from the `NewMovieController` function (described on page 2-29).

theClip
: Contains a pointer to a field that is to receive a handle to the clipping region of the entire movie controller. You must dispose of this region when you are done with it. If you are not interested in this information, you may set this parameter to `nil`.

movieClip
: Contains a pointer to a field that is to receive a handle to the clipping region of the controller's movie. You must dispose of this region when you are done with it. If you are not interested in this information, you may set this parameter to `nil`.

RESULT CODES

Memory Manager errors

SEE ALSO

You can set a controller's clipping information by calling the `MCSetClip` function, which is described in the previous section.

MCSetControllerPort

The `MCSetControllerPort` function allows your application to set the graphics port for a movie controller. You can use this function to place a movie and its associated movie controller in different graphics ports. If you are using an attached controller, both the controller and the movie's graphics ports are changed. If you are using a detached

CHAPTER 2

Movie Controller Components

controller, this function changes only the graphics port of the control portion of the controller. You must use the Movie Toolbox's `SetMovieGWorld` function followed by the `MCMovieChanged` function to change other portions.

```
pascal ComponentResult MCSetControllerPort (MovieController mc,
                                            CGrafPtr gp);
```

mc Specifies the movie controller for the operation. You obtain this identifier from the Component Manager's `OpenComponent` or `OpenDefaultComponent` function, or from the `NewMovieController` function (described on page 2-29).

gp Points to the new graphics port for the movie controller. Set this parameter to `nil` to use the current graphics port.

DESCRIPTION

The movie controller component may use the foreground and background colors from the graphics port at the time the `MCSetController` function is called to colorize the movie controller.

Movie controller components use the `MCSetControllerPort` function each time you create a new movie controller. Hence, your component must be set to a valid port before creating a new movie controller.

MCGetControllerPort

The `MCGetControllerPort` function returns a movie controller's color graphics port.

```
pascal CGrafPtr MCGetControllerPort (MovieController mc);
```

mc Specifies the movie controller for the operation. You obtain this identifier from the Component Manager's `OpenComponent` or `OpenDefaultComponent` function, or from the `NewMovieController` function (described on page 2-29).

Handling Movie Events

Movie controller components provide functions that handle movie controller actions. Your application must call these functions whenever an event occurs. Consider this event loop:

```
#if whatIsHandleEvent
   while (! gDoneFlag) {
      gResult = GetNextEvent (everyEvent, &gEventRec);
      if (( MCIsPlayerEvent(gMCPlay, &gEventRec) == 0 )) {
         if (gResult) {
```

Movie Controller Components

```
            /* player didn't handle the event */
            HandleEvent(gEventRec);
         }
      }
   }
#endif

#if 0
/* interface for application-defined routine: */
pascal Boolean MyPlayerFilter ( MovieController mc,
                                 short* action, long* params);
#endif
```

If the movie controller component handles the event, your application can loop to wait for the next event. Otherwise, your application must take care of the event as part of its normal event handling.

Movie controller components support an action filter. You can instruct the filter to invoke a function in your application whenever actions occur. This action filter function can then perform specialized processing or refer the action back to the movie controller component. The actions supported by movie controller components are discussed in "Movie Controller Actions," which begins on page 2-15.

The `MCIsPlayerEvent` function lets you pass events to a movie controller component. The `MCSetActionFilterWithRefCon` function allows you to specify your action filter function for a movie controller.

You can use the `MCDoAction` function to request action processing from a movie controller.

If you use any Movie Toolbox functions to change the characteristics of a movie that is associated with a movie controller, you must inform the movie controller—use the `MCMovieChanged` function.

You can obtain information about the current state of the movie controller and its movie by calling the `MCGetControllerInfo` function.

MCIsPlayerEvent

The `MCIsPlayerEvent` function handles all events for a movie controller. Your application should call this function in its main event loop. Call `MCIsPlayerEvent` for each active movie controller until the event is handled.

This function returns a long integer indicating whether the movie controller component handled the event. The component sets this long integer to 1 if it handled the event. Your application should then skip the rest of its event loop and wait for the next event. The return value is 0 otherwise. Your application must then handle the event as part of its normal event processing.

CHAPTER 2

Movie Controller Components

The movie controller component does everything necessary to support the movie controller and its associated movie. For example, the component calls the Movie Toolbox's `MoviesTask` function for each movie. The movie controller component also handles suspend and resume events. It treats suspend events as deactivate requests and resume events as activate requests.

You can provide an action filter function that is called by the movie controller component. See "Application-Defined Function," which begins on page 2-61, for details. The component calls your filter function after it decides to process a particular action, but before it actually does so. In this manner, your application can perform custom action processing for a movie controller. Set your action filter function with the `MCSetActionFilterWithRefCon` function, described on page 2-47.

```
pascal ComponentResult MCIsPlayerEvent (MovieController mc,
                                        const EventRecord *e);
```

mc Specifies the movie controller for the operation. You obtain this identifier from the Component Manager's `OpenComponent` or `OpenDefaultComponent` function, or from the `NewMovieController` function (described on page 2-29).

e Points to the current event structure.

DESCRIPTION

The `MCIsPlayerEvent` function returns a long integer indicating whether it handled the event. If the movie controller component handled the event, this function sets the returned value to 1. Your application should then skip the rest of its event loop and wait for the next event. If the component did not handle the event, the `MCIsPlayerEvent` function returns a value of 0. Your application must then handle the event.

MCDoAction

Your application can use the `MCDoAction` function to invoke a movie controller component and have it perform a specified action.

```
pascal ComponentResult MCDoAction (MovieController mc,
                                   short action, void *params;
```

mc Specifies the movie controller for the operation. You obtain this identifier from the Component Manager's `OpenComponent` or `OpenDefaultComponent` function, or from the `NewMovieController` function.

action Specifies the action to be taken. See "Movie Controller Actions," which begins on page 2-15, for descriptions of the actions supported by movie controller components.

Movie Controller Components

params   Points to the parameter data appropriate to the action. See the individual action descriptions in "Movie Controller Actions," which begins on page 2-15, for information about the parameters required for each supported action.

DESCRIPTION

For example, your application might define a menu item that stops all currently playing movies. When the user selects this menu item, your application could use the `MCDoAction` function to instruct each controller to stop playing. You would do so by specifying an `mcActionPlay` action with the parameters set to 0 to indicate that the controller should stop playing the movie.

MCSetActionFilterWithRefCon

The `MCSetActionFilterWithRefCon` function allows your application to establish an action filter function for a movie controller. The movie controller component calls your action filter function each time the component receives an action for its movie controller. Your filter function is then free to handle the action or to refer it back to the movie controller component. If you refer it back to the movie controller component, the component handles the action. See "Movie Controller Actions," which begins on page 2-15, for a description of the actions supported by movie controller components.

```
pascal ComponentResult MCSetActionFilterWithRefCon
                                (MovieController mc,
                                 MCActionFilter filter,
                                 long refCon);
```

mc   Specifies the movie controller for the operation. You obtain this identifier from the Component Manager's `OpenComponent` or `OpenDefaultComponent` function, or from the `NewMovieController` function (described on page 2-29).

filter   Points to your action filter function. Set this parameter to `nil` to remove your action filter function.

refCon   Contains a reference constant value. The movie controller component passes this reference constant to your action filter function each time it calls your function.

DESCRIPTION

Movie controller components allow your application to field movie controller actions. You define an action filter function in your application and assign it to a controller by calling the `MCSetActionFilterWithRefCon` function.

You can use the constants described in "Movie Controller Actions," which begins on page 2-15, to refer to movie controller actions.

Movie Controller Components

If your filter function handles an action, you can handle the action in any way you desire. For example, your filter function could change the operation of movie controller buttons. More commonly, applications use the action filter function to monitor actions of the controller. For instance, your filter function might enable you to find out when the user clicks the play button, so that your application can enable appropriate menu selections. Alternatively, you can use the filter function to detect when the user resizes the movie.

SEE ALSO

If you use any Movie Toolbox functions that modify the movie in your action filter function, be sure to call the `MCMovieChanged` function (described on page 2-49).

MCGetControllerInfo

Your application can use the `MCGetControllerInfo` function to determine the current status of a movie controller and its associated movie. You can use this information to control your application's menu highlighting.

```
pascal ComponentResult MCGetControllerInfo (MovieController mc,
                                            long *someFlags);
```

mc
: Specifies the movie controller for the operation. You obtain this identifier from the Component Manager's `OpenComponent` or `OpenDefaultComponent` function, or from the `NewMovieController` function (described on page 2-29).

someFlags
: Contains a pointer to flags that specify the current status and capabilities of the controller. The following flags are defined (more than one flag may be set to 1):

  mcInfoUndoAvailable
  : The user has edited the movie. If this flag is set to 1, you can call the `MCUndo` function (described on page 2-54).

  mcInfoCutAvailable
  : The user has selected some material in the movie and editing is enabled. If this flag is set to 1, you can call the `MCCut` function (described on page 2-52).

  mcInfoCopyAvailable
  : The user has selected some material in the movie. If this flag is set to 1, you can call the `MCCopy` function (described on page 2-52).

Movie Controller Components

mcInfoPasteAvailable
: There is movie data in the scrap and editing is enabled. If this flag is set to 1, you can call the `MCPaste` function (described on page 2-53).

    If your application maintains a private scrap, this flag does not reflect the state of that scrap.

mcInfoClearAvailable
: The user has selected some material in the movie and editing is enabled. If this flag is set to 1, you can call the `MCClear` function (described on page 2-54).

mcInfoHasSound
: The movie has sound. If this flag is set to 1, the controller can play a movie's sound.

mcInfoIsPlaying
: If this flag is set to 1, the movie is playing.

mcInfoIsLooping
: The controller is currently set to play its movie repeatedly. If this flag is set to 1, the movie is looping.

mcInfoIsInPalindrome
: The controller is currently set to play its movie repeatedly, alternating between forward and backward playback. If this flag is set to 1, the movie is in palindrome looping mode.

mcInfoEditingEnabled
: The user can edit the movie associated with this controller. If this flag is set to 1, you have enabled editing by calling the `MCEnableEditing` function (described on page 2-50).

MCMovieChanged

The `MCMovieChanged` function lets you inform a movie controller component that your application has used the Movie Toolbox to change the characteristics of its associated movie.

```
pascal ComponentResult MCMovieChanged (MovieController mc,
                                        Movie theMovie);
```

mc
: Specifies the movie controller for the operation. You obtain this identifier from the Component Manager's `OpenComponent` or `OpenDefaultComponent` function, or from the `NewMovieController` function (described on page 2-29).

theMovie
: Identifies the movie that has been changed.

Movie Controller Components Reference

CHAPTER 2

Movie Controller Components

DESCRIPTION

Your application should be able to make most movie changes using the `MCDoAction` function (described on page 2-46). However, if your application uses Movie Toolbox functions to change the characteristics of a movie that is associated with a movie controller, you must inform the controller so that it can update itself accordingly. For instance, if your application changes the size of the movie without informing the movie controller component, the control portion of the controller may no longer be the proper size for the movie.

RESULT CODES

Memory Manager errors

Editing Movies

Movie controller components can provide editing capabilities. This section describes the functions that your application can use to alter movies that are associated with movie controllers.

Your application can use the `MCEnableEditing` function to enable editing for a specified movie controller. Movie controller components may return an error code indicating that editing is not supported. Use the `MCIsEditingEnabled` function to find out if editing is enabled for a specified controller.

The `MCCopy`, `MCCut`, `MCPaste`, `MCClear`, and `MCUndo` functions support normal editing operations on movies associated with movie controllers. These functions operate on the current movie selection.

Two functions are also provided that facilitate work with Edit menus. You can use the `MCSetUpEditMenu` function to highlight and name the items in the Edit menu for your application. The `MCGetMenuString` function is provided for you to use with a non-standard Edit menu.

MCEnableEditing

The `MCEnableEditing` function allows your application to enable and disable editing for a movie controller. Once editing is enabled for a controller, the user may edit the movie associated with the controller.

```
pascal ComponentResult MCEnableEditing (MovieController mc,
                                        Boolean enabled);
```

Movie Controller Components

mc Specifies the movie controller for the operation. You obtain this identifier from the Component Manager's `OpenComponent` or `OpenDefaultComponent` function, or from the `NewMovieController` function (described on page 2-29).

enabled Specifies whether to enable or disable editing for the controller. Set this parameter to `true` to enable editing; set the `enabled` parameter to `false` to disable editing.

DESCRIPTION

By default, editing is turned off when you create a new movie controller. If you want to allow the user to edit, you must use the `MCEnableEditing` function to enable editing.

SPECIAL CONSIDERATIONS

Note that a movie controller component may not support editing. Therefore, your application should check the component result from this function before continuing with other movie-editing operations.

MCIsEditingEnabled

The `MCIsEditingEnabled` function allows your application to determine whether editing is currently enabled for a movie controller. The movie controller component returns a long value reflecting the edit state of the controller. Once editing is enabled for a controller, the user may edit the movie associated with the controller.

```
pascal long MCIsEditingEnabled (MovieController mc);
```

mc Specifies the movie controller for the operation. You obtain this identifier from the Component Manager's `OpenComponent` or `OpenDefaultComponent` function, or from the `NewMovieController` function (described on page 2-29).

DESCRIPTION

The `MCIsEditingEnabled` function returns a long integer that contains a value indicating the current edit state of the controller. This returned value is set to 1 if editing is enabled. This returned value is set to 0 if editing is disabled or if the controller component does not support editing.

CHAPTER 2

Movie Controller Components

MCCut

The `MCCut` function returns a copy of the current movie selection from the movie associated with a specified controller and then removes the current movie selection from the source movie. Your application is responsible for the returned movie. If you want to allow the user to paste the movie selection, use the Movie Toolbox's `PutMovieOnScrap` function to place the movie selection onto the scrap. Be sure to dispose of the movie afterward, using the Movie Toolbox's `DisposeMovie` function.

```
pascal Movie MCCut (MovieController mc);
```

mc Specifies the movie controller for the operation. You obtain this identifier from the Component Manager's `OpenComponent` or `OpenDefaultComponent` function, or from the `NewMovieController` function (described on page 2-29).

DESCRIPTION

The `MCCut` function returns a movie containing the current selection from the movie associated with the specified controller. If the user has not made a selection, the returned movie reference is set to `nil`.

SEE ALSO

The `MCCut` function is analogous to the Movie Toolbox's `CutMovieSelection` function.

MCCopy

The `MCCopy` function returns a copy of the current movie selection from the movie associated with a specified controller. The selection remains active after this operation. Your application is responsible for the returned movie.

If you want to allow the user to paste the movie selection, use the Movie Toolbox's `PutMovieOnScrap` function to place the movie selection onto the scrap. Be sure to dispose of the movie afterward, using the Movie Toolbox's `DisposeMovie` function.

```
pascal Movie MCCopy (MovieController mc);
```

mc Specifies the movie controller for the operation. You obtain this identifier from the Component Manager's `OpenComponent` or `OpenDefaultComponent` function, or from the `NewMovieController` function (described on page 2-29).

CHAPTER 2

Movie Controller Components

DESCRIPTION

The `MCCopy` function returns a movie containing the current selection from the movie associated with the specified controller. If the user has not made a selection, the returned movie reference is set to `nil`.

SEE ALSO

This function is analogous to the Movie Toolbox's `CopyMovieSelection` function.

MCPaste

The `MCPaste` function inserts a specified movie at the current movie time in the movie associated with a specified controller.

```
pascal ComponentResult MCPaste (MovieController mc,
                                Movie srcMovie);
```

mc Specifies the movie controller for the operation. You obtain this identifier from the Component Manager's `OpenComponent` or `OpenDefaultComponent` function, or from the `NewMovieController` function (described on page 2-29).

srcMovie Specifies the movie to be inserted into the current selection in the movie associated with the movie controller specified by the mc parameter. If you set this parameter to `nil`, the movie controller component retrieves the source movie from the scrap.

DESCRIPTION

All of the tracks from the source movie are placed in the destination movie. If the duration of the destination movie's current selection is 0, the source movie is inserted at the starting time of the current selection. If the current selection duration is nonzero, the function clears the current selection and then inserts the tracks from the source movie. After the paste operation, the current selection time is set to the start of the tracks that were inserted and the duration is set to the source movie's duration.

SEE ALSO

This function is analogous to the Movie Toolbox's `PasteMovieSelection` function.

SPECIAL CONSIDERATIONS

The preferred way to use the `MCPaste` function is to set the `srcMovie` parameter to `nil`. This causes the movie controller to use movie import components to paste other types of data than movies.

Movie Controller Components Reference

CHAPTER 2

Movie Controller Components

MCClear

The `MCClear` function removes the current movie selection from the movie associated with a specified controller.

```
pascal ComponentResult MCClear (MovieController mc);
```

mc   Specifies the movie controller for the operation. You obtain this identifier from the Component Manager's `OpenComponent` or `OpenDefaultComponent` function, or from the `NewMovieController` function.

DESCRIPTION

After removing the segment, the duration of the movie's current selection is set to 0. This function removes empty tracks from the resulting movie.

SEE ALSO

This function is analogous to the Movie Toolbox's `ClearMovieSelection` function.

MCUndo

The `MCUndo` function allows your application to discard the effects of the most recent edit operation.

```
pascal ComponentResult MCUndo (MovieController mc);
```

mc   Specifies the movie controller for the operation. You obtain this identifier from the Component Manager's `OpenComponent` or `OpenDefaultComponent` function, or from the `NewMovieController` function (described on page 2-29).

SEE ALSO

Your movie controller component could use the Movie Toolbox's edit state functions to implement this function. (See the chapter "Movie Toolbox" in *Inside Macintosh: QuickTime* for more information about the edit state functions.)

CHAPTER 2

Movie Controller Components

MCSetUpEditMenu

The `MCSetUpEditMenu` function correctly highlights and names the items in your application's Edit menu.

```
pascal ComponentResult MCSetUpEditMenu (MovieController mc,
                                        long modifiers,
                                        MenuHandle mh);
```

mc Specifies the movie controller for this operation. You obtain this identifier from the Component Manager's `OpenComponent` or `OpenDefaultComponent` function, or from the `NewMovieController` function.

modifiers Indicates the current modifiers from the mouse-down or key-down event to which you are responding.

mh Specifies a menu handler to your current Edit menu. The first six items in your Edit menu should be the standard editing commands: Undo, a blank line, Cut, Copy, Paste, and Clear.

DESCRIPTION

When your application is highlighting its menus, you should call `MCSetUpEditMenu` immediately before you use the Menu Manager's `MenuSelect` or `MenuKey` functions. For details on `MenuSelect` and `MenuKey`, see *Inside Macintosh: Macintosh Toolbox Essentials*.

MCGetMenuString

If your application has a non-standard Edit menu, you can use the `MCGetMenuString` function together with the `MCGetControllerInfo` function to assign names correctly to the items in your application's Edit menu.

```
pascal ComponentResult MCGetMenuString (MovieController mc,
                                        long modifiers,
                                        short item,
                                        Str255 aString);
```

mc Specifies the movie controller for this operation. You obtain this identifier from the Component Manager's `OpenComponent` or `OpenDefaultComponent` function, or from the `NewMovieController` function.

modifiers Indicates the current modifiers from the mouse-down or key-down event to which you are responding.

CHAPTER 2

Movie Controller Components

`item` Contains one of the appropriate movie controller Edit menu constants returned in the `aString` parameter.

`aString` Contains (on return) an appropriate string to set the menu item text. The following flags are available:

mcMenuUndo
: Contains the string to set the menu item text to the Undo command.

mcMenuCut Contains the string to set the menu item text to the Cut command.

mcMenuCopy
: Contains the string to set the menu item text to the Copy command.

mcMenuPaste
: Contains the string to set the menu item text to the Paste command.

mcMenuClear
: Contains the string to set the menu item text to the Clear command.

DESCRIPTION

The `MCGetMenuString` function is used by the `MCSetUpEditMenu` function, which is described in the previous section.

SEE ALSO

To highlight menu items, use the `MCGetControllerInfo` function, which is described on page 2-48, to determine which items should be enabled.

Getting and Setting Movie Controller Time

Movie controller components provide functions that allow your application to work with temporal aspects of movie controllers. You can use the `MCSetDuration` function to set the duration of a movie controller to some arbitrary value. The `MCGetCurrentTime` function lets you retrieve the time value represented by the indicator on the movie controller's slider.

MCSetDuration

The `MCSetDuration` function allows your application to set a controller's duration in the case where a controller does not have a movie associated with it.

```
pascal ComponentResult MCSetDuration (MovieController mc,
                                      TimeValue duration);
```

mc   Specifies the movie controller for the operation. You obtain this identifier from the Component Manager's `OpenComponent` or `OpenDefaultComponent` function, or from the `NewMovieController` function (described on page 2-29).

duration   Specifies the new duration for the movie. This duration value must be in the controller's time scale.

DESCRIPTION

The controller's duration remains at this new value until you assign a movie to the controller.

SEE ALSO

You can use the `MCGetCurrentTime` function, which is described in the next section, to obtain the time scale for the controller.

MCGetCurrentTime

Your application can use the `MCGetCurrentTime` function to obtain the time value represented by the indicator on the movie controller's slider. This time value is appropriate to the movie currently being affected by the movie controller. You can also obtain the time scale for this time value.

```
pascal TimeValue MCGetCurrentTime (MovieController mc,
                                   TimeScale *scale);
```

mc   Specifies the movie controller for the operation. You obtain this identifier from the Component Manager's `OpenComponent` or `OpenDefaultComponent` function, or from the `NewMovieController` function (described on page 2-29).

scale   Contains a pointer to a field that is to receive the time scale for the controller.

CHAPTER 2

Movie Controller Components

DESCRIPTION

The `MCGetCurrentTime` function returns the time value that corresponds to the current setting of the indicator on the movie controller's slider.

Customizing Event Processing

Movie controller components provide a number of functions that allow your application to customize event processing. If your application does not use the `MCIsPlayerEvent` function (described on page 2-45), you can use these functions to direct movie controller events to the appropriate movie controller component. The component then attempts to handle the event.

Your application obtains the values for many of the function parameters from the appropriate event structure.

Each function returns a value that indicates whether it handled the event. If the controller component completely handles the event, the function sets the return value to 1. If the controller component does not handle the event, the function sets the return value to 0. Your application must then handle the event.

MCActivate

Your application can use the `MCActivate` function in response to activate, deactivate, suspend, and resume events.

```
pascal ComponentResult MCActivate (MovieController mc,
                                    WindowPtr w,
                                    Boolean activate);
```

mc
: Specifies the movie controller for the operation. You obtain this identifier from the Component Manager's `OpenComponent` or `OpenDefaultComponent` function, or from the `NewMovieController` function (described on page 2-29).

w
: Specifies the window in which the event has occurred.

activate
: Indicates the nature of the event. Set this parameter to `true` for activate and resume events. Set it to `false` for deactivate and suspend events.

DESCRIPTION

The `MCActivate` function returns a value indicating whether it handled the event. The function sets the returned value to 1 if it handles the event. The function sets the returned value to 0 if it does not handle the event. In this case, your application is responsible for the event.

CHAPTER 2

Movie Controller Components

MCClick

Your application should call the `MCClick` function when the user clicks in a movie controller window.

```
pascal ComponentResult MCClick (MovieController mc, WindowPtr w,
                                Point where, long when,
                                long modifiers);
```

mc
: Specifies the movie controller for the operation. You obtain this identifier from the Component Manager's `OpenComponent` or `OpenDefaultComponent` function, or from the `NewMovieController` function (described on page 2-29).

w
: Specifies the window in which the event has occurred.

where
: Indicates the location of the click. This value is expressed in the local coordinates of the window specified by the w parameter. Your application must convert this value from the global coordinates returned in the event structure.

when
: Indicates when the user pressed the mouse button. You obtain this value from the event structure.

modifiers
: Specifies modifier flags for the event. You obtain this value from the event structure.

DESCRIPTION

The `MCClick` function returns a value indicating whether it handled the event. The function sets the returned value to 1 if it handles the event. The function sets the returned value to 0 if it does not handle the event. In this case, your application is responsible for the event.

MCDraw

Your application should call the `MCDraw` function in response to an update event. The movie controller component updates the movie controller if the controller is in the window that received the update event. The controller component updates the movie associated with the controller only if the movie is contained in the window that received the event.

```
pascal ComponentResult MCDraw (MovieController mc, WindowPtr w);
```

Movie Controller Components Reference

CHAPTER 2

Movie Controller Components

mc
Specifies the movie controller for the operation. You obtain this identifier from the Component Manager's `OpenComponent` or `OpenDefaultComponent` function, or from the `NewMovieController` function (described on page 2-29).

w
Points to the window in which the update event has occurred.

DESCRIPTION

The `MCDraw` function returns a value indicating whether it handled the event. The function sets the returned value to 1 if it handles the event. The function sets the returned value to 0 if it does not handle the event. In this case, your application is responsible for the event.

MCIdle

The `MCIdle` function performs idle processing for a movie controller. This idle processing includes calling the Movie Toolbox's `MoviesTask` function for each movie that is associated with the controller. Your application should call the `MCIdle` function as often as possible, in order to ensure consistent movie play behavior.

```
pascal ComponentResult MCIdle (MovieController mc);
```

mc
Specifies the movie controller for the operation. You obtain this identifier from the Component Manager's `OpenComponent` or `OpenDefaultComponent` function, or from the `NewMovieController` function (described on page 2-29).

DESCRIPTION

The `MCIdle` function returns a value indicating whether it handled the event. The function sets the returned value to 1 if it handles the event. The function sets the returned value to 0 if it does not handle the event. In this case, your application is responsible for the event.

Movie Controller Components

MCKey

The `MCKey` function handles keyboard events for a movie controller. You can call this function only if you have enabled keystroke processing in the controller. By default, keystroke processing is turned off when you create a movie controller. You can enable and disable keystroke processing using the `mcActionSetKeysEnabled` action with the `MCDoAction` function (described on page 2-46).

```
pascal ComponentResult MCKey (MovieController mc, char key,
                              long modifiers);
```

mc
: Specifies the movie controller for the operation. You obtain this identifier from the Component Manager's `OpenComponent` or `OpenDefaultComponent` function, or from the `NewMovieController` function (described on page 2-29).

key
: Specifies the keystroke. You obtain this value from the event structure.

modifiers
: Specifies modifier flags for the event. You obtain this value from the event structure.

DESCRIPTION

The `MCKey` function returns a value indicating whether it handled the event. The function sets the returned value to 1 if it handles the event. The function sets the returned value to 0 if it does not handle the event. In this case, your application is responsible for the event.

Application-Defined Function

Movie controller components provide an action filter function that you establish with the `MCSetActionFilterWithRefCon` function (described on page 2-47).

MyPlayerFilterWithRefCon

Your action filter function, `MyPlayerFilterWithRefCon`, should be in this form:

```
Boolean MyPlayerFilterWithRefCon (MovieController mc,
                                  short action,
                                  void *params, long refCon);
```

mc
: Specifies the movie controller for the operation.

Movie Controller Components

`action`
: A short integer containing the action code. The movie controller component sets this parameter to point to the `what` field in the appropriate action structure. (Although this action is passed as a variable, it should not be changed by the filter.) See "Movie Controller Actions," which begins on page 2-15, for a description of the actions supported by movie controller components.

`params`
: Contains a pointer to the parameter data appropriate to the action—for example, setting the playback rate. See the individual descriptions of the actions beginning on page 2-15 for information about the parameters supplied for each supported action.

`refCon`
: Contains a reference constant value. The movie controller component passes this reference constant to your action filter function each time it calls your function.

DESCRIPTION

Your filter function must return a Boolean value indicating whether it handled the action. Set the returned Boolean value to `true` if your function completely handles the action. In this case, the movie controller component performs no additional processing for the action. Set the returned value to `false` if your function does not handle the action. The movie controller component then performs the appropriate processing for the action.

Summary of Movie Controller Components

C Summary

Constants

```
enum {
    kMCSetMovieSelect              = 2,   /* MCSetMovie */
    kMCRemoveMovieSelect           = 3,   /* MCRemoveMovie */
    kMCIsPlayerEventSelect         = 7,   /* MCIsPlayerEvent */
    kMCSetActionFilterSelect       = 8,   /* MCSetActionFilter */
    kMCDoActionSelect              = 9,   /* MCDoAction */
    kMCSetControllerAttachedSelect = 10,  /* MCSetControllerAttached */
    kMCIsControllerAttachedSelect  = 11,  /* MCIsControllerAttached */
    kMCSetControllerPortSelect     = 12,  /* MCSetControllerPort */
    kMCGetControllerPortSelect     = 13,  /* MCGetControllerPort */
    kMCGetVisibleSelect            = 14,  /* MCGetVisible */
    kMCSetVisibleSelect            = 15,  /* MCSetVisible */
    kMCGetControllerBoundsRectSelect
                                   = 16,  /* MCGetControllerBoundsRect */
    kMCSetControllerBoundsRectSelect
                                   = 17,  /* MCSetControllerBoundsRect */
    kMCGetControllerBoundsRgnSelect
                                   = 18,  /* MCGetControllerBoundsRgn */
    kMCGetWindowRgnSelect          = 19,  /* MCGetWindowRgn */
    kMCMovieChangedSelect          = 20,  /* MCMovieChanged */
    kMCSetDurationSelect           = 21,  /* MCSetDuration */
    kMCGetCurrentTimeSelect        = 22,  /* MCGetCurrentTime */
    kMCNewAttachedControllerSelect = 23,  /* MCNewAttachedController */
    kMCDrawSelect                  = 24,  /* MCDraw */
    kMCActivateSelect              = 25,  /* MCActivate */
    kMCIdleSelect                  = 26,  /* MCIdle */
    kMCKeySelect                   = 27,  /* MCKey */
    kMCClickSelect                 = 28,  /* MCClick */
    kMCEnableEditingSelect         = 29,  /* MCEnableEditing */
    kMCIsEditingEnabledSelect      = 30,  /* MCIsEditingEnabled*/
    kMCCopySelect                  = 31,  /* MCCopy */
    kMCCutSelect                   = 32,  /* MCCut */
```

CHAPTER 2

Movie Controller Components

```
    kMCPasteSelect                   = 33,  /* MCPaste */
    kMCClearSelect                   = 34,  /* MCClear */
    kMCUndoSelect                    = 35,  /* MCUndo */
    kMCPositionControllerSelect      = 36,  /* MCPositionController */
    kMCGetControllerInfoSelect       = 37,  /* MCGetControllerInfo */
    kMCSetClipSelect                 = 40,  /* MCSetClip */
    kMCGetClipSelect                 = 41,  /* MCGetClip */
    kMCDrawBadgeSelect               = 42,  /* MCDrawBadge */
    kMCSetUpEditMenuSelect           = 43,  /* MCSetUpEditMenu */
    kMCGetMenuStringSelect           = 44,  /* MCGetMenuString */
    kMCSetActionFilterWithRefConSelect
                                     = 45
                                            /* SetActionFilterWithRefConSelect */
};

enum {
    mcActionIdle                     = 1,   /* give event-processing time to
                                                movie controller */
    mcActionDraw                     = 2,   /* send update event to movie
                                                controller */
    mcActionActivate                 = 3,   /* activate movie controller */
    mcActionDeactivate               = 4,   /* deactivate controller */
    mcActionMouseDown                = 5,   /* pass mouse-down event */
    mcActionKey                      = 6,   /* pass key-down or auto-key event */
    mcActionPlay                     = 8,   /* start playing movie */
    mcActionGoToTime                 = 12,  /* move to specific time in a movie */
    mcActionSetVolume                = 14,  /* set a movie's volume */
    mcActionGetVolume                = 15,  /* retrieve a movie's volume */
    mcActionStep                     = 18,  /* play a movie a specified number
                                                of frames at a time */
    mcActionSetLooping               = 21,  /* enable or disable looping */
    mcActionGetLooping               = 22,  /* find out if movie is looping */
    mcActionSetLoopIsPalindrome      = 23,  /* enable palindrome looping */
    mcActionGetLoopIsPalindrome      = 24,  /* find out if palindrome looping
                                                is on */
    mcActionSetGrowBoxBounds         = 25,  /* set limits for resizing a movie */
    mcActionControllerSizeChanged    = 26,  /* user has resized movie
                                                controller */
    mcActionSetSelectionBegin        = 29,  /* start time of movie's current
                                                selection */
    mcActionSetSelectionDuration     = 30,  /* set duration of movie's current
                                                selection */
    mcActionSetKeysEnabled           = 32,  /* enable or disable keystrokes for
                                                movie */
```

Movie Controller Components

```
    mcActionGetKeysEnabled      = 33,  /* find out if keystrokes are
                                          enabled */
    mcActionSetPlaySelection    = 34,  /* constrain playing to the current
                                          selection */
    mcActionGetPlaySelection    = 35,  /* find out if movie is constrained to
                                          playing within selection */
    mcActionSetUseBadge         = 36,  /* enable or disable movie's
                                          playback badge */
    mcActionGetUseBadge         = 37,  /* find out if movie controller is
                                          using playback badge */
    mcActionSetFlags            = 38,  /* set movie's control flags */
    mcActionGetFlags            = 39,  /* retrieve movie's control flags */
    mcActionSetPlayEveryFrame   = 40,  /* instruct controller to play all
                                          frames in movie */
    mcActionGetPlayEveryFrame   = 41,  /* find out if controller is playing
                                          every frame in movie */
    mcActionGetPlayRate         = 42,  /* determine playback rate */
    mcActionShowBalloon         = 43,  /* find out if controller wants to
                                          display Balloon Help */
    mcActionBadgeClick          = 44,  /* user clicked movie's badge */
    mcActionMovieClick          = 45,  /* user clicked movie */
    mcActionSuspend             = 46,  /* suspend action */
    mcActionResume              = 47   /* resume action */
};


enum {
    mcTopLeftMovie      = 1<<0,     /* places movie in upper-left corner of
                                       display rectangle */
    mcScaleMovieToFit   = 1<<1,     /* resizes movie to fit into display
                                       rectangle */
    mcWithBadge         = 1<<2,     /* controls whether badge is displayed */
    mcNotVisible        = 1<<3,     /* controls whether controller portion
                                       is visible */
    mcWithFrame         = 1<<4      /* specifies whether component shows
                                       frame around movie */
};


enum {
    mcFlagSuppressMovieFrame    = 1<<0,  /* controls display of frame */
    mcFlagSuppressStepButtons   = 1<<1,  /* controls display of step
                                            buttons */
```

```
    mcFlagSuppressSpeakerButton   = 1<<2,  /* controls display of speaker
                                              button */
    mcFlagsUseWindowPalette       = 1<<3   /* controls display of window
                                              palette */
};

enum {
    mcInfoUndoAvailable     = 1<<0,  /* MCUndo function available */
    mcInfoCutAvailable      = 1<<1,  /* MCCut function available */
    mcInfoCopyAvailable     = 1<<2,  /* MCCopy function available */
    mcInfoPasteAvailable    = 1<<3,  /* MCPaste function available */
    mcInfoClearAvailable    = 1<<4,  /* MCClear function available */
    mcInfoHasSound          = 1<<5,  /* controller can play movie's
                                        sound */
    mcInfoIsPlaying         = 1<<6,  /* movie is playing */
    mcInfoIsLooping         = 1<<7,  /* movie is looping */
    mcInfoIsInPalindrome    = 1<<8,  /* movie is alternating between
                                        forward and backward playback */
    mcInfoEditingEnabled    = 1<<9   /* MCEnableEditing function
                                        available */
};

enum {
    mcMenuUndo  = 1,  /* Undo command */
    mcMenuCut   = 3,  /* Cut command */
    mcMenuCopy  = 4,  /* Copy command */
    mcMenuPaste = 5,  /* Paste command */
    mcMenuClear = 6   /* Clear command */
};

enum {
    mcPositionDontInvalidate = 1<<5  /* do not invalidate areas of window
                                        changed due to repositioning of movie
                                        or controller */
};
```

Data Types

```
typedef short mcAction;

typedef unsigned long MCFlags;
```

Movie Controller Functions

Associating Movies With Controllers

```
pascal MovieController NewMovieController
                            (Movie theMovie, const Rect *movieRect,
                             long someFlags);
pascal ComponentResult MCNewAttachedController
                            (MovieController mc, Movie theMovie,
                             WindowPtr w, Point where);
pascal ComponentResult MCSetMovie
                            (MovieController mc, Movie theMovie,
                             WindowPtr movieWindow, Point where);
pascal Movie MCGetMovie     (MovieController mc);
pascal void DisposeMovieController
                            (MovieController mc);
```

Managing Controller Attributes

```
pascal ComponentResult MCPositionController
                            (MovieController mc, const Rect *movieRect,
                             const Rect *controllerRect, long someFlags);
pascal ComponentResult MCSetControllerAttached
                            (MovieController mc, Boolean attach);
pascal ComponentResult MCIsControllerAttached
                            (MovieController mc);
pascal ComponentResult MCSetVisible
                            (MovieController mc, Boolean visible);
pascal ComponentResult MCGetVisible
                            (MovieController mc);
pascal ComponentResult MCDrawBadge
                            (MovieController mc, RgnHandle movieRgn,
                             RgnHandle *badgeRgn);
pascal ComponentResult MCSetControllerBoundsRect
                            (MovieController mc, const Rect *bounds);
pascal ComponentResult MCGetControllerBoundsRect
                            (MovieController mc, Rect *bounds);
pascal RgnHandle MCGetControllerBoundsRgn
                            (MovieController mc);
pascal RgnHandle MCGetWindowRgn
                            (MovieController mc, WindowPtr w);
pascal ComponentResult MCSetClip
                            (MovieController mc, RgnHandle theClip,
                             RgnHandle movieClip);
```

```
pascal ComponentResult MCGetClip
                            (MovieController mc, RgnHandle *theClip,
                             RgnHandle *movieClip);
pascal ComponentResult MCSetControllerPort
                            (MovieController mc, CGrafPtr gp);
pascal CGrafPtr MCGetControllerPort
                            (MovieController mc);
```

Handling Movie Events

```
pascal ComponentResult MCIsPlayerEvent
                            (MovieController mc, const EventRecord *e);
pascal ComponentResult MCDoAction
                            (MovieController mc, short action,
                             void *params);
pascal ComponentResult MCSetActionFilterWithRefCon
                            (MovieController mc, MCActionFilter filter,
                             long refCon);
pascal ComponentResult MCGetControllerInfo
                            (MovieController mc, long *someFlags);
pascal ComponentResult MCMovieChanged
                            (MovieController mc, Movie theMovie);
```

Editing Movies

```
pascal ComponentResult MCEnableEditing
                            (MovieController mc, Boolean enabled);
pascal long MCIsEditingEnabled
                            (MovieController mc);
pascal Movie MCCut        (MovieController mc);
pascal Movie MCCopy       (MovieController mc);
pascal ComponentResult MCPaste
                            (MovieController mc, Movie srcMovie);
pascal ComponentResult MCClear
                            (MovieController mc);
pascal ComponentResult MCUndo
                            (MovieController mc);
pascal ComponentResult MCSetUpEditMenu
                            (MovieController mc, long modifiers,
                             MenuHandle mh);
pascal ComponentResult MCGetMenuString
                            (MovieController mc, long modifiers, short item,
                             Str255 aString);
```

CHAPTER 2

Movie Controller Components

Getting and Setting Movie Controller Time

```
pascal ComponentResult MCSetDuration
                        (MovieController mc, TimeValue duration);
pascal TimeValue MCGetCurrentTime
                        (MovieController mc, TimeScale *scale);
```

Customizing Event Processing

```
pascal ComponentResult MCActivate
                        (MovieController mc, WindowPtr w,
                         Boolean activate);
pascal ComponentResult MCClick
                        (MovieController mc, WindowPtr w, Point where,
                         long when, long modifiers);
pascal ComponentResult MCDraw
                        (MovieController mc, WindowPtr w);
pascal ComponentResult MCIdle
                        (MovieController mc);
pascal ComponentResult MCKey
                        (MovieController mc, char key, long modifiers);
```

Application-Defined Function

```
Boolean MyPlayerFilterWithRefCon
                        (MovieController mc, short *action,
                         void *params, long refCon);
```

Pascal Summary

Constants

```
CONST
   MovieControllerComponentType = 'play';

   {movie controller selectors}
   kMCSetMovieSelect                = 2;   {MCSetMovie}
   kMCGetMovie                      = 5;   {MCGetMovie}
   kMCIsPlayerEventSelect           = 7;   {MCIsPlayerEvent}
   kMCSetActionFilterSelect         = 8;   {MCSetActionFilter}
   kMCDoActionSelect                = 9;   {MCDoAction}
   kMCSetControllerAttachedSelect   = $A;  {MCSetControllerAttached}
```

```
kMCIsControllerAttachedSelect        = $B; {MCIsControllerAttached}
kMCSetControllerPortSelect           = $C; {MCSetControllerPort}
kMCGetControllerPortSelect           = $D; {MCGetControllerPort}
kMCGetVisibleSelect                  = $E; {MCGetVisible}
kMCSetVisibleSelect                  = $F; {MCSetVisible}
kMCGetControllerBoundsRectSelect     = $10;{MCGetControllerBoundsRect}
kMCSetControllerBoundsRectSelect     = $11;{MCSetControllerBoundsRect}
kMCGetControllerBoundsRgnSelect      = $12;{MCGetControllerBoundsRgn}
kMCGetWindowRgnSelect                = $13;{MCGetWindowRgn}
kMCMovieChangedSelect                = $14;{MCMovieChanged}
kMCSetDurationSelect                 = $15;{MCSetDuration}
kMCGetCurrentTimeSelect              = $16;{MCGetCurrentTime}
kMCNewAttachedControllerSelect       = $17;{MCNewAttachedController}
kMCDrawSelect                        = $18;{MCDraw}
kMCActivateSelect                    = $19;{MCActivate}
kMCIdleSelect                        = $1A;{MCIdle}
kMCKeySelect                         = $1B;{MCKey}
kMCClickSelect                       = $1C;{MCClick}
kMCEnableEditingSelect               = $1D;{MCEnableEditing}
kMCIsEditingEnabledSelect            = $1E;{MCIsEditingEnabled}
kMCCopySelect                        = $1F;{MCCopy}
kMCCutSelect                         = $20;{MCCut}
kMCPasteSelect                       = $21;{MCPaste}
kMCClearSelect                       = $22;{MCClear}
kMCUndoSelect                        = $23;{MCUndo}
kMCPositionControllerSelect          = $24;{MCPositionController}
kMCGetControllerInfoSelect           = $25;{MCGetControllerInfo}
kMCSetClipSelect                     = $28;{MCSetClip}
kMCGetClipSelect                     = $29;{MCGetClip}
kMCDrawBadgeSelect                   = $2A;{MCDrawBadge}
kMCSetUpEditMenuSelect               = $2B;{MCSetUpEditMenu}
kMCGetMenuStringSelect               = $2C;{MCGetMenuString}
kMCSetActionFilterWithRefConSelect
                                     = $2D;{MCSetActionFilterWithRefConSelect}

{movie controller actions}
mcActionIdle                         = 1;  {give event-processing }
                                           { time to movie controller}
mcActionDraw                         = 2;  {send update event to movie }
                                           { controller}
mcActionActivate                     = 3;  {activate controller}
mcActionDeactivate                   = 4;  {deactivate controller}
mcActionMouseDown                    = 5;  {pass mouse-down event}
mcActionKey                          = 6;  {pass key-down or auto-key event}
```

CHAPTER 2

Movie Controller Components

```
mcActionPlay                   = 8;  {start playing movie}
mcActionGoToTime               = 12; {move to specific time in }
                                     { a movie}
mcActionSetVolume              = 14; {set a movie's volume}
mcActionGetVolume              = 15; {retrieve a movie's volume}
mcActionStep                   = 18; {play movie skipping specified }
                                     { number of frames at a time}
mcActionSetLooping             = 21; {enable/disable looping }
                                     { for a movie}
mcActionGetLooping             = 22; {determine whether a }
                                     { movie is looping}
mcActionSetLoopIsPalindrome    = 23; {enable palindrome looping}
mcActionGetLoopIsPalindrome    = 24; {is palindrome looping on?}
mcActionSetGrowBoxBounds       = 25; {set limits for resizing a movie}
mcActionControllerSizeChanged  = 26; {user has resized movie controller}
mcActionSetSelectionBegin      = 29; {start time of movie's }
                                     { current selection}
mcActionSetSelectionDuration   = 30; {set duration of movie's }
                                     { current selection}
mcActionSetKeysEnabled         = 32; {enable/disable }
                                     { keystrokes for movie}
mcActionGetKeysEnabled         = 33; {are keystrokes enabled?}
mcActionSetPlaySelection       = 34; {constrain playing to the }
                                     { current selection}
mcActionGetPlaySelection       = 35; {is movie constrained to }
                                     { playing within selection}
mcActionSetUseBadge            = 36; {enable/disable movie's }
                                     { playback badge}
mcActionGetUseBadge            = 37; {is movie controller }
                                     { using playback badge?}
mcActionSetFlags               = 38; {set movie's control flags}
mcActionGetFlags               = 39; {get movie's control flags}
mcActionSetPlayEveryFrame      = 40; {instruct controller to }
                                     { play all frames in movie}
mcActionGetPlayEveryFrame      = 41; {is controller playing }
                                     { every frame in movie?}
mcActionGetPlayRate            = 42; {determine playback rate}
mcActionShowBalloon            = 43; {controller wants to }
                                     { display balloon help}
mcActionBadgeClick             = 44; {user clicked movie's badge}
mcActionMovieClick             = 45; {user clicked movie}
mcActionSuspend                = 46; {suspend action}
mcActionResume                 = 47; {resume action}
```

Summary of Movie Controller Components

Movie Controller Components

```
{controller creation flags}
mcTopLeftMovie                  = $1;  {places movie in upper-left }
                                       { corner of display rectangle}
mcScaleMovieToFit               = $2;  {resizes movie to fit into }
                                       { display rectangle}
mcWithBadge                     = $4;  {controls whether badge }
                                       { is displayed}
mcNotVisible                    = $8;  {controls whether controller }
                                       { portion is visible}
mcWithFrame                     = $10; {specifies whether component }
                                       { shows frame around movie}

{movie control flags}
mcFlagSuppressMovieFrame        = $1;  {controls display of frame}
mcFlagSuppressStepButtons       = $2;  {controls display of step buttons}
mcFlagSuppressSpeakerButton     = $4;  {controls display of speaker }
                                       { button}
mcFlagsUseWindowPalette         = $5;  {controls display of window }
                                       { palette}

{movie controller information flags}
mcInfoUndoAvailable             = $1;   {MCUndo function available}
mcInfoCutAvailable              = $2;   {MCCut function available}
mcInfoCopyAvailable             = $4;   {MCCopy function available}
mcInfoPasteAvailable            = $8;   {MCPaste function available}
mcInfoClearAvailable            = $10;  {MCClear function available}
mcInfoHasSound                  = $20;  {controller can play movie's }
                                        { sound}
mcInfoIsPlaying                 = $40;  {movie is playing}
mcInfoIsLooping                 = $80;  {movie is looping}
mcInfoIsInPalindrome            = $100; {movie is alternating between }
                                        { forward and backward playback}
mcInfoEditingEnabled            = $200; {MCEnableEditing function }
                                        { available}


mcMenuUndo  = 1;   {Undo command}
mcMenuCut   = 3;   {Cut command}
mcMenuCopy  = 4;   {Copy command}
mcMenuPaste = 5;   {Paste command}
mcMenuClear = 6;   {Clear commmand}
```

```
    mcPositionDontInvalidate = 32;    {do not invalidate areas of window }
                                      { changed due to repositioning of }
                                      { movie or controller}
```

Data Types

```
TYPE
    mcAction                          = Integer;
    mcFlags                           = LongInt;
```

Movie Controller Routines

Associating Movies With Controllers

```
FUNCTION NewMovieController  (theMovie: Movie; movieRect: Rect;
                              someFlags: LongInt): MovieController;
FUNCTION MCNewAttachedController
                             (mc: MovieController; theMovie: theMovie;
                              w: WindowPtr; where: Point): ComponentResult;
FUNCTION MCSetMovie          (mc: MovieController; theMovie: Movie;
                              movieWindow: WindowPtr; where: Point):
                              ComponentResult;
FUNCTION MCGetMovie          (mc: MovieController): Movie;
PROCEDURE DisposeMovieController
                             (mc: MovieController);
```

Managing Controller Attributes

```
FUNCTION MCPositionController
                             (mc: MovieController; VAR movieRect: Rect;
                              VAR controllerRect: Rect; someFlags: LongInt):
                              ComponentResult;
FUNCTION MCSetControllerAttached
                             (mc: MovieController;
                              attach: Boolean): ComponentResult;
FUNCTION MCIsControllerAttached
                             (mc: MovieController): ComponentResult;
FUNCTION MCSetVisible        (mc: MovieController; visible: Boolean):
                              ComponentResult;
FUNCTION MCGetVisible        (mc: MovieController): ComponentResult;
FUNCTION MCDrawBadge         (mc: MovieController; movieRgn: RgnHandle;
                              VAR badgeRgn: RgnHandle): ComponentResult;
```

```
FUNCTION MCSetControllerBoundsRect
                                (mc: MovieController; bounds: Rect):
                                    ComponentResult;
FUNCTION MCGetControllerBoundsRect
                                (mc: MovieController; VAR bounds: Rect):
                                    ComponentResult;
FUNCTION MCGetControllerBoundsRgn
                                (mc: MovieController): RgnHandle;
FUNCTION MCGetWindowRgn         (mc: MovieController; w: WindowPtr): RgnHandle;
FUNCTION MCSetClip              (mc: MovieController; theClip: RgnHandle;
                                    movieClip: RgnHandle): ComponentResult;
FUNCTION MCGetClip              (mc: MovieController; VAR theClip: RgnHandle;
                                    VAR movieClip: RgnHandle): ComponentResult;
FUNCTION MCSetControllerPort
                                (mc: MovieController; gp: CGrafPtr):
                                    ComponentResult;
FUNCTION MCGetControllerPort
                                (mc: MovieController): CGrafPtr;
```

Handling Movie Events

```
FUNCTION MCIsPlayerEvent        (mc: MovieController; e: EventRecord):
                                    ComponentResult;
FUNCTION MCDoAction             (mc: MovieController; action: Integer;
                                    params: Ptr): ComponentResult;
PROCEDURE MCSetActionFilterWithRefCon
                                (mc: MovieController; filter: MCActionFilter;
                                    refCon: LongInt);
FUNCTION MCGetControllerInfo
                                (mc: MovieController; VAR someFlags: LongInt):
                                    ComponentResult;
FUNCTION MCMovieChanged         (mc: MovieController; theMovie: Movie):
                                    ComponentResult;
```

Editing Movies

```
FUNCTION MCEnableEditing        (mc: MovieController; enabled: Boolean):
                                    ComponentResult;
FUNCTION MCIsEditingEnabled
                                (mc: MovieController): LongInt;
FUNCTION MCCut                  (mc: MovieController): Movie;
FUNCTION MCCopy                 (mc: MovieController): Movie;
FUNCTION MCPaste                (mc: MovieController; srcMovie: Movie):
                                    ComponentResult;
```

```
FUNCTION MCClear          (mc: MovieController): ComponentResult;
FUNCTION MCUndo           (mc: MovieController): ComponentResult;
FUNCTION MCSetUpEditMenu  (mc: MovieController; modifiers: LongInt;
                           mh: MenuHandle): ComponentResult;
FUNCTION MCGetMenuString  (mc: MovieController; modifiers: LongInt;
                           item: Integer; VAR aString: Str255):
                           ComponentResult;
```

Getting and Setting Movie Controller Time

```
FUNCTION MCSetDuration    (mc: MovieController; duration: TimeValue):
                           ComponentResult;
FUNCTION MCGetCurrentTime (mc: MovieController; VAR scale: TimeScale):
                           TimeValue;
```

Customizing Event Processing

```
FUNCTION MCActivate       (mc: MovieController; w: WindowPtr;
                           activate: Boolean): ComponentResult;
FUNCTION MCClick          (mc: MovieController; w: WindowPtr;
                           where: Point; when: LongInt;
                           modifiers: LongInt): ComponentResult;
FUNCTION MCDraw           (mc: MovieController; w: WindowPtr):
                           ComponentResult;
FUNCTION MCIdle           (mc: MovieController): ComponentResult;
FUNCTION MCKey            (mc: MovieController; key: Byte;
                           modifiers: LongInt): ComponentResult;
```

Application-Defined Routine

```
FUNCTION MyPlayerFilterWithRefCon
                          (mc: MovieController; VAR action: Integer;
                           VAR params: LongInt; refCon: LongInt): Boolean;
```

Result Codes

badControllerHeight	–9994	Invalid height
editingNotAllowed	–9995	Controller does not support editing
controllerBoundsNotExact	–9996	Boundary rectangle not exact
cannotSetWidthOfAttachedController	–9997	Cannot change controller width
controllerHasFixedHeight	–9998	Cannot change controller height
cannotMoveAttachedController	–9999	Cannot move attached controllers

Standard Image-Compression Dialog Components

Contents

About Standard Image-Compression Dialog Components   3-4
Using Standard Image-Compression Dialog Components   3-6
   Opening a Connection to a Standard Image-Compression Dialog Component   3-8
   Displaying the Dialog Box to the User   3-8
      Setting Default Parameters   3-8
      Designating a Test Image   3-9
      Displaying the Dialog Box and Retrieving Parameters   3-10
   Extending the Basic Dialog Box   3-11
Creating a Standard Image-Compression Dialog Component   3-14
Standard Image-Compression Dialog Components Reference   3-15
   Request Types   3-15
      The Spatial Settings Request Type   3-15
      The Temporal Settings Request Type   3-17
      The Data-Rate Settings Request Type   3-19
      The Color Table Settings Request Type   3-20
      The Progress Function Request Type   3-20
      The Extended Functions Request Type   3-21
      The Preference Flags Request Type   3-22
      The Settings State Request Type   3-24
      The Sequence ID Request Type   3-24
      The Window Position Request Type   3-25
      The Control Flags Request Type   3-25

Standard Image-Compression Dialog Component Functions 3-25
  Getting Default Settings for an Image or a Sequence 3-26
  Displaying the Standard Image-Compression Dialog Box 3-28
  Compressing Still Images 3-29
  Compressing Image Sequences 3-31
  Working With Image or Sequence Settings 3-34
  Specifying a Test Image 3-37
  Positioning Dialog Boxes and Rectangles 3-42
  Utility Function 3-44
 Application-Defined Function 3-45
Summary of Standard Image-Compression Dialog Components 3-47
 C Summary 3-47
  Constants 3-47
  Data Types 3-49
  Standard Image-Compression Dialog Component Functions 3-50
  Application-Defined Function 3-52
 Pascal Summary 3-52
  Constants 3-52
  Data Types 3-54
  Standard Image-Compression Dialog Component Routines 3-55
  Application-Defined Routine 3-57
 Result Codes 3-57

Standard Image-Compression Dialog Components

This chapter discusses standard image-compression dialog components. **Standard image-compression dialog components** provide a consistent user interface for selecting parameters that govern the compression of an image or image sequence and the management of the compression operation. Applications that use these components are freed from many of the details of obtaining and validating image-compression parameters and interacting with the Image Compression Manager to compress an image or sequence.

This chapter is divided into the following sections:

- "About Standard Image-Compression Dialog Components" provides a general introduction to components of this type.
- "Using Standard Image-Compression Dialog Components" discusses the facilities provided to applications by these components.
- "Creating a Standard Image-Compression Dialog Component" describes how to create one of these components.
- "Standard Image-Compression Dialog Components Reference" presents detailed information about the functions that are supported by these components.
- "Summary of Standard Image-Compression Dialog Components" contains a condensed listing of the constants, data structures, and functions supported by these components in C and in Pascal.

If you want to use a standard image-compression dialog component in your application, you should read the first two sections of this chapter, and then use the reference section as appropriate. If you want to create your own standard image-compression dialog component, you should be familiar with all of the information in this chapter.

As components, standard image-compression dialog components rely on the facilities of the Component Manager. In order to use any component, your application must also use the Component Manager. If you are not familiar with this manager, see the chapter "Component Manager" in *Inside Macintosh: More Macintosh Toolbox*. In addition, you should be familiar with image compression in general and the Image Compression Manager in particular. See the chapter "Image Compression Manager" in *Inside Macintosh: QuickTime* for more information.

Note
Throughout this chapter, the term *standard dialog component* refers to the standard image-compression dialog component. The term *standard dialog box* refers to one or both of the two dialog boxes presented by the standard image-compression dialog component. These dialog boxes are shown in Figure 3-1 and Figure 3-2. ◆

Standard Image-Compression Dialog Components

About Standard Image-Compression Dialog Components

Standard image-compression dialog components provide a consistent user interface for specifying the parameters that control the compression of an image or image sequence. Your application specifies a test image for the dialog box and then calls the standard-image compression component. The component then presents a dialog box to the user, manages the dialog box, validates the user's settings, and stores those settings for your application. The standard dialog component also provides numerous facilities for determining reasonable default settings for a given image or sequence. Finally, this component manages the process of compressing the image or image sequence, using the parameter settings provided by the user or your application.

By using a standard image-compression dialog component, you can reduce the amount of work you need to do in your application in order to compress an image or an image sequence. For example, you can eliminate the need to manage interactions with the user and to validate the image-compression parameters specified by the user. Furthermore, the standard dialog component simplifies the process of compressing images or sequences. This, in turn, allows you to focus on the problem at hand, rather than on the details of image-compression parameters. In addition, the standard image-compression dialog component supplied by Apple supports many features that are helpful to the user, including Balloon Help and a test image. Finally, Apple's component will be localized by Apple, so that you need not worry about international issues relating to this dialog box.

Standard image-compression dialog components support two basic dialog boxes. One dialog box provides a minimal interface and is suitable for compressing single images. Figure 3-1 shows an example of this dialog box. Using this dialog box, the user can select a compressor component, the pixel depth for the operation, and the desired spatial quality.

Figure 3-1   Dialog box for single-frame compression

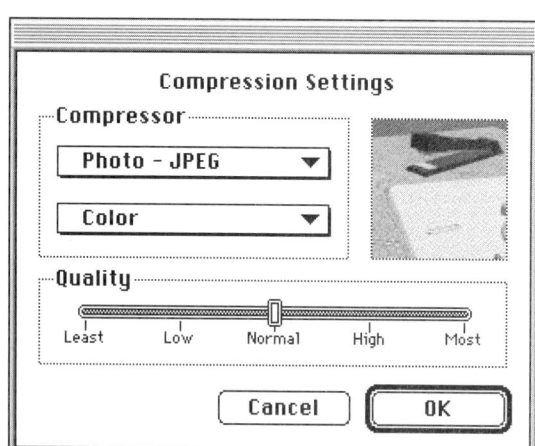

Standard Image-Compression Dialog Components

The other dialog box allows the user to set compression parameters for image sequences. In addition to the parameters supported by the single-frame dialog box, this dialog box supports frame rate, key frame rate, spatial and temporal quality settings, and data rate settings (for more information about these aspects of image compression, see the chapter "Image Compression Manager" in *Inside Macintosh: QuickTime*). Figure 3-2 shows an example of this dialog box.

Figure 3-2   Dialog box for image-sequence compression

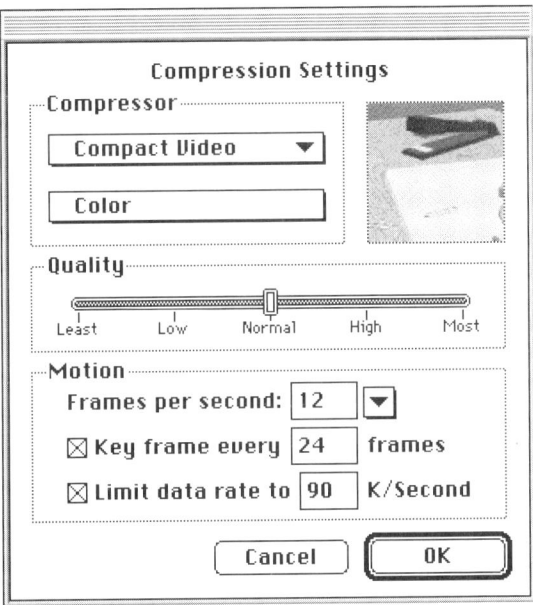

Your application can control which dialog box is presented to the user.

By using standard dialog components, you can avoid many of the details of obtaining, validating, and using image-compression parameters. The process of validating image-compression parameters can be very involved, depending upon the capabilities of the selected compressor component. Apple's standard image-compression dialog component verifies that the user's settings are valid for the selected compressor. In addition, this component uses a test image to demonstrate the effects of the user's compression settings.

Using Standard Image-Compression Dialog Components

You can use the standard image-compression dialog component to obtain image or image sequence compression parameters from the user and to manage the process of compressing the image or sequence. This component presents a consistent interface to the user and eliminates the need for you to worry about the details of managing this dialog box. Once you have collected the parameter information from the user, you can use the component to instruct the Image Compression Manager to perform the image or sequence compression. Again, the component manages the details for you.

Because the standard image-compression dialog component is a component, you use the Component Manager to open and close your connection. If you are unfamiliar with components or the Component Manager, see the chapter "Component Manager" in *Inside Macintosh: More Macintosh Toolbox*.

Before you can open a connection to a standard image-compression dialog component, be sure that the Component Manager, Image Compression Manager, and 32-bit Color QuickDraw are available. You can use the Gestalt Manager to determine if these facilities are available. For more information about the Gestalt Manager, see the chapter "Gestalt Manager" in *Inside Macintosh: Operating System Utilities*. For details on 32-bit Color QuickDraw, see the chapter "Color QuickDraw" in *Inside Macintosh: Imaging*.

Once you have established a connection to a standard image-compression dialog component, your application can present the dialog box to the user. The user selects the desired compression parameters and clicks the OK button. The component then stores these parameters for your application, using them, when appropriate, to work with the Image Compression Manager to compress the image or sequence. Figure 3-1 on page 3-4 shows one of the dialog boxes that is supported by the standard image-compression dialog component provided by Apple.

Every standard image-compression dialog box has its own set of parameter information. This information identifies the compressor component to be used, determines which dialog box is used, and specifies the parameters to be used during the compression operation. This information is stored by the component. You can use functions provided by the component to examine or modify these parameters.

The standard image-compression dialog component provided by Apple allows you to augment or extend the interface provided by its dialog boxes. This component supports a single custom button. Your application enables this button when it instructs the component to display the dialog box to the user. You provide the code that supports this

CHAPTER 3

Standard Image-Compression Dialog Components

button in a hook function in your application. In addition, this component allows you to define a filter function—you can use this function to process dialog box events before the component. Figure 3-3 identifies the parts of the dialog box supported by Apple's standard dialog component.

Figure 3-3 Elements of the standard image-compression dialog box

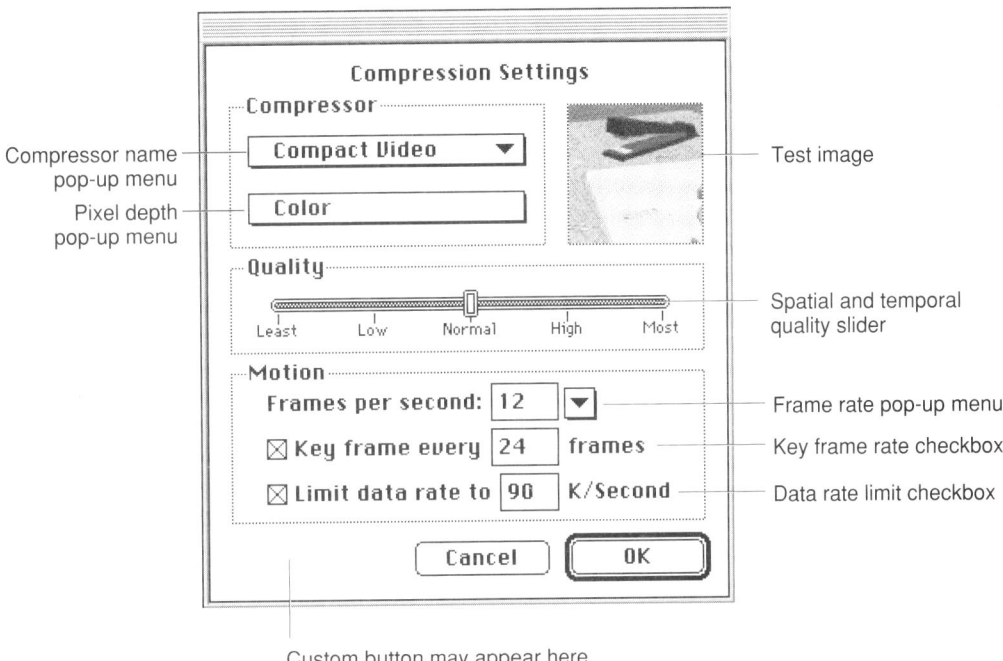

The following sections provide more detailed information about using the standard image-compression dialog component.

- "Opening a Connection to a Standard Image-Compression Dialog Component" tells you how to establish a connection between your application and the standard dialog component.

- "Displaying the Dialog Box to the User" describes the steps you must follow to display the standard dialog box to the user, retrieve the user's settings, and compress an image or sequence.

- "Extending the Basic Dialog Box" discusses several ways your application can customize the basic dialog box.

Using Standard Image-Compression Dialog Components

Opening a Connection to a Standard Image-Compression Dialog Component

As is the case with all components, your application must establish a connection to a standard image-compression dialog component before you can use its services. As with other components, you use the Component Manager's `OpenDefaultComponent` functions to connect to a component. You must use the Component Manager's `CloseComponent` function to close your application's connection when you are done.

Apple provides constants that define the component type and subtype values for standard image-compression dialog components. All of these components have a type value of 'scdi'; you can use the `StandardCompressionType` constant to specify this value. These components have a subtype value of 'imag'; the `StandardCompressionSubType` constant defines this value.

Displaying the Dialog Box to the User

Once you have opened a connection to a standard image-compression dialog component, you can proceed to display the dialog box to the user. In preparation, you might establish default parameter settings and specify a test image. Your application may then instruct the component to display the dialog box to the user. The following sections discuss each of these steps in more detail.

Setting Default Parameters

The standard dialog component stores and manages a set of compression parameters for your application. Before presenting the dialog box to the user, you may want to set default values for these parameters. The standard dialog component provides a number of options for establishing these default values:

1. You may supply an image to the component from which it can derive default settings. The component examines the characteristics of the image and sets appropriate default values. The `SCDefaultPictHandleSettings` function works with images stored in picture handles; the `SCDefaultPictFileSettings` function works with images stored in picture files; and the `SCDefaultPixMapSettings` function works with pixel maps. These functions are discussed in "Getting Default Settings for an Image or a Sequence" beginning on page 3-26.

2. If you have not set any defaults, but you do supply a test image for the dialog, the component examines the test image and derives appropriate default values based upon its characteristics. The next section discusses how to assign a test image to the user dialog box.

3. If you have not set any defaults and do not supply a test image, the component uses its own default values.

4. You may modify the settings by using the `SCSetInfo` function, which is described on page 3-36. This function gives you a great deal of freedom—you can use it to modify any of the parameters stored by the component.

Standard Image-Compression Dialog Components

If you supply either a test or a default image, the standard dialog component extracts default compression settings from that image, including color table, grayscale information (if appropriate), and compression defaults (if the source image is already compressed). If any of these default values differ from your needs, use the `SCSetInfo` function to modify the value.

Designating a Test Image

The standard image-compression dialog component provided by Apple supports a test image in its dialog box. The component uses this test image to show the user the effect of the current set of compression parameters. Whenever the user changes the dialog box settings, the component applies those parameters to the test image and displays the results in its dialog box. In addition, the standard dialog component may sometimes use the test image to obtain hints about the type of compression operation you expect to perform. In some cases, the component may derive default parameter values by examining the test image.

The component provides three functions that allow you to specify a dialog box's test image. Each of these functions uses a different image source—a handle, a picture file, or a pixel map. Your application is responsible for obtaining the image and for disposing of it after you are done.

The test image portion of the dialog box supported by Apple's standard image-compression dialog component is a square measuring 80 pixels by 80 pixels. In order to deal with test images that are larger than this area, Apple's component allows you to specify a part of the image to display. You can specify an **area of interest,** which indicates a portion of the test image that is to be displayed in the dialog box. If the area of interest is still larger than the display area in the dialog box, the component may shrink the image or crop it (or both) until the image fits.

Listing 3-1 shows one way to specify a test image. This code fragment uses an image that is stored in a picture file. The program asks the user to specify the file, using the `SFGetFilePreview` function. The program then opens the image file and instructs the standard image-compression dialog component to use the picture that is stored in the file.

Listing 3-1   Specifying a test image

```
Point               where;
ComponentInstance   ci;
SFTypeList          typeList;
SFReply             inReply;
short               srcPictFRef;

where.h = where.v = -2;              /* center dialog box on the
                                        best screen */
typeList[0] = 'PICT';                /* set file type */
```

Standard Image-Compression Dialog Components

```
SFGetFilePreview (where, "\p", nil, 1, typeList, nil,
          &inReply);
if (!inReply.good) { /* handle error */
}


result = FSOpen (inReply.fName, inReply.vRefNum, &srcPictFRef);
if (result) {       /* handle error */
}


result = SCSetTestImagePictFile
      (ci,                     /* component connection */
      srcPictFRef,             /* source picture file */
      nil,                     /* use the entire image */
      scPreferScalingAndCropping);
                               /* shrink image and crop it */
if (result) {                  /* handle error */
}
```

Displaying the Dialog Box and Retrieving Parameters

Standard image-compression dialog components provide two functions that display the dialog box to the user and retrieve the user's compression settings: SCRequestImageSettings and SCRequestSequenceSettings. Both of these functions start with your default parameter settings. Any changes made by the user are stored by the component. You may use the SCGetInfo function to examine these settings.

The SCRequestImageSettings function obtains image-compression parameters from the user and displays the dialog box that is shown in Figure 3-1 on page 3-4. The SCRequestSequenceSettings function works with sequence-compression parameters, using the dialog box shown in Figure 3-2 on page 3-5. Both of these functions allow you to augment or extend the interface in the dialog box—see "Extending the Basic Dialog Box," which begins on page 3-11, for more information about extending the basic dialog boxes.

Listing 3-2 shows how to use the SCRequestImageSettings function to display the dialog box to the user and obtain the resulting image-compression settings. This code fragment obtains the compression parameters from the user and then uses those parameters to compress the image that is stored in the file the user selected in Listing 3-1. The program then stores the compressed image in a different file—this fragment assumes that the destination file has already been selected.

CHAPTER 3

Standard Image-Compression Dialog Components

Listing 3-2 Displaying the dialog box to the user and compressing an image

```
ComponentInstance    ci;                /* component connection */
short                srcPictFRef;       /* source file */
short                dstPictFRef;       /* destination file */

result = SCRequestImageSettings(ci);
if (result < 0) {                       /* handle error */
}
if (result == scUserCancelled) {        /* user clicked Cancel
                                           button */
}
result = SCCompressPictureFile
        (ci,                            /* component connection */
         srcPictFRef,                   /* source picture file */
         dstPictFRef);                  /* dest picture file */
if (result < 0) {                       /* handle error */
}
```

Note that, because the standard dialog component stores the compression parameters for you, the new user settings become the default values the next time your application interacts with the user. If this is inappropriate, use one of the mechanisms discussed in "Setting Default Parameters" on page 3-8 to modify those defaults.

Extending the Basic Dialog Box

Apple's standard image-compression dialog component allows you to customize the operation of the user dialog box in a number of ways. First, you can define a filter function. This function, which is a modal-dialog filter function, can process dialog box events before the component does. Your filter function can then perform custom processing that is appropriate to your application. Because the compression dialog box is a movable modal dialog box, you must provide a filter to process update events for your application windows.

Second, you can define a hook function. This function receives item hits before the standard image-compression dialog component does, and can therefore augment the basic dialog box. For example, your hook function can provide additional validation of the user's selections.

Finally, you can define a custom button in the dialog box. You can then use your hook function to detect when the user clicks this button. Your hook function can then extend the dialog box interface by displaying additional dialog boxes, for example.

Standard Image-Compression Dialog Components

You use the `scExtendedProcsType` request type with the `SCSetInfo` function to take advantage of these mechanisms for customizing the user dialog box. Listing 3-3 contains code that uses this function to define a custom button in the dialog box. Listing 3-4 contains this application's hook function.

Listing 3-3 Defining a custom button in the dialog box

```
SCExtendedProcs ep;

ep.filterProc = MyFilter;      /* custom filter function */
ep.hookProc = MyHook;          /* custom hook function */
ep.refcon = 0;                 /* reference constant for filter
                                  and hook functions */
BlockMove("\pDefaults",ep.customName,32);
                               /* custom button name */
SCSetInfo(ci,scExtendedProcsType,&ep);
                               /* set new extended functions */
```

Listing 3-4 shows a hook function that returns the dialog box to its default settings whenever the user clicks the custom button. The standard dialog component calls this function each time the user selects an item in the dialog box. On entry, the hook function receives information about the current dialog box, a pointer to the appropriate standard image-compression dialog parameter block, and a reference constant that is supplied by your application.

This hook function first checks to see whether the user clicked the custom button. If so, the function changes the current compression settings.

Listing 3-4 A sample hook function

```
pascal short MyHook(DialogPtr theDialog,short itemHit,
                    void *params,long refcon)
{
   SCSpatialSettings ss;

   if (itemHit == scCustomItem) {   /* check for custom item */
      ss.codecType = 'jpeg';        /* create new settings */
      ss.codec = anyCodec;
      ss.depth = 32;
      ss.spatialQuality = codecNormalQuality;
```

```
    SCSetInfo(params,              /* component connection */
        scSpatialSettingsType,     /* set spatial settings */
        &ss);                      /* new spatial settings */
  }
  return (itemHit);
}
```

In your hook function, you may want to display additional user dialog boxes. Apple's standard image-compression dialog component provides two functions that help you position your dialog box on the screen. The `SCPositionDialog` function places a dialog box in a specified location; the `SCPositionRect` function positions a rectangle. By using these functions you can position your dialog boxes near the standard dialog box.

Listing 3-5 contains code that uses the `SCPositionDialog` function to place a Standard File Package dialog box onto the same screen as the standard image-compression dialog box.

Listing 3-5   Positioning related dialog boxes

```
Point    where;                    /* positions dialog boxes */
ComponentInstance ci;              /* component connection */

where.h = where.v = -2;            /* center dialog box on the
                                      best screen */

result = SCPositionDialog (ci,     /* component connection */
        -3999,                     /* resource number of dialog box */
        &where);                   /* returns upper-left point */

SFPutFile (where,                  /* positions the dialog box */
    "\pSave compressed picture as:",
    "\pUntitled",
    nil,
    &outReply);
```

Creating a Standard Image-Compression Dialog Component

Apple's standard image-compression dialog component fully implements the functional interface for components of this type. As a result, this component allows you to customize the dialog box by enabling the custom button or by defining a filter function. In most cases your application should be able to use the component that is supplied by Apple. However, if you want to create your own standard image-compression dialog component, you should read this section.

Apple has defined a component type value for standard image-compression dialog components. All components of this type have the same type and subtype values. You can use the following constants to specify the type and subtype.

```
#define    StandardCompressionType      'scdi'
#define    StandardCompressionSubType 'imag'
```

Apple has defined a functional interface for standard image-compression dialog components. For information about the functions your component must support, see the next section, "Standard Image-Compression Dialog Components Reference." You can use the following constants to refer to the request codes for each of the functions your component must support.

```
#define    scPositionRect              2    /* SCPositionRect */
#define    scPositionDialog            3    /* SCPositionDialog */
#define    scSetTestImagePictHandle    4    /* SCSetTestImagePictHandle */
#define    scSetTestImagePictFile      5    /* SCSetTestImagePictFile */
#define    scSetTestImagePixMap        6    /* SCSetTestImagePixMap */
#define    scGetBestDeviceRect         7    /* SCGetBestDeviceRect */
#define    scRequestImageSettings      10   /* SCRequestImageSettings */
#define    scCompressImage             11   /* SCCompressImage */
#define    scCompressPicture           12   /* SCCompressPicture */
#define    scCompressPictureFile       13   /* SCCompressPictureFile */
#define    scRequestSequenceSettings   14   /* SCRequestSequenceSettings */
#define    scCompressSequenceBegin     15   /* SCCompressSequenceBegin */
#define    scCompressSequenceFrame     16   /* SCCompressSequenceFrame */
#define    scCompressSequenceEnd       17   /* SCCompressSequenceEnd */
#define    scDefaultPictHandleSettings 18   /* SCDefaultPictHandleSettings */
#define    scDefaultPictFileSettings   19   /* SCDefaultPictFileSettings */
#define    scDefaultPixMapSettings     20   /* SCDefaultPixMapSettings */
#define    scGetInfo                   21   /* SCGetInfo */
#define    scSetInfo                   22   /* SCSetInfo */
#define    scNewGWorld                 23   /* SCNewGWorld */
```

Standard Image-Compression Dialog Components Reference

This section describes the request types and functions associated with the standard image-compression dialog components and an application-defined function.

Request Types

This section describes the request types used by two standard dialog component functions that allow you to work with the current compression settings for an image or a sequence of images. (You can establish these settings in a number of ways; see "Setting Default Parameters" on page 3-8 for more information about your options.)

You use the `SCGetInfo` function (described on page 3-34) to retrieve settings information. The `SCSetInfo` function (described on page 3-36) enables you to modify the settings.

These functions can work with a number of different types of settings information. When you call either function, you specify the type of data you want to work with. The following request types are defined:

```
#define    scSpatialSettingsType    'sptl'    /* spatial options */
#define    scTemporalSettingsType   'tprl'    /* temporal options */
#define    scDataRateSettingsType   'drat'    /* data rate */
#define    scColorTableType         'clut'    /* color table */
#define    scProgressProcType       'prog'    /* progress function */
#define    scExtendedProcsType      'xprc'    /* extended dialog */
#define    scPreferenceFlagsType    'pref'    /* preferences */
#define    scSettingsStateType      'ssta'    /* all settings */
#define    scSequenceIDType         'sequ'    /* sequence ID */
#define    scWindowPositionType     'wndw'    /* window position */
#define    scCodecFlagsType         'cflg'    /* compression flags */
```

Each of these request types requires different parameter data. The following sections discuss each of these request types and their data requirements.

The Spatial Settings Request Type

Use the spatial settings request to retrieve or modify the current spatial compression parameters. These parameters control how each image is compressed.

You supply a pointer to a spatial settings structure. If you are retrieving these settings, the standard dialog component places the current settings into the specified structure; if you are changing the settings, place the new values into the structure—the component uses those values to update its settings.

Standard Image-Compression Dialog Components

The `SCSpatialSettings` data type defines the format and content of the spatial settings structure:

```
typedef struct {
    CodecType       codecType;       /* compressor type */
    CodecComponent  codec;           /* compressor */
    short           depth;           /* pixel depth */
    CodecQ          spatialQuality;  /* desired quality */
} SCSpatialSettings;
```

Field descriptions

codecType
: Specifies the default compressor type that is displayed in the pop-up menu of compressors in the dialog box. The standard image-compression dialog component uses this field to return the compressor type that was selected by the user.

  You must set this parameter to one of the compressor types supported by the Image Compression Manager, or to `nil`.

  If you set the field to `nil`, the standard image-compression dialog component uses as the default value the first compressor or compressor type that it retrieves from the Image Compression Manager.

codec
: Provides additional information about the default compressor that is displayed in the pop-up menu of compressors in the dialog box. If the user selects a specific compressor component, the standard image-compression dialog component returns the appropriate compressor identifier in this field.

  The `scListEveryCodec` bit in the flag in the `scPreferenceFlagsType` request influences the operation of the compressor list in the dialog box and, therefore, the way the component uses this field.

  Set the flag to 1 to have the list contain an entry for each compressor component in the system. If the flag is set to 1, the standard image-compression dialog component uses this field along with the `codecType` field to select the default compressor that appears in the dialog box. To specify a default image compressor component, set this field to the appropriate compressor identifier. When the user clicks OK in the dialog box, the standard image-compression dialog component returns the compressor identifier that corresponds to the selected image compressor component.

  If you set the field to `nil`, the standard image-compression dialog component uses as the default value the first compressor of the specified type that it retrieves from the Image Compression Manager.

CHAPTER 3

Standard Image-Compression Dialog Components

If you have set the flag to 0, the list contains only one entry for each type of compressor in the system. The standard image-compression dialog component ignores this field when creating the list of compressor types. In this case, the standard image-compression dialog component does not change the value of this field when the user clicks OK.

However, you may use this field to specify additional selection criteria by setting this field to one of the special compressor identifiers supported by the Image Compression Manager (see the chapter "Image Compression Manager" in *Inside Macintosh: QuickTime* for these special values). The standard image-compression dialog component may use this value when it validates the compression parameters selected by the user.

`depth`   Specifies the default value of the pixel depth pop-up menu in the dialog box. This menu allows the user to select the color or gray scale resolution value to be used when compressing the image or image sequence. If you set this field to 0, the component chooses an appropriate depth for the default compressor you specified with the `theCodec` field. See the chapter "Image Compression Manager" in *Inside Macintosh: QuickTime* for other valid pixel depth values.

When the user clicks OK, the standard image-compression dialog component sets this field to the pixel depth value selected by the user. Note that the standard image-compression dialog component may adjust the depth value so that it corresponds to a value that is supported by the compressor that has been selected by the user.

The depth returned could be 0 if the `scShowBestDepth` flag is set.

`spatialQuality`
Specifies the default setting of the quality slider in the dialog box. This slider controls the spatial quality of the compressed image sequence, which influences the amount of spatial compression that can be achieved. Spatial compression eliminates redundant information within each frame in a sequence. See the chapter "Image Compression Manager" in *Inside Macintosh: QuickTime* for valid compression quality values.

When the user clicks OK, the standard image-compression dialog component sets this field to the spatial quality value selected by the user. Note that the standard image-compression dialog component may adjust the quality value so that it corresponds to a value that is supported by the compressor that has been selected by the user.

The Temporal Settings Request Type

Use the temporal settings request to retrieve or modify the current temporal compression parameters. These parameters govern sequence-compression operations.

You supply a pointer to a temporal settings structure. If you are retrieving these settings, the standard dialog component places the current settings into the specified structure; if you are changing the settings, place the new values into the structure—the component uses those values to update its settings.

Standard Image-Compression Dialog Components

The `SCTemporalSettings` data type defines the format and content of the temporal settings structure:

```
typedef struct {
   CodecQ   temporalQuality;            /* desired quality */
   Fixed    frameRate;                  /* frame rate */
   long     keyFrameRate;               /* key frame rate */
} SCTemporalSettings;
```

Field descriptions

temporalQuality
: Specifies the default setting of the motion quality slider in the dialog box. This slider controls the temporal quality of the compressed image, which influences the amount of temporal compression that can be achieved (note that Apple's component uses the same slider for both spatial and temporal quality). Temporal compression eliminates redundant information between frames in an image sequence. See the chapter "Image Compression Manager" in *Inside Macintosh: QuickTime* for valid compression quality values.

   When the user clicks OK, the standard image-compression dialog component sets this field to the temporal quality value selected by the user. Note that the standard image-compression dialog component may adjust the quality value so that it corresponds to a value that is supported by the compressor that has been selected by the user.

frameRate
: Specifies the default value of the text-edit box that controls the number of frames per second in the image sequence to be compressed. This dialog item allows the user to select the frame rate to be used when compressing the image sequence. Note that this field is stored as a fixed-point number, allowing the user to specify fractional frame rates.

   When the user clicks OK, the standard image-compression dialog component sets this field to the frame rate value specified by the user. If you have set the `scAllowZeroFrameRate` flag to 1 in the `scPreferenceFlagsType` request, and the user specifies nothing or 0, the component sets this field to 0.

   This dialog item can be useful in cases where your application cannot determine the frame rate of the source movie. For example, movies stored in PICT files do not include frame rate information. Therefore, the user must specify a frame rate for you. Alternatively, some users may want to create movies with different frame rates. This item allows the user to specify a rate for the compressed sequence.

Standard Image-Compression Dialog Components

keyFrameRate	Specifies the default value of the text-edit box that controls the frequency with which key frames are inserted into the compressed image sequence. Key frames provide points from which a temporally compressed sequence may be decompressed. For a more complete discussion of key frames, see the chapter "Image Compression Manager" in *Inside Macintosh: QuickTime*.

When the user clicks OK, the standard image-compression dialog component sets this field to the key frame rate value specified by the user. If you have set the scAllowZeroKeyFrameRate flag to 1 in the scPreferenceFlagsType request, and the user specifies nothing or 0, the component sets this field to 0.

The Data-Rate Settings Request Type

Use the data-rate settings request to retrieve or modify the current temporal compression parameters that govern the data rate. These parameters affect sequence-compression operations.

You supply a pointer to a data-rate settings structure. If you are retrieving these settings, the standard dialog component places the current settings into the specified structure; if you are changing the settings, place the new values into the structure—the component uses those values to update its settings.

The SCDataRateSettings data type defines the format and content of the data-rate settings structure:

```
typedef struct {
    long     dataRate;              /* desired data rate */
    long     frameDuration;         /* frame duration */
    CodecQ   minSpatialQuality;     /* minimum value */
    CodecQ   minTemporalQuality;    /* minimum value */
} SCDataRateSettings;
```

Field descriptions

dataRate	Specifies the maximum number of bytes of compressed data your application wants to receive per second. Use this parameter to modulate the rate at which the component passes compressed data to your application. This can be useful to account for hardware limitations during sequence playback.

frameDuration	Indicates the duration of each frame, in milliseconds. Set this parameter to 0 to allow the standard dialog component to calculate the duration based upon the frame rate you specify in an scTemporalSettingsType request. However, if you allow the user to specify a 0 frame rate (that is, you set the scAllowZeroFrameRate flag to 1 in your scPreferenceFlagsType request), you must set the frame duration each time you compress a frame, because the component does not have sufficient information to determine an appropriate rate.

Standard Image-Compression Dialog Components

`minSpatialQuality`
: Specifies the minimum acceptable spatial quality. In order to meet your specified data rate, the standard dialog component may have to adjust the spatial quality setting. Use this parameter to set a minimum level, which the component may not exceed. See the chapter "Image Compression Manager" in *Inside Macintosh: QuickTime* for values for both this parameter and the `minTemporalQuality` parameter.

`minTemporalQuality`
: Specifies the minimum acceptable temporal quality. As with spatial quality, in order to meet your specified data rate, the standard dialog component may have to adjust the temporal quality setting. Use this parameter to set a minimum level, which the component may not exceed.

The Color Table Settings Request Type

Use the color table settings request to retrieve or modify the color table that the standard dialog component uses with all compression operations. Unless you specify otherwise, the component extracts the color table from the source image or sequence.

You supply a pointer to a color table handle (`CTabHandle` data type). Your application is responsible for disposing of this handle when you are done with it. Set the pointer to `nil` to clear the current color table; this may be useful if the current color table is inappropriate for the image or sequence you are working with.

The Progress Function Request Type

Use the progress function request to assign a progress function for use by the standard dialog component. The progress function is a part of your application. The standard dialog component calls this function during time-consuming operations, and reports its progress. Your progress function can use the information it receives from the standard dialog component to keep the user informed about the progress of the operation.

You supply a pointer to an Image Compression Manager progress function structure (see the chapter "Image Compression Manager" in *Inside Macintosh: QuickTime* for information about the format and content of this structure, as well as complete information about progress functions). Set the pointer to `nil` to clear the current progress function; in this case, the standard dialog component does not report its progress to the user. Set the pointer to –1 to use the component's default progress function.

The Extended Functions Request Type

Use the extended functions request to extend the interface provided in the standard image or sequence dialog boxes. You may specify a filter function, a hook function, and a custom button; you may retrieve the current settings for these options using the `SCGetInfo` function.

You supply a pointer to an extended functions structure. If you are retrieving these settings, the standard dialog component places the current settings into the specified structure; if you are changing the settings, place the new values into the structure—the component uses those values to update its settings. Set this pointer to `nil` to remove the current functions.

By default, none of these extended interface elements are used.

The `SCExtendedProcs` data type defines the format and content of the extended functions structure:

```
typedef struct {
   SCModalFilterProcPtr    filterProc; /* filter function */
   SCModalHookProcPtr      hookProc;   /* hook function */
   long                    refcon;     /* reference constant */
   Str31                   customName; /* custom button name */
} SCExtendedProcs;
```

Field descriptions

filterProc   Contains a pointer to a modal-dialog filter function in your application. Because the compression dialog box is a movable modal dialog box, you must provide a filter to process update events for your application windows. The standard component calls your filter function before it processes the event. You can use this function to control events in the dialog box. For example, you might use the filter function to release processing time to other windows displayed by your application while the standard image-compression dialog box is being displayed.

This is how to declare a filter function named `MyFilter`:

```
pascal Boolean MyFilter (DialogPtr theDialog,
         EventRecord *theEvent, short *itemHit,
         long refcon);
```

The operation of modal-dialog filter functions is described in the chapter "Dialog Manager" in *Inside Macintosh: Macintosh Toolbox Essentials*. The `refcon` parameter contains the reference constant you supply in the `refcon` field of this structure.

If you do not want to specify a filter function, set this parameter to `nil`.

Standard Image-Compression Dialog Components

hookProc Contains a pointer to a dialog hook function in your application. The standard component calls your hook function whenever the user selects an item in the dialog box. You can use this function to customize the operation of the standard image-compression dialog box. For example, you might want to support a custom button that activates a secondary dialog box. Another possibility would be to provide additional validation support when the user clicks OK. For an example of defining a custom button, see "Extending the Basic Dialog Box" beginning on page 3-11.

This is how to declare a hook function named MyHook:

```
pascal short MyHook (DialogPtr theDialog,
                    short *itemHit, SCParams *params,
                    long refcon);
```

The operation of this dialog hook function is described in "Application-Defined Function," beginning on page 3-45.

If you do not want to specify a hook function, set this parameter to nil.

refcon Specifies a reference constant that is to be passed to the dialog hook function and the modal-dialog filter function.

customName Specifies the string to be displayed in the custom button in the dialog box.

If you are not using a custom button, set this parameter to nil.

The Preference Flags Request Type

Use the preference flags request to specify or retrieve the standard dialog component's preference flags. These flags govern some of the details of the dialog box that are presented to the user.

You supply a pointer to a long integer. If you are retrieving these flags, the standard dialog component places the current settings into the specified field; if you are changing the flags, set the field with your desired flag values—the component uses those values to update its settings.

By default, the SCRequestImageSettings function operates with the scShowBestDepth and scUseMovableModal flags set to 1. The SCRequestSequenceSettings function operates with the scUseMovableModal flag set to 1. You should never need to change the values of the scListEveryCodec or scUseMovableModal flags.

Standard Image-Compression Dialog Components

The following flags are defined:

```
#define   scListEveryCodec      (1L<<1)   /* list every component */
#define   scAllowZeroFrameRate  (1L<<2)   /* allow 0 frame rate */
#define   scAllowZeroKeyFrameRate
                                (1L<<3)   /* 0 key frame rate OK */
#define   scShowBestDepth       (1L<<4)   /* use best image depth */
#define   scUseMovableModal     (1L<<5)   /* use movable dialog */
```

Flag descriptions

`scListEveryCodec`
: Controls the contents of the pop-up menu of compressors. If you set this flag to 1, the standard image-compression dialog component lists every compressor component that is present in the system. Each entry in the list contains the name of a compressor component. The user may then select a specific component from the list.

  If you set this flag to 0, the list contains one entry for each type of compressor component that is present in the system. Each list entry contains the name of a compressor type (for example, a list entry might contain "Animation" for the animation compressor). The user may then select a type of compressor—it is your application's responsibility to select an appropriate compressor of that type.

`scAllowZeroFrameRate`
: Determines whether the component allows the user to specify a value of 0 for the frame rate. If you set this flag to 1, the component allows the user to specify either 0 or nothing for the frame rate. The component then includes a "best rate" entry in the pop-up menu. If the user specifies 0, the component sets the `frameRate` field in the `SCTemporalSettings` structure to 0. Your application must then determine the best frame rate for the movie.

  If you set this flag to 0, the component does not allow the user to enter 0 for the frame rate. In this case, the user must select a specific frame rate.

`scAllowZeroKeyFrameRate`
: Similar to the `scAllowZeroFrameRate` flag, this flag determines whether the component allows the user to specify a value of 0 for the key frame rate. If you set this flag to 1, the component allows the user to specify 0 for the frame rate. If the user specifies 0, the component sets the `keyFrameRate` field in the `SCTemporalSettings` structure to 0. Your application must then determine the best key frame rate for the movie.

  If you set this flag to 0, the component does not allow the user to specify 0 for the frame rate. In this case, if the user has enabled temporal compression by checking the key frame checkbox, the user must also select a specific key frame rate.

`scShowBestDepth`
: Determines whether the component includes a "best depth" entry in the pop-up menu for pixel depth. If you set this flag to 1, the component includes a "best depth" entry in the pop-up menu. If the user selects "best depth," the component sets the depth to 0. Your application must then determine the best pixel depth for the movie.

    If you set this flag to 0, the component does not include a "best depth" entry in the pop-up menu. The user must select a depth from among the other available choices.

`scUseMovableModal`
: Determines whether the standard compression dialog is a movable or a stationary dialog. Set this flag to 1 to create a movable dialog. In this case, you should provide an event filter function to handle update events (use the `scExtendedProcsType` request).

The Settings State Request Type

Use the settings state request to set or retrieve the configuration of the standard dialog component. You may use this request to retrieve the configuration information so that you can save it for later use, or to reconfigure the component based on a saved configuration.

Your application is not concerned with the content of the configuration information that is returned. The standard dialog component saves its configuration in a format that it understands. This request affects only those settings that are valid across system restarts, such as the spatial and temporal compression parameters and the data-rate settings.

You supply a pointer to a handle. When you retrieve the settings, the standard dialog component creates an appropriately-sized handle and places its current configuration information into the handle. Your application is responsible for disposing of the handle when you are done with it.

When you modify the settings, you supply the configuration information in the handle. The component copies the data out of this handle. Your application is responsible for disposing of the handle when you are done with it. Set the pointer to `nil` to reset the component to its default configuration.

The Sequence ID Request Type

Use the sequence ID request type to retrieve the sequence identifier being used by the component's `SCCompressSequenceFrame` function. You may not use this request to set the sequence identifier.

You supply a pointer to a field of type `ImageSequence` (this is an Image Compression Manager data type). The standard dialog component returns the current sequence identifier in that field.

The Window Position Request Type

Use the window position request to position the user's dialog box.

You supply a pointer to a point. If you are retrieving this information, the standard dialog component places the coordinates of the upper-left corner of the dialog box into this point; if you are changing the dialog box's position, place the new coordinates into the point structure—the component uses those coordinates to position the dialog box.

Normally you should not need to use this request. By default, the standard dialog component centers the dialog box on the screen that is best-suited to display your test image. The component also saves the last window position for movable modal dialogs.

The Control Flags Request Type

Use the control flags request to retrieve or modify the control flags used by the standard dialog component. The standard dialog component passes these flags through to the image compressor it uses to compress your image or sequence. These flags are Image Compression Manager control flags, as described in the chapter "Image Compression Manager" in *Inside Macintosh: QuickTime*.

You supply a pointer to a flags field of data type `CodecFlags` (this is an Image Compression Manager data type). If you are retrieving the flags, the standard dialog component places the current flags into this field. If you are setting new flag values, place your desired settings into the field—the component uses these new flag settings.

By default, the standard dialog component sets all flags to 0 when it compresses still images. When it is compressing sequences, the component sets the `codecFlagsPreviousUpdate` and `codecFlagsUpdatePreviousComp` flags to 1. Typically, you should not need to change these flag settings.

Standard Image-Compression Dialog Component Functions

This section describes the functions that are supported by standard image-compression dialog components. It is divided into the following topics:

- "Getting Default Settings for an Image or a Sequence" discusses how you can use the standard dialog component to derive default compression settings for an image or a sequence.

- "Displaying the Standard Image-Compression Dialog Box" tells you how to present the standard dialog box to the user.

- "Compressing Still Images" discusses functions that allow you to compress still images.

- "Compressing Image Sequences" discusses functions that allow you to compress image sequences.

- "Working With Image or Sequence Settings" describes the functions and data structures you can use to modify the compression settings stored by the standard dialog component.

- "Specifying a Test Image" tells you how you can specify the image that is displayed to the user in the standard dialog box.
- "Positioning Dialog Boxes and Rectangles" provides information about a number of functions that allow you to position dialog boxes and rectangles that may be related to the standard dialog box.
- "Utility Function" discusses a utility function that the standard dialog component provides to your application.

Getting Default Settings for an Image or a Sequence

This section describes the functions that allow you to derive sensible default compression settings for an image or a sequence. The standard dialog component examines an image you provide and selects appropriate default settings based on the image's characteristics. The component stores those settings for you and uses them with other functions, including not only functions governing image or sequence compression, but also utility functions such as SCNewGWorld. If you choose to display a dialog box to the user, the component uses these settings as the default dialog box settings.

Any of these functions may be used with a single image or an image that is part of a sequence. You tell the standard dialog component whether the image is part of a sequence when you call the function.

If there is a custom color table associated with the image or the sequence, these functions retrieve and store it. You can use the color table settings request (described on page 3-20) to retrieve the custom color table and obtain as much color and depth information as possible from the image or sequence of images.

You can retrieve these settings using the SCGetInfo function, or modify them using the SCSetInfo function, which are described on page 3-34 and page 3-36, respectively.

There are three functions available: SCDefaultPictHandleSettings works with pictures, SCDefaultPictFileSettings works with picture files, and SCDefaultPixMapSettings works with pixel maps.

SCDefaultPixMapSettings

The SCDefaultPixMapSettings function allows you to derive default compression settings for an image that is stored in a pixel map.

```
pascal ComponentResult SCDefaultPixMapSettings
                (ComponentInstance ci, PixMapHandle src,
                 short motion);
```

ci   Identifies your application's connection to a standard image-compression dialog component. You obtain this identifier from the Component Manager's OpenDefaultComponent function.

CHAPTER 3

Standard Image-Compression Dialog Components

src   Contains a handle to the pixel map to be analyzed.

motion   Specifies whether the image is part of a sequence. Set this parameter to
                `true` if the image is part of a sequence; set it to `false` if you are working
                with a single still image.

SCDefaultPictHandleSettings

The `SCDefaultPictHandleSettings` function allows you to derive default compression settings for a picture that is stored in a handle.

```
pascal ComponentResult SCDefaultPictHandleSettings
                            (ComponentInstance ci,
                                PicHandle srcPicture,
                                short motion);
```

ci   Identifies your application's connection to a standard image-compression
                dialog component. You obtain this identifier from the Component
                Manager's `OpenDefaultComponent` function.

srcPicture
                Contains a handle to the picture to be analyzed.

motion   Specifies whether the image is part of a sequence. Set this parameter to
                `true` if the image is part of a sequence; set it to `false` if you are working
                with a single still image.

SCDefaultPictFileSettings

The `SCDefaultPictFileSettings` function allows you to derive default compression settings for a picture that is stored in a file.

```
pascal ComponentResult SCDefaultPictFileSettings
                            (ComponentInstance ci, short srcRef,
                                short motion);
```

ci   Identifies your application's connection to a standard image-compression
                dialog component. You obtain this identifier from the Component
                Manager's `OpenDefaultComponent` function.

srcRef   Contains a reference to the file to be analyzed.

motion   Specifies whether the image is part of a sequence. Set this parameter to
                `true` if the image is part of a sequence; set it to `false` if you are working
                with a single still image.

CHAPTER 3

Standard Image-Compression Dialog Components

RESULT CODES

File Manager errors

Displaying the Standard Image-Compression Dialog Box

Standard image-compression dialog components provide two functions that allow you to display the standard dialog box to the user and retrieve the compression parameters specified by the user.

Use the `SCRequestImageSettings` function to retrieve the user's preferences for compressing a single image; use the `SCRequestSequenceSettings` functions when you are working with an image sequence.

Both of these functions manipulate the compression settings that the component stores for you. The component may derive the current settings from a number of different sources:

- You may supply an image to the component from which it can derive default settings. You do this by using one of the functions discussed in "Getting Default Settings for an Image or a Sequence" beginning on page 3-26.

- If you have not set any defaults, but you do supply a test image for the dialog, the component examines the test image and derives appropriate default values based upon its characteristics.

- If you have not set any defaults and do not supply a test image, the component uses its own default values.

- You may modify the settings by using the `SCSetInfo` function, which is described on page 3-36.

- You may allow the user to modify those settings by calling one of the functions discussed in this section.

You may customize the dialog boxes by specifying a modal-dialog hook function or a custom button. You may use the custom button to invoke an ancillary dialog box that is specific to your application. See "Request Types" beginning on page 3-15 for more information.

SCRequestImageSettings

The `SCRequestImageSettings` function displays the standard image dialog box to the user; the dialog box is populated with the default settings you have established.

```
pascal ComponentResult SCRequestImageSettings
                                (ComponentInstance ci);
```

ci   Identifies your application's connection to a standard image-compression dialog component.

DESCRIPTION

The standard dialog component retrieves and validates the user's selections, and saves the resulting settings for use later.

Use this function when you are working with a single still image.

RESULT CODES

`scUserCancelled`	1	Dialog box canceled—user clicked Cancel
`paramErr`	–50	Invalid parameter value

SCRequestSequenceSettings

The `SCRequestSequenceSettings` function displays the standard sequence dialog box to the user; the dialog box uses the default settings you have established.

```
pascal ComponentResult SCRequestSequenceSettings
                                (ComponentInstance ci);
```

ci   Identifies your application's connection to a standard image-compression dialog component.

DESCRIPTION

The standard dialog component retrieves and validates the user's selections, and saves the resulting settings for use later.

Use this function when you are working with an image sequence.

RESULT CODES

`scUserCancelled`	1	Dialog box canceled—user clicked Cancel
`paramErr`	–50	Invalid parameter value

Compressing Still Images

The standard dialog component provides three functions you may use to compress a still image. These functions differ based on how the image is stored: `SCCompressImage` works with pixel maps; `SCCompressPicture` compresses a picture that is stored in a handle; and `SCCompressPictureFile` works with pictures stored in files.

All of these functions use the current compression settings. See "Displaying the Standard Image-Compression Dialog Box" beginning on page 3-28 for detailed information about establishing these current settings.

If there are no default settings, each of these functions could potentially display the dialog box for single-frame compression operations shown in Figure 3-1 on page 3-4.

CHAPTER 3

Standard Image-Compression Dialog Components

SCCompressImage

The `SCCompressImage` function compresses an image that is stored in a pixel map.

```
pascal ComponentResult SCCompressImage (ComponentInstance ci,
                                        PixMapHandle src,
                                        Rect *srcRect,
                                        ImageDescriptionHandle *desc,
                                        Handle *data);
```

ci Identifies your application's connection to a standard image-compression dialog component.

src Contains a handle to the pixel map to be compressed.

srcRect Contains a pointer to a portion of the pixel map to compress. This rectangle must be in the pixel map's coordinate system. If you want to compress the entire pixel map, set this parameter to `nil`.

desc Contains a pointer to an image description handle. The standard dialog component creates an image description structure when it compresses the image, and returns a handle to that structure in the field referred to by this parameter. The component sizes that handle appropriately. Your application is responsible for disposing of that handle when you are done with it.

data Contains a pointer to a handle. The standard dialog component returns a handle to the compressed image data in the field referred to by this parameter. The component sizes that handle appropriately. Your application is responsible for disposing of that handle when you are done with it.

RESULT CODES

scUserCancelled   1   Dialog box canceled—user clicked Cancel

Image Compression Manager errors (from `FCompressImage` function)

SCCompressPicture

The `SCCompressPicture` function compresses a picture that is stored in a handle.

```
pascal ComponentResult SCCompressPicture (ComponentInstance ci,
                                          PicHandle srcPicture,
                                          PicHandle dstPicture);
```

ci Identifies your application's connection to a standard image-compression dialog component.

CHAPTER 3

Standard Image-Compression Dialog Components

`srcPicture`
: Contains a handle to the picture to be compressed.

`dstPicture`
: Contains a handle to the compressed picture. The standard dialog component resizes this handle to accommodate the compressed picture. Your application is responsible for creating and disposing of this handle when you are done with it.

RESULT CODES

`scUserCancelled`   1   Dialog box canceled—user clicked Cancel

Image Compression Manager errors (from `FCompressPicture` function)

SCCompressPictureFile

The `SCCompressPictureFile` function compresses a picture that is stored in a file.

```
pascal ComponentResult SCCompressPictureFile
                        (ComponentInstance ci,
                         short srcRefNum, short dstRefNum);
```

`ci`
: Identifies your application's connection to a standard image-compression dialog component.

`srcRefNum`
: Contains a reference to the file to be compressed.

`dstRefNum`
: Contains a reference to the file that is to receive the compressed data. This may be the same as the source file. The standard dialog component places the compressed image data into the file identified by this reference. Your application is responsible for this file after the compression operation.

RESULT CODES

`scUserCancelled`   1   Dialog box canceled—user clicked Cancel

Image Compression Manager errors (from `FCompressPictureFile` function)

Compressing Image Sequences

The standard dialog component provides three functions you may use to compress an image sequence. The `SCCompressSequenceBegin` function allows you to start a sequence-compression operation; use the `SCCompressSequenceFrame` function for each image in the sequence; you end the sequence by calling the `SCCompressSequenceEnd` function. The standard dialog component manages all of the compression details for you. Your application may have only one sequence-compression operation active on any given connection; naturally, you may have more than one connection active at a time.

CHAPTER 3

Standard Image-Compression Dialog Components

All of these functions use the current compression settings. See "Displaying the Standard Image-Compression Dialog Box" beginning on page 3-28 for detailed information about establishing these current settings.

If there are no default settings, each of these functions could potentially display the dialog box for sequence-compression operations shown in Figure 3-2 on page 3-5.

SCCompressSequenceBegin

The `SCCompressSequenceBegin` function initiates a sequence-compression operation. You supply the first image in the sequence so that the component can determine its spatial and graphical characteristics.

```
pascal ComponentResult SCCompressSequenceBegin
                        (ComponentInstance ci,
                            PixMapHandle src, Rect *srcRect,
                            ImageDescriptionHandle *desc);
```

ci
: Identifies your application's connection to a standard image-compression dialog component.

src
: Contains a handle to the pixel map to be compressed. This pixel map must contain the first image in the sequence.

srcRect
: Contains a pointer to a portion of the pixel map to compress. This rectangle must be in the pixel map's coordinate system. If you want to compress the entire pixel map, set this parameter to `nil`.

desc
: Contains a pointer to an image description handle. The standard dialog component creates an image description structure when it compresses the image, and returns a handle to that structure in the field referred to by this parameter. The component sizes the handle appropriately. If you do not want this information, set this parameter to `nil`.

    The returned structure is valid for the entire sequence. The standard dialog component disposes of the handle when you end the sequence by calling the `SCCompressSequenceEnd` function. Your application must not dispose of this handle by any other means.

RESULT CODES

Memory Manager errors
Image Compression Manager errors (from `CompressSequenceBegin` function)

SCCompressSequenceFrame

The `SCCompressSequenceFrame` function continues a sequence-compression operation. You must call this function once for each frame in the sequence, including the first frame.

```
pascal ComponentResult SCCompressSequenceFrame
                (ComponentInstance ci, PixMapHandle src,
                Rect *srcRect, Handle *data,
                long *dataSize, short *notSyncFlag);
```

ci
: Identifies your application's connection to a standard image-compression dialog component.

src
: Contains a handle to the pixel map to be compressed.

srcRect
: Contains a pointer to a portion of the pixel map to compress. This rectangle must be in the pixel map's coordinate system. If you want to compress the entire pixel map, set this parameter to `nil`.

data
: Contains a pointer to a handle. The standard dialog component returns a handle to the compressed image data in the field referred to by this parameter. The component sizes that handle appropriately for the sequence.

    Your application must not dispose of this handle. The standard dialog component disposes of the handle when you end the sequence by calling the `SCCompressSequenceEnd` function. If you need to lock the handle, be sure to save and restore the handle's state.

dataSize
: Contains a pointer to a long integer. The standard dialog component returns a value that indicates the number of bytes of compressed image data that it returns. Note that this value will differ from the size of the handle referred to by the `data` parameter, because the handle is allocated to accommodate the largest image in the sequence.

notSyncFlag
: Contains a pointer to a short integer that indicates whether the compressed frame is a key frame. If the frame is a key frame, the standard dialog component sets the field referred to by this parameter to 0; otherwise, the component sets this field to `mediaSampleNotSync`. You may use this field to set the `sampleFlags` parameter of the Movie Toolbox's `AddMediaSample` function.

RESULT CODES

scUserCancelled   1   Dialog box canceled—user clicked Cancel

Image Compression Manager errors (from `CompressSequenceFrame` function)

SCCompressSequenceEnd

The `SCCompressSequenceEnd` function ends a sequence-compression operation. The standard dialog component disposes of any memory it used to compress the image sequence, including the data and image description buffers. You must call this function once for each sequence you start.

```
pascal ComponentResult SCCompressSequenceEnd
                            (ComponentInstance ci);
```

ci   Identifies your application's connection to a standard image-compression dialog component.

Working With Image or Sequence Settings

The standard dialog component provides two functions that allow you to work with the current compression settings for an image or a sequence of images. You can establish these settings in a number of ways: see "Setting Default Parameters" on page 3-8 for more information about your options.

You use the `SCGetInfo` function to retrieve settings information. The `SCSetInfo` function enables you to modify the settings.

These functions can work with a number of different types of settings information. When you call either function, you specify the type of data you want to work with. Each of these request types requires different parameter data. See "Request Types" beginning on page 3-15 for a description of each of these request types and their data requirements.

SCGetInfo

The `SCGetInfo` function allows you to retrieve configuration information from the standard dialog component.

```
pascal ComponentResult SCGetInfo (ComponentInstance ci,
                            OSType type, void *info);
```

ci   Identifies your application's connection to a standard image-compression dialog component.

Standard Image-Compression Dialog Components

type
: Specifies the type of information you want to retrieve. The following values are valid:

  scSpatialSettingsType
  : The component returns its spatial compression parameters.

  scTemporalSettingsType
  : The component returns its temporal compression parameters.

  scDataRateSettingsType
  : The component returns information about its compression data rate.

  scColorTableType
  : The component returns its color table.

  scProgressProcType
  : The component returns a pointer to its progress function.

  scExtendedProcsType
  : The component returns information about how you have extended the standard dialog box.

  scPreferenceFlagsType
  : The component returns its current preference flags settings.

  scSettingsStateType
  : The component returns its complete configuration.

  scSequenceIDType
  : The component returns its current image-compression sequence identifier.

  scWindowPositionType
  : The component returns information about where the standard dialog is positioned.

  scCodecFlagsType
  : The component returns its current image-compression control flags.

info
: Contains a pointer to a field that is to receive the information.

DESCRIPTION

You use the `type` parameter to specify the type of information you want to retrieve. The `info` parameter contains a pointer to a location to receive the information (see this section's introductory text for information about the format of the data that is returned for each request type). If the component cannot satisfy your request, it returns a result code of `scTypeNotFoundErr`.

RESULT CODE

scTypeNotFoundErr –8971 Component does not have the information you want

SCSetInfo

The `SCSetInfo` function allows you to modify the standard dialog component's configuration information.

```
pascal ComponentResult SCSetInfo (ComponentInstance ci,
                                  OSType type, void *info);
```

ci
: Identifies your application's connection to a standard image-compression dialog component.

type
: Specifies the type of information you want to modify. The following values are valid:

    scSpatialSettingsType
    : Modifies the component's spatial compression parameters.

    scTemporalSettingsType
    : Modifies the component's temporal compression parameters.

    scDataRateSettingsType
    : Modifies the component's compression data rate.

    scColorTableType
    : Modifies the component's color table.

    scProgressProcType
    : Modifies the component's progress function.

    scExtendedProcsType
    : Allows you to extend the standard dialog box.

    scPreferenceFlagsType
    : Modifies the component's preference flags settings.

    scSettingsStateType
    : Configures the component, based on a saved configuration.

    scWindowPositionType
    : Positions the standard dialog box.

    scCodecFlagsType
    : Modifies the component's image-compression control flags.

info
: Contains a pointer to a field that contains the new configuration information.

DESCRIPTION

You use the `type` parameter to specify the type of information you want to modify. The `info` parameter contains a pointer to a location that contains the new information (see "Request Types" beginning on page 3-15 for information about the format of the data you must supply for each request type). If the component cannot satisfy your request, it returns a result code of `scTypeNotFoundErr`.

CHAPTER 3

Standard Image-Compression Dialog Components

RESULT CODE

scTypeNotFoundErr   –8971   Component does not have the information you want

Specifying a Test Image

The standard image-compression dialog component provided by Apple supports a test image. As you can see in Figure 3-3 on page 3-7, the dialog box contains a small image along with the other parts of the dialog box. The component uses this image to display the effect of the user's image-compression settings. In this manner, the user can experiment with different settings and see the results of those settings immediately.

The component provides three functions that allow you to specify the test image. Use the SCSetTestImagePictHandle function if your test image is stored in a handle. Use the SCSetTestImagePictFile function if your test image is in a picture file. The SCSetTestImagePixMap function sets the test image from a pixel map.

SCSetTestImagePictHandle

The SCSetTestImagePictHandle function sets the dialog box's test image from a picture that is stored in a handle.

```
pascal ComponentResult SCSetTestImagePictHandle
                (ComponentInstance ci, PicHandle testPict,
                 Rect *testRect, short testFlags);
```

ci
: Identifies your application's connection to a standard image-compression dialog component.

testPict
: Identifies a handle that contains the new test image. Your application is responsible for disposing of this handle when you are done with it. You must clear the image or close your connection to the standard image-compression dialog component before you dispose of this handle or close the corresponding resource file. You must set this handle as nonpurgeable.

  Set this parameter to nil to clear the test image.

testRect
: Contains a pointer to a rectangle structure. This rectangle specifies, in the coordinate system of the source image, the area of interest or point of interest in the test image. The area of interest defines a portion of the test image that is to be shown to the user in the dialog box. Use this parameter to direct the component to a specific portion of the test image. The component uses the value of the testFlags parameter to determine how it transforms this image before displaying it to the user. The component uses the testFlags parameter only when the test image is larger than the test image portion of the dialog box.

CHAPTER 3

Standard Image-Compression Dialog Components

You may specify a point of interest by setting the points in the rectangle structure so that they enclose a single point—for example, (0,0) and (1,1). The component centers this point in the image that is displayed in the dialog box, and displays the part of the image that fits in the test image portion of the dialog box.

To use the entire picture, specify `nil` in this parameter.

`testFlags` Specifies how the component is to display a test image that is larger than the test image portion of the dialog box. If you set this parameter to 0, the component uses a default method of its own choosing. In all cases, the component centers the area or point of interest in the test image portion of the dialog box, and then displays some part of the test image.

You may indicate your display preference by setting this parameter to one of the following values:

`scPreferCropping`
: Indicates that the component should crop the test image to fit the test image portion of the dialog box. The component displays the part of the image that fits in the test image portion of the box. If the image is smaller than the space allotted in the dialog box, the component does not alter the image before displaying it—the resulting image is smaller than the available space.

`scPreferScaling`
: Indicates that the component should scale the test image to fit the test image portion of the dialog box. The component shrinks the image to fit the test image portion of the dialog box.

`scPreferScalingAndCropping`
: Indicates that the component should both scale and crop the test image. This option is useful with very large test images. The component first shrinks the image to approximately the size of the test image portion of the dialog box, and then trims the image so that it fits the available space.

RESULT CODE

`paramErr`   –50   Invalid parameter specified

CHAPTER 3

Standard Image-Compression Dialog Components

SCSetTestImagePictFile

The `SCSetTestImagePictFile` function sets the dialog box's test image from a picture that is stored in a picture file.

```
pascal ComponentResult SCSetTestImagePictFile
                    (ComponentInstance ci, short testFileRef,
                    Rect *testRect, short testFlags);
```

`ci`
: Identifies your application's connection to a standard image-compression dialog component.

`testFileRef`
: Identifies the file that contains the new test image. Your application is responsible for opening this file before calling this function. You must also close the file when you are done with it. You must clear the image or close your connection to the standard image-compression dialog component before you close the file. If the file contains a large image, the component may take some time to display the standard image-compression dialog box. In this case, the component displays the watch cursor while it loads the test image.

  Set this parameter to 0 to clear the test image.

`testRect`
: Contains a pointer to a rectangle structure. This rectangle specifies, in the coordinate system of the source image, the area of interest or point of interest in the test image. The area of interest defines a portion of the test image that is to be shown to the user in the dialog box. Use this parameter to direct the component to a specific portion of the test image. The component uses the value of the `testFlags` parameter to determine how it transforms large images before displaying them to the user.

  You may specify a point of interest by setting the points in the rectangle structure so that they enclose a single point—for example, (0,0) and (1,1). The component centers this point in the image that is displayed in the dialog box, and displays the part of the image that fits in the test image portion of the dialog box.

  To use the entire picture file, pass `nil` in this parameter.

`testFlags`
: Specifies how the component is to display a test image that is larger than the test image portion of the dialog box. If you set this parameter to 0, the component uses a default method of its own choosing. In all cases, the component centers the area or point of interest in the test image portion of the dialog box, and then displays some part of the test image.

  You may indicate your display preference by setting this parameter to one of the following values:

  `scPreferCropping`
  : Indicates that the component should crop the test image to fit the test image portion of the dialog box. The component displays the part of the image that fits in the test image portion of the box. If the image is smaller than the space

Standard Image-Compression Dialog Components

alloted in the dialog box, the component does not alter the image before displaying it—the resulting image is smaller than the available space.

`scPreferScaling`
: Indicates that the component should scale the test image to fit the test image portion of the dialog box. The component shrinks the image to fit the test image portion of the dialog box.

`scPreferScalingAndCropping`
: Indicates that the component should both scale and crop the test image. This option is useful with very large test images. The component first shrinks the image to approximately the size of the test image portion of the dialog box, then trims the image so that it fits the available space.

RESULT CODES

`paramErr`   –50   Invalid parameter specified

File Manager errors

SCSetTestImagePixMap

The `SCSetTestImagePixMap` function sets the dialog box's test image from a picture that is stored in a pixel map.

```
pascal ComponentResult SCSetTestImagePixMap (ComponentInstance ci,
                                PixMapHandle testPixMap,
                                Rect *testRect,
                                short testFlags);
```

`ci`
: Identifies your application's connection to a standard image-compression dialog component.

`testPixMap`
: Contains a handle to a pixel map that contains the new test image. Your application is responsible for creating this pixel map before calling this function. You must also dispose of the pixel map when you are done with it. You must clear the image or close your connection to the standard image-compression dialog component before you dispose of the pixel map.

  Set this parameter to `nil` to clear the test image.

testRect   Contains a pointer to a rectangle structure. This rectangle specifies, in the coordinate system of the source image, the area of interest or point of interest in the test image. The area of interest defines a portion of the test image that is to be shown to the user in the dialog box. Use this parameter to direct the component to a specific portion of the test image. The component uses the value of the `testFlags` parameter to determine how it transforms large images before displaying them to the user.

You may specify a point of interest by setting the points in the rectangle structure so that they enclose a single point—for example, (0,0) and (1,1). The component centers this point in the image that is displayed in the dialog box, and displays the part of the image that fits in the test image portion of the dialog box.

To use the entire pixel map, specify `nil` in this parameter.

testFlags   Specifies how the component is to display a test image that is larger than the test image portion of the dialog box. If you set this parameter to 0, the component uses a default method of its own choosing. In all cases, the component centers the area or point of interest in the test image portion of the dialog box, and then displays some part of the test image.

You may indicate your display preference by setting this parameter to one of the following values:

scPreferCropping
: Indicates that the component should crop the test image to fit the test image portion of the dialog box. The component displays the part of the image that fits in the test image portion of the box. If the image is smaller than the space alloted in the dialog box, the component does not alter the image before displaying it—the resulting image is smaller than the available space.

scPreferScaling
: Indicates that the component should scale the test image to fit the test image portion of the dialog box. The component shrinks the image to fit the test image portion of the dialog box.

scPreferScalingAndCropping
: Indicates that the component should both scale and crop the test image. This option is useful with very large test images. The component first shrinks the image to approximately the size of the test image portion of the dialog box, then trims the image so that it fits the available space.

RESULT CODE

paramErr   –50   Invalid parameter specified

Positioning Dialog Boxes and Rectangles

Standard image-compression dialog components provide functions that allow you to position rectangles and dialog boxes. These functions are most useful in helping you to manage dialog boxes that are related to the standard image-compression dialog. For example, your application might support a custom button that initiates a dialog box with the user to specify additional compression parameters. You can use these functions to position that dialog box in relation to the standard image-compression dialog box.

There are two positioning functions: the `SCPositionRect` function positions a rectangle; the `SCPositionDialog` positions a dialog box. The `SCGetBestDeviceRect` function returns information about the best available display device.

SCPositionRect

The `SCPositionRect` function positions a rectangle on the screen. You indicate where you want to put the rectangle by specifying the desired coordinates of the upper-left corner of the rectangle.

```
pascal ComponentResult SCPositionRect (ComponentInstance ci,
                                       Rect *rp, Point *where);
```

ci   Identifies your application's connection to a standard image-compression dialog component.

rp   Contains a pointer to a rectangle structure. When you call the `SCPositionRect` function, this structure should contain the rectangle's current global coordinates. The `SCPositionRect` function adjusts the coordinates in the structure to reflect the rectangle's new position.

where   Contains a pointer to a point in global coordinates identifying the desired location of the upper-left corner of the rectangle. This parameter allows your application to position the rectangle on the screen.

The standard image-compression dialog component supports two special values for this parameter. If you set this parameter to (–1,–1), the component places the rectangle on the display device that has the menu bar. The component centers the rectangle horizontally on that device. The component vertically positions the rectangle so that 1/3 of the vertical space that is not used by the rectangle remains above the rectangle, and the remaining 2/3 of the unused space is below the rectangle.

If you set this parameter to (–2,–2), the component places the rectangle on the display device that supports the highest color or grayscale resolution. The component positions the rectangle as it does for the other special value. This option displays images most clearly and is the recommended value for most cases.

The `SCPositionRect` function adjusts the coordinates of this point to correspond to the upper-left corner of the rectangle.

Standard Image-Compression Dialog Components

RESULT CODE

    `paramErr`   –50   Invalid parameter specified

SCPositionDialog

The `SCPositionDialog` function helps you to position a dialog box on the screen.

```
pascal ComponentResult SCPositionDialog (ComponentInstance ci,
                                    short id, Point *where);
```

`ci`   Identifies your application's connection to a standard image-compression dialog component.

`id`   Specifies the resource number of a `'DLOG'` resource. The `SCPositionDialog` function positions the dialog box that corresponds to this resource.

`where`   Contains a pointer to a point in global coordinates identifying the desired location of the upper-left corner of the dialog box. This parameter allows you to indicate how you want to position the dialog box on the screen.

The standard image-compression dialog component supports two special values for this parameter. If you set this parameter to (–1,–1), the component places the dialog box on the display device that has the menu bar. The component centers the dialog box horizontally on that device. The component vertically positions the dialog box so that 1/3 of the vertical space that is not used by the box remains above the box, and the remaining 2/3 of the unused space is below the box.

If you set this parameter to (–2,–2), the component places the dialog box on the display device that supports the highest color or gray scale resolution. The component positions the dialog box as it does for the other special value. This option displays images most clearly and is the recommended value for most cases.

The `SCPositionDialog` function adjusts the coordinates of this point to correspond to the upper-left corner of the dialog box.

DESCRIPTION

You indicate where you want to put the dialog box by specifying the desired coordinates of the upper-left corner of the box. The component then derives appropriate location information for the dialog box based upon its size and the display characteristics of the destination device, and returns that location information to your program. You can then pass that information to the Dialog Manager when you want to display the dialog box.

RESULT CODES

    `paramErr`   –50   Invalid parameter specified
    Resource Manager errors

SCGetBestDeviceRect

The `SCGetBestDeviceRect` function determines the boundary rectangle that surrounds the display device that supports the largest color or grayscale palette.

```
pascal ComponentResult SCGetBestDeviceRect (ComponentInstance ci,
                                            Rect *r);
```

ci   Identifies your application's connection to a standard image-compression dialog component.

r   Contains a pointer to a rectangle structure. The `SCGetBestDeviceRect` function returns the global coordinates of a rectangle that surrounds the appropriate display device.

DESCRIPTION

The `SCGetBestDeviceRect` function determines the boundary rectangle that surrounds the display device that supports the largest color or grayscale palette. If more than one device supports the same pixel depth, the function returns information about the device that has the highest resolution.

Note that the function subtracts the menu bar from the returned rectangle if the best device is also the main display device.

The standard image-compression dialog component uses this function to position rectangles and dialog boxes when you indicate that the component is to choose the best display device. In general, your application does not need to use this function.

RESULT CODE

paramErr   –50   Invalid parameter specified

Utility Function

The standard dialog component provides a single utility function that you can use to create a graphics world that is appropriate for the current compression settings. This function is described next.

SCNewGWorld

The `SCNewGWorld` function creates a graphics world based on the current compression settings.

```
pascal ComponentResult SCNewGWorld (ComponentInstance ci,
                                    GWorldPtr *gwp, Rect *rp,
                                    GWorldFlags flags);
```

`ci`
: Identifies your application's connection to a standard image-compression dialog component.

`gwp`
: Contains a pointer to a pointer to a graphics world. The standard dialog component places a pointer to the new graphics world into the field referred to by this parameter. If the component cannot create the graphics world, it sets this field to `nil`.

  Your application is responsible for disposing of the graphics world when you are done with it.

`rp`
: Contains a pointer to the boundaries of the graphics world. If you set this parameter to `nil`, the standard dialog component uses the test image's boundary rectangle. If you don't specify a boundary rectangle and there is no test image, the component does not create the graphics world.

`flags`
: Contains flags that are passed to QuickDraw's `NewGWorld` function. See the chapter "Basic QuickDraw" in *Inside Macintosh: Imaging* for more information about this function.

DESCRIPTION

The `SCNewGWorld` function creates a graphics world that can accommodate the current compression settings, including color table and grayscale settings (if appropriate). If the selected color table is inappropriate for the pixel depth, the standard dialog component uses a standard color for the depth.

RESULT CODE

`scTypeNotFoundErr`   –8971   Component cannot create a graphics world

Application-Defined Function

The standard image-compression dialog component supplied by Apple allows you to extend the interface of the standard dialog box by defining a hook function. This section describes how that hook function operates.

CHAPTER 3

Standard Image-Compression Dialog Components

MyHook

This function is called by the standard dialog component whenever the user selects an item in the standard image-compression dialog box. You define the function in your application and assign it to a dialog box with the `hookProc` field of the `scExtendedProcsType` request, which is discussed on page 3-21.

This is how you would define a hook function called `MyHook`:

```
pascal short MyHook (DialogPtr theDialog, short itemHit,
                void *params, long refcon);
```

`theDialog` Contains a pointer to the dialog structure that identifies the current dialog box.

`itemHit` Identifies the item clicked by the user.

`params` Contains a pointer to a field that contains the identifier for your connection to the standard dialog component. You can use this identifier to call the dialog component's `SCGetInfo` or `SCSetInfo` functions.

`refcon` Contains the reference constant value you supplied to the `SCGetCompressionExtended` function.

DESCRIPTION

Your hook function returns a short integer that identifies the item selected by the user. In general, your hook function should return the same item number it receives in the `itemHit` parameter. By returning a specific value, you can affect how the component handles the user selection. The following values are defined:

`scOKItem` Indicates that the user clicked the OK button.

`scCancelItem`
    Indicates that the user clicked the Cancel button.

`scCustomItem`
    Indicates that the user clicked the custom button.

If you set the returned value to 0, you cancel the user selection; the dialog box remains on the screen awaiting further action by the user.

The hook function allows your application to tailor or extend the operation of the standard image-compression dialog box. By attaching your hook function to the dialog box, you intercept all user selections. For example, your hook function could perform additional parameter checking whenever the user clicks the OK button. In this case, whenever you detect an incorrect parameter value, you could display a message to the user and then set the returned value to 0, thereby canceling the user's selection. The user would then either cancel the dialog box or try again.

As another example, you could support additional parameters by implementing the dialog box's custom button. You could use your hook function to display a secondary dialog box whenever the user clicks the custom button. For an example of defining and using a custom button, see "Extending the Basic Dialog Box" beginning on page 3-11.

Summary of Standard Image-Compression Dialog Components

C Summary

Constants

```c
/* component type value */
#define  StandardCompressionType     'scdi' /* standard image-compression
                                               dialog component type */
#define  StandardCompressionSubType  'imag' /* standard image-compression
                                               dialog component subtype */

/* preference flags */
#define  scListEveryCodec            (1L<<1)    /* list all components */
#define  scAllowZeroFrameRate        (1L<<2)    /* allow 0 frame rate */
#define  scAllowZeroKeyFrameRate     (1L<<3)    /* allow 0 key frame rate */
#define  scShowBestDepth             (1L<<4)    /* allow "best depth" */
#define  scUseMovableModal           (1L<<5)    /* use movable dialog */

/* values for testFlags parameter of functions that set test image */
#define  scPreferCropping            (1<<0)     /* crop image to fit */
#define  scPreferScaling             (1<<1)     /* shrink image to fit */
#define  scPreferScalingAndCropping  (scPreferScaling + scPreferCropping)
                                                /* shrink then crop */

/* dimensions of the test image portion of the dialog box */
#define  scTestImageWidth            80     /* test width of image */
#define  scTestImageHeight           80     /* test height of image */

/* possible items returned by hook function */
#define  scOKItem                    1      /* user clicked OK */
#define  scCancelItem                2      /* user clicked Cancel */
#define  scCustomItem                3      /* user clicked custom button */

/* result returned when user canceled */
#define  scUserCancelled             1      /* user canceled dialog */
```

Standard Image-Compression Dialog Components

```c
/* selectors for standard image-compression dialog components */
#define     scPositionRect              2       /* SCPositionRect */
#define     scPositionDialog            3       /* SCPositionDialog */
#define     scSetTestImagePictHandle    4       /* SCSetTestImagePictHandle */
#define     scSetTestImagePictFile      5       /* SCSetTestImagePictFile */
#define     scSetTestImagePixMap        6       /* SCSetTestImagePixMap */
#define     scGetBestDeviceRect         7       /* SCGetBestDeviceRect */
#define     scRequestImageSettings      10      /* SCRequestImageSettings */
#define     scCompressImage             11      /* SCCompressImage */
#define     scCompressPicture           12      /* SCCompressPicture */
#define     scCompressPictureFile       13      /* SCCompressPictureFile */
#define     scRequestSequenceSettings   14      /* SCRequestSequenceSettings */
#define     scCompressSequenceBegin     15      /* SCCompressSequenceBegin */
#define     scCompressSequenceFrame     16      /* SCCompressSequenceFrame */
#define     scCompressSequenceEnd       17      /* SCCompressSequencEnd */
#define     scDefaultPictHandleSettings 18      /* SCDefaultPictHandleSettings */
#define     scDefaultPictFileSettings   19      /* SCDefaultPictFileSettings */
#define     scDefaultPixMapSettings     20      /* SCDefaultPixMapSettings */
#define     scGetInfo                   21      /* SCGetInfo */
#define     scSetInfo                   22      /* SCSetInfo */
#define     scNewGWorld                 23      /* SCNewGWorld */

/* selectors included for compatibility with earlier linked version
   of standard image-compression dialog component */
#define     scGetCompression            1       /* SCGetCompression */
#define     scShowMotionSettings        (1L<<0) /* SCShowMotionSettings */
#define     scSettingsChangedItem       -1      /* SCSettingsChangedItem */

/* SCSetInfo and SCGetInfo request types */
#define     scSpatialSettingsType       'sptl'  /* spatial options */
#define     scTemporalSettingsType      'tprl'  /* temporal options */
#define     scDataRateSettingsType      'drat'  /* data rate */
#define     scColorTableType            'clut'  /* color table */
#define     scProgressProcType          'prog'  /* progress function */
#define     scExtendedProcsType         'xprc'  /* extended dialog */
#define     scPreferenceFlagsType       'pref'  /* preferences */
#define     scSettingsStateType         'ssta'  /* all settings */
#define     scSequenceIDType            'sequ'  /* sequence ID */
#define     scWindowPositionType        'wndw'  /* window position */
#define     scCodecFlagsType            'cflg'  /* compression flags */
```

CHAPTER 3

Standard Image-Compression Dialog Components

Data Types

```
/* SCModelFilterProcPtr is a pointer to a filter function */
typedef pascal Boolean (*SCModalFilterProcPtr) (DialogPtr theDialog,
        EventRecord *theEvent, short *itemHit, long refcon);

/* SCModalHookProcPtr is a pointer to a hook function */
typedef pascal short (*SCModalHookProcPtr) (DialogPtr theDialog,
        short itemHit, SCParams *params, long refcon);

/* spatial options structure with the spatial settings request */
typedef struct {
   CodecType       codecType;         /* compressor type */
   CodecComponent  codec;             /* compressor */
   short           depth;             /* pixel depth */
   CodecQ          spatialQuality;    /* desired quality */
} SCSpatialSettings;

/* temporal options structure with the temporal settings request */
typedef struct {
   CodecQ  temporalQuality;           /* desired quality */
   Fixed   frameRate;                 /* frame rate */
   long    keyFrameRate;              /* key frame rate */
} SCTemporalSettings;

/* data rate options with the data rate settings request */
typedef struct {
   long    dataRate;                  /* desired data rate */
   long    frameDuration;             /* frame duration */
   CodecQ  minSpatialQuality;         /* minimum value */
   CodecQ  minTemporalQuality;        /* minimum value */
} SCDataRateSettings;

/* extending the dialog box with the extended functions request */
typedef struct {
   SCModalFilterProcPtr  filterProc;  /* filter function */
   SCModalHookProcPtr    hookProc;    /* hook function */
   long                  refcon;      /* reference constant */
   Str31                 customName;  /* custom button name */
} SCExtendedProcs;

/* standard compression parameter block for compatibility with earlier
   linked version of standard image-compression dialog components */
```

```
typedef struct {
    long            flags;           /* control flags */
    CodecType       theCodecType;    /* compressor type */
    CodecComponent  theCodec;        /* specific compressor */
    CodecQ          spatialQuality;  /* spatial quality value */
    CodecQ          temporalQuality; /* temporal quality value */
    short           depth;           /* pixel depth */
    Fixed           frameRate;       /* desired frame rate */
    long            keyFrameRate;    /* desired key frame rate */
    long            reserved1;       /* reserved--set to 0) */
    long            reserved2;       /* reserved--set to 0 */
} SCParams;
```

Standard Image-Compression Dialog Component Functions

Getting Default Settings for an Image or a Sequence

```
pascal ComponentResult SCDefaultPixMapSettings
                        (ComponentInstance ci, PixMapHandle src,
                         short motion);
pascal ComponentResult SCDefaultPictHandleSettings
                        (ComponentInstance ci, PicHandle srcPicture,
                         short motion);
pascal ComponentResult SCDefaultPictFileSettings
                        (ComponentInstance ci, short srcRef,
                         short motion);
```

Displaying the Standard Image-Compression Dialog Box

```
pascal ComponentResult SCRequestImageSettings
                        (ComponentInstance ci);
pascal ComponentResult SCRequestSequenceSettings
                        (ComponentInstance ci);
```

Compressing Still Images

```
pascal ComponentResult SCCompressImage
                        (ComponentInstance ci, PixMapHandle src,
                         Rect *srcRect, ImageDescriptionHandle *desc,
                         Handle *data);
pascal ComponentResult SCCompressPicture
                        (ComponentInstance ci, PicHandle srcPicture,
                         PicHandle dstPicture);
```

```
pascal ComponentResult SCCompressPictureFile
                        (ComponentInstance ci, short srcRefNum,
                         short dstRefNum);
```

Compressing Image Sequences

```
pascal ComponentResult SCCompressSequenceBegin
                        (ComponentInstance ci, PixMapHandle src,
                         Rect *srcRect, ImageDescriptionHandle *desc);
pascal ComponentResult SCCompressSequenceFrame
                        (ComponentInstance ci, PixMapHandle src,
                         Rect *srcRect, Handle *data, long *dataSize,
                         short *notSyncFlag);
pascal ComponentResult SCCompressSequenceEnd
                        (ComponentInstance ci);
```

Working With Image or Sequence Settings

```
pascal ComponentResult SCGetInfo
                        (ComponentInstance ci, OSType type, void *info);
pascal ComponentResult SCSetInfo
                        (ComponentInstance ci, OSType type, void *info);
```

Specifying a Test Image

```
pascal ComponentResult SCSetTestImagePictHandle
                        (ComponentInstance ci, PicHandle testPict,
                         Rect *testRect, short testFlags);
pascal ComponentResult SCSetTestImagePictFile
                        (ComponentInstance ci, short testFileRef,
                         Rect *testRect, short testFlags);
pascal ComponentResult SCSetTestImagePixMap
                        (ComponentInstance ci, PixMapHandle testPixMap,
                         Rect *testRect, short testFlags);
```

Positioning Dialog Boxes and Rectangles

```
pascal ComponentResult SCPositionRect
                        (ComponentInstance ci, Rect *rp, Point *where);
pascal ComponentResult SCPositionDialog
                        (ComponentInstance ci, short id, Point *where);
pascal ComponentResult SCGetBestDeviceRect
                        (ComponentInstance ci, Rect *r);
```

Utility Function

```
pascal ComponentResult SCNewGWorld
                        (ComponentInstance ci, GWorldPtr *gwp,
                         Rect *rp, GWorldFlags flags);
```

Application-Defined Function

```
pascal short MyHook      (DialogPtr theDialog, short itemHit,
                          void *params, long refcon);
```

Pascal Summary

Constants

```
CONST
   {component type value}
   StandardCompressionType    = 'scdi';   {standard image-compression }
                                          { dialog component type}
   StandardCompressionSubType = 'imag';   {standard image-compression }
                                          { dialog component subtype}

   {preference flags}
   scListEveryCodec        = $2;    {list all components}
   scAllowZeroFrameRate    = $4;    {allow 0 frame rate}
   scAllowZeroKeyFrameRate = $8;    {allow 0 key frame rate}
   scShowBestDepth         = $10;   {allow "best depth"}
   scUseMovableModal       = $20;   {use movable dialog box}

   {values for testFlags parameter of functions that set test image}
   scPreferCropping           = 1;  {crop image to fit}
   scPreferScaling            = 2;  {shrink image to fit}
   scPreferScalingAndCropping = 3;  {shrink then crop}

   {dimensions of the test image portion of the dialog box}
   scTestImageWidth    = 80; {test width of image}
   scTestImageHeight   = 80; {test height of image}

   {possible items returned by hook function}
   scOKItem       = 1;     {user clicked OK}
   scCancelItem   = 2;     {user clicked Cancel}
   scCustomItem   = 3;     {user clicked custom button}
```

CHAPTER 3

Standard Image-Compression Dialog Components

```
{result returned when user canceled}
scUserCancelled    = 1; {user canceled dialog}

{selectors for standard image-compression dialog components}
kScPositionRect             = 2;    {SCPositionRect}
kScPositionDialog           = 3;    {SCPositionDialog}
kScSetTestImagePictHandle   = 4;    {SCSetTestImagePictHandle}
kScSetTestImagePictFile     = 5;    {SCSetTestImagePictFile}
kScSetTestImagePixMap       = 6;    {SCSetTestImagePixMap}
kScGetBestDeviceRect        = 7;    {SCGetBestDeviceRect}
kScRequestImageSettings     = $A;   {SCRequestImageSettings}
kScCompressImage            = $B;   {SCCompressImage}
kScCompressPicture          = $C;   {SCCompressPicture}
kScCompressPictureFile      = $D;   {SCCompressPictureFile}
kScRequestSequenceSettings  = $E;   {SCRequestSequenceSettings}
kScCompressSequenceBegin    = $F;   {SCCompressSequenceBegin}
kScCompressSequenceFrame    = $10;  {SCCompressSequenceFrame}
kScCompressSequenceEnd      = $11;  {SCCompressSequenceEnd}
kScDefaultPictHandleSettings = $12; {SCDefaultPictHandleSettings}
kScDefaultPictFileSettings  = $13;  {SCDefaultPictFileSettings}
kScDefaultPixMapSettings    = $14;  {SCDefaultPixMapSettings}
kScGetInfo                  = $15;  {SCGetInfo}
kScSetInfo                  = $16;  {SCSetInfo}
kScNewGWorld                = $17;  {SCNewGWorld}

{selectors included for compatibility with earlier linked version }
{ of standard image-compression dialog component}
kScShowMotionSettings       = 1;    {SCShowMotionSettings}
kScGetCompression           = 1;    {SCGetCompression}
kScSettingsChangedItem      = -1;   {SCSettingsChangedItem}

{SCSetInfo and SCGetInfo request types}
scSpatialSettingsType     = 'sptl'; {spatial options}
scTemporalSettingsType    = 'tprl'; {temporal options}
scDataRateSettingsType    = 'drat'; {data rate}
scColorTableType          = 'clut'; {color table}
scProgressProcType        = 'prog'; {progress function}
scExtendedProcsType       = 'xprc'; {extended dialog}
scPreferenceFlagsType     = 'pref'; {preferences}
scSettingsStateType       = 'ssta'; {all settings}
scSequenceIDType          = 'sequ'; {sequence ID}
scWindowPositionType      = 'wndw'; {window position}
scCodecFlagsType          = 'cflg'; {compression flags}
```

CHAPTER 3

Standard Image-Compression Dialog Components

Data Types

```
TYPE
   {SCModelFilterProcPtr is a pointer to a filter function}
   SCModalFilterProcPtr = ProcPtr;

   {SCModalHookProcPtr is a pointer to a hook function}
   SCModalHookProcPtr = ProcPtr;

   {spatial options structure with the spatial settings request}
   SCSpatialSettings =
   RECORD
      cType:             CodecType;         {compressor type}
      codec:             CodecComponent;    {compressor}
      depth:             Integer;           {pixel depth}
      spatialQuality:    CodecQ;            {desired quality}
   END;

   {temporal options structure with the temporal settings request}
   SCTemporalSettings =
   RECORD
      temporalQuality:   CodecQ;            {desired quality}
      frameRate:         Fixed;             {frame rate}
      keyFrameRate:      LongInt;           {key frame rate}
   END;

   {data rate options with the data rate settings request}
   SCDataRateSettings =
   RECORD
      dataRate:          LongInt;           {desired data rate}
      frameDuration:     LongInt;           {frame duration}
      minSpatialQuality: CodecQ;            {minimum value}
      minTemporalQuality:CodecQ;            {minimum value}
   END;

   {extending the dialog box with the extended functions request}
   SCExtendedProcs =
   RECORD
      filterProc:    SCModalFilterProcPtr;{filter function}
      hookProc:      SCModalHookProcPtr;  {hook function}
      refCon:        LongInt;             {reference constant}
      customName:    Str31;               {custom button name}
   END;
```

```
{standard compression parameter block included for compatibility }
{ with earlier linked version of standard-image compression dialog }
{ component}
SCParams =
RECORD
    flags :             LongInt;            {control flags}
    theCodecType:       CodecType;          {compressor type}
    theCodec:           CodecComponent;     {specific compressor}
    spatialQuality:     CodecQ;             {spatial quality value}
    temporalQuality:    CodecQ;             {temporal quality value}
    depth:              Integer;            {pixel depth}
    frameRate:          Fixed;              {desired frame rate}
    keyFrameRate:       LongInt;            {desired key frame rate}
    reserved1:          LongInt;            {reserved--set to 0}
    reserved2:          LongInt;            [reserved--set to 0}
END;
```

Standard Image-Compression Dialog Component Routines

Getting Default Settings for an Image or a Sequence

```
FUNCTION SCDefaultPixMapSettings
                    (ci: ComponentInstance; src: PixMapHandle;
                     motion: Boolean): ComponentResult;
FUNCTION SCDefaultPictHandleSettings
                    (ci: ComponentInstance; src: PicHandle;
                     motion: Boolean): ComponentResult;
FUNCTION SCDefaultPictFileSettings
                    (ci: ComponentInstance; srcRef: Integer;
                     motion: Boolean): ComponentResult;
```

Displaying the Standard Image-Compression Dialog Box

```
FUNCTION SCRequestImageSettings
                    (ci: ComponentInstance): ComponentResult;
FUNCTION SCRequestSequenceSettings
                    (ci: ComponentInstance): ComponentResult;
```

Compressing Still Images

```
FUNCTION SCCompressImage    (ci: ComponentInstance; src: PixMapHandle;
                             srcRect: Rect;
                             VAR desc: ImageDescriptionHandle;
                             VAR data: Handle): ComponentResult;
```

```
FUNCTION SCCompressPicture    (ci: ComponentInstance; src, dst: PicHandle):
                                    ComponentResult;
FUNCTION SCCompressPictureFile
                              (ci: ComponentInstance; srcRef,
                                  dstRef: Integer): ComponentResult;
```

Compressing Image Sequences

```
FUNCTION SCCompressSequenceBegin
                              (ci: ComponentInstance; src: PixMapHandle;
                                  srcRect: Rect;
                                  VAR desc: ImageDescriptionHandle):
                                  ComponentResult;
FUNCTION SCCompressSequenceFrame
                              (ci: ComponentInstance; src: PixMapHandle;
                                  srcRect: Rect; VAR data: Handle;
                                  VAR dataSize: LongInt;
                                  VAR notSyncFlag: Boolean): ComponentResult;
FUNCTION SCCompressSequenceEnd
                              (ci: ComponentInstance): ComponentResult;
```

Working With Image or Sequence Settings

```
FUNCTION SCGetInfo            (ci: ComponentInstance; infoType: OSType;
                                  info: Ptr): ComponentResult;
FUNCTION SCSetInfo            (ci: ComponentInstance; infoType: OSType;
                                  info: Ptr): ComponentResult;
```

Specifying a Test Image

```
FUNCTION SCSetTestImagePictHandle
                              (ci: ComponentInstance; testPict: PicHandle;
                                  testRect: RectPtr; testFlags: Integer):
                                  ComponentResult;
FUNCTION SCSetTestImagePictFile
                              (ci: ComponentInstance; testFileRef: Integer;
                                  testRect: RectPtr; testFlags: Integer):
                                  ComponentResult;
FUNCTION SCSetTestImagePixMap
                              (ci: ComponentInstance;
                                  testPixMap: PixMapHandle; testRect: RectPtr;
                                  testFlags: Integer): ComponentResult;
```

Positioning Dialog Boxes and Rectangles

```
FUNCTION SCPositionRect     (ci: ComponentInstance; r: RectPtr;
                             VAR where: Point): ComponentResult;
FUNCTION SCPositionDialog   (ci: ComponentInstance; id: Integer;
                             VAR where: Point): ComponentResult;
FUNCTION SCGetBestDeviceRect
                            (ci: ComponentInstance; r: RectPtr):
                             ComponentResult;
```

Utility Function

```
FUNCTION SCNewGWorld        (ci: ComponentInstance; VAR gwp: GWorldPtr;
                             VAR rp: Rect; flags: GWorldFlags):
                             ComponentResult;
```

Application-Defined Routine

```
FUNCTION MyHook             (theDialog: DialogPtr; itemHit: Integer;
                             params Ptr; refcon: LongInt): Integer;
```

Result Codes

scTypeNotFoundErr	–8971	Component does not have the information you want

CHAPTER 4

Image Compressor Components

Contents

About Image Compressor Components   4-3
   Banding and Extending Images   4-4
   Spooling of Compressed Data   4-6
      Data Loading   4-6
      Data Unloading   4-7
   Compressing or Decompressing Images Asynchronously   4-8
   Progress Functions   4-9
Using Image Compressor Components   4-10
   Performing Image Compression   4-10
      Choosing a Compressor   4-10
      Compressing a Horizontal Band of an Image   4-13
   Decompressing an Image   4-16
      Choosing a Decompressor   4-17
      Decompressing a Horizontal Band of an Image   4-21
Image Compressor Components Reference   4-26
   Constants   4-26
      Image Compressor Component Capabilities   4-26
      Format of Compressed Data and Files   4-32
   Data Types   4-35
      The Compressor Capability Structure   4-35
      The Compression Parameters Structure   4-40
      The Decompression Parameters Structure   4-46
   Functions   4-53
      Direct Functions   4-54
      Indirect Functions   4-62
   Image Compression Manager Utility Functions   4-65

Summary of Image Compressor Components 4-69
    C Summary 4-69
        Constants 4-69
        Data Types 4-72
        Functions 4-76
        Image Compression Manager Utility Functions 4-77
    Pascal Summary 4-77
        Constants 4-77
        Data Types 4-80
        Routines 4-83
        Image Compression Manager Utility Functions 4-84
    Result Codes 4-84

CHAPTER 4

Image Compressor Components

This chapter discusses the attributes of image compressor components and the functional interfaces these components must support. An **image compressor component** is a code resource that provides compression or decompression services for image data. Throughout this chapter, the term *image compressor component* is used to describe both compressor and decompressor components.

Note
The information in this chapter is intended for developers of image compressor components. Application developers normally do not need to be familiar with this material to use the Image Compression Manager. ◆

This chapter has been divided into the following sections:

- "About Image Compressor Components" presents general information about image compressor components.
- "Using Image Compressor Components" discusses how the Image Compression Manager uses image compressor components to compress and decompress images.
- "Image Compressor Components Reference" describes the data structures used by the Image Compression Manager to communicate with image compressor components. It also provides a comprehensive reference to the functions that your image compressor component must support.
- "Summary of Image Compressor Components" presents a summary of image compressor components in C and in Pascal.

If you are developing an image compressor component, you should read all the material in this chapter. In addition, you should read the appropriate sections of the chapter "Component Manager" in *Inside Macintosh: More Macintosh Toolbox*.

About Image Compressor Components

Image compressor components are registered by the Component Manager, and they present a standard interface to the Image Compression Manager (see "Functions" beginning on page 4-53 for a detailed description of the functions that image compressor components must provide). An image compressor component can be a systemwide resource, or it can be local to a particular application.

Applications never communicate directly with these components. Applications request compression and decompression services by issuing the appropriate Image Compression Manager functions. The Image Compression Manager then performs its necessary processing before invoking the component. Of course, an application could install its own image compressor component. However, any interaction between the application and the component is still managed by the Image Compression Manager.

Image Compressor Components

The Image Compression Manager knows about two types of image compressor components. Components that can compress image data carry a component type of `'imco'` and are called *image compressors*. Components that can decompress images have a component type of `'imdc'` and are called *image decompressors*.

```
#define compressorComponentType 'imco'     /* compressor component
                                              type */

#define decompressorComponentType 'imdc'   /* decompressor
                                              component type */
```

The value of the component subtype indicates the compression algorithm supported by the component. For example, the graphics compressor has the component subtype `'cvid'`. (A **component subtype** is an element in the classification hierarchy used by the Component Manager to define the services provided by a component.) All compressor components with the same subtype must be able to handle the same format of compressed data. During decompression, a component should handle all variations of the data specified for a subtype. While compressing an image, a compressor must not produce data that decompressors of the same subtype cannot handle during decompression.

The Image Compression Manager provides a set of utility functions for compressor components. These functions allow compressors and decompressors to create custom color lookup tables, among other things. For a complete description of these utility functions, along with the functions that must be supported by compressor components, see "Image Compression Manager Utility Functions," which begins on page 4-65.

The Image Compression Manager defines four callback functions that may be provided to compressors and decompressors by applications. These callback functions are data-loading functions, data-unloading functions, completion functions, and progress functions. Data-loading functions and data-unloading functions support spooling of compressed data. Completion functions allow components to report that asynchronous operations have completed. Progress functions provide a mechanism for components to report their progress toward completing an operation. For more information about these callback functions, see the chapter "Image Compression Manager" in *Inside Macintosh: QuickTime*.

Banding and Extending Images

QuickTime handles images in **bands,** which are horizontal strips of an image. Bands allow large images to be accommodated even if the entire image cannot fit into memory. The Image Compression Manager calls the image compressor component once for each band as the image is compressed or decompressed.

The Image Compression Manager determines the height of a band based on the amount of available memory and the `bandMin` and `bandInc` parameters provided by the compressor component in the compressor capability structure (described in "The Compressor Capability Structure" beginning on page 4-35). The `bandMin` field specifies the minimum band height supported by a decompressor component. By providing a minimum height, decompressor components that operate on blocks of pixels can operate more efficiently since the minimum height ensures that a band has at least one row of pixel blocks. The `bandInc` field specifies the increment in pixels by which the height of a band is increased above the minimum when sufficient memory is available. This specification allows easier processing by ensuring that a band is an integral number of rows of blocks. The larger these two parameters, the more memory is required for the band buffer, which may limit the size of images used with a given amount of memory. By specifying a minimum height that is the size of the image, the compressor component can indicate that it cannot handle banded images. However, the specification of a full size is not recommended unless required by the compression format, since it requires large amounts of memory for large images.

For decompressing sequences of images with temporal compression, the Image Compression Manager always allocates the band to include the full image. The entire image must be available whenever the screen needs updating and the current frame does not have information for all pixels. The entire image is needed to make the comparison with the previous frame.

The depth of the band is determined by the Image Compression Manager and the `wantedPixelSize` field of the compressor capability structure (described on page 4-35). That field is filled in by the image compressor component's `CDPreCompress` or `CDPreDecompress` function (described on page 4-62 and page 4-63, respectively). The Image Compression Manager requests the depth that it decides is best for the image, and the compressor component can return the `wantedPixelSize` field set to that depth or another appropriate depth if the compressor cannot handle the one requested.

The width of the band is usually the width of the image, but the compressor can extend the measurement if it cannot easily handle partial blocks of pixels at the edge of the image. For compression operations, the Image Compression Manager sets the extra pixels added to the right edge of the band to the same value as the last pixel in each scan line. For decompression operations, the Image Compression Manager ignores the pixels that were added to the right edge for the extension.

Image compressor components can also use extension for the height of the last (or the only) band in the image (the other bands should always be an integral multiple of the `bandInc` field set by the decompressor component). The extended pixels are added to the bottom of the band. For compression operations, the added pixels have the same value as the pixel at the same location in the last scan line of the image. For decompression operations, the added pixels are ignored. If an image compressor component does not want to deal with partial blocks of pixels, either horizontally or vertically, it can use this extension technique. However, it would be more efficient for the compressor to handle those blocks itself.

Spooling of Compressed Data

If available memory is insufficient to hold the entire image that is being compressed or decompressed, the image compressor component must call data-loading or data-unloading functions to spool—that is, read or write the data from storage in stages. The calling application indicates this in the data-loading or data-unloading structure, as described in the following sections.

Data Loading

Decompressor components use data loading. The data buffer still exists when the calling application supplies a data-loading function; however, the data buffer holds only part of the data and you must use the data-loading function to load the remaining data into this buffer. The `bufferSize` parameter of the decompression parameters structure (described on page 4-46) indicates the size of the data buffer.

To use the data-loading function, the decompressor component calls it with the pointer to the current position in the data buffer as a parameter. The decompressor specifies the number of bytes it needs (this number must be less than or equal to the size of the data buffer). The data-loading function fills in the data buffer with the number of bytes requested and may adjust the pointer as necessary to remove some of the used data and make room for new data.

If the decompressor component needs to skip data in the compressed stream or go back to data earlier in the stream, the decompressor should call the data-loading function with a `nil` pointer (instead of the pointer to the data buffer of the data-loading function) and with the `size` parameter set to the number of bytes that the decompressor wants to skip relative to the current position in the stream. A positive number seeks forward and a negative one seeks backward. To ensure that the position in the stream is known by the data-loading function, the decompressor should call the function before specifying a seek operation with an actual pointer to the current position in the data buffer and a 0 byte count. After the seek operation, the decompressor component should call the data-loading function again with the number of bytes needed from the new position to make sure the needed bytes are read into the buffer.

A decompressor component should not depend on the ability to skip backward in the data stream since not all applications are able to take advantage of this feature. The decompressor should check the error from the data-loading function during a seek operation and should not use the seek feature if an error code is returned. Seeking forward works in most situations; however, it may entail reading the data and throwing it out. Hence, seeking forward may not always be faster than reading the data.

CHAPTER 4

Image Compressor Components

Figure 4-1 shows several image bands and their measurements.

Figure 4-1 Image bands and their measurements

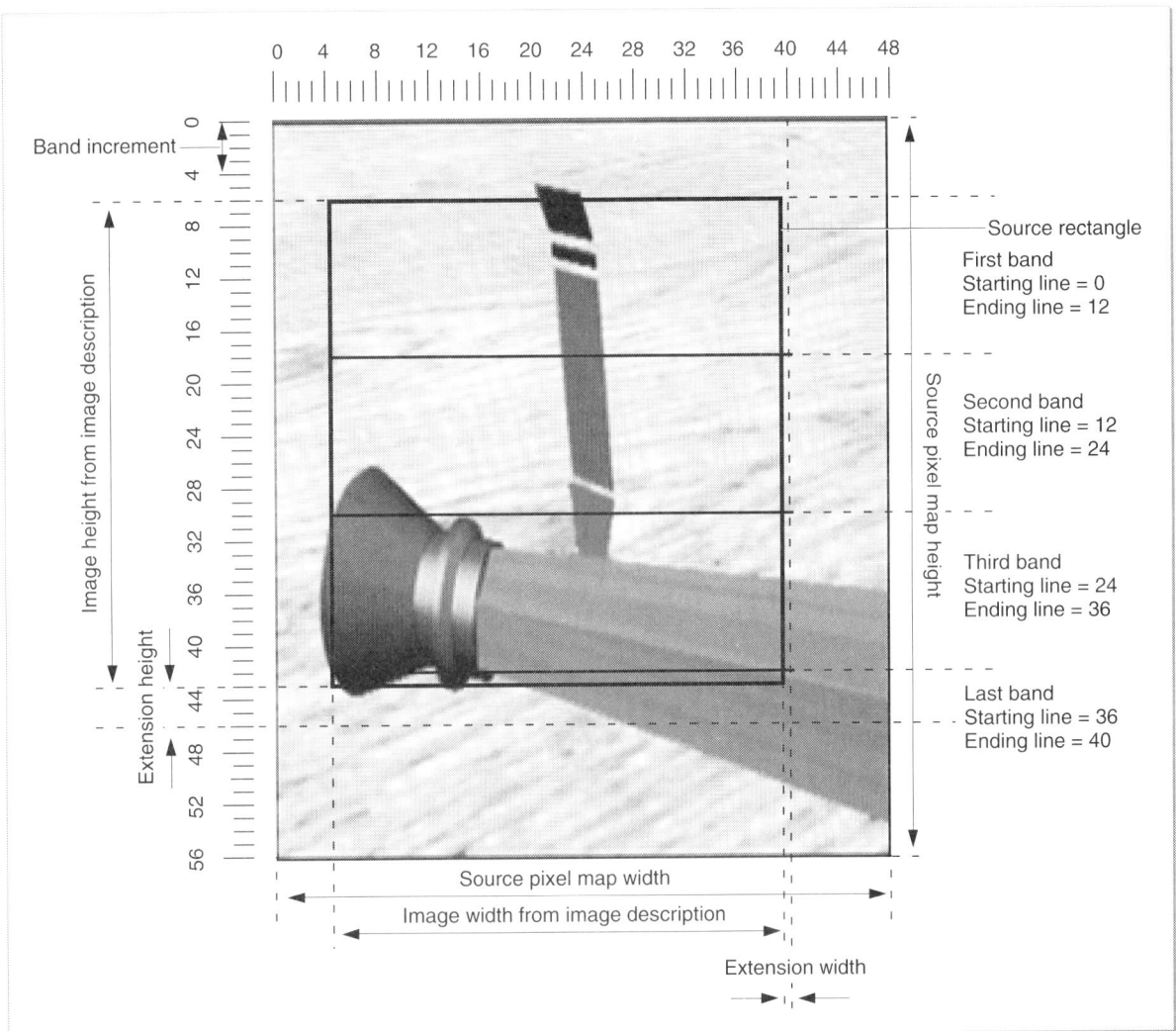

Data Unloading

Data-unloading functions are used by compressor components when there is insufficient memory to hold the buffer for the compressed data produced by the compressor component. The compressor component needs to use a data-unloading function if the `flushProcRecord` field in the compression parameters structure is not `nil`. (For details on the compression parameters structure, see page 4-40). A data buffer is provided even if the data-unloading function is present, and it should be used to hold the data to be unloaded by the data-unloading function. The size of the data buffer is indicated by the `bufferSize` field in the parameters.

About Image Compressor Components

To use the data-unloading function, the compressor fills the data buffer with as much data as possible (within the size limitations of the data buffer). The compressor component then calls the data-unloading function with a pointer to the start of the data buffer and the number of bytes written. The data-unloading function then unloads the data from the buffer. The compressor should then use the entire buffer for the next piece of data—and continue in this manner until all the data is unloaded.

If the compressor component needs to skip forward or backward in the data stream, it should call the data-unloading function with a `nil` data pointer, and the compressor should specify the number of bytes to seek relative to the current position in the `size` parameter. A positive number seeks forward and a negative one seeks backward. The compressor component should make sure that all data is unloaded from the buffer before commencing the seek operation. After the seek operation, the next data unloaded from the buffer with the data-unloading function is written starting at the new location. The new data overwrites any data previously written at that location in the data stream.

Not all applications support the ability to seek forward or backward with a data-unloading function. The compressor component should check the error result when performing such an operation.

Compressing or Decompressing Images Asynchronously

With the appropriate hardware, image compressor components can handle asynchronous compression and decompression of images using the `CDBandCompress` and `CDBandDecompress` functions, which are described on page 4-63 and page 4-64, respectively. *Asynchronous* refers to the fact that the compression or decompression hardware performs its operations while the Macintosh computer simultaneously continues its activities. For example, the Macintosh can read a movie for the next frame while the current frame is decompressed. The Image Compression Manager ensures that any asynchronous operation in progress is completed before starting the next operation.

If the Image Compression Manager wants the image compressor component to perform an operation asynchronously, then the `completionProcRecord` field in the compression or decompression parameters structure that the Image Compressor Manager sends to the image compressor component should be set to a nonzero value. If the value is –1, then the component should perform the operation asynchronously, but it does not need to call a completion function. If the value is not `nil` and not –1, then the component should perform the operation asynchronously, and it should call the completion function when the operation is done. For details on the compression parameters structure, see page 4-40. For more on the decompression parameters structure, see page 4-46.

To provide synchronization for the Image Compression Manager, an image compressor component provides the `CDCodecBusy` function (described on page 4-61). `CDCodecBusy` should always return 1 if an asynchronous operation is in progress; it should return 0 if there is no asynchronous operation in progress or if the image compressor component does not perform asynchronous operations. If the Image Compression Manager provided a completion function, the image compressor component must call the completion function as well.

Image Compressor Components

IMPORTANT

If the Image Compression Manager provided a completion function, then the compressor component must call it; otherwise, the memory for that operation may become increasingly stranded in the system and difficult to deallocate. ▲

There are two distinct steps to an asynchronous compression or decompression operation. The first step depends on the source data, and the second step depends on the destination data.

- For a compression operation, the first step indicates when the compressor is finished with the pixels of the source image, and the second step specifies that the compressed data is fully written to memory.
- For a decompression operation, the first step is complete when the compressed data is read into the hardware or the decompressor's local buffers, and the second step is complete when all the pixels of the image have been written to the destination.

Depending on the design of the hardware used by your image compressor component, the two steps in the asynchronous operations may be independent of each other or tied together. To indicate to the completion function which steps have been completed, you use the `codecCompletionSource` and `CodecCompletionDest` flags for the first and second steps, respectively. If both parts of the asynchronous operation are completed together, the image compressor component can call the completion function once with both flags set. The memory used for each part of the operation remains valid and locked while asynchronous operations are in progress. It is the responsibility of image compressor components to make sure that they remain resident in RAM if virtual memory is active (this is only an issue for hardware image compressor components that perform direct memory access).

Progress Functions

Progress functions provide the calling application an indication of how much of an operation is complete and a way for the user to cancel an operation. If the `progressProcRecord` field is set either in the compression parameters structure or the decompression parameters structure, then the image compressor component should call the progress function as it performs the operation. The progress function is typically called once for each scan line or row of pixel blocks processed, and it returns a completion value that is the percentage of the band that is complete, represented as a fixed-point number from 0 to 1.0.

If the result returned from a progress function is not 0, then the image compressor component should return as soon as possible (without completing the band that is being processed) with a return value of `codecAbortErr`.

Note

For efficiency, many image compressor components have a streamlined path used for cases that do not require data-loading, data-unloading, or progress functions, and a slower path that supports any or all these application-defined functions when required. ◆

Using Image Compressor Components

This section shows how to use compressors and decompressors in conjunction with the Image Compression Manager.

Performing Image Compression

This section describes what the Image Compression Manager does that affects compressors. It then provides sample code that shows how the compressor components prepare for image compression and how to compress an entire image or a horizontal band of an image.

When compressing an image, the Image Compression Manager performs three major tasks:

1. The Image Compression Manager first determines which compressor is best able to compress the image. To do so, the Image Compression Manager examines the source image as well as the parameters specified by the application. If the application requested a specific compressor, the Image Compression Manager uses that compressor (unless it is not installed, in which case the Image Compression Manager returns an error to the application). If the application did not request a compressor, the Image Compression Manager chooses the compressor that will do the best job. The Image Compression Manager collects the information it needs to choose a compressor by issuing the `CDPreCompress` request to each qualifying compressor (see page 4-62 for a detailed description of the `CDPreCompress` function).

2. If the chosen compressor can handle the image directly, the Image Compression Manager passes the request through to the compressor. The compressor then processes the image and returns the compressed data to the specified location.

3. If none of the compressors can handle it directly, the Image Compression Manager allocates an offscreen buffer and passes image bands to the compressor by issuing a `CDBandCompress` request. (For more on the `CDBandCompress` function, see page 4-63.) The compressor processes each band, accumulating the compressed data as it goes. When the image has been completely compressed, the Image Compression Manager returns control to the application.

Choosing a Compressor

Listing 4-1 on page 4-12 shows how the Image Compression Manager calls the `CDPreCompress` function before an image is compressed. The compressor component returns information about how it is able to compress the image to the Image Compression Manager, so that it can fit the destination data to the requirements of the compressor component. This information includes compressor capabilities for

- depth of input pixels
- minimum buffer band size

Image Compressor Components

- band increment size
- extension width and height

When your compressor component is called with the `CDPreCompress` function (described on page 4-62), it can handle all aspects of the function itself, or only the most common ones. All image compressor components must handle at least one case.

Here is a list of some of the operations your compressor component can perform during compression. It describes parameters in the compression parameters structure (described on page 4-40) and indicates the operations that are required and which flags in the compressor capabilities flags field of the compressor capabilities structure (described on page 4-35) must be set to allow your compressor to handle them.

- **Depth conversion.** If your compressor component can compress from the pixel depth indicated by the `pixelSize` field (in the pixel map structure pointed to by the `srcPixmap` field of the compression parameters structure), it should set the `wantedPixelSize` field of the compressor capability structure to the same value. If it cannot handle that depth, it should specify the closest depth it can support in the `wantedPixelSize` field. The Image Compression Manager will convert the source image to that depth.

- **Extension.** If the format for the compressed data is block oriented, the compressor component can request that the Image Compression Manager allocate a buffer that is a multiple of the proper block size by setting the `extendWidth` and `extendHeight` parameters of the compressor capability structure. The new pixels are replicated from the left and bottom edges to fill the extended area. If your compressor can perform this extension itself, it should leave the `extendWidth` and `extendHeight` fields set to 0. In this case, the Image Compression Manager can avoid copying the source image to attain more efficient operation.

- **Pixel shifting.** For pixel sizes less than 8 bits per pixel, it may be necessary to shift the source pixels so that they are at an aligned address. If the `pixelSize` field of the source pixel map structure is less than 8, and your compressor component handles that depth directly, and the left address of the image (`srcRect.left − srcPixMap.bounds.left`) is not aligned and your compressor component can handle these pixels directly, then it should set the `codecCanShift` flag in the `flags` field of the compressor capabilities structure. If your compressor component does not set this flag, then the data will be copied to a buffer with the image shifted so the first pixel is in the most significant bit of an aligned long-word address.

- **Updating previous pixel maps.** Compressors that perform temporal compression may keep their own copy of the previous frame's pixel map, or they may update the previous frame's pixel map as they perform the compression. In these cases, the compressor component should set the `codecCanCopyPrev` flag if it updates the previous pixel map with the original data from the current frame, or it should set the `codecCanCopyPrevComp` flag if it updates the previous pixel map with a compressed copy of the current frame.

Image Compressor Components

Listing 4-1 Preparing for simple compression operations

```
pascal long
CDPreCompress (Handle storage, register CodecCompressParams *p)
{
   CodecCapabilities *capabilities = p->capabilities;
/*
   First the compressor returns which depth input pixels it
   supports based on what the application has available. This
   compressor can only work with 32-bit input pixels.
*/
   switch ( (*p->imageDescription)->depth )  {
      case 16:
         capabilities->wantedPixelSize = 32;
         break;
      default:
         return(codecConditionErr);
         break;
   }

   /*
      If the buffer gets banded, return the smallest one the
      compressor can handle.
   */
   capabilities->bandMin = 2;

   /*
      If the buffer gets banded, return the increment
      by which it should increase.
   */
   capabilities->bandInc = 2;

   capabilities->extendWidth = (*p->imageDescription)->width & 1;
   capabilities->extendHeight = (*p->imageDescription)->height &
                                 1;

/*
   For efficiency, if the compressor could perform extension,
   these flags would be set to 0.
*/

   return(noErr);
}
```

Image Compressor Components

Compressing a Horizontal Band of an Image

Listing 4-2 shows how the Image Compression Manager calls the `CDBandCompress` function when it wants the compressor to compress a horizontal band of an image.

Note
This example does not perform compression on bands with a bit depth of more than 1 or an extension of width and height. If the example did do so, it would handle these cases faster. ◆

Listing 4-2 Performing simple compression on a horizontal band of an image

```
pascal long
CDBandCompress (Handle storage, register CodecCompressParams *p)
{
    short           width,height;
    Ptr             cDataPtr,dataStart;
    short           depth;
    Rect            sRect;
    long            offsetH,offsetV;
    Globals         **glob = (Globals **)storage;
    register char   *baseAddr;
    long            numLines,numStrips;
    short           rowBytes;
    long            stripBytes;
    char            mmuMode = 1;
    register short  y;
    ImageDescription **desc = p->imageDescription;
    OSErr           result = noErr;

    /*
    If there is a progress function, give it an open call at
       the start of this band.
    */

    if (p->progressProcRecord.progressProc)
       p->progressProcRecord.progressProc (codecProgressOpen, 0,
          p->progressProcRecord.progressRefCon);

    width = (*desc)->width;
    height = (*desc)->height;
    depth = (*desc)->depth;
    dataStart = cDataPtr = p->data;
```

Image Compressor Components

```
/*
   Figure out offset to first pixel in baseAddr from the
   pixel size and bounds.
 */

rowBytes = p->srcPixMap.rowBytes;
sRect =   p->srcPixMap.bounds;

numLines = p->stopLine - p->startLine; /* number of scan
                                          lines */
numStrips = (numLines+1)>>1;           /* number of strips
                                          in */
stripBytes = ((width+1)>>1) * 5;

/*
   Adjust the source baseAddress to be at the beginning
   of the desired rect.
*/

switch ( p->srcPixMap.pixelSize ) {
case 32:
   offsetH = sRect.left<<2;
   break;
case 16:
   offsetH = sRect.left<<1;
   break;
case 8:
   offsetH = sRect.left;
   break;

/*
   This compressor does not handle the other cases directly.
*/

default:
   result = codecErr;
   goto bail;
}

offsetV = sRect.top * rowBytes;
baseAddr = p->srcPixMap.baseAddr + offsetH + offsetV;

/*
   If there is not a data-unloading function,
```

CHAPTER 4

Image Compressor Components

```
      adjust the pointer to the next band.
   */

   if (  p->flushProcRecord.flushProc == nil ) {
      cDataPtr += (p->startLine>>1) * stripBytes;
   }
   else { /*
            Make sure the compressor can deal with the
            data-unloading function in this case.
         */
      if ( p->bufferSize < stripBytes ) {
         result = codecSpoolErr;
         goto bail;
      }
   }
   /*
      Perform the slower data-loading or progress operation, as
      required.
   */

   if (  p->flushProcRecord.flushProc ||
      p->progressProcRecord.progressProc ) {

      SharedGlobals *sg = (*glob)->sharedGlob;

      for ( y=0; y < numStrips; y++) {
         SwapMMUMode(&mmuMode);
         CompressStrip(cDataPtr,baseAddr,rowBytes,width,sg);
         SwapMMUMode(&mmuMode);
         baseAddr += rowBytes<<1;
         if ( p->flushProcRecord.flushProc ) {
            if ( (result=
            p->flushProcRecord.flushProc(cDataPtr,stripBytes,
            p->flushProcRecord.flushRefCon)) != noErr) {
               result = codecSpoolErr;
               goto bail;
            }
         } else {
            cDataPtr += stripBytes;
         }
         if (p->progressProcRecord.progressProc) {
            if ( (result=
               p->progressProcRecord.progressProc)
```

Using Image Compressor Components 4-15

```
                    codecProgressUpdatePercent,
                    FixDiv(y,numStrips),
                    p->progressProcRecord.progressRefCon)
                ) != noErr ) {
                    result = codecAbortErr;
                    goto bail;
                }
            }
        }
    } else {
        SharedGlobals *sg = (*glob)->sharedGlob;
        short tRowBytes = rowBytes<<1;

        SwapMMUMode(&mmuMode);
        for ( y=numStrips; y--; ) {
            CompressStrip(cDataPtr,baseAddr,rowBytes,width,sg);
            cDataPtr += stripBytes;
            baseAddr += tRowBytes;
        }
        SwapMMUMode(&mmuMode);
    }
}
```

Decompressing an Image

When decompressing an image, the Image Compression Manager performs these three major tasks:

1. The Image Compression Manager first determines which decompressor is best able to decompress the image. To do so, the Image Compression Manager examines the source image as well as the parameters specified by the application. If the application requested a specific decompressor, the Image Compression Manager uses that decompressor (unless it is not installed, in which case the Image Compression Manager returns an error to the application). If the application did not request a decompressor, the Image Compression Manager chooses the decompressor that will do the best job. The Image Compression Manager collects the information it needs to choose a decompressor by issuing the CDPreDecompress request to each qualifying decompressor (see page 4-63 for a detailed description of the CDPreDecompress function).

Image Compressor Components

2. If the chosen decompressor can handle the image directly, the Image Compression Manager passes the request through to the decompressor. The decompressor then processes the image and returns the image to the specified location.

3. If none of the decompressors can handle all of the conditions (matrix mapping, masking or matting, depth conversion, and so on) the Image Compression Manager allocates an offscreen buffer and passes image bands to the decompressor at a depth that the decompressor can handle by issuing a `CDBandDecompress` request. (For details on the `CDBandDecompress` function, see page 4-64). The decompressor processes each band, building the image as it goes. When the image has been completely decompressed, the Image Compression Manager returns control to the application.

Choosing a Decompressor

Listing 4-3 on page 4-20 provides an example of how a decompressor is chosen. The Image Compression Manager calls the `CDPreDecompress` function (described on page 4-63) before an image is decompressed. The decompressor returns information about how it can decompress an image. The Image Compression Manager can fit the destination pixel map to your decompressor's requirements if it is not able to support decompression to the destination directly. The capability information the decompressor returns includes

- depth of pixels for the destination pixel map
- minimum band size handled
- extension width and height required
- band increment size

When your decompressor component is called with the `CDPreDecompress` function, it can handle all aspects of the call itself, or only the most common ones. All decompressors must handle at least one case.

This section contains a bulleted list of some of the operations your decompressor component can perform during the decompression operation. The list describes which parameters in the decompression parameters structure (described on page 4-46) indicate the operations are required and which flags in the flags field of the compressor capabilities structure (described on page 4-35) must be set to allow your decompressor to handle them.

For sequences of images the `conditionFlags` field in the decompression parameters structure can be used to determine which parameters may have changed since the last decompression operation. These parameters are also indicated in the bulleted list.

Image Compressor Components

Since your decompressor's capabilities depend on the full combination of parameters, it must inspect all the relevant parameters before indicating that it will perform one of the operations itself. For instance, if your decompressor has hardware that can perform scaling only if the destination pixel depth is 32 and there is no clipping, then the pre-decompression operation would have to check the following fields in the decompression parameters structure: the `matrix` field, the `pixelSize` field of the destination pixel map structure pointed to by the `destPixMap` field, and the `maskBits` fields. Only then could the decompressor decide whether to set the `codecCanScale` flag in the `capabilities` field of the decompression parameters structure.

- **Scaling.** The decompressor component can look at the matrix and selectively decide which scaling operations it wishes to handle. If the scaling factor specified by the matrix is not unity and your decompressor can perform the scaling operation, it must set the `codecCanScale` flag in the `capabilities` field. If it does not, then the decompressor is asked to decompress without scaling, and the Image Compression Manager performs the scaling operation afterward.

- **Depth conversion.** If your component can decompress to the pixel depth indicated by the `pixelSize` field (of the pixel map structure pointed to by the `dstPixmap` field of the decompression parameters structure), it should set the `wantedPixelSize` field of the compressor capability structure to the same value. If it cannot handle that depth, it should specify the closest depth it can handle in the `wantedPixelSize` field.

- **Dithering.** When determining whether depth conversion can be performed (for converting an image to a lower bit depth, or to a similar bit depth with a different color table), dithering may be required. This is specified by the dither bit in the `transferMode` field (`0x40`) of the decompression parameters structure being set. The `accuracy` field of the decompression parameters structure indicates whether fast dithering is acceptable (`accuracy <= codecNormalQuality`) or whether true error diffusion dithering should be used (`accuracy > codecNormalQuality`). Most decompressors do not perform true error diffusion dithering, although they can. When a decompressor cannot perform the dither operation, it should specify the higher bit depth in the `wantedPixelSize` field of the compressor capability structure and let the Image Compression Manager perform the depth conversion with dithering. Dithering to 16-bit destinations is normally done only if the `accuracy` field is set to the `codecNormalQuality` value. However, if your decompressor component can perform dithering fast enough, it could be performed at the lower accuracy settings as well. To indicate that your decompressor can perform dithering as specified, it should set the `codecCanTransferMode` flag in the `capabilities` field of the decompression parameters structure.

- **Color remapping.** If the compressed data has an associated color lookup table that is different from the color lookup table of the destination pixel map, then the decompressor can remap the color indices to the closest available ones in the destination itself, or it can let the Image Compression Manager do the remapping. If the decompressor can do the mapping itself, it should set the `codecCanRemap` flag in the `capabilities` flags field of the decompression parameters structure.

- **Extending.** If the format for the compressed data is block-oriented, the decompressor can ask that the Image Compression Manager to allocate a buffer which is a multiple of the proper block size by setting the `extendWidth` and `extendHeight` fields of the compressor capabilities structure. If the right and bottom edges of the destination image (as determined by the transformed `srcRect` and `dstPixMap.bounds` fields of the decompression parameters structure) are not a multiple of the block size that your decompressor handles, and your decompressor cannot handle partial blocks (writing only the pixels that are needed for blocks that cross the left or bottom edge of the destination), then your decompressor component must set the `extendWidth` and `extendHeight` fields in the compressor capabilities structure. In this case, the Image Compression Manager creates a buffer large enough so that no partial blocks are needed. Your component can decompress into that buffer. This is then copied to the destination by the Image Compression Manager. Your component can avoid this extra step if it can handle partial blocks. In this case, it should leave the `extendWidth` and `extendHeight` fields set to 0.

- **Clipping.** If clipping must be performed on the image to be decompressed, the `maskBits` field of the decompression parameters structure is nonzero. In the `CDPreDecompress` function, it will be a region handle to the actual clipping region. If your decompressor can handle the clipping operation as specified by this region, it should set the `codecCanMask` bit in the `capabilities` flags field of the decompression parameters structure. If it does this, then the parameter passed to the `CDBandDecompress` function in the `maskBits` field will be a bitmap instead of a region. If desired, your decompressor can save a copy of the actual region structure during the pre-decompression operation.

- **Matting.** If a matte must be applied to the decompressed image, the `transferMode` field of the decompression parameters structure is set to blend and the `mattePixMap` field is a handle to the pixel map to be used as the matte. If your decompressor can perform the matte operation, then it should set the `codecCanMatte` field in the compressor capabilities structure. If it does not, then the Image Compression Manager will perform the matte operation after the decompression is complete.

- **Pixel shifting.** For pixel sizes less than 8 bits per pixel, it may be necessary to shift the destination pixels so that they are at an aligned address. If the pixel size of the destination pixel map is less than 8 and your component handles that depth directly, and the left address of the image is not aligned and your component can handle these pixels directly, then it should set the `codecCanShift` flag in the `capabilities` field of the decompression parameters structure. If your component does not set this flag, the Image Compression Manager allocates a buffer for and performs the shifting after the decompression is completed.

- **Partial extraction.** If the source rectangle is not the entire image and the component can decompress only the part of the image specified by the source rectangle, it should set the `codecCanSrcExtract` flag in the `capabilities` field of the decompression parameters structure. If it does not, the Image Compression Manger asks the component to decompress the entire image and copy only the required part to the destination.

Image Compressor Components

Listing 4-3 Preparing for simple decompression

```
pascal long
CDPreDecompress(Handle storage, register CodecDecompressParams *p)

{
   register CodecCapabilities*capabilities = p->capabilities;
   RectdRect = p->srcRect;

   /*
      Check if the matrix is OK for this decompressor.
      This decompressor doesn't do anything fancy.
   */

   if ( !TransformRect(p->matrix,&dRect,nil) )
      return(codecConditionErr);

   /*
      Decide which depth compressed data this decompressor can
      deal with.
   */

   switch ( (*p->imageDescription)->depth )  {
      case 16:
         break;
      default:
         return(codecConditionErr);
         break;
   }

      /*
         This decompressor can deal only with 32-bit pixels.
      */

   capabilities->wantedPixelSize = 32;

   /*
      The smallest possible band the decompressor can handle is
      2 scan lines.
   */

   capabilities->bandMin = 2;

   /* This decompressor can deal with 2 scan line high bands. */
```

Image Compressor Components

```
    capabilities->bandInc = 2;

    /*
       If this decompressor needed its pixels be aligned on
       some integer multiple, you would set extendWidth and
       extendHeight to the number of pixels by which you need the
       destination extended. If you don't have such requirements
       or if you take care of them yourself, you set extendWidth
       and extendHeight to 0.
    */

    capabilities->extendWidth = p->srcRect.right & 1;
    capabilities->extendHeight = p->srcRect.bottom & 1;

    return(noErr);
}
```

Decompressing a Horizontal Band of an Image

Listing 4-4 shows how to decompress the horizontal band of an image. The Image Compression Manager calls the `CDBandDecompress` function when it wants a decompressor to decompress an image or a horizontal band of an image. The pixel data indicated by the `baseAddr` field is guaranteed to conform to the criteria your decompressor specified in the `CDPreDecompress` function.

Note
This example does not perform decompression on bands with a bit depth of more than one or an extension of width and height. If the example did do so, it would handle these cases faster. ◆

Listing 4-4 Performing a decompression operation

```
pascal long
CDBandDecompress(Handle storage,register CodecDecompressParams *p)
{
    Rect            dRect;
    long            offsetH,offsetV;
    Globals         **glob = (Globals **)storage;
    long            numLines,numStrips;
    short           rowBytes;
    long            stripBytes;
    short           width;
    register short y;
```

CHAPTER 4

Image Compressor Components

```
    register char*  baseAddr;
    char            *cDataPtr;
    char            mmuMode = 1;
    OSErr           result = noErr;

    /*
        Calculate the real base address based on the boundary
        rectangle. If it's not a linear transformation, this
        decompressor does not perform the operation.
    */

    dRect = p->srcRect;
    if ( !TransformRect(p->matrix,&dRect,nil) )
        return(paramErr);

    /* If there is a progress function, give it an open call at
       the start of this band.
    */

    if (p->progressProcRecord.progressProc)
        p->progressProcRecord.progressProc(codecProgressOpen,0,
            p->progressProcRecord.progressRefCon);

    /*
        Initialize some local variables.
    */

    width = (*p->imageDescription)->width;
    rowBytes = p->dstPixMap.rowBytes;
    numLines = p->stopLine - p->startLine; /* number of scan lines
                                              in this band */
    numStrips = (numLines+1)>>1;           /* number of strips in
                                              this band */
    stripBytes = ((width+1)>>1) * 5;       /* number of bytes in
                                              1 strip of blocks */

    cDataPtr = p->data;

    /*
        Adjust the destination base address to be at the beginning
        of the desired rectangle.
    */

    offsetH = (dRect.left - p->dstPixMap.bounds.left);
```

Image Compressor Components

```
    switch ( p->dstPixMap.pixelSize ) {
       case 32:
          offsetH <<=2;   /* 1 pixel = 4 bytes */
          break;
       case 16:
          offsetH <<=1;   /* 1 pixel = 2 bytes */
          break;
       case 8:
          break;                /* 1 pixel = 1 byte */
       default:
          result = codecErr;   /* This decompressor doesn't handle
                                  these cases, although it
                                  could. */
          goto bail;
    }
    offsetV = (dRect.top - p->dstPixMap.bounds.top) * rowBytes;
    baseAddr = p->dstPixMap.baseAddr + offsetH + offsetV;

    /*
       If your decompressor component is skipping some data,
       it just skips it here. You can tell because
       firstBandInFrame indicates this is the first band for a new
       frame, and if startLine is not 0, then that many lines were
       clipped out.
     */
    if ( (p->conditionFlags & codecConditionFirstBand) &&
         p->startLine != 0 ) {
       if ( p->dataProcRecord.dataProc ) {
          for ( y=0; y  < p->startLine>>1; y++ )  {
             if ( (result=p->dataProcRecord.dataProc
                    (&cDataPtr,stripBytes,
                     p->dataProcRecord.dataRefCon)) != noErr ) {
                result = codecSpoolErr;
                goto bail;
             }
             cDataPtr += stripBytes;
          }
       } else
          cDataPtr += (p->startLine>>1) * stripBytes;
    }
/*
   If there is a data-loading function spooling the data to your
   decompressor, then you have to decompress the data in the
```

CHAPTER 4

Image Compressor Components

```
      chunk size that is specified, or, if there is a progress
      function, you must make sure to call it as you go along.
*/

   if ( p->dataProcRecord.dataProc ||
      p->progressProcRecord.progressProc ) {

      SharedGlobals *sg = (*glob)->sharedGlob;

      for (y=0; y < numStrips; y++) {
         if (p->dataProcRecord.dataProc) {
            if ( (result=p->dataProcRecord.dataProc
                  (&cDataPtr,stripBytes,
                  p->dataProcRecord.dataRefCon)) != noErr ) {
               result = codecSpoolErr;
               goto bail;
            }
         }
         SwapMMUMode(&mmuMode);
         DecompressStrip(cDataPtr,baseAddr,rowBytes,width,sg);
         SwapMMUMode(&mmuMode);
         baseAddr += rowBytes<<1;
         cDataPtr += stripBytes;

         if (p->progressProcRecord.progressProc) {
            if ( (result=p->progressProcRecord.progressProc
                  (codecProgressUpdatePercent,
                  FixDiv(y, numStrips),
                  p->progressProcRecord.progressRefCon)) != noErr ) {
               result = codecAbortErr;
                goto bail;
            }
         }
      }

/*
   Otherwise, do the fast case.
*/
   } else {
```

Image Compressor Components

```
        SharedGlobals *sg = (*glob)->sharedGlob;
        shorttRowBytes = rowBytes<<1;


        SwapMMUMode(&mmuMode);
        for ( y=numStrips; y--; ) {
            DecompressStrip(cDataPtr,baseAddr,rowBytes,width,sg);
            baseAddr += tRowBytes;
            cDataPtr += stripBytes;
        }
        SwapMMUMode(&mmuMode);
    }
/*
    IMPORTANT-- Update the pointer to data in the decompression
    parameters structure, so that when your decompressor gets the
    next band, you'll be at the right place in your data.
*/

    p->data = cDataPtr;

    if ( p->conditionFlags & codecConditionLastBand ) {
        /*
            Tie up any loose ends on the last band of the frame.
        */
    }

bail:
    /*
        If there is a progress function, give it a close call
        at the end of this band.
    */

    if (p->progressProcRecord.progressProc)
        p->progressProcRecord.progressProc(codecProgressClose,0,
            p->progressProcRecord.progressRefCon);
    return(result);
}
```

CHAPTER 4

Image Compressor Components

Image Compressor Components Reference

This section describes the constants, data structures, and functions that are specific to image compression components.

Constants

This section provides details on the image compressor component capability and format flags.

Image Compressor Component Capabilities

Apple has defined several component flags for image compressor components. These flags specify information about the capabilities of the component. You set these flags in the `componentFlags` field of your component's component description structure. The Image Compression Manager uses these same flags in the compressor information structure to describe the capabilities of image compressors and decompressors. For a complete description of this structure, see the chapter "Image Compression Manager" in *Inside Macintosh: QuickTime*.

The `compressFlags` and `decompressFlags` fields of the compressor information structure contain a number of flags that define the capabilities of your component.

Note
If the compressor information structure is shared, the compressor component uses the component flags that are the same as the compression flags for the component description structure, and the decompressor component uses the component flags that are the same as the decompression flags for the component description structure. ◆

The flag bits for those fields are defined as follows (each flag is valid for both fields unless the description states otherwise):

```
#define codecInfoDoes1          (1L<<0)  /* works with 1-bit pixel
                                            maps */
#define codecInfoDoes2          (1L<<1)  /* works with 2-bit pixel
                                            maps */
#define codecInfoDoes4          (1L<<2)  /* works with 4-bit pixel
                                            maps */
#define codecInfoDoes8          (1L<<3)  /* works with 8-bit pixel
                                            maps */
#define codecInfoDoes16         (1L<<4)  /* works with 16-bit pixel
                                            maps */
```

Image Compressor Components

```
#define codecInfoDoes32          (1L<<5)   /* works with 32-bit pixel
                                              maps */
#define codecInfoDoesDither      (1L<<6)   /* supports fast dithering */
#define codecInfoDoesStretch     (1L<<7)   /* stretches to arbitrary
                                              sizes */
#define codecInfoDoesShrink      (1L<<8)   /* shrinks to arbitrary sizes */
#define codecInfoDoesMask        (1L<<9)   /* handles clipping regions */
#define codecInfoDoesTemporal    (1L<<10)  /* sequential temporal
                                              compression */
#define codecInfoDoesDouble      (1L<<11)  /* stretches to double size
                                              exactly */
#define codecInfoDoesQuad        (1L<<12)  /* stretches to quadruple
                                              size */
#define codecInfoDoesHalf        (1L<<13)  /* shrinks to half size */
#define codecInfoDoesQuarter     (1L<<14)  /* shrinks to one-quarter
                                              size */
#define codecInfoDoesRotate      (1L<<15)  /* rotates during
                                              decompression */
#define codecInfoDoesHorizFlip   (1L<<16)  /* flips horizontally during
                                              decompression */
#define codecInfoDoesVertFlip    (1L<<17)  /* flips vertically during
                                              decompression */
#define codecInfoDoesSkew        (1L<<18)  /* skews image during
                                              decompression */
#define codecInfoDoesBlend       (1L<<19)  /* blends image with matte
                                              during decompression */
#define codecInfoDoesWarp        (1L<<20)  /* warps image arbitrarily
                                              during decompression */
#define codecInfoDoesRecompress  (1L<<21)  /* recompresses images without
                                              accumulating errors */
#define codecInfoDoesSpool       (1L<<22)  /* uses data-loading or
                                              data-unloading function */
#define codecInfoDoesRateConstrain (1L<<23) /* constrains amount of
                                              generated data to
                                              caller-defined limit */
```

Image Compressor Components

Flag descriptions

`codecInfoDoes1`
: Indicates whether the component can work with pixel maps that contain 1-bit pixels. If this flag is set to 1, then the component can compress or decompress images that contain 1-bit pixels. If this flag is set to 0, then the component cannot handle such images.

`codecInfoDoes2`
: Indicates whether the component can work with pixel maps that contain 2-bit pixels. If this flag is set to 1, then the component can compress or decompress images that contain 2-bit pixels. If this flag is set to 0, then the component cannot handle such images.

`codecInfoDoes4`
: Indicates whether the component can work with pixel maps that contain 4-bit pixels. If this flag is set to 1, then the component can compress or decompress images that contain 4-bit pixels. If this flag is set to 0, then the component cannot handle such images.

`codecInfoDoes8`
: Indicates whether the component can work with pixel maps that contain 8-bit pixels. If this flag is set to 1, then the component can compress or decompress images that contain 8-bit pixels. If this flag is set to 0, then the component cannot handle such images.

`codecInfoDoes16`
: Indicates whether the component can work with pixel maps that contain 16-bit pixels. If this flag is set to 1, then the component can compress or decompress images that contain 16-bit pixels. If this flag is set to 0, then the component cannot handle such images.

`codecInfoDoes32`
: Indicates whether the component can work with pixel maps that contain 32-bit pixels. If this flag is set to 1, then the component can compress or decompress images that contain 32-bit pixels. If this flag is set to 0, then the component cannot handle such images.

`codecInfoDoesDither`
: Indicates whether the component supports dithering. If this flag is set to 1, the component supports dithering of colors. If this flag is set to 0, the component does not support dithering. This flag is only available for decompressor components.

`codecInfoDoesStretch`
: Indicates whether the component can stretch images to arbitrary sizes. If this flag is set to 1, the component can stretch images. If this flag is set to 0, the component does not support stretching. This flag is only available for decompressor components.

`codecInfoDoesShrink`
: Indicates whether the component can shrink images to arbitrary sizes. If this flag is set to 1, the component can shrink images. If this flag is set to 0, the component does not support shrinking. This flag is only available for decompressor components.

Image Compressor Components

`codecInfoDoesMask`

> Indicates whether the component can handle clipping regions. If this flag is set to 1, the component can mask to an arbitrary clipping region. If this flag is set to 0, the component does not support clipping regions. This flag is only available for decompressor components.

`codecInfoDoesTemporal`

> Indicates whether the component supports temporal compression in sequences. If this flag is set to 1, the component supports time compression. If this flag is set to 0, the component does not support time compression.

`codecInfoDoesDouble`

> Indicates whether the component supports stretching to double size during decompression. Since images are in two dimensions (height and width), this means a total of four times as many pixels. The parameters for the stretch operation are specified in the matrix structure for the request—the component modifies the scaling attributes of the matrix (see the chapter "Movie Toolbox" in *Inside Macintosh: QuickTime* for information about transformation matrices). If this flag is set to 1, the component can stretch an image to exactly four times its original size, up to the maximum size supported by the decompressor. If this flag is set to 0, the component does not support stretching to double size. This flag is valid only for the `decompressFlags` field.

`codecInfoDoesQuad`

> Indicates whether the component supports stretching an image to four times its original size during decompression. Since images are in two dimensions (height and width), this means a total of sixteen times as many pixels. The parameters for the stretch operation are specified in the matrix structure (defined by the `MatrixRecord` data type) for the request—the component modifies the scaling attributes of the matrix (see the chapter "Movie Toolbox" in *Inside Macintosh: QuickTime* for information about transformation matrices). If this flag is set to 1, the component can stretch an image to exactly sixteen times its original size, up to the maximum size supported by the decompressor. If this flag is set to 0, the component does not support this capability. This flag is valid only for the `decompressFlags` field.

`codecInfoDoesHalf`

> Indicates whether the component supports shrinking an image to half of its original size during decompression. Since images are in two dimensions (height and width), this means a total of one-fourth the number of pixels. The parameters for the shrink operation are specified in the matrix structure for the request—the component modifies the scaling attributes of the matrix (see the chapter "Movie Toolbox" in *Inside Macintosh: QuickTime* for information about transformation matrices). If this flag is set to 1, the component can shrink an image to half size, down to the minimum size specified by the `minimumHeight` and `minimumWidth` fields in the compressor information structure. If this flag is set to 0, the component does not

CHAPTER 4

Image Compressor Components

codecInfoDoesQuarter
: support this capability. This flag is valid only for the `decompressFlags` field.

codecInfoDoesQuarter
: Indicates whether the component can shrink an image to one-quarter of its original size during decompression. Since images are in two dimensions (height and width), this means a total of one-sixteenth the number of pixels. The parameters for the shrink operation are specified in the matrix structure for the request—the component modifies the scaling attributes of the matrix (see the chapter "Movie Toolbox" in *Inside Macintosh: QuickTime* for information about transformation matrices). If this flag is set to 1, the component can shrink an image to exactly one-quarter of its original size, down to the minimum size specified by the `minimumHeight` and `minimumWidth` fields in the compressor information structure. If this flag is set to 0, the component does not support this capability. This flag is valid only for the `decompressFlags` field.

codecInfoDoesRotate
: Indicates whether the component can rotate an image during decompression. The parameters for the rotation are specified in the matrix structure for a decompression operation. If this flag is set to 1, the component can rotate the image at decompression time. If this flag is set to 0, the component cannot rotate the resulting image. This flag is valid only for the `decompressFlags` field.

codecInfoDoesHorizFlip
: Indicates whether the component can flip an image horizontally during decompression. The parameters for the horizontal flip are specified in the matrix structure for a decompression operation. If this flag is set to 1, the component can flip the image at decompression time. If this flag is set to 0, the component cannot flip the resulting image. This flag is valid only for the `decompressFlags` field.

codecInfoDoesVertFlip
: Indicates whether the component can flip an image vertically during decompression. The parameters for the vertical flip are specified in the matrix structure for a decompression operation. If this flag is set to 1, the component can flip the image at decompression time. If this flag is set to 0, the component cannot flip the resulting image. This flag is valid only for the `decompressFlags` field.

codecInfoDoesSkew
: Indicates whether the component can skew an image during decompression. Skewing an image distorts it linearly along only a single axis—for example, drawing a rectangular image into a parallelogram-shaped region. The parameters for the skew operation are specified in the matrix structure for the

decompression request. If this flag is set to 1, the component can skew an image at decompression time. If this flag is set to 0, the component does not support this capability. This flag is valid only for the `decompressFlags` field.

`codecInfoDoesBlend`
Indicates whether the component can blend the resulting image with a matte during decompression. The matte is provided by the application in the decompression request. If this flag is set to 1, the component can blend during decompression. If this flag is set to 0, the component does not support this capability. This flag is valid only for the `decompressFlags` field.

`codecInfoDoesWarp`
Indicates whether the component can warp an image during decompression. Warping an image distorts it along one or more axes, perhaps in a nonlinear fashion, in effect "bending" the resulting region. The parameters for the warp operation are specified in the matrix structure for the decompression request. If this flag is set to 1, the component can warp an image at decompression time. If this flag is set to 0, the component does not support this capability. This flag is valid only for the `decompressFlags` field.

`codecInfoDoesRecompress`
Indicates whether the component can recompress images it has previously compressed without losing image quality. Many compression algorithms cause image degradation when you apply them repeatedly to the same image. If this flag is set to 1, the component uses an algorithm that does not compromise image quality after repeated compressions. If this flag is set to 0, you should not use the component for repeated compressions of the same image. This flag is only available for compressor components.

`codecInfoDoesSpool`
Indicates whether the component uses data-loading or data-unloading functions. Your application can define data-loading and data-unloading functions to help the component work with images that are too large to be stored in memory (see the chapter "Image Compression Manager" in *Inside Macintosh: QuickTime* for more information about data-loading and data-unloading functions). If this flag is set to 1, the component uses these functions if needed for a given operation. If this flag is set to 0, the component does not use these functions under any circumstances.

`codecInfoDoesRateConstrain`
Indicates the compressor is able to constrain the amount of data it generates when compressing sequences of images to a limit defined by the caller. See the chapter "Image Compression Manager" in *Inside Macintosh: QuickTime* for details on data rate constraint functions. This flag is only available for compressor components.

Chapter 4

Image Compressor Components

Format of Compressed Data and Files

The `formatFlags` field of the compressor information structure contains a number of flags that define the possible format of compressed data produced by the component and the format of compressed files that the component can handle during decompression. The defined flags are as follows:

```
#define codecInfoDepth1      (1L<<0)   /* compressed images with 1-bit color
                                          depth available */
#define codecInfoDepth2      (1L<<1)   /* compressed images with 2-bit color
                                          depth available */
#define codecInfoDepth4      (1L<<2)   /* compressed images with 4-bit color
                                          depth available */
#define codecInfoDepth8      (1L<<3)   /* compressed images with 8-bit color
                                          depth available */
#define codecInfoDepth16     (1L<<4)   /* compressed images with 16-bit color
                                          depth available */
#define codecInfoDepth32     (1L<<5)   /* compressed images with 32-bit color
                                          depth available */
#define codecInfoDepth24     (1L<<6)   /* compressed images with 24-bit color
                                          depth available */
#define codecInfoDepth33     (1L<<7)   /* compressed data with monochrome images
                                          of 1-bit color depth */
#define codecInfoDepth34     (1L<<8)   /* compressed images with 2-bit grayscale
                                          depth available */
#define codecInfoDepth36     (1L<<9)   /* compressed images with 4-bit grayscale
                                          depth available */
#define codecInfoDepth40     (1L<<10)  /* compressed images with 8-bit grayscale
                                          depth available */
#define codecInfoStoresClut  (1L<<11)  /* compressed data with custom color
                                          tables */
#define codecInfoDoesLossless
                             (1L<<12)  /* compressed data stored lossless
                                          format */
#define codecInfoSequenceSensitive
                             (1L<<13)  /* compressed data requires non-key
                                          frames to be decompressed in same
                                          order as compressed */
```

Flag descriptions

`codecInfoDepth1`
>Indicates whether the component can work with files containing color images with a color depth of 1 bit. If this flag is set to 1, the component can compress into and decompress from files at this depth. If this flag is set to 0, the component cannot handle such files.

`codecInfoDepth2`
>Indicates whether the component can work with files containing color images with a color depth of 2 bits. If this flag is set to 1, the component can compress into and decompress from files at this depth. If this flag is set to 0, the component cannot handle such files.

`codecInfoDepth4`
>Indicates whether the component can work with files containing color images with a color depth of 4 bits. If this flag is set to 1, the component can compress into and decompress from files at this depth. If this flag is set to 0, the component cannot handle such files.

`codecInfoDepth8`
>Indicates whether the component can work with files containing color images with a color depth of 8 bits. If this flag is set to 1, the component can compress into and decompress from files at this depth. If this flag is set to 0, the component cannot handle such files.

`codecInfoDepth16`
>Indicates whether the component can work with files containing color images with a color depth of 16 bits. If this flag is set to 1, the component can compress into and decompress from files at this depth. If this flag is set to 0, the component cannot handle such files.

`codecInfoDepth32`
>Indicates whether the component can work with files containing color images with a color depth of 32 bits. If this flag is set to 1, the component can compress into and decompress from files at this depth. If this flag is set to 0, the component cannot handle such files. This flag is the same as the `codecInfoDepth24` flag except it contains one extra byte used as an alpha channel.

`codecInfoDepth24`
>Indicates whether the component can work with files containing color images with a color depth of 24 bits. If this flag is set to 1, the component can compress into and decompress from files at this depth. If this flag is set to 0, the component cannot handle such files.

`codecInfoDepth33`
>Indicates whether the component can work with files containing monochrome images, which have a grayscale depth of 1 bit. If this flag is set to 1, the component can compress into and decompress from files at this depth. If this flag is set to 0, the component cannot handle such files.

Image Compressor Components

`codecInfoDepth34`
: Indicates whether the component can work with files containing grayscale images with a grayscale depth of 2 bits. If this flag is set to 1, the component can compress into and decompress from files at this depth. If this flag is set to 0, the component cannot handle such files.

`codecInfoDepth36`
: Indicates whether the component can work with files containing grayscale images with a grayscale depth of 4 bits. If this flag is set to 1, the component can compress into and decompress from files at this depth. If this flag is set to 0, the component cannot handle such files.

`codecInfoDepth40`
: Indicates whether the component can work with files containing grayscale images with a grayscale depth of 8 bits. If this flag is set to 1, the component can compress into and decompress from files at this depth. If this flag is set to 0, the component cannot handle such files.

`codecInfoStoresClut`
: Indicates whether the component can accommodate compressed data with custom color tables. If this flag is set to 1, the component can create compressed files with custom color tables and can decompress files that contain custom color tables. If this flag is set to 0, the component cannot handle such files.

`codecInfoDoesLossless`
: Indicates whether the component can perform lossless compression or decompression operations. Lossless compression results in a decompressed image that is exactly the same as the original, uncompressed image. If this flag is set to 1, the component can perform lossless compression or decompression. If this flag is set to 0, the component cannot perform lossless operations. The application specifies a lossless operation by setting the desired quality level to `codecLosslessQuality` (see *Inside Macintosh: QuickTime* for more information about quality levels).

`codecInfoSequenceSensitive`
: Indicates that the compressed data generated by this image compressor component has the requirement that non-key frames in a sequence be decompressed in the same order that they were compressed.

Data Types

This section discusses the data structures that the Image Compression Manager uses to communicate with image compressor and decompressor components.

The Compressor Capability Structure

Image compressor components use the compressor capability structure to report their capabilities to the Image Compression Manager. Before compressing or decompressing an image, the Image Compression Manager requests this capability information from the component that will be handling the operation by calling the `CDPreCompress` or `CDPreDecompress` function provided by that component. The compressor component examines the compression or decompression parameters and indicates any restrictions on its ability to satisfy the request in a formatted compressor capability structure. The Image Compression Manager then manages the operation according to the capabilities of the component.

The `CodecCapabilities` data type defines the compressor capability structure.

```
typedef struct {
    long          flags;            /* control information */
    short         wantedPixelSize;  /* pixel depth for component
                                       to use with image */
    short         extendWidth;      /* extension width of image
                                       in pixels */
    short         extendHeight;     /* extension height of image
                                       in pixels */
    short         bandMin;          /* supported minimum
                                       image band height */
    short         bandInc;          /* common factor of
                                       supported band heights */
    short         pad;              /* reserved */
    unsigned long time;             /* milliseconds operation
                                       takes to complete */
} CodecCapabilities;

typedef CodecCapabilities *CodecCapabilitiesPtr;
```

CHAPTER 4

Image Compressor Components

Field descriptions

`flags` Contains flags that contain control information that is used by both the Image Compression Manager and the compressor component. The defined bit positions for this field are discussed later in this section.

`wantedPixelSize`
 Indicates the pixel depth the component can use with the specified image. The component determines the pixel depth of the image for the operation by examining the appropriate pixel map.

`extendWidth` Specifies the number of pixels the image must be extended in width. If the component cannot accommodate the image at its given width, the component may request that the Image Compression Manager extend the width of the image by adding pixels to the right edge of the image. This is sometimes necessary to accommodate the component's block size.

`extendHeight` Specifies the number of pixels the image must be extended in height. If the component cannot accommodate the image at its given height the component may request that the Image Compression Manager extend the height of the image by adding pixels to the bottom of the image. This is sometimes necessary to accommodate the component's block size.

`bandMin` Contains the minimum image band height supported by the component. Components that can tolerate small values operate under a wider set of memory conditions.

`bandInc` Specifies a common factor of supported image band heights. A component may support only image bands that are an even multiple of some number of pixels high. These components report this common factor in the `bandInc` field. Set this field to 1 if your component supports bands of any size.

`pad` Reserved for use by Apple.

`time` Indicates the number of milliseconds the operation will take to complete. If the compressor cannot determine this value, it sets this field to 0.

The `flags` field of the compressor capability structure contains flags that exchange control information between the Image Compression Manager and the compressor component. Components use flags in the low-order 16 bits to indicate their capabilities to the manager. The Image Compression Manager may use flags in the high-order 16 bits to pass control information to the component.

CHAPTER 4

Image Compressor Components

The following flags are defined:

```
#define codecCanScale          (1L<<0)   /* decompressor scales
                                            information */
#define codecCanMask           (1L<<1)   /* decompressor applies mask to
                                            image */
#define codecCanMatte          (1L<<2)   /* decompressor blends image using
                                            matte */
#define codecCanTransform      (1L<<3)   /* decompressor works with complex
                                            placement matrices */
#define codecCanTransferMode   (1L<<4)   /* decompressor accepts transfer
                                            mode */
#define codecCanCopyPrev       (1L<<5)   /* compressor updates previous
                                            image buffer */
#define codecCanSpool          (1L<<6)   /* component can use functions to
                                            spool data */
#define codecCanClipVertical   (1L<<7)   /* decompressor clips image
                                            vertically */
#define codecCanClipRectangular (1L<<8)  /* decompressor clips image
                                            vertically & horizontally */
#define codecCanRemapColor     (1L<<9)   /* compressor remaps color */
#define codecCanFastDither     (1L<<10)  /* compressor supports fast
                                            dithering */
#define codecCanSrcExtract     (1L<<11)  /* compressor extracts portion
                                            of source image */
#define codecCanCopyPrevComp   (1L<<12)  /* compressor updates previous
                                            image buffer */
#define codecCanAsync          (1L<<13)  /* component can work
                                            asynchronously */
#definecodecCanMakeMask        (1L<<14)  /* decompressor makes
                                            modification masks */
#define codecCanShift          (1L<<15)  /* component works with pixels
                                            that are not byte-aligned */
```

IMPORTANT

The following flags are currently unused by the Image Compression Manager: `codecCanClipVertical`, `codecCanClipRectangular`, and `codecCanFastDither`. ▲

Image Compressor Components

Flag descriptions

`codecCanScale` Indicates whether the decompressor can scale the image during decompression. The decompressor sets this flag to 1 to indicate that it can scale the image during decompression. The decompressor sets this flag to 0 if it cannot scale the decompressed image.

`codecCanMask` Indicates whether the decompressor can apply a mask to the decompressed image. The decompressor sets this flag to 1 to indicate that it can use a mask to control the image that results from a decompression operation. The decompressor sets this flag to 0 if it cannot work with masks.

`codecCanMatte` Indicates whether the decompressor can blend the decompressed image using a matte. The decompressor sets this flag to 1 to indicate that it can use a blend matte during decompression. The decompressor sets this flag to 0 if it cannot use a blend matte.

`codecCanTransform`
Indicates whether the decompressor can work with complex placement matrixes. The decompressor sets this flag to 1 to indicate that it can work with transformation matrixes during decompression. The decompressor sets this flag to 0 if it cannot work with matrixes.

`codecCanTransferMode`
Indicates whether the decompressor can accept a transfer mode other than source copy or dither copy when displaying a decompressed image. The decompressor sets this flag to 1 to indicate that it can accept transfer modes; otherwise, the decompressor sets this flag to 0.

`codecCanCopyPrev`
Indicates whether the compressor can update the previous image buffer during sequence compression. The compressor sets this flag to 1 to indicate that it can update the previous image buffer. The compressor sets this flag to 0 if it cannot update the buffer.

`codecCanSpool` Indicates whether the component can use data-loading and data-unloading functions to spool data during decompression and compression operations, respectively. Applications may define data-loading and data-unloading functions to handle images that cannot fit into memory (see the chapter "Image Compression Manager" in *Inside Macintosh: QuickTime* for more information on data-loading and data-unloading functions). The component sets this flag to 1 to indicate that it can use these functions. The component sets this flag to 0 to indicate that it cannot use these functions.

`codecCanClipVertical`
Indicates whether the decompressor can clip an image vertically during decompression. The decompressor sets this flag to 1 to indicate that it can clip an image vertically. The decompressor sets this flag to 0 to indicate that it cannot clip an image vertically.

Image Compressor Components

`codecCanClipRectangular`
: Indicates whether the decompressor can clip both vertically and horizontally during decompression. The decompressor sets this flag to 1 to indicate that it can clip along both axes. The decompressor sets this flag to 0 to indicate that it cannot clip an image both vertically and horizontally.

`codecCanRemapColor`
: Indicates whether the compressor can remap the colors for an image using color tables. The compressor sets this flag to 1 if it can remap colors. The compressor sets this flag to 0 if it cannot remap colors.

`codecCanFastDither`
: Indicates whether the compressor supports fast dithering. The compressor sets this flag to 1 if it supports fast dithering. The compressor sets this flag to 0 if it does not support fast dithering. See the chapter "Image Compression Manager" in *Inside Macintosh: QuickTime* for more information about fast dithering.

`codecCanSrcExtract`
: Indicates whether the compressor can extract a portion of the source image. The compressor sets this flag to 1 if it can extract a portion of the source image. The compressor sets the flag to 0 if it cannot.

`codecCanCopyPrevComp`
: Indicates whether the compressor can update the previous image buffer during sequence compression using compressed data. The compressor sets this flag to 1 to indicate that it can update the previous image buffer. The compressor sets this flag to 0 if it cannot update the buffer.

`codecCanAsync`
: Indicates whether the component can work asynchronously. The compressor sets this flag to 1 if it can compress and decompress asynchronously; otherwise, it sets this flag to 0.

`codecCanMakeMask`
: Indicates whether the decompressor creates modification masks during decompression. These masks indicate which pixels in the decompressed image differ from the previous image and must therefore be displayed. Such masks are useful only when processing sequences. The decompressor sets this flag to 1 to indicate that it creates modification masks. The decompressor sets this flag to 0 if it does not create such masks.

`codecCanShift`
: Indicates whether the component can work with pixels that are not byte-aligned. This flag is valid only when the source or destination uses fewer than 8 bits per pixel. Components set this flag to 1 if they can read or write pixels that are not byte-aligned. Components set this flag to 0 if pixels must be byte-aligned.

The Compression Parameters Structure

Compressor components accept the parameters that govern a compression operation in the form of a data structure. This data structure is called a *compression parameters structure*. This structure is used by the `CDBandCompress` and `CDPreCompress` functions (described on page 4-63 and page 4-62, respectively).

The compression parameters structure is defined by the `CodecCompressParams` data type as follows:

```
typedef struct {
   ImageSequence           sequenceID;         /* sequence identifier ID
                                                  (precompress or
                                                  bandcompress) */
   ImageDescriptionHandle  imageDescription;   /* handle to image
                                                  description structure
                                                  (precompress or
                                                  bandcompress) */
   Ptr                     data;               /* location for receipt of
                                                  compressed image data */
   long                    bufferSize;         /* size of buffer for data */
   long                    frameNumber;        /* frame identifier */
   long                    startLine;          /* starting line for band */
   long                    stopLine;           /* ending line for band */
   long                    conditionFlags;     /* condition flags */
   CodecFlags              callerFlags;        /* control information
                                                  flags */
   CodecCapabilitiesPtr    *capabilities;      /* pointer to compressor
                                                  capability structure */
   ProgressProcRecord      progressProcRecord; /* progress function
                                                  structure */
   CompletionProcRecord    completionProcRecord;/* completion function
                                                  structure */
   FlushProcRecord         flushProcRecord;    /* data-unloading function
                                                  structure */
   PixMap                  srcPixMap;          /* pointer to image
                                                  (precompress or
                                                  bandcompress) */
   PixMap                  prevPixMap;         /* pointer to pixel map
                                                  for previous image */
   CodecQ                  spatialQuality;     /* compressed image
                                                  quality */
   CodecQ                  temporalQuality;    /* sequence temporal
                                                  quality */
```

Image Compressor Components

```
    Fixed              similarity;         /* similarity between
                                              adjacent frames */
    DataRateParamsPtr  dataRateParams;     /* data constraint
                                              parameters */
    long               reserved;           /* reserved */
} CodecCompressParams;

typedef CodecCompressParams *CodecCompressParamsPtr;
```

Field descriptions

sequenceID
: Contains a unique sequence identifier. If the image to be compressed is part of a sequence, this field contains the sequence identifier that was assigned by the CompressSequenceBegin function. If the image is not part of a sequence, this field is set to 0.

imageDescription
: Contains a handle to the image description structure that describes the image to be compressed.

data
: Points to a location to receive the compressed image data. This is a 32-bit clean address—do not call StripAddress. If there is not sufficient memory to store the compressed image, the application may choose to write the compressed data to mass storage during the compression operation. The flushProc field identifies the data-unloading function that the application provides for this purpose.

  This field is used only by the CDBandCompress function.

bufferSize
: Contains the size of the buffer specified by the data field. Your component sets the value of the bufferSize field to the number of bytes of compressed data written into the buffer. Your component should not return more data than the buffer can hold—it should return a nonzero result code instead.

  This field is used only by the CDBandCompress function.

frameNumber
: Contains a frame identifier. Indicates the relative frame number within the sequence. The Image Compression Manager increments this value for each frame in the sequence.

  This field is used only by the CDBandCompress function.

startLine
: Contains the starting line for the band. This field indicates the starting line number for the band to be compressed. The line number refers to the pixel row in the image, starting from the top of the image. The first row is row number 0.

  This field is used only by the CDBandCompress function.

stopLine
: Contains the ending line for the band. This field indicates the ending line number for the band to be compressed. The line number refers to the pixel row in the image, starting from the top of the image. The first row in the image is row number 0.

Image Compressor Components

> The image band includes the row specified by this field. So, to define a band that contains one row of pixels at the top of an image, you set the `startLine` field to 0 and the `stopLine` field to 1.

`conditionFlags`

> Contains flags that identify the condition under which your component has been called. This field is used only by the `CDBandCompress` function. In addition, these fields contain information about actions taken by your component. Condition flags fields contain the following flags:
>
> ```
> #define codecConditionFirstBand      (1L<<0)
> #define codecConditionLastBand       (1L<<1)
> ```
>
> The `codecConditionFirstBand` constant is an input flag that indicates if this is the first band in the frame. If this flag is set to 1, then your component is being called for the first time for the current frame.
>
> The `codecConditionLastBand` constant is an input flag that indicates if this is the last band in the frame. If this flag is set to 1, then your component is being called for the last time for the current frame. If the `codecConditionFirstBand` flag is also set to 1, this is the only time the Image Compression Manager is calling your component for the current frame.
>
> The `codecConditionCodecChangedMask` constant is an output flag that indicates that the component has changed the mask bits. If your image decompressor component can mask decompressed images and if some of the image pixels should not be written to the screen, set to 0 the corresponding bits in the mask defined by the `maskBits` field in the decompression parameter structure. In addition, set this flag to 1. Otherwise, set this flag to 0.

`callerFlags`

> The `callerFlags` constant is an output flag that contains flags providing further control information. See the chapter "Image Compression Manager" in *Inside Macintosh: QuickTime* for information about the Image Compression Manager function control flags. The following flags are available:
>
> `codecFlagUpdatePrevious`
>
> > Controls whether your compressor updates the previous image during compression. This flag is only used with sequences that are being temporally compressed.
> > If this flag is set to 1, your compressor should copy the current frame into the previous frame buffer at the end of the frame-compression sequence. Use the source image.

Image Compressor Components

    codecFlagWasCompressed

        Indicates to your compressor that the image to be compressed has been compressed before. This information may be useful to compressors that can compensate for the image degradation that may otherwise result from repeated compression and decompression of the same image. This flag is set to 1 to indicate that the image was previously compressed. This flag is set to 0 if the image was not previously compressed.

    codecFlagUpdatePreviousComp

        Controls whether your compressor updates the previous image buffer with the compressed image. This flag is only used with temporal compression. If this flag is set to 1, your compressor should update the previous frame buffer at the end of the frame-compression sequence, allowing your compressor to perform frame differencing against the compression results. Use the image that results from the compression operation. If this flag is set to 0, your compressor should not modify the previous frame buffer during compression.

    codecFlagLiveGrab

        Indicates whether the current sequence results from grabbing live video. When working with live video, your compressor should operate as quickly as possible and disable any additional processing, such as compensation for previously compressed data. This flag is set to 1 when you are compressing from a live video source.

        This field is used only by the `CDBandCompress` function (described on page 4-63).

capabilities

    Points to a compressor capability structure. The Image Compression Manager uses this field to determine the capabilities of your compressor component.

    This field is used only by the `CDPreCompress` function (described on page 4-62).

progressProcRecord

    Contains a progress function structure. During the compression operation, your compressor may occasionally call a function that the application provides in order to report your progress (see the chapter "Image Compression Manager" in *Inside Macintosh: QuickTime* for more information about progress functions). This field contains a structure that identifies the progress function. If the `progressProc` field in this structure is set to `nil`, the application has not supplied a progress function.

    This structure is used only by the `CDBandCompress` function (described on page 4-63).

`completionProcRecord`
: Contains a completion function structure. This structure governs whether you perform the compression asynchronously. If the `completionProc` field in this structure is set to `nil`, perform the compression synchronously. If this field is not `nil`, it specifies an application completion function. Perform the compression asynchronously and call that completion function when your component is finished. See the chapter "Image Compression Manager" in *Inside Macintosh: QuickTime* for information on calling completion functions. If the `completionProc` field in this structure has a value of –1, perform the operation asynchronously but do not call the application's completion function.

  This structure is used only by the `CDBandCompress` function.

`flushProcRecord`
: Contains a data-unloading function structure. If there is not enough memory to store the compressed image, the application may provide a function that unloads some of the compressed data (see the chapter "Image Compression Manager" in *Inside Macintosh: QuickTime* for more information about data-unloading functions). This field contains a structure that identifies that data-unloading function.

  If the application did not provide a data-unloading function, the `flushProc` field in this structure is set to `nil`. In this case, your component writes the entire compressed image into the memory location specified by the `data` field.

  The data-unloading function structure is defined by the `flushProcRecord` data type as follows:

```
struct FlushProcRecord {
    FlushProcPtr flushProc; /* pointer to
                                    data-unloading
                                    function */
    long flushRefCon;       /* data-unloading
                                    function reference
                                    constant */
};
typedef struct FlushProcRecord FlushProcRecord;
typedef FlushProcRecord *FlushProcRecordPtr;
```

  The data-unloading function structure is used only by the `CDBandCompress` function (described on page 4-63).

`srcPixMap`
: Points to the image to be compressed. The image must be stored in a pixel map structure. The contents of this pixel map differ from a standard pixel map in two ways. First, the `rowBytes` field is a full 16-bit value—the high-order bit is not necessarily set to 1. Second, the `baseAddr` field must contain a 32-bit clean address.

  This field is used only by the `CDBandCompress` function.

Image Compressor Components

prevPixMap
: Points to a pixel map containing the previous image. If the image to be compressed is part of a sequence that is being temporally compressed, this field defines the previous image for temporal compression. Your component should then use this previous image as the basis of comparison for the image to be compressed.

    If the `temporalQuality` field is set to 0, do not perform temporal compression. If the `codecFlagUpdatePrevious` flag or the `codecFlagUpdatePreviousComp` flag in the `flags` field is set to 1, update the previous image at the end of the compression operation.

    The contents of this pixel map differ from a standard pixel map in two ways. First, the `rowBytes` field is a full 16-bit value—the high-order bit is not necessarily set to 1. Second, the `baseAddr` field must contain a 32-bit clean address.

    This field is used only by the `CDBandCompress` function.

spatialQuality
: Specifies the desired compressed image quality. See the chapter "Image Compression Manager" in *Inside Macintosh: QuickTime* for valid values.

    This field is used only by the `CDBandCompress` function.

    Check to see if the value of this parameter is `nil` and, if so, do not write to location 0.

temporalQuality
: Specifies the desired sequence temporal quality. This field governs the level of compression the application desires with respect to information in successive frames in the sequence. If this field is set to 0, do not perform temporal compression on this frame. See the chapter "Image Compression Manger" in *Inside Macintosh: QuickTime* for other available values.

    This field is used only by the `CDBandCompress` function (described on page 4-63).

    Check to see if the value of this parameter is `nil` and, if so, do not write to location 0.

similarity
: Indicates the similarity between adjacent frames when performing temporal compression. Your component returns a fixed-point number in this field. That value indicates the relative similarity between the frame just compressed and the previous frame. Valid values range from 0 (key frame) to 1 (identical).

    This field is used only by the `CDBandCompress` function.

    Check to see if the value of this parameter is `nil` and, if so, do not write to location 0.

dataRateParams
: Points to the parameters used when performing data rate constraint.

reserved
: Reserved for use by Apple.

The Decompression Parameters Structure

Decompressors accept the parameters that govern a decompression operation in the form of a data structure. This data structure is called a *decompression parameters structure*. It is used by the `CDBandDecompress` and `CDPreDecompress` functions, which are described on page 4-64 and page 4-63, respectively.

The decompression parameters structure is defined by the `CodecDecompressParams` data type as follows:

```
typedef struct {
    ImageSequence           sequenceID;       /* unique sequence ID
                                                 (predecompress,
                                                 band decompress) */
    ImageDescriptionHandle  imageDescription; /* handle to image description
                                                 structure (predecompress,
                                                 band decompress) */
    Ptr                     data;             /* compressed image data */
    long                    bufferSize;       /* size of data buffer */
    long                    frameNumber;      /* frame identifier */
    long                    startLine;        /* starting line for band */
    long                    stopLine;         /* ending line for band */
    long                    conditionFlags;   /* condition flags */
    CodecFlags              callerFlags;      /* control flags */
    CodecCapabilitiesPtr    *capabilities;    /* pointer to compressor
                                                 capability structure
                                                 (predecompress,
                                                 band decompress) */
    ProgressProcRecord      progressProcRecord;
                                              /* progress function
                                                 structure */
    CompletionProcRecord    completionProcRecord;
                                              /* completion function
                                                 structure */
    DataProcRecord          dataProcRecord;   /* data-loading function
                                                 structure */
    CGrafPtr                port;             /* pointer to color
                                                 graphics port for image
                                                 (predecompress,
                                                 band decompress) */
    PixMap                  dstPixMap;        /* destination pixel map
                                                 (predecompress,
                                                 band decompress) */
    BitMapPtr               maskBits;         /* update mask */
    PixMapPtr               mattePixMap;      /* blend matte pixel map */
```

Image Compressor Components

```
    Rect                srcRect;        /* source rectangle
                                            (predecompress,
                                            band decompress) */
    MatrixRecordPtr     *matrix;        /* pointer to matrix structure
                                            (predecompress,
                                            band decompress) */
    CodecQ              accuracy;       /* desired accuracy
                                            (predecompress,
                                            band decompress) */
    short               transferMode;   /* transfer mode(predecompress,
                                            band decompress) */
    long                reserved[2];    /* reserved */
} CodecDecompressParams;

typedef CodecDecompressParams *CodecDecompressParamsPtr;
```

Field descriptions

`sequenceID` Contains the unique sequence identifier. If the image to be decompressed is part of a sequence, this field contains the sequence identifier that was assigned by the Image Compression Manager's `DecompressSequenceBegin` function. If the image is not part of a sequence, this field is set to 0.

`imageDescription`
 Contains a handle to the image description structure that describes the image to be decompressed.

`data` Points to the compressed image data. This must be a 32-bit clean address. The `bufferSize` field indicates the size of this data buffer. If the entire compressed image does not fit in memory, the application should provide a data-loading function, identified by the `dataProc` field of the data-loading function structure stored in the `dataProcRecord` field.

 This field is used only by the `CDBandDecompress` function (described on page 4-64).

`bufferSize` Specifies the size of the image data buffer.

 This field is used only by the `CDBandDecompress` function.

`frameNumber` Contains a frame identifier. Indicates the relative frame number within the sequence. The Image Compression Manager increments this value for each frame in the sequence.

 This field is used only by the `CDBandDecompress` function (described on page 4-64).

`startLine` Specifies the starting line for the band. This field indicates the starting line number for the band to be decompressed. The line number refers to the pixel row in the image, starting from the top of the image. The first row in the image is row number 0.

 This field is used only by the `CDBandDecompress` function.

Image Compressor Components

stopLine
: Specifies the ending line for the band. This field indicates the ending line number for the band to be decompressed. The line number refers to the pixel row in the image, starting from the top of the image. The first row is row number 0.

  The image band includes the row specified by this field. So, to define a band that contains one row of pixels at the top of an image, you set the `startLine` field to 0 and the `stopLine` field to 1.

  This field is used only by the `CDBandDecompress` function.

conditionFlags
: Contains flags that identify the condition under which your component has been called (in order to save the component some work). The flags in this field are passed to the component in the `CDBandCompress` and `CDPreDecompress` functions when conditions change to save it some work. In addition, these fields contain information about actions taken by your component. Condition flags fields contain the following flags:

```
#define codecConditionFirstFrame      (1L<<2)
#define codecConditionNewDepth        (1L<<3)
#define codecConditionNewTransform    (1L<<4)
#define codecConditionNewSrcRect      (1L<<5)
#define codecConditionNewMatte        (1L<<7)
#define codecConditionNewTransferMode (1L<<8)
#define codecConditionNewClut         (1L<<9)
#define codecConditionNewAccuracy     (1L<<10)
#define codecConditionNewDestination  (1L<<11)
#define codecConditionCodecChangedMask (1L<<31)
```

  The `codecConditionFirstBand` constant is an input flag that indicates if this is the first band in the frame. If this flag is set to 1, then your component is being called for the first time for the current frame.

  The `codecConditionLastBand` constant is an input flag that indicates if this is the last band in the frame. If this flag is set to 1, then your component is being called for the last time for the current frame. If the `codecConditionFirstBand` flag is also set to 1, this is the only time the Image Compression Manager is calling your component for the current frame.

  The `codecConditionFirstFrame` constant is an input flag that indicates that this is the first frame to be decompressed for this image sequence.

CHAPTER 4

Image Compressor Components

The `codecConditionNewDepth` constant is an input flag that indicates that the depth of the destination has changed for this image sequence.

The `codecConditionNewTransform` constant is an input flag that indicates that the transformation matrix has changed for this sequence.

The `codecConditionNewSrcRect` constant is an input flag that indicates that the source rectangle has changed for this sequence.

The `codecConditionNewMatte` is an input flag that indicates that the matte pixel map has changed for this sequence.

The `codecConditionNewTransferMode` constant is an input flag that indicates that the transfer mode has changed for this sequence.

The `codecConditionNewClut` constant is an input flag that indicates that the color lookup table has changed for this sequence.

The `codecConditionNewAccuracy` constant is an input flag that indicates to the component that the accuracy parameter has changed for this sequence.

The `codecConditionNewDestination` constant is an input flag that indicates to the component that the destination pixel map has changed for this sequence.

The `codecConditionCodecChangedMask` constant is an output flag that indicates that the component has changed the mask bits. If your image decompressor component can mask decompressed images and if some of the image pixels should not be written to the screen, set the corresponding bits in the mask (defined by the `maskBits` field in the decompression parameter structure) to 0. In addition, set this flag to 1. Otherwise, set this flag to 0.

`callerFlags`   Contains flags providing further control information. See the chapter "Image Compression Manager" in *Inside Macintosh: QuickTime* for information about the Image Compression Manager function control flags. Four flags are available:

The `codecFlagUpdatePrevious` flag controls whether your compressor updates the previous image during compression. This flag is only used with sequences that are being temporally compressed. If this flag is set to 1, your compressor should copy the current frame into the previous frame buffer at the end of the frame-compression sequence. Use the source image.

The `codecFlagWasCompressed` flag indicates to your compressor that the image to be compressed has been compressed before. This information may be useful to compressors that can compensate for the image degradation that may otherwise result from repeated compression and decompression of the same image. This flag is set to 1 to indicate that the image was previously compressed. This flag is set to 0 if the image was not previously compressed.

Image Compressor Components Reference   4-49

Image Compressor Components

The `codecFlagUpdatePreviousComp` flag controls whether your compressor updates the previous image buffer with the compressed image. This flag is only used with temporal compression. If this flag is set to 1, your compressor should update the previous frame buffer at the end of the frame compression sequence, allowing your compressor to perform frame differencing against the compression results. Use the image that results from the compression operation. If this flag is set to 0, your compressor should not modify the previous frame buffer during compression.

The `codecFlagLiveGrab` flag indicates whether the current sequence results from grabbing live video. When working with live video, your compressor should operate as quickly as possible and disable any additional processing, such as compensation for previously compressed data. This flag is set to 1 when you are compressing from a live video source. This field is used only by the `CDBandCompress` function (described on page 4-63).

`capabilities`
Points to a compressor capability structure (described on page 4-35). The Image Compression Manager uses this parameter to determine the capabilities of your decompressor component.

This field is used only by the `CDPreDecompress` function (described on page 4-63).

`progressProcRecord`
Contains a progress function structure. During the decompression operation, your decompressor may occasionally call a function that the application provides in order to report your progress (see the chapter "Image Compression Manager" in *Inside Macintosh: QuickTime* for more information about progress functions). This field contains a structure that identifies the progress function. If the `progressProc` field of this structure is set to `nil`, the application did not provide a progress function.

The progress function structure is defined by the `progressProcRecord` data type as follows:

```
struct ProgressProcRecord {
    ProgressProcPtr progressProc;   /* pointer to
                                        progress
                                        function */
    long            progressRefCon; /* reference
                                        constant */
};
typedef struct ProgressProcRecord ProgressProcRecord;
typedef ProgressProcRecord *ProgressProcRecordPtr;
```

This field is used only by the `CDBandDecompress` function (described on page 4-64).

`completionProcRecord`
Contains a completion function structure. This field governs whether you perform the decompression asynchronously. If the

completionProc field in this structure is set to nil, perform the decompression synchronously. If this field is not nil, it specifies an application completion function. Perform the decompression asynchronously and call that completion function when your component is finished. See the chapter "Image Compression Manager" in *Inside Macintosh: QuickTime* for information on calling completion functions. If this field has a value of –1, perform the operation asynchronously but do not call the application's completion function.

The completion function structure is defined by the CompletionProcRecord data type as follows:

```
struct CompletionProcRecord {
  CompletionProcPtr completionProc;  /* pointer to
                                        completion
                                        function */
  long              completionRefCon; /* reference
                                        constant */
};
typedef struct CompletionProcRecord CompletionProcRecord;
typedef CompletionProcRecord *CompletionProcRecordPtr;
```

This field is used only by the CDBandDecompress function (described on page 4-64).

dataProcRecord

Contains a data-loading function structure. If the data stream is not all in memory, your component may call an application function that loads more compressed data (see the chapter "Image Compression Manager" in *Inside Macintosh: QuickTime* for more information about data-loading functions). This field contains a structure that identifies that data-loading function. If the application did not provide a data-loading function, the dataProc field in this structure is set to nil. In this case, the entire image must be in memory at the location specified by the data field.

The data-loading function structure is defined by the dataProcRecord data type as follows:

```
struct DataProcRecord {
   DataProcPtr dataProc;/* pointer to data-loading
                           function */
   long dataRefCon;     /* reference constant */
};
typedef struct DataProcRecord DataProcRecord;
typedef DataProcRecord *DataProcRecordPtr;
```

This field is used only by the CDBandDecompress function.

port	Points to the color graphics port that receives the decompressed image.
dstPixMap	Points to the pixel map where the decompressed image is to be displayed. The GDevice global variable is set to the destination graphics device.

The contents of this pixel map differ from a standard pixel map in two ways. First, the rowBytes field is a full 16-bit value—the high-order bit is not necessarily set to 1. Second, the baseAddr field must contain a 32-bit clean address. |
| maskBits | Contains an update mask. If your component can mask result data, use this mask to indicate which pixels in the destination pixel map to update. Your component indicates whether it can mask with the codecCanMask flag in the flags field of the compressor capability structure referred to by the capabilities field. This field is updated in response to the CDPreDecompress request (described on page 4-63). See "The Compressor Capability Structure" beginning on page 4-35 for a description of the compressor capability structure.

If the mask has not changed since the last CDBandDecompress request, the codecConditionCodecChangedMask flag in the conditionFlags field is set to 0.

This field is used only by the CDBandDecompress function. |
| mattePixMap | Points to a pixel map that contains a blend matte. The matte can be defined at any supported pixel depth—the matte depth need not correspond to the source or destination depths. The matte must be in the coordinate system of the source image. If the application does not want to apply a blend matte, this field is set to nil.

The contents of this pixel map differ from a standard pixel map in two ways. First, the rowBytes field is a full 16-bit value—the high-order bit is not necessarily set to 1. Second, the baseAddr field must contain a 32-bit clean address.

This field is used only by the CDBandDecompress function (described on page 4-64). |
srcRect	Points to a rectangle defining the portion of the image to decompress. This rectangle must lie within the boundary rectangle of the compressed image, which is defined by the width and height fields of the image description structure referred to by the imageDescription field.
matrix	Points to a matrix structure that specifies how to transform the image during decompression.
accuracy	Specifies the accuracy desired in the decompressed image. Values for this parameter are on the same scale as compression quality. See the chapter "Image Compression Manager" in *Inside Macintosh: QuickTime* for valid values.

Image Compressor Components

`transferMode`	Specifies the QuickDraw transfer mode for the operation. For details on QuickDraw's transfer modes, see the chapter "Basic QuickDraw" in *Inside Macintosh: Imaging*.
`reserved`	Reserved for use by Apple.

Functions

This section describes the external interface that image compressor components must support. It also discusses the utility functions that the Image Compression Manager provides for use by compressors and decompressors.

This discussion has been divided into two parts. They discuss the image compressor component functions that are called by the Image Compression Manager. "Direct Functions" deals with image compressor component functions that are called by the Image Compression Manager in response to application requests. "Indirect Functions" discusses image compressor component functions that may be called by the Image Compression Manager at any time. The next section, "Image Compression Manager Utility Functions," defines a number of Image Compression Manager utility functions that are available to image compressor components.

Apple has defined a functional interface for image compressor components. For information about the functions your component must support, see the individual function descriptions that follow.

You can use the following constants to refer to the request codes for each of the functions that your component must support.

```
#define codecGetCodecInfo           0x00   /* CDGetCodecInf */
#define codecGetCompressionTime     0x01   /* CDGetCompressionTime */
#define codecGetMaxCompressionSize  0x02   /* CDGetMaxCompressionSize */
#define codecPreCompress            0x03   /* CDPreCompress */
#define codecBandCompress           0x04   /* CDBandCompress */
#define codecPreDecompress          0x05   /* CDPreDeCompress */
#define codecBandDecompress         0x06   /* CDBandDeCompress */
#define codecCDSequenceBusy         0x07   /* CDSequenceBusy */
#define codecGetCompressedImageSize 0x08   /* CDGetCompressedImageSize */
#define codecGetSimilarity          0x09   /* CDGetSimilarity */
#define codecTrimImage              0x0A   /* CDTrimImage */
```

Note
Code selectors 0 through 127 are reserved for use by Apple. Code selectors 128 through 191 are subtype specific. Code selectors 192 through 255 are vendor specific. Code selectors 256 through 32767 are available for general use. Negative selectors are reserved by the Component Manager. ◆

Direct Functions

These functions are invoked by the Image Compression Manager in direct response to application functions. Refer to the chapter "Image Compression Manager" in *Inside Macintosh: QuickTime* for descriptions of the functions that applications call.

CDGetCodecInfo

Your component receives the `CDGetCodecInfo` request whenever an application calls the Image Compression Manager's `GetCodecInfo` function.

```
pascal ComponentResult CDGetCodecInfo (CodecInfo *info);
```

info   Contains a pointer to the compressor information structure (defined by the `CodecInfo` data type) to update. Your component should report its capabilities by formatting a compressor information structure in the location specified by this parameter.

DESCRIPTION

Your component returns a formatted compressor information structure defining its capabilities.

Both compressors and decompressors may receive this request.

RESULT CODES

```
noErr              0      No error
codecUnimpError   –8962   Feature not implemented by this compressor
```

SEE ALSO

See the chapter "Image Compression Manager" in *Inside Macintosh: QuickTime* for a description of the compressor information structure.

Image Compressor Components

CDGetMaxCompressionSize

Your component receives the `CDGetMaxCompressionSize` request whenever an application calls the Image Compression Manager's `GetMaxCompressionSize` function. The caller uses this function to determine the maximum size the data will become for a given parameter.

```
pascal ComponentResult CDGetMaxCompressionSize (PixMapHandle src,
                                                const Rect *srcRect,
                                                short depth,
                                                CodecQ quality,
                                                long *size);
```

src Contains a handle to the source image. The source image is stored in a pixel map structure. Applications use the size information you return to allocate buffers that may be used for more than one image. Consequently, your compressor should not consider the contents of the image when determining the maximum compressed size. Rather, you should consider only the quality level, pixel depth, and image size.

This parameter may be set to `nil`. In this case the application has not supplied a source image—your component should use the other parameters to determine the characteristics of the image to be compressed.

srcRect Contains a pointer to a rectangle defining the portion of the source image to compress.

depth Specifies the depth at which the image is to be compressed. Values of 1, 2, 4, 8, 16, 24, and 32 indicate the number of bits per pixel for color images. Values of 33, 34, 36, and 40 indicate 1-bit, 2-bit, 4-bit, and 8-bit grayscale, respectively, for grayscale images.

quality Specifies the desired compressed image quality. See the chapter "Image Compression Manager" in *Inside Macintosh: QuickTime* for valid values.

size Contains a pointer to a field to receive the maximum size, in bytes, of the compressed image.

DESCRIPTION

Your component returns a long integer indicating the maximum number of bytes of compressed data that results from compressing the specified image.

Only compressors receive this request.

RESULT CODES

noErr   0   No error
paramErr   –50   Invalid parameter specified

CDGetCompressionTime

Your component receives the `CDGetCompressionTime` request whenever an application calls the Image Compression Manager's `GetCompressionTime` function.

```
pascal ComponentResult CDGetCompressionTime (PixMapHandle src,
                                        const Rect *srcRect,
                                        short depth, CodecQ
                                        *spatialQuality,
                                        CodecQ *temporalQuality,
                                        unsigned long *time);
```

src
Contains a handle to the source image. The source image is stored in a pixel map. Applications may use the time information you return for more than one image. Consequently, your compressor should not consider the contents of the image when determining the maximum compression time. Rather, you should consider only the quality level, pixel depth, and image size.

This parameter may be set to `nil`. In this case the application has not supplied a source image—your component should use the other parameters to determine the characteristics of the image to be compressed.

srcRect
Contains a pointer to a rectangle defining the portion of the source image to compress.

depth
Specifies the depth at which the image is to be compressed. Values of 1, 2, 4, 8, 16, 24, and 32 indicate the number of bits per pixel for color images. Values of 33, 34, 36, and 40 indicate 1-bit, 2-bit, 4-bit, and 8-bit grayscale, respectively, for grayscale images.

spatialQuality
Contains a pointer to a field containing the desired compressed image quality. The compressor sets this field to the closest actual quality that it can achieve. See the chapter "Image Compression Manager" in *Inside Macintosh: QuickTime* for valid values. Check to see if the value of this field is `nil` and, if so, do not write to location 0.

temporalQuality
Contains a pointer to a field containing the desired sequence temporal quality. The compressor sets this field to the closest actual quality that it can achieve. See the chapter "Image Compression Manager" in *Inside Macintosh: QuickTime* for valid values. Check to see if the value of this field is `nil` and, if so, do not write to location 0.

time
Contains a pointer to a field to receive the compression time, in milliseconds. If your component cannot determine the amount of time required to compress the image, set this field to 0. Check to see if the value of this field is `nil` and, if so, do not write to location 0.

Image Compressor Components

DESCRIPTION

Your component returns a long integer indicating the maximum number of milliseconds it would require to compress the specified image.

Only compressors receive this request.

RESULT CODES

```
noErr            0      No error
paramErr        –50     Invalid parameter specified
codecUnimpError –8962   Feature not implemented by this compressor
```

CDGetSimilarity

Your component receives the `CDGetSimilarity` request whenever an application calls the Image Compression Manager's `GetSimilarity` function. Your component compares the specified compressed image to a picture stored in a pixel map and returns a value indicating the relative similarity of the two images.

Note
The `CDGetSimilarity` function is optional. If your component doesn't support it, it should return the `codecUnimpError` result code. ◆

```
pascal ComponentResult CDGetSimilarity (PixMapHandle src,
                                        const Rect *srcRect,
                                        ImageDescriptionHandle desc,
                                        Ptr data,
                                        Fixed *similarity);
```

`src`
: Contains a handle to the noncompressed image. The image is stored in a pixel map structure.

`srcRect`
: Contains a pointer to a rectangle defining the portion of the image to compare to the compressed image.

`desc`
: Contains a handle to the image description structure that defines the compressed image for the operation.

`data`
: Contains a pointer to the compressed image data.

`similarity`
: Contains a pointer to a field that is to receive the similarity value. Your component sets this field to reflect the relative similarity of the two images. Valid values range from 0 (key frame) to 1 (identical).

DESCRIPTION

If the source image has been temporally compressed and is not a key frame (that is, the image relies on other frames that are not available to your component at this time), your component should return a result value of `paramErr`.

Only decompressors receive this request.

RESULT CODES

`noErr`	0	No error
`paramErr`	–50	Invalid parameter specified
`memFullErr`	–108	Not enough memory available
`codecUnimpError`	–8962	Feature not implemented by this compressor

CDGetCompressedImageSize

Your component receives the `CDGetCompressedImageSize` request whenever an application calls the Image Compression Manager's `GetCompressedImageSize` function.

You can use the `CDGetCompressedImageSize` function when you are extracting a single image from a sequence; therefore, you don't have an image description structure and don't know the exact size of one frame. In this case, the Image Compression Manager calls the component to determine the size of the data.

```
pascal ComponentResult CDGetCompressedImageSize
                    (ImageDescriptionHandle desc,
                    Ptr data, long bufferSize,
                    DataProcRecordPtr dataProc,
                    long *dataSize);
```

desc
: Contains a handle to the image description structure that defines the compressed image for the operation.

data
: Points to the compressed image data.

bufferSize
: Specifies the size of the buffer to be used by the data-loading function specified by the `dataProc` parameter. If the application did not specify a data-loading function this parameter is `nil`.

dataProc
: Points to a data-loading function structure. If the data stream is not all in memory when the application calls `GetCompressedImageSize`, your component may call an application function that loads more compressed data (see the chapter "Image Compression Manager" in *Inside Macintosh: QuickTime* for more information about data-loading functions). This parameter contains a pointer to a structure that identifies the data-loading

Image Compressor Components

function. If the application did not provide a data-loading function, this parameter is `nil`. In this case, the entire image must be in memory at the location specified by the `data` parameter.

`dataSize`   Contains a pointer to a field that is to receive the size, in bytes, of the compressed image.

DESCRIPTION

Your component returns a long integer indicating the number of bytes of data in the compressed image. You may want to store the image size somewhere in the image description structure, so that you can respond to this request quickly. See the chapter "Image Compression Manager" in *Inside Macintosh: QuickTime* for more information about image description structures.

Only decompressors receive this request.

RESULT CODES

```
noErr            0      No error
paramErr        -50     Invalid parameter specified
codecSpoolErr   -8966   Error loading or unloading data
```

CDTrimImage

Your component receives the `CDTrimImage` request whenever an application calls the `TrimImage` function. Your component adjusts a compressed image to the boundaries defined by a rectangle specified by your application. The resulting image data is still compressed and is in the same compression format as the source image.

Note
The `CDTrimImage` function is optional. If your component doesn't support it, it should return the `codecUnimpError` result code. ◆

```
pascal ComponentResult CDTrimImage
            (ImageDescriptionHandle desc, Ptr inData,
             long inBufferSize, DataProcRecordPtr dataProc,
             Ptr outData, long outBufferSize,
             FlushProcRecordPtr flushProc, Rect *trimRect,
             ProgressProcRecordPtr progressProc);
```

`desc`   Contains a handle to the image description structure that describes the compressed image. Your component updates this image description to refer to the resized image.

inData
: Points to the compressed image data. If the entire compressed image cannot be stored at this location, the application may provide a data-loading function (see the description of the `dataProc` parameter to this function for details). This is a 32-bit clean address.

inBufferSize
: Specifies the size of the buffer to be used by the data-loading function specified by the `dataProc` parameter. If the application did not specify a data-loading function, this parameter is `nil`.

dataProc
: Points to a data-loading function structure. If the data stream is not all in memory when the application calls the Image Compression Manager's `GetCompressedImageSize` function, your component may call an application function that loads more compressed data (see the chapter "Image Compression Manager" in *Inside Macintosh: QuickTime* for more information about data-loading functions). This parameter contains a pointer to a structure that identifies the data-loading function. If the application did not provide a data-loading function, this parameter is `nil`. In this case, the entire image must be in memory at the location specified by the `inData` parameter.

outData
: Points to a buffer to receive the trimmed image. If there is not sufficient memory to store the compressed image, the application may choose to write the compressed data to mass storage during the compression operation. The `flushProc` parameter identifies the data-unloading function. This is a 32-bit clean address.

    Your component should place the actual size of the resulting image into the `dataSize` field of the image description referred to by the `desc` parameter.

outBufferSize
: Specifies the size of the buffer to be used by the data-unloading function specified by the `flushProc` parameter. If the application did not specify a data-unloading function, this parameter is `nil`.

flushProc
: Points to a data-unloading function structure. If there is not enough memory to store the compressed image, your component may call an application function that unloads some of the compressed data (see the chapter "Image Compression Manager" in *Inside Macintosh: QuickTime* for more information about data-unloading functions). This parameter contains a pointer to a structure that identifies that data-unloading function. If the application did not provide a data-unloading function, this parameter is `nil`. In this case, your component writes the entire compressed image into the memory location specified by the `outData` parameter.

trimRect
: Contains a pointer to a rectangle that defines the desired image dimensions. Your component adjusts the rectangle values so that they refer to the same rectangle in the resulting image (this is necessary whenever data is removed from the beginning of the image).

Image Compressor Components

`progressProc`
: Points to a progress function structure. During the operation, your component should occasionally call an application function to report its progress (see the chapter "Image Compression Manager" in *Inside Macintosh: QuickTime* for more information about progress functions). This parameter contains a pointer to a structure that identifies that progress function. If the application did not provide a progress function, this parameter is `nil`.

DESCRIPTION

Only decompressors receive this request. If the `TrimImage` function has been called by an application, the resulting picture should be modified.

RESULT CODES

`noErr`	0	No error
`paramErr`	−50	Invalid parameter specified
`memFullErr`	−108	Not enough memory available
`noCodecErr`	−8961	Image Compression Manager could not find the specified compressor
`codecUnimpErr`	−8962	Feature not implemented by this compressor
`codecSpoolErr`	−8966	Error loading or unloading data
`codecAbortErr`	−8967	Operation aborted by the progress function

CDCodecBusy

Your component receives the `CDCodecBusy` request whenever an application calls the `CDSequenceBusy` function. Your component must report whether it is performing an asynchronous operation.

```
pascal ComponentResult CDCodecBusy (ImageSequence seq);
```

`seq`
: Contains the unique sequence identifier assigned by the Image Compression Manager's `CompressSequenceBegin` or `DecompressSequenceBegin` function.

DESCRIPTION

Your component should return a result code value of 1 if an asynchronous operation is in progress; it should return a result code value of 0 if the component is not performing an asynchronous operation. You can indicate an error by returning a negative result code.

Both compressors and decompressors may receive this request.

RESULT CODES

noErr	0	No error
codecUnimpError	–8962	Feature not implemented by this compressor

Indirect Functions

This section describes functions that are invoked by the Image Compression Manager but do not correspond to functions called by applications. The Image Compression Manager may call these functions at any time.

CDPreCompress

Your component receives the `CDPreCompress` request before compressing an image or a band of an image. The Image Compression Manager also calls this function when processing a sequence. In that case, the Image Compression Manager calls this function whenever the parameters governing the sequence operation have changed substantially. Your component indicates whether it can perform the requested compression operation.

```
pascal ComponentResult CDPreCompress
                            (CodecCompressParams *params);
```

params   Contains a pointer to a compression parameters structure. The Image Compression Manager places the appropriate parameter information in that structure. See "The Compression Parameters Structure" beginning on page 4-40 for details.

DESCRIPTION

Your component should return a 0 result code to indicate that it can handle the request. In addition, your component indicates any limitations on its capabilities in a compressor capability structure (see "The Compressor Capability Structure" beginning on page 4-35 for details). Your component should return a result code of `codecConditionError` if it cannot field the compression request.

Only compressors receive this request.

RESULT CODES

noErr	0	No error
paramErr	–50	Invalid parameter specified
codecConditionErr	–8972	Component cannot perform requested operation

CDBandCompress

Your component receives the `CDBandCompress` request to compress an image or a band of an image. The image may be part of a sequence.

```
pascal ComponentResult CDBandCompress
                            (CodecCompressParams *params);
```

params   Contains a pointer to a compression parameters structure. The Image Compression Manager places the appropriate parameter information in that structure. See "The Compression Parameters Structure" beginning on page 4-40 for a complete description of the compression parameters structure.

DESCRIPTION

Only compressors receive this request.

RESULT CODES

noErr	0	No error
paramErr	–50	Invalid parameter specified
codecSpoolErr	–8966	Error loading or unloading data
codecAbortErr	–8967	Operation aborted by the progress function

CDPreDecompress

Your component receives the `CDPreDecompress` request before decompressing an image or a band of an image. The Image Compression Manager also calls this function when processing a sequence. In that case, the Image Compression Manager calls this function whenever the parameters governing the sequence operation have changed substantially. Your component indicates whether it can perform the requested decompression operation.

```
pascal ComponentResult CDPreDecompress
                            (CodecDecompressParams *params);
```

params   Contains a pointer to a decompression parameters structure. The Image Compression Manager places the appropriate parameter information in that structure. See "The Decompression Parameters Structure" beginning on page 4-46 for a complete description of the decompression parameters structure.

CHAPTER 4

Image Compressor Components

DESCRIPTION

Your component should return a 0 result code to indicate that it can handle the request. In addition, your component indicates any limitations on its capabilities in a compressor capability structure (see page 4-35 for a description of that structure). Return a result code of `codecConditionError` if your component cannot field the decompression request.

Only decompressors receive this request.

RESULT CODES

noErr	0	No error
paramErr	–50	Invalid parameter specified
codecConditionErr	–8972	Component cannot perform requested operation

CDBandDecompress

Your component receives the `CDBandDecompress` request to decompress an image or a band of an image. The image may be part of a sequence.

```
pascal ComponentResult CDBandDecompress
                            (CodecDecompressParams *params);
```

params
Contains a pointer to a decompression parameters structure. The Image Compression Manager places the appropriate parameter information in that structure. See "The Decompression Parameters Structure" beginning on page 4-46 for a complete description of the decompression parameters structure.

DESCRIPTION

Only decompressors receive these requests.

RESULT CODES

noErr	0	No error
paramErr	–50	Invalid parameter specified
codecSpoolErr	–8966	Error loading or unloading data
codecAbortErr	–8967	Operation aborted by the progress function

Image Compressor Components

Image Compression Manager Utility Functions

The Image Compression Manager provides a number of utility functions for use by your compressor component. These utility functions allow compressor components to manipulate the Image Compression Manager's image description structures.

SetImageDescriptionExtension

Your component may use the `SetImageDescriptionExtension` function to create or update the extended data for an image.

```
pascal OSErr SetImageDescriptionExtension
                        (ImageDescriptionHandle desc,
                         Handle extension,
                         long idType);
```

desc
: Contains a handle to the appropriate image description structure. The `SetImageDescriptionExtension` function updates the size of the image description to accommodate the new extended data.

extension
: Contains a handle to the new extended data. The `SetImageDescriptionExtension` function uses this data to update the extended data for the image described by the image description referred to by the `desc` parameter.

idType
: Specifies the extension's type value. Use this parameter to assign a data type to the extension. Use a four-character code, similar to an `OSType` field value.

DESCRIPTION

The Image Compression Manager appends the extended data for an image to the appropriate image description structure (see the chapter "Image Compression Manager" in *Inside Macintosh: QuickTime* for information about image description structures). Note that each compressor type may have its own format for the extended data that is stored with an image. The extended data is similar in concept to the user data that applications can associate with QuickTime movies—see the chapter "Movie Toolbox" in *Inside Macintosh: QuickTime* for more information about user data in QuickTime movies. Once you have added extended data to an image, you cannot delete it.

Image Compressor Components

RESULT CODES

noErr	0	No error
paramErr	–50	Invalid parameter specified
memFullErr	–108	Not enough memory available
noCodecErr	–8961	Image Compression Manager could not find the specified compressor
codecExtensionNotFoundErr	–8971	Requested extension is not in the image description

GetImageDescriptionExtension

Your component may use the `GetImageDescriptionExtension` function to obtain the extended data for an image.

```
pascal OSErr GetImageDescriptionExtension
                            (ImageDescriptionHandle desc,
                            Handle *extension,
                            long idType, long index);
```

desc Contains a handle to the appropriate image description structure.

extension Contains a pointer to a field to receive a handle to the returned data. The `GetImageDescriptionExtension` function returns the extended data for the image described by the image description referred to by the `desc` parameter. The function correctly sizes the handle for the data it returns.

idType Specifies the extension's type value. Use this parameter to determine the data type of the extension. This parameter contains a four-character code, similar to an `OSType` field value.

index Specifies the extension's index value.

DESCRIPTION

The Image Compression Manager appends the extended data for an image to the appropriate image description structure (see the chapter "Image Compression Manager" in *Inside Macintosh: QuickTime* for information about image description structures). Note that each compressor type may have its own format for the extended data that is stored with an image. The extended data is similar in concept to the user data that applications can associate with QuickTime movies—see the chapter "Movie Toolbox" in *Inside Macintosh: QuickTime* for more information about user data in QuickTime movies. Once you have added extended data to an image, you cannot delete it.

RESULT CODES

`noErr`	0	No error
`paramErr`	–50	Invalid parameter specified
`memFullErr`	–108	Not enough memory available
`noCodecErr`	–8961	The Image Compression Manager could not find the specified compressor
`codecExtensionNotFoundErr`	–8971	Requested extension is not in the image description

RemoveImageDescriptionExtension

The `RemoveImageDescriptionExtension` function allows you to remove an extension based on its type or index.

```
pascal OSErr RemoveImageDescriptionExtension
                            (ImageDescription **desc,
                             long type, long index);
```

`desc` Contains a handle to the appropriate image description structure.

`type` Specifies the extension's type, starting at 1. Use this parameter to specify the data type of the extension to be removed. This parameter contains a four-character code, similar to an `OSType` field value. Set the value of this parameter to 0 to indicate that any extension should be matched, with the `index` parameter becoming an index into all of the extensions.

`index` Specifies the extension's index value.

RESULT CODE

`codecExtensionNotFoundErr`	–8971	Requested extension is not in the image description

CountImageDescriptionExtensionType

The `CountImageDescriptionExtensionType` function counts the number of image description extensions in a specified image description structure.

```
pascal OSErr CountImageDescriptionExtensionType
                            (ImageDescription **desc,
                             long type, long *count);
```

`desc` Contains a handle to the image description structure with the extensions to be counted.

Image Compressor Components

type
: Indicates the type of extension to be counted in the specified image description structure. Set the value of this parameter to 0 to match any extension, and return a count of all of the extensions.

count
: Contains a pointer to an integer that indicates how many extensions of the given type are in the given image description structure.

GetNextImageDescriptionExtensionType

The `GetNextImageDescriptionExtensionType` function retrieves the next extension type encountered after the one you specify.

```
pascal OSErr GetNextImageDescriptionExtensionType
                        (ImageDescription **desc, long *type);
```

desc
: Contains a handle to the image description structure with the extension under scrutiny.

type
: Contains a pointer to an integer that indicates the type of the extension after which this function is to return the next extension type. Set the value of this parameter to 0 to return the first type found. Point to a value of 0 to return the first type found.

DESCRIPTION

If `GetNextImageDescriptionExtensionType` returns a value of 0 in the type parameter, no more types could be found.

Summary of Image Compressor Components

C Summary

Constants

```
#define compressorComponentType      'imco' /* compressor component type */
#define decompressorComponentType    'imdc' /* decompressor component type */

/* selector values */
#define codecGetCodecInfo            0x00   /* CDGetCodecInfo */
#define codecGetCompressionTime      0x01   /* CDGetCompressionTime */
#define codecGetMaxCompressionSize   0x02   /* CDGetMaxCompressionSize */
#define codecPreCompress             0x03   /* CDPreCompress */
#define codecBandCompress            0x04   /* CDBandCompress */
#define codecPreDecompress           0x05   /* CDPreDecompress */
#define codecBandDecompress          0x06   /* CDBandDecompress */
#define codecCDSequenceBusy          0x07   /* CDSequenceBusy */
#define codecGetCompressedImageSize  0x08   /* CDGetCompressedImageSize */
#define codecGetSimilarity           0x09   /* CDGetSimilarity */
#define codecTrimImage               0x0A   /* CDTrimImage */

/* image compressor component capabilities flags */
#define codecCanScale         (1L<<0)  /* decompressor scales
                                          information */
#define codecCanMask          (1L<<1)  /* decompressor applies mask to
                                          image */
#define codecCanMatte         (1L<<2)  /* decompressor blends image using
                                          matte */
#define codecCanTransform     (1L<<3)  /* decompressor works with complex
                                          placement matrices */
#define codecCanTransferMode  (1L<<4)  /* decompressor accepts transfer
                                          mode */
#define codecCanCopyPrev      (1L<<5)  /* compressor updates previous
                                          image buffer */
#define codecCanSpool         (1L<<6)  /* component can use functions to
                                          spool data */
#define codecCanClipVertical  (1L<<7)  /* decompressor clips image
                                          vertically */
```

CHAPTER 4

Image Compressor Components

```c
#define codecCanClipRectangular   (1L<<8)   /* decompressor clips image
                                               vertically & horizontally */
#define codecCanRemapColor        (1L<<9)   /* compressor remaps color */
#define codecCanFastDither        (1L<<10)  /* compressor supports fast
                                               dithering */
#define codecCanSrcExtract        (1L<<11)  /* compressor extracts portion
                                               of source image */
#define codecCanCopyPrevComp      (1L<<12)  /* compressor updates previous
                                               image buffer */
#define codecCanAsync             (1L<<13)  /* component can work
                                               asynchronously */
#definecodecCanMakeMask           (1L<<14)  /* decompressor makes
                                               modification masks */
#define codecCanShift             (1L<<15)  /* component works with pixels
                                               that are not byte-aligned */

/* compressor component condition flags passed to component in
   CDBandDecompress and CDPreDecompress functions indicate changes */
#define codecConditionFirstBand        (1L<<0)   /* (input) first band
                                                    in frame */
#define codecConditionLastBand         (1L<<1)   /* (input) last band
                                                    in frame */
#define codecConditionFirstFrame       (1L<<2)   /* (input) first frame to be
                                                    decompressed in this
                                                    sequence */
#define codecConditionNewDepth         (1L<<3)   /* (input) depth of
                                                    destination */
#define codecConditionNewTransform     (1L<<4)   /* (input) transformation
                                                    matrix has changed */
#define codecConditionNewSrcRect       (1L<<5)   /* (input) source rectangle */
#define codecConditionNewMask          (1L<<6)   /* (input) mask bitmap has
                                                    changed */
#define codecConditionNewMatte         (1L<<7)   /* (input) matte pixel map */
#define codecConditionNewTransferMode  (1L<<8)   /* (input) transfer mode */
#define codecConditionNewClut          (1L<<9)   /* (input) color lookup
                                                    table */
#define codecConditionNewAccuracy      (1L<<10)  /* accuracy parameter has
                                                    changed */
#define codecConditionNewDestination   (1L<<11)  /*(input) destination pixel
                                                    map */
#define codecConditionCodecChangedMask (1L<<31)  /* (output) component has
                                                    changed mask bits */
```

Image Compressor Components

```c
/* compressor and decompressor flag bits */
#define codecInfoDoes1          (1L<<0)   /* works with 1-bit pixel maps */
#define codecInfoDoes2          (1L<<1)   /* works with 2-bit pixel maps */
#define codecInfoDoes4          (1L<<2)   /* works with 4-bit pixel maps */
#define codecInfoDoes8          (1L<<3)   /* works with 8-bit pixel maps */
#define codecInfoDoes16         (1L<<4)   /* works with 16-bit pixel maps */
#define codecInfoDoes32         (1L<<5)   /* works with 32-bit pixel maps */
#define codecInfoDoesDither     (1L<<6)   /* supports fast dithering */
#define codecInfoDoesStretch    (1L<<7)   /* stretches to arbitrary sizes */
#define codecInfoDoesShrink     (1L<<8)   /* shrinks to arbitrary sizes */
#define codecInfoDoesMask       (1L<<9)   /* handles clipping regions */
#define codecInfoDoesTemporal   (1L<<10)  /* sequential temporal
                                             compression */
#define codecInfoDoesDouble     (1L<<11)  /* stretches to double size
                                             exactly */
#define codecInfoDoesQuad       (1L<<12)  /* stretches to quadruple size */
#define codecInfoDoesHalf       (1L<<13)  /* shrinks to half size */
#define codecInfoDoesQuarter    (1L<<14)  /* shrinks to one quarter size */
#define codecInfoDoesRotate     (1L<<15)  /* rotates during decompression */
#define codecInfoDoesHorizFlip  (1L<<16)  /* flips horizontally during
                                             decompression */
#define codecInfoDoesVertFlip   (1L<<17)  /* flips vertically during
                                             decompression */
#define codecInfoDoesSkew       (1L<<18)  /* skews image during
                                             decompression */
#define codecInfoDoesBlend      (1L<<19)  /* blends image with matte during
                                             decompression */
#define codecInfoDoesWarp       (1L<<20)  /* warps image arbitrarily during
                                             decompression */
#define codecInfoDoesRecompress (1L<<21)  /* recompresses images without
                                             accumulating errors */
#define codecInfoDoesSpool      (1L<<22)  /* uses data-loading or
                                             data-unloading function */
#define codecInfoDoesRateConstrain
                                (1L<<23)  /* constrains amount of generated
                                             data to caller-defined limit */

/* compressor and decompressor format flag bits */
#define codecInfoDepth1 (1L<<0)   /* compressed images with 1-bit
                                     color depth available */
#define codecInfoDepth2 (1L<<1)   /* compressed images with 2-bit
                                     color depth available */
#define codecInfoDepth4 (1L<<2)   /* compressed images with 4-bit
                                     color depth available */
```

```
#define codecInfoDepth8 (1L<<3)    /* compressed images with 8-bit
                                      color depth available */
#define codecInfoDepth16(1L<<4)    /* compressed images with 16-bit
                                      color depth available */
#define codecInfoDepth32(1L<<5)    /* compressed images with 32-bit
                                      color depth available */
#define codecInfoDepth24(1L<<6)    /* compressed images with 24-bit
                                      color depth available */
#define codecInfoDepth33(1L<<7)    /* compressed data with monochrome images of
                                      1-bit color depth */
#define codecInfoDepth34(1L<<8)    /* compressed images with
                                      2-bit grayscale depth available */
#define codecInfoDepth36(1L<<9)    /* compressed images with 4-bit grayscale
                                      depth available */
#define codecInfoDepth40(1L<<10)   /* compressed images with 8-bit grayscale
                                      depth available */
#define codecInfoStoresClut
                    (1L<<11) /* compressed data with custom color
                                tables */
#define codecInfoDoesLossless
                    (1L<<12) /* compressed data stored lossless format */
#define codecInfoSequenceSensitive
                    (1L<<13) /* compressed data requires non-key frames
                                to be compressed in same order as
                                compressed */
```

Data Types

```
typedef struct {
   long              flags;            /* control information */
   short             wantedPixelSize;  /* pixel depth for component to use
                                          with image */
   short             extendWidth;      /* extension width of image in pixels */
   short             extendHeight;     /* extension height of image in pixels */
   short             bandMin;          /* supported minimum image band height */
   short             bandInc;          /* common factor of supported band
                                          heights */
   short             pad;              /* reserved */
   unsigned long     time;             /* milliseconds operation takes to
                                          complete */
} CodecCapabilities;
typedef CodecCapabilities *CodecCapabilitiesPtr;
```

```c
typedef struct {
    ImageSequence           sequenceID;         /* sequence identifier ID
                                                    (precompress or
                                                    bandcompress) */
    ImageDescriptionHandle  imageDescription;   /* handle to image
                                                    description structure
                                                    (precompress or
                                                    bandcompress) */
    Ptr                     data;               /* location for receipt of
                                                    compressed image data */
    long                    bufferSize;         /* size of buffer for data */
    long                    frameNumber;        /* frame identifier */
    long                    startLine;          /* starting line for band */
    long                    stopLine;           /* ending line for band */
    long                    conditionFlags;     /* condition flags */
    CodecFlags              callerFlags;        /* control info flags */
    CodecCapabilities       *capabilities;      /* pointer to compressor
                                                    capability structure */
    ProgressProcRecord      progressProcRecord; /* progress function
                                                    structure */
    CompletionProcRecord    completionProcRecord;/* completion function
                                                    structure */
    FlushProcRecord         flushProcRecord;    /* data-unloading function
                                                    structure */
    PixMap                  srcPixMap;          /* pointer to image
                                                    (precompress or
                                                    bandcompress) */
    PixMap                  prevPixMap;         /* pointer to pixel map
                                                    for previous image */
    CodecQ                  spatialQuality;     /* compressed image
                                                    quality */
    CodecQ                  temporalQuality;    /* sequence temporal
                                                    quality */
    Fixed                   similarity;         /* similarity between
                                                    adjacent frames */
    DataRateParamsPtr       dataRateParams;     /* pointer to the data rate
                                                    parameters structure */
    long                    reserved;           /* reserved */
} CodecCompressParams;
typedef CodecCompressParams *CodecCompressParamsPtr;
```

CHAPTER 4

Image Compressor Components

```c
typedef struct {
    ImageSequence          sequenceID;          /* unique sequence ID
                                                    (predecompress,
                                                    band decompress) */
    ImageDescriptionHandle imageDescription;    /* handle to image
                                                    description structure
                                                    (predecompress,
                                                    band decompress) */
    Ptr                    data;                /* compressed image data */
    long                   bufferSize;          /* size of data buffer */
    long                   frameNumber;         /* frame identifier */
    long                   startLine;           /* starting line for band */
    long                   stopLine;            /* ending line for band */
    long                   conditionFlags;      /* condition flags */
    CodecFlags             callerFlags;         /* control flags */
    CodecCapabilities      *capabilities;       /* pointer to compressor
                                                    capability structure
                                                    (predecompress,
                                                    band decompress) */
    ProgressProcRecord     progressProcRecord;  /* progress function
                                                    structure */
    CompletionProcRecord   completionProcRecord;/* completion function
                                                    structure */
    DataProcRecord         dataProcRecord;      /* data-loading function
                                                    structure */
    CGrafPtr               port;                /* pointer to color
                                                    graphics port for image
                                                    (predecompress,
                                                    band decompress) */
    PixMap                 dstPixMap;           /* destination pixel map
                                                    (predecompress,
                                                    band decompress) */
    BitMapPtr              maskBits;            /* update mask */
    PixMapPtr              mattePixMap;         /* blend matte pixel map */
    Rect                   srcRect;             /* source rectangle
                                                    (predecompress,
                                                    band decompress) */
    MatrixRecord           *matrix;             /* pointer to matrix
                                                    structure
                                                    (predecompress,
                                                    band decompress) */
```

```
    CodecQ               accuracy;            /* desired accuracy
                                                  (predecompress,
                                                   band decompress) */
    short                transferMode;        /* transfer mode
                                                  (predecompress,
                                                   band decompress) */
    long                 reserved[2];         /* reserved */
} CodecDecompressParams;

typedef CodecDecompressParams *CodecDecompressParamsPtr;

/* progress function structure */
typedef struct ProgressProcRecord ProgressProcRecord;
typedef ProgressProcRecord *ProgressProcRecordPtr;

struct ProgressProcRecord {
    ProgressProcPtr progressProc; /* pointer to your progress function */
    long progressRefCon;          /* reference constant for use by
                                     your progress function */
};

/* completion function structure */
typedef struct CompletionProcRecord CompletionProcRecord;
typedef CompletionProcRecord *CompletionProcRecordPtr;

struct CompletionProcRecord {
    CompletionProcPtr completionProc;/* pointer to completion function */
    long completionRefCon;           /* reference constant used by
                                        completion function */
};

/* data-loading structure */
typedef struct DataProcRecord DataProcRecord;
typedef DataProcRecord *DataProcRecordPtr;

struct DataProcRecord {
    DataProcPtr dataProc;         /* pointer to data-loading function */
    long dataRefCon;              /* reference constant used by
                                     data-loading function */
};

/* data-unloading structure */
typedef struct FlushProcRecord FlushProcRecord;
typedef FlushProcRecord *FlushProcRecordPtr;
```

Image Compressor Components

```
struct FlushProcRecord {
    FlushProcPtr flushProc; /* pointer to data-unloading function */
    long flushRefCon;       /* reference constant used by data-unloading
                               function */
};
```

Functions

Direct Functions

```
pascal ComponentResult CDGetCodecInfo
                        (CodecInfo *info);
pascal ComponentResult CDGetMaxCompressionSize
                        (PixMapHandle src, const Rect *srcRect,
                         short depth, CodecQ quality, long *size);
pascal ComponentResult CDGetCompressionTime
                        (PixMapHandle src, const Rect *srcRect,
                         short depth, CodecQ *spatialQuality,
                         CodecQ *temporalQuality, unsigned long *time);
pascal ComponentResult CDGetSimilarity
                        (PixMapHandle src, const Rect *srcRect,
                         ImageDescriptionHandle desc, Ptr data,
                         Fixed *similarity);
pascal ComponentResult CDGetCompressedImageSize
                        (ImageDescriptionHandle desc, Ptr data,
                         long bufferSize, DataProcRecordPtr dataProc,
                         long *dataSize);
pascal ComponentResult CDTrimImage
                        (ImageDescriptionHandle desc, Ptr inData,
                         long inBufferSize, DataProcRecordPtr dataProc,
                         Ptr outData, long outBufferSize,
                         FlushProcRecordPtr flushProc, Rect *trimRect,
                         ProgressProcRecordPtr progressProc);
pascal ComponentResult CDCodecBusy
                        (ImageSequence seq);
```

Indirect Functions

```
pascal ComponentResult CDPreCompress
                        (CodecCompressParams *params);
pascal ComponentResult CDBandCompress
                        (CodecCompressParams *params);
pascal ComponentResult CDPreDecompress
                        (CodecDecompressParams *params);
```

```
pascal ComponentResult CDBandDecompress
                        (CodecDecompressParams *params);
```

Image Compression Manager Utility Functions

```
pascal OSErr SetImageDescriptionExtension
                        (ImageDescriptionHandle desc, Handle extension,
                         long idType);
pascal OSErr GetImageDescriptionExtension
                        (ImageDescriptionHandle desc,
                         Handle *extension, long idType, long index);
pascal OSErr RemoveImageDescriptionExtension
                        (ImageDescription **desc, long type,
                         long index);
pascal OSErr CountImageDescriptionExtensionType
                        (ImageDescription **desc, long type,
                         long *count);
pascal OSErr GetNextImageDescriptionExtensionType
                        (ImageDescription **desc, long *type);
```

Pascal Summary

Constants

```
CONST
compressorComponentType          ='imco';   {compressor component type}
decompressorComponentType        ='imdc';   {decompressor component type}

    {selector values}
    codecGetCodecInfo            = $00;     {CDGetCodecInfo}
    codecGetCompressionTime      = $01;     {CDGetCompressionTime}
    codecGetMaxCompressionSize   = $02;     {CDGetMaxCompressionSize}
    codecPreCompress             = $03;     {CDPreCompress}
    codecBandCompress            = $04;     {CDBandCompress}
    codecPreDecompress           = $05;     {CDPreDeCompress}
    codecBandDecompress          = $06;     {CDBandDeCompress}
    codecCDSequenceBusy          = $07;     {CDSequenceBusy}
    codecGetCompressedImageSize  = $08;     {CDGetCompressedImageSize}
    codecGetSimilarity           = $09;     {CDGetSimilarity}
    codecTrimImage               = $0a;     {CDTrimImage}
```

Image Compressor Components

```
{image compressor component capabilities flags}
codecCanScale              = $1;     {decompressor scales information}
codecCanMask               = $2;     {decompressor applies mask to image}
codecCanMatte              = $4;     {decompressor blends using matte}
codecCanTransform          = $8;     {decompressor works with complex }
                                     { placement matrices}
codecCanTransferMode       = $10;    {decompressor accepts transfer mode}
codecCanCopyPrev           = $20;    {compressor updates previous buffer}
codecCanSpool              = $40;    {component uses functions to spool }
                                     { data}
codecCanClipVertical       = $80;    {decompressor clips vertically}
codecCanClipRectangular    = $100;   {decompressor clips vertically }
                                     { & horizontally}
codecCanRemapColor         = $200;   {compressor remaps color}
codecCanFastDither         = $400;   {compressor does fast dithering}
codecCanSrcExtract         = $800;   {compressor extracts portion of }
                                     { source image}
codecCanCopyPrevComp       = $1000;  {compressor updates previous buffer}
codecCanAsync              = $2000;  {component works asynchronously}
codecCanMakeMask           = $4000;  {decompressor makes masks}
codecCanShift              = $8000;  {component works with pixels }
                                     { that are not byte-aligned}

{condition flags}
codecConditionFirstBand          = $1;    {first band in frame}
codecConditionLastBand           = $2;    {last band in frame}
codecConditionFirstFrame         = $4;    {(input) first frame to be }
                                          { decompressed in this }
                                          { sequence}
codecConditionNewDepth           = $8;    {(input) depth of }
                                          { destination}
codecConditionNewTransform       = $10;   {(input) transformation }
                                          { matrix has changed}
codecConditionNewSrcRect         = $20;   {(input) source rectangle}
codecConditionNewMask            = $40;   {(input) mask bitmap }
                                          { has changed}
codecConditionNewMatte           = $80;   {(input) matte pixel map)
codecConditionNewTransferMode    = $100;  {(input) transfer mode}
codecConditionNewClut            = $200;  {(input) color lookup table}
codecConditionNewAccuracy        = $400;  {accuracy parameter has }
                                          { changed}
codecConditionNewDestination     = $800;  {(input) destination pixel }
                                          { map}
codecConditionCodecChangedMask   = $80000000;{changed mask bits}
```

```
{CodecInfo compressFlags and deCompressFlags bits}
codecInfoDoes1            = $1;     {works with 1-bit pixel maps}
codecInfoDoes2            = $2;     {works with 2-bit pixel maps}
codecInfoDoes4            = $4;     {works with 4-bit pixel maps}
codecInfoDoes8            = $8;     {works with 8-bit pixel maps}
codecInfoDoes16           = $10;    {works with 16-bit pixel maps}
codecInfoDoes32           = $20;    {works with 32-bit pixel maps}
codecInfoDoesDither       = $40;    {supports fast dithering}
codecInfoDoesStretch      = $80;    {stretches to arbitrary sizes}
codecInfoDoesShrink       = $100;   {shrinks to arbitrary sizes}
codecInfoDoesMask         = $200;   {handles clipping regions}
codecInfoDoesTemporal     = $400;   {sequential temporal }
                                    { compression}
codecInfoDoesDouble       = $800;   {stretches to double size}
codecInfoDoesQuad         = $1000;  {stretches to quadruple size}
codecInfoDoesHalf         = $2000;  {shrinks to half size}
codecInfoDoesQuarter      = $4000;  {shrinks to one-quarter size}
codecInfoDoesRotate       = $8000;  {rotates during decompression}
codecInfoDoesHorizFlip    = $10000; {flips horizontally}
codecInfoDoesVertFlip     = $20000; {flips vertically}
codecInfoDoesSkew         = $40000; {skews image during }
                                    { decompression}
codecInfoDoesBlend        = $80000; {blends image with matte }
                                    { during decompression}
codecInfoDoesWarp         = $100000;{warps image during }
                                    { decompression}
codecInfoDoesRecompress   = $200000;{recompresses images}
codecInfoDoesSpool        = $400000;{uses data-loading }
                                    { or unloading functions}
codecInfoDoesRateConstrain = $800000;{constrains amount of generated }
                                    { data to caller-defined limit}

{codecInfo formatFlags bits}
codecInfoDepth1           = $1;     {color images with 1-bit color depth}
codecInfoDepth2           = $2;     {color images with 2-bit color depth}
codecInfoDepth4           = $4;     {color images with 4-bit color depth}
codecInfoDepth8           = $8;     {color images with 8-bit color depth}
codecInfoDepth16          = $10;    {color images with 16-bit color depth}
codecInfoDepth32          = $20;    {color images with 32-bit color depth}
codecInfoDepth24          = $40;    {color images with 24-bit color depth}
codecInfoDepth33          = $80;    {monochrome images with 1-bit color }
                                    { depth}
codecInfoDepth34          = $100;   {grayscale images with 2-bit }
                                    { grayscale depth}
```

Image Compressor Components

```
codecInfoDepth36              = $200;   {grayscale images with 4-bit }
                                        { grayscale depth}
codecInfoDepth40              = $400;   {grayscale images with 8-bit }
                                        { grayscale depth}
codecInfoStoresClut           = $800;   {custom color tables}
codecInfoDoesLossless         = $1000;  {lossless compression or }
                                        { decompression operations}
codecInfoSequenceSensitive    = $2000;  {compression data requires non-key }
                                        { frames to be decompressed in same }
                                        { order as compressed}
```

Data Types

```
TYPE  CodecCapabilities =
      RECORD
        flags:           LongInt;    {control information}
        wantedPixelSize: Integer;    {pixel depth for component to use }
                                     { with image}
        extendWidth:     Integer;    {extension width of image}
        extendHeight:    Integer;    {extension height of image}
        bandMin:         Integer;    {supported minimum band height}
        bandInc:         Integer;    {common factor of band heights}
        pad:             Integer;    {reserved}
        time:            Integer;    {milliseconds to completion}
      END;

      CodecCapabilitiesPtr         =^CodecCapabilities;

      CodecCompressParams =
      RECORD
        sequenceID:       ImageSequence; {sequence identifier ID}
        imageDescription: ImageDescriptionHandle;
                                         {handle to image }
                                         { description record}
        data:             Ptr;           {location for receipt of }
                                         { compressed image data}
        bufferSize:       LongInt;       {size of buffer for data}
        frameNumber:      LongInt;       {frame identifier}
        startLine:        LongInt;       {starting line for band}
        stopLine:         LongInt;       {ending line for band}
        conditionFlags:   LongInt;       {condition flags}
        callerFlags:      CodecFlags;    {control information flags}
```

Image Compressor Components

```
        capabilities:        CodecCapabilitiesPtr;
                                            {pointer to compressor }
                                            { capability record
    progressProcRecord:      ProgressProcRecord;
                                            {progress function record}
    completionProcRecord:CompletionProcRecord;
                                            {completion function }
                                            { record}
        flushProcRecord:     FlushProcRecord;
                                            {data-unloading function }
                                            { record}
        srcPixMap:           PixMap;         {pointer to image}
        prevPixMap:          PixMap;         {pointer to pixel map }
                                            { for previous image}
        spatialQuality:      CodecQ;         {compressed image quality}
        temporalQuality:     CodecQ;         {sequence temporal quality}
        similarity:          Fixed;          {similarity between }
                                            { adjacent frames}
        dataRateParams       dataRateParamsPtr;
                                            {pointer to the data rate }
                                            { parameters record}
        reserved:            ARRAY[0..1] OF LongInt;
                                            {reserved}
END;

CodecCompressParamsPtr            = ^CodecCompressParams;

CodecDecompressParams =
RECORD
    sequenceID:              ImageSequence; {unique sequence ID}
    imageDescription:        ImageDescriptionHandle;
                                            {handle to image }
                                            { description record}
    data:                    Ptr;           {compressed image data}
    bufferSize:              LongInt;       {size of data buffer}
    frameNumber:             LongInt;       {frame identifier}
    startLine:               LongInt;       {starting line for band}
    stopLine:                LongInt;       {ending line for band}
    conditionFlags:          LongInt;       {condition flags}
    callerFlags:             CodecFlags;    {control flags}
    capabilities:            CodecCapabilitiesPtr;
                                            {pointer to compressor }
                                            { capability record}
```

CHAPTER 4

Image Compressor Components

```pascal
        progressProcRecord:     ProgressProcRecord;
                                            {progress function record}
        completionProcRecord:   CompletionProcRecord;
                                            {completion function record}
        dataProcRecord:         DataProcRecord;{data-loading function }
                                            { record}
        port:                   CGrafPtr;   {pointer to color }
                                            { grafport for image}
        dstPixMap:              PixMap;     {destination pixel map}
        maskBits:               BitMapPtr;  {update mask}
        mattePixMap:            PixMapPtr;  {blend matte pixel map}
        srcRect:                Rect;       {source rectangle}
        matrix:                 MatrixRecordPtr;
                                            {pointer to matrix }
                                            { structure}
        accuracy:               CodecQ;     {desired accuracy}
        transferMode:           Integer;    {transfer mode}
        reserved:               ARRAY[0..1] OF LongInt;
                                            {reserved}
    END;

CodecDecompressParamsPtr        = ^CodecDecompressParams;


ProgressProcRecordPtr           = ^ProgressProcRecord;
ProgressProcRecord =
RECORD
    progressProc:    ProgressProcPtr;  {pointer to progress function}
    progressRefCon:  LongInt;          {progress function }
                                       { reference constant}
END;

CompletionProcRecordPtr         = ^CompletionProcRecord;
CompletionProcRecord =
RECORD
    completionProc:   CompletionProcPtr;{pointer to completion function}
    completionRefCon: LongInt;         {completion function reference }
                                       { constant}
END;

DataProcRecordPtr    = ^DataProcRecord;
DataProcRecord =
RECORD
    dataProc:    DataProcPtr;      {pointer to data-loading function}
```

Image Compressor Components

```
        dataRefCon:      LongInt;           {data-loading function }
                                            { reference constant}
    END;

FlushProcRecordPtr    = ^FlushProcRecord;
FlushProcRecord =
RECORD
    flushProc:       FlushProcPtr;      {pointer to data-unloading function}
    flushRefCon:     LongInt;           {data-unloading function reference }
                                        { constant}
END;
```

Routines

Direct Functions

```
FUNCTION CDGetCodecInfo       (VAR info: CodecInfo): ComponentResult;
FUNCTION CDGetMaxCompressionSize
                              (src: PixMapHandle; srcRect: Rect;
                               depth: Integer; quality: CodecQ;
                               VAR size: LongInt): ComponentResult;
FUNCTION CDGetCompressionTime
                              (src: PixMapHandle; srcRect: Rect;
                               depth: Integer; VAR spatialQuality: CodecQ;
                               VAR temporalQuality: CodecQ;
                               VAR time: LongInt): ComponentResult;
FUNCTION CDGetSimilarity      (src: PixMapHandle; srcRect: Rect;
                               desc: ImageDescriptionHandle; data: Ptr;
                               VAR similarity: Fixed): ComponentResult;
FUNCTION CDGetCompressedImageSize
                              (desc: ImageDescriptionHandle; data: Ptr;
                               bufferSize: LongInt;
                               dataProc: DataProcRecordPtr;
                               VAR dataSize: LongInt): ComponentResult;
FUNCTION CDTrimImage          (desc: ImageDescriptionHandle; inData: Ptr;
                               inBufferSize: LongInt;
                               dataProc: DataProcRecordPtr; outData: Ptr;
                               outBufferSize: LongInt;
                               flushProc: FlushProcRecordPtr;
                               VAR trimRect: Rect;
                               progressProc: ProgressProcRecordPtr):
                               ComponentResult;
FUNCTION CDCodecBusy          (seq: ImageSequence): ComponentResult;
```

Indirect Functions

```
FUNCTION CDPreCompress       (params: CodecCompressParamsPtr):
                              ComponentResult;
FUNCTION CDBandCompress      (params: CodecCompressParamsPtr):
                              ComponentResult;
FUNCTION CDPreDecompress     (params: CodecCompressParamsPtr):
                              ComponentResult;
FUNCTION CDBandDecompress    (params: CodecCompressParamsPtr):
                              ComponentResult;
```

Image Compression Manager Utility Functions

```
FUNCTION SetImageDescriptionExtension
                    (desc: ImageDescriptionHandle;
                     extension: Handle; idType: LongInt): OSErr;
FUNCTION GetImageDescriptionExtension
                    (desc: ImageDescriptionHandle;
                     VAR extension: Handle; idType: LongInt;
                     index: LongInt): OSErr;
FUNCTION RemoveImageDescriptionExtension
                    (desc: ImageDescriptionHandle; idType: LongInt;
                     index: LongInt): OSErr;
FUNCTION CountImageDescriptionExtensionType
                    (desc: ImageDescriptionHandle; idType: LongInt;
                     VAR count: LongInt): OSErr;
FUNCTION GetNextImageDescriptionExtensionType
                    (desc: ImageDescriptionHandle;
                     VAR idType: LongInt): OSErr;
```

Result Codes

`codecErr`	–8960	General error returned by compressor; can be returned by any function that gets handled by the compressor
`noCodecErr`	–8961	Image Compression Manager could not find specified error
`codecUnimpErr`	–8962	Feature not implemented by this compressor
`codecSpoolErr`	–8966	Error loading or unloading data
`codecAbortErr`	–8967	Operation aborted by progress function
`codecExtensionNotFoundErr`	–8971	Requested extension is not in the image description structure
`codecOpenErr`	–8973	Compressor component could not be opened by the Image Compression Manager

CHAPTER 5

Sequence Grabber Components

Contents

About Sequence Grabber Components   5-3
Using Sequence Grabber Components   5-5
    Previewing and Recording Captured Data   5-9
        Previewing   5-9
        Recording   5-10
    Playing Captured Data and Saving It in a QuickTime Movie   5-11
        Initializing a Sequence Grabber Component   5-11
        Creating a Sound Channel and a Video Channel   5-12
        Previewing Sound and Video Sequences in a Window   5-14
        Capturing Sound and Video Data   5-18
        Setting Up the Video Bottleneck Functions   5-19
        Drawing Information Over Video Frames During Capture   5-20
Sequence Grabber Components Reference   5-22
    Data Types   5-22
        The Compression Information Structure   5-22
        The Frame Information Structure   5-23
    Sequence Grabber Component Functions   5-24
        Configuring Sequence Grabber Components   5-24
        Controlling Sequence Grabber Components   5-36
        Working With Sequence Grabber Settings   5-47
        Working With Sequence Grabber Characteristics   5-53
        Working With Channel Characteristics   5-58
        Working With Channel Devices   5-72
        Working With Video Channels   5-77
        Working With Sound Channels   5-92
        Video Channel Callback Functions   5-99

CHAPTER 5

　　　　　　Utility Functions for Video Channel Callback Functions　　5-102
　　　　　Application-Defined Functions　　5-111
　Summary of Sequence Grabber Components　　5-123
　　　C Summary　　5-123
　　　　Constants　　5-123
　　　　Data Types　　5-127
　　　　　Sequence Grabber Component Functions　　5-129
　　　　　Application-Defined Functions　　5-135
　　　Pascal Summary　　5-136
　　　　Constants　　5-136
　　　　Data Types　　5-140
　　　　　Sequence Grabber Component Routines　　5-141
　　　　　Application-Defined Routines　　5-148
　　Result Codes　　5-149

CHAPTER 5

Sequence Grabber Components

This chapter discusses sequence grabber components. **Sequence grabber components** allow applications to obtain digitized data from external sources. Applications can then request that the sequence grabber display that data or store it in QuickTime movie files. If you are writing an application that needs to acquire data from sources external to the Macintosh computer, or if you are developing a sequence grabber channel component, you should read this chapter. If you are developing a channel component, you should also read the chapter "Sequence Grabber Channel Components."

Note that the information in this chapter is presented from the perspective of a developer of an application that uses sequence grabber components. If you are developing a sequence grabber component, your component must support the interfaces described in this chapter.

This chapter has been divided into the following sections:

- "About Sequence Grabber Components" presents general information about sequence grabber components.

- "Using Sequence Grabber Components" discusses how to use the sequence grabber component to preview and record captured data. It then provides a sample program that shows how to play captured data and save it in a QuickTime movie.

- "Sequence Grabber Components Reference" describes the constants and data structures that an application needs to communicate with sequence grabber components as well as the functions that your sequence grabber component must support.

- "Summary of Sequence Grabber Components" supplies a summary of the sequence grabber component constants, data types, and functions in C and in Pascal.

About Sequence Grabber Components

Sequence grabber components allow applications to obtain digitized data from sources that are external to a Macintosh computer. For example, you can use a sequence grabber component to record video data from a video digitizer. Your application can then request that the sequence grabber store the captured video data in a QuickTime movie. In this manner, you can acquire movie data from various sources that can augment the movie data you create by other means, such as computer animation. You can also use sequence grabber components to obtain and display data from external sources, without saving the captured data in a movie.

The sequence grabber component provided by Apple allows applications to capture both audio and video data easily, without concern for the details of how the data is acquired. When capturing video data, this sequence grabber uses a video digitizer component to supply the digitized video images (see the chapter "Video Digitizer Components" in this book for more information about video digitizer components). When working with audio data, Apple's sequence grabber component retrieves its sound data from a sound input device (see *Inside Macintosh: More Macintosh Toolbox* for more information about sound input devices).

CHAPTER 5

Sequence Grabber Components

Sequence grabber components use sequence grabber channel components (or, simply, channel components) to obtain data from the audio- or video-digitizing equipment. These components isolate the sequence grabber from the details of working with the various types of data that can be collected. The features that a sequence grabber component supplies are dependent on the services provided by sequence grabber channel components. The channel components, in turn, may use other components to interact with the digitizing equipment. For example, the video channel component supplied by Apple uses a video digitizer component. Figure 5-1 shows the relationship between these components and your application.

Figure 5-1 Relationships among your application, a sequence grabber component, and channel components

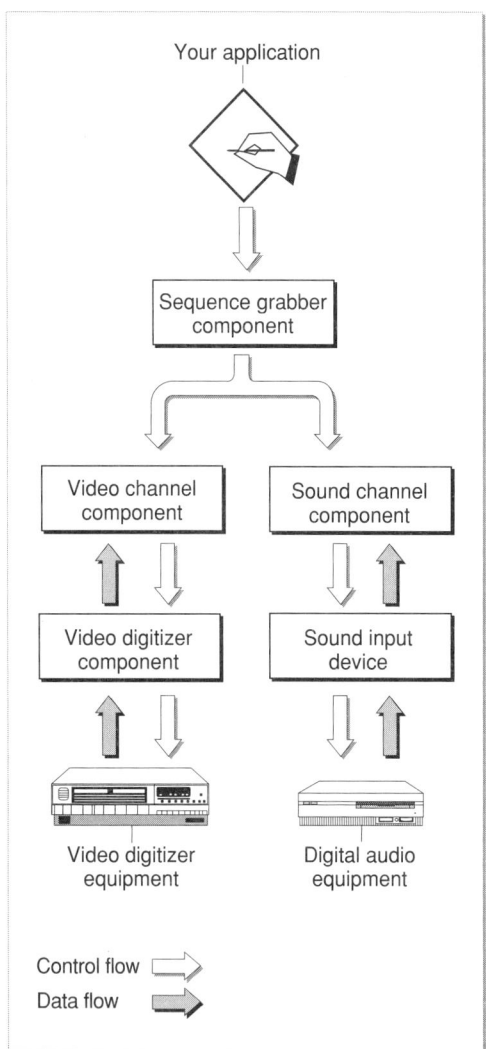

Sequence grabber panel components augment the capabilities of sequence grabber components and sequence grabber channel components by allowing sequence grabbers to obtain configuration information from the user for a particular digitizing source. Sequence grabbers present a settings dialog box to the user whenever an application calls the `SGSettingsDialog` function (see "Working With Sequence Grabber Settings" beginning on page 5-47 for more information about this sequence grabber function). Applications never call sequence grabber panel components directly; application developers use panel components only by calling the sequence grabber component. See the chapter "Sequence Grabber Panel Components" in this book for more information about the sequence grabber configuration dialog box and the relationships of sequence grabbers, sequence grabber channels, and sequence grabber panels.

If you are developing digitizing equipment and you want to allow applications to use the services of your equipment with a sequence grabber component, you should create an appropriate video digitizer component or sound input device driver. See the chapter "Video Digitizer Components" later in this book for a description of video digitizer components. See *Inside Macintosh: More Macintosh Toolbox* for information about sound input device drivers.

If you are developing equipment that provides a new type of data to QuickTime, you should develop a new sequence grabber channel component. See the chapter "Sequence Grabber Channel Components" in this book for a complete description of sequence grabber channel components.

Using Sequence Grabber Components

You can use the sequence grabber component to play captured data for the user or to save captured data in a QuickTime movie. The sequence grabber component provides functions that give your application precise control over the display of the captured data.

This section describes how to use the basic sequence grabber component functions as well as the functions that allow you to configure video and sound channels.

Sequence grabber components are standard components that are managed by the Component Manager. See the chapter "Component Manager" in *Inside Macintosh: More Macintosh Toolbox* for more information about the Component Manager and about how to use components.

Apple has defined a component type value for sequence grabber components—that type value is `'barg'`. You can use the following constant to specify this type value.

```
#define SeqGrabComponentType 'barg' /* sequence grabber
                                       component type */
```

Sequence Grabber Components

Apple has defined a functional interface for basic sequence grabber components. For information about the functions a sequence grabber component may support, see "Sequence Grabber Component Functions," which begins on page 5-24.

You can use the following constants to refer to the request codes for each of the functions that a sequence grabber component may support.

```
enum {
    /* selectors for basic sequence grabber component functions */
    kSGInitializeSelect                 = 0x1;    /* SGInitialize */
    kSGSetDataOutputSelect              = 0x2;    /* SGSetDataOutput */
    kSGGetDataOutputSelect              = 0x3;    /* SGGetDataOutput */
    kSGSetGWorldSelect                  = 0x4;    /* SGSetGWorld */
    kSGGetGWorldSelect                  = 0x5;    /* SGGetGWorld */
    kSGNewChannelSelect                 = 0x6;    /* SGNewChannel */
    kSGDisposeChannelSelect             = 0x7;    /* SGDisposeChannel */
    kSGStartPreviewSelect               = 0x10;   /* SGStartPreview */
    kSGStartRecordSelect                = 0x11;   /* SGStartRecord */
    kSGIdleSelect                       = 0x12;   /* SGIdle */
    kSGStopSelect                       = 0x13;   /* SGStop */
    kSGPauseSelect                      = 0x14;   /* SGPause */
    kSGPrepareSelect                    = 0x15;   /* SGPrepare */
    kSGReleaseSelect                    = 0x16;   /* SGRelease */
    kSGGetMovieSelect                   = 0x17;   /* SGGetMovie */
    kSGSetMaximumRecordTimeSelect       = 0x18;   /* SGSetMaximumRecordTime */
    kSGGetMaximumRecordTimeSelect       = 0x19;   /* SGGetMaximumRecordTime */
    kSGGetStorageSpaceRemainingSelect   = 0x1a;   /* SGGetStorageSpaceRemaining */
    kSGGetTimeRemainingSelect           = 0x1b;   /* SGGetTimeRemaining */
    kSGGrabPictSelect                   = 0x1c;   /* SGGrabPict */
    kSGGetLastMovieResIDSelect          = 0x1d;   /* SGGetLastMovieResID */
    kSGSetFlagsSelect                   = 0x1e;   /* SGSetFlags */
    kSGGetFlagsSelect                   = 0x1f;   /* SGGetFlags */
    kSGSetDataProcSelect                = 0x20;   /* SGSetDataProc */
    kSGNewChannelFromComponentSelect    = 0x21;   /* SGNewChannelFromComponent */
    kSGDisposeDeviceListSelect          = 0x22;   /* SGDisposeDeviceList */
    kSGAppendDeviceListToMenuSelect     = 0x23;   /* SGAppendDeviceListToMenu */
    kSGSetSettingsSelect                = 0x24;   /* SGSetSettings */
    kSGGetSettingsSelect                = 0x25;   /* SGGetSettings */
    kSGGetIndChannelSelect              = 0x26;   /* SGGetIndChannel */
    kSGUpdateSelect                     = 0x27;   /* SGUpdate */
    kSGGetPauseSelect                   = 0x28;   /* SGGetPause */
    kSGSettingsDialogSelect             = 0x29;   /* SGSettingsDialog */
    kSGGetAlignmentProcSelect           = 0x2A;   /* SGGetAlignmentProc */
    kSGSetChannelSettingsSelect         = 0x2B;   /* SGSetChannelSettings */
    kSGGetChannelSettingsSelect         = 0x2C;   /* SGGetChannelSettings */
```

Sequence Grabber Components

```
/* selectors for common channel configuration functions */
kSGCSetChannelUsageSelect           = 0x80;   /* SGCSetChannelUsage */
kSGCGetChannelUsageSelect           = 0x81;   /* SGCGetChannelUsage */
kSGCSetChannelBoundsSelect          = 0x82;   /* SGCSetChannelBounds */
kSGCGetChannelBoundsSelect          = 0x83;   /* SGCGetChannelBounds */
kSGCSetChannelVolumeSelect          = 0x84;   /* SGCSetChannelVolume */
kSGCGetChannelVolumeSelect          = 0x85;   /* SGCGetChannelVolume */
kSGCGetChannelInfoSelect            = 0x86;   /* SGCGetChannelInfo */
kSGCSetChannelPlayFlagsSelect       = 0x87;   /* SGCSetChannelPlayFlags */
kSGCGetChannelPlayFlagsSelect       = 0x88;   /* SGCGetChannelPlayFlags */
kSGCSetChannelMaxFramesSelect       = 0x89;   /* SGCSetChannelMaxFrames */
kSGCGetChannelMaxFramesSelect       = 0x8a;   /* SGCGetChannelMaxFrames */
kSGCSetChannelRefConSelect          = 0x8b;   /* SGCSetChannelRefCon */
kSGCSetChannelClipSelect            = 0x8C;   /* SGCSetChannelClip */
kSGCGetChannelClipSelect            = 0x8D;   /* SGCGetChannelClip */
kSGCGetChannelSampleDescriptionSelect = 0x8E;
                                    /* SGCGetChannelSampleDescription */
kSGCGetChannelDeviceListSelect      = 0x8F;   /* SGCGetChannelDeviceList */
kSGCSetChannelDeviceSelect          = 0x90;   /* SGCSetChannelDevice */
kSGCSetChannelMatrixSelect          = 0x91;   /* SGCSetChannelMatrix */
kSGCGetChannelMatrixSelect          = 0x92;   /* SGCGetChannelMatrix */
kSGCGetChannelTimeScaleSelect       = 0x93;   /* SGCGetChannelTimeScale */

/* selectors for video channel configuration functions */
kSGCGetSrcVideoBoundsSelect         = 0x100;  /* SGCGetSrcVideoBounds */
kSGCSetVideoRectSelect              = 0x101;  /* SGCSetVideoRect */
kSGCGetVideoRectSelect              = 0x102;  /* SGCGetVideoRect */
kSGCGetVideoCompressorTypeSelect    = 0x103;  /* SGCGetVideoCompressorType */
kSGCSetVideoCompressorTypeSelect    = 0x104;  /* SGCSetVideoCompressorType */
kSGCSetVideoCompressorSelect        = 0x105;  /* SGCSetVideoCompressor */
kSGCGetVideoCompressorSelect        = 0x106;  /* SGCGetVideoCompressor */
kSGCGetVideoDigitizerComponentSelect
                                    = 0x107;
                                        /* SGCGetVideoDigitizerComponent */
kSGCSetVideoDigitizerComponentSelect
                                    = 0x108;
                                        /* SGCSetVideoDigitizerComponent */
kSGCVideoDigitizerChangedSelect     = 0x109;  /* SGCVideoDigitizerChanged */
kSGCSetVideoBottlenecksSelect       = 0x10a;  /* SGCSetVideoBottlenecks */
kSGCGetVideoBottlenecksSelect       = 0x10b;  /* SGCGetVideoBottlenecks */
kSGCGrabFrameSelect                 = 0x10c;  /* SGCGrabFrame */
kSGCGrabFrameCompleteSelect         = 0x10d;  /* SGCGrabFrameComplete */
```

Using Sequence Grabber Components

```c
    kSGCDisplayFrameSelect              = 0x10e; /* SGCDisplayFrame */
    kSGCCompressFrameSelect             = 0x10f; /* SGCCompressFrame */
    kSGCCompressFrameCompleteSelect     = 0x110; /* SGCCompressFrameComplete */
    kSGCAddFrameSelect                  = 0x111; /* SGCAddFrameSelect */
    kSGCTransferFrameForCompressSelect  = 0x112;
                                        /* SGCTransferFrameForCompress */
    kSGCSetCompressBufferSelect         = 0x113; /* SGCSetCompressBuffer */
    kSGCGetCompressBufferSelect         = 0x114; /* SGCGetCompressBuffer */
    kSGCGetBufferInfoSelect             = 0x115; /* SGCGetBufferInfo */
    kSGCSetUseScreenBufferSelect        = 0x116; /* SGCSetUseScreenBuffer */
    kSGCGetUseScreenBufferSelect        = 0x117; /* SGCGetUseScreenBuffer */
    kSGCGrabCompressCompleteSelect      = 0x118; /* SGCGrabCompressComplete */
    kSGCDisplayCompressSelect           = 0x119; /* SGCDisplayCompress */
    kSGCSetFrameRateSelect              = 0x11A; /* SGCSetFrameRate */
    kSGCGetFrameRateSelect              = 0x11B; /* SGCGetFrameRate */

    /* selectors for sound channel configuration functions */
    kSGCSetSoundInputDriverSelect       = 0x100;/* SGCSetSoundInputDriver */
    kSGCGetSoundInputDriverSelect       = 0x101;/* SGCGetSoundInputDriver */
    kSGCSoundInputDriverChangedSelect   = 0x102;
                                        /* SGCSoundInputDriverChanged */
    kSGCSetSoundRecordChunkSizeSelect   = 0x103;
                                        /* SGCSetSoundRecordChunkSize */
    kSGCGetSoundRecordChunkSizeSelect   = 0x104;
                                        /* SGCGetSoundRecordChunkSize */
    kSGCSetSoundInputRateSelect         = 0x105; /* SGCSetSoundInputRate */
    kSGCGetSoundInputRateSelect         = 0x106; /* SGCGetSoundInputRate */
    kSGCSetSoundInputParametersSelect   = 0x107;
                                        /* SGCSetSoundInputParameters */
    kSGCGetSoundInputParametersSelect   = 0x108;
                                        /* SGCGetSoundInputParameters */
    /* selectors for utility functions provided to channel components */
    kSGWriteMovieData                   = 0x100; /* SGWriteMovieData */
    kSGAddFrameReferenceSelect          = 0x101; /* SGAddFrameReference */
    kSGGetNextFrameReferenceSelect      = 0x102; /* SGGetNextFrameReference */
    kSGGetTimeBaseSelect                = 0x103; /* SGGetTimeBase */
    kSGSortDeviceListSelect             = 0x104; /* SGSortDeviceList */
    kSGAddMovieDataSelect               = 0x105; /* SGAddMovieData */
    kSGChangedSourceSelect              = 0x106; /* SGChangedSource */
};
```

Previewing and Recording Captured Data

You can use sequence grabber components in two ways: to play digitized data for the user or to save captured data in a QuickTime movie. The process of displaying data that is to be captured is called *previewing*; saving captured data in a movie is called *recording*. You can use previewing to allow the user to prepare to make a recording. If you do so, your application can move directly from the preview operation to a record operation, without stopping the process.

Previewing

Previewing captured data involves playing that data for the user as it is captured. For video data, this means displaying the video images on the computer screen. For audio data, this means playing the sound through the computer's sound system. The following paragraphs outline the steps you must follow to preview captured data.

1. First, you must open a connection to the sequence grabber component. Use the Component Manager's `OpenDefaultComponent` or `OpenComponent` function.

2. Once you have a connection to a sequence grabber component, you must configure the component for the preview operation. Use the `SGSetGWorld` function (described on page 5-29) to set the graphics world in which the preview is to be displayed. Allocate the appropriate channels by calling the `SGNewChannel` function (described on page 5-31). You must call this function once for each channel to be used by the sequence grabber component. Use the `SGSetChannelUsage` function (described on page 5-59) to specify that each channel is to be used for previewing. You can then use the appropriate channel configuration functions to prepare the channel for the preview operation. For video channels, use the functions discussed in "Working With Video Channels" beginning on page 5-77. For sound channels, use the functions discussed in "Working With Sound Channels" beginning on page 5-92.

3. You start the preview operation by calling the `SGStartPreview` function (see page 5-37). The sequence grabber component then begins collecting data from the channels that you have created and plays that data appropriately. You can pause and restart the preview by calling the `SGPause` function (see page 5-41). Use the `SGStop` function (see page 5-40) to stop the preview. During the preview operation, be sure to call the `SGIdle` function (see page 5-39) frequently, so that the sequence grabber and its channels can perform the operation.

4. When you are done previewing, you can start recording or close your connection to the sequence grabber component. When you close the sequence grabber component, it automatically disposes of the channels you created.

See the sample program in Listing 5-1 on page 5-11 for an example of the preview operation.

Recording

During a record operation, a sequence grabber component collects the data it captures and formats that data into a QuickTime movie. During a record operation, the sequence grabber can also play the captured data for the user. However, the sequence grabber tries to prevent the playback from interfering with the quality of the recording process.

The following paragraphs discuss the steps you must follow to record captured data.

1. As with a preview operation, your application must establish a connection to a sequence grabber component. Use the Component Manager's `OpenDefaultComponent` or `OpenComponent` function.

2. Once you have a connection to a sequence grabber component, you must configure the component for the record operation. Use the `SGSetGWorld` function (see page 5-29) to set the graphics world in which the data is to be displayed. Allocate the appropriate channels by calling the `SGNewChannel` function (see page 5-31). You must call this function once for each channel to be used by the sequence grabber component. Use the `SGSetChannelUsage` function (see page 5-59) to specify that each channel is to be used for recording. At this time, you can specify whether the sequence grabber is to play that channel's data while recording. You can then use the appropriate channel configuration functions to prepare the channel for the record operation. For video channels, use the functions discussed in "Working With Video Channels" beginning on page 5-77. For sound channels, use the functions discussed in "Working With Sound Channels" beginning on page 5-92.

3. You must specify a movie file for use by the sequence grabber during the record operation. Use the `SGSetDataOutput` function (see page 5-26) to specify this movie file. This function also allows you to control whether the sequence grabber adds the movie resource to the movie file and whether it replaces existing data or appends the new movie to the file.

4. You can limit the amount of data that is captured during a record operation. The `SGSetMaximumRecordTime` function (see page 5-53) establishes a time limit for the record operation. The `SGSetChannelMaxFrames` function (see page 5-63) limits the number of frames of data that the sequence grabber collects from a specific channel.

5. You start the record operation by calling the `SGStartRecord` function (see page 5-38). The sequence grabber component then begins collecting data from the channels you have created, stores the data in a QuickTime movie, and, optionally, plays that data appropriately. You can pause and restart the record process by calling the `SGPause` function (see page 5-41). During the record operation, be sure to call the `SGIdle` function (see page 5-39) frequently, so that the sequence grabber and its channels can perform the operation. Use the `SGStop` function (see page 5-40) to stop recording. At this time, the sequence grabber saves the movie in your movie file, if you have chosen to do so.

6. When you are done recording, you can go back to previewing or close your connection to the sequence grabber component. When you close the sequence grabber component, it automatically disposes of the channels you created as well as any movies it has created.

Playing Captured Data and Saving It in a QuickTime Movie

This section supplies a sample program that shows how to use a sequence grabber component to preview and record captured data. The program is divided into groups of functions that do the following tasks:

- initialization
- video and sound channel creation
- sequence preview
- capture of sound and video sequences
- drawing over video frames during a capture operation

Initializing a Sequence Grabber Component

Listing 5-1 provides a sample function that creates and initializes a default sequence grabber component for a specified window (using the `OpenDefaultComponent` and `SGInitialize` functions, respectively). It then sets the graphics world of the sequence grabber component to the specified window with the `SGSetGWorld` function. Note that the `CloseComponent` function is called for housekeeping purposes in case the sequence grabber component fails. For more on `OpenDefaultComponent` and `CloseComponent`, see the chapter "Component Manager" in *Inside Macintosh: More Macintosh Toolbox*. For details on `SGInitialize` and `SGSetGWorld`, see page 5-25 and page 5-29, respectively.

Listing 5-1 Initializing a sequence grabber component

```
SeqGrabComponent MakeSequenceGrabber (WindowPtr aWindow)
{
    SeqGrabComponent anSG;
    OSErr err = noErr;

    /* open up the default sequence grabber */
    anSG = OpenDefaultComponent (SeqGrabComponentType, 0);
    if (anSG) {
```

Sequence Grabber Components

```
    /* initialize the default sequence grabber component */
    err = SGInitialize (anSG);
    if (!err) {
    /* set the sequence grabber's graphics world to the
       specified window */
        err = SGSetGWorld (anSG, (CGrafPtr) aWindow, nil);
    }
  }
  if (err && anSG) {
    /* clean up on failure */
    CloseComponent (anSG);
    anSG = nil;
  }
  return anSG;
}
```

Creating a Sound Channel and a Video Channel

Listing 5-2 supplies a sample function that attempts to create a video channel and a sound channel for the sequence grabber component that was created in Listing 5-1. The boundaries of the video channel are set to the specifications of the bounds parameter. The channel's usage is always set to allow previewing. If the value of the willRecord parameter is true, then the usage of the channel is set to allow recording also.

The SGNewChannel function (described on page 5-31) uses the VideoMediaType constant to create a video channel and the SoundMediaType constant to create a sound channel. The SGSetChannelBounds function (described on page 5-65) specifies the boundaries of the video channel. The SGSetChannelUsage function (described on page 5-59) specifies whether the video and the sound channels are used for preview or record operations. The SGDisposeChannel function (described on page 5-34) cleans up upon failure for each of the channels.

Listing 5-2 Creating a sound channel and a video channel

```
void MakeGrabChannels (SeqGrabComponent anSG,
                       SGChannel *videoChannel,
                       SGChannel *soundChannel,
                       const Rect *bounds, Boolean willRecord)
{
  OSErr err;
  long usage;
  /* figure out the usage */
```

Sequence Grabber Components

```c
    usage = seqGrabPreview;        /* always previewing */
    if (willRecord)
        usage |= seqGrabRecord;    /* sometimes recording */

    /* create a video channel */
    err = SGNewChannel (anSG, VideoMediaType, videoChannel);
    if (!err) {

    /* set boundaries for new video channel */
        err = SGSetChannelBounds (*videoChannel, bounds);

    /* set usage for new video channel */
        if (!err)
            err = SGSetChannelUsage (*videoChannel,
                                    usage | seqGrabPlayDuringRecord);
        if (err) {

            /* clean up on failure */
            SGDisposeChannel (anSG, *videoChannel);
            *videoChannel = nil;
        }
    }

    /* create a sound channel */
    err = SGNewChannel (anSG, SoundMediaType, soundChannel);
    if (!err) {

        /* set usage of new sound channel */
        err = SGSetChannelUsage (*soundChannel, usage);
        if (err) {

            /* clean up on failure */
            SGDisposeChannel(anSG, *soundChannel);
            *soundChannel = nil;
        }
    }
}
```

Using Sequence Grabber Components

Previewing Sound and Video Sequences in a Window

Listing 5-3 shows how to use the sequence grabber component to preview sound and video sequences in a window. Clicking the content area of the window causes the sequence grabber to pause until the mouse button is released.

The Image Compression Manager's `GetBestDeviceRect` function helps you determine the best monitor for the window. The `SGStartPreview` function (described on page 5-37) begins the preview of the sound and video sequences. The `SGIdle` function (described on page 5-39) grants the sequence grabber component the time it needs to preview data. The `SGUpdate` function (described on page 5-39) informs the sequence grabber of the update event. The Window Manager's `BeginUpdate` and `EndUpdate` functions respond to the event. The `SGPause` function (described on page 5-41) instructs the sequence grabber to suspend and resume its preview operation. In this example, it is used to suspend the preview operation while the mouse button is held down. Finally, the `SGStop` function (described on page 5-40) halts the action of the sequence grabber component. The Component Manager's `CloseComponent` function closes the component connection. The Window Manager's `DisposeWindow` function disposes of the window.

Listing 5-3   Previewing sound and video sequences in a window

```
void CheckError(OSErr error, Str255 displayString)
{
   if (error == noErr) return;
   if (displayString[0] > 0)
      DebugStr(displayString);
   ExitToShell();
}

Boolean IsQuickTimeInstalled (void)
{
   short    error;
   long     result;
   error = Gestalt (gestaltQuickTime, &result);
   return (error == noErr);
}

void initialize (void)
{
   OSErr err;
```

Sequence Grabber Components

```c
    InitGraf (&qd.thePort);
    InitFonts ();
    InitWindows ();
    InitMenus ();
    TEInit ();
    InitDialogs (nil);
    MaxApplZone();

    if (!IsQuickTimeInstalled())
        CheckError(-1,"\pPlease install QuickTime and try again.");

    err = EnterMovies ();
    CheckError(err,"\pUnable to initialize Movie Toolbox.");
}

WindowPtr makeWindow(void)
{
    WindowPtr aWindow;
    Rect windowRect = {0, 0, 120, 160};
    Rect bestRect;

    /* figure out the best monitor for the window */
    GetBestDeviceRect (nil, &bestRect);

    /* put the window in the top left corner of that monitor */
    OffsetRect(&windowRect, bestRect.left + 10, bestRect.top + 50);

    /* create the window */
    aWindow = NewCWindow (nil, &windowRect, "\pGrabber",
                        true, noGrowDocProc, (WindowPtr)-1,
                        true, 0);

    /* and set the port to the new window */
    SetPort(aWindow);

    return aWindow;
}
```

CHAPTER 5

Sequence Grabber Components

```c
main (void)
{
   WindowPtr theWindow;
   SeqGrabComponent theSG;
   SGChannel videoChannel, soundChannel;
   Boolean done = false;
   OSErr err;

   initialize();
   theWindow = makeWindow();
   theSG = makeSequenceGrabber(theWindow);
   if (!theSG) return;

   makeGrabChannels(theSG, &videoChannel, &soundChannel,
               &theWindow->portRect, false);
   if ((videoChannel == nil) && (soundChannel == nil))
      CheckError(-1,"\pNo sound or video available.");

   err = SGStartPreview(theSG);
   CheckError(err, "\pCan't start preview");

   while (!done) {
      AlignmentProcRecord alignProc;
      short part;
      WindowPtr whichWindow;
      EventRecord theEvent;

      GetNextEvent(everyEvent, &theEvent);

      switch (theEvent.what) {
         case nullEvent:   /* give the sequence grabber time */
               err = SGIdle (theSG);
               if (err) done = true;
               break;

         case updateEvt:if (theEvent.message == (long)theWindow) {
                        /* inform the sequence grabber of the
                           update */
            SGUpdate(theSG,((WindowPeek)
                        theWindow)->updateRgn);
            /* and swallow the update event */
            BeginUpdate(theWindow);
            EndUpdate(theWindow);
         }
```

```
            break;

        case mouseDown:part = FindWindow (theEvent.where,
                                    &whichWindow);
            if (whichWindow != theWindow) break;
            switch (part) {
                case inContent:
                    /* pause until mouse button is
                        released */
                    SGPause (theSG, true);
                    while (StillDown())
                        ;
                    SGPause(theSG, false);
                    break;
                case inGoAway:
                    done = TrackGoAway (theWindow,
                                    theEvent.where);
                    break;
                case inDrag:
                    /* pause when dragging window so video
                        doesn't draw in the wrong place */
                    SGPause (theSG, true);
                    SGGetAlignmentProc (theSG, &alignProc);
                    DragAlignedWindow (theWindow,
                                    theEvent.where,
                                    &screenBits.bounds,
                                    nil, &alignProc);
                    SGPause (theSG, false);
                    break;
            }
            break;
        }
    }
    /* clean up */
    SGStop (theSG);
    CloseComponent (theSG);
    DisposeWindow (theWindow);
}
```

CHAPTER 5

Sequence Grabber Components

Capturing Sound and Video Data

Listing 5-4 uses the sequence grabber component to capture ten seconds of sound and video data. It prompts the user for the name of the file to create. The SGSettingsDialog function (described on page 5-48) is issued to invoke the default sound and video capture settings dialog boxes. These default dialog boxes allow the user to configure the settings for the capture operations. The SGSetMaximumRecordTime function (described on page 5-53) indicates how long the capture operations will last. The SGStartRecord function (described on page 5-38) specifies the time at which the capture operations will begin. The SGIdle function (described on page 5-39) grants the time needed to confirm the capture operations. Finally, the SGStop function (described on page 5-40) and the Window Manager's DisposeWindow routine are called in order to complete the capture of the sequences.

Listing 5-4   Capturing sound and video

```
main (void)
{
   WindowPtr theWindow;
   CGrafPort tempPort;
   SeqGrabComponent theSG;
   SGChannel videoChannel, soundChannel;
   OSErr err;

   initialize();
   theWindow = makeWindow();

   theSG = makeSequenceGrabber(theWindow);
   if (!theSG) return;
   err = setGrabFile(theSG);
   CheckError(err, "\pNo output file");

   makeGrabChannels (theSG, &videoChannel, &soundChannel,
                     &theWindow->portRect, true);
   if ((videoChannel == nil) && (soundChannel == nil))
      CheckError(-1,"\pNo sound or video available.");
```

```
    if (videoChannel)
        SGSettingsDialog (theSG, videoChannel, 0, nil,
                            DoTheRightThing, nil, 0);
    if (soundChannel)
        SGSettingsDialog(theSG, soundChannel, 0, nil,
                            DoTheRightThing, nil, 0);

    err = SGSetMaximumRecordTime(theSG, 10 * 60);
    CheckError(err, "\pCan't set max record time");

    err = SGStartRecord (theSG);
    CheckError(err, "\pCan't start record");

    while (!err)
        err = SGIdle (theSG);
    if (err == grabTimeComplete)
        err = noErr;
    CheckError(err, "\pError while recording");

    err = SGStop(theSG);
    CheckError(err, "\pError creating movie");

    CloseComponent(theSG);
    DisposeWindow(theWindow);
}
```

Setting Up the Video Bottleneck Functions

Listing 5-5 shows how to set up the video bottleneck functions of the sequence grabber video channel component. For more information on the video bottleneck functions, see "Utility Functions for Video Channel Callback Functions" beginning on page 5-102. Inside the main event loop in Listing 5-4, you should add the following lines after you call the SGSetMaximumRecordTime function (described on page 5-53).

Listing 5-5   Setting up the video bottleneck functions

```
    if (videoChannel) {

        err = setupVideoBottlenecks (videoChannel, theWindow,
                                    &tempPort);
        CheckError(err, "\pCouldn't set video bottlenecks");
    }
```

Drawing Information Over Video Frames During Capture

Listing 5-6 shows how to use the video bottleneck functions of the sequence grabber video channel component to draw the letters "QT" over each video frame as it is captured.

Listing 5-6 Drawing information over video frames during capture

```
pascal ComponentResult myGrabFrameComplete (SGChannel c,
                                            short bufferNum,
                                            Boolean *done,
                                            long refCon)
{
    ComponentResult err;

    /* call the default grab-complete function */
    err = SGGrabFrameComplete (c, bufferNum, done);
    if (*done) {

        /* frame is done */
        CGrafPtr savePort;
        GDHandle saveGD;
        PixMapHandle bufferPM, savePM;
        Rect bufferRect;
        CGrafPtr tempPort = (CGrafPtr)refCon;

        /* set to our temporary port */
        GetGWorld (&savePort, &saveGD);
        SetGWorld (tempPort, nil);

        /* find out about this buffer */
        err = SGGetBufferInfo (c, bufferNum, &bufferPM, &bufferRect,
                               nil, nil);
        if (!err) {

            /* set up to draw into this buffer */
            savePM = tempPort->portPixMap;
            SetPortPix(bufferPM);

            /* draw some text into the buffer */
            TextMode (srcXor);
```

Sequence Grabber Components

```
            MoveTo (bufferRect.right - 20, bufferRect.bottom - 14);
            DrawString ("\pQT");
            TextMode(srcOr);
            /* restore temporary port */
            SetPortPix (savePM);
         }
         SetGWorld (savePort, saveGD);
      }
      return err;
   }

   OSErr setupVideoBottlenecks (SGChannel videoChannel, WindowPtr w,
                                CGrafPtr tempPort)
   {
      OSErr err;
      err = SGSetChannelRefCon (videoChannel, (long)tempPort);
      if (!err) {
         VideoBottles vb;

         /* get the current bottlenecks */
         vb.procCount = 9;
         err = SGGetVideoBottlenecks (videoChannel, &vb);
         if (!err) {
            /* add our GrabFrameComplete function */
            vb.grabCompleteProc = myGrabFrameComplete;
            err = SGSetVideoBottlenecks (videoChannel, &vb);

            /* set up the temporary port */
            OpenCPort (tempPort);   /* create a temporary port
                                       for drawing */
            SetRectRgn (tempPort->visRgn, -32000, -32000, 32000,
                     32000);   /* with a wide open visible
                                  and clip region . . . */
            CopyRgn (tempPort->visRgn, tempPort->clipRgn);
                                    /* so that you can use it in
                                       any video buffer */
            PortChanged ((GrafPtr)tempPort);
                                    /* tell QuickDraw about the
                                       changes */
         }
      }

      return err;
   }
```

Using Sequence Grabber Components

Sequence Grabber Components Reference

This section describes the data structures and functions that are specific to sequence grabber components.

Data Types

This section describes the compression information structure and the sequence grabber frame information structure.

Note
You only need to know about the frame information structure if you are creating a sequence grabber component. If you are not creating a sequence grabber component, you may skip this section. ◆

The Compression Information Structure

The compression information structure defines the characteristics of a buffer that contains a captured image that has been compressed. Callback functions use compression information structures to exchange information about compressed images. For example, the compress-complete function must format a compression information record whenever a video frame is compressed (see "Video Channel Callback Functions" beginning on page 5-99 for more information about the compress-complete callback function). The SGCompressInfo data type defines a compression information structure.

```
struct SGCompressInfo {
    Ptr             buffer;     /* buffer for compressed image */
    unsigned long   bufferSize; /* bytes of image data in buffer */
    unsigned char   similarity; /* relative similarity */
    unsigned char   reserved;   /* reserved--set to 0 */
};
typedef struct SGCompressInfo SGCompressInfo;
```

Field descriptions

buffer   Points to the buffer that contains the compressed image. This pointer must contain a 32-bit clean address.

bufferSize   Specifies the number of bytes of image data in the buffer.

Sequence Grabber Components

similarity   Indicates the relative similarity of this image to the previous image in a sequence. A value of 0 indicates that the current frame is a key frame in the sequence. A value of 255 indicates that the current frame is identical to the previous frame. Values from 1 through 254 indicate relative similarity, ranging from very different (1) to very similar (254).

reserved   Reserved for use by Apple. Set this field to 0.

The Frame Information Structure

The frame information structure defines a frame for a sequence grabber component and sequence grabber channel components. The `SeqGrabFrameInfo` data type defines the format of a frame information structure.

```
struct SeqGrabFrameInfo {
    long        frameOffset;    /* offset to the sample */
    long        frameTime;      /* time that frame was captured */
    long        frameSize;      /* number of bytes in sample */
    SGChannel   frameChannel;   /* current connection to channel */
    long        frameRefCon;    /* reference constant for channel */
};
```

Field descriptions

frameOffset   Specifies the offset to the sample.

frameTime   Specifies the time at which a sequence grabber channel component captured the frame. This time value is relative to the data sequence. That is, this time is not represented in the context of any fixed time scale. Rather, the channel component must choose and use a time scale consistently for all sample references.

frameSize   Specifies the number of bytes in the sample described by the sample reference.

frameChannel   Identifies the current connection to the channel component.

frameRefCon   Contains a reference constant for use by the channel component. A channel component can use this value in any way that is appropriate. For example, video channel components may use this value to store a reference to frame differencing information for a temporally compressed image sequence.

Sequence Grabber Component Functions

This section describes the functions that are provided by sequence grabber components. These functions are described from the perspective of an application developer. If you are developing a sequence grabber component, your component must behave as described here.

This section discusses the following groups of functions:

- "Configuring Sequence Grabber Components" describes the functions that allow you to configure a sequence grabber component, including creating channels for the component.

- "Controlling Sequence Grabber Components" discusses the functions that allow you to control a record or preview operation.

- "Working With Sequence Grabber Settings" discusses the functions that allow you to obtain sequence grabber configuration data from the user.

- "Working With Sequence Grabber Characteristics" describes functions that allow you to manage some of the detailed characteristics of a sequence grabber component.

- "Working With Channel Characteristics" describes functions that allow you to configure the general characteristics of a sequence grabber channel.

- "Working With Channel Devices" discusses functions that allow you to determine the device that is attached to a sequence grabber channel.

- "Working With Video Channels" describes functions that allow you to configure video channels.

- "Working With Sound Channels" discusses functions that allow you to configure sound channels.

- "Video Channel Callback Functions" describes the callback functions that are supported by video channels.

- "Utility Functions for Video Channel Callback Functions" discusses a number of utility functions that sequence grabber components provide for use by callback functions.

Configuring Sequence Grabber Components

Sequence grabber components provide a number of functions that allow you to establish the environment for grabbing or previewing digitized data. Before you can start a record or a preview operation, you must initialize the sequence grabber component, establish the channels that will be used, define the display environment for the operation, and determine the optimum screen position for the sequence grabber. In addition, if you are performing a record operation, you must define a destination movie file. This section describes the sequence grabber component functions that allow you to perform these tasks.

You can use the `SGInitialize` function to initialize a sequence grabber component. Before you can call this function, you must establish a connection to the sequence

CHAPTER 5

Sequence Grabber Components

grabber by calling the Component Manager's `OpenDefaultComponent` or `OpenComponent` function.

The `SGNewChannel` function allows you to create channels for the sequence grabber for an operation. You can use the `SGNewChannelFromComponent` function to create a new channel using a specified channel component. Use the `SGDisposeChannel` function to dispose of those channels that you are no longer using.

You can use the `SGGetIndChannel` function to retrieve information about the channels that are currently in use by the sequence grabber.

You can use the `SGSetGWorld` and `SGGetGWorld` functions to establish the display environment for the sequence grabber. These functions affect only those channels that work with data that has visual information.

The `SGSetDataOutput` and `SGGetDataOutput` functions allow you to identify the movie file that is currently assigned to the sequence grabber. You only use these functions when you are performing a record operation.

The `SGSetDataProc` function allows you to assign a data function to a channel. The sequence grabber calls your data function whenever it writes movie data to the output file.

The `SGGetAlignmentProc` function allows you to determine a sequence grabber's optimum screen position to ensure the best performance and appearance.

SGInitialize

The `SGInitialize` function allows you to initialize the sequence grabber component. Before you can call this function you must establish a connection to the sequence grabber component. Use the Component Manager's `OpenDefaultComponent` or `OpenComponent` function to establish a component connection.

```
pascal ComponentResult SGInitialize (SeqGrabComponent s);
```

s   Specifies the component instance that identifies your connection to the sequence grabber component. You obtain this value from the Component Manager's `OpenDefaultComponent` or `OpenComponent` function.

DESCRIPTION

You must call the `SGInitialize` function before you call any other sequence grabber component functions. If this function returns a nonzero result code, you should close your connection to the sequence grabber component.

RESULT CODES

Memory Manager errors

CHAPTER 5

Sequence Grabber Components

SGSetDataOutput

The `SGSetDataOutput` function allows you to specify the movie file for a record operation and to specify other options that govern the operation. The sequence grabber component stores the data that is obtained during the record operation as a QuickTime movie in this file. This function also allows you to control some aspects of the record operation, which are related to output, by specifying control flags. These flags are discussed in the function description that follows.

```
pascal ComponentResult SGSetDataOutput (SeqGrabComponent s,
                                        FSSpec *movieFile,
                                        long whereFlags);
```

s
Specifies the component instance that identifies your connection to the sequence grabber component. You obtain this value from the Component Manager's `OpenDefaultComponent` or `OpenComponent` function.

movieFile
Contains a pointer to the movie file for this record operation.

whereFlags
Contains flags that control the record operation. The following flags are defined by the `SeqGrabDataOutputEnum` data type; you must set either the `seqGrabToDisk` flag or the `seqGrabToMemory` flag to 1 (set unused flags to 0).

seqGrabToDisk
Instructs the sequence grabber component to write the recorded data to a QuickTime movie in the movie file specified by the `movieFile` parameter. If you set this flag to 1, the sequence grabber writes the data to the file as the data is recorded. Set this flag to 0 if you set the `seqGrabToMemory` flag to 1 (only one of these two flags may be set to 1).

seqGrabToMemory
Instructs the sequence grabber component to store the recorded data in memory until the recording process is complete. The sequence grabber then writes the recorded data to the movie file specified by the `movieFile` parameter. This technique provides better performance than recording directly to the movie file, but it limits the amount of data you can record. Set this flag to 1 to record to memory. Set this flag to 0 if you set the `seqGrabToDisk` flag to 1 (only one of these two flags may be set to 1).

seqGrabDontUseTempMemory
Prevents the sequence grabber component from using temporary memory during the record operation. By default, the sequence grabber component and its channel components use as much temporary memory as necessary

Sequence Grabber Components

> to perform the record operation. Set this flag to 1 to prevent the sequence grabber component and its channel components from using temporary memory.

`seqGrabAppendToFile`
> Directs the sequence grabber component to add the recorded data to the data fork of the movie file specified by the `movieFile` parameter. By default, the sequence grabber component deletes the movie file and creates a new file containing one movie and the corresponding movie resource. Set this flag to 1 to cause the sequence grabber component to append the recorded data to the data fork of the movie file and create a new movie resource in that file.

`seqGrabDontAddMovieResource`
> Prevents the sequence grabber component from adding the new movie resource to the movie file specified by the `movieFile` parameter. By default, the sequence grabber component creates a new movie resource and adds that resource to the movie file. Set this flag to 1 to prevent the sequence grabber component from adding the movie resource to the movie file. You are then responsible for adding the resource to a file, if you so desire.

`seqGrabDontMakeMovie`
> Prevents the sequence grabber component from creating a movie. By default, the sequence grabber component creates a new movie resource and adds the captured data to that movie. If you set this flag to 1, the sequence grabber still calls your data function, but does not write any data to the movie file.

DESCRIPTION

If you are performing a preview operation, you do not need to use the `SGSetDataOutput` function.

RESULT CODES

`notEnoughMemoryToGrab`	–9403	Insufficient memory for record operation
`notEnoughDiskSpaceToGrab`	–9404	Insufficient disk space for record operation

File Manager errors
Memory Manager errors

CHAPTER 5

Sequence Grabber Components

SGGetDataOutput

The `SGGetDataOutput` function allows you to determine the movie file that is currently assigned to a sequence grabber component and the control flags that would govern a record operation.

```
pascal ComponentResult SGGetDataOutput (SeqGrabComponent s,
                                        FSSpec *movieFile,
                                        long *whereFlags);
```

s
Specifies the component instance that identifies your connection to the sequence grabber component. You obtain this value from the Component Manager's `OpenDefaultComponent` or `OpenComponent` function.

movieFile
Contains a pointer to a file system specification record that is to receive information about the movie file for this record operation.

whereFlags
Contains a pointer to a long integer that is to receive flags that control the record operation. The following flags are defined (unused flags are set to 0):

seqGrabToDisk
Instructs the sequence grabber component to write the recorded data to a QuickTime movie in the movie file specified by the `movieFile` parameter. If this flag is set to 1, the sequence grabber writes the data to the file as the data is recorded.

seqGrabToMemory
Instructs the sequence grabber component to store the recorded data in memory until the recording process is complete. The sequence grabber then writes the recorded data to the movie file specified by the `movieFile` parameter. This technique provides better performance than recording directly to the movie file, but it limits the amount of data you can record. If this flag is set to 1, the sequence grabber component is recording to memory.

seqGrabDontUseTempMemory
Prevents the sequence grabber component from using temporary memory during the record operation. By default, the sequence grabber component and its channel components use as much temporary memory as necessary to perform the record operation. If this flag is set to 1, the sequence grabber component and its channel components do not use temporary memory.

seqGrabAppendToFile
Directs the sequence grabber component to add the recorded data to the data fork of the movie file specified by the `movieFile` parameter. By default, the sequence grabber component deletes the movie file and creates a

CHAPTER 5

Sequence Grabber Components

new file containing one movie and its movie resource. If this flag is set to 1, the sequence grabber component appends the recorded data to the data fork of the movie file and creates a new movie resource in that file.

seqGrabDontAddMovieResource
: Prevents the sequence grabber component from adding the new movie resource to the movie file specified by the `movieFile` parameter. By default, the sequence grabber component creates a new movie resource and adds that resource to the movie file. If this flag is set to 1, the sequence grabber component does not add the movie resource to the movie file. You are then responsible for adding the resource to a file, if you so desire.

seqGrabDontMakeMovie
: Prevents the sequence grabber component from creating a movie. By default, the sequence grabber component creates a new movie resource and adds the captured data to that movie. If this flag is set to 1, the sequence grabber still calls your data function, but does not write any data to the movie file.

DESCRIPTION

You set these characteristics by calling the `SGSetDataOutput` function, which is described in the previous section. If you have not set these characteristics before calling the `SGGetDataOutput` function, the returned data is meaningless.

SGSetGWorld

The `SGSetGWorld` function allows you to establish the graphics port and device for a sequence grabber component. The sequence grabber component displays the recorded or previewed data in this graphics world.

```
pascal ComponentResult SGSetGWorld (SeqGrabComponent s,
                                    CGrafPtr gp, GDHandle gd);
```

s
: Specifies the component instance that identifies your connection to the sequence grabber component. You obtain this value from the Component Manager's `OpenDefaultComponent` or `OpenComponent` function.

gp
: Specifies the destination graphics port. The specified graphics port must be a color graphics port. Set this parameter to `nil` to use the current graphics port.

gd
: Specifies the destination graphics device. Set this parameter to `nil` to use the current device. If the `gp` parameter specifies a graphics world, set this parameter to `nil` to use that graphics world's graphics device.

CHAPTER 5

Sequence Grabber Components

DESCRIPTION

You must call this function if you are working with any channels that collect visual data. If you are working only with data that has no visual representation, you do not need to call this function. The sequence grabber component performs this operation implicitly when you call the `SGInitialize` function (described on page 5-25), and the component uses your application's current graphics port.

You cannot call this function during a record or preview operation or after you have prepared the sequence grabber component for a record or preview operation (by calling the `SGPrepare` function, which is described on page 5-43).

IMPORTANT

The window in which the sequence grabber is to draw video frames as defined by `SGSetGWorld` must be visible before you call the `SGPrepare` function. Otherwise, the sequence grabber does not display the frames properly. For details, see the discussion of `SGPrepare` beginning on page 5-43. ▲

RESULT CODE

cantDoThatInCurrentMode   –9402   Request invalid in current mode

SGGetGWorld

The `SGGetGWorld` function allows you to determine the graphics port and device for a sequence grabber component.

```
pascal ComponentResult SGGetGWorld (SeqGrabComponent s,
                                    CGrafPtr *gp, GDHandle *gd);
```

s   Specifies the component instance that identifies your connection to the sequence grabber component. You obtain this value from the Component Manager's `OpenDefaultComponent` or `OpenComponent` function.

gp   Contains a pointer to a location that is to receive a pointer to the destination graphics port. Set this parameter to `nil` if you are not interested in this information.

gd   Contains a pointer to a location that is to receive a handle to the destination graphics device. Set this parameter to `nil` if you are not interested in this information.

DESCRIPTION

The sequence grabber component displays the recorded or previewed data in this graphics world.

SEE ALSO

You can establish the graphics port and device for a sequence grabber component by calling the `SGSetGWorld` function, which is described in the previous section.

SGNewChannel

The `SGNewChannel` function creates a sequence grabber channel and assigns a channel component to the channel. The channel component is responsible for providing digitized data to the sequence grabber component. You specify the type of channel component to be added to the sequence grabber component.

```
pascal ComponentResult SGNewChannel (SeqGrabComponent s,
                                     OSType channelType,
                                     SGChannel *ref);
```

s
: Specifies the component instance that identifies your connection to the sequence grabber component. You obtain this value from the Component Manager's `OpenDefaultComponent` or `OpenComponent` function.

channelType
: Specifies the type of channel to open. This value corresponds to the component subtype value of the channel component. The following values are valid:

    VideoMediaType
    : Video channel

    SoundMediaType
    : Sound channel

ref
: Contains a pointer to the `frameChannel` field in the sequence grabber information structure that is to receive a reference to the channel that is added to the sequence grabber component. If the sequence grabber component successfully locates and connects to an appropriate channel component, the sequence grabber component returns a reference to the channel component into the field referred to by this parameter. If the sequence grabber component cannot open a connection, it sets the result code to a nonzero value.

DESCRIPTION

The sequence grabber component locates, and attempts to connect to, an appropriate channel component. If the sequence grabber component cannot locate or connect to a channel component, it returns a nonzero result code.

CHAPTER 5

Sequence Grabber Components

RESULT CODES

couldntGetRequiredComponent   –9405   Component not found

Memory Manager errors

SEE ALSO

When you are done with the sequence grabber component, you can dispose of the channels you have used by calling the SGDisposeChannel function, which is described on page 5-34. However, when you close the sequence grabber component, it automatically disposes of all its channels, so this function is usually unnecessary.

If you want to use a specific channel component, you may use the SGNewChannelFromComponent function, which is described next.

SGNewChannelFromComponent

The SGNewChannelFromComponent function creates a sequence grabber channel and assigns a channel component to the channel. The channel component is responsible for providing digitized data to the sequence grabber component. You specify the channel component to be used.

```
pascal ComponentResult SGNewChannelFromComponent
                (SeqGrabComponent s, SGChannel *newChannel,
                Component sgChannelComponent);
```

s   Specifies the component instance that identifies your connection to the sequence grabber component. You obtain this value from the Component Manager's OpenDefaultComponent or OpenComponent function.

newChannel
           Contains a pointer to a channel component that is to receive a reference to the channel that is added to the sequence grabber component. If the sequence grabber component successfully locates and connects to the specified channel component, the sequence grabber component returns a reference to the channel component into the field referred to by this parameter. If the sequence grabber component cannot open a connection, it sets the result code to a nonzero value.

sgChannelComponent
           Identifies the channel component to use. You supply a component ID value to the sequence grabber. The sequence grabber then opens a connection to that channel component and returns your connection ID in the field specified by the newChannel parameter. You may obtain a component ID value by calling the Component Manager's FindNextComponent function.

CHAPTER 5

Sequence Grabber Components

DESCRIPTION

The sequence grabber component locates and connects to the specified channel component. If the sequence grabber component cannot locate or connect to the channel component, it returns a nonzero result code.

This function is similar to the `SGNewChannel` function, except that this function allows you to specify a particular component rather than just a component subtype value. Use this function if you want to connect to a specific component.

RESULT CODES

`couldntGetRequiredComponent`   –9405   Component not found

Memory Manager errors

SEE ALSO

You may also use the `SGNewChannel` function to establish a new channel. That function requires only a component subtype value, and is described on page 5-31.

When you are done with the sequence grabber component, you can dispose of the channels you have used by calling the `SGDisposeChannel` function, which is described on page 5-34.

SGGetIndChannel

The `SGGetIndChannel` function allows you to collect information about all of the channel components currently in use by a sequence grabber component.

```
pascal ComponentResult SGGetIndChannel (SeqGrabComponent s,
                                        short index,
                                        SGChannel *ref,
                                        OSType *chanType);
```

s   Specifies the component instance that identifies your connection to the sequence grabber component. You obtain this value from the Component Manager's `OpenDefaultComponent` or `OpenComponent` function.

index   Specifies an index value. This value identifies the channel to be queried. The first channel has an index value of 1.

ref   Contains a pointer to a field to receive a value identifying your connection to the channel. If you do not want to receive this information, set this parameter to `nil`.

CHAPTER 5

Sequence Grabber Components

chanType Contains a pointer to a field to receive the channel's subtype value. This value indicates the media type supported by the channel component. The following values are valid:

VideoMediaType
: Video channel

SoundMediaType
: Sound channel

If you do not want to receive this information, set this parameter to `nil`.

DESCRIPTION

You may use the `SGGetIndChannel` function to retrieve information about each of the channel components currently in use by a sequence grabber component. You identify the channel in which you are interested by specifying an index value. These index values start at 1 and increase sequentially; each channel has its own index value.

RESULT CODE

paramErr   –50   Component not found

SGDisposeChannel

The `SGDisposeChannel` function removes a channel from a sequence grabber component.

```
pascal ComponentResult SGDisposeChannel
                    (SeqGrabComponent s, SGChannel c);
```

s Specifies the component instance that identifies your connection to the sequence grabber component. You obtain this value from the Component Manager's `OpenDefaultComponent` or `OpenComponent` function.

c Specifies the reference that identifies the channel you want to close. You obtain this reference from the `SGNewChannel` function, described in the previous section.

DESCRIPTION

You can use this function to remove a channel that you are no longer using. However, you cannot dispose of a channel that is currently active—if you are recording or previewing data, this function returns a nonzero result code.

CHAPTER 5

Sequence Grabber Components

RESULT CODE

badSGChannel   –9406   Invalid channel specified

SEE ALSO

The sequence grabber component automatically disposes of any open channels when you close your connection to the component, so you do not need to call this function prior to calling the Component Manager's `CloseComponent` function.

SGSetDataProc

The `SGSetDataProc` function allows you to specify a data function for use by the sequence grabber. Whenever any channel assigned to the sequence grabber writes data, your data function is called as well. Your data function may then write the data to another destination.

```
pascal ComponentResult SGSetDataProc (SeqGrabComponent sg,
                                      SGDataProc proc,
                                      long refCon);
```

sg
: Identifies your connection to the sequence grabber component. You obtain this value from the Component Manager's `OpenDefaultComponent` or `OpenComponent` function.

proc
: Contains a pointer to your data function. To remove your data function, set this parameter to `nil`. The interface that your data function must support is described in "Application-Defined Functions" beginning on page 5-111.

refCon
: Contains a reference constant. The sequence grabber provides this value to your data function.

DESCRIPTION

Your application may use the `SGSetDataProc` function to assign a data function to a sequence grabber. The sequence grabber calls your data function whenever any channel component writes data to the destination movie. You may use your data function to store the digitized data in some format other than a QuickTime movie.

SEE ALSO

You can instruct the sequence grabber not to write its data to a QuickTime movie by calling the `SGSetDataOutput` function and setting the `seqGrabDontMakeMovie` flag to 1. This can save processing time in cases where you do not want to create a movie. This function is discussed beginning on page 5-26.

SGGetAlignmentProc

The `SGGetAlignmentProc` function allows you to obtain information about the best screen positions for a sequence grabber's video image in terms of appearance and maximum performance.

```pascal
pascal ComponentResult SGGetAlignmentProc (SeqGrabComponent s,
                            AlignmentProcRecordPtr alignmentProc);
```

s Specifies the component instance that identifies your connection to the sequence grabber component. You obtain this value from the Component Manager's `OpenDefaultComponent` or `OpenComponent` function.

alignmentProc
   Contains a pointer to an Image Compression Manager alignment function structure. The sequence grabber places its alignment information into this structure.

DESCRIPTION

You may use the `SGGetAlignmentProc` function to retrieve information about the best screen positions for the sequence grabber's window. The sequence grabber returns information that can be used by the Image Compression Manager's alignment functions (see the chapter "Image Compression Manager" in *Inside Macintosh: QuickTime* for more information about these functions). By using this alignment information, you can place the sequence grabber's window in a position that allows for optimal display performance.

Controlling Sequence Grabber Components

Sequence grabber components provide a full set of functions that allow your application to control the preview or record operation. You can use these functions to start and stop the operation, to pause data collection, and to retrieve a reference to the movie that is created during a record operation. This section describes these functions.

Use the `SGStartPreview` function to start a preview operation. The `SGStartRecord` function lets you start a record operation. The `SGStop` function allows you to stop a sequence grabber component.

You can instruct the sequence grabber to pause by calling the `SGPause` function. You can determine whether the sequence grabber is paused by calling the `SGGetPause` function.

You grant processing time to the sequence grabber by calling the `SGIdle` function. Be sure to call this function often during record and preview operations. If your application receives an update event during a record or preview operation, you should call the `SGUpdate` function.

You can prepare the sequence grabber for an upcoming preview or record operation by calling the `SGPrepare` function. This function also allows the sequence grabber to verify that it can support the parameters you have specified. By verifying the parameters you

CHAPTER 5

Sequence Grabber Components

want to use, you can improve the startup of preview and record operations. Use the `SGRelease` function to release system resources after calling the `SGPrepare` function.

You can retrieve a reference to the movie created by a record operation by calling the `SGGetMovie` function. You can determine the resource ID value assigned to the last movie resource created by the sequence grabber by calling the `SGGetLastMovieResID` function.

You can extract a picture from the video source data by calling the `SGGrabPict` function.

SGStartPreview

The `SGStartPreview` function instructs the sequence grabber to begin processing data from its channels.

```
pascal ComponentResult SGStartPreview (SeqGrabComponent s);
```

s   Specifies the component instance that identifies your connection to the sequence grabber component. You obtain this value from the Component Manager's `OpenDefaultComponent` or `OpenComponent` function.

DESCRIPTION

The sequence grabber immediately presents the data to the user in the appropriate format, according to the channel configuration parameters you have specified (see "Working With Channel Characteristics" beginning on page 5-58 for information about configuring channels). Video data is displayed in the destination display region; sound data is played at the specified volume settings.

RESULT CODES

`cantDoThatInCurrentMode`	–9402	Request invalid in current mode
`deviceCantMeetRequest`	–9408	Device cannot support grabber

File Manager errors
Memory Manager errors

SEE ALSO

You stop the preview process by calling the `SGStop` function, which is described on page 5-40.

In preview mode, the sequence grabber does not save any of the data it gathers from its channels. If you want to record the data, use record mode. You start a record operation by calling the `SGStartRecord` function, which is described in the next section.

Sequence Grabber Components Reference

SGStartRecord

The `SGStartRecord` function instructs the sequence grabber component to begin collecting data from its channels.

```
pascal ComponentResult SGStartRecord (SeqGrabComponent s);
```

s   Specifies the component instance that identifies your connection to the sequence grabber component. You obtain this value from the Component Manager's `OpenDefaultComponent` or `OpenComponent` function.

DESCRIPTION

The sequence grabber stores the collected data according to the recording parameters you specify with the `SGSetDataOutput` function, which is described on page 5-26. Before calling this function, you must correctly configure the sequence grabber's channels—see "Working With Channel Characteristics" beginning on page 5-58 for information about configuring sequence grabber channels.

RESULT CODES

`cantDoThatInCurrentMode`	−9402	Request invalid in current mode
`notEnoughMemoryToGrab`	−9403	Insufficient memory for record operation
`notEnoughDiskSpaceToGrab`	−9404	Insufficient disk space for record operation
`deviceCantMeetRequest`	−9408	Device cannot support grabber

File Manager errors
Memory Manager errors

SEE ALSO

You can switch from previewing to recording by calling this function during a preview operation—you need not stop the preview operation first. You stop the recording process by calling the `SGStop` function, which is described on page 5-40.

You can cause the sequence grabber to display the data it obtains from its channels without storing any of the data by calling the `SGStartPreview` function, which is described in the previous section.

CHAPTER 5

Sequence Grabber Components

SGIdle

The `SGIdle` function provides processing time to the sequence grabber component and its channel components. After starting a preview or record operation, you should call this function as often as possible, until you stop the operation by calling `SGStop`.

▲ **WARNING**
If you do not call `SGIdle` frequently enough, you may lose data. ▲

```
pascal ComponentResult SGIdle (SeqGrabComponent s);
```

s   Specifies the component instance that identifies your connection to the sequence grabber component. You obtain this value from the Component Manager's `OpenDefaultComponent` or `OpenComponent` function.

DESCRIPTION

The `SGIdle` function reports several status and error conditions by means of its result code. If you have established a time limit for a record operation by calling the `SGSetMaximumRecordTime` function (described on page 5-53), `SGIdle` returns a result code of `grabTimeComplete` when the time limit expires. In addition, `SGIdle` reports errors that are specific to the channels that are active for a given operation. If `SGIdle` returns a nonzero result code during a record operation, you should still call the `SGStop` function (described on page 5-40) so that the sequence grabber can store the data it has collected.

RESULT CODES

`grabTimeComplete`	–9401	Time for record operation has expired
`cantDoThatInCurrentMode`	–9402	Request invalid in current mode

File Manager errors
Memory Manager errors

SGUpdate

The `SGUpdate` function allows you to tell the sequence grabber that it must refresh its display.

```
pascal ComponentResult SGUpdate (SeqGrabComponent s,
                                 RgnHandle updateRgn);
```

CHAPTER 5

Sequence Grabber Components

s   Specifies the component instance that identifies your connection to the sequence grabber component. You obtain this value from the Component Manager's `OpenDefaultComponent` or `OpenComponent` function.

updateRgn   Indicates the part of the window that has been changed. You may use this parameter to specify a portion of the window that you know has been changed. You can obtain this information by examining the appropriate window record. For example:

```
SGUpdate (theSG, ((WindowPeek)updateWindow)->updateRgn);
```

If you set this parameter to `nil`, the sequence grabber uses the window's current visible region.

DESCRIPTION

You may use the `SGUpdate` function to tell the sequence grabber that it must refresh its display. You should call this function whenever you receive an update event for a window that contains a sequence grabber display. You should call this function before calling the Window Manager's `BeginUpdate` function.

Your application should avoid drawing where the sequence grabber is displaying video. Doing so may cause some video digitizer components to stop displaying video.

SPECIAL CONSIDERATIONS

It is dangerous to allow an update event to occur during recording. Many digitizers capture directly to the screen; thus, an update event will result in data loss.

RESULT CODES

paramErr	–50	Component not found
deviceCantMeetRequest	–9408	Device cannot support grabber

SGStop

The `SGStop` function stops a preview or record operation.

```
pascal ComponentResult SGStop (SeqGrabComponent s);
```

s   Specifies the component instance that identifies your connection to the sequence grabber component. You obtain this value from the Component Manager's `OpenDefaultComponent` or `OpenComponent` function.

DESCRIPTION

The sequence grabber releases any system resources it used during the operation, such as temporary memory. In the case of a record operation, the sequence grabber stores the

CHAPTER 5

Sequence Grabber Components

collected movie data in the assigned movie file—you specify the movie file by calling the `SGSetDataOutput` function, which is described on page 5-26.

RESULT CODES

`cantDoThatInCurrentMode`   –9402   Request invalid in current mode

File Manager errors
Memory Manager errors

SGPause

You can suspend or restart a record or preview operation by calling the `SGPause` function. You supply a byte value that instructs the sequence grabber whether to pause or restart the current operation.

```
pascal ComponentResult SGPause (SeqGrabComponent s,
                                Byte pause);
```

s
: Specifies the component instance that identifies your connection to the sequence grabber component. You obtain this value from the Component Manager's `OpenDefaultComponent` or `OpenComponent` function.

pause
: Instructs the sequence grabber whether to suspend or restart the current operation. The following values are valid:

    `seqGrabUnpause`
    : Restarts the current operation.

    `seqGrabPause`
    : Pauses the current operation.

    `seqGrabPauseForMenu`
    : Pauses the current operation so that you may display a menu. Use this option only in preview mode, just before you call the Menu Manager's `MenuSelect` or `PopUpMenuSelect` function. In this case, the sequence grabber may not pause all channels, depending upon the ability of the sequence grabber to play with acceptable quality. For example, sound channels may continue to play while video channels are paused.

DESCRIPTION

The `SGPause` function does not release any system resources or temporary memory associated with the current operation. Consequently, it is generally much faster than using the `SGStop` and `SGStartRecord` functions or the `SGStartPreview` function to suspend an operation.

CHAPTER 5

Sequence Grabber Components

SPECIAL CONSIDERATIONS

When you restart the operation, the sequence grabber component may be unable to satisfy your request. This can occur, for example, if the user has moved the display window to a location that the digitizing hardware cannot support.

RESULT CODES

`cantDoThatInCurrentMode`	–9402	Request invalid in current mode
`notEnoughMemoryToGrab`	–9403	Insufficient memory for record operation
`deviceCantMeetRequest`	–9408	Device cannot support grabber

File Manager errors
Memory Manager errors

SEE ALSO

You may determine whether the sequence grabber is paused by calling the `SGGetPause` function, which is described next.

SGGetPause

You can determine whether the sequence grabber is paused by calling the `SGGetPause` function.

```
pascal ComponentResult SGGetPause (SeqGrabComponent s,
                                    Byte *paused);
```

s
: Specifies the component instance that identifies your connection to the sequence grabber component. You obtain this value from the Component Manager's `OpenDefaultComponent` or `OpenComponent` function.

paused
: Contains a pointer to a field that is to receive a value that indicates whether the sequence grabber is currently paused. The following values are valid:

    seqGrabUnpause
    : The sequence grabber is not paused.

    seqGrabPause
    : The sequence grabber is paused—all channels are stopped.

    seqGrabPauseForMenu
    : The sequence grabber is paused in order to display a menu—some or all of the channels may be stopped.

DESCRIPTION

The `SGGetPause` function allows you to determine whether the sequence grabber is paused.

CHAPTER 5

Sequence Grabber Components

SEE ALSO

You may pause or restart the sequence grabber by calling the `SGPause` function, which is described in the previous section.

SGPrepare

The `SGPrepare` function instructs the sequence grabber to get ready to begin a preview or record operation (or to commence both operations). You specify the operations.

```
pascal ComponentResult SGPrepare (SeqGrabComponent s,
                                  Boolean prepareForPreview,
                                  Boolean prepareForRecord);
```

s
: Specifies the component instance that identifies your connection to the sequence grabber component. You obtain this value from the Component Manager's `OpenDefaultComponent` or `OpenComponent` function.

prepareForPreview
: Instructs the sequence grabber component to prepare for a preview operation. Set this parameter to `true` to prepare for a preview operation. You may set both the `prepareForPreview` and `prepareForRecord` parameters to `true`.

prepareForRecord
: Instructs the sequence grabber component to prepare for a record operation. Set this parameter to `true` to prepare for a record operation. You may set both the `prepareForPreview` and `prepareForRecord` parameters to `true`.

DESCRIPTION

The sequence grabber component does whatever is necessary to get ready to start the preview or record operation. This may involve allocating memory, readying hardware, and notifying the sequence grabber's channels. By calling this function, you ensure that the `SGStartRecord` or `SGStartPreview` function starts as quickly as possible.

If you do not call this function before starting a record or preview operation, the sequence grabber component makes these preparations when you start the operation. You cannot call this function after you start a preview or record operation.

If you call `SGPrepare` without subsequently starting a record or preview operation, you should call the `SGRelease` function (described in the next section). This allows the sequence grabber component to release any system resources it allocated when you called `SGPrepare`.

Sequence Grabber Components

SPECIAL CONSIDERATIONS

The window in which the sequence grabber is to draw video frames (as defined by the `SGSetGWorld` function, described on page 5-29) must be visible before you call the `SGPrepare` function. Otherwise, the sequence grabber does not display the frames properly. If the window isn't visible and `SGPrepare` is called with the `prepareForPreview` parameter set to `true` and the `prepareForRecord` parameter set to `false`, and the window is subsequently shown via the Window Manager's `ShowWindow` routine, the sequence grabber won't display frames properly in the video window. The visible region of the window wasn't valid when the `SGPrepare` call was made.

RESULT CODES

`paramErr`	–50	Invalid parameter specified
`cantDoThatInCurrentMode`	–9402	Request invalid in current mode
`notEnoughMemoryToGrab`	–9403	Insufficient memory for record operation
`notEnoughDiskSpaceToGrab`	–9404	Insufficient disk space for record operation
`deviceCantMeetRequest`	–9408	Device cannot support grabber

File Manager errors
Memory Manager errors

SGRelease

The `SGRelease` function instructs the sequence grabber to release any system resources it allocated when you called the `SGPrepare` function, which is described in the previous section. You should call `SGRelease` whenever you call `SGPrepare` without subsequently starting a record or preview operation.

```
pascal ComponentResult SGRelease (SeqGrabComponent s);
```

s   Specifies the component instance that identifies your connection to the sequence grabber component. You obtain this value from the Component Manager's `OpenDefaultComponent` or `OpenComponent` function.

DESCRIPTION

When you stop a record or preview operation by calling the `SGStop` function, the sequence grabber component automatically releases the resources it uses during the operation. Consequently, you do not have to call this function after a record or preview operation.

You cannot call the `SGRelease` function during a record or preview operation.

SGGetMovie

The `SGGetMovie` function returns a reference to the movie that contains the data collected during a record operation. You can use this movie identifier with Movie Toolbox functions. However, you should not dispose of this movie—it is owned by the sequence grabber component. Furthermore, the sequence grabber component disposes of this movie when you prepare for or start the next record or preview operation, or when you close the connection to the sequence grabber. If you want to work with a movie containing the collected data, use the Movie Toolbox's `NewMovieFromFile` function (see the chapter "Movie Toolbox" in *Inside Macintosh: QuickTime* for more information).

You can call this function only after you have stopped the record operation by calling the `SGStop` function.

```
pascal Movie SGGetMovie (SeqGrabComponent s);
```

s Specifies the component instance that identifies your connection to the sequence grabber component. You obtain this value from the Component Manager's `OpenDefaultComponent` or `OpenComponent` function.

DESCRIPTION

The `SGGetMovie` function returns a reference to the movie that contains the data collected during a record operation. If there is no current movie, either because you are in preview mode or because you have not yet stopped the record operation, the sequence grabber component sets this returned reference to `nil`.

RESULT CODE

seqGrabInfoNotAvailable   –9407   Sequence grabber cannot support request

SGGetLastMovieResID

The `SGGetLastMovieResID` allows you to retrieve the last resource ID used by the sequence grabber component. The sequence grabber component assigns a new resource ID to each movie resource it creates. The sequence grabber creates the movie resource when you stop a record operation by calling the `SGStop` function, unless you have instructed the sequence grabber not to add the movie resource to the movie file (see the description of the `SGSetDataOutput` function beginning on page 5-26 for more information).

```
pascal ComponentResult SGGetLastMovieResID (SeqGrabComponent s,
                                            short *resID) ;
```

CHAPTER 5

Sequence Grabber Components

s Specifies the component instance that identifies your connection to the sequence grabber component. You obtain this value from the Component Manager's `OpenDefaultComponent` or `OpenComponent` function.

resID Contains a pointer to an integer that is to receive the resource ID the sequence grabber assigned to the movie resource it just created.

DESCRIPTION

If you want this information, you should call this function before you prepare for or start another record or preview operation—because the sequence grabber component resets this value when you start the next operation.

RESULT CODE

seqGrabInfoNotAvailable   –9407   Sequence grabber cannot support request

SGGrabPict

The `SGGrabPict` function provides a simple interface that allows your application to obtain a QuickDraw picture from a sequence grabber component. The sequence grabber can display the picture directly, or it can write the picture to an offscreen buffer. This function is limited in scope, however, and does not allow you to control all of the parameters that govern the operation. When you call this function, the sequence grabber component obtains and configures appropriate sequence grabber channel components (if necessary), grabs the data, and then releases any components it obtained.

```
pascal ComponentResult SGGrabPict (SeqGrabComponent s,
                                   PicHandle *p,
                                   const Rect *bounds,
                                   short offscreenDepth,
                                   long grabPictFlags);
```

s Specifies the component instance that identifies your connection to the sequence grabber component. You obtain this value from the Component Manager's `OpenDefaultComponent` or `OpenComponent` function.

p Contains a pointer to a field that is to receive a handle to the picture. If the `SGGrabPict` function cannot create the picture, it sets this handle to `nil`.

bounds Contains a pointer to the boundary region for the picture. By default, this rectangle lies in the current graphics port. If you set the `grabPictOffScreen` flag in the `grabPictFlags` parameter to 1, the sequence grabber places the picture in an offscreen graphics world. In this case, the rectangle is interpreted in that offscreen world.

offscreenDepth

Specifies the pixel depth for the offscreen graphics world. This parameter is typically set to 0, which chooses the best available depth. If you set the

Sequence Grabber Components

        `grabPictOffScreen` flag in the `grabPictFlags` parameter to 1, the sequence grabber places the picture in an offscreen graphics world. You specify the pixel depth of this offscreen graphics world with this parameter. If you are displaying the picture, this parameter is ignored.

`grabPictFlags`
    Contains flags that control the operation. The following flags are defined (set unused flags to 0):

    `grabPictOffScreen`
        Instructs the sequence grabber to place the picture in an offscreen graphics world. Set this flag to 1 to use an offscreen graphics world. In this case, you use the `offscreenDepth` parameter to specify the pixel depth in the offscreen buffer. In addition, the rectangle specified by the `bounds` parameter is applied to the offscreen buffer.

    `grabPictIgnoreClip`
        Instructs the sequence grabber to ignore any clipping regions you may have defined for the sequence grabber's channels. Set this flag to 1 to have the sequence grabber ignore these clipping regions.

DESCRIPTION

    If you have created any channels for the sequence grabber component, the `SGGrabPict` function uses those channels to obtain the data for the captured image.

SPECIAL CONSIDERATIONS

    Some digitizer sources do not support grabbing offscreen, so the `SGGrabPict` function may fail. In this case, try again grabbing onscreen.

RESULT CODES

`notEnoughMemoryToGrab`	–9403	Insufficient memory for record operation
`deviceCantMeetRequest`	–9408	Device cannot support grabber

File Manager errors
Memory Manager errors

Working With Sequence Grabber Settings

Sequence grabber components can work with channel components and panel components to collect configuration settings from the user. The functions discussed in this section allow you to direct the sequence grabber to display its settings dialog box to the user and to work with the configuration of each of the grabber's channels. See "About Sequence Grabber Components" on page 5-3 for more information about the relationship between the sequence grabber and panel components.

Sequence Grabber Components

Use the `SGSettingsDialog` function to instruct the sequence grabber to display its settings dialog box to the user.

The `SGSetSettings` and `SGGetSettings` functions allow you to retrieve or set the sequence grabber's configuration.

The `SGSetChannelSettings` and `SGGetChannelSettings` functions work with the configuration of an individual channel.

SGSettingsDialog

You may cause the sequence grabber to display its settings dialog box to the user by calling the `SGSettingsDialog` function. The user can use this dialog box to specify the configuration of a sequence grabber channel.

```
pascal ComponentResult SGSettingsDialog (SeqGrabComponent s,
                SGChannel c, short numPanels,
                Component *panelList, long flags,
                SGModalFilterProcPtr proc, long procRefNum);
```

s
: Specifies the component instance that identifies your connection to the sequence grabber component. You obtain this value from the Component Manager's `OpenDefaultComponent` or `OpenComponent` function.

c
: Identifies the channel to be configured. You provide your connection identifier. You connect to a channel component by calling the `SGNewChannel` or `SGNewChannelFromComponent` function, discussed on page 5-31 and page 5-32, respectively.

numPanels
: Specifies the number of panel components to be listed in the panel component pop-up menu. You specify the panel components with the `panelList` parameter. You may use these parameters to limit the user's choice of panel components. If you set this parameter to 0 and the `panelList` parameter to `nil`, the sequence grabber lists all available panel components.

panelList
: Contains a pointer to an array of component identifiers. The sequence grabber presents only these components in the panel component pop-up menu. You specify the number of identifiers in the array with the `numPanels` parameter. If you set this parameter to `nil`, the sequence grabber lists all available panel components.

flags
: Reserved for Apple Computer. Set this parameter to 0.

proc
: Specifies an event filter function. Because the sequence grabber's settings dialog box is a movable modal dialog box, you must supply an event filter function to process update events in your window. The interface that your filter function must support is described in "Application-Defined Functions" beginning on page 5-111.

procRefNum
: Contains a reference constant for use by your filter function.

CHAPTER 5

Sequence Grabber Components

IMPORTANT
Because the settings dialog box is a movable modal dialog box, you must provide an event filter function. ▲

DESCRIPTION

The `SGSettingsDialog` function instructs the sequence grabber to display its settings dialog box to the user. The sequence grabber works with one or more panel components to configure a specified channel component.

If the user clicks OK and the settings are acceptable to the panel and channel components, this function returns a result code of `noErr`. Because the user may change several channel configuration parameters, your application should retrieve new configuration information from the channel so that you can update any values you save, such as the channel's display boundaries or the channel device. In particular, the video rectangle for the channels may be adjusted.

RESULT CODE

userCanceledErr   –128   User canceled the dialog

SEE ALSO

You may retrieve or set the configuration of one or more channel components by using the `SGGetSettings` (described in the next section), `SGSetSettings` (described on page 5-50), `SGGetChannelSettings` (described on page 5-51), or `SGSetChannelSettings` function (described on page 5-52).

SGGetSettings

The `SGGetSettings` function retrieves the current settings of all channels used by the sequence grabber. The sequence grabber places all of this configuration information into a Movie Toolbox user data list.

```
pascal ComponentResult SGGetSettings (SeqGrabComponent s,
                                      UserData *ud, long flags);
```

s   Specifies the component instance that identifies your connection to the sequence grabber component. You obtain this value from the Component Manager's `OpenDefaultComponent` or `OpenComponent` function.

ud   Contains a pointer. The sequence grabber returns a pointer to a Movie Toolbox user data list that contains the configuration information. Your application is responsible for disposing of this user data list when you are done with it.

flags   Reserved for Apple. Set this parameter to 0.

DESCRIPTION

The `SGGetSettings` function allows you to retrieve the sequence grabber's configuration information. The sequence grabber, in turn, retrieves configuration information for each of its channels and stores that information in a Movie Toolbox user data list. You may subsequently use the `SGSetSettings` function (described in the next section) to reconfigure the sequence grabber. You can store the settings (for example, in a Preferences file) by using the Movie Toolbox's `PutUserDataIntoHandle` function.

RESULT CODES

Memory Manager errors

SEE ALSO

You may retrieve the configuration of one channel component by using the `SGGetChannelSettings` function (described on page 5-51).

SGSetSettings

The `SGSetSettings` function allows you to configure a sequence grabber and its channels.

```
pascal ComponentResult SGSetSettings (SeqGrabComponent s,
                                      UserData ud, long flags);
```

s   Specifies the component instance that identifies your connection to the sequence grabber component. You obtain this value from the Component Manager's `OpenDefaultComponent` or `OpenComponent` function.

ud   Specifies a Movie Toolbox user data list that contains the configuration information to be used by the sequence grabber.

flags Reserved for Apple. Set this parameter to 0.

DESCRIPTION

The `SGSetSettings` function allows you to configure a sequence grabber. You provide this configuration information in a Movie Toolbox user data list. Typically, you obtain this configuration data from the `SGGetSettings` function, which is discussed in the previous section.

Note that the sequence grabber disposes of any of its current channels before applying this configuration information. It then opens connections to new channels as appropriate.

You can restore saved settings by using the Movie Toolbox's `NewUserDataFromHandle` function.

CHAPTER 5

Sequence Grabber Components

RESULT CODES

`noDeviceForChannel`	–9400	Channel component cannot find its device
`couldntGetRequiredComponent`	–9405	Component not found
`deviceCantMeetRequest`	–9408	Device cannot support grabber

SEE ALSO

You may set the configuration of one channel component by using the `SGSetChannelSettings` function (described on page 5-52).

You may use the `SGGetIndChannel` function (described on page 5-33) to obtain information about each channel that the sequence grabber is using as a result of applying this new configuration.

SGGetChannelSettings

The `SGGetChannelSettings` function retrieves the current settings of one channel used by the sequence grabber. The sequence grabber places this configuration information into a Movie Toolbox user data list.

```
pascal ComponentResult SGGetChannelSettings (SeqGrabComponent s,
                                              SGChannel c,
                                              UserData *ud,
                                              long flags);
```

s
: Specifies the component instance that identifies your connection to the sequence grabber component. You obtain this value from the Component Manager's `OpenDefaultComponent` or `OpenComponent` function.

c
: Identifies the channel for this operation. You pass your connection identifier. You connect to a channel component by calling the `SGNewChannel` or `SGNewChannelFromComponent` function, discussed on page 5-31 and page 5-32, respectively.

ud
: Contains a pointer. The sequence grabber returns a pointer to a Movie Toolbox user data list that contains the configuration information.

flags
: Reserved for Apple. Set this parameter to 0.

DESCRIPTION

The `SGGetChannelSettings` function allows you to retrieve the configuration information for a single channel component. The channel component stores that information in a Movie Toolbox user data list. You may subsequently use the `SGSetChannelSettings` function to reconfigure the channel (this function is described next).

CHAPTER 5

Sequence Grabber Components

RESULT CODES

Memory Manager errors

SEE ALSO

You may retrieve the configuration of the entire sequence grabber, including all of its channels, by using the `SGGetSettings` function, described on page 5-49.

SGSetChannelSettings

The `SGSetChannelSettings` function allows you to configure a sequence grabber channel.

```
pascal ComponentResult SGSetChannelSettings (SeqGrabComponent s,
                                             SGChannel c,
                                             UserData ud,
                                             long flags);
```

s   Specifies the component instance that identifies your connection to the sequence grabber component. You obtain this value from the Component Manager's `OpenDefaultComponent` or `OpenComponent` function.

c   Identifies the channel to be configured. You provide your connection identifier. You connect to a channel component by calling the `SGNewChannel` or `SGNewChannelFromComponent` function, discussed on page 5-31 and page 5-32, respectively.

ud   Specifies a Movie Toolbox user data list that contains the configuration information to be used by the channel component.

flags   Reserved for Apple. Set this parameter to 0.

DESCRIPTION

The `SGSetChannelSettings` function allows you to configure a sequence grabber channel. You provide this configuration information in a Movie Toolbox user data list. Typically, you obtain this configuration data from the `SGGetChannelSettings` function, which is discussed in the previous section.

CHAPTER 5

Sequence Grabber Components

RESULT CODES

`noDeviceForChannel`	–9400	Channel component cannot find its device
`couldntGetRequiredComponent`	–9405	Component not found
`deviceCantMeetRequest`	–9408	Device cannot support grabber

SEE ALSO

You may set the configuration of all of the sequence grabber's channels by using the `SGSetSettings` function. This function is described on page 5-50.

Working With Sequence Grabber Characteristics

The characteristics that govern a sequence grabber operation fall into two main categories: those that apply to the sequence grabber component, and those that apply to an individual channel that has been created for the sequence grabber. Sequence grabber components provide a number of functions in each category. This section describes the functions that allow you to configure the characteristics of the sequence grabber component. See "Working With Channel Characteristics" beginning on page 5-58 for information about functions that apply to a single channel.

Use the `SGSetMaximumRecordTime` function to limit the duration of a record operation. You can retrieve this time limit by calling the `SGGetMaximumRecordTime` function.

The `SGSetFlags` function allows you to set control flags that govern an operation. Use the `SGGetFlags` function to retrieve those flags.

You can obtain information about the progress of a record operation by calling the `SGGetStorageSpaceRemaining` and `SGGetTimeRemaining` functions.

You can retrieve a reference to the time base used by a sequence grabber component by calling the `SGGetTimeBase` function.

SGSetMaximumRecordTime

You can limit the duration of a record operation by calling the `SGSetMaximumRecordTime` function. You specify the time limit as an exact number of Macintosh system ticks (each is approximately a sixtieth of a second). The most efficient technique for monitoring this time limit is to examine the result code from the `SGIdle` function, which is described on page 5-39. When the time limit expires, the sequence grabber component sets that result code to `grabTimeComplete`.

```
pascal ComponentResult SGSetMaximumRecordTime (SeqGrabComponent s,
                                               unsigned long ticks);
```

Sequence Grabber Components

s Specifies the component instance that identifies your connection to the sequence grabber component. You obtain this value from the Component Manager's `OpenDefaultComponent` or `OpenComponent` function.

ticks Specifies the maximum duration for the record operation, in system ticks. Set this parameter to 0 to remove the time limit from the operation.

DESCRIPTION

By default, there is no time limit on a record operation. If you do not set a limit, a record operation will run until it exhausts the Operating System resources or you call the `SGStop` function (described on page 5-40). Memory and disk space are the two major limiting factors.

You must call the `SGSetMaximumRecordTime` function before you start the record operation.

SGGetMaximumRecordTime

The `SGGetMaximumRecordTime` function allows you to determine the time limit you have set for a record operation.

```
pascal ComponentResult SGGetMaximumRecordTime (SeqGrabComponent s,
                                               unsigned long *ticks);
```

s Specifies the component instance that identifies your connection to the sequence grabber component. You obtain this value from the Component Manager's `OpenDefaultComponent` or `OpenComponent` function.

ticks Contains a pointer to a long integer that is to receive a value indicating the maximum duration for the record operation, in system ticks. A value of 0 indicates that there is no time limit.

SEE ALSO

You set this time limit by calling the `SGSetMaximumRecordTime` function, which is described in the previous section.

SGGetStorageSpaceRemaining

The `SGGetStorageSpaceRemaining` function allows you to monitor the amount of space remaining for use during a record operation. You can use this function to monitor the space being used so that you can limit the amount of space consumed by an operation. Alternatively, you can use the information you receive from this function to update a status display for the user.

```
pascal ComponentResult SGGetStorageSpaceRemaining
                                    (SeqGrabComponent s,
                                    unsigned long *bytes);
```

s   Specifies the component instance that identifies your connection to the sequence grabber component. You obtain this value from the Component Manager's `OpenDefaultComponent` or `OpenComponent` function.

bytes   Contains a pointer to a long integer that is to receive a value indicating the amount of space remaining for the current record operation. If you are recording to memory, this value contains information about the amount of memory remaining. If you are recording to a movie file, this value contains information about the amount of storage space available on the device that holds the file.

DESCRIPTION

The `SGGetStorageSpaceRemaining` function returns information that is appropriate for the output conditions you establish with the `SGSetDataOutput` function, which is described on page 5-26. If you are recording to memory, this function returns information about the amount of memory remaining. If you are recording to a movie file, this function returns information about the amount of storage space available on the device that holds the file.

You can call this function only after you have started a record operation.

RESULT CODE

seqGrabInfoNotAvailable   −9407   Sequence grabber does not have this information at this time

SGGetTimeRemaining

The `SGGetTimeRemaining` function allows you to obtain an estimate of the amount of recording time that remains for the current record operation. The sequence grabber component estimates this value based on the amount of storage remaining and the speed with which the record operation is consuming that space. This estimate improves as the record process continues. If you have limited the record time by calling the `SGSetMaximumRecordTime` function (see page 5-53 for details), `SGGetTimeRemaining` does not return a value that is greater than the limit you have set.

```
pascal ComponentResult SGGetTimeRemaining (SeqGrabComponent s,
                                            long *ticksLeft);
```

s   Specifies the component instance that identifies your connection to the sequence grabber component. You obtain this value from the Component Manager's `OpenDefaultComponent` or `OpenComponent` function.

ticksLeft   Contains a pointer to a long integer that is to receive a value indicating an estimate of the amount of time remaining for the current record operation. This value is expressed in system ticks.

DESCRIPTION

You can call the `SGGetTimeRemaining` function only after you have started a record operation.

SPECIAL CONSIDERATIONS

This function may take a relatively long time to execute. You should not call it too frequently—once per second is reasonable.

RESULT CODE

seqGrabInfoNotAvailable   –9407   Sequence grabber cannot support request

SGGetTimeBase

The `SGGetTimeBase` function allows you to retrieve a reference to the time base that is being used by a sequence grabber component.

```
pascal ComponentResult SGGetTimeBase (SeqGrabComponent s,
                                       TimeBase *tb);
```

CHAPTER 5

Sequence Grabber Components

s   Specifies the component instance that identifies your connection to the sequence grabber component. You obtain this value from the Component Manager `OpenDefaultComponent` or `OpenComponent` function.

tb Contains a pointer to a time base record that is to receive information about the sequence grabber's time base.

DESCRIPTION

You can examine the time base to monitor an operation or to schedule events based on time values. However, you should not change this time base in any way.

SGSetFlags

The `SGSetFlags` function allows you to pass control information about the current operation to the sequence grabber component.

```
pascal ComponentResult SGSetFlags (SeqGrabComponent s,
                                    long sgFlags);
```

s   Specifies the component instance that identifies your connection to the sequence grabber component. You obtain this value from the Component Manager's `OpenDefaultComponent` or `OpenComponent` function.

sgFlags   Contains flags for the current operation. The following flag is defined (set unused flags to 0):

sgFlagControlledGrab
  Informs the sequence grabber component that you are working with a frame-addressable device to perform a controlled record operation. The sequence grabber and its channel components optimize their operation for this situation. This flag allows the sequence grabber component to trade off speed and quality. Set this flag to 1 if you are performing a controlled grab using a frame-addressable source device.

SGGetFlags

You can retrieve a sequence grabber's control flags by calling the `SGGetFlags` function.

```
pascal ComponentResult SGGetFlags (SeqGrabComponent s,
                                    long *sgFlags) ;
```

s   Specifies the component instance that identifies your connection to the sequence grabber component. You obtain this value from the Component Manager's `OpenDefaultComponent` or `OpenComponent` function.

Sequence Grabber Components

sgFlags   Contains a pointer to a long integer that is to receive the control flags for the current operation. The following flag is defined (unused flags are set to 0):

sgFlagControlledGrab
    Informs the sequence grabber component that you are working with a frame-addressable device to perform a controlled record operation. The sequence grabber and its channel components optimize their operation for this situation. This flag allows the sequence grabber component to trade off speed and quality. This flag is set to 1 if you are performing a controlled grab using a frame-addressable source device.

SEE ALSO

You set these flags by calling the `SGSetFlags` function, which is described in the previous section.

Working With Channel Characteristics

Sequence grabber components use channel components to obtain digitized data from external media. After you create a channel for a sequence grabber component (by calling the `SGNewChannel` function, which is described on page 5-31), you must configure that channel before you start a preview or record operation. The sequence grabber component provides a number of functions that allow you to configure the characteristics of a channel component. Several of these functions work on any channel component. This section discusses these general channel configuration functions.

In addition, sequence grabber components provide functions that are specific to the channel type. Apple currently provides two types of channel components: video channel components and sound channel components. See "Working With Video Channels" beginning on page 5-77 for information about the sequence grabber configuration functions that work only with video channels. See "Working With Sound Channels" beginning on page 5-92 for information about the sequence grabber configuration functions that work only with sound channels.

Use the `SGSetChannelUsage` function to specify how a channel is to be used. You can restrict a channel to use during record or preview operations. In addition, this function allows you to specify whether a channel plays during a record operation. The `SGGetChannelUsage` function enables you to determine a channel's usage.

The `SGGetChannelInfo` function allows you to determine whether a channel has a visual or an audio representation.

The `SGSetChannelPlayFlags` function allows you to influence the speed and quality with which the sequence grabber displays captured data. The `SGGetChannelPlayFlags` function lets you determine these flag settings.

Sequence Grabber Components

The `SGSetChannelMaxFrames` function establishes a limit on the number of frames that the sequence grabber will capture from a channel. The `SGGetChannelMaxFrames` function allows you to determine that limit.

The `SGSetChannelBounds` function allows you to set the display boundary rectangle for a channel. Use the `SGGetChannelBounds` function to determine a channel's boundary rectangle.

The `SGSetChannelVolume` function allows you to control a channel's sound volume. Use the `SGGetChannelVolume` function to determine a channel's volume.

The `SGSetChannelRefCon` function allows you to set the value of a reference constant that is passed to your callback functions (see "Video Channel Callback Functions" beginning on page 5-99 for information about the callback functions that are supported by video channels).

Use the `SGGetChannelSampleDescription` function to retrieve a channel's sample description. The `SGGetChannelTimeScale` function allows you to obtain the channel's time scale.

You can modify or retrieve the channel's clipping region by calling the `SGSetChannelClip` or `SGGetChannelClip` function, respectively. You can work with a channel's transformation matrix by calling the `SGSetChannelMatrix` and `SGGetChannelMatrix` functions.

SGSetChannelUsage

The `SGSetChannelUsage` function specifies how a channel is to be used by the sequence grabber component. The sequence grabber component does not use a channel until you specify how it is to be used. You can specify that a channel is to be used for recording or previewing, or both. In addition, you can control whether the data captured by a channel is displayed during the record or preview operation.

```
pascal ComponentResult SGSetChannelUsage (SGChannel c,
                                          long usage);
```

c Specifies the reference that identifies the channel for this operation. You obtain this reference from the `SGNewChannel` function, described on page 5-31.

usage Contains flags (defined by the `SeqGrabUsageEnum` data type) specifying how the channel is to be used. You may set more than one of these flags to 1. Set unused flags to 0. The following flags are defined:

   seqGrabRecord
      Indicates that the channel is to be used during record operations. Set this flag to 1 to use a channel for recording.

   seqGrabPreview
      Indicates that the channel is to be used during preview operations. Set this flag to 1 to use a channel for previewing.

CHAPTER 5

Sequence Grabber Components

seqGrabPlayDuringRecord
: Indicates that the sequence grabber may play the data captured by this channel during a record operation. If you set this flag to 1, the data from the channel may be played during the record operation, if the destination buffer is onscreen. Video data is displayed; sound data is played through the computer's speaker. However, playing the data may affect the quality of the recorded sequence by causing frames to be dropped. Set this flag to 0 to prevent the channel's data from being played during a record operation.

DESCRIPTION

You cannot call the `SGSetChannelUsage` function during a record or preview operation.

RESULT CODES

notEnoughMemoryToGrab	–9403	Insufficient memory for record operation
notEnoughDiskSpaceToGrab	–9404	Insufficient disk space for record operation
deviceCantMeetRequest	–9408	Device cannot support grabber

SGGetChannelUsage

The `SGGetChannelUsage` function allows you to determine how a channel is to be used by the sequence grabber component.

```
pascal ComponentResult SGGetChannelUsage (SGChannel c,
                                          long *usage);
```

c
: Specifies the reference that identifies the channel for this operation. You obtain this reference from the `SGNewChannel` function, described on page 5-31.

usage
: Contains a pointer to flags indicating how the channel is to be used. More than one flag may be set to 1; unused flags are set to 0. The following flags are defined:

    seqGrabRecord
    : Indicates that the channel is used during record operations.

    seqGrabPreview
    : Indicates that the channel is used during preview operations.

    seqGrabPlayDuringRecord
    : Indicates that the sequence grabber component plays the data captured by this channel during a record operation.

CHAPTER 5

Sequence Grabber Components

SEE ALSO

You establish a channel's usage by calling the `SGSetChannelUsage` function, described in the previous section.

SGGetChannelInfo

The `SGGetChannelInfo` function allows you to determine how a channel's data is represented to the user—as visual or audio data, or both.

```
pascal ComponentResult SGGetChannelInfo (SGChannel c,
                                         long *channelInfo);
```

c   Specifies the reference that identifies the channel for this operation. You obtain this reference from the `SGNewChannel` function, described on page 5-31.

channelInfo
            Contains a pointer to a long integer that is to receive channel information flags. More than one flag may be set to 1. Unused flags are set to 0. The following flags are defined:

    seqGrabHasBounds
            Indicates that the channel has a visual representation. If this flag is set to 1, the channel has a visual representation.

    seqGrabHasVolume
            Indicates that the channel has an audio representation. If this flag is set to 1, the channel has an audio representation.

    seqGrabHasDiscreteSamples
            Indicates that the channel data is organized into discrete frames. If this flag is set to 1, you can use the `SGSetChannelMaxFrames` function (see page 5-63) to limit the number of frames processed in a record operation or the rate at which those frames are processed. If this flag is set to 0, the channel data is not organized into frames. Therefore, you can only limit a record operation by setting the maximum time for the operation.

SGSetChannelPlayFlags

The `SGSetChannelPlayFlags` function allows you to influence the speed and quality with which the sequence grabber displays data from a channel.

```
pascal ComponentResult SGSetChannelPlayFlags (SGChannel c,
                                              long playFlags);
```

Sequence Grabber Components Reference

CHAPTER 5

Sequence Grabber Components

c
: Specifies the reference that identifies the channel for this operation. You obtain this reference from the `SGNewChannel` function, described on page 5-31.

playFlags
: Specifies a long integer that contains flags that influence channel playback. The following values are defined—you must use one of these values:

    channelPlayNormal
    : Instructs the channel component to use its default playback methodology.

    channelPlayFast
    : Instructs the channel component to sacrifice playback quality in order to achieve the specified playback rate.

    channelPlayHighQuality
    : Instructs the channel component to play the channel's data at the highest possible quality—this option sacrifices playback rate for the sake of image quality. This option may reduce the amount of processor time available for recording. This option does not affect the quality of the recorded data, however.

    The following flag is defined—you may use this flag with any of the values defined for this parameter (set unused flags to 0):

    channelPlayAllData
    : Instructs the channel component to try to play all of the data it captures, even the data that is stored in offscreen buffers. This option is useful when you want to be sure that the user sees as much of the captured data as possible. Set this flag to 1 to play all the captured data. You may combine this flag with any of the values defined for the `playFlags` parameter.

DESCRIPTION

The `SGSetChannelPlayFlags` function does not affect the quality of a record operation.

SPECIAL CONSIDERATIONS

You cannot call this function during a record operation; you can call it during a preview operation.

SGGetChannelPlayFlags

The `SGGetChannelPlayFlags` function allows you to retrieve the playback control flags that you set with the `SGSetChannelPlayFlags` function, which is described in the previous section.

```
pascal ComponentResult SGGetChannelPlayFlags (SGChannel c,
                                              long *playFlags);
```

c Specifies the reference that identifies the channel for this operation. You obtain this reference from the `SGNewChannel` function, described on page 5-31.

playFlags Contains a pointer to a long integer that is to receive flags that influence channel playback. The following values are defined:

channelPlayNormal
: The channel component uses its default playback methodology.

channelPlayFast
: The channel component sacrifices playback quality in order to achieve the specified playback rate.

channelPlayHighQuality
: The channel component plays the channel's data at the highest possible quality—this option sacrifices playback rate for the sake of image quality. This option may reduce the amount of processor time available for recording. This option does not affect the quality of the recorded data, however.

The following flag is defined and may be used with any of the values defined for this parameter (unused flags are set to 0):

channelPlayAllData
: The channel component tries to play all of the data it captures, even the data that is stored in offscreen buffers. This option is useful when you want to be sure that the user sees as much of the captured data as possible.

SGSetChannelMaxFrames

The `SGSetChannelMaxFrames` function allows you to limit the number of frames that the sequence grabber will capture from a specified channel. This function works only with channels that have data that is organized into frames, such as video data from a video disc.

```
pascal ComponentResult SGSetChannelMaxFrames (SGChannel c,
                                              long frameCount);
```

CHAPTER 5

Sequence Grabber Components

c   Specifies the reference that identifies the channel for this operation. You obtain this reference from the `SGNewChannel` function, described on page 5-31.

frameCount
              Specifies the maximum number of frames to capture during the preview or record operation. Set this value to –1 to remove the limit.

DESCRIPTION

You can use the `SGSetChannelMaxFrames` function in the context of a time-based function to control the number of frames you collect for each unit of time. For example, if you want to collect one frame of data per second, you can create a function that executes once per second. That function should call `SGSetChannelMaxFrames` to set the maximum frame count to 1. Your application can determine when the frame is captured by calling the `SGGetChannelMaxFrames` function and detecting when that function returns a value of 0. The `SGGetChannelMaxFrames` function is described in the next section.

You may use this function only after you have prepared the sequence grabber component for a record operation or during an active record operation. Note that sequence grabber components clear this value when you prepare for a record operation.

SEE ALSO

You can determine whether a channel's data is organized into frames by calling the `SGGetChannelInfo` function, which is described on page 5-61.

RESULT CODES

| paramErr | –50 | Invalid parameter specified |
| cantDoThatInCurrentMode | –9402 | Request invalid in current mode |

SGGetChannelMaxFrames

The `SGGetChannelMaxFrames` function allows you to determine the number of frames left to be captured from a specified channel.

```
pascal ComponentResult SGGetChannelMaxFrames (SGChannel c,
                                              long *frameCount);
```

c   Specifies the reference that identifies the channel for this operation. You obtain this reference from the `SGNewChannel` function, described on page 5-31.

Sequence Grabber Components

`frameCount`
Contains a pointer to a long integer that is to receive a value specifying the number of frames left to be captured during the preview or record operation. If the returned value is –1, the sequence grabber captures as many frames as it can.

SEE ALSO

You set the starting value by calling the `SGSetChannelMaxFrames` function, which is described in the previous section.

RESULT CODE

`seqGrabInfoNotAvailable`   –9407   Sequence grabber component cannot support request

SGSetChannelBounds

The `SGSetChannelBounds` function allows you to specify a channel's display boundary rectangle. This rectangle defines the destination for data from this channel. This rectangle is defined in the graphics world you establish by calling the `SGSetGWorld` function, described on page 5-29.

```
pascal ComponentResult SGSetChannelBounds (SGChannel c,
                                           const Rect *bounds);
```

`c`
Specifies the reference that identifies the channel for this operation. You obtain this reference from the `SGNewChannel` function, described on page 5-31.

`bounds`
Contains a pointer to a rectangle that defines the channel's display boundary rectangle. This rectangle is defined in the graphics world you establish when you call the `SGSetGWorld` function, described on page 5-29.

DESCRIPTION

You cannot call the `SGSetChannelBounds` function during a record operation.

SPECIAL CONSIDERATIONS

The `SGSetChannelBounds` function adjusts the channel matrix, as appropriate.

CHAPTER 5

Sequence Grabber Components

RESULT CODES

`cantDoThatInCurrentMode`	–9402	Request invalid in current mode
`notEnoughMemoryToGrab`	–9403	Insufficient memory for record operation
`deviceCantMeetRequest`	–9408	Device cannot support grabber component

SGGetChannelBounds

The `SGGetChannelBounds` function allows you to determine a channel's display boundary rectangle.

```
pascal ComponentResult SGGetChannelBounds (SGChannel c,
                                            Rect *bounds);
```

c
: Specifies the reference that identifies the channel for this operation. You obtain this reference from the `SGNewChannel` function, described on page 5-31.

bounds
: Contains a pointer to a rectangle structure that is to receive information about the channel's display boundary rectangle. This rectangle is defined in the graphics world that you establish when you call the `SGSetGWorld` function.

DESCRIPTION

You set the boundary rectangle by calling the `SGSetChannelBounds` function, which is described in the previous section. This rectangle is defined in the graphics world that you establish by calling the `SGSetGWorld` function, described on page 5-29.

SGSetChannelVolume

The `SGSetChannelVolume` function sets a channel's sound volume.

```
pascal ComponentResult SGSetChannelVolume (SGChannel c,
                                            short volume);
```

c
: Specifies the reference that identifies the channel for this operation. You obtain this reference from the `SGNewChannel` function, described on page 5-31.

volume
: Specifies the volume setting of the channel represented as a 16-bit, fixed-point number. The high-order 8 bits contain the integer part of the value; the low-order 8 bits contain the fractional part. Volume values range from –1.0 to 1.0. Negative values play no sound but preserve the absolute value of the volume setting.

CHAPTER 5

Sequence Grabber Components

DESCRIPTION

The sequence grabber component uses this volume setting during playback—this setting does not affect the record level or the volume of the track in the recorded QuickTime movie.

SGGetChannelVolume

The `SGGetChannelVolume` function allows you to determine a channel's sound volume setting.

```
pascal ComponentResult SGGetChannelVolume (SGChannel c,
                                            short *volume);
```

c Specifies the reference that identifies the channel for this operation. You obtain this reference from the `SGNewChannel` function, described on page 5-31.

volume Contains a pointer to an integer that is to receive the volume setting of the channel represented as a 16-bit, fixed-point number. The high-order 8 bits contain the integer part of the value; the low-order 8 bits contain the fractional part. Volume values range from –1.0 to 1.0. Negative values play no sound but preserve the absolute value of the volume setting.

SEE ALSO

You establish the volume setting by calling the `SGSetChannelVolume` function, described in the previous section.

SGSetChannelRefCon

The `SGSetChannelRefCon` function allows you to set the value of a reference constant that is passed to your callback functions (see "Video Channel Callback Functions" beginning on page 5-99 for information about the callback functions that are supported by video channels).

```
pascal ComponentResult SGSetChannelRefCon (SGChannel c,
                                            long refCon);
```

c Specifies the reference that identifies the channel for this operation. You obtain this reference from the `SGNewChannel` function, described on page 5-31.

Sequence Grabber Components Reference   5-67

CHAPTER 5

Sequence Grabber Components

refCon Specifies a reference constant value that is to be passed to your callback functions for this channel. See "Video Channel Callback Functions" on page 5-99 for information about the callback functions that are supported by video channels. Sound channels do not support callback functions.

SPECIAL CONSIDERATIONS

Sound channels do not support callback functions.

SGGetChannelSampleDescription

The SGGetChannelSampleDescription function allows you to retrieve a channel's sample description.

```
pascal ComponentResult SGGetChannelSampleDescription
                        (SGChannel c, Handle sampleDesc);
```

c Identifies the channel for this operation. You provide your connection identifier. You connect to a channel component by calling the SGNewChannel or SGNewChannelFromComponent function, described on page 5-31 and page 5-32, respectively.

sampleDesc Specifies a handle that is to receive the sample description.

DESCRIPTION

The SGGetChannelSampleDescription function allows you to retrieve a channel's current sample description. You may call this function only when the channel is prepared to record or is actually recording.

The channel returns a sample description that is appropriate to the type of data being captured. For video channels, the channel component returns an Image Compression Manager image description structure; for sound channels, you receive a sound description structure, as defined by the Movie Toolbox.

RESULT CODE

cantDoThatInCurrentMode   –9402   Request invalid in current mode

SGGetChannelTimeScale

The SGGetChannelTimeScale function allows you to retrieve a channel's time scale.

```
pascal ComponentResult SGGetChannelTimeScale (SGChannel c,
                                              TimeScale *scale);
```

CHAPTER 5

Sequence Grabber Components

c	Identifies the channel for this operation. You provide your connection identifier. You connect to a channel component by calling the SGNewChannel or SGNewChannelFromComponent function; these functions are described on page 5-31 and page 5-32, respectively.

scale	Contains a pointer to a time scale structure. The channel component places information about its time scale into this structure.

DESCRIPTION

The time scale you obtain by calling the SGGetChannelTimeScale typically corresponds to the time scale of the media that has been created by the channel. You can use this time scale in your data function, which you assign with the SGSetDataProc function (discussed on page 5-35).

SGSetChannelClip

The SGSetChannelClip function allows you to set a channel's clipping region.

```
pascal ComponentResult SGSetChannelClip (SGChannel c,
                                         RgnHandle theClip);
```

c	Identifies the channel for this operation. You provide your connection identifier. You connect to a channel component by calling the SGNewChannel or SGNewChannelFromComponent function, described on page 5-31 and page 5-32, respectively.

theClip	Contains a handle to the new clipping region. Set this parameter to nil to remove the current clipping region. The channel component makes a copy of this handle; it is your application's responsibility to dispose of this handle when you are finished with it.

DESCRIPTION

The SGSetChannelClip function allows you to apply a clipping region to a channel's display region. By default, channel components do not apply a clipping region to their displayed image.

SEE ALSO

You may retrieve a channel's clipping region by calling the SGGetChannelClip function, described in the next section.

CHAPTER 5

Sequence Grabber Components

SGGetChannelClip

The `SGGetChannelClip` function allows you to retrieve a channel's clipping region.

```
pascal ComponentResult SGGetChannelClip (SGChannel c,
                                         RgnHandle *theClip);
```

c   Identifies the channel for this operation. You provide your
            connection identifier. You connect to a channel component by calling the
            `SGNewChannel` or `SGNewChannelFromComponent` function, described
            on page 5-31 and page 5-32, respectively.

theClip   Contains a pointer to a handle that is to receive the clipping region. Your
            application is responsible for disposing of this handle. If there is no
            clipping region, the channel component sets this handle to `nil`.

Note
Some devices may not support clipping. ◆

SEE ALSO

You may set a channel's clipping region by calling the `SGSetChannelClip` function, which is discussed in the previous section.

SGSetChannelMatrix

The `SGSetChannelMatrix` function allows you to set a channel's display transformation matrix.

```
pascal ComponentResult SGSetChannelMatrix (SGChannel c,
                                           const MatrixRecord *m);
```

c   Identifies the channel for this operation. You provide your
            connection identifier. You connect to a channel component by calling the
            `SGNewChannel` or `SGNewChannelFromComponent` function, discussed
            on page 5-31 and page 5-32, respectively.

m   Contains a pointer to a matrix structure, as defined by the Movie Toolbox
            (see the chapter "Movie Toolbox" in *Inside Macintosh: QuickTime* for more
            information about matrix structures). Set this parameter to `nil` to select
            the identity matrix.

Sequence Grabber Components

DESCRIPTION

The `SGSetChannelMatrix` function allows you to specify a display transformation matrix for a video channel. The channel uses this matrix to transform its video image into the destination window. If the channel cannot accommodate your matrix, it returns an appropriate result code. Note that you may not call this function when you are recording.

Other channel component functions may affect this matrix. The `SGSetChannelBounds` function sets the matrix values so that the matrix maps the channel's output to the channel's boundary rectangle (this function is discussed beginning on page 5-65). The `SGSetVideoRect` function modifies the matrix so that the specified video rectangle appears in the existing destination rectangle (see page 5-78 for more information about this function).

RESULT CODES

```
matrixErr                -2203    Invalid matrix
deviceCantMeetRequest    -9408    Device cannot support grabber
```

SEE ALSO

You may retrieve a channel's matrix by calling the `SGGetChannelMatrix` function, which is discussed next.

SGGetChannelMatrix

The `SGGetChannelMatrix` function allows you to retrieve a channel's display transformation matrix.

```
pascal ComponentResult SGGetChannelMatrix (SGChannel c,
                                           MatrixRecord *m);
```

c   Identifies the channel for this operation. You provide your connection identifier. You connect to a channel component by calling the `SGNewChannel` or `SGNewChannelFromComponent` function, described on page 5-31 and page 5-32, respectively.

m   Contains a pointer to a matrix structure, as defined by the Movie Toolbox (see "Movie Toolbox" in *Inside Macintosh: QuickTime* for more information about matrix structures). The channel component places its current matrix values into this matrix structure.

SEE ALSO

You may set a channel's matrix by calling the `SGSetChannelMatrix` function, which is discussed in the previous section.

Working With Channel Devices

Sequence grabbers provide a number of functions that allow you to determine the device that is attached to a given sequence grabber channel. These devices allow the channel component to control the digitizing equipment. For example, video channels use video digitizer components, and sound channels use sound input drivers. Your application can use these routines to present a list of available devices to the user, allowing the user to select a specific device for each channel.

You may use the SGGetChannelDeviceList function to retrieve a list of devices that may be used with a specified channel. You dispose of this device list by calling the SGDisposeDeviceList function. You can place one or more device names into a menu by calling the SGAppendDeviceListToMenu function. You can use the SGSetChannelDevice function to assign a device to a channel.

Some of these functions use a device list structure to pass information about one or more channel devices. The SGDeviceListRecord data type defines the format of the device list structure.

```
typedef struct SGDeviceListRecord {
    short           count;              /* count of devices */
    short           selectedIndex;      /* current device */
    long            reserved;           /* set to 0 */
    SGDeviceName    entry[1];           /* device names */
} SGDeviceListRecord, *SGDeviceListPtr, **SGDeviceList;
```

Field descriptions

count
: Indicates the number of devices described by this structure. The value of this field corresponds to the number of entries in the device name array defined by the entry field.

selectedIndex
: Identifies the currently active device. The value of this field corresponds to the appropriate entry in the device name array defined by the entry field. Note that this value is 0-relative; that is, the first entry has an index number of 0, the second's value is 1, and so on.

reserved
: Reserved for Apple. Always set to 0.

entry
: Contains an array of device name structures. Each structure corresponds to one valid device. The count field indicates the number of entries in this array. The SGDeviceName data type defines the format of a device name structure; this data type is discussed next.

Device list structures contain an array of device name structures. Each device name structure identifies a single device that may be used by the channel. The SGDeviceName data type defines the format of a device name structure.

Sequence Grabber Components

```
typedef struct SGDeviceName {
    Str63       name;        /* device name */
    Handle      icon;        /* device icon */
    long        flags;       /* flags */
    long        refCon;      /* set to 0 */
    long        reserved;    /* set to 0 */
} SGDeviceName;
```

Field descriptions

`name` Contains the name of the device. For video digitizer components, this field contains the component's name as specified in the component resource. For sound input drivers, this field contains the driver name.

`icon` Contains a handle to the device's icon. Some devices may support an icon, which you may choose to present to the user. If the device does not support an icon, or if you choose not to retrieve this information (by setting the `sgDeviceListWithIcons` flag to 0 when you call the `SGGetChannelDeviceList` function), this field is set to `nil`.

`flags` Reflects the current status of the device. The sequence grabber sets these flags when you retrieve a device list. The following flag is defined:

`sgDeviceNameFlagDeviceUnavailable`
When set to 1, this flag indicates that this device is not currently available.

`refCon` Reserved for Apple. Always set to 0.

`reserved` Reserved for Apple. Always set to 0.

SGGetChannelDeviceList

The `SGGetChannelDeviceList` function allows you to retrieve a list of the devices that are valid for a specified channel.

```
pascal ComponentResult SGGetChannelDeviceList (SGChannel c,
                                               long selectionFlags,
                                               SGDeviceList *list);
```

`c` Identifies the channel for this operation. You provide your connection identifier. You connect to a channel component by calling the `SGNewChannel` or `SGNewChannelFromComponent` function, discussed on page 5-31 and page 5-32, respectively.

Sequence Grabber Components

selectionFlags
: Controls the data returned for each device. The following flags are defined:

    sgDeviceListWithIcons
    : Specifies whether you want to retrieve an icon for each device. If you set this flag to 1, the sequence grabber returns an icon for each device in the list, in the `icon` field. If you set this flag to 0, the sequence grabber sets the `icon` fields to 0.

    sgDeviceListDontCheckAvailability
    : Controls whether the sequence grabber verifies that each device is currently available. If you set this flag to 1, the sequence grabber does not check the availability of each device. Otherwise, the sequence grabber checks each device's availability, and sets the `sgDeviceNameFlagDeviceUnavailable` flag appropriately in each device name structure that is returned.

        Note that checking device availability slows this function. In general, however, you should check availability if you plan to present a list of devices to the user. Otherwise, the user may select a device that is unavailable.

list
: Defines a pointer to a device list structure pointer. The sequence grabber creates a device name structure and returns a pointer to that structure in the field referred to by this parameter. When you are done with the list, use the `SGDisposeDeviceList` function (described in the next section) to dispose of the memory used by the list.

DESCRIPTION

This function allows you to retrieve a list of the devices that may be used with a channel. Each entry in this list identifies a valid device by name. Your application may then place these device names into a menu using the `SGAppendDeviceListToMenu` function, which is described on page 5-75.

This function can be useful for retrieving the name of the current device. Retrieve the device list and use the `selectedIndex` field to determine which device is currently in use.

RESULT CODES

Memory Manager errors

SEE ALSO

When you are done with the list, use the `SGDisposeDeviceList` function to dispose of the memory used by the list. This function is discussed next.

CHAPTER 5

Sequence Grabber Components

SGDisposeDeviceList

The `SGDisposeDeviceList` function allows you to dispose of a device list.

```
pascal ComponentResult SGDisposeDeviceList (SeqGrabComponent s,
                                            SGDeviceList list);
```

s
: Specifies the component instance that identifies your connection to the sequence grabber component. You obtain this value from the Component Manager's `OpenDefaultComponent` or `OpenComponent` function.

list
: Defines a pointer to a device list structure pointer. The sequence grabber disposes of the memory used by the device list structure.

DESCRIPTION

You must use this function to dispose of the memory used by a device list structure. Do not use Memory Manager functions to do so.

RESULT CODES

Memory Manager errors

SGAppendDeviceListToMenu

The `SGAppendDeviceListToMenu` function allows you to place a list of device names into a specified menu.

```
pascal ComponentResult SGAppendDeviceListToMenu
                        (SeqGrabComponent s,
                        SGDeviceList list, MenuHandle mh);
```

s
: Specifies the component instance that identifies your connection to the sequence grabber component. You obtain this value from the Component Manager's `OpenDefaultComponent` or `OpenComponent` function.

list
: Defines a pointer to a device list structure pointer. The sequence grabber appends the name of each device in the list to the menu specified by the mh parameter. If the `sgDeviceNameFlagDeviceUnavailable` flag is set to 1 for a device in the list, the sequence grabber disables the menu item corresponding to that device.

mh
: Specifies the menu to which the device names are to be appended.

CHAPTER 5

Sequence Grabber Components

DESCRIPTION

You may use the `SGAppendDeviceListToMenu` function to present a list of valid devices to the user. The user may then select a device from the list. You can assign that device to a channel by calling the `SGSetChannelDevice` function. Note that, if you choose to have the sequence grabber check the availability of each device (by setting the `sgDeviceListDontCheckAvailability` flag to 0 with the `SGGetChannelDeviceList` function), the sequence grabber will disable menu items that correspond to unavailable devices. This prevents the user from selecting a device that cannot be used.

RESULT CODE

paramErr   –50   Invalid parameter value

SEE ALSO

You obtain the device list by calling the `SGGetChannelDeviceList` function, which is discussed on page 5-73.

SGSetChannelDevice

The `SGSetChannelDevice` function allows you to assign a device to a channel.

```
pascal ComponentResult SGSetChannelDevice (SGChannel c,
                                            StringPtr name);
```

c   Identifies the channel for this operation. You provide your connection identifier. You connect to a channel component by calling the `SGNewChannel` or `SGNewChannelFromComponent` function, discussed on page 5-31 and page 5-32, respectively.

name   Points to the device's name string. This name is contained in the `name` field of the appropriate device name structure in the device list.

DESCRIPTION

When you call the `SGSetChannelDevice` function, the sequence grabber channel tries to use the specified device, in place of the device currently in use. You must obtain the device name from the channel's device list.

CHAPTER 5

Sequence Grabber Components

RESULT CODES

`paramErr`	−50	Invalid parameter value
`deviceCantMeetRequest`	−9408	Device cannot support grabber

SEE ALSO

You obtain the device list by calling the `SGGetChannelDeviceList` function, which is described on page 5-73.

Working With Video Channels

Sequence grabber components provide a number of functions that allow you to configure the grabber's video channels. This section describes these configuration functions, which you can use only with video channels. You can determine whether a channel has a visual representation by calling the `SGGetChannelInfo` function, which is described on page 5-61. If you want to configure a sound channel, use the functions described in "Working With Sound Channels" beginning on page 5-92. If you want to configure general attributes of a channel, use the functions described in "Working With Channel Characteristics" beginning on page 5-58.

The `SGGetSrcVideoBounds` function allows you to determine the coordinates of the source video boundary rectangle. This rectangle defines the size of the source video image being captured by the video channel. You can use the `SGSetVideoRect` function to specify a part of the source video boundary rectangle to be captured by the channel. The `SGGetVideoRect` function allows you to determine the active source video rectangle.

Typically, the sequence grabber component uses the Image Compression Manager to compress the video data it captures. You can control many aspects of this image-compression process. Use the `SGSetVideoCompressorType` function to specify the type of image compressor to use. You can determine the type of image compressor currently in use by calling the `SGGetVideoCompressorType` function. You can specify a particular image compressor and set many image-compression parameters by calling the `SGSetVideoCompressor` function. You can determine which image compressor is being used and its parameter settings by calling the `SGGetVideoCompressor` function.

The channel components that supply video data to a sequence grabber component typically work with a video digitizer component (see the chapter "Video Digitizer Components" in this book for a complete description of video digitizer components). Sequence grabber components provide functions that allow you to work with a channel's video digitizer component. You can use the `SGGetVideoDigitizerComponent` function to determine which video digitizer component is supplying data to a specified channel component. You can set a channel's video digitizer by calling the `SGSetVideoDigitizerComponent` function. If you change any video digitizer settings by calling the video digitizer component directly, you should inform the sequence grabber component by calling the `SGVideoDigitizerChanged` function.

Some video source data may contain unacceptable levels of visual noise or artifacts. One technique for removing this noise is to capture the image and then reduce it in size. During the size reduction process, the noise can be filtered out. Sequence grabber components provide functions that allow you to filter the input video data. The `SGSetCompressBuffer` function sets a filter buffer for a video channel. The `SGGetCompressBuffer` function returns information about your filter buffer.

You can work with a video channel's frame rate by calling the `SGSetFrameRate` and `SGGetFrameRate` functions. You can control whether a channel uses an offscreen buffer by calling the `SGSetUseScreenBuffer` and `SGGetUseScreenBuffer` functions.

SGGetSrcVideoBounds

The `SGGetSrcVideoBounds` function allows you to determine the size of the source video boundary rectangle. This rectangle defines the size of the source video image. For video channel components that work with video digitizer components, this rectangle corresponds to the video digitizer's active source rectangle (see the chapter "Video Digitizer Components" in this book for more information).

```
pascal ComponentResult SGGetSrcVideoBounds (SGChannel c, Rect *r);
```

c Specifies the reference that identifies the channel for this operation. You obtain this reference from the `SGNewChannel` function, described on page 5-31.

r Contains a pointer to a rectangle structure that is to receive information about the source video boundary rectangle.

RESULT CODE

paramErr   –50   Invalid parameter specified

SGSetVideoRect

The `SGSetVideoRect` function allows you to specify a part of the source video image that is to be captured by the sequence grabber component. This rectangle must reside within the boundaries of the source video boundary rectangle. You obtain the dimensions of the source video boundary rectangle by calling the `SGGetSrcVideoBounds` function, described in the previous section. If you do not use this function to set a source rectangle, the sequence grabber component captures the entire video image, as defined by the source video boundary rectangle.

```
pascal ComponentResult SGSetVideoRect (SGChannel c, Rect *r);
```

CHAPTER 5

Sequence Grabber Components

c Specifies the reference that identifies the channel for this operation. You obtain this reference from the `SGNewChannel` function, described on page 5-31.

r Contains a pointer to the dimensions of the rectangle that defines the portion of the source video image to be captured. This rectangle must lie within the boundaries of the source video boundary rectangle, which you can obtain by calling the `SGGetSrcVideoBounds` function.

DESCRIPTION

For video channel components that receive their data from video digitizer components, this function sets the video digitizer component's digitizer rectangle. See the chapter "Video Digitizer Components" in this book for information about video digitizer components.

You cannot call this function during a record operation.

RESULT CODES

`cantDoThatInCurrentMode`	–9402	Request invalid in current mode
`notEnoughMemoryToGrab`	–9403	Insufficient memory for record operation

SGGetVideoRect

The `SGGetVideoRect` function allows you to determine the portion of the source video image that is to be captured. Use the `SGSetVideoRect` function, which is described in the previous section, to set the dimensions of this rectangle.

```
pascal ComponentResult SGGetVideoRect (SGChannel c, Rect *r);
```

c Specifies the reference that identifies the channel for this operation. You obtain this reference from the `SGNewChannel` function, described on page 5-31.

r Contains a pointer to a rectangle structure that is to receive the dimensions of the rectangle that defines the portion of the source video image to be captured.

DESCRIPTION

If you have not set a source rectangle, the sequence grabber captures the entire source video image, as defined by the source video boundary rectangle.

SEE ALSO

You can obtain the dimensions of the source video boundary rectangle by calling the `SGGetSrcVideoBounds` function, described on page 5-78.

SGSetVideoCompressorType

The `SGSetVideoCompressorType` function allows you to specify the type of image compression to be applied to the captured video images.

```
pascal ComponentResult SGSetVideoCompressorType (SGChannel c,
                                    OSType compressorType);
```

c
: Specifies the reference that identifies the channel for this operation. You obtain this reference from the `SGNewChannel` function, described on page 5-31.

compressorType
: Specifies the type of image compression to use. The value of this parameter must correspond to one of the image compressor types supported by the Image Compression Manager. Currently, six `CodecType` values are provided by Apple. You should use the `GetCodecNameList` function to retrieve these names, so that your application can take advantage of new compressor types that may be added in the future. For each `CodecType` value in the following list, the corresponding compression method is also identified by its text string name.

Compressor type	Compressor name
`'rpza'`	video compressor
`'jpeg'`	photo compressor
`'rle '`	animation compressor
`'raw '`	raw compressor
`'smc '`	graphics compressor
`'cvid'`	compact video compressor

See the chapter "Image Compression Manager" in *Inside Macintosh: QuickTime* for information about valid compressor types. If this value is set to 0, the default compression type is selected.

DESCRIPTION

In addition, the `SGSetVideoCompressorType` function resets all image-compression parameters to their default values. You can then use the `SGSetVideoCompressor` function, described on page 5-82, to change the compression parameters.

SPECIAL CONSIDERATIONS

You cannot call the `SGSetVideoCompressorType` function during a record operation or after you have prepared the sequence grabber component for a record operation (by calling the `SGPrepare` function, described on page 5-43).

CHAPTER 5

Sequence Grabber Components

RESULT CODES

`cantDoThatInCurrentMode`	–9402	Request invalid in current mode
`notEnoughMemoryToGrab`	–9403	Insufficient memory for record operation
`deviceCantMeetRequest`	–9408	Device cannot support grabber

SGGetVideoCompressorType

The `SGGetVideoCompressorType` function allows you to determine the type of image compression that is being applied to a channel's video data.

```
pascal ComponentResult SGGetVideoCompressorType (SGChannel c,
                                    OSType *compressorType);
```

c
: Specifies the reference that identifies the channel for this operation. You obtain this reference from the `SGNewChannel` function, described on page 5-31.

compressorType
: Contains a pointer to an `OSType` field that is to receive information about the type of image compression to use. The returned value must correspond to one of the image compressor types supported by the Image Compression Manager. Currently, six `CodecType` values are provided by Apple. You should use the `GetCodecNameList` function to retrieve these names, so that your application can take advantage of new compressor types that may be added in the future. For each `CodecType` value in the following list, the corresponding compression method is also identified by its text string name.

Compressor type	Compressor name
`'rpza'`	video compressor
`'jpeg'`	photo compressor
`'rle '`	animation compressor
`'raw '`	raw compressor
`'smc '`	graphics compressor
`'cvid'`	compact video compressor

See the chapter "Image Compression Manager" in *Inside Macintosh: QuickTime* for information about valid compressor types.

SEE ALSO

You can set the image-compression type by calling the `SGSetVideoCompressorType` function, which is described in the previous section.

SGSetVideoCompressor

The `SGSetVideoCompressor` function allows you to specify many of the parameters that control image compression of the video data captured by a video channel.

```
pascal ComponentResult SGSetVideoCompressor (SGChannel c,
                            short depth,
                            CompressorComponent compressor,
                            CodecQ spatialQuality,
                            CodecQ temporalQuality,
                            long keyFrameRate);
```

`c`
: Specifies the reference that identifies the channel for this operation. You obtain this reference from the `SGNewChannel` function, described on page 5-31.

`depth`
: Specifies the depth at which the image is likely to be viewed. Image compressors may use this as an indication of the color or grayscale resolution of the compressed images. If you set this parameter to 0, the sequence grabber component determines the appropriate value for the source image. Values of 1, 2, 4, 8, 16, 24, and 32 indicate the number of bits per pixel for color images. Values of 33, 34, 36, and 40 indicate 1-bit, 2-bit, 4-bit, and 8-bit grayscale, respectively, for grayscale images. Your program can determine which depths are supported by a given compressor by examining the compressor information structure returned by the Image Compression Manager's `GetCodecInfo` function (see the chapter "Image Compression Manager" in *Inside Macintosh: QuickTime* for more information on the `GetCodecInfo` function).

  Set this parameter to 0 to leave the depth unchanged.

`compressor`
: Specifies the image compressor identifier. Specify a particular compressor by setting this parameter to its compressor identifier. You can obtain this identifier from the Image Compression Manager's `GetCodecNameList` function. Set this parameter to 0 to leave the compressor unchanged.

`spatialQuality`
: Specifies the desired compressed image quality. See the chapter "Image Compression Manager" in *Inside Macintosh: QuickTime* for valid values.

`temporalQuality`
: Specifies the desired sequence temporal quality. This parameter governs the level of compression you desire with respect to information between successive frames in the sequence. Set this parameter to 0 to prevent the image compressor from applying temporal compression to the sequence. See the chapter "Image Compression Manager" in *Inside Macintosh: QuickTime* for other valid values.

`keyFrameRate`
: Specifies the maximum number of frames allowed between key frames. Key frames provide points from which a temporally compressed sequence may be decompressed. Use this parameter to control the

frequency at which the image compressor places key frames into the compressed sequence. For more information about key frames, see the chapter "Image Compression Manager" in *Inside Macintosh: QuickTime*.

The compressor determines the optimum placement for key frames based upon the amount of redundancy between adjacent images in the sequence. Consequently, the compressor may insert key frames more frequently than you have requested. However, the compressor will never place key frames less often than is indicated by the setting of the `keyFrameRate` parameter. The compressor ignores this parameter if you have not requested temporal compression (that is, you have set the `temporalQuality` parameter to 0).

DESCRIPTION

Typically, you are interested in setting only one or two of these parameters. You can call the `SGGetVideoCompressor` function to retrieve the values of all of the parameters, and you can then use that information to supply values for the parameters you do not wish to change.

SPECIAL CONSIDERATIONS

You may call this function during a record operation or after you have prepared the sequence grabber component for a record operation only if you set the `depth` and `compressor` parameters to 0. This allows you to work with the quality or key frame rate configuration while you are capturing a sequence.

RESULT CODES

paramErr	–50	Invalid parameter specified
cantDoThatInCurrentMode	–9402	Request invalid in current mode
notEnoughMemoryToGrab	–9403	Insufficient memory for record operation
deviceCantMeetRequest	–9408	Device cannot support grabber

SGGetVideoCompressor

The `SGGetVideoCompressor` function allows you to determine a channel's current image-compression parameters.

```
pascal ComponentResult SGGetVideoCompressor (SGChannel c,
                        short *depth,
                        compressorComponent *compressor,
                        CodecQ *spatialQuality,
                        CodecQ *temporalQuality,
                        long *keyFrameRate);
```

Sequence Grabber Components

`c`
: Specifies the reference that identifies the channel for this operation. You obtain this reference from the `SGNewChannel` function, described on page 5-31.

`depth`
: Contains a pointer to a field that is to receive the depth at which the image is likely to be viewed. Image compressors may use this as an indication of the color or grayscale resolution of the compressed images. If the value returned by this function is 0, the sequence grabber component determines the appropriate value for the source image. Values of 1, 2, 4, 8, 16, 24, and 32 indicate the number of bits per pixel for color images. Values of 33, 34, 36, and 40 indicate 1-bit, 2-bit, 4-bit, and 8-bit grayscale, respectively, for grayscale images. Your program can determine which depths are supported by a given compressor by examining the compressor information record (defined by the `CodecInfo` data type) returned by the Image Compression Manager's `GetCodecInfo` function (see the chapter "Image Compression Manager" in *Inside Macintosh: QuickTime* for more information on the `GetCodecInfo` function).

    If you are not interested in this information, set this parameter to `nil`.

`compressor`
: Contains a pointer a field that is to receive an image compressor identifier. If you are not interested in this information, set this parameter to `nil`.

`spatialQuality`
: Contains a pointer to a field that is to receive the desired compressed image quality. See the chapter "Image Compression Manager" in *Inside Macintosh: QuickTime* for valid values. If you are not interested in this information, set this parameter to `nil`.

`temporalQuality`
: Contains a pointer to a field that is to receive the desired sequence temporal quality. This parameter governs the level of compression you desire with respect to information between successive frames in the sequence. If the returned value is set to 0, the image compressor is not performing temporal compression on the source video. See the chapter "Image Compression Manager" in *Inside Macintosh: QuickTime* for other valid values.

    If you are not interested in this information, set this parameter to `nil`.

`keyFrameRate`
: Contains a pointer to a field that is to receive the maximum number of frames allowed between key frames. Key frames provide points from which a temporally compressed sequence may be decompressed. This value controls the frequency at which the image compressor places key frames into the compressed sequence. The compressor determines the optimum placement for key frames based upon the amount of redundancy between adjacent images in the sequence. Consequently, the compressor may insert key frames more frequently than you have

Sequence Grabber Components

requested. However, the compressor will never place key frames less often than is indicated by the setting of the `keyFrameRate` parameter. The compressor ignores this value if you have not requested temporal compression (that is, you have set the `temporalQuality` parameter of the `SGSetVideoCompressor` function to 0).

If you are not interested in this information, set this parameter to `nil`.

SEE ALSO

You can set these parameters by calling the `SGSetVideoCompressor` function, which is described in the previous section.

SGSetVideoDigitizerComponent

The `SGSetVideoDigitizerComponent` function allows you to assign a video digitizer component to a video channel.

```
pascal ComponentResult SGSetVideoDigitizerComponent
                        (SGChannel c, ComponentInstance vdig);
```

c   Specifies the reference that identifies the channel for this operation. You obtain this reference from the `SGNewChannel` function, described on page 5-31.

vdig   Contains a component instance that identifies a connection to a video digitizer component. The specified video channel component uses this video digitizer component to obtain its source video data. For more information about video digitizer components, see the chapter "Video Digitizer Components" in this book.

DESCRIPTION

Typically, the video channel component locates its own video digitizer component. Consequently, you may not need to use the `SGSetVideoDigitizerComponent` function.

SPECIAL CONSIDERATIONS

You cannot use the `SGSetVideoDigitizerComponent` function during a record operation. Many values are reinitialized as a result of changing digitizers.

RESULT CODE

cantDoThatInCurrentMode   –9402   Request invalid in current mode

Sequence Grabber Components Reference

SGGetVideoDigitizerComponent

The `SGGetVideoDigitizerComponent` function allows you to determine the video digitizer component that is providing source video to a video channel component. You can use this function to obtain access to the video digitizer component so that you can set its parameters, if you so desire. See the chapter "Video Digitizer Components" in this book for information about video digitizer components.

```
pascal ComponentInstance SGGetVideoDigitizerComponent
                                                    (SGChannel c);
```

c   Specifies the reference that identifies the channel for this operation. You obtain this reference from the `SGNewChannel` function, described on page 5-31.

DESCRIPTION

The `SGGetVideoDigitizerComponent` function returns a component instance that identifies the connection between the video channel component and its video digitizer component. If the video channel component does not use a video digitizer component, this returned value is set to `nil`.

SPECIAL CONSIDERATIONS

If you change any video digitizer component parameters, be sure to notify the sequence grabber component by calling the `SGVideoDigitizerChanged` function, which is described in the next section. In addition, you should not change any video digitizer component parameters during a record operation.

SGVideoDigitizerChanged

The `SGVideoDigitizerChanged` function allows you to notify the sequence grabber component whenever you change the configuration of a video channel's video digitizer.

```
pascal ComponentResult SGVideoDigitizerChanged (SGChannel c);
```

c   Specifies the reference that identifies the channel for this operation. You obtain this reference from the `SGNewChannel` function, described on page 5-31.

DESCRIPTION

The sequence grabber and its video channels maintain information about the configuration of any video digitizer components that are currently in use.

CHAPTER 5

Sequence Grabber Components

IMPORTANT
It is very important to notify the sequence grabber of any configuration changes you make. ▲

SPECIAL CONSIDERATIONS

You should not change the configuration of the video digitizer during a record operation.

SEE ALSO

You can obtain access to a video channel's video digitizer component by calling the `SGGetVideoDigitizerComponent` function, which is described in the previous section.

RESULT CODE

cantDoThatInCurrentMode   –9402   Request invalid in current mode

SGSetCompressBuffer

Some video source data may contain unacceptable levels of visual noise or artifacts. One technique for removing this noise is to capture the image and then reduce it in size. During the size reduction process, the noise can be filtered out.

The `SGSetCompressBuffer` function creates a filter buffer for a video channel. Logically, this buffer sits between the source video buffer and the destination rectangle you set with the `SGSetChannelBounds` function, described on page 5-65. The filter buffer should be larger than the area enclosed by the destination rectangle.

```
pascal ComponentResult SGSetCompressBuffer (SGChannel c,
                                            short depth,
                                            const Rect *compressSize);
```

c   Specifies the reference that identifies the channel for this operation. You obtain this reference from the `SGNewChannel` function, described on page 5-31.

depth   Specifies the pixel depth of the filter buffer. If you set this parameter to 0, the sequence grabber component uses the depth of the video buffer.

compressSize
            Contains a pointer to the dimensions of the filter buffer. This buffer should be larger than the destination buffer. Set this parameter to `nil`, or set the coordinates of this rectangle to 0 (specifying an empty rectangle), to stop filtering the input source video data.

DESCRIPTION

If you establish a filter buffer for a channel, the sequence grabber component places the captured video image into the filter buffer, then copies the image into the destination buffer. This process may be too slow for some record operations, but can be useful during controlled record operations (where the source video can be read on a frame-by-frame basis). Be sure to call this function before you prepare the sequence grabber component for the record or playback operation.

Figure 5-2 demonstrates the process by which the `SGSetCompressBuffer` function creates a filter buffer for a video channel.

Figure 5-2 The effect of the `SGSetCompressBuffer` function

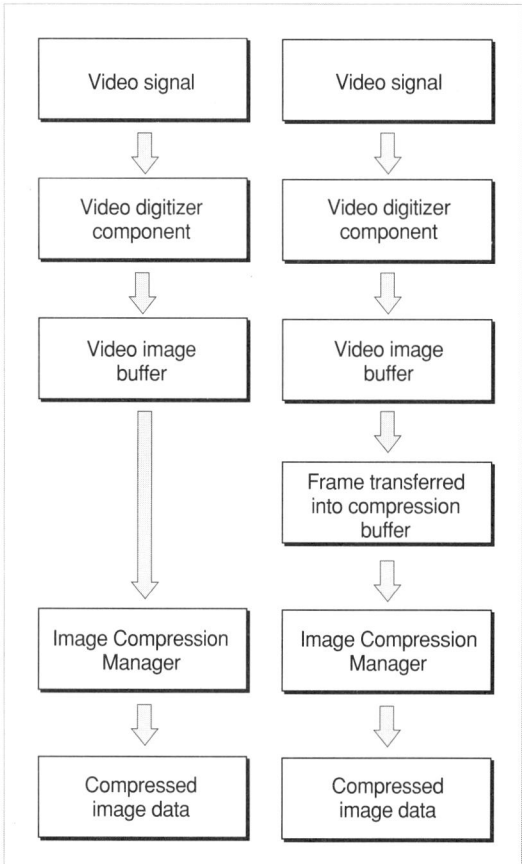

SEE ALSO

If you want to perform some more elaborate image filtering, you may define a transfer-frame function. See "Video Channel Callback Functions" beginning on page 5-99 for more information about transfer-frame functions.

RESULT CODE

cantDoThatInCurrentMode   –9402   Request invalid in current mode

SGGetCompressBuffer

The `SGGetCompressBuffer` function returns information about the filter buffer you have established for a video channel.

```
pascal ComponentResult SGGetCompressBuffer (SGChannel c,
                                            short *depth,
                                            Rect *compressSize);
```

c
: Specifies the reference that identifies the channel for this operation. You obtain this reference from the `SGNewChannel` function, described on page 5-31.

depth
: Contains a pointer to a field that is to receive the pixel depth of the filter buffer. If the returned value is set to 0, the sequence grabber is not filtering the input video data.

compressSize
: Contains a pointer to a rectangle structure that is to receive the dimensions of the filter buffer. If the sequence grabber is not filtering the input video data, it returns an empty rectangle (all coordinates set to 0).

SEE ALSO

You set a filter buffer by calling the `SGSetCompressBuffer` function, which is described in the previous section.

SGSetFrameRate

The `SGSetFrameRate` function allows you to specify a video channel's frame rate for recording.

```
pascal ComponentResult SGSetFrameRate (SGChannel c,
                                       Fixed frameRate);
```

c
: Identifies the channel for this operation. You provide your connection identifier. You connect to a channel component by calling the `SGNewChannel` or `SGNewChannelFromComponent` function, discussed on page 5-31 and page 5-32, respectively.

frameRate
: Specifies the desired frame rate. Set this parameter to 0 to select the channel's default frame rate. Typically, this corresponds to the fastest rate that the channel can support.

CHAPTER 5

Sequence Grabber Components

DESCRIPTION

The `SGSetFrameRate` function allows you to control a video channel's frame rate. Note that the digitizing hardware may not be able to support the full rate you specify. If you specify too high a rate, the sequence grabber operates at the highest rate that it can support. Note that you may not call this function when you are recording.

RESULT CODES

paramErr	–50	Invalid parameter value
cantDoThatInCurrentMode	–9402	Request invalid in current mode

SEE ALSO

You can retrieve a channel's current frame rate by calling the `SGGetFrameRate` function, which is described next.

SGGetFrameRate

The `SGGetFrameRate` function allows you to retrieve a video channel's frame rate for recording.

```
pascal ComponentResult SGGetFrameRate (SGChannel c,
                                       Fixed *frameRate);
```

c   Identifies the channel for this operation. You provide your connection identifier. You connect to a channel component by calling the `SGNewChannel` or `SGNewChannelFromComponent` function, discussed on page 5-31 and page 5-32, respectively.

frameRate   Contains a pointer to a field to receive the current frame rate. The sequence grabber returns the channel's current frame rate.

DESCRIPTION

The `SGGetFrameRate` function returns the channel's current rate. By default, the channel records at the fastest rate it can support. In this case, the channel sets the field referred to by the `frameRate` parameter to 0.

SEE ALSO

You can set a channel's frame rate by calling the `SGSetFrameRate` function, which is described in the previous section.

SGSetUseScreenBuffer

The `SGSetUseScreenBuffer` function allows you to control whether a video channel uses an offscreen buffer.

```
pascal ComponentResult SGSetUseScreenBuffer (SGChannel c,
                                             Boolean useScreenBuffer);
```

c Identifies the channel for this operation. You provide your connection identifier. You connect to a channel component by calling the `SGNewChannel` or `SGNewChannelFromComponent` function, discussed on page 5-31 and page 5-32, respectively.

useScreenBuffer
Indicates whether to use an offscreen buffer. If you set this parameter to `true`, the channel draws directly to the screen. If you set it to `false`, the channel may use an offscreen buffer. If the channel cannot work with offscreen buffers, it ignores this parameter.

DESCRIPTION

By default, video channels try to draw directly to the screen. The `SGSetUseScreenBuffer` function allows you to direct a video channel to draw to an offscreen buffer. If the channel cannot draw offscreen, it ignores this function. Note that you may not call this function when you are recording.

Directing a channel to draw offscreen may be useful if you are performing transformations on the data before displaying it (such as blending it with another graphical image).

RESULT CODES

paramErr	–50	Invalid parameter value
cantDoThatInCurrentMode	–9402	Request invalid in current mode

SEE ALSO

You can determine whether you have allowed a channel to draw offscreen by calling the `SGGetUseScreenBuffer` function, which is described next.

SGGetUseScreenBuffer

The `SGGetUseScreenBuffer` function allows you to determine whether a video channel is allowed to use an offscreen buffer.

```
pascal ComponentResult SGGetUseScreenBuffer (SGChannel c,
                                             Boolean *useScreenBuffer);
```

CHAPTER 5

Sequence Grabber Components

c
: Identifies the channel for this operation. You provide your connection identifier. You connect to a channel component by calling the `SGNewChannel` or `SGNewChannelFromComponent` function, discussed on page 5-31 and page 5-32, respectively.

useScreenBuffer
: Contains a pointer to a Boolean value. The sequence grabber sets this field to reflect whether you have allowed the channel to draw offscreen. If this field is set to `true`, the channel draws directly to the screen. If it is set to `false`, the channel may use an offscreen buffer. If the channel cannot work with offscreen buffers, it ignores this value.

DESCRIPTION

By default, video channels draw directly to the screen. You can direct a channel to draw to an offscreen buffer by calling the `SGSetUseScreenBuffer` function. Channels that can work offscreen then allocate and draw to an offscreen buffer.

SEE ALSO

You can allow a channel to draw offscreen by calling the `SGSetUseScreenBuffer` function, which is described in the previous section.

Working With Sound Channels

Sequence grabber components provide a number of functions that allow you to configure the grabber's sound channels. This section describes these configuration functions, which you can use only with sound channels. You can determine whether a channel has a sound representation by calling the `SGGetChannelInfo` function, described on page 5-61. If you want to configure a video channel, use the functions described in "Working With Video Channels" beginning on page 5-77. If you want to configure general attributes of a channel, use the functions described in "Working With Channel Characteristics" beginning on page 5-58.

Use the `SGSetSoundInputDriver` function to specify a channel's sound input device. You can determine a channel's sound input device by calling the `SGGetSoundInputDriver` function. If you change any attributes of the sound input device, you should notify the sequence grabber component by calling the `SGSoundInputDriverChanged` function. By default, the sequence grabber component uses the sound driver's best settings.

You can control the amount of sound data the sequence grabber works with at one time by calling the `SGSetSoundRecordChunkSize` function. You can determine this value by calling the `SGGetSoundRecordChunkSize` function.

You can control the rate at which the sound channel samples the input data by calling the `SGSetSoundInputRate` function. You can determine the sample rate by calling the `SGGetSoundInputRate` function.

Sequence Grabber Components

You can control other sound input parameters by using the SGSetSoundInputParameters and SGGetSoundInputParameters functions.

SGSetSoundInputDriver

Some sound channel components may use sound input devices to obtain their source data. The SGSetSoundInputDriver function allows you to assign a sound input device to a sound channel.

```
pascal ComponentResult SGSetSoundInputDriver (SGChannel c,
                                    const Str255 driverName);
```

c Specifies the reference that identifies the channel for this operation. You obtain this reference from the SGNewChannel function, described on page 5-31.

driverName
   Specifies the name of the sound input device. This is a Pascal string, and it must correspond to a valid sound input device.

DESCRIPTION

If the sound channel component does not use sound input devices, it returns a nonzero result code. For more information about sound input devices, see *Inside Macintosh: More Macintosh Toolbox*—in particular, refer to the discussion of the Sound Manager's SPBGetIndexedDevice routine.

SPECIAL CONSIDERATIONS

You cannot call the SGSetSoundInputDriver function during a record operation.

RESULT CODES

noDeviceForChannel	–9400	Channel component cannot find its device
cantDoThatInCurrentMode	–9402	Request invalid in current mode
deviceCantMeetRequest	–9408	Device cannot support grabber

SGGetSoundInputDriver

The SGGetSoundInputDriver function allows you to determine the sound input device currently in use by a sound channel component.

```
pascal long SGGetSoundInputDriver (SGChannel c);
```

CHAPTER 5

Sequence Grabber Components

c Specifies the reference that identifies the channel for this operation. You obtain this reference from the `SGNewChannel` function, described on page 5-31.

DESCRIPTION

The `SGGetSoundInputDriver` function returns a reference to the sound input device. If the sound channel is not using a sound input device, this returned value is set to `nil`.

You may want to gain access to the sound input device if you want to change the device's configuration.

SPECIAL CONSIDERATIONS

If you change any of the device's operating parameters, be sure to inform the sequence grabber component by calling the `SGSoundInputDriverChanged` function, which is described in the next section.

SEE ALSO

You can assign a sound input device to a sound channel by calling the `SGSetSoundInputDriver` function, described in the previous section.

SGSoundInputDriverChanged

The `SGSoundInputDriverChanged` function allows you to notify the sequence grabber component whenever you change the configuration of a sound channel's sound input device.

```
pascal ComponentResult SGSoundInputDriverChanged (SGChannel c);
```

c Specifies the reference that identifies the channel for this operation. You obtain this reference from the `SGNewChannel` function, described on page 5-31.

DESCRIPTION

The sequence grabber's sound channels maintain information about the configuration of any sound input devices that are currently in use. It is very important to notify the sequence grabber component of any configuration changes you make.

SPECIAL CONSIDERATIONS

You should not change the configuration of the sound input device during a record operation.

CHAPTER 5

Sequence Grabber Components

SEE ALSO

You can obtain access to a sound channel's sound input device by calling the `SGGetSoundInputDriver` function, which is described in the previous section.

SGSetSoundRecordChunkSize

During record operations, the sequence grabber works with groups of sound samples. These groups are referred to as *chunks*. By default, each chunk contains two seconds of sound data. Smaller chunks use less memory. You can control the amount of sound data in each chunk by calling the `SGSetSoundRecordChunkSize` function.

```
pascal ComponentResult SGSetSoundRecordChunkSize (SGChannel c,
                                                  long seconds);
```

c　　　　　　Specifies the reference that identifies the channel for this operation. You obtain this reference from the `SGNewChannel` function, described on page 5-31.

seconds　　　Specifies the number of seconds of sound data the sequence grabber is to work with at a time. To specify a fraction of a second, set this parameter to a negative fixed-point number. For example, to set the duration to half a second, pass in –0.5 in this parameter.

DESCRIPTION

You specify the number of seconds of sound data the sequence grabber is to work with at a time.

SPECIAL CONSIDERATIONS

You cannot call the `SGSetSoundRecordChunkSize` function during a record or preview operation, or after you have prepared the sequence grabber for a record or preview operation (by calling the `SGPrepare` function, described on page 5-43).

This function may return a fraction (for details, see the discussion of the `seconds` parameter above).

RESULT CODES

paramErr	–50	Invalid parameter specified
cantDoThatInCurrentMode	–9402	Request invalid in current mode

SGGetSoundRecordChunkSize

The `SGGetSoundRecordChunkSize` function allows you to determine the amount of sound data the sequence grabber component works with at a time.

```
pascal long SGGetSoundRecordChunkSize (SGChannel c);
```

c   Specifies the reference that identifies the channel for this operation. You obtain this reference from the `SGNewChannel` function, described on page 5-31.

DESCRIPTION

`SGGetSoundRecordChunkSize` returns a long integer that specifies the number of seconds of sound data the sequence grabber works with at a time.

SEE ALSO

You set the amount of sound data the sequence grabber component works with at any given time by calling the `SGSetSoundRecordChunkSize` function, which is described in the previous section.

SGSetSoundInputRate

The `SGSetSoundInputRate` function allows you to set the rate at which the sound channel obtains its sound data.

```
pascal ComponentResult SGSetSoundInputRate (SGChannel c,
                                            Fixed rate);
```

c   Specifies the reference that identifies the channel for this operation. You obtain this reference from the `SGNewChannel` function, described on page 5-31.

rate   Specifies the rate at which the sound channel is to acquire data. This parameter specifies the number of samples the sound channel is to generate per second. If the sound channel cannot support the rate you specify, it uses the closest available rate that it supports—you can use the `SGGetSoundInputRate` function, described in the next section, to retrieve the rate being used by the channel. Set this parameter to 0 to cause the sound channel to use its default rate.

            You can determine the rates that are valid for a sound channel that uses a sound input device by calling the Sound Manager (see *Inside Macintosh: More Macintosh Toolbox* for more information about the Sound Manager).

CHAPTER 5

Sequence Grabber Components

RESULT CODES

`cantDoThatInCurrentMode`	–9402	Request invalid in current mode
`deviceCantMeetRequest`	–9408	Device cannot support grabber

SGGetSoundInputRate

The `SGGetSoundInputRate` function allows you to determine the rate at which the sound channel is collecting sound data.

```
pascal Fixed SGGetSoundInputRate (SGChannel c);
```

c   Specifies the reference that identifies the channel for this operation. You obtain this reference from the `SGNewChannel` function, described on page 5-31.

DESCRIPTION

`SGGetSoundInputRate` returns a fixed-point number that indicates the number of samples the sound channel collects per second.

SEE ALSO

You set the rate at which the sound channel is collecting data by calling the `SGSetSoundInputRate` function, which is described in the previous section.

SGSetSoundInputParameters

The `SGSetSoundInputParameters` function allows you to set some parameters that relate to sound recording.

```
pascal ComponentResult SGSetSoundInputParameters (SGChannel c,
                                        short sampleSize,
                                        short numChannels,
                                        OSType compressionType);
```

c   Identifies the channel for this operation. You provide your connection identifier. You connect to a channel component by calling the `SGNewChannel` or `SGNewChannelFromComponent` function, discussed on page 5-31 and page 5-32, respectively.

sampleSize
        Specifies the number of bits in each sound sample. Set this field to 8 for 8-bit sound; set it to 16 for 16-bit sound.

CHAPTER 5

Sequence Grabber Components

numChannels
: Indicates the number of sound channels used by the sound sample. Set this field to 1 for monaural sounds; set it to 2 for stereo sounds.

compressionType
: Describes the format of the sound data. The following values are supported:

   `'raw '`   Sound samples are uncompressed, in offset-binary format (that is, sample data values range from 0 to 255).

   `'MAC3'`   Sound samples have been compressed by the Sound Manager at a ratio of 3:1.

   `'MAC6'`   Sound samples have been compressed by the Sound Manager at a ratio of 6:1.

DESCRIPTION

You may use the `SGSetSoundInputParameters` function to control many parameters relating to sound recording. All of the sound parameters support two special values. If you set any of these parameters to 0, the sequence grabber does not change the current value of that parameter. If you set any of them to –1, the sequence grabber returns that parameter to its default value.

If you select a parameter value that the sound device cannot support, the sequence grabber returns an appropriate Sound Manager result code.

RESULT CODES

Sound Manager errors

SGGetSoundInputParameters

The `SGGetSoundInputParameters` function allows you to retrieve some parameters that relate to sound recording.

```
pascal ComponentResult SGGetSoundInputParameters (SGChannel c,
                                    short *sampleSize,
                                    short *numChannels,
                                    OSType *compressionType);
```

c
: Identifies the channel for this operation. You provide your connection identifier. You connect to a channel component by calling the `SGNewChannel` or `SGNewChannelFromComponent` function, discussed on page 5-31 and page 5-32, respectively.

CHAPTER 5

Sequence Grabber Components

sampleSize
: Contains a pointer to a field to receive the sample size. The sequence grabber sets this field to 8 for 8-bit sound; it sets the field to 16 for 16-bit sound.

numChannels
: Contains a pointer to a field to receive the number of sound channels used by the sound sample. The sequence grabber sets this field to 1 for monaural sounds; it sets the field to 2 for stereo sounds.

compressionType
: Contains a pointer to a field that is to receive the format of the sound data. The following values may be returned:

  `'raw'`   Sound samples are uncompressed, in offset-binary format (that is, sample data values range from 0 to 255).

  `'MAC3'`   Sound samples have been compressed by the Sound Manager at a ratio of 3:1.

  `'MAC6'`   Sound samples have been compressed by the Sound Manager at a ratio of 6:1.

DESCRIPTION

You may use the `SGGetSoundInputParameters` function to retrieve many parameters relating to sound recording. If you set any of the sound parameters to `nil`, the sequence grabber does not return that value.

Video Channel Callback Functions

Sequence grabber components allow you to define a number of callback functions in your application. The sequence grabber calls your functions at specific points in the process of collecting, compressing, and displaying the source video data. By defining callback functions, you can control the process more precisely or customize the operation of the sequence grabber component.

For example, you could use a callback function to draw a frame number on each video frame as it is collected. You could use either a compress callback function or a grab-complete callback function to accomplish this. The compress callback function is called after each frame is collected, in order to compress the frame. The grab-complete callback function is called just before the compress callback function, as soon as the frame has been captured.

The `SGSetVideoBottlenecks` function lets you assign callback functions to a video channel. You can use the `SGGetVideoBottlenecks` function to determine the callback functions that have been assigned to a video channel.

The `SGSetVideoBottlenecks` function accepts a video bottlenecks structure that identifies the callback functions to be assigned to the channel. In addition, the `SGGetVideoBottlenecks` function contains a pointer to this structure.

Sequence Grabber Components

The video bottlenecks structure is defined by the `VideoBottles` data type as follows:

```
struct VideoBottles {
    short                       procCount;          /* count of callbacks */
    GrabProc                    grabProc;           /* grab function */
    GrabCompleteProc            grabCompleteProc;   /* grab-complete function */
    DisplayProc                 displayProc;        /* display function */
    CompressProc                compressProc;       /* compress function */
    CompressCompleteProc        compressCompleteProc;
                                                    /* compress-complete
                                                       function */
    AddFrameProc                addFrameProc;       /* add-frame function */
    TransferFrameProc           transferFrameProc;  /* transfer-frame function */
    GrabCompressCompleteProc    grabCompressCompleteProc;
                                                    /* grab-compress—complete
                                                       function */
    DisplayCompressProc         displayCompressProc;
                                                    /* display-compress
                                                       function */
};
typedef struct VideoBottles VideoBottles;
```

Field descriptions

procCount Specifies the number of callback functions that may be identified in the structure. Set this field to 9.

grabProc Identifies the grab function. If you are setting a grab function, set this field so that it points to the function's entry point. If you are not setting a grab function, set this field to `nil`.

grabCompleteProc
 Identifies the grab-complete function. If you are setting a grab-complete function, set this field so that it points to the function's entry point. If you are not setting a grab-complete function, set this field to `nil`.

displayProc Identifies the display function. If you are setting a display function, set this field so that it points to the function's entry point. If you are not setting a display function, set this field to `nil`.

compressProc Identifies the compress function. If you are setting a compress function, set this field so that it points to the function's entry point. If you are not setting a compress function, set this field to `nil`.

compressCompleteProc
 Identifies the compress-complete function. If you are setting a compress-complete function, set this field so that it points to the function's entry point. If you are not setting a compress-complete function, set this field to `nil`.

Sequence Grabber Components

`addFrameProc`
: Identifies the add-frame function. If you are setting an add-frame function, set this field so that it points to the function's entry point. If you are not setting an add-frame function, set this field to `nil`.

`transferFrameProc`
: Identifies the transfer-frame function. If you are setting a transfer-frame function, set this field so that it points to the function's entry point. If you are not setting a transfer-frame function, set this field to `nil`.

`grabCompressCompleteProc`
: Identifies the grab-compress–complete function. If you are setting a grab-compress–complete function, set this field so that it points to the function's entry point. If you are not setting a grab-compress–complete function, set this field to `nil`.

`displayCompressProc`
: Identifies the display-compress function. If you are setting a display-compress function, set this field so that it points to the function's entry point. If you are not setting a display-compress function, set this field to `nil`.

SGSetVideoBottlenecks

The `SGSetVideoBottlenecks` function assigns callback functions to a video channel.

```
pascal ComponentResult SGSetVideoBottlenecks (SGChannel c,
                                              VideoBottles *vb);
```

`c`
: Specifies the reference that identifies the channel for this operation. You obtain this reference from the `SGNewChannel` function, described on page 5-31.

`vb`
: Contains a pointer to a video bottlenecks structure (defined by the `VideoBottles` data type). That structure identifies the callback functions to be assigned to this video channel. The video bottlenecks structure is described on page 5-100.

DESCRIPTION

The `SGSetVideoBottlenecks` function accepts a video bottlenecks structure that identifies the callback functions to be assigned to the channel.

SPECIAL CONSIDERATIONS

Your application should not call this function during a record or playback operation.

SGGetVideoBottlenecks

The `SGGetVideoBottlenecks` function allows you to determine the callback functions that have been assigned to a video channel.

```
pascal ComponentResult SGGetVideoBottlenecks (SGChannel c,
                                              VideoBottles *vb);
```

c Specifies the reference that identifies the channel for this operation. You obtain this reference from the `SGNewChannel` function, described on page 5-31.

vb Contains a pointer to a video bottlenecks structure, described on page 5-100. The `SGGetVideoBottlenecks` function sets the fields of that structure to indicate the callback functions that have been assigned to this video channel. You must set the `procCount` field in the video bottlenecks structure to 9.

SEE ALSO

You assign callback functions to a video channel by calling the `SGSetVideoBottlenecks` function, which is described in the previous section.

Utility Functions for Video Channel Callback Functions

Sequence grabber components provide a number of functions that your callback functions can use. This section describes those functions.

Use the `SGGetBufferInfo` function to obtain information about a buffer that contains data to be manipulated by your callback function.

The remaining functions described here provide default behavior for your callback functions.

SGGetBufferInfo

You can use the `SGGetBufferInfo` function to obtain information about a buffer that has been passed to your callback function.

```
pascal ComponentResult SGGetBufferInfo (SGChannel c,
                                        short bufferNum,
                                        PixMapHandle *bufferPM,
                                        Rect *bufferRect,
                                        GWorldPtr *compressBuffer,
                                        Rect *compressBufferRect);
```

CHAPTER 5

Sequence Grabber Components

c
Specifies the reference that identifies the channel for this operation.

bufferNum
Identifies the buffer. The sequence grabber component provides this value to your callback function.

bufferPM
Contains a pointer to a location that is to receive a handle to the pixel map that contains the image. Note that this pixel map may be offscreen. Do not dispose of this pixel map. If you do not want this information, set this parameter to `nil`.

bufferRect
Contains a pointer to a rectangle structure that is to receive the dimensions of the image's boundary rectangle. If you do not want this information, set this parameter to `nil`.

compressBuffer
Contains a pointer to a location that is to receive a pointer to the filter buffer for the image. The sequence grabber component returns this information only if your application has assigned a filter buffer to this video channel. You assign a filter buffer by calling the `SGSetCompressBuffer` function, which is described on page 5-87. Do not dispose of this buffer.

If you have not assigned a filter buffer, the sequence grabber sets the returned value to `nil`. If you do not want this information, set this parameter to `nil`.

compressBufferRect
Contains a pointer to a rectangle structure that is to receive the dimensions of the filter buffer for the image. The sequence grabber component returns this information only if your application has assigned a filter buffer to this video channel. You assign a filter buffer by calling the `SGSetCompressBuffer` function, which is described on page 5-87. If you have not assigned a filter buffer, the sequence grabber component returns an empty rectangle. If you do not want this information, set this parameter to `nil`.

RESULT CODE

paramErr   –50   Invalid parameter specified

SGGrabFrame

The `SGGrabFrame` function provides the default behavior for your grab function.

```
pascal ComponentResult SGGrabFrame (SGChannel c, short bufferNum);
```

c
Specifies the reference that identifies the channel for this operation. The sequence grabber component provides this value to your grab function.

bufferNum
Identifies the buffer. The sequence grabber component provides this value to your grab function.

CHAPTER 5

Sequence Grabber Components

SPECIAL CONSIDERATIONS

You should call the `SGGrabFrame` function only from your grab function. If you call it at any other time, results are unpredictable.

SEE ALSO

See "Application-Defined Functions," which begins on page 5-111, for information about grab-complete functions.

RESULT CODE

cantDoThatInCurrentMode   –9402   Request invalid in current mode

SGGrabFrameComplete

The `SGGrabFrameComplete` function provides the default behavior for your grab-complete function.

```
pascal ComponentResult SGGrabFrameComplete (SGChannel c,
                                            short bufferNum,
                                            Boolean *done);
```

c   Specifies the reference that identifies the channel for this operation. The sequence grabber provides this value to your grab-complete function.

bufferNum   Identifies the buffer. The sequence grabber provides this value to your grab-complete function.

done   Contains a pointer to a Boolean value. The `SGGrabFrameComplete` function sets this Boolean value to indicate whether the frame has been completely captured. The function sets the Boolean value to `true` if the capture is complete, and sets it to `false` if the capture is incomplete. The sequence grabber provides this pointer to your grab-complete function.

SPECIAL CONSIDERATIONS

You should call the `SGGrabFrameComplete` function only from your grab-complete function. If you call it at any other time, results are unpredictable.

RESULT CODE

cantDoThatInCurrentMode   –9402   Request invalid in current mode

SEE ALSO

See "Application-Defined Functions," which begins on page 5-111, for details about grab-complete functions.

SGDisplayFrame

The `SGDisplayFrame` function provides the default behavior for your display function.

```
pascal ComponentResult SGDisplayFrame (SGChannel c,
                                        short bufferNum,
                                        MatrixRecord *mp,
                                        RgnHandle clipRgn);
```

c
    Specifies the reference that identifies the channel for this operation. The sequence grabber component provides this value to your display function.

bufferNum
    Identifies the buffer. The sequence grabber component provides this value to your display function.

mp
    Contains a pointer to a transformation matrix for the display operation. If there is no matrix for the operation, set this parameter to `nil`.

clipRgn
    Contains a handle to the clipping region for the destination image. This region is defined in the destination coordinate system. If there is no clipping region, set this parameter to `nil`.

SPECIAL CONSIDERATIONS

You should call the `SGDisplayFrame`function only from your display function. If you call it at any other time, results are unpredictable.

RESULT CODE

    cantDoThatInCurrentMode   –9402   Request invalid in current mode

SEE ALSO

See "Application-Defined Functions," which begins on page 5-111, for details about display functions.

SGCompressFrame

The `SGCompressFrame` function provides the default behavior for your compress function.

```
pascal ComponentResult SGCompressFrame (SGChannel c,
                                         short bufferNum);
```

c
    Specifies the reference that identifies the channel for this operation. The sequence grabber provides this value to your compress function.

Sequence Grabber Components

bufferNum   Identifies the buffer. The sequence grabber provides this value to your compress function.

SPECIAL CONSIDERATIONS

You should call the `SGCompressFrame` function only from your compress function. If you call it at any other time, results are unpredictable.

RESULT CODES

cantDoThatInCurrentMode   –9402   Request invalid in current mode

Image Compression Manager errors

SEE ALSO

See "Application-Defined Functions," which begins on page 5-111, for information about compress functions.

SGCompressFrameComplete

The `SGCompressFrameComplete` function provides the default behavior for your compress-complete function.

```
pascal ComponentResult SGCompressFrameComplete (SGChannel c,
                                                short bufferNum,
                                                Boolean *done,
                                                SGCompressInfo *ci);
```

c   Specifies the reference that identifies the channel for this operation. The sequence grabber component provides this value to your compress-complete function.

bufferNum   Identifies the buffer. The sequence grabber component provides this value to your compress-complete function.

done   Contains a pointer to a Boolean value. The `SGCompressFrameComplete` function sets this Boolean value to indicate whether the frame has been completely compressed. The function sets the Boolean value to `true` if the compression is complete; it sets the Boolean value to `false` if the operation is incomplete. The sequence grabber component provides this pointer to your compress-complete function.

Sequence Grabber Components

ci Contains a pointer to a compression information structure (defined by the `SGCompressInfo` data type). If the compression is complete, the function completely formats this structure with information that is appropriate to the frame just compressed. See "The Compression Information Structure" beginning on page 5-22 for a description of this structure. The sequence grabber component provides this pointer to your compress-complete function.

SPECIAL CONSIDERATIONS

You should call the `SGCompressFrameComplete` function only from your compress-complete function. If you call it at any other time, results are unpredictable.

RESULT CODES

cantDoThatInCurrentMode   –9402   Request invalid in current mode
Image Compression Manager errors

SEE ALSO

See "Application-Defined Functions," which begins on page 5-111, for information about compress-complete functions.

SGAddFrame

The `SGAddFrame` function provides the default behavior for your add-frame function.

```
pascal ComponentResult SGAddFrame (SGChannel c, short bufferNum,
                                   TimeValue atTime,
                                   TimeScale scale,
                                   const SGCompressInfo *ci);
```

c Specifies the reference that identifies the channel for this operation. The sequence grabber component provides this value to your add-frame function.

bufferNum Identifies the buffer. The sequence grabber component provides this value to your add-frame function.

atTime Specifies the time at which the frame was captured, in the time scale specified by the `scale` parameter. The sequence grabber component provides this value to your add-frame function. Your add-frame function can change this value before calling the `SGAddFrame` function. You can determine the duration of a frame by subtracting its capture time from the capture time of the next frame in the sequence.

scale Specifies the time scale of the movie. The sequence grabber component provides this value to your add-frame function.

CHAPTER 5

Sequence Grabber Components

ci   Contains a pointer to a compression information structure (defined by the `SGCompressInfo` data type). This structure contains information describing the compression characteristics of the image to be added to the movie. See "The Compression Information Structure" beginning on page 5-22 for a description of this structure. The sequence grabber component provides this structure to your add-frame function.

SPECIAL CONSIDERATIONS

You should call the `SGAddFrame` function only from your add-frame function. If you call it at any other time, results are unpredictable.

RESULT CODES

cantDoThatInCurrentMode   –9402   Request invalid in current mode
Memory Manager errors

SEE ALSO

See "Application-Defined Functions," which begins on page 5-111, for information about add-frame functions.

SGTransferFrameForCompress

The `SGTransferFrameForCompress` function provides the default behavior for your transfer-frame function.

```
pascal ComponentResult SGTransferFrameForCompress (SGChannel c,
                                                    short bufferNum,
                                                    MatrixRecord *mp,
                                                    RgnHandle clipRgn);
```

c   Specifies the reference that identifies the channel for this operation. The sequence grabber component provides this value to your transfer-frame function.

bufferNum   Identifies the buffer. The sequence grabber component provides this value to your transfer-frame function.

mp   Contains a pointer to a transformation matrix for the transfer operation. If there is no matrix for the operation, set this parameter to `nil`.

clipRgn   Contains a handle to the clipping region for the destination image. This region is defined in the destination coordinate system. If there is no clipping region, set this parameter to `nil`.

CHAPTER 5

Sequence Grabber Components

SPECIAL CONSIDERATIONS

You should call the `SGTransferFrameForCompress` function only from your transfer-frame function. If you call it at any other time, results are unpredictable.

RESULT CODE

cantDoThatInCurrentMode   –9402   Request invalid in current mode

SEE ALSO

See "Application-Defined Functions," which begins on page 5-111, for information about transfer-frame functions.

SGGrabCompressComplete

The `SGGrabCompressComplete` function provides the default behavior for your grab-compress–complete function.

```
pascal ComponentResult SGGrabCompressComplete (SGChannel c,
                                               Boolean *done,
                                               SGCompressInfo *ci,
                                               TimeRecord *tr);
```

c   Identifies the channel for this operation. The sequence grabber provides this value to your grab-compress–complete function.

done   Contains a pointer to a Boolean value. The `SGGrabCompressComplete` function sets this value to true when it is done; it sets it to false if the operation is incomplete. The sequence grabber provides this pointer to your grab-compress–complete function.

ci   Contains a pointer to a compression information structure. When the operation is complete, the `SGGrabCompressComplete` function fills in this structure with information about the compression operation. The format and content of this structure are discussed earlier in this chapter, beginning on page 5-22.

The sequence grabber provides this pointer to your grab-compress–complete function.

tr   Contains a pointer to a time record. When the operation is complete, the `SGGrabCompressComplete` function uses this structure to indicate when the frame was grabbed. The format and content of this structure are discussed in the chapter "Movie Toolbox" in *Inside Macintosh: QuickTime*.

The sequence grabber provides this pointer to your grab-compress–complete function.

CHAPTER 5

Sequence Grabber Components

SPECIAL CONSIDERATIONS

You should call the `SGGrabCompressComplete` function only from your grab-compress–complete function. If you call it at other times, results are unpredictable.

RESULT CODE

cantDoThatInCurrentMode   –9402   Request invalid in current mode

SEE ALSO

See "Application-Defined Functions" beginning on page 5-111 for information about grab-compress–complete functions.

SGDisplayCompress

The `SGDisplayCompress` function provides the default behavior for your display-compress function.

```
pascal ComponentResult SGDisplayCompress (SGChannel c,
                                          Ptr dataPtr,
                                          ImageDescriptionHandle desc,
                                          MatrixRecord *mp,
                                          RgnHandle clipRgn);
```

c
: Identifies the channel for this operation. The sequence grabber provides this value to your display-compress function.

dataPtr
: Contains a pointer to the compressed image data. The sequence grabber provides this pointer to your display-compress function.

desc
: Specifies a handle to the image description structure to use for the decompression operation. The sequence grabber provides this handle to your display-compress function.

mp
: Contains a pointer to a matrix structure. This matrix structure contains the transformation matrix to use when displaying the image. If there is no matrix for the operation, set this parameter to `nil`.

clipRgn
: Contains a handle to the clipping region for the destination image. This region is defined in the destination coordinate system. If there is no clipping region, set this parameter to `nil`.

CHAPTER 5

Sequence Grabber Components

SPECIAL CONSIDERATIONS

You should call the `SGDisplayCompress` function only from your display-compress function. If you call it at other times, results are unpredictable.

RESULT CODE

cantDoThatInCurrentMode   –9402   Request invalid in current mode

SEE ALSO

See the next section, "Application-Defined Functions," for information about display-compress functions.

Application-Defined Functions

This section describes the functions that your application may supply to sequence grabber components.

Your grab function is used by the sequence grabber component to begin the capture of a frame of video data. Your grab-complete function allows the sequence grabber component to determine whether the current frame-capture operation is complete.

Your display function enables the sequence grabber component to move a captured video image in an offscreen buffer into the destination buffer for the video channel.

The sequence grabber component uses your compress function to commence the compression of a captured video image. Your compress-complete function helps the sequence grabber component to find out if the current frame-compression operation is finished.

Your add-frame function lets the sequence grabber component add a frame to a movie.

The sequence grabber component uses your transfer-frame function to move a video frame from the capture buffer into the channel's filter buffer.

You may provide two functions for use with compressed-source devices. Your grab-compress–complete function determines when the current capture and compress operation is complete. Your display-compress function decompresses and displays a frame.

The sequence grabber calls your data function whenever any of the grabber's channels write data to the movie file.

If you call the `SGSettingsDialog` function, described on page 5-48, you must supply a modal-dialog filter function. The interface that your function must provide is discussed on page 5-122.

MyGrabFunction

The sequence grabber component calls your grab function in order to start capturing a frame of video data.

Your grab function must present the following interface:

```
pascal ComponentResult MyGrabFunction (SGChannel c,
                                       short bufferNum,
                                       long refCon);
```

c
  Specifies the reference that identifies the channel for this operation.

bufferNum
  Identifies the buffer for this operation. You can obtain information about this buffer by calling the SGGetBufferInfo function, which is described on page 5-102.

refCon
  Contains a reference constant value. You can set this value by calling the SGSetChannelRefCon function, which is described on page 5-67.

RESULT CODE

cantDoThatInCurrentMode   –9402   Request invalid in current mode

SEE ALSO

Your grab function can use the sequence grabber component's SGGrabFrame function to support the default behavior. SGGrabFrame is described on page 5-103.

MyGrabCompleteFunction

The sequence grabber component calls your grab-complete function in order to determine whether the current frame-capture operation is complete. Once a frame has been completely captured, you can modify its contents to suit your needs. For example, you can overlay text onto the video image.

Your function must present the following interface:

```
pascal ComponentResult MyGrabCompleteFunction (SGChannel c,
                                               short bufferNum,
                                               Boolean *done,
                                               long refCon);
```

c
  Specifies the reference that identifies the channel for this operation.

bufferNum
  Identifies the buffer for this operation. You can obtain information about this buffer by calling the SGGetBufferInfo function, which is described on page 5-102.

CHAPTER 5

Sequence Grabber Components

done
: Contains a pointer to a Boolean value. Your function sets this Boolean value to indicate whether the frame has been completely captured. Set the Boolean value to `true` if the capture is complete; set it to `false` if it is incomplete.

refCon
: Contains a reference constant value. You can set this value by calling the `SGSetChannelRefCon` function, which is described on page 5-67.

RESULT CODE

cantDoThatInCurrentMode   –9402   Request invalid in current mode

SEE ALSO

Your grab-complete function can use the sequence grabber component's `SGGrabFrameComplete` function to support the default behavior. `SGGrabFrameComplete` is described on page 5-104.

See Listing 5-6 on page 5-20 for a sample grab-complete function. This function draws the letters "QT" over each video frame in the sequence.

MyDisplayFunction

The sequence grabber component calls your display function in order to transfer a captured video image in an offscreen buffer into the destination buffer for the video channel.

Your display function must support the following interface:

```
pascal ComponentResult MyDisplayFunction (SGChannel c,
                                          short bufferNum,
                                          MatrixRecord *mp,
                                          RgnHandle clipRgn,
                                          long refCon);
```

c
: Specifies the reference that identifies the channel for this operation.

bufferNum
: Identifies the buffer for this operation. You can obtain information about this buffer by calling the `SGGetBufferInfo` function, which is described on page 5-102.

mp
: Contains a pointer to a transformation matrix for the display operation. If there is no matrix for the operation, this parameter is set to `nil`.

clipRgn
: Contains a handle to the clipping region for the destination image. This region is defined in the destination coordinate system. Apply the clipping region after applying the transformation matrix. If there is no clipping region, this parameter is set to `nil`.

refCon
: Contains a reference constant value. You can set this value by calling the `SGSetChannelRefCon` function, which is described on page 5-67.

CHAPTER 5

Sequence Grabber Components

RESULT CODE

cantDoThatInCurrentMode   –9402   Request invalid in current mode

SEE ALSO

Your application sets the destination buffer by calling the `SGSetChannelBounds` function, which is described on page 5-65.

Your display function can use the sequence grabber component's `SGDisplayFrame` function to support the default behavior. `SGDisplayFrame` is described on page 5-105.

MyCompressFunction

The sequence grabber component calls your compress function in order to start compressing the captured video image.

Your compress function must support the following interface:

```
pascal ComponentResult MyCompressFunction (SGChannel c,
                                           short bufferNum,
                                           long refCon);
```

c   Specifies the reference that identifies the channel for this operation.

bufferNum   Identifies the buffer for this operation. You can obtain information about this buffer by calling the `SGGetBufferInfo` function, which is described on page 5-102.

refCon   Contains a reference constant value. You can set this value by calling the `SGSetChannelRefCon` function, which is described on page 5-67.

RESULT CODES

cantDoThatInCurrentMode   –9402   Request invalid in current mode
Image Compression Manager errors

SEE ALSO

Your compress function can use the sequence grabber component's `SGCompressFrame` function to support the default behavior. `SGCompressFrame` is described on page 5-105. This function uses the Image Compression Manager to compress the video image. For more on the Image Compression Manager, see *Inside Macintosh: QuickTime*.

MyCompressCompleteFunction

The sequence grabber component calls your compress-complete function in order to determine whether the current frame-compression operation is complete.

Your compress-complete function must support the following interface:

```
pascal ComponentResult MyCompressCompleteFunction (SGChannel c,
                                        short bufferNum,
                                        Boolean *done,
                                        SGCompressInfo *ci,
                                        long refCon);
```

c
: Specifies the reference that identifies the channel for this operation.

bufferNum
: Identifies the buffer for this operation. You can obtain information about this buffer by calling the `SGGetBufferInfo` function, which is described on page 5-102.

done
: Contains a pointer to a Boolean value. Your function sets this Boolean value to indicate whether the frame has been completely compressed. Set the Boolean value to `true` if the compression is complete; set it to `false` if it is incomplete.

ci
: Contains a pointer to a compression information structure (defined by the `SGCompressInfo` data type). If the compression is complete, your function must completely format this structure with information that is appropriate to the frame just compressed. See "The Compression Information Structure" beginning on page 5-22, for a description of this structure.

refCon
: Contains a reference constant value. You can set this value by calling the `SGSetChannelRefCon` function, which is described on page 5-67.

DESCRIPTION

Once a frame has been completely compressed, you can add it to the movie.

SEE ALSO

Your compress-complete function can use the sequence grabber component's `SGCompressFrameComplete` function to support the default behavior. `SGCompressFrameComplete` is described on page 5-106.

RESULT CODES

cantDoThatInCurrentMode   –9402   Request invalid in current mode
Image Compression Manager errors

CHAPTER 5

Sequence Grabber Components

MyAddFrameFunction

The sequence grabber component calls your add-frame function in order to add a frame to a movie. Your add-frame function must support the following interface:

```
pascal ComponentResult MyAddFrameFunction (SGChannel c,
                                           short bufferNum,
                                           TimeValue atTime,
                                           TimeScale scale,
                                           SGCompressInfo *ci,
                                           long refCon);
```

c
: Specifies the reference that identifies the channel for this operation.

bufferNum
: Identifies the buffer for this operation. You can obtain information about this buffer by calling the `SGGetBufferInfo` function, which is described on page 5-102.

atTime
: Specifies the time at which the frame was captured, in the time scale specified by the `scale` parameter. Your add-frame function can change this value before adding the frame to the movie or before calling the `SGAddFrame` function, which is described on page 5-107. You can determine the duration of a frame by subtracting its capture time from the capture time of the next frame in the sequence.

scale
: Specifies the time scale of the movie. You must not change this value.

ci
: Contains a pointer to a compression information structure (defined by the `SGCompressInfo` data type). This structure contains information describing the compression characteristics of the image to be added to the movie. See "The Compression Information Structure" beginning on page 5-22 for a description of this structure.

refCon
: Contains a reference constant value. You can set this value by calling the `SGSetChannelRefCon` function, which is described on page 5-67.

DESCRIPTION

You can use your add-frame function to modify the contents of the frame before it is added to the movie. This can be useful if you want to place frame numbers onto frames you are recording.

RESULT CODES

cantDoThatInCurrentMode   –9402   Request invalid in current mode
Memory Manager errors

SEE ALSO

Your add-frame function can use the sequence grabber component's SGAddFrame function to support the default behavior. SGAddFrame is described on page 5-107.

MyTransferFrameFunction

The sequence grabber component calls your transfer-frame function in order to move a video frame from the capture buffer into the channel's filter buffer.

Your transfer-frame function must support the following interface:

```
pascal ComponentResult MyTransferFrameFunction (SGChannel c,
                                                short bufferNum,
                                                MatrixRecord *mp,
                                                RgnHandle clipRgn,
                                                long refCon);
```

c
: Specifies the reference that identifies the channel for this operation.

bufferNum
: Identifies the buffer for this operation. You can obtain information about this buffer by calling the SGGetBufferInfo function, which is described on page 5-102.

mp
: Contains a pointer to a transformation matrix for the transfer operation. If there is no matrix for the operation, this parameter is set to nil.

clipRgn
: Contains a handle to the clipping region for the destination image. This region is defined in the destination coordinate system. Apply the clipping region after applying the transformation matrix. If there is no clipping region, this parameter is set to nil.

refCon
: Contains a reference constant value. You can set this value by calling the SGSetChannelRefCon function, which is described on page 5-67.

DESCRIPTION

The sequence grabber component calls this function only when you are filtering the video data. By filtering the video data through a filter buffer, you can eliminate some visual artifacts that result from noisy input video sources. Your application sets a filter buffer by calling the SGSetCompressBuffer function, which is described on page 5-87.

If you are using a grab-complete function to determine when frames have been grabbed, you should also implement a grab-compress–complete function (described in the next section). Otherwise, the channel will decompress the specified image before calling your grab-complete function, which will result in significantly lower performance. For details on grab-complete functions, see page 5-112.

CHAPTER 5

Sequence Grabber Components

RESULT CODE

cantDoThatInCurrentMode   –9402   Request invalid in current mode

SEE ALSO

Your transfer-frame function can use the sequence grabber component's `SGTransferFrameForCompress` function to support the default behavior—`SGTransferFrameForCompress` is described on page 5-108.

MyGrabCompressCompleteFunction

The sequence grabber calls your grab-compress–complete function when it is working with a video digitizer that supports compressed source data. Your grab-compress–complete function is responsible for determining whether the current compressed frame has been completely captured and compressed, essentially combining your grab-complete, compress, and compress-complete functions into one function.

Your function must support the following interface:

```
pascal ComponentResult MyGrabCompressCompleteFunction
                            (SGChannel c,
                             Boolean *done,
                             SGCompressInfo *ci,
                             TimeRecord *tr,
                             long refCon);
```

c
: Identifies the channel for this operation.

done
: Contains a pointer to a Boolean value. Set this Boolean value to indicate whether you are finished. Set it to `true` when you are done; set it to `false` if the operation is incomplete.

ci
: Contains a pointer to a compression information structure. When the operation is complete, fill in this structure with information about the compression operation. The format and content of this structure are discussed earlier in this chapter, beginning on page 5-22.

tr
: Contains a pointer to a time record. When the operation is complete, fill in this structure with information indicating when the frame was grabbed. The format and content of this structure are discussed in the chapter "Movie Toolbox" in *Inside Macintosh: QuickTime*.

refCon
: Contains a reference constant value. You can set this value by calling the `SGSetChannelRefCon` function, which is described on page 5-67.

CHAPTER 5

Sequence Grabber Components

RESULT CODE

cantDoThatInCurrentMode   –9402   Request invalid in current mode

SEE ALSO

Your grab-compress–complete function may use the sequence grabber's SGGrabCompressComplete function to support the default behavior. SGGrabCompressComplete is discussed beginning on page 5-109.

MyDisplayCompressFunction

The sequence grabber calls your display-compress function when it is working with a video digitizer component that supports compressed source data. Your display-compress function is responsible for decompressing and displaying a compressed image.

```
pascal ComponentResult MyDisplayCompressFunction (SGChannel c,
                                Ptr dataPtr,
                                ImageDescriptionHandle desc,
                                MatrixRecord *mp,
                                RgnHandle clipRgn,
                                long refCon);
```

c
: Identifies the channel for this operation. The sequence grabber provides this value to your display-compress function.

dataPtr
: Contains a pointer to the compressed image data.

desc
: Specifies a handle to the image description structure to use for the decompression operation. See the chapter "Image Compression Manager" in *Inside Macintosh: QuickTime* for more information about this data structure.

mp
: Contains a pointer to a matrix structure. This matrix structure contains the transformation matrix to use when displaying the image. If there is no matrix for the operation, this parameter is set to nil.

clipRgn
: Contains a handle to the clipping region for the destination image. This region is defined in the destination coordinate system. Apply the clipping region after the transformation matrix. If there is no clipping region, this parameter is set to nil.

refCon
: Contains a reference constant value. You can set this value by calling the SGSetChannelRefCon function, which is described on page 5-67.

CHAPTER 5

Sequence Grabber Components

RESULT CODE

cantDoThatInCurrentMode   –9402   Request invalid in current mode

SEE ALSO

Your display-compress function may use the sequence grabber's `SGDisplayCompress` function to support the default behavior. `SGDisplayCompress` is discussed beginning on page 5-110.

MyDataFunction

The sequence grabber calls your data function whenever any of the grabber's channels write digitized data to the destination movie file. You assign a data function to the sequence grabber by calling the `SGSetDataProc` function, which is discussed on page 5-35.

Your data function must support the following interface:

```
pascal OSErr MyDataFunction (SGChannel c, Ptr p, long len,
                              long *offset, long chRefCon,
                              TimeValue time, short writeType,
                              long refCon);
```

c	Identifies the channel component that is writing the digitized data.
p	Contains a pointer to the digitized data.
len	Indicates the number of bytes of digitized data.
offset	Contains a pointer to a field that may specify where you are to write the digitized data, and that is to receive a value indicating where you wrote the data. You must update the field referred to by this parameter, supplying the value indicated by the `writeType` parameter.
chRefCon	Contains control information. The low-order 16 bits contain sample flags for use by the Movie Toolbox's `AddMediaSample` function (see the chapter "Movie Toolbox" in *Inside Macintosh: QuickTime* for information about these flags). The sequence grabber sets these flags as appropriate. The high-order 16 bits are reserved for Apple and are always set to 0.
time	Identifies the starting time of the data, in the channel's time scale. You may use the `SGGetChannelTimeScale` function to retrieve the channel's time scale (discussed on page 5-68).

CHAPTER 5

Sequence Grabber Components

`writeType`   Indicates the type of write operation being performed. The following values are defined:

`seqGrabWriteAppend`
Append the new data to the end of the file. Set the field referred to by the offset parameter to reflect the location at which you added the data.

`seqGrabWriteReserve`
Do not write any data to the output file. Instead, reserve space in the output file for the amount of data indicated by the `len` parameter. Set the field referred to by the `offset` parameter to the location of the reserved space.

`seqGrabWriteFill`
Write the data into the location specified by the field referred to by the `offset` parameter. Set that field to the location of the byte following the last byte you wrote.

This option is used to fill the space reserved previously when the `writeType` parameter was set to `seqGrabWriteReserve`. Note that the sequence grabber may call your data function several times to fill a single reserved location.

`refCon`   Contains the reference constant you specified when you assigned your data function to the sequence grabber.

DESCRIPTION

The sequence grabber calls your data function whenever any channel component writes data to the destination movie. You may use your data function to store the digitized data in some format other than a QuickTime movie.

RESULT CODES

File Manager errors
Memory Manager errors

SEE ALSO

You can instruct the sequence grabber not to write its data to a QuickTime movie by calling the `SGSetDataOutput` function and setting the `seqGrabDontMakeMovie` flag to 1. This can save processing time in cases where you do not want to create or update a movie. `SGSetDataOutput` is discussed on page 5-26.

CHAPTER 5

Sequence Grabber Components

MyModalFilter

The `SGSettingsDialog` function causes the sequence grabber to present its settings dialog box to the user. This is a movable modal dialog box, so you must provide a filter function to handle update events in your window. You specify your filter function with the `proc` parameter.

A modal-dialog filter function whose address is passed to `SGSettingsDialog` should support the following interface:

```
pascal Boolean MyModalFilter (DialogPtr theDialog,
                              EventRecord *theEvent,
                              short *itemHit, long refCon);
```

theDialog
: Points to the settings dialog box's dialog structure.

theEvent
: Contains a pointer to an event structure. This event structure contains information identifying the nature of the event.

itemHit
: Contains a pointer to a field that contains the item selected by the user. If you handle the event, you should update this field to reflect the item number of the selected item.

refCon
: Contains a reference constant. You provide this reference constant to the sequence grabber in the `procRefNum` parameter of the `SGSettingsDialog` function, which is described on page 5-48.

DESCRIPTION

Your modal-dialog filter function returns a Boolean value that indicates whether you handled the event. Set this value to `true` if you handled the event; otherwise, set it to `false`. If you handle the event, be sure to update the value of the field referred to by the `itemHit` parameter.

SEE ALSO

See *Inside Macintosh: Files* for a sample modal-dialog filter function.

Summary of Sequence Grabber Components

C Summary

Constants

```
/* sequence grabber component type */
#define SeqGrabComponentType 'barg'

/* sequence grabber channel type */
#define SeqGrabChannelType 'sgch'

/* SGGrabPict function grabPictFlags parameter flags */
enum {
     grabPictOffScreen = 1,     /* place in offscreen graphics world */
     grabPictIgnoreClip = 2     /* ignore channel clipping regions */
  };

/* flag for SGSetFlags and SGGetFlags functions */
#define sgFlagControlledGrab (1)/* controlled grab */

/* flags for SGSetChannelPlayFlags and SGGetChannelPlayFlags functions */
#define channelPlayNormal 0        /* use default playback methodology */
#define channelPlayFast 1          /* achieve fast playback rate */
#define channelPlayHighQuality 2   /* achieve high quality image */
#define channelPlayAllData 4       /* play all captured data */

/* flags for SGSetDataOutput and SGGetDataOutput functions */
enum {
   seqGrabToDisk                = 1,  /* write recorded data to movie */
   seqGrabToMemory              = 2,  /* store recorded data in memory */
   seqGrabDontUseTempMemory     = 4,  /* no temporary memory for recorded
                                         data */
   seqGrabAppendToFile          = 8,  /* add recorded data to file's data
                                         fork */
   seqGrabDontAddMovieResource = 16, /* don't add movie resource to file */
   seqGrabDontMakeMovie         = 32  /* don't put data into movie */
};
typedef unsigned char SeqGrabDataOutputEnum;
```

CHAPTER 5

Sequence Grabber Components

```c
/* usage flags for SGSetChannelUsage and SGGetChannelUsage functions */
enum {
    seqGrabRecord           = 1,  /* used during record operations */
    seqGrabPreview          = 2,  /* used during preview operations */
    seqGrabPlayDuringRecord = 4   /* plays data during record operation */
};
typedef unsigned char SeqGrabUsageEnum;

/* SGGetChannelInfo function flags */
enum {
    seqGrabHasBounds         = 1,  /* visual representation of data */
    seqGrabHasVolume         = 2,  /* audio representation of data */
    seqGrabHasDiscreteSamples = 4  /* data organized in discrete frames */
};typedef unsigned char SeqGrabChannelInfoEnum;


/* device list structure flags */

#define sgDeviceListWithIcons (1)             /* include icons */
#define sgDeviceListDontCheckAvailability (2) /* don't check available */

/* data function write operation types */

enum {
    seqGrabWriteAppend,    /* append to file */
    seqGrabWriteReserve,   /* reserve space in file */
    seqGrabWriteFill       /* fill reserved space */
};

/* SGPause and SGGetPause options */

enum {
    seqGrabUnpause = 0,            /* release grabber */
    seqGrabPause = 1,              /* pause all playback */
    seqGrabPauseForMenu = 3        /* pause for menu display */
};

/* selectors for basic sequence grabber component functions */
    kSGInitializeSelect       = 0x1;  /* SGInitialize */
    kSGSetDataOutputSelect    = 0x2;  /* SGSetDataOutput */
    kSGGetDataOutputSelect    = 0x3;  /* SGGetDataOutput */
    kSGSetGWorldSelect        = 0x4;  /* SGSetGWorld */
    kSGGetGWorldSelect        = 0x5;  /* SGGetGWorld */
    kSGNewChannelSelect       = 0x6;  /* SGNewChannel */
```

CHAPTER 5

Sequence Grabber Components

```
    kSGDisposeChannelSelect            = 0x7;   /* SGDisposeChannel */
    kSGStartPreviewSelect              = 0x10;  /* SGStartPreview */
    kSGStartRecordSelect               = 0x11;  /* SGStartRecord */
    kSGIdleSelect                      = 0x12;  /* SGIdle */
    kSGStopSelect                      = 0x13;  /* SGStop */
    kSGPauseSelect                     = 0x14;  /* SGPause */
    kSGPrepareSelect                   = 0x15;  /* SGPrepare */
    kSGReleaseSelect                   = 0x16;  /* SGRelease */
    kSGGetMovieSelect                  = 0x17;  /* SGGetMovie */
    kSGSetMaximumRecordTimeSelect      = 0x18;  /* SGSetMaximumRecordTime */
    kSGGetMaximumRecordTimeSelect      = 0x19;  /* SGGetMaximumRecordTime */
    kSGGetStorageSpaceRemainingSelect  = 0x1a;  /* SGGetStorageSpaceRemaining */
    kSGGetTimeRemainingSelect          = 0x1b;  /* SGGetTimeRemaining */
    kSGGrabPictSelect                  = 0x1c;  /* SGGrabPict */
    kSGGetLastMovieResIDSelect         = 0x1d;  /* SGGetLastMovieResID */
    kSGSetFlagsSelect                  = 0x1e;  /* SGSetFlags */
    kSGGetFlagsSelect                  = 0x1f;  /* SGGetFlags */
    kSGSetDataProcSelect               = 0x20;  /* SGSetDataProc */
    kSGNewChannelFromComponentSelect   = 0x21;  /* SGNewChannelFromComponent */
    kSGDisposeDeviceListSelect         = 0x22;  /* SGDisposeDeviceList */
    kSGAppendDeviceListToMenuSelect    = 0x23;  /* SGAppendDeviceListToMenu */
    kSGSetSettingsSelect               = 0x24;  /* SGSetSettings */
    kSGGetSettingsSelect               = 0x25;  /* SGGetSettings */
    kSGGetIndChannelSelect             = 0x26;  /* SGGetIndChannel */
    kSGUpdateSelect                    = 0x27;  /* SGUpdate */
    kSGGetPauseSelect                  = 0x28;  /* SGGetPause */
    kSGSettingsDialogSelect            = 0x29;  /* SGSettingsDialog */
    kSGGetAlignmentProcSelect          = 0x2A;  /* SGGetAlignmentProc */
    kSGSetChannelSettingsSelect        = 0x2B;  /* SGSetChannelSettings */
    kSGGetChannelSettingsSelect        = 0x2C;  /* SGGetChannelSettings */

/* selectors for common channel configuration functions */
    kSGCSetChannelUsageSelect          = 0x80;  /* SGCSetChannelUsage */
    kSGCGetChannelUsageSelect          = 0x81;  /* SGCGetChannelUsage */
    kSGCSetChannelBoundsSelect         = 0x82;  /* SGCSetChannelBounds */
    kSGCGetChannelBoundsSelect         = 0x83;  /* SGCGetChannelBounds */
    kSGCSetChannelVolumeSelect         = 0x84;  /* SGCSetChannelVolume */
    kSGCGetChannelVolumeSelect         = 0x85;  /* SGCGetChannelVolume */
    kSGCGetChannelInfoSelect           = 0x86;  /* SGCGetChannelInfo */
    kSGCSetChannelPlayFlagsSelect      = 0x87;  /* SGCSetChannelPlayFlags */
    kSGCGetChannelPlayFlagsSelect      = 0x88;  /* SGCGetChannelPlayFlags */
    kSGCSetChannelMaxFramesSelect      = 0x89;  /* SGCSetChannelMaxFrames */
    kSGCGetChannelMaxFramesSelect      = 0x8a;  /* SGCGetChannelMaxFrames */
```

CHAPTER 5

Sequence Grabber Components

```
kSGCSetChannelRefConSelect      = 0x8b;   /* SGCSetChannelRefCon */
kSGCSetChannelClipSelect        = 0x8C;   /* SGCSetChannelClip */
kSGCGetChannelClipSelect        = 0x8D;   /* SGCGetChannelClip */
kSGCGetChannelSampleDescriptionSelect = 0x8E;
                                          /* SGCGetChannelSampleDescription */
kSGCGetChannelDeviceListSelect  = 0x8F;   /* SGCGetChannelDeviceList */
kSGCSetChannelDeviceSelect      = 0x90;   /* SGCSetChannelDevice */
kSGCSetChannelMatrixSelect      = 0x91;   /* SGCSetChannelMatrix */
kSGCGetChannelMatrixSelect      = 0x92;   /* SGCGetChannelMatrix */
kSGCGetChannelTimeScaleSelect   = 0x93;   /* SGCGetChannelTimeScale */

/* selectors for video channel configuration functions */
kSGCGetSrcVideoBoundsSelect     = 0x100;  /* SGCGetSrcVideoBounds */
kSGCSetVideoRectSelect          = 0x101;  /* SGCSetVideoRect */
kSGCGetVideoRectSelect          = 0x102;  /* SGCGetVideoRect */
kSGCGetVideoCompressorTypeSelect = 0x103; /* SGCGetVideoCompressorType */
kSGCSetVideoCompressorTypeSelect = 0x104; /* SGCSetVideoCompressorType */
kSGCSetVideoCompressorSelect    = 0x105;  /* SGCSetVideoCompressor */
kSGCGetVideoCompressorSelect    = 0x106;  /* SGCGetVideoCompressor */
kSGCGetVideoDigitizerComponentSelect
                                = 0x107;
                                          /* SGCGetVideoDigitizerComponent */
kSGCSetVideoDigitizerComponentSelect
                                = 0x108;
                                          /* SGCSetVideoDigitizerComponent */
kSGCVideoDigitizerChangedSelect = 0x109;  /* SGCVideoDigitizerChanged */
kSGCSetVideoBottlenecksSelect   = 0x10a;  /* SGCSetVideoBottlenecks */
kSGCGetVideoBottlenecksSelect   = 0x10b;  /* SGCGetVideoBottlenecks */
kSGCGrabFrameSelect             = 0x10c;  /* SGCGrabFrame */
kSGCGrabFrameCompleteSelect     = 0x10d;  /* SGCGrabFrameComplete */
kSGCDisplayFrameSelect          = 0x10e;  /* SGCDisplayFrame */
kSGCCompressFrameSelect         = 0x10f;  /* SGCCompressFrame */
kSGCCompressFrameCompleteSelect = 0x110;  /* SGCCompressFrameComplete */
kSGCAddFrameSelect              = 0x111;  /* SGCAddFrame */
kSGCTransferFrameForCompressSelect = 0x112;
                                          /* SGCTransferFrameForCompress */
kSGCSetCompressBufferSelect     = 0x113;
                                          /* SGCSetCompressBuffer */
kSGCGetCompressBufferSelect     = 0x114;
                                          /* SGCGetCompressBuffer */
kSGCGetBufferInfoSelect         = 0x115;  /* SGCGetBufferInfo */
kSGCSetUseScreenBufferSelect    = 0x116;  /* SGCSetUseScreenBuffer */
kSGCGetUseScreenBufferSelect    = 0x117;  /* SGCGetUseScreenBuffer */
```

Sequence Grabber Components

```
    kSGCGrabCompressCompleteSelect      = 0x118; /* SGCGrabCompressComplete */
    kSGCDisplayCompressSelect           = 0x119; /* SGCDisplayCompress */
    kSGCSetFrameRateSelect              = 0x11A; /* SGCSetFrameRate */
    kSGCGetFrameRateSelect              = 0x11B; /* SGCGetFrameRate */

    /* selectors for sound channel configuration functions */
    kSGCSetSoundInputDriverSelect       = 0x100; /* SGCSetSoundInputDriver */
    kSGCGetSoundInputDriverSelect       = 0x101; /* SGCGetSoundInputDriver */
    kSGCSoundInputDriverChangedSelect   = 0x102;
                                        /* SGCSoundInputDriverChanged */
    kSGCSetSoundRecordChunkSizeSelect   = 0x103;
                                        /* SGCSetSoundRecordChunkSize */
    kSGCGetSoundRecordChunkSizeSelect   = 0x104;
                                        /* SGCGetSoundRecordChunkSize */
    kSGCSetSoundInputRateSelect         = 0x105; /* SGCSetSoundInputRate */
    kSGCGetSoundInputRateSelect         = 0x106; /* SGCGetSoundInputRate */
    kSGCSetSoundInputParametersSelect   = 0x107;
                                            /* SGCSetSoundInputParameters */
    kSGCGetSoundInputParametersSelect   = 0x108;
                                            /* SGCGetSoundInputParameters */

    /* selectors for utility functions provided to channel components */
    kSGWriteMovieDataSelect             = 0x100; /* SGWriteMovieData */
    kSGAddFrameReferenceSelect          = 0x101; / *SGAddFrameReference */
    kSGGetNextFrameReferenceSelect      = 0x102; /* SGGetNextFrameReference */
    kSGGetTimeBaseSelect                = 0x103; /* SGGetTimeBase */
    kSGSortDeviceListSelect             = 0x104; /* SGSortDeviceList */
    kSGAddMovieDataSelect               = 0x105; /* SGAddMovieData */
    kSGChangedSourceSelect              = 0x106; /* SGChangedSource */
```

Data Types

```
struct SGCompressInfo {
    Ptr             buffer;     /* buffer for compressed image */
    unsigned long   bufferSize; /* bytes of image data in buffer */
    unsigned char   similarity; /* relative similarity */
    unsigned char   reserved;   /* reserved--set to 0 */
};
typedef struct SGCompressInfo SGCompressInfo;

struct SeqGrabFrameInfo {
    long            frameOffset;    /* offset to the sample */
    long            frameTime;      /* time that frame was captured */
```

```
    long        frameSize;      /* number of bytes in sample */
    SGChannel   frameChannel;   /* current connection to channel */
    long        frameRefCon;    /* reference constant for channel */
};

struct VideoBottles {
    short                     procCount;              /* count of callbacks */
    GrabProc                  grabProc;               /* grab function */
    GrabCompleteProc          grabCompleteProc;       /* grab-complete
                                                         function */
    DisplayProc               displayProc;            /* display function */
    CompressProc              compressProc;           /* compress function */
    CompressCompleteProc      compressCompleteProc;
                                                      /* compress-complete
                                                         function */
    AddFrameProc              addFrameProc;           /* add-frame function */
    TransferFrameProc         transferFrameProc;      /* transfer-frame
                                                         function */
    GrabCompressCompleteProc  grabCompressCompleteProc;
                                                      /* grab-compress-complete
                                                         function */
    DisplayCompressProc       displayCompressProc;    /* display-compress
                                                         function */
};
typedef struct VideoBottles VideoBottles;

typedef struct SGDeviceListRecord {
    short         count;          /* count of devices */
    short         selectedIndex;  /* current device */
    long          reserved;       /* set to 0 */
    SGDeviceName  entry[1];       /* device names */
} SGDeviceListRecord, *SGDeviceListPtr, **SGDeviceList;

typedef struct SGDeviceName {
    Str63    name;       /* device name */
    Handle   icon;       /* device icon */
    long     flags;      /* flags */
    long     refCon;     /* set to 0 */
    long     reserved;   /* set to 0 */
} SGDeviceName;
```

Sequence Grabber Component Functions

Configuring Sequence Grabber Components

```
pascal ComponentResult SGInitialize
                    (SeqGrabComponent s);
pascal ComponentResult SGSetDataOutput
                    (SeqGrabComponent s, FSSpec *movieFile,
                     long whereFlags);
pascal ComponentResult SGGetDataOutput
                    (SeqGrabComponent s,
                     FSSpec *movieFile, long *whereFlags);
pascal ComponentResult SGSetGWorld
                    (SeqGrabComponent s, CGrafPtr gp, GDHandle gd);
pascal ComponentResult SGGetGWorld
                    (SeqGrabComponent s, CGrafPtr *gp,
                     GDHandle *gd);
pascal ComponentResult SGNewChannel
                    (SeqGrabComponent s, OSType channelType,
                     SGChannel *ref);
pascal ComponentResult SGNewChannelFromComponent
                    (SeqGrabComponent s, SGChannel *newChannel,
                     Component sgChannelComponent);
pascal ComponentResult SGGetIndChannel
                    (SeqGrabComponent s, short index,
                     SGChannel *ref, OSType *chanType);
pascal ComponentResult SGDisposeChannel
                    (SeqGrabComponent s, SGChannel c);
pascal ComponentResult SGSetDataProc
                    (SeqGrabComponent sg, SGDataProc proc,
                     long refCon);
pascal ComponentResult SGGetAlignmentProc
                    (SeqGrabComponent s,
                     AlignmentProcRecordPtr alignmentProc);
```

Controlling Sequence Grabber Components

```
pascal ComponentResult SGStartPreview
                    (SeqGrabComponent s);
pascal ComponentResult SGStartRecord
                    (SeqGrabComponent s);
pascal ComponentResult SGIdle
                    (SeqGrabComponent s);
```

CHAPTER 5

Sequence Grabber Components

```
pascal ComponentResult SGUpdate
                        (SeqGrabComponent s, RgnHandle updateRgn);
pascal ComponentResult SGStop
                        (SeqGrabComponent s);
pascal ComponentResult SGPause
                        (SeqGrabComponent s, Byte pause);
pascal ComponentResult SGGetPause
                        (SeqGrabComponent s, Byte *paused);
pascal ComponentResult SGPrepare
                        (SeqGrabComponent s, Boolean prepareForPreview,
                         Boolean prepareForRecord);
pascal ComponentResult SGRelease
                        (SeqGrabComponent s);
pascal Movie SGGetMovie    (SeqGrabComponent s);
pascal ComponentResult SGGetLastMovieResID
                        (SeqGrabComponent s, short *resID);
pascal ComponentResult SGGrabPict
                        (SeqGrabComponent s, PicHandle *p,
                         const Rect *bounds, short offscreenDepth,
                         long grabPictFlags);
```

Working With Sequence Grabber Settings

```
pascal ComponentResult SGSettingsDialog
                        (SeqGrabComponent s, SGChannel c,
                         short numPanels, Component *panelList,
                         long flags, SGModalFilterProcPtr proc,
                         long procRefNum);
pascal ComponentResult SGGetSettings
                        (SeqGrabComponent s, UserData *ud, long flags);
pascal ComponentResult SGSetSettings
                        (SeqGrabComponent s, UserData ud, long flags);
pascal ComponentResult SGGetChannelSettings
                        (SeqGrabComponent s, SGChannel c, UserData *ud,
                         long flags);
pascal ComponentResult SGSetChannelSettings
                        (SeqGrabComponent s, SGChannel c, UserData ud,
                         long flags);
```

Working With Sequence Grabber Characteristics

```
pascal ComponentResult SGSetMaximumRecordTime
                        (SeqGrabComponent s, unsigned long ticks);
```

```
pascal ComponentResult SGGetMaximumRecordTime
                        (SeqGrabComponent s, unsigned long *ticks);
pascal ComponentResult SGGetStorageSpaceRemaining
                        (SeqGrabComponent s, unsigned long *bytes);
pascal ComponentResult SGGetTimeRemaining
                        (SeqGrabComponent s, long *ticksLeft);
pascal ComponentResult SGGetTimeBase
                        (SeqGrabComponent s, TimeBase *tb);
pascal ComponentResult SGSetFlags
                        (SeqGrabComponent s, long sgFlags);
pascal ComponentResult SGGetFlags
                        (SeqGrabComponent s, long *sgFlags);
```

Working With Channel Characteristics

```
pascal ComponentResult SGSetChannelUsage
                        (SGChannel c, long usage);
pascal ComponentResult SGGetChannelUsage
                        (SGChannel c, long *usage);
pascal ComponentResult SGGetChannelInfo
                        (SGChannel c, long *channelInfo);
pascal ComponentResult SGSetChannelPlayFlags
                        (SGChannel c, long playFlags);
pascal ComponentResult SGGetChannelPlayFlags
                        (SGChannel c, long *playFlags);
pascal ComponentResult SGSetChannelMaxFrames
                        (SGChannel c, long frameCount);
pascal ComponentResult SGGetChannelMaxFrames
                        (SGChannel c, long *frameCount);
pascal ComponentResult SGSetChannelBounds
                        (SGChannel c, const Rect *bounds);
pascal ComponentResult SGGetChannelBounds
                        (SGChannel c, Rect *bounds);
pascal ComponentResult SGSetChannelVolume
                        (SGChannel c, short volume);
pascal ComponentResult SGGetChannelVolume
                        (SGChannel c, short *volume);
pascal ComponentResult SGSetChannelRefCon
                        (SGChannel c, long refCon);
pascal ComponentResult SGGetChannelSampleDescription
                        (SGChannel c, Handle sampleDesc);
pascal ComponentResult SGGetChannelTimeScale
                        (SGChannel c, TimeScale *scale);
```

```
pascal ComponentResult SGSetChannelClip
                        (SGChannel c, RgnHandle theClip);
pascal ComponentResult SGGetChannelClip
                        (SGChannel c, RgnHandle *theClip);
pascal ComponentResult SGSetChannelMatrix
                        (SGChannel c, const MatrixRecord *m);
pascal ComponentResult SGGetChannelMatrix
                        (SGChannel c, MatrixRecord *m);
```

Working With Channel Devices

```
pascal ComponentResult SGGetChannelDeviceList
                        (SGChannel c, long selectionFlags,
                         SGDeviceList *list);
pascal ComponentResult SGDisposeDeviceList
                        (SeqGrabComponent s, SGDeviceList list);
pascal ComponentResult SGAppendDeviceListToMenu
                        (SeqGrabComponent s, SGDeviceList list,
                         MenuHandle mh);
pascal ComponentResult SGSetChannelDevice
                        (SGChannel c, StringPtr name);
```

Working With Video Channels

```
pascal ComponentResult SGGetSrcVideoBounds
                        (SGChannel c, Rect *r);
pascal ComponentResult SGSetVideoRect
                        (SGChannel c, Rect *r);
pascal ComponentResult SGGetVideoRect
                        (SGChannel c, Rect *r);
pascal ComponentResult SGSetVideoCompressorType
                        (SGChannel c, OSType compressorType);
pascal ComponentResult SGGetVideoCompressorType
                        (SGChannel c, OSType *compressorType);
pascal ComponentResult SGSetVideoCompressor
                        (SGChannel c, short depth,
                         CompressorComponent compressor,
                         CodecQ spatialQuality,
                         CodecQ temporalQuality, long keyFrameRate);
pascal ComponentResult SGGetVideoCompressor
                        (SGChannel c, short *depth,
                         CompressorComponent *compressor,
                         CodecQ *spatialQuality,
                         CodecQ *temporalQuality, long *keyFrameRate);
```

Sequence Grabber Components

```
pascal ComponentResult SGSetVideoDigitizerComponent
                    (SGChannel c, ComponentInstance vdig);
pascal ComponentInstance SGGetVideoDigitizerComponent
                    (SGChannel c);
pascal ComponentResult SGVideoDigitizerChanged
                    (SGChannel c);
pascal ComponentResult SGSetCompressBuffer
                    (SGChannel c, short depth,
                     const Rect *compressSize);
pascal ComponentResult SGGetCompressBuffer
                    (SGChannel c, short *depth, Rect *compressSize);
pascal ComponentResult SGSetFrameRate
                    (SGChannel c, Fixed frameRate);
pascal ComponentResult SGGetFrameRate
                    (SGChannel c, Fixed *frameRate);
pascal ComponentResult SGSetUseScreenBuffer
                    (SGChannel c, Boolean useScreenBuffer);
pascal ComponentResult SGGetUseScreenBuffer
                    (SGChannel c, Boolean *useScreenBuffer);
```

Working With Sound Channels

```
pascal ComponentResult SGSetSoundInputDriver
                    (SGChannel c, const Str255 driverName);
pascal long SGGetSoundInputDriver
                    (SGChannel c);
pascal ComponentResult SGSoundInputDriverChanged
                    (SGChannel c);
pascal ComponentResult SGSetSoundRecordChunkSize
                    (SGChannel c, long seconds);
pascal long SGGetSoundRecordChunkSize
                    (SGChannel c);
pascal ComponentResult SGSetSoundInputRate
                    (SGChannel c, Fixed rate);
pascal Fixed SGGetSoundInputRate
                    (SGChannel c);
pascal ComponentResult SGSetSoundInputParameters
                    (SGChannel c, short sampleSize,
                     short numChannels, OSType compressionType);
pascal ComponentResult SGGetSoundInputParameters
                    (SGChannel c, short *sampleSize,
                     short *numChannels, OSType *compressionType);
```

Video Channel Callback Functions

```
pascal ComponentResult SGSetVideoBottlenecks
                    (SGChannel c, VideoBottles *vb);
pascal ComponentResult SGGetVideoBottlenecks
                    (SGChannel c, VideoBottles *vb);
```

Utility Functions for Video Channel Callback Functions

```
pascal ComponentResult SGGetBufferInfo
                    (SGChannel c, short bufferNum,
                     PixMapHandle *bufferPM, Rect *bufferRect,
                     GWorldPtr *compressBuffer,
                     Rect *compressBufferRect);
pascal ComponentResult SGGrabFrame
                    (SGChannel c, short bufferNum);
pascal ComponentResult SGGrabFrameComplete
                    (SGChannel c, short bufferNum, Boolean *done);
pascal ComponentResult SGDisplayFrame
                    (SGChannel c, short bufferNum,
                     MatrixRecord *mp, RgnHandle clipRgn);
pascal ComponentResult SGCompressFrame
                    (SGChannel c, short bufferNum);
pascal ComponentResult SGCompressFrameComplete
                    (SGChannel c, short bufferNum, Boolean *done,
                     SGCompressInfo *ci);
pascal ComponentResult SGAddFrame
                    (SGChannel c, short bufferNum,
                     TimeValue atTime, TimeScale scale,
                     const SGCompressInfo *ci);
pascal ComponentResult SGTransferFrameForCompress
                    (SGChannel c, short bufferNum, MatrixRecord *mp,
                     RgnHandle clipRgn);
pascal ComponentResult SGGrabCompressComplete
                    (SGChannel c, Boolean *done,
                     SGCompressInfo *ci, TimeRecord *tr);
pascal ComponentResult SGDisplayCompress
                    (SGChannel c, Ptr dataPtr,
                     ImageDescriptionHandle desc, MatrixRecord *mp,
                     RgnHandle clipRgn);
```

CHAPTER 5

Sequence Grabber Components

Application-Defined Functions

```
pascal ComponentResult MyGrabFunction
                        (SGChannel c, short bufferNum, long refCon);
pascal ComponentResult MyGrabCompleteFunction
                        (SGChannel c, short bufferNum, Boolean *done,
                          long refCon);
pascal ComponentResult MyDisplayFunction
                        (SGChannel c, short bufferNum,
                          MatrixRecord *mp, RgnHandle clipRgn,
                          long refCon);
pascal ComponentResult MyCompressFunction
                        (SGChannel c, short bufferNum, long refCon);
pascal ComponentResult MyCompressCompleteFunction
                        (SGChannel c, short bufferNum, Boolean *done,
                          SGCompressInfo *ci, long refCon);
pascal ComponentResult MyAddFrameFunction
                        (SGChannel c, short bufferNum,
                          TimeValue atTime, TimeScale scale,
                          SGCompressInfo ci, long refCon);
pascal ComponentResult MyTransferFrameFunction
                        (SGChannel c, short bufferNum, MatrixRecord *mp,
                          RgnHandle clipRgn, long refCon);
pascal ComponentResult MyGrabCompressCompleteFunction
                        (SGChannel c, Boolean *done,
                          SGCompressInfo *ci, TimeRecord *tr,
                          long refCon);
pascal ComponentResult MyDisplayCompressFunction
                        (SGChannel c, Ptr dataPtr,
                          ImageDescriptionHandle desc, MatrixRecord *mp,
                          RgnHandle clipRgn, long refCon);
pascal OSErr MyDataFunction    (SGChannel c, Ptr p, long len, long *offset,
                          long chRefCon, TimeValue time,
                          short writeType, long refCon);
pascal Boolean MyModalFilter
                        (DialogPtr theDialog, EventRecord *theEvent,
                          short *itemHit, long refCon);
```

Pascal Summary

Constants

```
CONST
   {sequence grabber component type}
   SeqGrabComponentType        = 'barg';

   {sequence grabber channel type}
   SeqGrabChannelType          = 'sgch'

   {SGGrabPict function grabPictFlags parameter flags}
   grabPictOffScreen           = 1;  {place in offscreen graphics world}
   grabPictIgnoreClip          = 2;  {ignore channel clipping regions}

   {flag for SGSetFlags and SGGetFlags functions}
   sgFlagControlledGrab        = 1;  {controlled grab}


   {flags for SGSetChannelPlayFlags and SGGetChannelPlayFlags functions}
   channelPlayNormal           = 0;  {use default playback methodology}
   channelPlayFast             = 1;  {achieve fast playback rate}
   channelPlayHighQuality      = 2;  {achieve high quality image}
   channelPlayAllData          = 4;  {play all captured data}

   {flags for SGSetDataOutput and SGGetDataOutput functions}
   seqGrabToDisk               = 1;  {write recorded data to specified }
                                     { QuickTime movie}
   seqGrabToMemory             = 2;  {store recorded data in memory until }
                                     { completion of recording process}
   seqGrabDontUseTempMemory    = 4;  {don't use temporary memory to store }
                                     { recorded data}
   seqGrabAppendToFile         = 8;  {add recorded data to data fork of }
                                     { specified movie file}
   seqGrabDontAddMovieResource = 16; {don't add movie resource to }
                                     { specified movie file}

   {usage flags for SGSetChannelUsage and SGGetChannelUsage functions}
   seqGrabRecord               = 1;  {used during record operations}
   seqGrabPreview              = 2;  {used during preview operations}
   seqGrabPlayDuringRecord     = 4;  {used during record operations}
```

Sequence Grabber Components

```
{SGGetChannelInfo function flags}
seqGrabHasBounds                     = 1;    {visual representation of data}
seqGrabHasVolume                     = 2;    {audio representation of data}
seqGrabHasDiscreteSamples            = 4;    {data organized in discrete frames}

{device list structure flags}
sgDeviceListWithIcons                = 1;    {include icons}
sgDeviceListDontCheckAvailability    = 2;    {do not check availability }
                                             { of device}

{data function write operation types}
seqGrabWriteAppend      = 0;    {append to file}
seqGrabWriteReserve     = 1;    {reserve space in file}
seqGrabWrite            = 2;    {fill reserved space}

{SGPause and SGGetPause options}
seqGrabUnpause          = 0;    {release grabber}
seqGrabPause            = 1;    {pause all playback}
seqGrabPauseForMenu     = 3;    {pause for menu display}

{selectors for basic sequence grabber component functions}
kSGInitializeSelect                  = $1;   {SGInitialize}
kSGSetDataOutputSelect               = $2;   {SGSetDataOutput}
kSGGetDataOutputSelect               = $3;   {SGGetDataOutput}
kSGSetGWorldSelect                   = $4;   {SGSetGWorld}
kSGGetGWorldSelect                   = $5;   {SGGetGWorld}
kSGNewChannelSelect                  = $6;   {SGNewChannel}
kSGDisposeChannelSelect              = $7;   {SGDisposeChannel}
kSGStartPreviewSelect                = $10;  {SGStartPreview}
kSGStartRecordSelect                 = $11;  {SGStartRecord}
kSGIdleSelect                        = $12;  {SGIdle}
kSGStopSelect                        = $13;  {SGStop}
kSGPauseSelect                       = $14;  {SGPause}
kSGPrepareSelect                     = $15;  {SGPrepare}
kSGReleaseSelect                     = $16;  {SGRelease}
kSGGetMovieSelect                    = $17;  {SGGetMovie}
kSGSetMaximumRecordTimeSelect        = $18;  {SGSetMaximumRecordTime}
kSGGetMaximumRecordTimeSelect        = $19;  {SGGetMaximumRecordTime}
kSGGetStorageSpaceRemainingSelect    = $1A;  {SGGetStorageSpaceRemaining}
kSGGetTimeRemainingSelect            = $1B;  {SGGetTimeRemaining}
kSGGrabPictSelect                    = $1C;  {SGGrabPict}
kSGGetLastMovieResIDSelect           = $1D;  {SGGetLastMovieResID}
kSGSetFlagsSelect                    = $1E;  {SGSetFlags}
kSGGetFlagsSelect                    = $1F;  {SGGetFlags}
```

CHAPTER 5

Sequence Grabber Components

```
kSGSetDataProcSelect               = $20;   {SGSetDataProc}
kSGNewChannelFromComponentSelect   = $21;   {SGNewChannelFromComponent}
kSGDisposeDeviceListSelect         = $22;   {SGDisposeDeviceList}
kSGAppendDeviceListToMenuSelect    = $23;   {SGAppendDeviceListToMenu}
kSGSetSettingsSelect               = $24;   {SGSetSettings}
kSGGetSettingsSelect               = $25;   {SGGetSettings}
kSGGetIndChannelSelect             = $26;   {SGGetIndChannel}
kSGUpdateSelect                    = $27;   {SGUpdate}
kSGGetPauseSelect                  = $28;   {SGGetPause}
kSGSettingsDialogSelect            = $29;   {SGSettingsDialog}
kSGGetAlignmentProcSelect          = $2A;   {SGGetAlignmentProc}
kSGSetChannelSettingsSelect        = $2B;   {SGSetChannelSettings}
kSGGetChannelSettingsSelect        = $2C;   {SGGetChannelSettings}

{selectors for common channel configuration functions}
kSGCSetChannelUsageSelect             = $80;   {SGCSetChannelUsage}
kSGCGetChannelUsageSelect             = $81;   {SGCGetChannelUsage}
kSGCSetChannelBoundsSelect            = $82;   {SGCSetChannelBounds}
kSGCGetChannelBoundsSelect            = $83;   {SGCGetChannelBounds}
kSGCSetChannelVolumeSelect            = $84;   {SGCSetChannelVolume}
kSGCGetChannelVolumeSelect            = $85;   {SGCGetChannelVolume}
kSGCGetChannelInfoSelect              = $86;   {SGCGetChannelInfo}
kSGCSetChannelPlayFlagsSelect         = $87;   {SGCSetChannelPlayFlags}
kSGCGetChannelPlayFlagsSelect         = $88;   {SGCGetChannelPlayFlags}
kSGCSetChannelMaxFramesSelect         = $89;   {SGCSetChannelMaxFrames}
kSGCGetChannelMaxFramesSelect         = $8A;   {SGCGetChannelMaxFrames}
kSGCSetChannelRefConSelect            = $8B;   {SGCSetChannelRefCon}
kSGCSetChannelClipSelect              = $8C;   {SGCSetChannelClip}
kSGCGetChannelClipSelect              = $8D;   {SGCGetChannelClip}
kSGCGetChannelSampleDescriptionSelect = $8E;
                                            {SGCGetChannelSampleDescription}
kSGCGetChannelDeviceListSelect        = $8F;   {SGCGetChannelDeviceList}
kSGCSetChannelDeviceSelect            = $90;   {SGCSetChannelDevice}
kSGCSetChannelMatrixSelect            = $91;   {SGCSetChannelMatrix}
kSGCGetChannelMatrixSelect            = $92;   {SGCGetChannelMatrix}
kSGCGetChannelTimeScaleSelect         = $93;   {SGCGetChannelTimeScale}

{selectors for video channel configuration functions}
kSGCGetSrcVideoBoundsSelect        = $100;  {SGCGetSrcVideoBounds}
kSGCSetVideoRectSelect             = $101;  {SGCSetVideoRect}
kSGCGetVideoRectSelect             = $102;  {SGCGetVideoRect}
kSGCGetVideoCompressorTypeSelect   = $103;
                                            {SGCGetVideoCompressorType}
```

Sequence Grabber Components

```
kSGCSetVideoCompressorTypeSelect         = $104;
                                         {SGCSetVideoCompressorType}
kSGCSetVideoCompressorSelect             = $105;  {SGCSetVideoCompressor}
kSGCGetVideoCompressorSelect             = $106;  {SGCGetVideoCompressor}
kSGCGetVideoDigitizerComponentSelect     = $107;
                                         {SGCGetVideoDigitizerComponent}
kSGCSetVideoDigitizerComponentSelect     = $108;
                                         {SGCSetVideoDigitizerComponent}
kSGCVideoDigitizerChangedSelect          = $109;  {SGCVideoDigitizerChanged}
kSGCSetVideoBottlenecksSelect            = $10A;  {SGCSetVideoBottlenecks}
kSGCGetVideoBottlenecksSelect            = $10B;  {SGCGetVideoBottlenecks}
kSGCGrabFrameSelect                      = $10C;  {SGCGrabFrame}
kSGCGrabFrameCompleteSelect              = $10D;  {SGCGrabFrameComplete}
kSGCDisplayFrameSelect                   = $10E;  {SGCDisplayFrame}
kSGCCompressFrameSelect                  = $10F;  {SGCCompressFrame}
kSGCCompressFrameCompleteSelect          = $110;  {SGCCompressFrameComplete}
kSGCAddFrameSelect                       = $111;  {SGCAddFrame}
kSGCTransferFrameForCompressSelect       = $112;
                                         {SGCTransferFrameForCompress}
kSGCSetCompressBufferSelect              = $113;  {SGCSetCompressBuffer}
kSGCGetCompressBufferSelect              = $114;  {SGCGetCompressBuffer}
kSGCGetBufferInfoSelect                  = $115;  {SGCGetBufferInfo}
kSGCSetUseScreenBufferSelect             = $116;  {SGCSetUseScreenBuffer}
kSGCGetUseScreenBufferSelect             = $117;  {SGCGetUseScreenBuffer}
kSGCGrabCompressCompleteSelect           = $118;  {SGCGrabCompressComplete}
kSGCDisplayCompressSelect                = $119;  {SGCDisplayCompress}
kSGCSetFrameRateSelect                   = $11A;  {SGCSetFrameRate}
kSGCGetFrameRateSelect                   = $11B;  {SGCGetFrameRate}

{selectors for sound channel configuration functions}
kSGCSetSoundInputDriverSelect            = $100;  {SGCSetSoundInputDriver}
kSGCGetSoundInputDriverSelect            = $101;  {SGCGetSoundInputDriver}
kSGCSoundInputDriverChangedSelect        = $102;  {SGCSoundInputDriverChanged}
kSGCSetSoundRecordChunkSizeSelect        = $103;  {SGCSetSoundRecordChunkSize}
kSGCGetSoundRecordChunkSizeSelect        = $104;  {SGCGetSoundRecordChunkSize}
kSGCSetSoundInputRateSelect              = $105;  {SGCSetSoundInputRate}
kSGCGetSoundInputRateSelect              = $106;  {SGCGetSoundInputRate}
kSGCSetSoundInputParametersSelect        = $107;  {SGCSetSoundInputParameters}
kSGCGetSoundInputParametersSelect        = $108;  {SGCGetSoundInputParameters}

{selectors for utility functions provided to channel components}
kSGWriteMovieDataSelect                  = $100;  {SGWriteMovieData}
kSGAddFrameReferenceSelect               = $101;  {SGAddFrameReference}
kSGGetNextFrameReferenceSelect           = $102;  {SGGetNextFrameReference}
```

CHAPTER 5

Sequence Grabber Components

```
kSGGetTimeBaseSelect            = $103;   {SGGetTimeBase}
kSGSortDeviceListSelect         = $104;   {SGSortDeviceList}
kSGAddMovieDataSelect           = $105;   {SGAddMovieData}
kSGChangedSourceSelect          = $106;   {SGChangedSource}
```

Data Types

```
TYPE SGCompressInfo =
   PACKED RECORD
      buffer:         Ptr;       {buffer containing compressed image}
      bufferSize:     LongInt;   {bytes of image data in buffer}
      similarity:     Char;      {relative similarity of image }
                                 { to previous image in sequence}
      reserved:       Char;      {reserved}
END;

   VideoBottles =
   RECORD
      procCount:              Integer;              {number of callback }
                                                    { routines in record}
      grabProc:               GrabProc;             {grab function}
      grabCompleteProc:       GrabCompleteProc;     {grab-complete function}
      displayProc:            DisplayProc;          {display function}
      compressProc:           CompressProc;         {compress function}
      compressCompleteProc:   CompressCompleteProc;
                                                    {compress-complete }
                                                    { function}
      addFrameProc:           AddFrameProc;         {add-frame function}
      transferFrameProc:      TransferFrameProc;    {transfer-frame }
                                                    { function}
   END;

   SeqGrabFrameInfo =
   RECORD
      frameOffset:    LongInt;     {offset to the sample}
      frameTime:      LongInt;     {time that frame was captured}
      frameSize:      LongInt;     {number of bytes in sample}
      frameChannel:   SGChannel;   {current connection to channel}
      frameRefCon:    LongInt;     {reference constant for channel}
   END;
```

Sequence Grabber Components

```
SGDeviceName =
RECORD
   name:    Str63;        {device name}
   icon:    Handle;        {device icon}
   flags:   LongInt;       {flags}
   refCon:  LongInt;       {set to 0}
   reserved: LongInt;      {reserved--set to 0}
END;

SGDeviceListPtr = ^SGDeviceListRecord;
SGDeviceList = ^SGDeviceListPtr;

SGDeviceListRecord =
RECORD
   count:         Integer;                       {count of devices}
   selectedIndex: Integer;                       {current device}
   reserved:      LongInt;                       {reserved--set to 0}
   entry:         ARRAY[0..0] OF SGDeviceName;   {device names}
END;
```

Sequence Grabber Component Routines

Configuring Sequence Grabber Components

```
FUNCTION SGInitialize        (s: SeqGrabComponent): ComponentResult;
FUNCTION SGSetDataOutput     (s: SeqGrabComponent; movieFile: FSSpec;
                               whereFlags: LongInt): ComponentResult;
FUNCTION SGGetDataOutput     (s: SeqGrabComponent; VAR movieFile: FSSpec;
                               VAR whereFlags: LongInt): ComponentResult;
FUNCTION SGSetGWorld         (s: SeqGrabComponent; gp: CGrafPtr;
                               gd: GDHandle): ComponentResult;
FUNCTION SGGetGWorld         (s: SeqGrabComponent; VAR gp: CGrafPtr;
                               VAR gd: GDHandle): ComponentResult;
FUNCTION SGNewChannel        (s: SeqGrabComponent; channelType: OSType;
                               VAR ref: SGChannel): ComponentResult;
FUNCTION SGNewChannelFromComponent
                             (s: SeqGrabComponent;
                               VAR newChannel: SGChannel;
                               sgChannelComponent: Component):
                               ComponentResult;
FUNCTION SGGetIndChannel     (s: SeqGrabComponent; index: Integer;
                               VAR ref: SGChannel;
                               VAR chanType: OSType): ComponentResult;
```

```
FUNCTION SGDisposeChannel     (s: SeqGrabComponent;
                               c: SGChannel): ComponentResult;
FUNCTION SGSetDataProc        (s: SeqGrabComponent; proc: SGDataProc;
                               refCon: LongInt): ComponentResult;
FUNCTION SGGetAlignmentProc
                              (s: SeqGrabComponent;
                               alignmentProc: AlignmentProcRecordPtr):
                               ComponentResult;
```

Controlling Sequence Grabber Components

```
FUNCTION SGStartPreview       (s: SeqGrabComponent): ComponentResult;
FUNCTION SGStartRecord        (s: SeqGrabComponent): ComponentResult;
FUNCTION SGIdle               (s: SeqGrabComponent): ComponentResult;
FUNCTION SGUpdate             (s: SeqGrabComponent; updateRgn: RgnHandle):
                               ComponentResult;
FUNCTION SGStop               (s: SeqGrabComponent): ComponentResult;
FUNCTION SGPause              (s: SeqGrabComponent;
                               paused: Byte): ComponentResult;
FUNCTION SGGetPause           (s: SeqGrabComponent;
                               VAR paused: Byte): ComponentResult;
FUNCTION SGPrepare            (s: SeqGrabComponent;
                               prepareForPreview: Boolean;
                               prepareForRecord: Boolean): ComponentResult;
FUNCTION SGRelease            (s: SeqGrabComponent): ComponentResult;
FUNCTION SGGetMovie           (s: SeqGrabComponent): Movie;
FUNCTION SGGetLastMovieResID
                              (s: SeqGrabComponent;
                               VAR resID: Integer): ComponentResult;
FUNCTION SGGrabPict           (s: SeqGrabComponent; VAR p: PicHandle;
                               bounds: Rect; offscreenDepth: Integer;
                               grabPictFlags: LongInt): ComponentResult;
```

Working With Sequence Grabber Settings

```
FUNCTION SGSettingsDialog     (s: SeqGrabComponent; c: SGChannel;
                               numPanels: Integer; VAR panelList: Component;
                               flags: LongInt; proc: SGModalFilterProcPtr;
                               procRefNum: LongInt): ComponentResult;
FUNCTION SGGetSettings        (s: SeqGrabComponent; VAR ud: UserData;
                               flags: LongInt): ComponentResult;
FUNCTION SGSetSettings        (s: SeqGrabComponent; ud: UserData;
                               flags: LongInt): ComponentResult;
```

Sequence Grabber Components

```
FUNCTION SGGetChannelSettings
                        (s: SeqGrabComponent; c: SGChannel;
                         VAR ud: UserData; flags: LongInt):
                         ComponentResult;
FUNCTION SGSetChannelSettings
                        (s: SeqGrabComponent; c: SGChannel;
                         ud: UserData; flags: LongInt): ComponentResult;
```

Working With Sequence Grabber Characteristics

```
FUNCTION SGSetMaximumRecordTime
                        (s: SeqGrabComponent; ticks: LongInt):
                         ComponentResult;
FUNCTION SGGetMaximumRecordTime
                        (s: SeqGrabComponent; VAR ticks: LongInt):
                         ComponentResult;
FUNCTION SGGetStorageSpaceRemaining
                        (s: SeqGrabComponent; VAR bytes: LongInt):
                         ComponentResult;
FUNCTION SGGetTimeRemaining  (s: SeqGrabComponent; VAR ticksLeft: LongInt):
                         ComponentResult;
FUNCTION SGGetTimeBase       (s: SeqGrabComponent; VAR tb: TimeBase):
                         ComponentResult;
FUNCTION SGSetFlags          (s: SeqGrabComponent; sgFlags: LongInt):
                         ComponentResult;
FUNCTION SGGetFlags          (s: SeqGrabComponent; VAR sgFlags: LongInt):
                         ComponentResult;
```

Working With Channel Characteristics

```
FUNCTION SGSetChannelUsage   (c: SGChannel; usage: LongInt): ComponentResult;
FUNCTION SGGetChannelUsage   (c: SGChannel; VAR usage: LongInt):
                         ComponentResult;
FUNCTION SGGetChannelInfo    (c: SGChannel; VAR channelInfo: LongInt):
                         ComponentResult;
FUNCTION SGSetChannelPlayFlags
                        (c: SGChannel; playFlags: LongInt):
                         ComponentResult;
FUNCTION SGGetChannelPlayFlags
                        (c: SGChannel; VAR playFlags: LongInt):
                         ComponentResult;
FUNCTION SGSetChannelMaxFrames
                        (c: SGChannel; frameCount: LongInt):
                         ComponentResult;
```

CHAPTER 5

Sequence Grabber Components

```
FUNCTION SGGetChannelMaxFrames
                            (c: SGChannel; VAR frameCount: LongInt):
                             ComponentResult;
FUNCTION SGSetChannelBounds
                            (c: SGChannel; bounds: Rect): ComponentResult;
FUNCTION SGGetChannelBounds
                            (c: SGChannel; VAR bounds: Rect):
                             ComponentResult;
FUNCTION SGSetChannelVolume
                            (c: SGChannel; volume: Integer):
                             ComponentResult;
FUNCTION SGGetChannelVolume
                            (c: SGChannel; VAR volume: Integer):
                             ComponentResult;
FUNCTION SGSetChannelRefCon
                            (c: SGChannel; refCon: LongInt):
                             ComponentResult;
FUNCTION SGGetChannelSampleDescription
                            (c: SGChannel; sampleDesc: Handle):
                             ComponentResult;
FUNCTION SGGetChannelTimeScale
                            (c: SGChannel; VAR scale: TimeScale):
                             ComponentResult;
FUNCTION SGGetChannelClip   (c: SGChannel; VAR theClip: RgnHandle):
                             ComponentResult;
FUNCTION SGGetChannelClip   (c: SGChannel; VAR theClip: RgnHandle):
                             ComponentResult;
FUNCTION SGGetChannelMatrix
                            (c: SGChannel; VAR m: MatrixRecord):
                             ComponentResult;
FUNCTION SGGetChannelMatrix
                            (c: SGChannel; VAR m: MatrixRecord):
                             ComponentResult;
```

Working With Channel Devices

```
FUNCTION SGGetChannelDeviceList
                            (c: SGChannel; selectionFlags: LongInt;
                             VAR list: SGDeviceList): ComponentResult;
FUNCTION SGDisposeDeviceList
                            (s: SeqGrabComponent; list: SGDeviceList):
                             ComponentResult;
```

```
FUNCTION SGAppendDeviceListToMenu
                              (s: SeqGrabComponent; list: SGDeviceList;
                               mh: MenuHandle): ComponentResult;
FUNCTION SGSetChannelDevice (c: SGChannel; name: StringPtr):
                              ComponentResult;
```

Working With Video Channels

```
FUNCTION SGGetSrcVideoBounds
                              (c: SGChannel; VAR r: Rect): ComponentResult;
FUNCTION SGSetVideoRect     (c: SGChannel; r: Rect): ComponentResult;
FUNCTION SGGetVideoRect     (c: SGChannel; VAR r: Rect): ComponentResult;
FUNCTION SGSetVideoCompressorType
                              (c: SGChannel; compressorType: OSType):
                              ComponentResult;
FUNCTION SGGetVideoCompressorType
                              (c: SGChannel; VAR compressorType: OSType):
                              ComponentResult;
FUNCTION SGSetVideoCompressor
                              (c: SGChannel; depth: Integer;
                               compressor: CompressorComponent;
                               spatialQuality: CodecQ;
                               temporalQuality: CodecQ;
                               keyFrameRate: LongInt): ComponentResult;
FUNCTION SGGetVideoCompressor
                              (c: SGChannel; VAR depth: Integer;
                               VAR compressor: CompressorComponent;
                               VAR spatialQuality: CodecQ;
                               VAR temporalQuality: CodecQ;
                               VAR keyFrameRate: LongInt): ComponentResult;
FUNCTION SGSetVideoDigitizerComponent
                              (c: SGChannel; vdig: ComponentInstance):
                              ComponentResult;
FUNCTION SGGetVideoDigitizerComponent
                              (c: SGChannel): ComponentInstance;
FUNCTION SGVideoDigitizerChanged
                              (c: SGChannel): ComponentResult;
FUNCTION SGSetCompressBuffer
                              (c: SGChannel; depth: Integer;
                               compressSize: Rect): ComponentResult;
FUNCTION SGGetCompressBuffer
                              (c: SGChannel; VAR depth: Integer;
                               VAR compressSize: Rect): ComponentResult;
```

```
FUNCTION SGSetFrameRate       (c: SGChannel;
                               frameRate: Fixed): ComponentResult;
FUNCTION SGGetFrameRate       (c: SGChannel;
                               VAR frameRate: Fixed): ComponentResult;
FUNCTION SGSetUseScreenBuffer
                              (c: SGChannel; useScreenBuffer: Boolean):
                               ComponentResult;
FUNCTION SGGetUseScreenBuffer
                              (c: SGChannel; VAR useScreenBuffer: Boolean):
                               ComponentResult;
```

Working With Sound Channels

```
FUNCTION SGSetSoundInputDriver
                              (c: SGChannel; driverName: Str255):
                               ComponentResult;
FUNCTION SGGetSoundInputDriver
                              (c: SGChannel): LongInt;
FUNCTION SGSoundInputDriverChanged
                              (c: SGChannel): ComponentResult;
FUNCTION SGSetSoundRecordChunkSize
                              (c: SGChannel; seconds: LongInt):
                               ComponentResult;
FUNCTION SGGetSoundRecordChunkSize
                              (c: SGChannel): LongInt;
FUNCTION SGSetSoundInputRate
                              (c: SGChannel; rate: Fixed): ComponentResult;
FUNCTION SGGetSoundInputRate
                              (c: SGChannel): Fixed;
FUNCTION SGSetSoundInputParameters
                              (c: SGChannel; sampleSize: Integer;
                               numChannels: Integer;
                               compressionType: OSType): ComponentResult;
FUNCTION SGGetSoundInputParameters
                              (c: SGChannel; VAR sampleSize: Integer;
                               VAR numChannels: Integer;
                               VAR compressionType: OSType): ComponentResult;
```

Video Channel Callback Routines

```
FUNCTION SGSetVideoBottlenecks
                              (c: SGChannel; VAR vb: VideoBottles):
                               ComponentResult;
```

```
FUNCTION SGGetVideoBottlenecks
                                (c: SGChannel; VAR vb: VideoBottles):
                                ComponentResult;
```

Utility Routines for Video Channel Callback Functions

```
FUNCTION SGGetBufferInfo        (c: SGChannel; bufferNum: Integer;
                                VAR bufferPM: PixMapHandle;
                                VAR bufferRect: Rect;
                                VAR compressBuffer: GWorldPtr;
                                VAR compressBufferRect: Rect): ComponentResult;
FUNCTION SGGrabFrame            (c: SGChannel; bufferNum: Integer):
                                ComponentResult;
FUNCTION SGGrabFrameComplete
                                (c: SGChannel; bufferNum: Integer;
                                VAR done: Boolean): ComponentResult;
FUNCTION SGDisplayFrame         (c: SGChannel; bufferNum: Integer;
                                mp: MatrixRecord; clipRgn: RgnHandle):
                                ComponentResult;
FUNCTION SGCompressFrame        (c: SGChannel; bufferNum: Integer):
                                ComponentResult;
FUNCTION SGCompressFrameComplete
                                (c: SGChannel; bufferNum: Integer;
                                VAR done: Boolean; VAR ci: SGCompressInfo):
                                ComponentResult;
FUNCTION SGAddFrame             (c: SGChannel; bufferNum: Integer;
                                atTime: TimeValue; scale: TimeScale;
                                ci: SGCompressInfo): ComponentResult;
FUNCTION SGTransferFrameForCompress
                                (c: SGChannel; bufferNum: Integer;
                                mp: MatrixRecord; clipRgn: RgnHandle):
                                ComponentResult;
FUNCTION SGGrabCompressComplete
                                (c: SGChannel; VAR done: Boolean;
                                VAR ci: SGCompressInfo; VAR tr: TimeRecord):
                                ComponentResult;
FUNCTION SGDisplayCompress      (c: SGChannel; dataPtr: Ptr;
                                desc: ImageDescriptionHandle;
                                VAR mp: MatrixRecord;
                                clipRgn: RgnHandle): ComponentResult;
```

CHAPTER 5

Sequence Grabber Components

Application-Defined Routines

```
FUNCTION MyGrabFunction         (c: SGChannel; bufferNum: Integer;
                                 refCon: LongInt): ComponentResult;
FUNCTION MyGrabCompleteFunction
                                (c: SGChannel; bufferNum: Integer;
                                 VAR done: Boolean; refCon: LongInt):
                                 ComponentResult;
FUNCTION MyDisplayFunction      (c: SGChannel; bufferNum: Integer;
                                 mp: MatrixRecord; clipRgn: RgnHandle;
                                 refCon: LongInt): ComponentResult;
FUNCTION MyCompressFunction
                                (c: SGChannel; bufferNum: Integer;
                                 refCon: LongInt): ComponentResult;
FUNCTION MyCompressCompleteFunction
                                (c: SGChannel; bufferNum: Integer;
                                 VAR done: Boolean; VAR ci: SGCompressInfo;
                                 refCon: LongInt): ComponentResult;
FUNCTION MyAddFrameFunction
                                (c: SGChannel; bufferNum: Integer;
                                 atTime: TimeValue; scale: TimeScale;
                                 ci: SGCompressInfo; refCon: LongInt):
                                 ComponentResult;
FUNCTION MyTransferFrameFunction
                                (c: SGChannel; bufferNum: Integer;
                                 mp: MatrixRecord; clipRgn: RgnHandle;
                                 refCon: LongInt): ComponentResult;
FUNCTION MyGrabCompressCompleteFunction
                                (c: SGChannel; VAR done: Boolean;
                                 VAR ci: SGCompressInfo; VAR tr: TimeRecord;
                                 refCon: LongInt): ComponentResult;
FUNCTION MyDisplayCompressFunction
                                (c: SGChannel; dataPtr; Ptr;
                                 desc: ImageDescriptionHandle;
                                 VAR mp: MatrixRecord; clipRgn: RgnHandle;
                                 refCon: LongInt): ComponentResult;
FUNCTION MyDataFunction         (c: SGChannel; p: Ptr; len: LongInt;
                                 VAR offset: LongInt; chRefCon: LongInt;
                                 time: TimeValue; writeType: Integer;
                                 refCon: LongInt): OSErr;
FUNCTION MyModalFilter          (theDialog: DialogPtr;
                                 VAR theEvent: EventRecord;
                                 VAR ItemHit: Integer; refCon: LongInt): OSErr;
```

Result Codes

`noDeviceForChannel`	−9400	Channel component cannot find its device
`grabTimeComplete`	−9401	Time limit for record operation has expired
`cantDoThatInCurrentMode`	−9402	Request invalid in current mode
`notEnoughMemoryToGrab`	−9403	Insufficient memory for record operation
`notEnoughDiskSpaceToGrab`	−9404	Insufficient disk space for record operation
`couldntGetRequiredComponent`	−9405	Component not found
`badSGChannel`	−9406	Invalid channel specified
`seqGrabInfoNotAvailable`	−9407	Sequence grabber does not have this information at this time
`deviceCantMeetRequest`	−9408	Device cannot support grabber

CHAPTER 6

Sequence Grabber Channel Components

Contents

About Sequence Grabber Channel Components   6-3
Creating Sequence Grabber Channel Components   6-5
   Component Type and Subtype Values   6-6
   Required Functions   6-6
   Component Manager Request Codes   6-7
   A Sample Sequence Grabber Channel Component   6-10
      Implementing the Required Component Functions   6-10
      Initializing the Sequence Grabber Channel Component   6-15
      Setting and Retrieving the Channel State   6-16
      Managing Spatial Properties   6-17
      Controlling Previewing and Recording Operations   6-20
      Managing Channel Devices   6-24
      Utility Functions for Recording Image Data   6-24
      Providing Media-Specific Functions   6-28
      Managing the Settings Dialog Box   6-29
      Displaying Channel Information in the Settings Dialog Box   6-31
Using Sequence Grabber Channel Components   6-33
   Previewing   6-33
   Recording   6-34
   Working With Callback Functions   6-35
      Using Callback Functions for Video Channel Components   6-35
      Using Utility Functions for Video Channel Component Callback Functions   6-36
Sequence Grabber Channel Components Reference   6-37
   Functions   6-37
      Configuring Sequence Grabber Channel Components   6-38
      Controlling Sequence Grabber Channel Components   6-39

              Configuration Functions for All Channel Components   6-46
              Working With Channel Devices   6-58
              Configuration Functions for Video Channel Components   6-61
              Configuration Functions for Sound Channel Components   6-77
              Utility Functions for Sequence Grabber Channel Components   6-84
    Summary of Sequence Grabber Channel Components   6-91
        C Summary   6-91
            Constants   6-91
            Data Types   6-94
            Functions   6-94
        Pascal Summary   6-99
            Constants   6-99
            Data Types   6-101
            Routines   6-102
        Result Codes   6-107

CHAPTER 6

Sequence Grabber Channel Components

This chapter discusses sequence grabber channel components. **Sequence grabber channel components** manipulate captured data for sequence grabber components.

This chapter has been divided into the following sections:

- "About Sequence Grabber Channel Components" presents general information about sequence grabber channel components and their relationship to sequence grabber components.
- "Creating Sequence Grabber Channel Components" lists issues you should consider when developing a sequence grabber component, including required functions and the Component Manager result codes that you should use. It then provides a sample program that illustrates how to implement a sequence grabber channel component.
- "Using Sequence Grabber Channel Components" gives details on how sequence grabber components can use channel components to play captured data for the user or to save captured data in a QuickTime movie.
- "Sequence Grabber Channel Components Reference" describes the data structures and functions associated with the Apple-supplied sequence grabber channel component.
- "Summary of Sequence Grabber Channel Components" presents a summary of sequence grabber channel components in C and in Pascal.

If you are writing an application that uses the sequence grabber component, you do not need to read this chapter. Read the chapter "Sequence Grabber Components" in this book for a description of the services provided by sequence grabber components. If you are writing a sequence grabber channel component, you should read this chapter and read the earlier chapter that discusses sequence grabber components.

Note
Information in this chapter is presented from the perspective of a developer of a sequence grabber channel component. If you are developing a sequence grabber channel component, your component must support the interfaces described in this chapter. ◆

About Sequence Grabber Channel Components

Sequence grabber components allow applications to obtain digitized data from sources that are external to a Macintosh computer. For example, applications can use a sequence grabber component to record video data from a video digitizer or a video disc player. The application can then request that the sequence grabber component store the captured video data in a QuickTime movie. In this manner users can acquire movie data from various sources. Applications can also use sequence grabber components to obtain and display data from external sources, without saving the captured data in a movie. For more information about sequence grabbers, see the chapter "Sequence Grabber Components" in this book.

Sequence Grabber Channel Components

Sequence grabber components use sequence grabber channel components (or, simply, channel components) to obtain data from audio- or video-digitizing equipment. These components isolate the sequence grabber component from the details of working with the various types of data that can be collected. The functionality provided by a sequence grabber component depends upon the services provided by sequence grabber channel components. The channel components, in turn, may use other components to interact with the digitizing equipment. For example, the video channel component supplied by Apple uses a video digitizer component. Figure 6-1 shows the relationship between these components and an application.

Figure 6-1 Relationships of an application, a sequence grabber component, and channel components

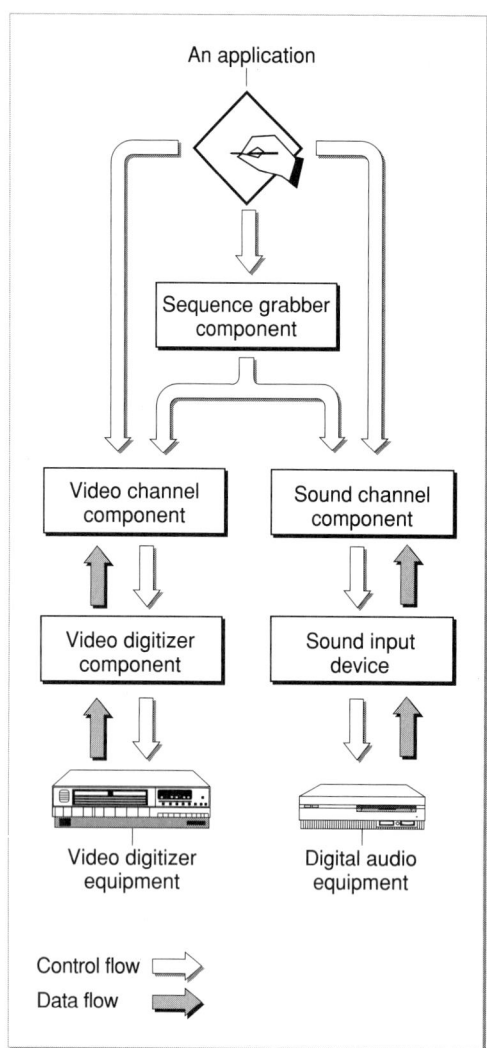

Sequence grabber panel components augment the capabilities of sequence grabber components and sequence grabber channel components by allowing sequence grabbers to obtain configuration information from the user for a particular digitizing source. Sequence grabbers present a settings dialog box to the user whenever an application calls the `SGSettingsDialog` function (see the chapter "Sequence Grabber Components" for more information about this sequence grabber function). Applications never call sequence grabber panel components directly; application developers use panel components only by calling the sequence grabber component.

Note that sequence grabber channel components may support all of the functions that are supported by sequence grabber panel components. For example, sequence grabbers obtain settings information from a channel component by calling the channel component's `SGPanelGetSettings` function. See the chapter "Sequence Grabber Panel Components" in this book for more information about the sequence grabber configuration dialog box; the relationship between sequence grabbers, sequence grabber channels, and sequence grabber panels; and the functional interface supported by sequence grabber panel components.

If you are developing digitizing equipment and you want to allow applications to use the services of your equipment with a sequence grabber component, you should create an appropriate video digitizer component or sound input device driver. See the chapter "Video Digitizer Components" in this book for a description of video digitizer components. See *Inside Macintosh: More Macintosh Toolbox* for information about sound input device drivers.

If you are developing equipment that provides a new type of data to QuickTime, you should develop a new sequence grabber channel component. See the next section, "Creating Sequence Grabber Channel Components," for more information about creating sequence grabber channel components.

Creating Sequence Grabber Channel Components

Sequence grabber channel components are the most convenient mechanism for extending the ability of the sequence grabber component to accommodate new types of source data. For example, if you are developing special-purpose hardware that generates a new kind of data, you should create a channel component for that kind of data.

Refer to the chapter "Component Manager" in *Inside Macintosh: More Macintosh Toolbox* for a general discussion of how to create a component.

This section discusses issues you should consider when creating a sequence grabber channel component. It also provides a sample program for the implementation of a sequence grabber channel component.

Sequence Grabber Channel Components

Component Type and Subtype Values

Apple has defined a component type value for sequence grabber channel components—that type value is `'sgch'`. You can use the following constant to specify this type value:

```
#define SeqGrabChannelType 'sgch';
```

Sequence grabber channel components use their component subtype value to indicate the media type created by the component. For example, a channel component that works with video data would have a subtype of `'vide'` (this value is defined by the Movie Toolbox's `VideoMediaType` constant).

Required Functions

At a minimum, your channel component should support the following functions:

SGGetChannelInfo	SGRelease
SGGetChannelUsage	SGSetChannelRefCon
SGGetDataRate	SGSetChannelUsage
SGIdle	SGStartPreview
SGInitChannel	SGStartRecord
SGPause	SGStop
SGPrepare	SGWriteSamples

In addition, if your channel component supports visual data, it should support at least the following functions:

SGGetChannelBounds
SGSetChannelBounds
SGSetGWorld

If your channel component supports audio data, it should support the following functions as well:

SGGetChannelVolume
SGSetChannelVolume

The remaining functions described in this section are optional. However, your channel component should support as many of these functions as possible, so that your component is more useful to applications and users.

Component Manager Request Codes

As with all components, your channel component receives its requests from the Component Manager in the form of request codes. Apple strongly recommends that you fully support all of the Component Manager's request codes in your channel component—especially the target request. Developers will want to extend the capabilities of the sequence grabber channel components. The Component Manager's `CaptureComponent` function, which uses the target request, is the most convenient mechanism for obtaining the services of a component and then extending those services. If your channel component does not support the target request, then it cannot be used by applications or other components in this manner. You can use the following constants to refer to the request codes for each of the functions that your channel component must support.

```
/*  basic sequence grabber channel component selectors */
kSGSetGWorldSelect              = 0x4;   /* SetGWorld */
kSGStartPreviewSelect           = 0x10;  /* SGStartPreview */
kSGStartRecordSelect            = 0x11;  /* SGStartRecord */
kSGIdleSelect                   = 0x12;  /* SGIdle */
kSGStopSelect                   = 0x13;  /* SGStop */
kSGPauseSelect                  = 0x14;  /* SGPause */
kSGPrepareSelect                = 0x15;  /* SGPrepare */
kSGReleaseSelect                = 0x16;  /* SGRelease */
kSGUpdateSelect                 = 0x27;  /* SGUpdate */

/*  selectors for common channel configuration functions */
kSGCSetChannelUsageSelect       = 0x80; /* SGCSetChannelUsage */
kSGCGetChannelUsageSelect       = 0x81; /* SGCGetChannelUsage */
kSGCSetChannelBoundsSelect      = 0x82; /* SGCSetChannelBounds */
kSGCGetChannelBoundsSelect      = 0x83; /* SGCGetChannelBounds */
kSGCSetChannelVolumeSelect      = 0x84; /* SGCSetChannelVolume */
kSGCGetChannelVolumeSelect      = 0x85; /* SGCGetChannelVolume */
kSGCGetChannelInfoSelect        = 0x86; /* SGCGetChannelInfo */
kSGCSetChannelPlayFlagsSelect   = 0x87; /* SGCSetChannelPlayFlags */
kSGCGetChannelPlayFlagsSelect   = 0x88; /* SGCGetChannelPlayFlags */
kSGCSetChannelMaxFramesSelect   = 0x89; /* SGCSetChannelMaxFrames */
kSGCGetChannelMaxFramesSelect   = 0x8a; /* SGCGetChannelMaxFrames */
kSGCSetChannelRefConSelect      = 0x8b; /* SGCSetChannelRefCon */
kSGCSetChannelClipSelect        = 0x8C; /* SGCSetChannelClip */
kSGCGetChannelClipSelect        = 0x8D; /* SGCGetChannelClip */
```

Sequence Grabber Channel Components

```
kSGCGetChannelSampleDescriptionSelect = 0x8E;
                                        /* SGCGetChannelSampleDescription */
kSGCGetChannelDeviceListSelect     = 0x8F;  /* SGCGetChannelDeviceList */
kSGCSetChannelDeviceSelect         = 0x90;  /* SGCSetChannelDevice */
kSGCSetChannelMatrixSelect         = 0x91;  /* SGCSetChannelMatrix */
kSGCGetChannelMatrixSelect         = 0x92;  /* SGCGetChannelMatrix */
kSGCGetChannelTimeScaleSelect      = 0x93;  /* SGCGetChannelTimeScale */

/*  selectors for video channel configuration functions */
kSGCGetSrcVideoBoundsSelect          = 0x100; /* SGCGetSrcVideoBounds */
kSGCSetVideoRectSelect               = 0x101; /* SGCSetVideoRect */
kSGCGetVideoRectSelect               = 0x102; /* SGCGetVideoRect */
kSGCGetVideoCompressorTypeSelect     = 0x103;
                                     /* SGCGetVideoCompressorType */

kSGCSetVideoCompressorTypeSelect     = 0x104;
                                     /* SGCSetVideoCompressorType */
kSGCSetVideoCompressorSelect         = 0x105; /* SGCSetVideoCompressor */
kSGCGetVideoCompressorSelect         = 0x106; /* SGCGetVideoCompressor */
kSGCGetVideoDigitizerComponentSelect= 0x107;
                                     /* SGCGetVideoDigitizerComponent */
kSGCSetVideoDigitizerComponentSelect= 0x108;
                                     /* SGCSetVideoDigitizerComponent */
kSGCVideoDigitizerChangedSelect      = 0x109;
                                     /* SGCVideoDigitizerChanged */
kSGCSetVideoBottlenecksSelect        = 0x10a;
                                     /* SGCSetVideoBottlenecks */
kSGCGetVideoBottlenecksSelect        = 0x10b;
                                     /* SGCGetVideoBottlenecks */
kSGCGrabFrameSelect                  = 0x10c; /* SGCGrabFrame */
kSGCGrabFrameCompleteSelect          = 0x10d;
                                     /* SGCGrabFrameComplete */
kSGCDisplayFrameSelect               = 0x10e; /* SGCDisplayFrame */
kSGCCompressFrameSelect              = 0x10f; /* SGCCompressFrame */
kSGCCompressFrameCompleteSelect      = 0x110;
                                         /* SGCCompressFrameComplete */
kSGCAddFrameSelect                   = 0x111; /* SGCAddFrame */
kSGCTransferFrameForCompressSelect   = 0x112;
                                     /* SGCTransferFrameForCompress */
```

Sequence Grabber Channel Components

```
    kSGCSetCompressBufferSelect         = 0x113;  /* SGCSetCompressBuffer */
    kSGCGetCompressBufferSelect         = 0x114;  /* SGCGetCompressBuffer */
    kSGCGetBufferInfoSelect             = 0x115;  /* SGCGetBufferInfo */
    kSGCSetUseScreenBufferSelect        = 0x116;  /* SGCSetUseScreenBuffer */
    kSGCGetUseScreenBufferSelect        = 0x117;  /* SGCGetUseScreenBuffer */
    kSGCGrabCompressCompleteSelect      = 0x118;
                                                  /* SGCGrabCompressComplete */
    kSGCDisplayCompressSelect           = 0x119;  /* SGCDisplayCompress */
    kSGCSetFrameRateSelect              = 0x11A;  /* SGCSetFrameRate */
    kSGCGetFrameRateSelect              = 0x11B;  /* SGCGetFrameRate */

    /*   selectors for sound channel configuration functions */
    kSGCSetSoundInputDriverSelect       = 0x100;  /* SGCSetSoundInputDriver */
    kSGCGetSoundInputDriverSelect       = 0x101;  /* SGCGetSoundInputDriver */
    kSGCSoundInputDriverChangedSelect
                                        = 0x102;  /* SGCSoundInputDriverChanged */
    kSGCSetSoundRecordChunkSizeSelect
                                        = 0x103;
                                                  /* SGCSetSoundRecordChunkSize */
    kSGCGetSoundRecordChunkSizeSelect   = 0x104;
                                                  /* SGCGetSoundRecordChunkSize */
    kSGCSetSoundInputRateSelect         = 0x105;  /* SGCSetSoundInputRate */
    kSGCGetSoundInputRateSelect         = 0x106;  /* SGCGetSoundInputRate */
    kSGCSetSoundInputParametersSelect   = 0x107;
                                                  /* SGCSetSoundInputParameters */
    kSGCGetSoundInputParametersSelect   = 0x108;
                                                  /* SGCGetSoundInputParameters */
    /*   selectors for channel control functions */
    kSGCInitChannelSelect               = 0x180;  /* SGCInitChannel */
    kSGCWriteSamplesSelect              = 0x181;  /* SGCWriteSamples */
    kSGCGetDataRateSelect               = 0x182;  /* SGCDataRate */
    kSGCAlignChannelRectSelect          = 0x183;  /* SGAlignChannelRect */
};
```

CHAPTER 6

Sequence Grabber Channel Components

A Sample Sequence Grabber Channel Component

This section describes a sample sequence grabber channel component for PICT image data.

Implementing the Required Component Functions

Listing 6-1 supplies the component dispatchers for the sequence grabber channel component together with the required functions.

Listing 6-1 Setting up global variables and implementing required functions

```
#define kMediaTimeScale 600

typedef struct {
    ComponentInstance self;
    SeqGrabComponent  grabber;
    long              usage;
    Boolean           paused;
    CGrafPtr          destPort;
    GDHandle          destGD;
    CGrafPort         tempPort;
    MatrixRecord      displayMatrix;
    Rect              destRect;
    Rect              srcRect;
    RgnHandle         clip;
    Boolean           inPreview;
    Boolean           inRecord;
    TimeBase          base;
    long              bytesWritten;
    Boolean           showTickCount;
    long              saveUsage;
} SGPictGlobalsRecord, *SGPictGlobals;

pascal ComponentResult SGPICTDispatcher
                (ComponentParameters *params, Handle storage)
{
    OSErr err = badComponentSelector;
    ComponentFunction componentProc = 0;
```

Sequence Grabber Channel Components

```
switch (params->what) {
   case kComponentOpenSelect:
         componentProc = SGPictOpen; break;
   case kComponentCloseSelect:
         componentProc = SGPictClose; break;
   case kComponentCanDoSelect:
         componentProc = SGPictCanDo; break;
   case kComponentVersionSelect:
         componentProc = SGPictVersion; break;
   case kSGSetGWorldSelect:
         componentProc = SGPictSetGWorld; break;
   case kSGStartPreviewSelect:
         componentProc = SGPictStartPreview; break;
   case kSGStartRecordSelect:
         componentProc = SGPictStartRecord; break;
   case kSGIdleSelect:
         componentProc = SGPictIdle; break;
   case kSGStopSelect:
         componentProc = SGPictStop; break;
   case kSGPauseSelect:
         componentProc = SGPictPause; break;
   case kSGPrepareSelect:
         componentProc = SGPictPrepare; break;
   case kSGReleaseSelect:
         componentProc = SGPictRelease; break;
   case kSGCSetChannelUsageSelect:
         componentProc = SGPictSetChannelUsage; break;
   case kSGCGetChannelUsageSelect:
         componentProc = SGPictGetChannelUsage; break;
   case kSGCSetChannelBoundsSelect:
         componentProc = SGPictSetChannelBounds; break;
   case kSGCGetChannelBoundsSelect:
         componentProc = SGPictGetChannelBounds; break;
   case kSGCGetChannelInfoSelect:
         componentProc = SGPictGetChannelInfo; break;
   case kSGCSetChannelMatrixSelect:
         componentProc = SGPictSetChannelMatrix; break;
   case kSGCGetChannelMatrixSelect:
         componentProc = SGPictGetChannelMatrix; break;
   case kSGCSetChannelClipSelect:
         componentProc = SGPictSetChannelClip; break;
   case kSGCGetChannelClipSelect:
         componentProc = SGPictGetChannelClip; break;
```

Creating Sequence Grabber Channel Components

```
        case kSGCGetChannelSampleDescriptionSelect:
            componentProc = SGPictGetChannelSampleDescription;
             break;
        case kSGCGetChannelDeviceListSelect:
          componentProc = SGPictGetChannelDeviceList; break;
        case kSGCSetChannelDeviceSelect:
          componentProc = SGPictSetChannelDevice; break;
        case kSGCGetChannelTimeScaleSelect:
          componentProc = SGPictGetChannelTimeScale; break;
        case kSGCInitChannelSelect:
          componentProc = SGPictInitChannel; break;
        case kSGCWriteSamplesSelect:
          componentProc = SGPictWriteSamples; break;
        case kSGCGetDataRateSelect:
            componentProc = SGPictGetDataRate; break;
        case kSGCPanelGetDitlSelect:
            componentProc = SGPictPanelGetDitl; break;
        case kSGCPanelInstallSelect:
            componentProc = SGPictPanelInstall; break;
        case kSGCPanelEventSelect:
            componentProc = SGPictPanelEvent; break;
        case kSGCPanelRemoveSelect:
            componentProc = SGPictPanelRemove; break;
        case kSGCPanelGetSettingsSelect:
            componentProc = SGPictPanelGetSettings; break;
        case kSGCPanelSetSettingsSelect:
            componentProc = SGPictPanelSetSettings; break;
        case 0x0100:
            componentProc = SGPictSetShowTickCount; break;
        case 0x0101:
            componentProc = SGPictGetShowTickCount; break;
    }

    if (componentProc)
        err = CallComponentFunctionWithStorage (storage, params,
                                        componentProc);

    return err;

}

pascal ComponentResult SGPictCanDo (SGPictGlobals store,
                                    short ftnNumber)
{
   switch (ftnNumber) {
```

Sequence Grabber Channel Components

```
        case kComponentOpenSelect:
        case kComponentCloseSelect:
        case kComponentCanDoSelect:
        case kComponentVersionSelect:

        case kSGSetGWorldSelect:

        case kSGStartPreviewSelect:
        case kSGStartRecordSelect:
        case kSGIdleSelect:
        case kSGStopSelect:
        case kSGPauseSelect:
        case kSGPrepareSelect:
        case kSGReleaseSelect:

        case kSGCSetChannelUsageSelect:
        case kSGCGetChannelUsageSelect:
        case kSGCSetChannelBoundsSelect:
        case kSGCGetChannelBoundsSelect:
        case kSGCGetChannelInfoSelect:

        case kSGCSetChannelMatrixSelect:
        case kSGCGetChannelMatrixSelect:
        case kSGCSetChannelClipSelect:
        case kSGCGetChannelClipSelect:

        case kSGCGetChannelSampleDescriptionSelect:
        case kSGCGetChannelDeviceListSelect:
        case kSGCSetChannelDeviceSelect:
        case kSGCGetChannelTimeScaleSelect:

        case kSGCInitChannelSelect:
        case kSGCWriteSamplesSelect:
        case kSGCGetDataRateSelect:

        case kSGCPanelGetDitlSelect:
        case kSGCPanelInstallSelect:
        case kSGCPanelEventSelect:
        case kSGCPanelRemoveSelect:
        case kSGCPanelGetSettingsSelect:
        case kSGCPanelSetSettingsSelect:

        /* private component functions */
        case 0x0100:
        case 0x0101:
            return true;
```

Creating Sequence Grabber Channel Components

Sequence Grabber Channel Components

```
        default:
            return false;
    }
}

pascal ComponentResult SGPictVersion (SGPictGlobals store)
{
    return 0x00020001;
}

pascal ComponentResult SGPictOpen (SGPictGlobals store,
                                    ComponentInstance self)
{
    OSErr err;
    GrafPtr savePort;

    /* allocate global variables */

    store =
    (SGPictGlobals)NewPtrClear(sizeof(SGPictGlobalsRecord));
    if (err = MemError()) goto bail;

    /* create a temporary port for drawing during the idle
       function */

    GetPort (&savePort);
    OpenCPort (&store->tempPort);
    SetPort ((GrafPtr)&store->tempPort);
    PortSize (4096, 4096);
    SetRectRgn (store->tempPort.visRgn, 0, 0, 4096, 4096);
    ClipRgn (store->tempPort.visRgn);
    SetPort (savePort);

    store->self = self;
    store->showTickCount = false;
    SetComponentInstanceStorage (self, (Handle)store);

bail:
    return err;
}
```

```
pascal ComponentResult SGPictClose (SGPictGlobals store,
                                    ComponentInstance self)
{
   /* disposal operations */
   if (store) {
      if (store->clip) DisposeRgn(store->clip);
      CloseCPort(&store->tempPort);
      DisposPtr((Ptr)store);
   }

   return noErr;
}
```

Initializing the Sequence Grabber Channel Component

To initialize the channel component, the sequence grabber component calls the SGInitChannel function, which is described on page 6-38.

The code in Listing 6-2 initializes channel variables. The grabber component calls the SGPictInitChannel function to initialize a sequence grabber channel component. The SGPictInitChannel function calls QuickDraw's SetRect routine and QuickTime's SetIdentityMatrix function to specify the size of the area (around a mouse-down event) in which the sequence grabber component will capture PICT images. For more on the SetRect routine, see the chapter "Basic QuickDraw" in *Inside Macintosh: Imaging*. For details on the SetIdentityMatrix function, see the chapter "Movie Toolbox" in *Inside Macintosh: QuickTime*.

Listing 6-2 Initializing the sequence grabber channel component

```
pascal ComponentResult SGPictInitChannel (SGPictGlobals store,
                                          SeqGrabComponent owner)

{

   /* initialize any variables here */
   SetRect(&store->srcRect, 0, 0, 160, 120);/* rectangle in which
                                                capture occurs */
   SetIdentityMatrix (&store->displayMatrix);

   store->grabber = owner;
   SGGetTimeBase (owner, &store->base);

   return noErr;
}
```

Sequence Grabber Channel Components

Setting and Retrieving the Channel State

Listing 6-3 supplies configuration functions that set the usage parameters and storage for the channel component. (See the descriptions of the SGSetChannelUsage and SGGetChannelUsage functions on page 6-48 and page 6-49, respectively, for details.)

The sample code illustrates how to retrieve usage information. (See the description of the SGGetChannelInfo function on page 6-49 for details.) In this case, you indicate that the sequence grabber component has spatial boundaries by using the seqGrabHasBounds constant in the channelInfo parameter.

Listing 6-3 Determining usage parameters and getting usage data

```
pascal ComponentResult SGPictSetChannelUsage(SGPictGlobals store,
                                             long usage)
{
   /* remember usage */
   store->usage = usage;

   return noErr;
}

pascal ComponentResult SGPictGetChannelUsage(SGPictGlobals store,
                                             long *usage)
{
   /* return usage */
   *usage = store->usage;

   return noErr;
}

pascal ComponentResult SGPictGetChannelInfo (SGPictGlobals store,
                                             long *channelInfo)
{
   /* indicate that you have spatial boundaries */
   *channelInfo = seqGrabHasBounds;

   return noErr;
}
```

Managing Spatial Properties

To set up an area in which the channel component displays image data, the sequence grabber should perform these tasks:

- Assign the destination graphics world and graphics device for the display of the captured image with the SGSetGWorld function (described on page 6-39).

- Specify a display transformation matrix for a video channel using the SGSetChannelMatrix function, which is described on page 6-57. Your function determines the matrix that is being set, validates it, and updates the matrix and destination rectangle. Your channel uses this matrix to transform its video image into the destination window.

- Obtain the channel's display transformation matrix by calling the SGGetChannelMatrix function, which is described on page 6-58.

- Specify the channel's display boundary rectangle with the SGSetChannelBounds function, which is described on page 6-63. The display boundary rectangle defines the destination for data from this channel and adjusts the channel matrix.

- Determine the channel's display boundary rectangle with the SGGetChannelBounds function (described on page 6-63).

- Dispose of the old clipping region and apply a new clipping region to the channel's display region using the SGSetChannelClip function, which is described on page 6-56.

- Retrieve the new clipping region by calling the SGGetChannelClip function (described on page 6-56).

The code in Listing 6-4 provides an example of how to manage the spatial characteristics of the area in which the channel component displays PICT image data.

Listing 6-4   Managing spatial characteristics

```
pascal ComponentResult SGPictSetGWorld (SGPictGlobals store,
                                        CGrafPtr gp, GDHandle gd)
{
   /* remember the destination graphics world */
   store->destPort = gp;
   store->destGD = gd;

   return noErr;
}
```

Sequence Grabber Channel Components

```
pascal ComponentResult SGPictSetChannelMatrix
                    (SGPictGlobals store, const MatrixRecord *m)
{
   OSErr err = noErr;
   MatrixRecord mat;
   short matType;

   /* determine the matrix being set */
   if (m)
      mat = *m;
   else
      SetIdentityMatrix (&mat);

   /* validate it */
   matType = GetMatrixType (&mat);

   if ((mat.matrix[0][0] < 0) || (mat.matrix[1][1] < 0) ||
   (matType >= linearMatrixType))
      return paramErr;

   /* update the matrix and destination rectangle */
   store->displayMatrix = mat;
   store->destRect = store->srcRect;
   TransformRect (&mat, &store->destRect, nil);

   return err;
}

pascal ComponentResult SGPictGetChannelMatrix
                    (SGPictGlobals store, MatrixRecord *m)
{
   /* return current matrix */
   *m = store->displayMatrix;

   return noErr;
}

pascal ComponentResult SGPictSetChannelBounds
                    (SGPictGlobals store, const Rect *bounds)
{
   /* remember destination rect */
   store->destRect = *bounds;
```

Sequence Grabber Channel Components

```
    /* recalculate display matrix from it */
    RectMatrix (&store->displayMatrix, &store->srcRect,
                &store->destRect);

    return noErr;
}

pascal ComponentResult SGPictGetChannelBounds
                                  (SGPictGlobals store, Rect *bounds)
{
    /* return current boundaries */
    *bounds = store->destRect;

    return noErr;
}

pascal ComponentResult SGPictSetChannelClip (SGPictGlobals store,
                                                 RgnHandle theClip)
{
    OSErr err = noErr;

    /* toss the old channel clipping */
    if (store->clip) {
        DisposeRgn (store->clip);
        store->clip = nil;
    }
    /* and remember the new one */
    if (theClip) {
        err = HandToHand ((Handle *)&theClip);
        store->clip = theClip;
    }

    return err;
}

pascal ComponentResult SGPictGetChannelClip
                            (SGPictGlobals store, RgnHandle *theClip)
{
    OSErr err = noErr;

    /* return clip, if there is one */
    if (*theClip = store->clip)
        err = HandToHand ((Handle *)theClip);
    return err;
}
```

Creating Sequence Grabber Channel Components

Controlling Previewing and Recording Operations

To preview and record image data in the channel component, the code in Listing 6-5 implements these tasks:

- The SGStartPreview function (described on page 6-40) instructs the channel to commence processing any source data. In preview mode, the component does not save any of the data it gathers from its source. Your channel component should immediately present the data to the user in the appropriate format for the channel's configuration and display video data in the destination display region.

- The SGStartRecord function (described on page 6-41) instructs the channel to begin recording data from its source. The sequence grabber component stores the collected data. The channel component should immediately begin recording data.

- The SGIdle function (described on page 6-42) allows the sequence grabber component to grant processing time to the channel component. The SGIdle function permits the processing time for the previewing and recording operations to take place. In the example shown in Listing 6-5, the work for the channel consists of getting the current time, adding data to the movie if recording, and showing the preview image if necessary.

- The SGStop function (described on page 6-43) stops the channel's preview and recording operations.

- The SGPause function (described on page 6-44) suspends or restarts the channel's preview and recording operations.

- The SGPrepare function (described on page 6-45) has the sequence grabber component prepare the channel for subsequent preview or record operations.

- The SGRelease function (described on page 6-46) releases any system resources that were allocated during preview or recording operations and that remain thereafter.

The code in Listing 6-5 illustrates a channel component's control of the previewing and recording of a PICT image.

Listing 6-5 Controlling previewing and recording operations

```
pascal ComponentResult SGPictStartPreview (SGPictGlobals store)
{
    /* into preview mode */

    store->inPreview = (store->usage & seqGrabPreview) != 0;
    return noErr;
}

pascal ComponentResult SGPictStartRecord (SGPictGlobals store)
{
    /* into record mode (also preview, if PlayDuringRecord) */
    store->inRecord = (store->usage & seqGrabRecord) != 0;
    store->inPreview = (store->usage & seqGrabPlayDuringRecord) !=
```

Sequence Grabber Channel Components

```c
         0;
      return noErr;
}

pascal ComponentResult SGPictIdle (SGPictGlobals store)
{
   OSErr err = noErr;

   /* this is where the work for preview and record happens */
   if (!store->paused && (store->inRecord || store->inPreview)) {
      Point mouseLoc;
      Rect r;
      PicHandle tempPict = nil;
      TimeRecord tr;
      CGrafPtr savePort;
      GDHandle saveGD;
      Rect maxR;

      GetGWorld (&savePort, &saveGD);

      /* get the current time */
      GetTimeBaseTime (store->base, kMediaTimeScale, &tr);

      /* figure the current area around the mouse
         (only on main screen) */
      SetGWorld (&store->tempPort, GetMainDevice());
      GetMouse (&mouseLoc);
      LocalToGlobal (&mouseLoc);
      r.top = r.bottom = mouseLoc.v;
      r.left = r.right = mouseLoc.h;
      InsetRect(&r, -(store->srcRect.right >> 1),
                    -(store->srcRect.bottom >> 1));
      maxR = (**GetMainDevice()).gdRect;
      if (r.left < maxR.left)
         OffsetRect (&r, -r.left + maxR.left, 0);
      if (r.top < maxR.top)
         OffsetRect (&r, 0, -r.top + maxR.top);
      if (r.right > maxR.right)
         OffsetRect(&r, maxR.right - r.right, 0);
      if (r.bottom > maxR.bottom)
         OffsetRect (&r, 0, maxR.bottom - r.bottom);

      /* copy the screen into a picture */
      tempPict = OpenPicture(&r);
         CopyBits ((BitMap *)&store->tempPort.portPixMap,
```

Creating Sequence Grabber Channel Components

Sequence Grabber Channel Components

```
                    (BitMap *)&store->tempPort.portPixMap, &r, &r,
                            srcCopy, nil);
        if (store->showTickCount) {
           /* if users want to see ticks, draw them */
           Str63 str;
           NumToString ( TickCount(), str);
           /* do some magic positioning */
           r.right = r.left + StringWidth(str) + 4;
           r.bottom = r.top + 14;
           EraseRect (&r);
           MoveTo(r.left + 2, r.bottom - 3);
           TextSize (12);
           DrawString (str);
        }
     ClosePicture();

     /* if recording, add data to movie */
     if (store->inRecord) {
        long offset;
        long pictSize = GetHandleSize ((Handle)tempPict);

        HLock ((Handle)tempPict);
        err = SGAddMovieData (store->grabber, store->self,
                       (Ptr)*tempPict, pictSize, &offset, 0,
                       tr.value.lo, seqGrabWriteAppend);
        store->bytesWritten += pictSize;
     }

     /* if you need to show the preview image, do that */
     if (store->inPreview) {
        RgnHandle saveClip;
        SetGWorld (store->destPort, store->destGD);
        if (store->clip) {
           saveClip = NewRgn();
           GetClip (saveClip);
           SetClip (store->clip);
        }
        DrawPicture (tempPict, &store->destRect);
        if (store->clip) {
           SetClip (saveClip);
           DisposeRgn (saveClip);
        }
     }
```

Sequence Grabber Channel Components

```
      KillPicture (tempPict);

      SetGWorld (savePort, saveGD);
   }

   return err;
}

pascal ComponentResult SGPictStop (SGPictGlobals store)
{
   /* stop all previewing and recording */
   store->inRecord = store->inPreview = false;

   return noErr;
}

pascal ComponentResult SGPictPause (SGPictGlobals store,
                                    Byte pause)
{
   /* pause */
   store->paused = pause;

   return noErr;
}

pascal ComponentResult SGPictPrepare (SGPictGlobals store,
                                      Boolean prepareForPreview,
                                      Boolean prepareForRecord)
{
   /* prepare for previewing and recording operations--
      all you do here is initialize a variable */
   store->bytesWritten = 0;

   return noErr;
}

pascal ComponentResult SGPictRelease (SGPictGlobals store)
{
   /* no resources to release after previewing or recording */
   return noErr;
}
```

Managing Channel Devices

To manage channel devices such as video digitizers or sound input drivers, you should

- let the sequence grabber retrieve a list of devices that are valid for the channel using the SGGetChannelDeviceList function (described on page 6-60)

- assign an appropriate channel device with the SGSetChannelDevice function (described on page 6-61)

Listing 6-6 provides examples of these required functions for channel device management. The SGPictGetChannelDeviceList function obtains a list of devices associated with the channel component. The SGPictSetChannelDevice function allows the sequence grabber to specify a channel device. In this code sample, there are no devices associated with the channel component.

Listing 6-6 Coordinating devices for the channel component

```
pascal ComponentResult SGPictGetChannelDeviceList
                    (SGPictGlobals store,
                     long selectionFlags,
                     SGDeviceList *list)
{
   *list = (SGDeviceList) NewHandleClear
                (sizeof (SGDeviceListRecord)); /* no devices */

   return MemError();
}

pascal ComponentResult SGPictSetChannelDevice
                    (SGPictGlobals store, StringPtr name)
{
   /* you have no devices, so no problem */
   return noErr;
}
```

Utility Functions for Recording Image Data

To record image data, the channel component must allow the sequence grabber to do the following:

- Obtain an appropriate time scale with the SGGetChannelTimeScale function (described on page 6-55).

- Retrieve the sample description of the image that is to be recorded with the SGGetChannelSampleDescription function (described on page 6-55).

- Create a track and media in which to record the sample image by calling the SGWriteSamples function (described on page 6-43). SGWriteSamples writes the captured data to a movie file after a record operation.

CHAPTER 6

Sequence Grabber Channel Components

- Obtain references from the sequence grabber and add them to the newly created media using the SGGetNextFrameReference function (described on page 6-88) so that the channel component can retrieve the sample references it stored.
- Determine how many bytes of captured data the channel is collecting each second using the SGGetDataRate function (described on page 6-54).

The code in Listing 6-7 shows how the channel component uses these utility functions to record PICT image data.

Listing 6-7 Recording image data

```
pascal ComponentResult SGPictGetChannelTimeScale
                        (SGPictGlobals store, TimeScale *scale)
{
   *scale = kMediaTimeScale; /* a reasonable default time scale */

   return noErr;
}

pascal ComponentResult SGPictGetChannelSampleDescription
                        (SGPictGlobals store, Handle sampleDesc)
{
   OSErr err;
   SampleDescriptionPtr sdp;

   SetHandleSize (sampleDesc, sizeof(SampleDescription));
   if (err = MemError()) goto bail;

   /* make up a minimal sample description */
   sdp = (SampleDescriptionPtr)*sampleDesc;
   sdp->descSize = sizeof(SampleDescription);
   sdp->dataFormat = 'PICT';
   sdp->resvd1 = 0;
   sdp->resvd2 = 0;
   sdp->dataRefIndex = 0;

bail:
   return err;
}

pascal ComponentResult SGPictWriteSamples (SGPictGlobals store,
                                Movie m, AliasHandle theFile)
{
   OSErr err = 0;
   Track pictT;
   Media pictM;
```

Creating Sequence Grabber Channel Components   6-25

CHAPTER 6

Sequence Grabber Channel Components

```
    long i;
    MatrixRecord aMatrix;
    Rect from, to;
    seqGrabFrameInfo fi;
    TimeRecord tr;
    TimeValue mediaDuration;
    SampleDescriptionHandle sampleDesc = 0;

    /* after SGStop, this function creates the track and media */
    if (!(store->usage & seqGrabRecord))
       return err;

    /* get the sample description */
    sampleDesc = (SampleDescriptionHandle)NewHandle(4);
    if (err = MemError()) goto bail;
    if (err = SGGetChannelSampleDescription (store->self,
                            (Handle)sampleDesc)) goto bail;

    /* figure out the track matrix */
    SetRect (&from, 0, 0, store->srcRect.right,
          store->srcRect.bottom);
    to = from;

    TransformRect (&store->displayMatrix, &to, nil);

    /* create the track and media */
    pictT = NewMovieTrack (m, (long)from.right << 16,
                          (long)from.bottom << 16, 0);
    pictM = NewTrackMedia (pictT, 'PICT', kMediaTimeScale,
                          (Handle)theFile, rAliasType);

    /* spin in a loop getting sample references from the
       sequence grabber and adding them to the media */
    fi.frameChannel = store->self;
    i = -1;
    do {
       TimeValue frameDuration;

       err = SGGetNextFrameReference (store->grabber,
                                     &fi, &frameDuration, &i);
       if (err) {
          if (err == paramErr)
             err = 0;
          break;
       }
```

6-26 Creating Sequence Grabber Channel Components

Sequence Grabber Channel Components

```
        err = AddMediaSampleReference (pictM,
            fi.frameOffset, fi.frameSize,
            frameDuration,
            sampleDesc, 1,
            0, 0);

        if (err == invalidDuration) {
            err = noErr;
            break;
        }
    } while (!err);

done:
    if (err) goto bail;

    GetTimeBaseTime (store->base, 0, &tr);
    ConvertTimeScale (&tr, kMediaTimeScale);/* trim media inserted
                                                to not extend
                                                beyond end time */

    mediaDuration = GetMediaDuration(pictM);

    /* add media to track */
    err = InsertMediaIntoTrack (pictT, 0, 0, tr.value.lo, kFix1);

    /* set track matrix */
    RectMatrix (&aMatrix, &from, &to);
    SetTrackMatrix (pictT, &aMatrix);

    /* set track clipping region */
    SetTrackClipRgn (pictT, store->clip);

bail:
    if (sampleDesc) DisposHandle ((Handle)sampleDesc);
    return err;
}

pascal ComponentResult SGPictGetDataRate (SGPictGlobals store,
                                                long *bytesPerSecond)
{
    /* take a guess at the data rate */
    *bytesPerSecond = 24 * 1024;
    if (store->bytesWritten) {
        TimeValue timeNow = GetTimeBaseTime (store->base, 8, nil);
                        /* one-eighth second resolution */
```

Creating Sequence Grabber Channel Components 6-27

```
        if (!timeNow)
            return seqGrabInfoNotAvailable;

        *bytesPerSecond = (store->bytesWritten / timeNow) * 8;
                                        /* convert back to seconds */
    }
    return noErr;
}
```

Providing Media-Specific Functions

The channel can provide media-specific functions for a particular channel type. These functions are analogous to the SGSetVideoCompressorType and SGGetVideoCompressorType functions (described on page 6-66 and page 6-67, respectively). These functions allow the sequence grabber to specify and determine the type of image compression the channel component is to apply to the captured video images.

The code in Listing 6-8 provides two specialized channel component functions, SGPictSetShowTickCount and SGPictGetShowTickCount, which set and retrieve the tick count, respectively. Note that both the functions refer to the showTickCount field in the SGPictGlobals structure.

Listing 6-8   Showing the tick count

```
pascal ComponentResult SGPictSetShowTickCount
                                (SGPictGlobals store, Boolean show)
{
    store->showTickCount = show;
    return noErr;
}

pascal ComponentResult SGPictGetShowTickCount
                                (SGPictGlobals store, Boolean *show)
{
    *show = store->showTickCount;
    return noErr;
}
```

Managing the Settings Dialog Box

The channel allows the sequence grabber to manage the placement of your channel data in the sequence grabber's settings dialog box.

- To prepare to add the channel component's items to the settings dialog box, the sequence grabber obtains your item list by calling the sequence grabber panel component's SGPanelGetDITL function. It retrieves and detaches the dialog box template from the sequence grabber panel component.

- Once it has installed the items, the sequence grabber uses the SGPanelInstall function so initial values can be set. This function resets the channel to use the dialog window and preview mode. It also updates the boundaries to match the size of the user item list.

- To provide idle time in which to draw the channel's information in the settings dialog box, the sequence grabber uses the SGPanelEvent function. It allows the sequence grabber component to receive and process dialog events in a manner similar to a modal-dialog filter function. In this example, the information is the tick count.

- Prior to the removal of items from the settings dialog box, the sequence grabber component calls the SGPanelRemove function. The sequence grabber supplies information that specifies the channel that the panel is to configure, the dialog box, and the offset of the panel's items into the dialog box.

For details on the SGPanelGetDITL, SGPanelInstall, SGPanelEvent, and SGPanelRemove functions, see the chapter "Sequence Grabber Panel Components" in this book.

The code in Listing 6-9 calls the sequence grabber panel component and indicates that the channel component will display a tick count checkbox in the panel settings.

Listing 6-9 Including a tick count checkbox in a dialog box in the panel component

```
pascal ComponentResult SGPictPanelGetDitl (SGPictGlobals store,
                                            Handle *ditl)
{
   /* get and detach your dialog template */
   *ditl = GetResource('DITL', 7000);
   if (!*ditl) return resNotFound;
   DetachResource(*ditl);
   return noErr;
}

pascal ComponentResult SGPictPanelInstall (SGPictGlobals store,
                                            SGChannel c,
                                            DialogPtr d,
                                            short itemOffset)
{
```

Sequence Grabber Channel Components

```
      Rect newBounds;
      short kind;
      Handle h;

      /* reset this channel to use the dialog window and be in
         preview mode with no clip */
      SGSetGWorld (store->self, (CGrafPtr)d, GetMainDevice());
      SGGetChannelUsage (store->self, &store->saveUsage);
      SGSetChannelUsage (store->self, seqGrabPreview);
      SGSetChannelClip (c, nil);

      /* update boundaries to match size of user item */
      GetDItem (d, 1 + itemOffset, &kind, &h, &newBounds);
      SGSetChannelBounds (c, &newBounds);
      SGStartPreview (store->self);
      return noErr;
   }

   pascal ComponentResult SGPictPanelEvent (SGPictGlobals store,
                                            SGChannel c, DialogPtr d,
                                            short itemOffset,
                                            EventRecord *theEvent,
                                            short *itemHit,
                                            Boolean *handled)
   {
      /* use idle time to draw */
      if (theEvent->what == nullEvent)
         return SGIdle (store->self);

      return noErr;
   }

   pascal ComponentResult SGPictPanelRemove (SGPictGlobals store,
                                             SGChannel c, DialogPtr d,
                                             short itemOffset)
   {
      /* stop playing */
      SGStop (store->self);
      SGRelease (store->self);

      /* note that the clip and bounds are automatically restored
         for you because you stored them using the SGGetSettings
         function */
```

Sequence Grabber Channel Components

```
   /* restore usage */
   SGSetChannelUsage(store->self, store->saveUsage);

   return noErr;
}
```

Displaying Channel Information in the Settings Dialog Box

The final step in the implementation of a sequence grabber channel component is the display of the channel preview in the settings dialog box. Two sequence grabber functions, SGSettingsDialog and SGGetSettingsDialog (described in the chapter "Sequence Grabber Components" in this book), facilitate this process.

- The channel component instructs the sequence grabber to display its settings dialog box to the user by calling the sequence grabber component's SGSettingsDialog function. The user can specify the configuration of a sequence grabber channel in this dialog box.

- To retrieve the current settings of all channels used by the sequence grabber, call the SGGetSettings function. The sequence grabber places all of this configuration information into a Movie Toolbox user data list.

Listing 6-10 provides code that creates a user data list to contain the tick count information for the sequence grabber's settings dialog box, adds a matrix to the list, and stores clipping information (if any exists). The sample code then restores the clipping and the matrix.

Listing 6-10 Displaying channel settings

```
pascal ComponentResult SGPictPanelGetSettings
                              (SGPictGlobals store, SGChannel c,
                               UserData *result, long flags)
{
   OSErr err = noErr;
   UserData ud = 0;
   MatrixRecord matrix;
   RgnHandle clip;

   /* create a user data list to hold your state */

   if (err = NewUserData (&ud)) goto bail;

   /* add matrix to user data */
```

Sequence Grabber Channel Components

```
        if (SGGetChannelMatrix (c, &matrix) == noErr) {
           if (err = SetUserDataItem (ud, &matrix, sizeof(matrix),
                                 sgMatrixType, 1))
              goto bail;
        }

        /* store clip, if there is one */
        if (SGGetChannelClip (c, &clip) == noErr) {
           if (clip)
              err = AddUserData (ud, (Handle)clip, sgClipType);

           else
              err = SetUserDataItem (ud, nil, 0, sgClipType, 1);
                              /* add a dummy to indicate none */
           DisposeRgn(clip);
           if (err) goto bail;
        }

bail:
     if (err) {
        DisposeUserData (ud);
        ud = 0;
     }
     *result = ud;

     return err;
}

pascal ComponentResult SGPictPanelSetSettings
                          (SGPictGlobals store,
                           SGChannel c, UserData ud, long flags)
{
     OSErr err;
     RgnHandle clip = NewRgn();
     MatrixRecord matrix;

     /* restore clip, if one was stored */
     if (GetUserData (ud, (Handle)clip, sgClipType, 1) == noErr) {
        if (err = SGSetChannelClip
                   (c, GetHandleSize ((Handle)clip) ? clip : 0))
           goto bail;
     }
```

```
    /* restore matrix */
    if (err = GetUserDataItem (ud, &matrix, sizeof(matrix),
                                sgMatrixType, 1)) goto bail;
    if (err = SGSetChannelMatrix (c, &matrix))
        goto bail;

bail:
    DisposeRgn (clip);
    return err;
}
```

Using Sequence Grabber Channel Components

In response to application requests, sequence grabber components can use channel components in two ways: to play digitized data for the user or to save captured data in a QuickTime movie. The process of playing digitized data is called *previewing*; saving captured data in a movie is called *recording*. Applications can use previewing to allow the user to prepare to make a recording. Applications that use previewing can move directly from the preview operation to a record operation, without stopping the process.

The next two sections provide an overview of preview and record operations. A third section discusses the callback functions that are supported by some channel components.

Previewing

Previewing captured data involves playing that data for the user as it is digitized. For video data, this means displaying the video images on the computer screen. For audio data, this means playing the sound through the computer's sound system. The following paragraphs outline the steps the sequence grabber component follows to preview captured data.

1. First, the sequence grabber component opens a connection to your channel component, using the Component Manager's OpenComponent function. The sequence grabber component then calls your SGInitChannel function to initialize your component. For more on SGInitChannel, see page 6-38.

2. The sequence grabber component then configures your channel component for the preview operation. The SGSetGWorld function (described on page 6-39) sets the graphics world in which the preview is to be displayed. The SGSetChannelUsage function (described on page 6-48) specifies that your channel is to be used for previewing. The application can then use the appropriate channel configuration functions to prepare your channel for the preview operation. For video channels, it uses the functions discussed in "Configuration Functions for Video Channel Components" beginning on page 6-61. For sound channels, the sequence grabber uses the functions discussed in "Configuration Functions for Sound Channel Components" beginning on page 6-77.

3. The sequence grabber component starts the preview operation by calling your `SGStartPreview` function (described on page 6-40). The sequence grabber component then begins collecting data from all of the channels participating in the preview and plays that data appropriately. The sequence grabber component can pause and restart the preview by calling the `SGPause` function (described on page 6-44). The sequence grabber component uses the `SGStop` function (described on page 6-43) to stop the preview. During the preview operation, the sequence grabber component calls your `SGIdle` function (described on page 6-42) frequently, so that your channel can perform its operation.

4. When the application is done previewing, the sequence grabber component can start recording or close its connection to your component.

Recording

During a record operation, a sequence grabber component collects the data it captures and formats that data into a QuickTime movie. During a record operation, the sequence grabber component can also play the captured data for the user.

The following paragraphs discuss the steps the sequence grabber component follows to record captured data.

1. As with a preview operation, the sequence grabber component establishes a connection to your channel component by calling the Component Manager's `OpenComponent` function. It then initializes your component by calling your `SGInitChannel` function (described on page 6-38).

2. The sequence grabber component then configures your component for the record operation. The `SGSetGWorld` function (described on page 6-39) sets the graphics world in which the data is to be displayed. The `SGSetChannelUsage` function (described on page 6-48) specifies each channel that is to be used for recording. At this time, the sequence grabber component can also specify whether your component is to play its data while recording. The application can then use the appropriate channel configuration functions to prepare your channel for the record operation. For video channels, it uses the functions discussed in "Configuration Functions for Video Channel Components" beginning on page 6-61. For sound channels, the sequence grabber uses the functions discussed in "Configuration Functions for Sound Channel Components" beginning on page 6-77.

3. The sequence grabber component starts the record operation by calling your `SGStartRecord` function (described on page 6-41). The sequence grabber component then begins collecting data from the channels it has assigned, stores the data in a QuickTime movie, and, optionally, plays that data appropriately. The sequence grabber can pause and restart the record process by calling the `SGPause` function (described on page 6-44). During the record operation, the sequence grabber component calls your `SGIdle` function (described on page 6-42) frequently, so that your channel can perform its operation. The sequence grabber component uses the `SGStop` function (described on page 6-43) to stop the record operation. At this time,

Sequence Grabber Channel Components

your component saves the movie in the appropriate movie file if the sequence grabber component instructs your component to do so by calling your `SGWriteSamples` function (described on page 6-43).

4. When the application is done recording, it either returns to previewing or closes its connection to your component.

Working With Callback Functions

Sequence grabber components provide callback functions that allow application developers to customize some aspects of capturing video data. It is your channel component's responsibility to call these callback functions at specified points in the data capture process. The application's function can then perform any special processing that is appropriate for the application. For example, an application can overlay text, such as a frame number, on each frame of video data as it is captured. These functions are discussed in detail in the next section.

Note
Sound channel components do not support any callback functions. ◆

Using Callback Functions for Video Channel Components

Sequence grabber components allow application developers to define a number of callback functions in their applications. Your channel component calls these functions at specific points in the process of collecting, compressing, and displaying the source visual data. By defining callback functions, a developer can control the process more precisely or customize the operation of the sequence grabber component and its channel components.

For example, a developer could use a callback function to draw a frame number on each video frame as it is collected. In this case, the developer could use either a compress callback function or a grab-complete callback function. You call the compress function after each frame is collected, in order to compress the frame. You call the grab-complete function just before the compress function or as soon as the frame has been captured.

Note that your channel component need not call each and every callback function. If some functions are inappropriate to the operation of your channel, do not call them. However, if your component calls one function of a pair, be sure to call the other. For example, if your component calls an application's grab function, you must also call its grab-complete function.

The sequence grabber component uses the `SGSetVideoBottlenecks` function to assign callback functions to your video channel. The `SGGetVideoBottlenecks` function allows the sequence grabber to determine the callback functions that have been assigned to your video channel. See the chapter "Sequence Grabber Components" in this book for details on `SGSetVideoBottlenecks` and `SGGetVideoBottlenecks`.

CHAPTER 6

Sequence Grabber Channel Components

The following application-defined functions are supported by video channels and are described in the chapter "Sequence Grabber Components" in this book.

MyAddFrameFunction   MyGrabCompressCompleteFunction
MyCompressCompleteFunction MyGrabFunction
MyCompressFunction   MyTransferFrameFunction
MyDisplayFunction
MyGrabCompleteFunction

Using Utility Functions for Video Channel Component Callback Functions

Sequence grabber components provide a number of functions that application-defined functions can use. Several channel functions support those sequence grabber component functions.

The sequence grabber component uses the SGGetBufferInfo function to obtain information about a buffer that contains data to be manipulated by a callback function. Application callback functions can use the SGGetBufferInfo function to obtain information about a buffer that you have passed. This information is valid only during record operations, or after your channel has been prepared to record. The SGGetBufferInfo function is described in detail in the chapter "Sequence Grabber Components" in this book.

The following functions provide default behavior for application-defined grab, grab-complete, display, compress, compress-complete, add-frame, transfer-frame, display-compress, and grab-compress–complete functions:

- Your video channel component's SGGrabFrame function provides the default behavior for an application's grab function. Applications should call this function only from their grab function.

- Your channel component's SGGrabFrameComplete function provides the default behavior for an application's grab-complete function. Applications should call this function only from their grab-complete functions.

- Your channel component's SGDisplayFrame function provides the default behavior for an application's display function. Applications should call this function only from their display functions.

- Your video channel component's SGCompressFrame function provides the default behavior for an application's compress function. Applications should call this function only from their compress functions.

- Your channel component's SGCompressFrameComplete function provides the default behavior for an application's compress-complete function. Applications should call this function only from their compress-complete functions.

- Your component's SGAddFrame function provides the default behavior for an application's add-frame function. Applications should call this function only from their add-frame functions.

Sequence Grabber Channel Components

- Your component's `SGTransferFrameForCompress` function provides the default behavior for an application's transfer-frame function. Applications should call this function only from their transfer-frame functions.

- Your component's `SGGrabCompressComplete` function provides the default behavior for an application's grab-compress–complete function. Applications should call this function only from their grab-compress–complete function.

- Your component's `SGDisplayCompress` function provides the default behavior for an application's display-compress function. Applications should call this function only from their display-compress function.

Sequence Grabber Channel Components Reference

This section describes the functions and associated data structures and constants that are specific to the Apple-supplied sequence grabber channel component. These functions are described from the perspective of a sequence grabber component—the most likely client of a sequence grabber channel component. If you are developing a sequence grabber channel component, your component must behave as described here.

Functions

This section has been divided into the following topics:

- "Configuring Sequence Grabber Channel Components" describes the functions that allow sequence grabber components to configure your channel component.

- "Controlling Sequence Grabber Channel Components" discusses the functions that allow sequence grabber components to control your channel component.

- "Configuration Functions for All Channel Components" describes configuration functions that may be supported by all sequence grabber channel components.

- "Working With Channel Devices" discusses functions that allow the sequence grabber to assign devices to your channel.

- "Configuration Functions for Video Channel Components" describes functions that are supported only by video channel components.

- "Configuration Functions for Sound Channel Components" discusses functions that are supported only by sound channel components.

- "Utility Functions for Sequence Grabber Channel Components" describes several utility functions that sequence grabber components provide to sequence grabber channel components.

Note
If your channel component will also receive any of the functions defined in the interface for sequence grabber panel components, see the chapter "Sequence Grabber Panel Components" in this book for more information about these functions. ◆

CHAPTER 6

Sequence Grabber Channel Components

Configuring Sequence Grabber Channel Components

Sequence grabber components use a number of functions to establish the environment for grabbing or previewing digitized data. This section describes the channel component functions that allow the sequence grabber component to establish the environment for recording or previewing captured data.

The sequence grabber component uses the `SGInitChannel` function to initialize your channel prior to a record or preview operation.

The `SGSetGWorld` function allows the sequence grabber component to assign a graphics world to your component.

SGInitChannel

A sequence grabber component calls the `SGInitChannel` function to initialize a sequence grabber channel component. Your component should perform its initialization processing here, rather than in response to the Component Manager's open request. The initialization processing may include allocating memory or checking for the availability of special-purpose hardware or software.

```
pascal ComponentResult SGInitChannel (SGChannel c,
                                      SeqGrabComponent owner);
```

c   Identifies the channel connection for this operation.

owner   Identifies the sequence grabber component that has connected to your channel component. You should save this value so that your channel component can call the utility functions that are provided by the sequence grabber component (see "Utility Functions for Sequence Grabber Channel Components," which begins on page 6-84, for information about these utility functions).

DESCRIPTION

If your component cannot gain access to the resources or equipment it needs to function properly, you should return a nonzero result code. If you return a nonzero result, the sequence grabber component closes its connection to your component and reports the error to the calling application.

RESULT CODES

noDeviceForChannel   –9400   Channel component cannot find its device
File Manager errors
Memory Manager errors

CHAPTER 6

Sequence Grabber Channel Components

SGSetGWorld

A sequence grabber component calls the `SGSetGWorld` function to establish the display environment for your channel component.

```
pascal ComponentResult SGSetGWorld (SeqGrabComponent s,
                                    CGrafPtr gp, GDHandle gd);
```

s
: Identifies the sequence grabber component that has connected to your channel component.

gp
: Specifies the destination graphics port. The sequence grabber component always sets this parameter to a valid value. The specified graphics port must be a color graphics port. The parameter is set to `nil` to use the current graphics port.

gd
: Specifies the destination graphics device. The sequence grabber component always sets this parameter to a valid value.

DESCRIPTION

Note that sequence grabber components may call this function for sound channel components as well as for video channel components.

RESULT CODE

cantDoThatInCurrentMode   –9402   Request invalid in current mode

Controlling Sequence Grabber Channel Components

Sequence grabber channel components must provide a full set of functions that allow the sequence grabber component to control the preview or record operation. The sequence grabber component can use these functions to start and stop the operation, to pause data collection, and to write captured data to a movie. This section describes these functions.

The sequence grabber component uses the `SGStartPreview` function to start a preview operation. The `SGStartRecord` function starts a record operation. The `SGStop` function stops your channel component after a preview or record operation.

The sequence grabber component grants processing time to your channel component by calling the `SGIdle` function. The sequence grabber notifies you of update events by calling your `SGUpdate` function.

The sequence grabber pauses the current operation by calling the `SGPause` function.

The sequence grabber component calls your `SGWriteSamples` function to write captured data to a movie file after a record operation.

CHAPTER 6

Sequence Grabber Channel Components

The sequence grabber component prepares your channel component for an upcoming preview or record operation by calling the `SGPrepare` function. This function also allows the sequence grabber component to verify that your component can support the parameters an application has specified. The `SGRelease` function releases system resources allocated during the `SGPrepare` function.

SGStartPreview

The `SGStartPreview` function instructs your channel to begin processing its source data. In preview mode, your component does not save any of the data it gathers from its source.

```
pascal ComponentResult SGStartPreview (SeqGrabComponent s);
```

s   Identifies the sequence grabber component that has connected to your channel component.

DESCRIPTION

Your channel component should immediately present the data to the user in the appropriate format, according to your channel's configuration (see "Configuration Functions for All Channel Components," which begins on page 6-46, for information about functions that configure channels). Display video data in the destination display region; play sound data at the specified volume settings.

RESULT CODES

`cantDoThatInCurrentMode`	–9402	Request invalid in current mode
`deviceCantMeetRequest`	–9408	Device cannot support grabber

File Manager errors
Memory Manager errors

SEE ALSO

The sequence grabber component stops the preview process by calling your `SGStop` function, which is described on page 6-43.

SGStartRecord

The `SGStartRecord` function instructs your channel component to begin recording data from its source. The sequence grabber component stores the collected data according to the recording parameters that the calling application specified with the sequence grabber component's `SGSetDataOutput` function (described in the chapter "Sequence Grabber Components" in this book). Your channel component should immediately begin recording data in the appropriate format, according to your channel's configuration (see "Configuration Functions for All Channel Components," which begins on page 6-46, for information about functions that configure channels).

```
pascal ComponentResult SGStartRecord (SeqGrabComponent s);
```

s   Identifies the sequence grabber component that has connected to your channel component.

DESCRIPTION

The sequence grabber component can switch from previewing to recording by calling this function during a preview operation—the sequence grabber need not stop the preview operation first.

RESULT CODES

cantDoThatInCurrentMode	–9402	Request invalid in current mode
notEnoughMemoryToGrab	–9403	Insufficient memory for record operation
notEnoughDiskSpaceToGrab	–9404	Insufficient disk space for record operation
deviceCantMeetRequest	–9408	Device cannot support grabber

File Manager errors
Memory Manager errors

SEE ALSO

The sequence grabber component stops the recording process by calling your `SGStop` function, which is described on page 6-43.

CHAPTER 6

Sequence Grabber Channel Components

SGIdle

The `SGIdle` function provides processing time to your channel component.

```
pascal ComponentResult SGIdle (SeqGrabComponent s);
```

s   Identifies the sequence grabber component that has connected to your channel component.

DESCRIPTION

After starting a preview or record operation, the application calls the sequence grabber component's `SGIdle` function as often as possible. The sequence grabber component then calls your `SGIdle` function. This continues until the calling application stops the operation by calling the `SGStop` sequence grabber function.

Your `SGIdle` function reports several status and error conditions by means of its result code. If your component returns a nonzero result code during a record operation, the application should still call the `SGStop` function (described on page 6-43) so that the sequence grabber component can store the data it has collected.

RESULT CODES

File Manager errors
Memory Manager errors

SGUpdate

The `SGUpdate` function allows you to learn about update events. This gives you an opportunity to update your display.

```
pascal ComponentResult SGUpdate (SeqGrabComponent s,
                                 RgnHandle updateRgn);
```

s   Identifies the sequence grabber component that has connected to your channel component.

updateRgn   Indicates the part of the window that has been changed. This parameter specifies a portion of the window that has been changed. Applications can obtain this information by examining the appropriate window record. For example, they may call the sequence grabber in this manner:

```
SGUpdate (theSG, ((WindowPeek)updateWindow)->updateRgn);
```

If this parameter is set to `nil`, use the window's current visible region.

CHAPTER 6

Sequence Grabber Channel Components

DESCRIPTION

Applications call the sequence grabber's `SGUpdate` function whenever they receive an update event for a window that contains a sequence grabber display. The sequence grabber then calls each affected channel. Applications should call this function before calling the Window Manager's `BeginUpdate` function.

RESULT CODE

`deviceCantMeetRequest`   –9408   Device cannot support grabber

SGStop

The `SGStop` function stops a preview or record operation.

```
pascal ComponentResult SGStop (SeqGrabComponent s);
```

s   Identifies the sequence grabber component that has connected to your channel component.

DESCRIPTION

In the case of a record operation, the sequence grabber component stores the collected movie data in the assigned movie file. The sequence grabber component then calls your `SGWriteSamples` function (described in the next section) to place the references to the captured data into the movie after it calls `SGStop`.

▲ **WARNING**
It is dangerous to allow an update event to occur during recording. Many digitizers capture directly to the screen, and an update event will result in data loss. ▲

RESULT CODES

File Manager errors
Memory Manager errors

SGWriteSamples

The sequence grabber component calls the `SGWriteSamples` function when it is ready to add recorded data to a movie.

```
pascal ComponentResult SGWriteSamples (SGChannel c, Movie m,
                                       AliasHandle theFile);
```

CHAPTER 6

Sequence Grabber Channel Components

c
: Identifies the channel connection for this operation.

m
: Identifies the movie to which your component should add the captured data. Your component should not make any other changes to the movie identified by this reference. Use the SGWriteMovieData function, described on page 6-86.

theFile
: Identifies the movie file. The sequence grabber component provides this alias so that you can supply it to the Movie Toolbox. You should not open this file or write to it directly. Use the SGWriteMovieData function.

DESCRIPTION

The sequence grabber component calls this function when the recording operation is complete, after calling your SGStop function (described on page 6-43). In this manner, your channel component can avoid unnecessary Movie Toolbox overhead during the record operation.

SPECIAL CONSIDERATIONS

Your component should dispose of any buffered data and add the captured data to the movie. If necessary, use the Movie Toolbox's functions to create a track and a media. See the chapter "Movie Toolbox" in *Inside Macintosh: QuickTime* for details.

RESULT CODES

File Manager errors
Memory Manager errors

SGPause

A sequence grabber component can suspend or restart a record or preview operation by calling the SGPause function.

```
pascal ComponentResult SGPause (SeqGrabComponent s, Byte pause);
```

s
: Identifies the sequence grabber component that has connected to your channel component.

pause
: Instructs your component to suspend or restart the current operation. The following values are valid:

    seqGrabUnpause
    : Restart the current operation.

    seqGrabPause
    : Pause the current operation.

CHAPTER 6

Sequence Grabber Channel Components

DESCRIPTION

The sequence grabber component supplies a constant value in the `paused` parameter that instructs your component to pause or restart the current operation.

SPECIAL CONSIDERATIONS

Your component should not release any system resources or temporary memory associated with the current operation—you should be ready to restart the operation immediately.

RESULT CODES

`deviceCantMeetRequest`	–9408	Device cannot support grabber

File Manager errors
Memory Manager errors

SGPrepare

The `SGPrepare` function instructs your component to get ready to begin a preview or record operation (or both)—the sequence grabber component specifies the operations.

```
pascal ComponentResult SGPrepare (SeqGrabComponent s,
                                  Boolean prepareForPreview,
                                  Boolean prepareForRecord);
```

s
: Identifies the sequence grabber component that has connected to your channel component.

prepareForPreview
: Instructs your component to prepare for a preview operation. The sequence grabber component sets this parameter to `true` to prepare for a preview operation. The sequence grabber component may set both the `prepareForPreview` and `prepareForRecord` parameters to `true`.

prepareForRecord
: Instructs your component to prepare for a record operation. The sequence grabber component sets this parameter to `true` to prepare for a record operation. The sequence grabber component may set both the `prepareForPreview` and `prepareForRecord` parameters to `true`.

DESCRIPTION

Your component should do whatever is necessary to get ready to start the operation. The goal is to reduce the delay between the time when the sequence grabber calls your `SGStartPreview` function (described on page 6-40) or `SGStartRecord` function (described on page 6-41) and the time when the operation actually begins. This may involve allocating memory or readying special hardware.

CHAPTER 6

Sequence Grabber Channel Components

SPECIAL CONSIDERATIONS

If the sequence grabber calls `SGPrepare` without subsequently starting a record or preview operation, it calls the `SGRelease` function (described in the next section) later. This allows your component to release any system resources it allocated during the `SGPrepare` function.

RESULT CODES

paramErr	–50	Invalid parameter specified
notEnoughDiskSpaceToGrab	–9404	Insufficient disk space for record operation
deviceCantMeetRequest	–9408	Device cannot support grabber

File Manager errors
Memory Manager errors

SGRelease

The `SGRelease` function instructs your component to release any system resources it allocated during the `SGPrepare` function, which is described in the previous section.

```
pascal ComponentResult SGRelease (SeqGrabComponent s);
```

s   Identifies the sequence grabber component that has connected to your channel component.

DESCRIPTION

The sequence grabber component calls your `SGRelease` function whenever it calls `SGPrepare` without subsequently starting a record or preview operation.

SPECIAL CONSIDERATIONS

Note that the sequence grabber component may call `SGRelease` more than once after calling `SGPrepare`.

Configuration Functions for All Channel Components

Sequence grabber components use channel components to obtain digitized data from external media. Your channel is assigned to a sequence grabber component when the application calls the sequence grabber component's `SGNewChannel` function, described in the chapter "Sequence Grabber Components" in this book. The sequence grabber component must configure your channel before a preview or record operation. Your channel component must provide a number of functions that allow the sequence grabber to configure the characteristics of your channel. Several of these functions work on any channel component. This section discusses these general channel configuration functions.

In addition, channel components provide functions that are specific to the channel type. The sequence grabber component supplied by Apple uses two types of channel components: video channel components and sound channel components. See "Configuration Functions for Video Channel Components," which begins on page 6-61, for information about the configuration functions that work only with video channels. See "Configuration Functions for Sound Channel Components," which begins on page 6-77, for information about the configuration functions that work only with sound channels.

The SGSetChannelUsage function specifies how your channel is to be used. The sequence grabber component can restrict a channel to use during record or preview operations. In addition, this function allows the sequence grabber component to specify whether your channel plays during a record operation. The SGGetChannelUsage function allows the sequence grabber component to determine a channel's usage.

The SGGetChannelInfo function allows the sequence grabber component to determine some of the characteristics of your channel. For example, this function returns information indicating whether your channel has a visual or an audio representation.

The SGSetChannelPlayFlags function lets the sequence grabber component influence the speed and quality with which your channel plays captured data. The SGGetChannelPlayFlags function allows the sequence grabber component to determine these flag settings.

The SGSetChannelMaxFrames function establishes a limit on the number of frames that your channel component will capture from a channel.

The SGGetChannelMaxFrames function enables the sequence grabber component to determine that limit.

The SGSetChannelRefCon function allows the sequence grabber component to set the value of a reference constant that your component passes to its callback functions (see "Using Callback Functions for Video Channel Components," which begins on page 6-35, for information about the callback functions that are supported by video channels).

The SGGetDataRate function allows the sequence grabber component to determine how many bytes of captured data your channel is collecting each second.

The SGGetChannelSampleDescription function allows the sequence grabber to retrieve your channel's sample description. The SGGetChannelTimeScale function allows it to obtain your channel's time scale.

The sequence grabber can modify or retrieve your channel's clipping region by calling the SGSetChannelClip or SGGetChannelClip function, respectively. The sequence grabber can work with your channel's transformation matrix by calling the SGSetChannelMatrix and SGGetChannelMatrix functions.

SGSetChannelUsage

The `SGSetChannelUsage` function specifies how your channel is to be used by the sequence grabber component.

```
pascal ComponentResult SGSetChannelUsage (SGChannel c,
                                          long usage);
```

c
Identifies the channel connection for this operation.

usage
Contains flags specifying how your channel is to be used. The sequence grabber component may set more than one of these flags to 1. It sets unused flags to 0. The following flags are defined by the `SeqGrabUsageEnum` data type:

seqGrabRecord
Indicates that your channel is to be used during record operations. The sequence grabber component sets this flag to 1 to use a channel for recording.

seqGrabPreview
Indicates that your channel is to be used during preview operations. The sequence grabber component sets this flag to 1 to use a channel for previewing.

seqGrabPlayDuringRecord
Indicates that your component is to play its captured data during a record operation. If the sequence grabber component sets this flag to 1, your channel should play its captured data during a record operation, if the destination buffer is onscreen.

DESCRIPTION

The sequence grabber component can specify that a channel is to be used for recording or previewing, or both. In addition, the sequence grabber component can control whether the data captured by a channel is displayed during the record or preview operation.

RESULT CODES

notEnoughMemoryToGrab	–9403	Insufficient memory for record operation
deviceCantMeetRequest	–9408	Device cannot support grabber

CHAPTER 6

Sequence Grabber Channel Components

SGGetChannelUsage

The `SGGetChannelUsage` function allows the sequence grabber to determine how your channel is to be used.

```
pascal ComponentResult SGGetChannelUsage (SGChannel c,
                                          long *usage);
```

c   Identifies the channel connection for this operation.

usage   Contains a pointer to a location that is to receive flags specifying how your channel is to be used. You may set more than one of these flags to 1. Set unused flags to 0. The following flags are defined by the `SeqGrabUsageEnum` data type:

   seqGrabRecord
              Indicates that your channel is to be used during record operations. Set this flag to 1 if your channel is being used for recording.

   seqGrabPreview
              Indicates that your channel is to be used during preview operations. Set this flag to 1 if your channel is being used for previewing.

   seqGrabPlayDuringRecord
              Indicates that your component is to play its captured data during a record operation. Set this flag to 1 if your channel plays its captured data during a record operation.

SEE ALSO

The sequence grabber component establishes your channel's usage by calling your `SGSetChannelUsage` function, described in the previous section.

SGGetChannelInfo

The `SGGetChannelInfo` function allows the sequence grabber to determine how a channel's data is represented to the user—as visual or audio data, or both.

```
pascal ComponentResult SGGetChannelInfo (SGChannel c,
                                         long *channelInfo);
```

c   Identifies the channel connection for this operation.

CHAPTER 6

Sequence Grabber Channel Components

channelInfo
: Contains a pointer to a long integer that is to receive channel information flags. You may set more than one flag to 1. Set unused flags to 0. The following flags are defined:

    seqGrabHasBounds
    : Indicates that your channel has a visual representation. If you set this flag to 1, the channel has a visual representation. The sequence grabber component may call your SGSetChannelBounds function (described on page 6-63).

    seqGrabHasVolume
    : Indicates that your channel has an audio representation. If you set this flag to 1, the channel has an audio representation. The sequence grabber component may call your SGSetChannelVolume function (described on page 6-77).

    seqGrabHasDiscreteSamples
    : Indicates that the data captured by your channel component is organized into discrete frames. If you set this flag to 1, the sequence grabber component may use the SGSetChannelMaxFrames function (described on page 6-52) to limit the number of frames processed in a record operation or the rate at which those frames are processed. If your channel's data is not organized into frames, set this flag to 0.

SGSetChannelPlayFlags

The `SGSetChannelPlayFlags` function allows the sequence grabber component to influence the speed and quality with which your channel component displays data from its source.

```
pascal ComponentResult SGSetChannelPlayFlags (SGChannel c,
                                              long playFlags);
```

c
: Identifies the channel connection for this operation.

playFlags
: Specifies a long integer that contains flags and values that influence channel playback. The following values are defined—the sequence grabber component must use one of these values:

    channelPlayNormal
    : Instructs your channel component to use its default playback methodology.

    channelPlayFast
    : Instructs your channel component to sacrifice playback quality in order to achieve the specified playback rate.

CHAPTER 6

Sequence Grabber Channel Components

`channelPlayHighQuality`
: Instructs your channel component to play the channel's data at the highest possible quality—this option sacrifices playback rate for the sake of image quality. This option may reduce the amount of processor time available to other programs in the computer. This option should not affect the quality of the recorded data, however.

The following flag is defined—the sequence grabber component may use this flag with any of the values defined for this parameter (unused flags are set to 0):

`channelPlayAllData`
: Instructs your channel component to try to play all of the data it captures, even the data that is stored in offscreen buffers. This option is useful when you want to be sure that the user sees as much of the captured data as possible. The sequence grabber component sets this flag to 1 to play all the captured data. The sequence grabber component may combine this flag with any of the values defined for the `playFlags` parameter.

DESCRIPTION

The `SGSetChannelPlayFlags` function should not affect the quality of a record operation.

SGGetChannelPlayFlags

The `SGGetChannelPlayFlags` function allows the sequence grabber component to retrieve the playback control flags that it set with the `SGSetChannelPlayFlags` function, which is described in the previous section.

```
pascal ComponentResult SGGetChannelPlayFlags (SGChannel c,
                                              long *playFlags);
```

c
: Identifies the channel connection for this operation.

playFlags
: Contains a pointer to a long integer that is to receive flags and values that influence channel playback. The following values are defined:

  `channelPlayNormal`
  : Your channel component uses its default playback methodology.

  `channelPlayFast`
  : Your channel component sacrifices playback quality in order to achieve the specified playback rate.

Sequence Grabber Channel Components Reference

CHAPTER 6

Sequence Grabber Channel Components

> channelPlayHighQuality
> > Your channel component plays the channel's data at the highest possible quality—this option sacrifices playback rate for the sake of image quality. This option may reduce the amount of processor time available to other programs in the computer. This option should not affect the quality of the recorded data, however.
>
> The following flag is defined—this flag may be used with any of the values defined for this parameter (unused flags are set to 0):
>
> channelPlayAllData
> > Your channel component tries to play all of the data it captures, even the data that is stored in offscreen buffers. This option is useful when you want to be sure that the user sees as much of the captured data as possible. The sequence grabber component sets this flag to 1 to play all the captured data. The sequence grabber component may combine this flag with any of the values defined for the `playFlags` parameter.

SGSetChannelMaxFrames

The `SGSetChannelMaxFrames` function allows the sequence grabber to limit the number of frames that your channel component will capture during a record operation.

```
pascal ComponentResult SGSetChannelMaxFrames (SGChannel c,
                                              long frameCount);
```

c   Identifies the channel connection for this operation.

frameCount
            Specifies the maximum number of frames to capture during the preview or record operation. The sequence grabber component sets this parameter to –1 to remove the limit.

DESCRIPTION

The `SGSetChannelMaxFrames` function works only with channels that have data that is organized into frames, such as video data from a video disc.

RESULT CODES

| paramErr | –50 | Invalid parameter specified |
| cantDoThatInCurrentMode | –9402 | Request invalid in current mode |

CHAPTER 6

Sequence Grabber Channel Components

SEE ALSO

You report whether your channel's data is organized into frames in your response to the `SGGetChannelInfo` function, which is described on page 6-49.

SGGetChannelMaxFrames

The `SGGetChannelMaxFrames` function allows the sequence grabber component to determine the number of frames left to be captured from your channel.

```
pascal ComponentResult SGGetChannelMaxFrames (SGChannel c,
                                              long *frameCount);
```

c   Identifies the channel connection for this operation.

frameCount
            Contains a pointer to a long integer that is to receive a value specifying the number of frames left to be captured during the preview or record operation. If the returned value is –1, the sequence grabber channel component captures as many frames as it can.

RESULT CODE

            `seqGrabInfoNotAvailable`   –9407   Channel component cannot support request

SEE ALSO

The sequence grabber component sets the starting value by calling the `SGSetChannelMaxFrames` function, which is described in the previous section.

SGSetChannelRefCon

The `SGSetChannelRefCon` function allows the sequence grabber component to set the value of a reference constant that your component passes to its callback functions.

```
pascal ComponentResult SGSetChannelRefCon (SGChannel c,
                                           long refCon);
```

c   Identifies the channel connection for this operation.

refCon   Specifies a reference constant value that your component should pass to the callback functions that have been assigned to this channel.

DESCRIPTION

Sound channels do not support callback functions.

Sequence Grabber Channel Components Reference   6-53

SEE ALSO

See "Using Callback Functions for Video Channel Components," which begins on page 6-36, for a description of the callback functions that are supported by video channel components.

SGGetDataRate

The sequence grabber component calls your component's `SGGetDataRate` function in order to determine how much recording time is left. The sequence grabber calls your component when an application calls the sequence grabber component's `SGGetTimeRemaining` function (see the chapter "Sequence Grabber Components" in this book for details).

```
pascal ComponentResult SGGetDataRate (SGChannel c,
                                      long *bytesPerSecond);
```

c   Identifies the channel connection for this operation.

bytesPerSecond
            Contains a pointer to a long integer that is to receive a value indicating the number of bytes your component is recording per second. Your component calculates this value based on its current operational parameters.

DESCRIPTION

Your component should calculate and return a value indicating the number of bytes of data your component is recording per second. The sequence grabber component uses this information, along with similar information gathered from other channels being used in the recording operation, to determine how many seconds of data may be recorded given the amount of space remaining.

SPECIAL CONSIDERATIONS

The sequence grabber component calls the `SGGetDataRate` function during the recording operation. Consequently, your component should service the request as quickly as possible.

SGGetChannelSampleDescription

The `SGGetChannelSampleDescription` function allows the sequence grabber to retrieve your channel's sample description.

```
pascal ComponentResult SGGetChannelSampleDescription
                            (SGChannel c, Handle sampleDesc);
```

c Identifies the channel connection for this operation.

sampleDesc
Specifies a handle that is to receive your sample description.

DESCRIPTION

The `SGGetChannelSampleDescription` function allows the sequence grabber to retrieve your channel's current sample description. The sequence grabber may call this function only when your channel is prepared to record or is actually recording.

Your channel returns a sample description that is appropriate to the type of data being captured. For video channels, your channel component returns an Image Compression Manager image description structure; for sound channels, you return a sound description structure, as defined by the Movie Toolbox.

RESULT CODE

cantDoThatInCurrentMode   –9402   Request invalid in current mode

SGGetChannelTimeScale

The `SGGetChannelTimeScale` function allows the sequence grabber to retrieve your channel's time scale.

```
pascal ComponentResult SGGetChannelTimeScale (SGChannel c,
                                        TimeScale *scale);
```

c Identifies the channel connection for this operation.

scale Contains a pointer to a time scale structure. Your channel component places information about its time scale into this structure.

DESCRIPTION

The time scale you return typically corresponds to the time scale of the media that has been created by your channel. Applications may use this time scale in their data functions (see the chapter "Sequence Grabber Components" in this book for more information about application-defined data functions).

SGSetChannelClip

The `SGSetChannelClip` function allows the sequence grabber to set your channel's clipping region.

```
pascal ComponentResult SGSetChannelClip (SGChannel c,
                                         RgnHandle theClip);
```

c   Identifies the channel connection for this operation.

theClip Contains a handle to the new clipping region. You should make a copy of this region; the application may dispose of the region immediately.

If this parameter is set to `nil`, remove the current clipping region.

DESCRIPTION

The `SGSetChannelClip` function allows the sequence grabber to apply a clipping region to your channel's display region. By default, channel components do not apply a clipping region to their displayed image.

SGGetChannelClip

The `SGGetChannelClip` function allows the sequence grabber to retrieve your channel's clipping region.

```
pascal ComponentResult SGGetChannelClip (SGChannel c,
                                         RgnHandle *theClip);
```

c   Identifies the channel connection for this operation.

theClip Contains a pointer to a handle that is to receive the clipping region. The application is responsible for disposing of this handle. If there is no clipping region, set this handle to `nil`.

Note

Some devices may not support clipping. ◆

SGSetChannelMatrix

The `SGSetChannelMatrix` function allows the sequence grabber to set your channel's display transformation matrix.

```
pascal ComponentResult SGSetChannelMatrix (SGChannel c,
                                           const MatrixRecord *m);
```

c   Identifies the channel connection for this operation.

m   Contains a pointer to a matrix structure, as defined by the Movie Toolbox (see the chapter "Movie Toolbox" in *Inside Macintosh: QuickTime* for more information about matrix structures). This parameter is set to `nil` to select the identity matrix.

DESCRIPTION

The `SGSetChannelMatrix` function allows the sequence grabber to specify a display transformation matrix for a video channel. Your channel uses this matrix to transform its video image into the destination window. If your channel cannot accommodate the matrix, return an appropriate result code. Note that the sequence grabber may not call this function when you are recording.

Other channel component functions may affect this matrix. The `SGSetChannelBounds` function sets the matrix values so that the matrix maps the channel's output to the channel's boundary rectangle (described on page 6-63). The `SGSetVideoRect` function modifies the matrix so that the specified video rectangle appears in the existing destination rectangle (see page 6-64 for more information about the `SGSetVideoRect` function).

RESULT CODES

`matrixErr`	–2203	Invalid matrix
`deviceCantMeetRequest`	–9408	Device cannot support grabber

SEE ALSO

The sequence grabber may retrieve your channel's matrix by calling the `SGGetChannelMatrix` function, which is discussed next.

SGGetChannelMatrix

The `SGGetChannelMatrix` function allows the sequence grabber to retrieve your channel's display transformation matrix.

```
pascal ComponentResult SGGetChannelMatrix (SGChannel c,
                                           MatrixRecord *m);
```

c   Identifies the channel connection for this operation.

m   Contains a pointer to a matrix structure, as defined by the Movie Toolbox (see "Movie Toolbox" in *Inside Macintosh: QuickTime* for more information about matrix structures). Place your current matrix values into this matrix structure.

SEE ALSO

The sequence grabber may set your channel's matrix by calling the `SGSetChannelMatrix` function, which is discussed in the previous section.

Working With Channel Devices

Sequence grabbers provide a number of functions that allow applications to determine the devices that can be, or the device that is, attached to a given sequence grabber channel. These devices, in turn, allow the channel component to control the digitizing equipment. For example, video channels use video digitizer components, and sound channels use sound input drivers. Applications can use these functions to present a list of available devices to the user, allowing the user to select a specific device for each channel. The sequence grabber passes these functions on to your channel component.

The sequence grabber may use the `SGGetChannelDeviceList` function to retrieve a list of devices that may be used by your channel.

The sequence grabber can use the `SGSetChannelDevice` function to assign a device to your channel.

The `SGGetChannelDeviceList` function uses a device list structure to pass information about one or more channel devices. The `SGDeviceListRecord` data type defines the format of the device list structure.

```
typedef struct SGDeviceListRecord {
    short         count;             /* count of devices */
    short         selectedIndex;     /* current device */
    long          reserved;          /* set to 0 */
    SGDeviceName  entry[1];          /* device names */
} SGDeviceListRecord, *SGDeviceListPtr, **SGDeviceList;
```

CHAPTER 6

Sequence Grabber Channel Components

Field descriptions

count
Indicates the number of devices described by this structure. The value of this field corresponds to the number of entries in the device name array defined by the `entry` field.

selectedIndex
Identifies the currently active device. The value of this field corresponds to the appropriate entry in the device name array defined by the `entry` field. Note that this value is 0-relative; that is, the first entry has an index number of 0, the second's value is 1, and so on.

reserved
Reserved for Apple. Always set to 0.

entry
Contains an array of device name structures. Each structure corresponds to one valid device. The `count` field indicates the number of entries in this array. The `SGDeviceName` data type defines the format of a device name structure; this data type is discussed next.

Device list structures contain an array of device name structures. Each device name structure identifies a single device that may be used by the channel. The `SGDeviceName` data type defines the format of a device name structure.

```
typedef struct SGDeviceName {
    Str63       name;           /* device name */
    Handle      icon;           /* device icon */
    long        flags;          /* flags */
    long        refCon;         /* set to 0 */
    long        reserved;       /* set to 0 */
} SGDeviceName;
```

Field descriptions

name
Contains the name of the device. For video digitizer components, this field contains the component's name as specified in the component resource. For sound input drivers, this field contains the driver name.

icon
Contains a handle to the device's icon. Some devices may support an icon, which applications may choose to present to the user. If the device does not support an icon, or if the sequence grabber chooses not to retrieve this information (by setting the `sgDeviceListWithIcons` flag to 0 when it calls the `SGGetChannelDeviceList` function, which is described in the next section), set this field to `nil`.

flags
Reflects the current status of the device. The following flag is defined:

sgDeviceNameFlagDeviceUnavailable
When set to 1, this flag indicates that this device is not currently available.

refCon
Reserved for Apple. Always set to 0.

reserved
Reserved for Apple. Always set to 0.

Sequence Grabber Channel Components Reference

SGGetChannelDeviceList

The `SGGetChannelDeviceList` function allows the sequence grabber to retrieve a list of the devices that are valid for your channel.

```
pascal ComponentResult SGGetChannelDeviceList (SGChannel c,
                                               long selectionFlags,
                                               SGDeviceList *list);
```

c
: Identifies the channel connection for this operation.

selectionFlags
: Controls the data you are to return for each device. The following flags are defined:

    sgDeviceListWithIcons
    : Specifies whether the sequence grabber wants to retrieve an icon for each device. If this flag is set to 1, return an icon for each device in the list, in the `icon` field. If this flag is set to 0, set the `icon` field to 0.

    sgDeviceListDontCheckAvailability
    : Controls whether you verify that each device is currently available. If this flag is set to 1, do not check the availability of each device. Otherwise, you should check each device's availability, and set the `sgDeviceNameFlagDeviceUnavailable` flag appropriately in each device name structure that you return.

list
: Contains a pointer to a device list structure pointer. The channel creates a device name structure and returns a pointer to that structure in the field referred to by this parameter. Applications use the sequence grabber's `SGDisposeDeviceList` function to dispose of the memory used by the list.

DESCRIPTION

This function allows the sequence grabber to retrieve a list of the devices that may be used by your channel. Each entry in this list identifies a valid device by name. Applications may then place these device names into a menu using the sequence grabber's `SGAppendDeviceListToMenu` function.

Applications may use this function in order to determine the device your channel is currently using. Be sure to set the `selectedIndex` field properly.

RESULT CODES

Memory Manager errors

CHAPTER 6

Sequence Grabber Channel Components

SEE ALSO

You may use the sequence grabber's `SGSortDeviceList` function to sort the entries in your device list structure. This function is discussed on page 6-89.

SGSetChannelDevice

The `SGSetChannelDevice` function allows the sequence grabber to assign a device to your channel.

```
pascal ComponentResult SGSetChannelDevice (SGChannel c,
                                           StringPtr name);
```

c Identifies the channel connection for this operation.

name Contains a pointer to the device's name string. This name is contained in the `name` field of the appropriate device name structure in the device list that your channel returns to the `SGGetChannelDeviceList` function.

DESCRIPTION

When the sequence grabber calls your `SGSetChannelDevice` function, your channel should try to use the specified device instead of the device currently in use. The device name must be derived from your channel's device list.

RESULT CODES

`paramErr`	–50	Invalid parameter value
`deviceCantMeetRequest`	–9408	Device cannot support grabber

SEE ALSO

The sequence grabber obtains the device list by calling your `SGGetChannelDeviceList` function, which is discussed in the previous section.

Configuration Functions for Video Channel Components

Video channel components provide a number of functions that allow the sequence grabber to configure the channel's video characteristics. This section describes these video channel configuration functions, which the sequence grabber component uses only with video channels.

The `SGSetChannelBounds` function allows the sequence grabber to set the display boundary rectangle for a video channel. The `SGGetChannelBounds` function determines a channel's boundary rectangle.

The sequence grabber component uses the `SGGetSrcVideoBounds` function to determine the coordinates of the source video boundary rectangle. This rectangle defines the size of the source video image being captured by a video channel. The `SGSetVideoRect` function specifies a part of the source video boundary rectangle to be captured by the channel. The `SGGetVideoRect` function retrieves this active source video rectangle.

Typically, video channel components use the Image Compression Manager to compress the video data they capture. The sequence grabber component can control many aspects of this image-compression process. The `SGSetVideoCompressorType` function specifies the type of image compressor to use. The sequence grabber can determine the type of image compressor currently in use by calling the `SGGetVideoCompressorType` function. The sequence grabber component can specify a particular image compressor and set many image-compression parameters by calling the `SGSetVideoCompressor` function. The sequence grabber component can determine which image compressor is being used and its parameter settings by calling the `SGGetVideoCompressor` function.

Video channel components typically work with a video digitizer component (see the chapter "Video Digitizer Components" in this book for a complete description of video digitizer components). Sequence grabber components provide functions that allow an application to work with a channel's video digitizer component. Video channel components, in turn, must provide support for these functions. The sequence grabber component uses the `SGGetVideoDigitizerComponent` function to determine which video digitizer component is supplying data to your video channel component. The sequence grabber component sets a channel's video digitizer component by calling the `SGSetVideoDigitizerComponent` function. If an application changes any video digitizer settings by calling the video digitizer component directly, the sequence grabber component informs your video channel component by calling the `SGVideoDigitizerChanged` function.

Some video source data may contain unacceptable levels of visual noise or artifacts. One technique for removing this noise is to capture the image and then reduce it in size. During the size reduction process, the noise can be filtered out. Some video channel components may provide functions that allow the sequence grabber component to filter the input video data. The `SGSetCompressBuffer` function sets a filter buffer for a video channel. The `SGGetCompressBuffer` function returns information about your filter buffer.

The sequence grabber can work with a video channel's frame rate by calling the `SGSetFrameRate` and `SGGetFrameRate` functions. The sequence grabber can control whether your channel uses an offscreen buffer by calling your `SGSetUseScreenBuffer` and `SGGetUseScreenBuffer` functions.

Your `SGAlignChannelRect` function allows the sequence grabber to determine a channel's optimum screen position.

SGSetChannelBounds

The `SGSetChannelBounds` function allows the sequence grabber component to specify your channel's display boundary rectangle.

```
pascal ComponentResult SGSetChannelBounds (SGChannel c,
                                           Rect *bounds);
```

c   Identifies the channel connection for this operation.

bounds   Contains a pointer to a rectangle that defines your channel's display boundary rectangle.

DESCRIPTION

This rectangle defines the destination for data from this channel. This rectangle is defined in the graphics world that the sequence grabber component establishes by calling the `SGSetGWorld` function, described on page 6-39.

SPECIAL CONSIDERATIONS

The `SGSetChannelBounds` function adjusts the channel matrix, as appropriate.

RESULT CODES

cantDoThatInCurrentMode	−9402	Request invalid in current mode
notEnoughMemoryToGrab	−9403	Insufficient memory for record operation
deviceCantMeetRequest	−9408	Device cannot support grabber

SGGetChannelBounds

The `SGGetChannelBounds` function allows the sequence grabber component to determine your channel's display boundary rectangle.

```
pascal ComponentResult SGGetChannelBounds (SGChannel c,
                                           const Rect *bounds);
```

c   Identifies the channel connection for this operation.

bounds   Contains a pointer to a rectangle structure that is to receive information about your channel's display boundary rectangle.

CHAPTER 6

Sequence Grabber Channel Components

DESCRIPTION

The sequence grabber component sets the boundary rectangle by calling the `SGSetChannelBounds` function, which is described in the previous section. This rectangle is defined in the graphics world that the sequence grabber establishes by calling the `SGSetGWorld` function, described on page 6-39.

SGGetSrcVideoBounds

The `SGGetSrcVideoBounds` function allows the sequence grabber component to determine the size of the source video boundary rectangle.

```
pascal ComponentResult SGGetSrcVideoBounds (SGChannel c, Rect *r);
```

c   Identifies the channel connection for this operation.

r   Contains a pointer to a rectangle structure that is to receive information about your channel's source video boundary rectangle.

DESCRIPTION

This rectangle defines the size of the source video image.

RESULT CODE

paramErr   –50   Invalid parameter specified

SEE ALSO

For video channel components that work with video digitizer components, this rectangle corresponds to the video digitizer's active source rectangle (see the chapter "Video Digitizer Components" in this book for more information about video digitizer components).

SGSetVideoRect

The `SGSetVideoRect` function allows the sequence grabber component to specify a part of the source video image that is to be captured by your channel component.

```
pascal ComponentResult SGSetVideoRect (SGChannel c, Rect *r);
```

c   Identifies the channel connection for this operation.

CHAPTER 6

Sequence Grabber Channel Components

r Contains a pointer to the dimensions of the rectangle that defines the portion of the source video image to be captured. This rectangle must lie within the boundaries of the source video boundary rectangle, which the sequence grabber can obtain by calling the `SGGetSrcVideoBounds` function, described in the previous section.

DESCRIPTION

This rectangle must reside within the boundaries of the source video boundary rectangle. The sequence grabber component obtains the dimensions of the source video boundary rectangle by calling the `SGGetSrcVideoBounds` function. By default, your component should capture the entire video image, as defined by the source video boundary rectangle.

RESULT CODES

`cantDoThatInCurrentMode`	–9402	Request invalid in current mode
`notEnoughMemoryToGrab`	–9403	Insufficient memory for record operation
`deviceCantMeetRequest`	–9408	Device cannot support grabber

SEE ALSO

For video channel components that receive their data from video digitizer components, this function sets the video digitizer component's digitizer rectangle. See the chapter "Video Digitizer Components" in this book for information about video digitizer components.

SGGetVideoRect

The `SGGetVideoRect` function allows the sequence grabber to determine the portion of the source video image that your component is going to capture.

```
pascal ComponentResult SGGetVideoRect (SGChannel c, Rect *r);
```

c Contains a pointer to the channel connection for this operation.

r Contains a pointer to a rectangle structure that is to receive the dimensions of the rectangle that defines the portion of the source video image your component is going to capture.

SEE ALSO

The sequence grabber uses the `SGSetVideoRect` function, which is described in the previous section, to set the dimensions of this rectangle.

SGSetVideoCompressorType

The `SGSetVideoCompressorType` function allows the sequence grabber component to specify the type of image compression your component is to apply to the captured video images.

```
pascal ComponentResult SGSetVideoCompressorType (SGChannel c,
                                                 OSType compressorType);
```

c
: Identifies the channel connection for this operation.

compressorType
: Specifies the type of image compression to use. The value of this parameter must correspond to one of the image compressor types supported by the Image Compression Manager. Currently, six `CodecType` values are provided by Apple. You should use the `GetCodecNameList` function to retrieve these names, so that your application can take advantage of new compressor types that may be added in the future. For each `CodecType` value in the following list, the corresponding compression method is also identified by its text string name.

Compressor type	Compressor name
`'rpza'`	video compressor
`'jpeg'`	photo compressor
`'rle '`	animation compressor
`'raw '`	raw compressor
`'smc '`	graphics compressor
`'cvid'`	compact video compressor

See the chapter "Image Compression Manager" in *Inside Macintosh: QuickTime* for information about valid compressor types. If this value is set to 0, its default compression type is selected.

DESCRIPTION

In addition, your component should reset all image-compression parameters to their default values. The sequence grabber component can then use the `SGSetVideoCompressor` function, described on page 6-68, to change those compression parameters.

RESULT CODES

`cantDoThatInCurrentMode`	–9402	Request invalid in current mode
`notEnoughMemoryToGrab`	–9403	Insufficient memory for record operation
`deviceCantMeetRequest`	–9408	Device cannot support grabber

SGGetVideoCompressorType

The `SGGetVideoCompressorType` function allows the sequence grabber component to determine the type of image compression that is being applied to your channel's video data.

```
pascal ComponentResult SGGetVideoCompressorType (SGChannel c,
                                        OSType *compressorType);
```

c
: Identifies the channel connection for this operation.

compressorType
: Contains a pointer to an `OSType` field that is to receive information about the type of image compression to use. Return a value that corresponds to one of the image-compression types supported by the Image Compression Manager. Currently, six `CodecType` values are provided by Apple. You should use the `GetCodecNameList` function to retrieve these names, so that your application can take advantage of new compressor types that may be added in the future. For each `CodecType` value in the following list, the corresponding compression method is also identified by its text string name.

Compressor type	Compressor name
`'rpza'`	video compressor
`'jpeg'`	photo compressor
`'rle '`	animation compressor
`'raw '`	raw compressor
`'smc '`	graphics compressor
`'cvid'`	compact video compressor

See the chapter "Image Compression Manager" in *Inside Macintosh: QuickTime* for information about valid compressor types. If this value is set to 0, its default compression type is selected.

SEE ALSO

The sequence grabber component can set the image-compression type by calling the `SGSetVideoCompressorType` function, which is described in the previous section.

SGSetVideoCompressor

The `SGSetVideoCompressor` function allows the sequence grabber component to specify many of the parameters that control image compression of the video data captured by your video channel.

```
pascal ComponentResult SGSetVideoCompressor (SGChannel c,
                            short depth,
                            CompressorComponent compressor,
                            CodecQ spatialQuality,
                            CodecQ temporalQuality,
                            long keyFrameRate);
```

`c`
: Identifies the channel connection for this operation.

`depth`
: Specifies the depth at which the image is likely to be viewed. Image compressors may use this as an indication of the color or grayscale resolution of the compressed images. If the sequence grabber component sets this parameter to 0, let the sequence grabber component determine the appropriate value for the source image. Values of 1, 2, 4, 8, 16, 24, and 32 indicate the number of bits per pixel for color images. Values of 33, 34, 36, and 40 indicate 1-bit, 2-bit, 4-bit, and 8-bit grayscale, respectively, for grayscale images. Your component can determine which depths are supported by a given compressor by examining the compression information record (defined by the `CodecInfo` data type) returned by the Image Compression Manager's `GetCodecInfo` function (see the chapter "Image Compression Manager" in *Inside Macintosh: QuickTime* for more information on the `GetCodecInfo` function).

`compressor`
: Specifies the image compressor identifier. The sequence grabber component may specify a particular compressor by setting this parameter to its compressor identifier. You can obtain these identifiers from the Image Compression Manager's `GetCodecNameList` function.

`spatialQuality`
: Specifies the desired quality of the compressed image. See the chapter "Image Compression Manager" in *Inside Macintosh: QuickTime* for valid values.

`temporalQuality`
: Specifies the desired temporal quality of the sequence. This parameter governs the level of compression the sequence grabber component desires with respect to information in successive frames in the sequence. The sequence grabber component sets this parameter to 0 to prevent the image compressor from applying temporal compression to the sequence. See the chapter "Image Compression Manager" in *Inside Macintosh: QuickTime* for other valid values.

Sequence Grabber Channel Components

keyFrameRate

>Specifies the maximum number of frames allowed between key frames. Key frames provide points from which a temporally compressed sequence may be decompressed. The sequence grabber component uses this parameter to control the frequency with which the image compressor places key frames into the compressed sequence. For more information about key frames, see the chapter "Image Compression Manager" in *Inside Macintosh: QuickTime*.

>The compressor determines the optimum placement for key frames based upon the amount of redundancy between adjacent images in the sequence. Consequently, the compressor may insert key frames more frequently than you have requested. However, the compressor will never place key frames less often than is indicated by the setting of the `keyFrameRate` parameter. The compressor ignores this parameter if you have not requested temporal compression (that is, you have set the `temporalQuality` parameter to 0).

RESULT CODES

paramErr	–50	Invalid parameter
cantDoThatInCurrentMode	–9402	Request invalid in current mode
notEnoughMemoryToGrab	–9403	Insufficient memory for record operation
deviceCantMeetRequest	–9408	Device cannot support grabber

SGGetVideoCompressor

The `SGGetVideoCompressor` function allows the sequence grabber component to determine your channel's current image-compression parameters.

```
pascal ComponentResult SGGetVideoCompressor (SGChannel c,
                            short *depth,
                            CompressorComponent *compressor,
                            CodecQ *spatialQuality,
                            CodecQ *temporalQuality,
                            long *keyFrameRate);
```

c
>Identifies the channel connection for this operation.

depth
>Contains a pointer to a field that is to receive the depth at which the image is likely to be viewed. Image compressor components may use the depth as an indication of the color or grayscale resolution of the compressed images. Return the depth value currently in use by your channel component. If this parameter is set to `nil`, the sequence grabber component is not interested in this information.

CHAPTER 6

Sequence Grabber Channel Components

compressor
: Contains a pointer to a field that is to receive an image compressor identifier. Return the identifier that corresponds to the image compressor your channel is using. If this parameter is set to `nil`, the sequence grabber component is not interested in this information.

spatialQuality
: Contains a pointer to a field that is to receive the desired compressed image quality. Return the current quality value. See the chapter "Image Compression Manager" in *Inside Macintosh: QuickTime* for valid values. If this parameter is set to `nil`, the sequence grabber component is not interested in this information.

temporalQuality
: Contains a pointer to a field that is to receive the desired temporal quality of the sequence. This parameter governs the level of compression you desire with respect to information between successive frames in the sequence. Return the current temporal quality value. If this parameter is set to `nil`, the sequence grabber component is not interested in this information.

keyFrameRate
: Contains a pointer to a field that is to receive the maximum number of frames allowed between key frames. Key frames provide points from which a temporally compressed sequence may be decompressed. This value controls the frequency at which the image compressor places key frames into the compressed sequence. Return the current key frame rate. If this parameter is set to `nil`, the sequence grabber component is not interested in this information.

SEE ALSO

The sequence grabber component can set these parameters by calling the `SGSetVideoCompressor` function, which is described in the previous section.

SGSetVideoDigitizerComponent

The `SGSetVideoDigitizerComponent` function allows the sequence grabber component to assign a video digitizer component to your video channel.

```
pascal ComponentResult SGSetVideoDigitizerComponent
                    (SGChannel c, ComponentInstance vdig);
```

c
: Identifies the channel connection for this operation.

Sequence Grabber Channel Components

vdig   Contains a component instance that identifies a connection to a video digitizer component. Your video channel component should use this video digitizer component to obtain its source video data.

DESCRIPTION

Typically, your video channel component locates its own video digitizer component. The sequence grabber component calls the `SGSetVideoDigitizerComponent` function if an application chooses to assign a video digitizer to a video channel.

RESULT CODE

cantDoThatInCurrentMode   –9402   Request invalid in current mode

SGGetVideoDigitizerComponent

The `SGGetVideoDigitizerComponent` function allows the sequence grabber component to determine the video digitizer component that is providing source video to your video channel component. For example, the sequence grabber component can use this function to obtain access to the video digitizer component so that the grabber component can set the digitizer's parameters. See the chapter "Video Digitizer Components" in this book for information about video digitizer components.

```
pascal ComponentInstance SGGetVideoDigitizerComponent
                                                    (SGChannel c);
```

c   Identifies the channel connection for this operation.

DESCRIPTION

The `SGGetVideoDigitizerComponent` function returns a component instance that identifies the connection between your video channel component and its video digitizer component. If your video channel component does not use a video digitizer component, set this returned value to `nil`.

SEE ALSO

If the sequence grabber component changes any video digitizer component parameters, it notifies your sequence grabber channel component by calling your `SGVideoDigitizerChanged` function, which is described in the next section.

CHAPTER 6

Sequence Grabber Channel Components

SGVideoDigitizerChanged

The `SGVideoDigitizerChanged` function allows the sequence grabber component to notify your component whenever an application changes the configuration of your video channel's video digitizer.

```
pascal ComponentResult SGVideoDigitizerChanged (SGChannel c);
```

c   Identifies the channel connection for this operation.

DESCRIPTION

You should update any status information you maintain regarding the video digitizer component used by your channel component.

RESULT CODE

cantDoThatInCurrentMode   –9402   Request invalid in current mode

SGSetCompressBuffer

Some video source data may contain unacceptable levels of visual noise or artifacts. One technique for removing this noise is to capture the image and then reduce it in size. During the size reduction process, the noise can be filtered out.

The `SGSetCompressBuffer` function allows the sequence grabber component to direct your component to create a filter buffer for your video channel. Logically, this buffer sits between the source video buffer and the destination rectangle that the sequence grabber component sets with the `SGSetChannelBounds` function, described on page 6-63. The filter buffer should be larger than the area enclosed by the destination rectangle.

```
pascal ComponentResult SGSetCompressBuffer (SGChannel c,
                                            short depth,
                                            const Rect *compressSize);
```

c   Identifies the channel connection for this operation.

depth   Specifies the pixel depth of the filter buffer. If the sequence grabber sets this parameter to 0, use the depth of the video buffer (which the sequence grabber sets with the `SGSetChannelBounds` function).

Sequence Grabber Channel Components

compressSize
: Contains a pointer to the dimensions of the filter buffer. This buffer should be larger than the destination buffer. The sequence grabber component sets this parameter to `nil`, or it sets the coordinates of this rectangle to 0 (specifying an empty rectangle), to stop filtering the input source video data.

DESCRIPTION

If the sequence grabber component establishes a filter buffer for a channel, your channel component should place its captured video image into the filter buffer and then copy the image into the destination buffer. This process may be too slow for some record operations, but it can be useful during controlled record operations (where the source video can be read on a frame-by-frame basis).

RESULT CODE

cantDoThatInCurrentMode   –9402   Request invalid in current mode

SGGetCompressBuffer

The `SGGetCompressBuffer` function returns information about the filter buffer that the sequence grabber component has established for your video channel.

```
pascal ComponentResult SGGetCompressBuffer (SGChannel c,
                                            short *depth,
                                            Rect *compressSize);
```

c
: Identifies the channel connection for this operation.

depth
: Contains a pointer to a field that is to receive the pixel depth of the filter buffer. If your component is not filtering the input video data, set the returned value to 0.

compressSize
: Contains a pointer to a rectangle structure that is to receive the dimensions of the filter buffer. If your component is not filtering the input video data, return an empty rectangle (all coordinates set to 0).

SEE ALSO

The sequence grabber component sets a filter buffer by calling the `SGSetCompressBuffer` function, which is described in the previous section.

CHAPTER 6

Sequence Grabber Channel Components

SGSetFrameRate

The `SGSetFrameRate` function allows the sequence grabber to specify a video channel's frame rate for recording.

```
pascal ComponentResult SGSetFrameRate (SGChannel c,
                                       Fixed frameRate);
```

c   Identifies the channel connection for this operation.

frameRate   Specifies the desired frame rate. If this parameter is set to 0, use your channel's default frame rate. Typically, this corresponds to the fastest rate that your channel can support.

DESCRIPTION

The `SGSetFrameRate` function allows the sequence grabber to control a video channel's frame rate. Note that the digitizing hardware may not be able to support the full rate that the sequence grabber specifies. If the rate is too high, operate at the highest rate you can support.

SPECIAL CONSIDERATIONS

Note that this function will not be called when you are recording.

RESULT CODES

paramErr	–50	Invalid parameter value
cantDoThatInCurrentMode	–9402	Request invalid in current mode

SEE ALSO

The sequence grabber can retrieve your channel's current frame rate by calling your `SGGetFrameRate` function, which is described next.

SGGetFrameRate

The `SGGetFrameRate` function allows you to retrieve a video channel's frame rate for recording.

```
pascal ComponentResult SGGetFrameRate (SGChannel c,
                                       Fixed *frameRate);
```

c   Identifies the channel connection for this operation.

frameRate   Contains a pointer to a field to receive the current frame rate. Return your channel's current frame rate.

CHAPTER 6

Sequence Grabber Channel Components

DESCRIPTION

The `SGGetFrameRate` function returns your channel's current rate. By default, your channel should record at the fastest rate that it can support. In this case, set the field referred to by the `frameRate` parameter to 0.

SEE ALSO

The sequence grabber can set your channel's frame rate by calling the `SGSetFrameRate` function, which is described in the previous section.

SGSetUseScreenBuffer

The `SGSetUseScreenBuffer` function allows the sequence grabber to control whether your video channel uses an offscreen buffer.

```
pascal ComponentResult SGSetUseScreenBuffer (SGChannel c,
                                             Boolean useScreenBuffer);
```

c   Identifies the channel connection for this operation.

useScreenBuffer
               Indicates whether to use an offscreen buffer. If this parameter is set to `true`, draw directly to the screen. If it is set to `false`, your channel may use an offscreen buffer. If your channel cannot work with offscreen buffers, ignore this parameter.

DESCRIPTION

By default, video channels try to draw directly to the screen. The `SGSetUseScreenBuffer` function allows the sequence grabber to direct your video channel to draw to an offscreen buffer. If your channel cannot draw offscreen, ignore this function. Note that this function will not be called when you are recording.

RESULT CODES

`paramErr`	–50	Invalid parameter value
`cantDoThatInCurrentMode`	–9402	Request invalid in current mode

SEE ALSO

The sequence grabber can determine whether it has allowed your channel to draw offscreen by calling your `SGGetUseScreenBuffer` function, which is described next.

SGGetUseScreenBuffer

The `SGGetUseScreenBuffer` function allows the sequence grabber to determine whether your video channel is allowed to use an offscreen buffer.

```
pascal ComponentResult SGGetUseScreenBuffer (SGChannel c,
                                     Boolean *useScreenBuffer);
```

c Identifies the channel connection for this operation.

useScreenBuffer
: Contains a pointer to a Boolean value. Set this field to `true` if your channel draws directly to the screen. Set it to `false` if your channel can use an offscreen buffer. If your channel cannot work with offscreen buffers, ignore this value.

DESCRIPTION

By default, video channels draw directly to the screen. The sequence grabber can direct a channel to draw to an offscreen buffer by calling your `SGSetUseScreenBuffer` function. If the channels can work offscreen, it then allocates and draws to an offscreen buffer.

SEE ALSO

You can allow a channel to draw offscreen by calling the `SGSetUseScreenBuffer` function, which is described in the previous section.

SGAlignChannelRect

The sequence grabber calls your `SGAlignChannelRect` function in order to determine whether your channel prefers to draw at a particular screen location.

```
pascal ComponentResult SGAlignChannelRect (SGChannel c, Rect *r);
```

c Identifies the connection to your channel.

r Contains a pointer to a rectangle. On entry, this rectangle contains coordinates at which the sequence grabber would like to draw your captured video image. If your component can draw more efficiently or at a higher frame rate at a different location, update the contents of this rectangle to reflect where you would prefer to draw. The rectangle will be passed in with global, not local, coordinates.

CHAPTER 6

Sequence Grabber Channel Components

DESCRIPTION

The sequence grabber uses your `SGAlignChannelRect` function to determine the best alignment for your captured image.

RESULT CODE

badComponentSelector   0x80008002   Function not supported

Configuration Functions for Sound Channel Components

Sound channel components provide a number of functions that allow sequence grabber components to configure the component's sound channel. This section describes these sound channel configuration functions. The sequence grabber component uses these functions only with sound channels.

The `SGSetChannelVolume` function allows the sequence grabber component to control a channel's sound volume. The sequence grabber component uses the `SGGetChannelVolume` function to determine a channel's volume.

The `SGSetSoundInputDriver` specifies a channel's sound input device. The sequence grabber component can determine a channel's sound input device by calling the `SGGetSoundInputDriver` function. If an application changes any attributes of the sound input device, the sequence grabber component notifies your sound component by calling the `SGSoundInputDriverChanged` function.

The sequence grabber component can control the amount of sound data your channel works with at one time by calling the `SGSetSoundRecordChunkSize` function. The sequence grabber component can determine this value by calling the `SGGetSoundRecordChunkSize` function.

The sequence grabber component controls the rate at which your sound channel samples the input data by calling the `SGSetSoundInputRate` function. The sequence grabber component can determine the sample rate by calling the `SGGetSoundInputRate` function.

The sequence grabber can control other sound input parameters by using your `SGSetSoundInputParameters` and `SGGetSoundInputParameters` functions.

SGSetChannelVolume

The `SGSetChannelVolume` function sets your channel's sound volume.

```
pascal ComponentResult SGSetChannelVolume (SGChannel c,
                                            short volume);
```

c   Identifies the channel connection for this operation.

CHAPTER 6

Sequence Grabber Channel Components

volume
: Specifies the volume setting of your channel represented as a 16-bit, fixed-point number. The high-order 8 bits contain the integer part of the value; the low-order 8 bits contain the fractional part. Volume values range from –1.0 to 1.0. Negative values play no sound but preserve the absolute value of the volume setting.

DESCRIPTION

Use this volume setting during playback—this setting should not affect the record level or the volume of the track in the recorded QuickTime movie.

SGGetChannelVolume

The `SGGetChannelVolume` function allows the sequence grabber component to determine your channel's sound volume setting.

```
pascal ComponentResult SGGetChannelVolume (SGChannel c,
                                           short *volume);
```

c
: Identifies the channel connection for this operation.

volume
: Contains a pointer to an integer that is to receive the volume setting of the channel represented as a 16-bit, fixed-point number. The high-order 8 bits contain the integer part of the value; the low-order 8 bits contain the fractional part. Volume values range from –1.0 to 1.0. Negative values play no sound but preserve the absolute value of the volume setting.

SEE ALSO

The sequence grabber component establishes the volume setting by calling the `SGSetChannelVolume` function, described in the previous section.

SGSetSoundInputDriver

Some sound channel components may use sound input devices to obtain their source data. The `SGSetSoundInputDriver` function allows the sequence grabber component to assign a sound input device to your sound channel.

```
pascal ComponentResult SGSetSoundInputDriver (SGChannel c,
                                              const Str255 driverName);
```

c
: Identifies the channel connection for this operation.

Sequence Grabber Channel Components

`driverName`
Specifies the name of the sound input device. This is a Pascal string, and it must correspond to a valid sound input device.

DESCRIPTION

If your sound channel component does not use sound input devices, return a nonzero result code.

RESULT CODES

`noDeviceForChannel`	–9400	Channel component cannot find its device
`cantDoThatInCurrentMode`	–9402	Request invalid in current mode
`deviceCantMeetRequest`	–9408	Device cannot support grabber

SEE ALSO

For more information about sound input devices, see *Inside Macintosh: More Macintosh Toolbox*—in particular, refer to the discussion of the `SPBGetIndexedDevice` function in the chapter "Sound Manager."

SGGetSoundInputDriver

The `SGGetSoundInputDriver` function allows the sequence grabber component to determine the sound input device currently in use by your sound channel component.

```
pascal long SGGetSoundInputDriver (SGChannel c);
```

c   Identifies the channel connection for this operation.

DESCRIPTION

The sequence grabber component may want to gain access to the sound input device if it wants to change the device's configuration. For example, the sequence grabber component may want to configure the device for stereo sound. If the sequence grabber component changes any of the device's operating parameters, it informs your sequence grabber channel component by calling your `SGSoundInputDriverChanged` function, which is described in the next section.

The `SGGetSoundInputDriver` function returns a reference to the sound input device. If your sound channel is not using a sound input device, set the returned value to `nil`.

CHAPTER 6

Sequence Grabber Channel Components

SEE ALSO

The sequence grabber component can assign a sound input device to a sound channel by calling the `SGSetSoundInputDriver` function, which is described in the previous section.

SGSoundInputDriverChanged

The `SGSoundInputDriverChanged` function allows the sequence grabber component to notify your sound channel component whenever an application changes the configuration of your sound channel's sound input device.

```
pascal ComponentResult SGSoundInputDriverChanged (SGChannel c);
```

c   Identifies the channel connection for this operation.

DESCRIPTION

Your component should update any sound device status information it maintains.

SGSetSoundRecordChunkSize

During record operations, the sequence grabber component and its sound channels work with groups of sound samples. These groups are referred to as *chunks*. By default, each chunk contains two seconds of sound data. Smaller chunks use less memory.

```
pascal ComponentResult SGSetSoundRecordChunkSize (SGChannel c,
                                                   long seconds);
```

c   Identifies the channel connection for this operation.
seconds   Specifies the number of seconds of sound data your sound channel component is to work with at a time. This parameter is set to a negative fixed-point number to specify a fraction of a second. For example, to set the duration to half a second, –0.5 is passed in.

DESCRIPTION

The sequence grabber component can control the amount of sound data in each chunk by calling the `SGSetSoundRecordChunkSize` function. The sequence grabber component specifies the number of seconds of sound data your channel is to work with at a time.

CHAPTER 6

Sequence Grabber Channel Components

SPECIAL CONSIDERATIONS

The `SGSetSoundRecordChunkSize` function may return a fraction of a second (see the discussion of the `seconds` parameter above).

RESULT CODES

paramErr	–50	Invalid parameter specified
cantDoThatInCurrentMode	–9402	Request invalid in current mode

SGGetSoundRecordChunkSize

The `SGGetSoundRecordChunkSize` function allows the sequence grabber component to determine the amount of sound data your sound channel component works with at a time.

```
pascal long SGGetSoundRecordChunkSize (SGChannel c);
```

c   Identifies the channel connection for this operation.

DESCRIPTION

The `SGGetSoundRecordChunkSize` function returns a long integer that specifies the number of seconds of sound data your channel works with at a time.

SEE ALSO

The sequence grabber component sets this value by calling the `SGSetSoundRecordChunkSize` function, which is described in the previous section.

SGSetSoundInputRate

The `SGSetSoundInputRate` function allows the sequence grabber component to set the rate at which your sound channel obtains its sound data.

```
pascal ComponentResult SGSetSoundInputRate (SGChannel c,
                                            Fixed rate);
```

c   Identifies the channel connection for this operation.

rate   Specifies the rate at which your sound channel is to acquire data. This parameter specifies the number of samples your sound channel is to generate per second. If your sound channel cannot support the specified rate, use the closest available rate that you can support. If this parameter is set to 0, use your default rate.

CHAPTER 6

Sequence Grabber Channel Components

RESULT CODES

`cantDoThatInCurrentMode`	–9402	Request invalid in current mode
`deviceCantMeetRequest`	–9408	Device cannot support grabber

SGGetSoundInputRate

The `SGGetSoundInputRate` function allows the sequence grabber component to determine the rate at which your sound channel is collecting sound data.

```
pascal Fixed SGGetSoundInputRate (SGChannel c);
```

c   Identifies the channel connection for this operation.

DESCRIPTION

The `SGGetSoundInputRate` function returns a fixed-point number that indicates the number of samples your sound channel collects per second.

SEE ALSO

The sequence grabber component sets this rate by calling the `SGSetSoundInputRate` function, which is described in the previous section.

SGSetSoundInputParameters

The `SGSetSoundInputParameters` function allows the sequence grabber to set some parameters that relate to sound recording.

```
pascal ComponentResult SGSetSoundInputParameters (SGChannel c,
                                        short sampleSize,
                                        short numChannels,
                                        OSType compressionType);
```

c   Identifies the channel connection for this operation.

sampleSize
        Specifies the number of bits in each sound sample. This field is set to 8 for 8-bit sound; it is set to 16 for 16-bit sound.

numChannels
        Indicates the number of sound channels to be used by the sound sample. This field is set to 1 for monaural sounds; it is set to 2 for stereo sounds.

Sequence Grabber Channel Components

`compressionType`
: Describes the format of the sound data. The following values are supported:

    `'raw '` Sound samples are uncompressed, in offset-binary format (that is, sample data values range from 0 to 255).

    `'MAC3'` Sound samples have been compressed by the Sound Manager at a ratio of 3:1.

    `'MAC6'` Sound samples have been compressed by the Sound Manager at a ratio of 6:1.

DESCRIPTION

Sequence grabbers may use the `SGSetSoundInputParameters` function to control many parameters relating to sound recording. All of the sound parameters support two special values. If any of these parameters are set to 0, your channel should not change the current value of that parameter. If any are set to –1, return that parameter to its default value.

If your sound device cannot support a specified parameter value, return an appropriate Sound Manager result code.

RESULT CODES

Sound Manager errors

SGGetSoundInputParameters

The `SGGetSoundInputParameters` function allows the sequence grabber to retrieve some parameters that relate to sound recording.

```
pascal ComponentResult SGGetSoundInputParameters (SGChannel c,
                                    short *sampleSize,
                                    short *numChannels,
                                    OSType *compressionType);
```

`c`
: Identifies the channel connection for this operation.

`sampleSize`
: Contains a pointer to a field to receive the sample size. Set this field to 8 for 8-bit sound; set the field to 16 for 16-bit sound.

`numChannels`
: Contains a pointer to a field to receive the number of sound channels used by the sound sample. Set this field to 1 for monaural sounds; set the field to 2 for stereo sounds.

compressionType
: Contains a pointer to a field to receive the format of the sound data. You may return the following values:

'raw '
: Sound samples are uncompressed, in offset-binary format (that is, sample data values range from 0 to 255).

'MAC3'
: Sound samples have been compressed by the Sound Manager at a ratio of 3:1.

'MAC6'
: Sound samples have been compressed by the Sound Manager at a ratio of 6:1.

DESCRIPTION

The sequence grabber may use the `SGGetSoundInputParameters` function to retrieve many parameters relating to sound recording. If any of the sound parameters are set to `nil`, do not return that value.

Utility Functions for Sequence Grabber Channel Components

Sequence grabber components provide several utility functions that your channel component can use. This section discusses those functions.

The `SGAddMovieData` function lets you add data and sample references to a movie.

Alternatively, you can use the `SGWriteMovieData` function to add data to a movie, and the `SGAddFrameReference` and `SGGetNextFrameReference` functions to keep track of sample references prior to creating a QuickTime movie from recorded data.

The `SGSortDeviceList` function allows you to sort the entries in the device list that you create for the sequence grabber when it calls your `SGGetChannelDeviceList` function (which is discussed on page 6-60).

The `SGChangedSource` function allows you to tell the sequence grabber that you have changed your source device.

The `SGAddFrameReference` and `SGGetNextFrameReference` functions take a pointer to a frame information structure as a parameter. The `SeqGrabFrameInfo` data type defines the format of a frame information structure.

```
struct SeqGrabFrameInfo {
    long        frameOffset;    /* offset to the sample */
    long        frameTime;      /* time that frame was captured */
    long        frameSize;      /* number of bytes in sample */
    SGChannel   frameChannel;   /* current connection to channel */
    long        frameRefCon;    /* reference constant for channel */
};
```

Field descriptions

frameOffset
Specifies the offset to the sample. Your channel component obtains this value from the SGWriteMovieData function, described on page 6-86.

frameTime
Specifies the time at which your channel component captured the frame. This time value is relative to the data sequence. That is, this time is not represented in the context of any fixed time scale. Rather, your channel component must choose and use a time scale consistently for all sample references.

frameSize
Specifies the number of bytes in the sample described by the sample reference.

frameChannel
Identifies the current connection to your channel.

frameRefCon
Contains a reference constant for use by your channel component. You can use this value in any way that is appropriate for your channel component. For example, video channel components may use this value to store a reference to frame differencing information for a temporally compressed image sequence.

SGAddMovieData

The SGAddMovieData function allows your channel component to add data to a movie. This function combines the services provided by the SGWriteMovieData and SGAddFrameReference functions. Your channel component should not write data directly to the movie file—use this function instead.

```
pascal ComponentResult SGAddMovieData (SeqGrabComponent s,
                                       SGChannel c, Ptr p,
                                       long len,
                                       long *offset,
                                       long chRefCon,
                                       TimeValue time,
                                       short writeType);
```

s
Specifies the component instance that identifies the sequence grabber component that is using your channel. The sequence grabber provides this to you when it calls your SGInitChannel function (described on page 6-38).

c
Identifies the connection to your channel.

p
Specifies the location of the data to be added to the movie.

len
Indicates the number of bytes of data to be added to the movie.

CHAPTER 6

Sequence Grabber Channel Components

offset
: Contains a pointer to a field that is to receive the offset to the new data in the movie. The sequence grabber component returns an offset that is correct in the context of the movie resource, even if the movie is currently stored in memory. That is, if the movie is in memory, the returned offset reflects the location that the data will have in a movie on a permanent storage device, such as a disk.

chRefCon
: Contains your channel's reference constant.

time
: Specifies the time at which your channel captured the frame. This time value is expressed in your channel's time scale.

writeType
: Specifies the type of write operation. The following values are valid:

    seqGrabWriteAppend
    : Append the new data to the end of the file. The sequence grabber sets the field referred to by the `offset` parameter to reflect the location at which it added the data.

    seqGrabWriteReserve
    : Do not write any data to the output file. Instead, reserve space in the output file for the amount of data indicated by the `len` parameter. The sequence grabber sets the field referred to by the `offset` parameter to the location of the reserved space.

    seqGrabWriteFill
    : Write the data into the location specified by the field referred to by the `offset` parameter. The sequence grabber sets that field to the location of the byte following the last byte it wrote.

        This option is used to fill the space reserved previously when the `writeType` parameter was set to `seqGrabWriteReserve`.

RESULT CODES

File Manager errors
Memory Manager errors

SGWriteMovieData

The `SGWriteMovieData` function allows your channel component to add data to a movie.

```
pascal ComponentResult SGWriteMovieData (SeqGrabComponent s,
                                         SGChannel c, Ptr p,
                                         long len, long *offset);
```

CHAPTER 6

Sequence Grabber Channel Components

s
: Contains a component instance that identifies the sequence grabber component that has connected to your channel component. The sequence grabber component provides this value to your channel component when it calls your `SGInitChannel` function (described on page 6-38).

c
: Identifies the connection to your channel.

p
: Specifies the location of the data to be added to the movie.

len
: Contains the number of bytes of data to be added to the movie.

offset
: Contains a pointer to a long integer that is to receive the offset to the new data in the movie. The sequence grabber component returns an offset that is correct in the context of a movie resource, even if the movie data is currently stored in memory. That is, if the movie is in memory, the returned offset reflects the location that the data will have in a movie on a permanent storage device, such as a disk.

DESCRIPTION

The `SGWriteMovieData` function behaves differently depending upon when you call it. If you call it from your `SGWriteSamples` function, this function writes the movie data to the device that contains the recording operation's movie file. If you call this function at other times, it may write the movie data to a movie in memory, depending upon the recording options that are in effect.

RESULT CODES

File Manager errors
Memory Manager errors

SGAddFrameReference

The `SGAddFrameReference` function allows your channel component to store sample references.

```
pascal ComponentResult SGAddFrameReference (SeqGrabComponent s,
                                             SeqGrabFrameInfo *frameInfo);
```

s
: Contains a component instance that identifies the sequence grabber component that has connected to your channel component. The sequence grabber component provides this value to your channel component when it calls your `SGInitChannel` function (described on page 6-38).

frameInfo
: Contains a pointer to a frame information structure (defined by the `SeqGrabFrameInfo` data type). Your component must completely specify the reference by placing the appropriate information into the record referred to by this parameter. The format and content of the frame information structure are described on page 6-84.

CHAPTER 6

Sequence Grabber Channel Components

DESCRIPTION

The sequence grabber component uses the information you provide to create a new sample reference in the movie that contains the captured data. You supply the information for the reference in a frame information structure.

RESULT CODES

Memory Manager errors

SEE ALSO

Your component can retrieve these references by calling the `SGGetNextFrameReference` function, which is described in the next section.

SGGetNextFrameReference

The `SGGetNextFrameReference` function allows your channel component to retrieve the sample references you stored by calling the `SGAddMovieData` or `SGAddFrameReference` function, described on page 6-85 and in the previous section, respectively.

```
pascal ComponentResult SGGetNextFrameReference
                            (SeqGrabComponent s,
                             SeqGrabFrameInfo *frameInfo,
                             TimeValue *frameDuration,
                             long *frameNumber);
```

s   Contains a component instance that identifies the sequence grabber component that has connected to your channel component. The sequence grabber component provides this value to your channel component when it calls your `SGInitChannel` function (described on page 6-38).

frameInfo   Contains a pointer to a frame information structure (defined by the `SeqGrabFrameInfo` data type), which is described on page 6-84. Your component must identify itself to the sequence grabber component by setting the `frameChannel` field of this structure to the component instance that identifies the current connection to your channel. The sequence grabber component then returns information about the specified frame in the remaining fields of this structure.

Sequence Grabber Channel Components

frameDuration
: Contains a pointer to a time value. The sequence grabber component calculates the duration of the specified frame and returns that duration in the structure referred to by this parameter. Note that the sequence grabber component cannot calculate the duration of the last frame in a sequence. In this case, the sequence grabber component sets the returned time value to –1.

frameNumber
: Contains a pointer to a long integer. Your channel component specifies the frame number corresponding to the frame about which you want to retrieve information. Frames are numbered starting at 0. However, frame numbers need not start at 0, and they may not be sequential. Set the field referred to by the frameNumber parameter to –1 to retrieve information about the first frame in a movie.

  The sequence grabber component returns the frame number of the movie's next frame into the field referred to by this parameter. You can use this value the next time you call SGGetNextFrameReference.

DESCRIPTION

The SGGetNextFrameReference function allows your channel component to process these references sequentially or randomly—you specify the relative frame for which you want to retrieve information. The sequence grabber component then retrieves and returns information for that frame. Typically, your channel component calls this function within its SGWriteSamples function (described on page 6-43).

RESULT CODE

paramErr   –50   Invalid parameter specified

SGSortDeviceList

The SGSortDeviceList function allows you to sort your device list alphabetically.

```
pascal ComponentResult SGSortDeviceList (SeqGrabComponent s,
                                         SGDeviceList list);
```

s
: Specifies the component instance that identifies the sequence grabber component that is using your channel. The sequence grabber provides this to you when it calls your SGInitChannel function (described on page 6-38).

list
: Contains a pointer to a device list structure pointer.

DESCRIPTION

Your component constructs its device list whenever the sequence grabber calls your `SGGetChannelDeviceList` function (described on page 6-60). You may add entries to the device list in any order you like. Once you have built up your device list, you may use the `SGSortDeviceList` function to sort that list alphabetically, by device name. The sequence grabber correctly updates the `selectedIndex` field in the device list structure, as well.

The format and content of the device list structure are discussed earlier in this chapter, in "Working With Channel Devices" beginning on page 6-58.

RESULT CODE

paramErr   –50   Invalid parameter value

SGChangedSource

The `SGChangedSource` function allows you to tell the sequence grabber that your component is now using a different device.

```
pascal ComponentResult SGChangedSource (SeqGrabComponent s,
                                        SGChannel c);
```

s   Specifies the component instance that identifies the sequence grabber component that is using your channel. The sequence grabber provides this to you when it calls your `SGInitChannel` function (described on page 6-38).

c   Identifies the connection to your channel.

DESCRIPTION

Applications can instruct your channel to change its input device, for example, by calling the sequence grabber's `SGSetChannelDevice` function. The sequence grabber passes this request on to your channel component. Whenever you successfully change your input device, you should tell the sequence grabber by calling its `SGChangedSource` function. This allows the sequence grabber to update the information it keeps about your channel.

Summary of Sequence Grabber Channel Components

C Summary

Constants

```c
/* sequence grabber channel component type */
#define SeqGrabChannelType 'sgch'

/* device list structure flags */
#define sgDeviceListWithIcons (1)              /* include icons */
#define sgDeviceListDontCheckAvailability (2)  /* don't check available */

/* data function write operation types */
enum {
    seqGrabWriteAppend,         /* append to file */
    seqGrabWriteReserve,        /* reserve space in file */
    seqGrabWriteFill            /* fill reserved space */
};
/* flags for SGSetChannelPlayFlags and SGGetChannelPlayFlags functions */
#define channelPlayNormal 0        /* use default playback methodology */
#define channelPlayFast 1          /* achieve fast playback rate */
#define channelPlayHighQuality 2   /* achieve high-quality image */
#define channelPlayAllData 4       /* play all captured data */

/* usage flags for SGSetChannelUsage and SGGetChannelUsage functions */
enum {
    seqGrabRecord           = 1,  /* used during record operations */
    seqGrabPreview          = 2,  /* used during preview operations */
    seqGrabPlayDuringRecord = 4   /* plays data during record operation */
};
typedef unsigned char SeqGrabUsageEnum;

/* SGGetChannelInfo function flags */
enum {
    seqGrabHasBounds         = 1,  /* visual representation of data */
    seqGrabHasVolume         = 2,  /* audio representation of data */
    seqGrabHasDiscreteSamples = 4  /* data organized in discrete frames */
```

```
};
typedef unsigned char SeqGrabChannelInfoEnum;

/* basic sequence grabber channel component selectors */
kSGSetGWorldSelect                   = 0x4;    /* SetGWorld */
kSGStartPreviewSelect                = 0x10;   /* SGStartPreview */
kSGStartRecordSelect                 = 0x11;   /* SGStartRecord */
kSGIdleSelect                        = 0x12;   /* SGIdle */
kSGStopSelect                        = 0x13;   /* SGStop */
kSGPauseSelect                       = 0x14;   /* SGPause */
kSGPrepareSelect                     = 0x15;   /* SGPrepare */
kSGReleaseSelect                     = 0x16;   /* SGRelease */
kSGUpdateSelect                      = 0x27;   /* SGUpdate */

/*   selectors for common channel configuration functions */
kSGCSetChannelUsageSelect            = 0x80;   /* SGSetChannelUsage */
kSGCGetChannelUsageSelect            = 0x81;   /* SGGetChannelUsage */
kSGCSetChannelBoundsSelect           = 0x82;   /* SGSetChannelBounds */
kSGCGetChannelBoundsSelect           = 0x83;   /* SGGetChannelBounds */
kSGCSetChannelVolumeSelect           = 0x84;   /* SGSetChannelVolume */
kSGCGetChannelVolumeSelect           = 0x85;   /* SGGetChannelVolume */
kSGCGetChannelInfoSelect             = 0x86;   /* SGGetChannelInfo */
kSGCSetChannelPlayFlagsSelect        = 0x87;   /* SGSetChannelPlayFlags */
kSGCGetChannelPlayFlagsSelect        = 0x88;   /* SGGetChannelPlayFlags */
kSGCSetChannelMaxFramesSelect        = 0x89;   /* SGSetChannelMaxFrames */
kSGCGetChannelMaxFramesSelect        = 0x8A;   /* SGGetChannelMaxFrames */
kSGCSetChannelRefConSelect           = 0x8B;   /* SGSetChannelRefCon */
kSGCSetChannelClipSelect             = 0x8C;   /* SGSetChannelClip */
kSGCGetChannelClipSelect             = 0x8D;   /* SGGetChannelClip */
kSGCGetChannelSampleDescriptionSelect = 0x8E;
                                    /* SGCGetChannelSampleDescription */
kSGCGetChannelDeviceListSelect       = 0x8F;   /* SGCGetChannelDeviceList */
kSGCSetChannelDeviceSelect           = 0x90;   /* SGCSetChannelDevice */
kSGCSetChannelMatrixSelect           = 0x91;   /* SGCSetChannelMatrix */
kSGCGetChannelMatrixSelect           = 0x92;   /* SGCGetChannelMatrix */
kSGCGetChannelTimeScaleSelect        = 0x93;   /* SGCGetChannelTimeScale */

/*   selectors for video channel configuration functions */
kSGCGetSrcVideoBoundsSelect          = 0x100;  /* SGCGetSrcVideoBounds */
kSGCSetVideoRectSelect               = 0x101;  /* SGCSetVideoRect */
kSGCGetVideoRectSelect               = 0x102;  /* SGCGetVideoRect */
kSGCGetVideoCompressorTypeSelect     = 0x103;  /* SGCGetVideoCompressorType */
```

```
kSGCSetVideoCompressorTypeSelect      = 0x104; /* SGCSetVideoCompressorType */
kSGCSetVideoCompressorSelect          = 0x105; /* SGCSetVideoCompressor */
kSGCGetVideoCompressorSelect          = 0x106; /* SGCGetVideoCompressor */
kSGCGetVideoDigitizerComponentSelect= 0x107;
                                               /* SGCGetVideoDigitizerComponent */
kSGCSetVideoDigitizerComponentSelect= 0x108;
                                               /* SGCSetVideoDigitizerComponent */
kSGCVideoDigitizerChangedSelect       = 0x109; /* SGCVideoDigitizerChanged */
kSGCSetVideoBottlenecksSelect         = 0x10a; /* SGCSetVideoBottlenecks */
kSGCGetVideoBottlenecksSelect         = 0x10b; /* SGCGetVideoBottlenecks */
kSGCGrabFrameSelect                   = 0x10c; /* SGCGrabFrame */
kSGCGrabFrameCompleteSelect           = 0x10d; /* SGCGrabFrameComplete */
kSGCDisplayFrameSelect                = 0x10e; /* SGCDisplayFrame */
kSGCCompressFrameSelect               = 0x10f; /* SGCCompressFrame */
kSGCCompressFrameCompleteSelect       = 0x110; /* SGCCompressFrameComplete */
kSGCAddFrameSelect                    = 0x111; /* SGCAddFrame */
kSGCTransferFrameForCompressSelect    = 0x112;
                                               /* SGCTransferFrameForCompress */
kSGCSetCompressBufferSelect           = 0x113; /* SGCSetCompressBuffer */
kSGCGetCompressBufferSelect           = 0x114; /* SGCGetCompressBuffer */
kSGCGetBufferInfoSelect               = 0x115; /* SGCGetBufferInfo */
kSGCSetUseScreenBufferSelect          = 0x116; /* SGCSetUseScreenBuffer */
kSGCGetUseScreenBufferSelect          = 0x117; /* SGCGetUseScreenBuffer */
kSGCGrabCompressCompleteSelect        = 0x118; /* SGCGrabCompressComplete */
kSGCDisplayCompressSelect             = 0x119; /* SGCDisplayCompress */
kSGCSetFrameRateSelect                = 0x11A; /* SGCSetFrameRate */
kSGCGetFrameRateSelect                = 0x11B; /* SGCGetFrameRate */

/* selectors for sound channel configuration functions */
kSGCSetSoundInputDriverSelect         = 0x100; /* SGCSetSoundInputDriver */
kSGCGetSoundInputDriverSelect         = 0x101; /* SGCGetSoundInputDriver */
kSGCSoundInputDriverChangedSelect     = 0x102; /* SGCSoundInputDriverChanged */
kSGCSetSoundRecordChunkSizeSelect     = 0x103; /* SGCSetSoundRecordChunkSize */
kSGCGetSoundRecordChunkSizeSelect     = 0x104; /* SGCGetSoundRecordChunkSize */
kSGCSetSoundInputRateSelect           = 0x105; /* SGCSetSoundInputRate */
kSGCGetSoundInputRateSelect           = 0x106; /* SGCGetSoundInputRate */
kSGCSetSoundInputParametersSelect     = 0x107; /* SGCSetSoundInputParameters */
kSGCGetSoundInputParametersSelect     = 0x108; /* SGCGetSoundInputParameters */

/* selectors for channel control functions */
kSGCInitChannelSelect                 = 0x180; /* SGCInitChannel */
kSGCWriteSamplesSelect                = 0x181; /* SGCWriteSamples */
```

```
    kSGCGetDataRateSelect              = 0x182; /* SGCDataRate */
    kSGCAlignChannelRectSelect         = 0x183; /* SGAlignChannelRect */
};

/* values for pause parameter of SGPause function */
enum {
    seqGrabUnpause = 0,  /* restart the current operation */
    seqGrabPause   = 1,  /* pause the current operation */
};
```

Data Types

```
struct SeqGrabFrameInfo {
    long         frameOffset;   /* offset to the sample */
    long         frameTime;     /* time that frame was captured */
    long         frameSize;     /* number of bytes in sample */
    SGChannel    frameChannel;  /* current connection to channel */
    long         frameRefCon;   /* reference constant for channel */
};

typedef struct SGDeviceListRecord {
    short         count;          /* count of devices */
    short         selectedIndex;  /* current device */
    long          reserved;       /* set to 0 */
    SGDeviceName  entry[1];       /* device names */
} SGDeviceListRecord, *SGDeviceListPtr, **SGDeviceList;

typedef struct SGDeviceName {
    Str63    name;        /* device name */
    Handle   icon;        /* device icon */
    long     flags;       /* flags */
    long     refCon;      /* set to 0 */
    long     reserved;    /* set to 0 */
} SGDeviceName;
```

Functions

Configuring Sequence Grabber Channel Components

```
pascal ComponentResult SGInitChannel
                        (SGChannel c, SeqGrabComponent owner);
pascal ComponentResult SGSetGWorld
                        (SeqGrabComponent s, CGrafPtr gp, GDHandle gd);
```

CHAPTER 6

Sequence Grabber Channel Components

Controlling Sequence Grabber Channel Components

```
pascal ComponentResult SGStartPreview
                        (SeqGrabComponent s);
pascal ComponentResult SGStartRecord
                        (SeqGrabComponent s);
pascal ComponentResult SGIdle
                        (SeqGrabComponent s);
pascal ComponentResult SGUpdate
                        (SeqGrabComponent s, RgnHandle updateRgn);
pascal ComponentResult SGStop
                        (SeqGrabComponent s);
pascal ComponentResult SGWriteSamples
                        (SGChannel c, Movie m, AliasHandle theFile);
pascal ComponentResult SGPause
                        (SeqGrabComponent s, Byte pause);
pascal ComponentResult SGPrepare
                        (SeqGrabComponent s, Boolean prepareForPreview,
                         Boolean prepareForRecord);
pascal ComponentResult SGRelease
                        (SeqGrabComponent s);
```

Configuration Functions for All Channel Components

```
pascal ComponentResult SGSetChannelUsage
                        (SGChannel c, long usage);
pascal ComponentResult SGGetChannelUsage
                        (SGChannel c, long *usage);
pascal ComponentResult SGGetChannelInfo
                        (SGChannel c, long *channelInfo);
pascal ComponentResult SGSetChannelPlayFlags
                        (SGChannel c, long playFlags);
pascal ComponentResult SGGetChannelPlayFlags
                        (SGChannel c, long *playFlags);
pascal ComponentResult SGSetChannelMaxFrames
                        (SGChannel c, long frameCount);
pascal ComponentResult SGGetChannelMaxFrames
                        (SGChannel c, long *frameCount);
pascal ComponentResult SGSetChannelRefCon
                        (SGChannel c, long refCon);
pascal ComponentResult SGGetDataRate
                        (SGChannel c, long *bytesPerSecond);
pascal ComponentResult SGGetChannelSampleDescription
                        (SGChannel c, Handle sampleDesc);
```

Summary of Sequence Grabber Channel Components

CHAPTER 6

Sequence Grabber Channel Components

```
pascal ComponentResult SGGetChannelTimeScale
                        (SGChannel c, TimeScale *scale);
pascal ComponentResult SGSetChannelClip
                        (SGChannel c, RgnHandle theClip);
pascal ComponentResult SGGetChannelClip
                        (SGChannel c, RgnHandle *theClip);
pascal ComponentResult SGSetChannelMatrix
                        (SGChannel c, const MatrixRecord *m);
pascal ComponentResult SGGetChannelMatrix
                        (SGChannel c, MatrixRecord *m);
```

Working With Channel Devices

```
pascal ComponentResult SGGetChannelDeviceList
                        (SGChannel c, long selectionFlags,
                         SGDeviceList *list);
pascal ComponentResult SGSetChannelDevice
                        (SGChannel c, StringPtr name);
```

Configuration Functions for Video Channel Components

```
pascal ComponentResult SGSetChannelBounds
                        (SGChannel c, Rect *bounds);
pascal ComponentResult SGGetChannelBounds
                        (SGChannel c, const Rect *bounds);
pascal ComponentResult SGGetSrcVideoBounds
                        (SGChannel c, Rect *r);
pascal ComponentResult SGSetVideoRect
                        (SGChannel c, Rect *r);
pascal ComponentResult SGGetVideoRect
                        (SGChannel c, Rect *r);
pascal ComponentResult SGSetVideoCompressorType
                        (SGChannel c, OSType compressorType);
pascal ComponentResult SGGetVideoCompressorType
                        (SGChannel c, OSType *compressorType);
pascal ComponentResult SGSetVideoCompressor
                        (SGChannel c, short depth,
                         CompressorComponent compressor,
                         CodecQ spatialQuality, CodecQ temporalQuality,
                         long keyFrameRate);
```

```
pascal ComponentResult SGGetVideoCompressor
                        (SGChannel c, short *depth,
                         CompressorComponent *compressor,
                         CodecQ *spatialQuality,
                         CodecQ *temporalQuality, long *keyFrameRate);
pascal ComponentResult SGSetVideoDigitizerComponent
                        (SGChannel c, ComponentInstance vdig);
pascal ComponentInstance SGGetVideoDigitizerComponent
                        (SGChannel c);
pascal ComponentResult SGVideoDigitizerChanged
                        (SGChannel c);
pascal ComponentResult SGSetCompressBuffer
                        (SGChannel c, short depth,
                         const Rect *compressSize);
pascal ComponentResult SGGetCompressBuffer
                        (SGChannel c, short *depth, Rect *compressSize);
pascal ComponentResult SGSetFrameRate
                        (SGChannel c, Fixed frameRate);
pascal ComponentResult SGGetFrameRate
                        (SGChannel c, Fixed *frameRate);
pascal ComponentResult SGSetUseScreenBuffer
                        (SGChannel c, Boolean useScreenBuffer);
pascal ComponentResult SGGetUseScreenBuffer
                        (SGChannel c, Boolean *useScreenBuffer);
pascal ComponentResult SGAlignChannelRect
                        (SGChannel c, Rect *r);
```

Configuration Functions for Sound Channel Components

```
pascal ComponentResult SGSetChannelVolume
                        (SGChannel c, short volume);
pascal ComponentResult SGGetChannelVolume
                        (SGChannel c, short *volume);
pascal ComponentResult SGSetSoundInputDriver
                        (SGChannel c, const Str255 driverName);
pascal long SGGetSoundInputDriver
                        (SGChannel c);
pascal ComponentResult SGSoundInputDriverChanged
                        (SGChannel c);
pascal ComponentResult SGSetSoundRecordChunkSize
                        (SGChannel c, long seconds);
pascal long SGGetSoundRecordChunkSize
                        (SGChannel c);
```

```
pascal ComponentResult SGSetSoundInputRate
                        (SGChannel c, Fixed rate);
pascal Fixed SGGetSoundInputRate
                        (SGChannel c);
pascal ComponentResult SGSetSoundInputParameters
                        (SGChannel c, short sampleSize,
                         short numChannels, OSType compressionType);
pascal ComponentResult SGGetSoundInputParameters
                        (SGChannel c, short *sampleSize,
                         short *numChannels, OSType *compressionType);
```

Utility Functions for Sequence Grabber Channel Components

```
pascal ComponentResult SGAddMovieData
                        (SeqGrabComponent s, SGChannel c, Ptr p,
                         long len, long *offset, long chRefCon,
                         TimeValue time, short writeType);
pascal ComponentResult SGWriteMovieData
                        (SeqGrabComponent s, SGChannel c,
                         Ptr p, long len, long *offset);
pascal ComponentResult SGAddFrameReference
                        (SeqGrabComponent s,
                         SeqGrabFrameInfo *frameInfo);
pascal ComponentResult SGGetNextFrameReference
                        (SeqGrabComponent s,
                         SeqGrabFrameInfo *frameInfo,
                         TimeValue *frameDuration,
                         long *frameNumber);
pascal ComponentResult SGSortDeviceList
                        (SeqGrabComponent s, SGDeviceList list);
pascal ComponentResult SGChangedSource
                        (SeqGrabComponent s, SGChannel c);
```

CHAPTER 6

Sequence Grabber Channel Components

Pascal Summary

Constants

```
CONST
  SeqGrabChannelType = 'sgch';{sequence grabber channel component type}


  {device list structure flags}
  sgDeviceListWithIcons            = 1;     {include icons}
  sgDeviceListDontCheckAvailability = 2;    {don't check available }
                                            { device list}

  {flags for SGSetChannelPlayFlags and SGGetChannelPlayFlags functions}
  channelPlayNormal                = 0      {use default play methodology}
  channelPlayFast                  = 1;     {sacrifice playback quality }
                                            { for specified rate}
  channelPlayHighQuality           = 2;     {sacrifice playback rate }
                                            { for image quality}
  channelPlayAllData               = 4;     {play all captured data }
                                            { including that stored in }
                                            { offscreen buffers}

  {flags for SGSetChannelUsage and SGGetChannelUsage functions}
  seqGrabRecord                    = 1;     {used during record operations}
  seqGrabPreview                   = 2;     {used during preview operations}
  seqGrabPlayDuringRecord          = 4;     {used during record operations}

  {SGGetChannelInfo function flags}
  seqGrabHasBounds                 = 1;     {visual representation of data}
  seqGrabHasVolume                 = 2;     {audio representation of data}
  seqGrabHasDiscreteSamples        = 4;     {data organized in discrete frames}

  {basic sequence grabber channel component selectors}
  kSGSetGWorldSelect               = $4;    {SGSetGWorld}
  kSGStartPreviewSelect            = $10;   {SGStartPreview}
  kSGStartRecordSelect             = $11;   {SGStartRecord}
  kSGIdleSelect                    = $12;   {SGIdle}
  kSGStopSelect                    = $13;   {SGStop}
  kSGPauseSelect                   = $14;   {SGPause}
  kSGPrepareSelect                 = $15;   {SGPrepare}
```

```
kSGReleaseSelect                      = $16;   {SGRelease}
kSGUpdateSelect                       = $27;   {SGUpdate}

{selectors for common channel configuration functions}
kSGCSetChannelUsageSelect             = $80;   {SGCSetChannelUsage}
kSGCGetChannelUsageSelect             = $81;   {SGCGetChannelUsage}
kSGCSetChannelBoundsSelect            = $82;   {SGCSetChannelBounds}
kSGCGetChannelBoundsSelect            = $83;   {SGCGetChannelBounds}
kSGCSetChannelVolumeSelect            = $84;   {SGCSetChannelVolume}
kSGCGetChannelVolumeSelect            = $85;   {SGCGetChannelVolume}
kSGCGetChannelInfoSelect              = $86;   {SGCGetChannelInfo}
kSGCSetChannelPlayFlagsSelect         = $87;   {SGCSetChannelPlayFlags}
kSGCGetChannelPlayFlagsSelect         = $88;   {SGCGetChannelPlayFlags}
kSGCSetChannelMaxFramesSelect         = $89;   {SGCSetChannelMaxFrames}
kSGCGetChannelMaxFramesSelect         = $8A;   {SGCGetChannelMaxFrames}
kSGCSetChannelRefConSelect            = $8B;   {SGCSetChannelRefCon}
kSGCSetChannelClipSelect              = $8C;   {SGSetChannelClip}
kSGCGetChannelClipSelect              = $8D;   {SGGetChannelClip}
kSGCGetChannelSampleDescriptionSelect
                                      = $8E;   {SGCGetChannelSampleDescription}
kSGCGetChannelDeviceListSelect        = $8F;   {SGCGetChannelDeviceList}
kSGCSetChannelDeviceSelect            = $90;   {SGCSetChannelDevice}
kSGCSetChannelMatrixSelect            = $91;   {SGCSetChannelMatrix}
kSGCGetChannelMatrixSelect            = $92;   {SGCGetChannelMatrix}
kSGCGetChannelTimeScaleSelect         = $93;   {SGCGetChannelTimeScale}

{selectors for video channel configuration functions}
kSGCGetSrcVideoBoundsSelect           = $100;  {SGCGetSrcVideoBounds}
kSGCSetVideoRectSelect                = $101;  {SGCSetVideoRect}
kSGCGetVideoRectSelect                = $102;  {SGCGetVideoRect}
kSGCGetVideoCompressorTypeSelect      = $103;  {SGCGetVideoCompressorType}
kSGCSetVideoCompressorTypeSelect      = $104;  {SGCSetVideoCompressorType}
kSGCSetVideoCompressorSelect          = $105;  {SGCSetVideoCompressor}
kSGCGetVideoCompressorSelect          = $106;  {SGCGetVideoCompressor}
kSGCGetVideoDigitizerComponentSelect  = $107;
                                               {SGCGetVideoDigitizerComponent}
kSGCSetVideoDigitizerComponentSelect  = $108;
                                               {SGCSetVideoDigitizerComponent}
kSGCVideoDigitizerChangedSelect       = $109;  {SGCVideoDigitizerChanged}
kSGCSetVideoBottlenecksSelect         = $10A;  {SGCSetVideoBottlenecks}
kSGCGetVideoBottlenecksSelect         = $10B;  {SGCGetVideoBottlenecks}
kSGCGrabFrameSelect                   = $10C;  {SGCGrabFrame}
kSGCGrabFrameCompleteSelect           = $10D;  {SGCGrabFrameComplete}
```

CHAPTER 6

Sequence Grabber Channel Components

```
kSGCDisplayFrameSelect              = $10E;  {SGCDisplayFrame}
kSGCCompressFrameSelect             = $10F;  {SGCCompressFrame}
kSGCCompressFrameCompleteSelect     = $110;  {SGCCompressFrameComplete}
kSGCAddFrameSelect                  = $111;  {SGCAddFrame}
kSGCTransferFrameForCompressSelect  = $112;  {SGCTransferFrameForCompress}
kSGCSetCompressBufferSelect         = $113;  {SGCSetCompressBuffer}
kSGCGetCompressBufferSelect         = $114;  {SGCGetCompressBuffer}
kSGCGetBufferInfoSelect             = $115;  {SGCGetBufferInfo}
kSGCSetUseScreenBufferSelect        = $116;  {SGCSetUseScreenBuffer}
kSGCGetUseScreenBufferSelect        = $117;  {SGCGetUseScreenBuffer}
kSGCGrabCompressCompleteSelect      = $118;  {SGCGrabCompressComplete}
kSGCDisplayCompressSelect           = $119;  {SGCDisplayCompress}
kSGCSetFrameRateSelect              = $11A;  {SGCSetFrameRate}
kSGCGetFrameRateSelect              = $11B;  {SGCGetFrameRate}

{selectors for sound channel configuration functions}
kSGCSetSoundInputDriverSelect       = $100;  {SGCSetSoundInputDriver}
kSGCGetSoundInputDriverSelect       = $101;  {SGCGetSoundInputDriver}
kSGCSoundInputDriverChangedSelect   = $102;  {SGCSoundInputDriverChanged}
kSGCSetSoundRecordChunkSizeSelect   = $103;  {SGCSetSoundRecordChunkSize}
kSGCGetSoundRecordChunkSizeSelect   = $104;  {SGCGetSoundRecordChunkSize}
kSGCSetSoundInputRateSelect         = $105;  {SGCSetSoundInputRate}
kSGCGetSoundInputRateSelect         = $106;  {SGCGetSoundInputRate}
kSGCSetSoundInputParametersSelect   = $107;  {SGCSetSoundInputParameters}
kSGCGetSoundInputParametersSelect   = $108;  {SGCGetSoundInputParameters}

{selectors for channel control functions}
kSGCInitChannelSelect               = $180; {SGCInitChannel}
kSGCWriteSamplesSelect              = $181; {SGCWriteSamples}
kSGCGetDataRateSelect               = $182; {SGCDataRate}

{values for the pause parameter of the SGPause function}
seqGrabUnpause    = 0;    {restart current operation}
seqGrabPause      = 1;    {pause the current operation}
```

Data Types

```
TYPE
   SeqGrabFrameInfo =
   RECORD
      frameOffset:     LongInt;    {offset to the sample}
      frameTime:       LongInt;    {time that frame was captured}
```

```
        frameChannel:    SGChannel;   {current connection to channel}
        frameRefCon:     LongInt;     {reference constant for channel}
    END;

SGDeviceListPtr = ^SGDeviceListRecord;
SGDeviceList = ^SGDeviceListPtr;

    SGDeviceListRecord =
    RECORD
        count:           Integer;                        {count of devices}
        selectedIndex:   Integer;                        {current device}
        reserved:        LongInt;                        {set to 0}
        entry:           ARRAY[0..] OF SGDeviceName;     {device names}
    END;

    SGDeviceName =
    RECORD
        name:    Str63;      {device name}
        icon:    Handle;     {device icon}
        flags:   LongInt;    {flags}
        refCon:  LongInt;    {set to 0}
        reserved: LongInt;   {set to 0}
}   END;
```

Routines

Configuring Sequence Grabber Channel Components

```
FUNCTION SGInitChannel       (c: SGChannel; owner: SeqGrabComponent):
                                ComponentResult;
FUNCTION SGSetGWorld         (s: SeqGrabComponent; gp: CGrafPtr;
                                gd: GDHandle): ComponentResult;
```

Controlling Sequence Grabber Channel Components

```
FUNCTION SGStartPreview      (s: SeqGrabComponent): ComponentResult;
FUNCTION SGStartRecord       (s: SeqGrabComponent): ComponentResult;
FUNCTION SGIdle              (s: SeqGrabComponent): ComponentResult;
FUNCTION SGUpdate            (s SeqGrabComponent; updateRgn RgnHandle):
                                ComponentResult;
FUNCTION SGStop              (s: SeqGrabComponent): ComponentResult;
FUNCTION SGWriteSamples      (c: SGChannel; m: Movie; theFile: AliasHandle):
                                ComponentResult;
```

```
FUNCTION SGPause              (s: SeqGrabComponent; pause: Byte):
                                ComponentResult;
FUNCTION SGPrepare            (s: SeqGrabComponent;
                                prepareForPreview: Boolean;
                                prepareForRecord: Boolean): ComponentResult;
FUNCTION SGRelease            (s: SeqGrabComponent): ComponentResult;
```

Configuration Routines for All Channel Components

```
FUNCTION SGSetChannelUsage    (c: SGChannel; usage: LongInt): ComponentResult;
FUNCTION SGGetChannelUsage    (c: SGChannel;
                                VAR usage: LongInt): ComponentResult;
FUNCTION SGGetChannelInfo     (c: SGChannel;
                                VAR channelInfo: LongInt): ComponentResult;
FUNCTION SGSetChannelPlayFlags
                              (c: SGChannel; playFlags: LongInt):
                                ComponentResult;
FUNCTION SGGetChannelPlayFlags
                              (c: SGChannel; VAR playFlags: LongInt):
                                ComponentResult;
FUNCTION SGSetChannelMaxFrames
                              (c: SGChannel; frameCount: LongInt):
                                ComponentResult;
FUNCTION SGGetChannelMaxFrames
                              (c: SGChannel; VAR frameCount: LongInt):
                                ComponentResult;
FUNCTION SGSetChannelRefCon
                              (c: SGChannel; refCon: LongInt):
                                ComponentResult;
FUNCTION SGGetDataRate        (c: SGChannel;
                                VAR bytesPerSecond: LongInt): ComponentResult;
FUNCTION SGGetChannelSampleDescription
                              (c: SGChannel; sampleDesc: Handle):
                                ComponentResult;
FUNCTION SGGetChannelTimeScale
                              (c: SGChannel; VAR scale: TimeScale):
                                ComponentResult;
FUNCTION SGSetChannelClip     (c: SGChannel; theClip: RgnHandle):
                                ComponentResult;
FUNCTION SGGetChannelClip     (c: SGChannel; VAR theClip: RgnHandle):
                                ComponentResult;
```

```
FUNCTION SGSetChannelMatrix
                              (c: SGChannel; VAR m: MatrixRecord):
                               ComponentResult;
FUNCTION SGGetChannelMatrix
                              (c: SGChannel; VAR m: MatrixRecord):
                               ComponentResult;
```

Working With Channel Devices

```
FUNCTION SGGetChannelDeviceList
                              (c: SGChannel; selectionFlags: LongInt;
                               VAR list: SGDeviceList): ComponentResult;
FUNCTION SGSetChannelDevice
                              (c: SGChannel; name: StringPtr):
                               ComponentResult;
```

Configuration Routines for Video Channel Components

```
FUNCTION SGSetChannelBounds  (c: SGChannel; bounds: Rect): ComponentResult;
FUNCTION SGGetChannelBounds  (c: SGChannel; VAR bounds: Rect):
                              ComponentResult;
FUNCTION SGGetSrcVideoBounds
                             (c: SGChannel; VAR r: Rect): ComponentResult;
FUNCTION SGSetVideoRect      (c: SGChannel; r: Rect): ComponentResult;
FUNCTION SGGetVideoRect      (c: SGChannel; VAR r: Rect): ComponentResult;
FUNCTION SGSetVideoCompressorType
                             (c: SGChannel;
                              compressorType: OSType): ComponentResult;
FUNCTION SGGetVideoCompressorType
                             (c: SGChannel;
                              VAR compressorType: OSType): ComponentResult;
FUNCTION SGSetVideoCompressor
                             (c: SGChannel; depth: Integer;
                              compressor: CompressorComponent;
                              spatialQuality: CodecQ;
                              temporalQuality: CodecQ;
                              keyFrameRate: LongInt): ComponentResult;
FUNCTION SGGetVideoCompressor
                             (c: SGChannel; VAR depth: Integer;
                              VAR compressor: CompressorComponent;
                              VAR spatialQuality: CodecQ;
                              VAR temporalQuality: CodecQ;
                              VAR keyFrameRate: LongInt): ComponentResult;
```

```
FUNCTION SGSetVideoDigitizerComponent
                            (c: SGChannel; vdig: ComponentInstance):
                             ComponentResult;
FUNCTION SGGetVideoDigitizerComponent
                            (c: SGChannel): ComponentInstance;
FUNCTION SGVideoDigitizerChanged
                            (c: SGChannel): ComponentResult;
FUNCTION SGSetCompressBuffer
                            (c: SGChannel; depth: Integer;
                             compressSize: Rect): ComponentResult;
FUNCTION SGGetCompressBuffer
                            (c: SGChannel; VAR depth: Integer;
                             VAR compressSize: Rect): ComponentResult;
FUNCTION SGSetFrameRate     (c: SGChannel; frameRate: Fixed):
                             ComponentResult;
FUNCTION SGGetFrameRate     (c: SGChannel; VAR frameRate: Fixed):
                             ComponentResult;
FUNCTION SGSetUseScreenBuffer
                            (c: SGChannel; useScreenBuffer: Boolean):
                             ComponentResult;
FUNCTION SGGetUseScreenBuffer
                            (c: SGChannel; VAR useScreenBuffer: Boolean):
                             ComponentResult;
FUNCTION SGAlignChannelRect
                            (c: SGChannel; VAR r: Rect): ComponentResult;
```

Configuration Routines for Sound Channel Components

```
FUNCTION SGSetChannelVolume
                            (c: SGChannel; volume: Integer):
                             ComponentResult;
FUNCTION SGGetChannelVolume
                            (c: SGChannel; VAR volume: Integer):
                             ComponentResult;
FUNCTION SGSetSoundInputDriver
                            (c: SGChannel; driverName: Str255):
                             ComponentResult;
FUNCTION SGGetSoundInputDriver
                            (c: SGChannel): LongInt;
FUNCTION SGSoundInputDriverChanged
                            (c: SGChannel): ComponentResult;
FUNCTION SGSetSoundRecordChunkSize
                            (c: SGChannel; seconds: LongInt):
                             ComponentResult;
```

```
FUNCTION SGGetSoundRecordChunkSize
                                (c: SGChannel): LongInt;
FUNCTION SGSetSoundInputRate
                                (c: SGChannel; rate: Fixed): ComponentResult;
FUNCTION SGGetSoundInputRate
                                (c: SGChannel): Fixed;
FUNCTION SGSetSoundInputParameters
                                (c: SGChannel; sampleSize: Integer;
                                 numChannels: Integer;
                                 compressionType: OSType): ComponentResult;
FUNCTION SGGetSoundInputParameters
                                (c: SGChannel; VAR sampleSize: Integer;
                                 VAR numChannels: Integer;
                                 VAR compressionType: OSType): ComponentResult;
```

Utility Routines for Sequence Grabber Channel Components

```
FUNCTION SGAddMovieData      (s: SeqGrabComponent; c: SGChannel; p: Ptr;
                              len: LongInt; VAR offset: LongInt;
                              chRefCon: LongInt; time: TimeValue;
                              writeType: Integer): ComponentResult;
FUNCTION SGWriteMovieData    (s: SeqGrabComponent; c: SGChannel; p: Ptr;
                              len: LongInt; VAR offset: LongInt):
                              ComponentResult;
FUNCTION SGAddFrameReference
                             (s: SeqGrabComponent;
                              VAR frameInfo: SeqGrabFrameInfo):
                              ComponentResult;
FUNCTION SGGetNextFrameReference
                             (s: SeqGrabComponent;
                              VAR frameInfo: SeqGrabFrameInfo;
                              VAR frameDuration: TimeValue;
                              VAR frameNumber: LongInt): ComponentResult;
FUNCTION SGSortDeviceList    (s: SeqGrabComponent; list: SGDeviceList):
                              ComponentResult;
FUNCTION SGChangedSource     (s: SeqGrabComponent; c: SGChannel):
                              ComponentResult;
```

CHAPTER 6

Sequence Grabber Channel Components

Result Codes

`noDeviceForChannel`	–9400	Channel component cannot find its device
`cantDoThatInCurrentMode`	–9402	Request invalid in current mode
`notEnoughMemoryToGrab`	–9403	Insufficient memory for record operation
`notEnoughDiskSpaceToGrab`	–9404	Insufficient disk space for record operation
`seqGrabInfoNotAvailable`	–9407	Channel component cannot support request
`deviceCantMeetRequest`	–9408	Device cannot support grabber

CHAPTER 7

Sequence Grabber Panel Components

Contents

About Sequence Grabber Panel Components 7-4
Creating Sequence Grabber Panel Components 7-7
   Implementing the Required Component Functions 7-9
   Managing the Dialog Box 7-11
   Managing Your Panel's Settings 7-13
Sequence Grabber Panel Components Reference 7-14
   Component Flags for Sequence Grabber Panel Components 7-15
   Functions 7-15
      Managing Your Panel Component 7-15
      Processing Your Panel's Events 7-21
      Managing Your Panel's Settings 7-24
Summary of Sequence Grabber Panel Components 7-27
   C Summary 7-27
      Constants 7-27
      Functions 7-28
   Pascal Summary 7-29
      Constants 7-29
      Routines 7-29
   Result Codes 7-30

CHAPTER 7

Sequence Grabber Panel Components

This chapter discusses sequence grabber panel components. Sequence grabber components create a settings dialog box that includes items that are managed by sequence grabber panel components and sequence grabber channel components. **Sequence grabber panel components** allow sequence grabber components to obtain configuration information from the user for a particular sequence grabber channel component. Applications never call sequence grabber panel components directly; application developers use panel components only by calling the sequence grabber component.

This chapter is divided into the following sections:

- "About Sequence Grabber Panel Components" provides a general introduction to components of this type.
- "Creating Sequence Grabber Panel Components" discusses how sequence grabbers use these components.
- "Sequence Grabber Panel Components Reference" presents detailed information about the functions that are supported by these components.
- "Summary of Sequence Grabber Panel Components" contains a condensed listing of the constants and functions supported by these components.

This chapter addresses developers of sequence grabber panel components. If you plan to create a sequence grabber panel component, you should read the entire chapter. If you are writing an application that uses components of this type, you do not need to read this chapter. Refer to the chapter "Sequence Grabber Components" in this book for information about sequence grabber components and how to display the settings dialog box to the user.

As components, sequence grabber panel components rely on the facilities of the Component Manager. In order to use any component, your application must also use the Component Manager. If you are not familiar with this manager, see the chapter "Component Manager" in *Inside Macintosh: More Macintosh Toolbox*. In addition, you should be familiar with sequence grabber components and sequence grabber channel components. See the chapters "Sequence Grabber Components" and "Sequence Grabber Channel Components" in this book for more information.

Note
The text in this chapter makes numerous references to sequence grabber components, sequence grabber channel components, and sequence grabber panel components. For the sake of brevity, shortened names have been adopted for each of these components. Consequently, you will often find sequence grabber components referred to as *sequence grabbers*; sequence grabber channel components as *channel components*; and sequence grabber panel components as *panel components*. ◆

About Sequence Grabber Panel Components

This section provides background information about sequence grabber panel components. After reading this section, you should understand why these components exist and whether you need to create one.

Sequence grabber panel components augment the capabilities of sequence grabber components and sequence grabber channel components by allowing sequence grabbers to obtain configuration information from the user for a particular digitizing source that is managed by a channel component. Consequently, sequence grabbers, channel components, and panel components have a close relationship. Figure 7-1 shows this relationship and how these components interact with one another to place digitized data into a QuickTime movie.

Sequence Grabber Panel Components

Figure 7-1 Sequence grabbers, channel components, and panel components

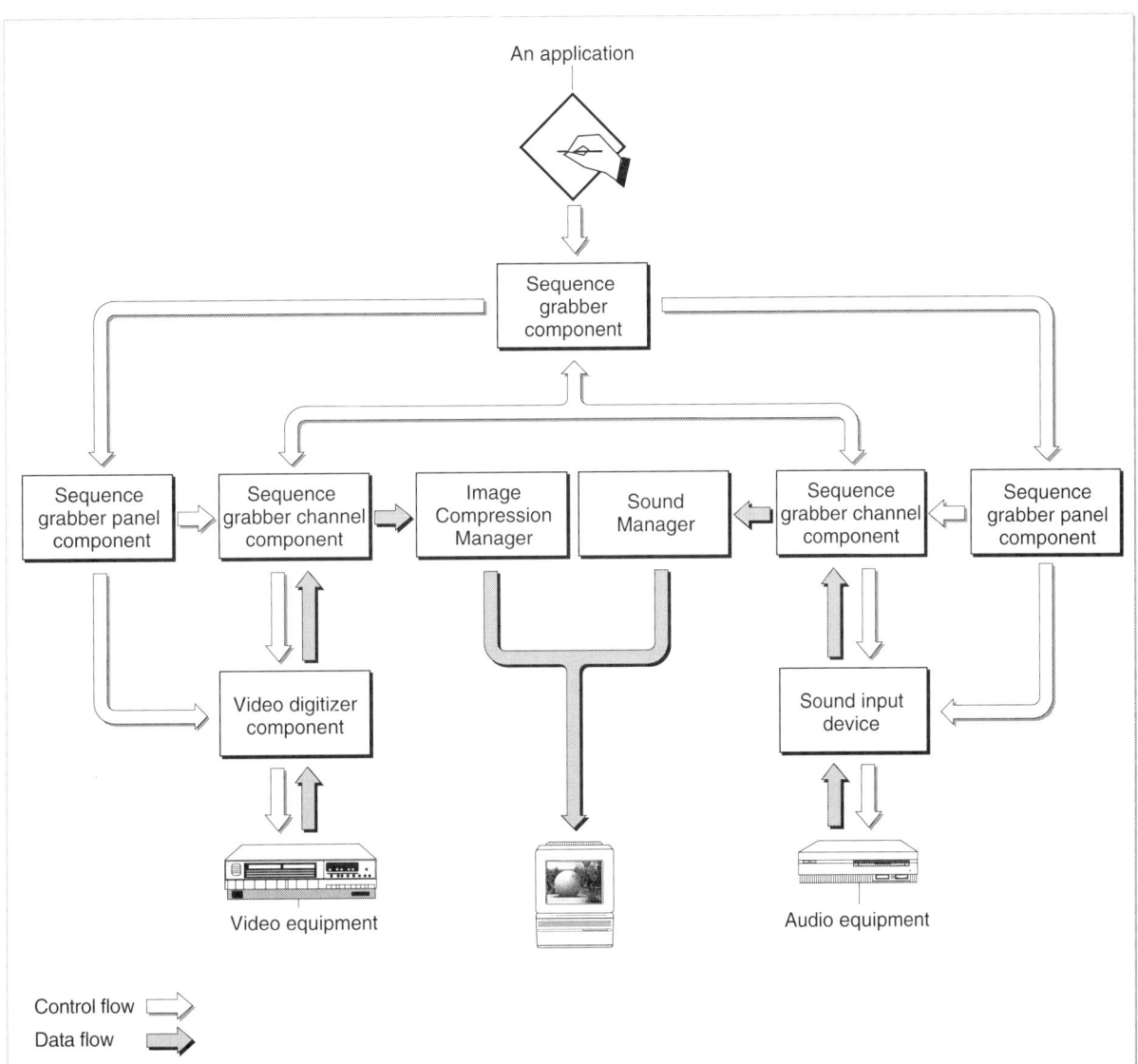

Sequence grabbers present a settings dialog box to the user whenever an application calls the SGSettingsDialog function (see the chapter "Sequence Grabber Components" in this book for more information about this sequence grabber function). Applications never call sequence grabber panel components directly; application developers use panel components only by calling the sequence grabber component.

CHAPTER 7

Sequence Grabber Panel Components

Although the sequence grabber creates the dialog box and manages its interactions with the user, portions of the dialog box are controlled by panel components and channel components. Figure 7-2 shows a sample dialog box and identifies the various parts of the dialog box.

Figure 7-2 A sample sequence grabber settings dialog box

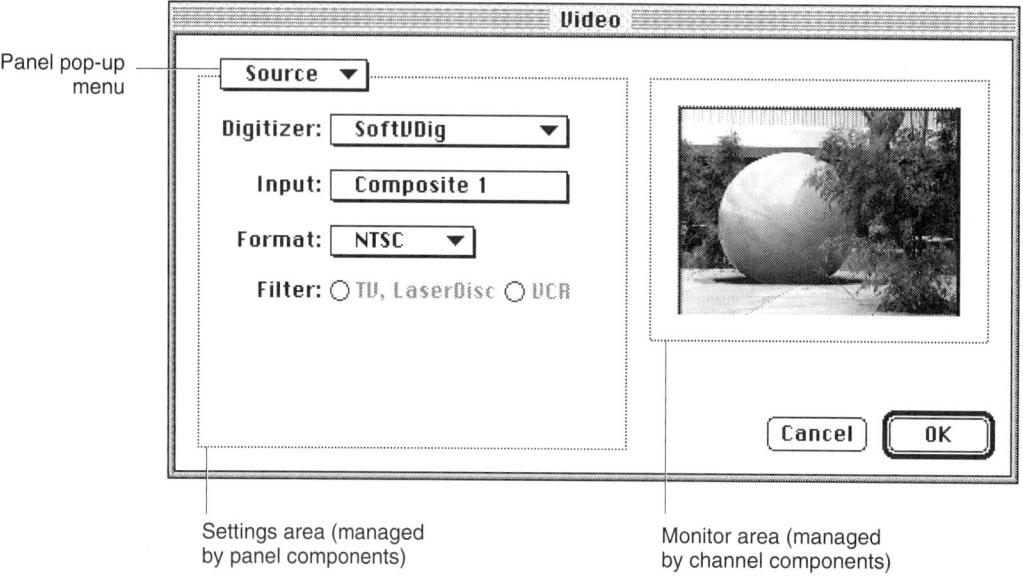

The sequence grabber creates the dialog box itself and manages the OK and Cancel buttons and the panel pop-up menu. Channel components are responsible for the monitor area on the right side of the dialog box. Panel components manage the settings area immediately below the panel pop-up menu. Only one panel component is active at any given time; the user selects a panel component by manipulating the panel pop-up menu.

When the user selects a specific panel component, the sequence grabber works with that component to build the panel settings dialog area and present it to the user. The panel component processes dialog events and mouse clicks as appropriate and validates the user's settings. The sequence grabber then retrieves the settings from the panel component and stores those settings.

There are two circumstances under which you should consider creating a sequence grabber panel component: first, if you want to support special digitizing equipment in the QuickTime environment; and, second, if you have created your own sequence grabber channel component.

Sequence Grabber Panel Components

If you have created special digitizing equipment, you may not have to create a special channel component for your equipment—the channel components provided by Apple may be sufficient for your needs. By providing a special panel component, however, you can allow the user to take advantage of your equipment's special capabilities.

If you have created your own channel component, you must create an accompanying panel component to allow the user to configure your channel.

Creating Sequence Grabber Panel Components

This section discusses how to create a sequence grabber panel component. You should read this section if you are creating a panel component.

Applications do not call panel components directly. Rather, they invoke a sequence grabber's settings dialog box by calling the SGSettingsDialog function. In response, the sequence grabber presents the settings dialog box to the user. When the user selects a specific settings panel, the sequence grabber invokes the appropriate panel component.

Panel components provide a number of functions that allow sequence grabbers to manage their relationships with panel components. See "Managing Your Panel Component" beginning on page 7-15 for complete descriptions of these functions.

Panel components are not responsible for saving their settings information. Sequence grabbers manage this information on behalf of panel components, and a sequence grabber may combine configuration information from several panel components in order to build up the complete configuration for an elaborate digitizing environment. Panel components provide functions that allow sequence grabbers to obtain this configuration information. See "Managing Your Panel's Settings" beginning on page 7-24 for more information about these functions.

Sequence grabbers store this configuration data in user data items. The Movie Toolbox provides a number of functions that allow you to create and manage user data items. If you are not familiar with these functions, see the chapter "Movie Toolbox" in *Inside Macintosh: QuickTime* for more information.

Apple has defined a component type value for sequence grabber panel components. You can use the following constant to specify this component type.

```
#define  SeqGrabPanelType  'sgpn'  /* panel component type */
```

Sequence grabber panel components use their component subtype and manufacturer values to indicate the type of configuration services they provide. The subtype value indicates the media type supported by the panel component. This value should correspond to the component subtype value of channel components that may be configured by the panel component. For example, a panel component that manages video settings would have a subtype of 'vide' (this value is defined by the Movie Toolbox's VideoMediaType constant).

CHAPTER 7

Sequence Grabber Panel Components

The manufacturer field contains a unique identifier for each panel component. The value should indicate something about the specific services provided by the component. For example, Apple has defined the following manufacturer values:

```
#define    SeqGrabCompressionPanelType    'sour'    /* input source
                                                      selection */
#define    SeqGrabSourcePanelType         'cmpr'    /* compression
                                                      settings */
```

In general, Apple has reserved all lowercase values of component subtypes and manufacturer codes.

Apple has defined a functional interface for sequence grabber panel components. For information about the functions that your component must support, see "Sequence Grabber Panel Components Reference" beginning on page 7-14. You may use the following constants to refer to the request codes for each of the functions that your component must support:

```
enum {
   /* sequence grabber panel request codes */

   kSGCPanelGetDitlSelect         = 0x200, /* SGPanelGetDITL */
   kSGCPanelCanRunSelect          = 0x202, /* SGPanelCanRun */
   kSGCPanelInstallSelect         = 0x203, /* SGPanelInstall */
   kSGCPanelEventSelect           = 0x204, /* SGPanelEvent */
   kSGCPanelItemSelect            = 0x205, /* SGPanelItem */
   kSGCPanelRemoveSelect          = 0x206, /* SGPanelRemove */
   kSGCPanelSetGrabberSelect      = 0x207, /* SGPanelSetGrabber */
   kSGCPanelSetResFileSelect      = 0x208, /* SGPanelSetResFile */
   kSGCPanelGetSettingsSelect     = 0x209, /* SGPanelGetSettings */
   kSGCPanelSetSettingsSelect     = 0x20A, /* SGPanelSetSettings */
   kSGCPanelValidateInputSelect   = 0x20B  /* SGPanelValidateInput */
};
```

Before reading the rest of this chapter, you should know how to create components. See the chapter "Component Manager" in *Inside Macintosh: More Macintosh Toolbox* for a complete discussion of components, how to use them, and how to create them.

The next section contains sample code for the creation of a sequence grabber panel component that acts as a settings dialog box for PICT images. To create a sequence grabber panel component, you set up the global variables and implement the required Component Manager request codes and the functions that are private to your particular component. Then you manage the dialog box and work with the settings in the dialog box.

Sequence Grabber Panel Components

Implementing the Required Component Functions

Listing 7-1 supplies the component dispatchers for the sequence grabber panel component together with the required functions for open, close, can do, and version.

Listing 7-1 Implementing the required functions

```
#define sgcPictShowTicksType 'TICK'

typedef struct {
   ComponentInstance    self;
   ControlHandle        ch;
} PictPanelGlobalsRecord, *PictPanelGlobals;

/* only for PICT channels */
pascal ComponentResult SGSetShowTickCount (SGChannel c,
            Boolean show) = {0x2f3c,2,0x100,0x7000,0xA82A};
pascal ComponentResult SGGetShowTickCount (SGChannel c,
            Boolean *show) = {0x2f3c,4,0x101,0x7000,0xA82A};
pascal ComponentResult PictPanelDispatcher
            (ComponentParameters *params, Handle storage)

{
   OSErr err = badComponentSelector;
   ComponentFunction componentProc = 0;
   switch (params->what) {

      case kComponentOpenSelect:
         componentProc = PictPanelOpen; break;
      case kComponentCloseSelect:
         componentProc = PictPanelClose; break;
      case kComponentCanDoSelect:
         componentProc = PictPanelCanDo; break;
      case kComponentVersionSelect:
         componentProc = PictPanelVersion; break;
      case kSGCPanelGetDitlSelect:
         componentProc = PictPanelPanelGetDitl; break;
      case kSGCPanelInstallSelect:
         componentProc = PictPanelPanelInstall; break;
      case kSGCPanelItemSelect:
         componentProc = PictPanelPanelItem; break;
      case kSGCPanelRemoveSelect:
         componentProc = PictPanelPanelRemove; break;
```

Sequence Grabber Panel Components

```
            case kSGCPanelGetSettingsSelect:
                componentProc = PictPanelPanelGetSettings; break;
            case kSGCPanelSetSettingsSelect:
                componentProc = PictPanelPanelSetSettings; break;
        }

        if (componentProc)
            err = CallComponentFunctionWithStorage (storage, params,
                                                    componentProc);

        return err;
    }

    pascal ComponentResult PictPanelCanDo (PictPanelGlobals store,
                                            short ftnNumber)
    {

        switch (ftnNumber) {
            case kComponentOpenSelect:
            case kComponentCloseSelect:
            case kComponentCanDoSelect:
            case kComponentVersionSelect:
            case kSGCPanelGetDitlSelect:
            case kSGCPanelInstallSelect:
            case kSGCPanelItemSelect:
            case kSGCPanelRemoveSelect:
            case kSGCPanelGetSettingsSelect:
            case kSGCPanelSetSettingsSelect:
                return true;
            default:
                return false;
        }
    }

    pascal ComponentResult PictPanelVersion (PictPanelGlobals store)
    {
        return 0x00020001;
    }
```

```
pascal ComponentResult PictPanelOpen (PictPanelGlobals store,
                                      ComponentInstance self)
{
   OSErr err;

   /* allocate global variables */
   store = (PictPanelGlobals) NewPtrClear
           (sizeof(PictPanelGlobalsRecord));
   if (err = MemError()) goto bail;
   SetComponentInstanceStorage (self, (Handle)store);

   /* remember the component instance identification number */
   store->self = self;

bail:
   return err;
}

pascal ComponentResult PictPanelClose (PictPanelGlobals store,
                                       ComponentInstance self)
{
   if (store) DisposePtr ((Ptr)store);
   return noErr;
}
```

Managing the Dialog Box

This section gives details on the functions that the panel component must provide so that the sequence grabber can load the component's items into the settings dialog box and receive and process dialog events.

1. To prepare to add the component's items to the settings dialog box, the sequence grabber obtains the item list by calling the SGPanelGetDITL function (described on page 7-18).

2. Once it has installed the items, the sequence grabber calls the SGPanelInstall function (described on page 7-19), which sets up the state of the dialog box (for example, a checkbox) and gives the panel component an opportunity to set initial values.

3. When the panel component is loaded into the settings dialog box and active, it may receive and process dialog events and mouse clicks. The component's SGPanelEvent function (described on page 7-22) processes individual dialog events.

4. Whenever the user clicks a dialog item, the sequence grabber calls the SGPanelItem function (described on page 7-21).

5. Before the sequence grabber removes the items from the settings dialog box, it calls the SGPanelRemove function (described on page 7-20).

CHAPTER 7

Sequence Grabber Panel Components

Listing 7-2 provides an example of the management of the settings dialog box for a sequence grabber that displays PICT images. The component item displayed in the dialog box in this case is a tick count checkbox.

Listing 7-2 Managing the settings dialog box

```
pascal ComponentResult PictPanelPanelGetDitl
                                    (PictPanelGlobals store,
                                     Handle *ditl)
{
   /*
      Get and detach the dialog box template. Note that
      the sequence grabber has already opened the resource file.
   */
   *ditl = GetResource ('DITL', 7001);
   if (!*ditl) return resNotFound;
   DetachResource (*ditl);
   return noErr;
}


pascal ComponentResult PictPanelPanelInstall
                        (PictPanelGlobals store, SGChannel c,
                         DialogPtr d, short itemOffset)
{
   Rect r;
   short kind;
   Handle h;
   Boolean ticksShowing;

   /* set up the initial state of the checkbox */
   GetDItem (d, 1 + itemOffset, &kind, &h, &r);
   store->ch = (ControlHandle)h;
   SGGetShowTickCount (c, &ticksShowing);
   SetCtlValue (store->ch, ticksShowing);

   return noErr;
}

pascal ComponentResult PictPanelPanelItem
                        (PictPanelGlobals store, SGChannel c,
                         DialogPtr d, short itemOffset,
                         short itemNum)
```

Sequence Grabber Panel Components

```
{
   /* if the item clicked was your checkbox, update its state */
   if ((itemNum - itemOffset) == 1) {
      Boolean showing = GetCtlValue (store->ch);
      SetCtlValue (store->ch, !showing);
      SGSetShowTickCount (c, !showing);
   }

   return noErr;
}

pascal ComponentResult PictPanelPanelRemove
                              (PictPanelGlobals store,
                               SGChannel c, DialogPtr d,
                               short itemOffset)
{
   /* forget that it ever had a control */
   store->ch = nil;
   return noErr;
}
```

Managing Your Panel's Settings

To allow the sequence grabber to work with your panel's settings, your panel component must allow the sequence grabber to

- retrieve the panel's current settings by calling your `SGPanelGetSettings` function (described on page 7-24)
- restore those settings to some previous values by using your `SGPanelSetSettings` function (described on page 7-25)

Listing 7-3 gives an example in which the settings are managed in a user list that contains tick count information for a panel component for PICT images.

Listing 7-3 Managing the settings for a panel component

```
pascal ComponentResult PictPanelPanelGetSettings
                  (PictPanelGlobals store, SGChannel c,
                   UserData *result, long flags)
{
   OSErr      err;
   UserData   ud;
   Boolean    ticksShowing;
```

Sequence Grabber Panel Components

```
    /* create a user data list containing your state */
    if (err = NewUserData (&ud)) goto bail;
    if (err = SGGetShowTickCount (c, &ticksShowing)) goto bail;
    if (err = SetUserDataItem (ud, &ticksShowing,
                               sizeof (ticksShowing),
                               sgcPictShowTicksType, 1)) goto bail;

bail:
    if (err) {
       DisposeUserData(ud);
       ud = 0;
    }
    *result = ud;

    return err;
}

pascal ComponentResult PictPanelPanelSetSettings
                           (PictPanelGlobals store, SGChannel c,
                            UserData ud, long flags)
{
    Boolean ticksShowing;

    /* restore the state from the specified user data list */
    if (GetUserDataItem (ud, &ticksShowing,
                         sizeof (ticksShowing),
                         sgcPictShowTicksType, 1) == noErr)
       SGSetShowTickCount (c, ticksShowing);

    return noErr;
}
```

Sequence Grabber Panel Components Reference

This section describes the constants and functions that your sequence grabber panel component may support. Some of these functions are optional—your component should support only those functions that are appropriate to it.

Component Flags for Sequence Grabber Panel Components

The Component Manager allows you to specify information about your component's capabilities in the `componentFlags` field of the component description record. Sequence grabber panel components use the `componentFlags` field to indicate specific information about their capabilities.

The following flags are currently defined:

```
enum {
    channelFlagDontOpenResFile = 2,   /* do not open resource
                                         file */
    channelFlagHasDependency = 4      /* needs special hardware */
};
```

These flags control how sequence grabbers manage their connection with your panel component. The `channelFlagDontOpenResFile` flag instructs the sequence grabber not to open your component's resource file. By default, the sequence grabber opens your component's resource file for you, and then provides you with the appropriate file reference number. In general, this is convenient. However, if your component is linked with your application and does not have its own resource file, you may not want the sequence grabber to try to open the resource file. In such cases, set this flag to 1.

The `channelFlagHasDependency` flag allows you to tell the sequence grabber that your panel component requires special digitizing hardware. If you set this flag to 1, the sequence grabber gives your component an opportunity to verify that it can work in the current hardware environment—by calling your component's `SGPanelCanRun` function (described on page 7-17).

Functions

This section describes the functions that may be supported by sequence grabber panel components. It is divided into the following topics:

- "Managing Your Panel Component" discusses the functions that allow sequence grabber components to load, configure, and unload your panel component.
- "Processing Your Panel's Events" describes the functions that allow your component to receive and process events in your panel.
- "Managing Your Panel's Settings" tells you about the functions that allow sequence grabber components to collect and reset your panel's settings.

Managing Your Panel Component

Sequence grabber components load, configure, and unload your panel component. As part of this process, the sequence grabber installs your panel's dialog items into the settings dialog box and may open your component's resource file. Panel components

Sequence Grabber Panel Components

provide a number of functions that allow the sequence grabber to manage its relationship with panel components. This section discusses those functions.

After opening a connection to your panel component, the sequence grabber identifies itself to your component by calling your `SGPanelSetGrabber` function. The sequence grabber then tries to determine whether your component can work with its associated channel component by calling your `SGPanelCanRun` function. The sequence grabber calls this function only if you have set the `channelFlagHasDependency` component flag to 1.

Once the sequence grabber has determined that your panel component can work with its channel component, the sequence grabber may open your component's resource file (unless you have set the `channelFlagDontOpenResFile` component flag to 1). Once it has opened the resource file, it passes the file's reference number to you by calling your `SGPanelSetResFile` function.

Next, the sequence grabber prepares to add your component's items to the settings dialog box. The sequence grabber obtains your item list by calling your `SGPanelGetDITL` function. Once it has installed the items, it calls your `SGPanelInstall` function, giving you an opportunity to set initial values.

Before the sequence grabber removes your items from the settings dialog box, it calls your `SGPanelRemove` function.

SGPanelSetGrabber

The `SGPanelSetGrabber` function allows a sequence grabber component to identify itself to your panel component. This is typically the first function the sequence grabber component calls after opening your panel component.

```
pascal ComponentResult SGPanelSetGrabber
                            (SeqGrabPanelComponent s,
                             SeqGrabComponent sg);
```

s Identifies the sequence grabber component's connection to your panel component.

sg Identifies a connection to the sequence grabber component that is using your panel component. Your component may use this connection to call sequence grabber component functions.

DESCRIPTION

A sequence grabber component calls your `SGPanelSetGrabber` function in order to identify itself to your panel component. Your component can use the provided connection to call sequence grabber functions, either to determine the characteristics of the current capture operation or to alter those characteristics.

RESULT CODE

    `badComponentSelector`   0x80008002   Function not supported

SGPanelCanRun

The `SGPanelCanRun` function allows a sequence grabber component to determine whether your panel component can work with the current sequence grabber channel component.

```
pascal ComponentResult SGPanelCanRun (SeqGrabPanelComponent s,
                                      SGChannel c);
```

s   Identifies the sequence grabber component's connection to your panel component.

c   Identifies a connection to a sequence grabber channel component. You must determine whether your panel component can operate with this channel component and its associated channel hardware.

DESCRIPTION

A sequence grabber component calls your `SGPanelCanRun` function in order to determine whether your component can work with a specified sequence grabber channel component and its associated hardware. If your component works only with certain hardware, you should support this function.

Set the `channelFlagHasDependency` component flag to 1 to cause the sequence grabber component to call this function.

The sequence grabber component provides you with a connection to the channel component in question. Your component should query the channel component to determine whether you can operate with it. You may want to use channel component functions to determine the characteristics of the digitization source attached to the channel. If your component can work with the specified channel, return a result code of `noErr`. Otherwise, return an appropriate sequence grabber or sequence grabber channel component result code.

If your panel component can only support a limited number of connections, you should regulate the number of active connections in your `SGPanelCanRun` function. Return a nonzero result code to indicate to the sequence grabber that your panel component cannot support the current connection.

RESULT CODES

    `noDeviceForChannel`   –9408   Cannot work with specified channel
    `badComponentSelector`   0x80008002   Function not supported

Other appropriate sequence grabber or sequence grabber channel result codes

SGPanelSetResFile

Unless you instruct it otherwise, the sequence grabber component opens your panel component's resource file for you. The `SGPanelSetResFile` function allows the sequence grabber to pass you the resource file's reference number. The sequence grabber also calls this function when it closes your resource file.

```
pascal ComponentResult SGPanelSetResFile
                                (SeqGrabPanelComponent s,
                                 short resRef);
```

s   Identifies the sequence grabber component's connection to your panel component.

resRef   Contains a reference number that identifies your component's resource file. After it closes your resource file, the sequence grabber component calls this function and sets this value to 0.

DESCRIPTION

A sequence grabber component calls your `SGPanelSetResFile` function in order to pass you your component's resource file reference number. By default, the sequence grabber component opens your component's resource file for you. You can use this reference number to retrieve resources from your resource file.

The sequence grabber component also calls this function when it closes your component's resource file. In this case, it sets the `resRef` parameter to 0. Note that the sequence grabber component may close your resource file at any time; you should not count on any particular calling sequence.

If you do not want the sequence grabber component to open your resource file, set the `channelFlagDontOpenResFile` component flag to 1.

SGPanelGetDITL

The `SGPanelGetDITL` function allows a sequence grabber component to determine the dialog items managed by your panel component. The sequence grabber uses this information to build the sequence grabber settings dialog box for the user.

```
pascal ComponentResult SGPanelGetDITL (SeqGrabPanelComponent s,
                                       Handle *ditl);
```

s   Identifies the sequence grabber component's connection to your panel component.

ditl   Contains a pointer to a handle that is to receive your component's item list. Your component should resize this handle as appropriate.

DESCRIPTION

A sequence grabber component calls your `SGPanelGetDITL` function in order to obtain the list of dialog items supported by your panel component. The sequence grabber then places these items into the settings dialog box and presents the dialog box to the user. When the sequence grabber builds the settings dialog box, it places your items appropriately—you do not need to specify particular locations for the items.

Your component returns the item list in a handle that is provided by the sequence grabber component. Note that the sequence grabber component will dispose of this handle after retrieving the item list, so make sure that the item list is not stored in a resource. If your item list is in a resource handle, you can use the Resource Manager's `DetachResource` routine to convert that resource handle into a handle that is suitable for use with the `SGPanelGetDITL` function.

The sequence grabber component will open your resource file before calling this function unless you have instructed the sequence grabber component not to open your resource file (that is, you have set the `channelFlagDontOpenResFile` component flag to 1).

SGPanelInstall

A sequence grabber component calls your `SGPanelInstall` function after adding your items to the settings dialog box, just before it displays the dialog box to the user.

```
pascal ComponentResult SGPanelInstall (SeqGrabPanelComponent s,
                                       SGChannel c, DialogPtr d,
                                       short itemOffset);
```

s   Identifies the sequence grabber component's connection to your panel component.

c   Identifies a connection to the sequence grabber channel associated with your panel component.

d   Contains a dialog pointer identifying the settings dialog box. Your component may use this value to manage its part of the dialog box.

`itemOffset`
            Specifies the offset to your panel's first item in the dialog box. Because sequence grabber components build your dialog items into a larger dialog box containing other items, this value may be different each time your panel component is installed; do not rely on it being the same.

DESCRIPTION

A sequence grabber component calls your `SGPanelInstall` function just before displaying the dialog box to the user. The sequence grabber provides you with information identifying the channel that your panel is to configure, the dialog box, and the offset of your panel's items into the dialog box. You may use this opportunity to set default dialog values or to initialize your control values.

CHAPTER 7

Sequence Grabber Panel Components

SEE ALSO

Sequence grabber components call your component's `SGPanelRemove` function before they remove your panel from the settings dialog box. That function is discussed next.

SGPanelRemove

Sequence grabber components call your component's `SGPanelRemove` function before removing your panel from the settings dialog box.

```
pascal ComponentResult SGPanelRemove (SeqGrabPanelComponent s,
                                      SGChannel c, DialogPtr d,
                                      short itemOffset);
```

s Identifies the sequence grabber component's connection to your panel component.

c Identifies a connection to the sequence grabber channel associated with your panel component.

d Contains a dialog pointer identifying the settings dialog box.

itemOffset
   Specifies the offset to your panel's first item in the dialog box.

DESCRIPTION

A sequence grabber component calls your `SGPanelRemove` function just before removing your items from the settings dialog box. The sequence grabber provides you with information identifying the channel your panel is to configure, the dialog box, and the offset of your panel's items into the dialog box. You may use this opportunity to save any changes you may have made to the dialog box or to retrieve the contents of TextEdit items.

If the sequence grabber opened your resource file, it will still be open when it calls this function.

SEE ALSO

Sequence grabbers call your `SGPanelInstall` function (described in the previous section) before displaying the settings dialog box to the user.

Processing Your Panel's Events

When your panel component is loaded into the settings dialog box and active, you may receive and process dialog events and mouse clicks.

Your component's `SGPanelEvent` function acts like a modal-dialog filter function, allowing you to process individual dialog events. The sequence grabber calls your `SGPanelItem` function whenever the user clicks a dialog item.

Whenever the user clicks the OK button, the sequence grabber calls your `SGPanelValidateInput` function. Your panel component may then validate the user's settings.

SGPanelItem

Your `SGPanelItem` function allows your component to receive and process mouse clicks in the settings dialog box.

```
pascal ComponentResult SGPanelItem (SeqGrabPanelComponent s,
                                    SGChannel c, DialogPtr d,
                                    short itemOffset,
                                    short itemNum);
```

s
Identifies the sequence grabber component's connection to your panel component.

c
Identifies a connection to the sequence grabber channel associated with your panel component.

d
Contains a dialog pointer identifying the settings dialog box.

itemOffset
Specifies the offset to your panel's first item in the dialog box.

itemNum
Contains the item number of the dialog item selected by the user. Note that this is an absolute item number; the sequence grabber does not adjust this value to account for the offset to your first dialog item.

DESCRIPTION

A sequence grabber component calls your `SGPanelItem` function whenever the user clicks an item in the settings dialog box. Your component may then perform whatever processing is appropriate, depending upon the item number. Note that the sequence grabber provides an absolute item number. It is your responsibility to adjust this value to account for the offset to your panel's first item in the dialog box.

CHAPTER 7

Sequence Grabber Panel Components

SEE ALSO

Your component can filter all dialog events with your `SGPanelEvent` function. This function is described next.

Sequence grabber components use your component's `SGPanelValidateInput` function to validate the current input settings as a whole. That function is discussed on page 7-23.

SGPanelEvent

Your `SGPanelEvent` function allows your component to receive and process dialog events. This function is similar to a modal-dialog filter function.

```
pascal ComponentResult SGPanelEvent (SeqGrabPanelComponent s,
                                     SGChannel c, DialogPtr d,
                                     short itemOffset,
                                     EventRecord *theEvent,
                                     short *itemHit,
                                     Boolean *handled);
```

`s` Identifies the sequence grabber component's connection to your panel component.

`c` Identifies a connection to the sequence grabber channel associated with your panel component.

`d` Contains a dialog pointer identifying the settings dialog box.

`itemOffset`
Specifies the offset to your panel's first item in the dialog box.

`theEvent` Contains a pointer to an event structure. This event structure contains information identifying the nature of the event.

`itemHit` Contains a pointer to a field that is to receive the item number in cases where your component handles the event. The number returned is an absolute, not a relative number, so it must be offset by the `itemOffset` parameter.

`handled` Contains a pointer to a Boolean value. Set this Boolean value to indicate whether your component handles the event: set it to `true` if you handle the event; set it to `false` if you do not.

DESCRIPTION

A sequence grabber component calls your `SGPanelEvent` function whenever an event occurs in the settings dialog box. Your `SGPanelEvent` function is similar to a modal-dialog filter function. The main difference is that, rather than returning a Boolean value to indicate whether you handled the event, your `SGPanelEvent` function sets a Boolean

CHAPTER 7

Sequence Grabber Panel Components

value that is provided by the calling function. If you handle the event, be sure to update the field referred to by the `itemHit` parameter.

SEE ALSO

Your component can process mouse clicks with your `SGPanelItem` function. This function is discussed on page 7-21.

SGPanelValidateInput

Sequence grabber components call your component's `SGPanelValidateInput` function in order to allow you to validate the contents of the user dialog box.

```
pascal ComponentResult SGPanelValidateInput
                        (SeqGrabPanelComponent s,
                         Boolean *ok);
```

s   Identifies the sequence grabber component's connection to your panel component.

ok   Contains a pointer to a Boolean value. You set this Boolean value to indicate whether the user's settings are acceptable. Set it to `true` if the settings are OK; otherwise, set it to `false`.

DESCRIPTION

A sequence grabber component calls your `SGPanelValidateInput` function in order to allow you to validate the settings chosen by the user. This is your opportunity to validate the settings in their entirety, including those for which you may not have received dialog events or mouse clicks. For example, if your panel component uses a TextEdit box, you should validate its contents at this time. Be sure to give the user some indication of what to do to fix the settings.

The sequence grabber calls this function when the user clicks the OK button. If the user clicks the Cancel button, the sequence grabber does not call this function.

You indicate whether the settings are acceptable by setting the Boolean value referred to by the `ok` parameter. If you set this Boolean value to `false`, the sequence grabber component ignores the OK button in the dialog box.

SEE ALSO

Your component can process mouse clicks with your `SGPanelItem` function, described on page 7-21. Your component can filter all dialog events with your `SGPanelEvent` function, described in the previous section.

Managing Your Panel's Settings

Sequence grabber components store their configuration information in Movie Toolbox user data items (see the chapter "Movie Toolbox" in *Inside Macintosh: QuickTime* for more information about user data items). This configuration information includes settings for each of the channels used by the sequence grabber. Because your panel component configures sequence grabber channels, your panel component is responsible for creating and formatting the contents of its user data items. The sequence grabber component calls your component whenever it wants to retrieve these settings. The sequence grabber may also use previously stored settings to restore your panel's settings. This section discusses the functions that allow the sequence grabber to work with your panel's settings.

The sequence grabber calls your `SGPanelGetSettings` function in order to retrieve your panel's current settings. The sequence grabber uses your `SGPanelSetSettings` function to restore those settings to some previous values.

SGPanelGetSettings

Sequence grabber components call your component's `SGPanelGetSettings` function in order to retrieve your panel's current settings.

```
pascal ComponentResult SGPanelGetSettings
                            (SeqGrabPanelComponent s,
                            SGChannel c, UserData *ud,
                            long flags);
```

s Identifies the sequence grabber component's connection to your panel component.

c Identifies a connection to the sequence grabber channel associated with your panel component.

ud Contains a pointer to a user data item. Your component is responsible for creating a new user data item and returning that item by means of this pointer. Your component is not responsible for disposing of the user data item.

flags Reserved for future use.

DESCRIPTION

A sequence grabber component calls your `SGPanelGetSettings` function in order to obtain a copy of your panel's current settings. The sequence grabber stores these settings for you and may use them to restore your panel's settings by calling your `SGPanelSetSettings` function (described next). Your component should store whatever values are necessary to properly configure your associated channel component. For example, Apple's video compression panel component saves such values as video compressor component type, compression quality, key frame rate, and frame rate values.

These settings may be stored as part of a larger sequence grabber configuration and may be stored for a long period of time. Therefore, you should not store values that may change without your knowledge (such as component ID or connection values).

You are free to format the data in the user data item in any way you desire. Make sure you can retrieve the settings information from the user data item when your `SGPanelGetSettings` function is called. You may choose to format the data in such a way that other components can parse it easily, thus allowing your component to operate with other panel components.

You create a new user data item by calling the Movie Toolbox's `NewUserData` function (see the chapter "Movie Toolbox" in *Inside Macintosh: QuickTime* for more information about this function). You may then use other Movie Toolbox functions to manipulate the user data item.

SEE ALSO

Sequence grabber components use your component's `SGPanelSetSettings` function to restore this configuration information. That function is discussed next.

SGPanelSetSettings

Sequence grabber components call your component's `SGPanelSetSettings` function in order to restore your panel's current settings.

```
pascal ComponentResult SGPanelSetSettings
                        (SeqGrabPanelComponent s,
                         SGChannel c, UserData ud,
                         long flags);
```

s   Identifies the sequence grabber component's connection to your panel component.

c   Identifies a connection to the sequence grabber channel associated with your panel component.

ud   Identifies a user data item that contains new settings information for your panel. Your component must not dispose of this user data item.

flags   Reserved for future use.

CHAPTER 7

Sequence Grabber Panel Components

DESCRIPTION

A sequence grabber component calls your `SGPanelSetSettings` function in order to restore your panel's settings. The sequence grabber may call this function when the user cancels the settings dialog box.

Your component originally creates the settings information when the sequence grabber calls your `SGPanelGetSettings` function (described in the previous section). The sequence grabber passes this configuration information back to you in the ud parameter to this function. Your component should parse the configuration information and use it to establish your panel's current settings.

Note that your component may not be able to accommodate the original settings. For example, because the settings may have been stored for some time, the hardware environment may not be able to support the values in the settings. You should try to make your new settings match the original settings as closely as possible. If you cannot get close enough, return an appropriate sequence grabber or sequence grabber channel result code.

You may use Movie Toolbox functions to manipulate the user data item (see the chapter "Movie Toolbox" in *Inside Macintosh: QuickTime* for more information about functions that work with user data items).

RESULT CODES

`noDeviceForChannel`   –9408   Device cannot support settings

Other appropriate sequence grabber or sequence grabber channel result codes

SEE ALSO

Sequence grabber components use your component's `SGPanelGetSettings` function (described in the previous section) to retrieve the configuration information.

Summary of Sequence Grabber Panel Components

C Summary

Constants

```
/* component type value */
#define   SeqGrabPanelType 'sgpn'      /* panel component type */

/* component manufacturer code values */
#define   SeqGrabCompressionPanelType   'sour'    /* input source selection */
#define   SeqGrabSourcePanelType        'cmpr'    /* compression settings */

/* componentFlags values for sequence grabber panel components */
enum {
   channelFlagDontOpenResFile = 2,  /* do not open resource file */
   channelFlagHasDependency   = 4   /* needs special hardware */
};

enum {
   /* sequence grabber panel request codes */
   kSGCPanelGetDitlSelect        = 0x200, /* SGPanelGetDITL */
   kSGCPanelCanRunSelect         = 0x202, /* SGPanelCanRun */
   kSGCPanelInstallSelect        = 0x203, /* SGPanelInstall */
   kSGCPanelEventSelect          = 0x204, /* SGPanelEvent */
   kSGCPanelItemSelect           = 0x205, /* SGPanelItem */
   kSGCPanelRemoveSelect         = 0x206, /* SGPanelRemove */
   kSGCPanelSetGrabberSelect     = 0x207, /* SGPanelSetGrabber */
   kSGCPanelSetResFileSelect     = 0x208, /* SGPanelSetResFile */
   kSGCPanelGetSettingsSelect    = 0x209, /* SGPanelGetSettings */
   kSGCPanelSetSettingsSelect    = 0x20A, /* SGPanelSetSettings */
   kSGCPanelValidateInputSelect  = 0x20B  /* SGPanelValidateInput */
};
```

Functions

Managing Your Panel Component

```
pascal ComponentResult SGPanelSetGrabber
                    (SeqGrabPanelComponent s, SeqGrabComponent sg);
pascal ComponentResult SGPanelCanRun
                    (SeqGrabPanelComponent s, SGChannel c);
pascal ComponentResult SGPanelSetResFile
                    (SeqGrabPanelComponent s, short resRef);
pascal ComponentResult SGPanelGetDITL
                    (SeqGrabPanelComponent s, Handle *ditl);
pascal ComponentResult SGPanelInstall
                    (SeqGrabPanelComponent s, SGChannel c,
                        DialogPtr d, short itemOffset);
pascal ComponentResult SGPanelRemove
                    (SeqGrabPanelComponent s, SGChannel c,
                        DialogPtr d, short itemOffset);
```

Processing Your Panel's Events

```
pascal ComponentResult SGPanelItem
                    (SeqGrabPanelComponent s, SGChannel c,
                        DialogPtr d, short itemOffset, short itemNum);
pascal ComponentResult SGPanelEvent
                    (SeqGrabPanelComponent s, SGChannel c,
                        DialogPtr d, short itemOffset,
                        EventRecord *theEvent, short *itemHit,
                        Boolean *handled);
pascal ComponentResult SGPanelValidateInput
                    (SeqGrabPanelComponent s, Boolean *ok);
```

Managing Your Panel's Settings

```
pascal ComponentResult SGPanelGetSettings
                    (SeqGrabPanelComponent s, SGChannel c,
                        UserData *ud, long flags);
pascal ComponentResult SGPanelSetSettings
                    (SeqGrabPanelComponent s, SGChannel c,
                        UserData ud, long flags);
```

Sequence Grabber Panel Components

Pascal Summary

Constants

```
CONST
  {component type value}
  SeqGrabPanelType                = 'sgpn';    {panel component type}
  {component manufacturer code values}
  SeqGrabCompressionPanelType     = 'comp';    {compression settings}
  SeqGrabSourcePanelType          = 'sour';    {input source slection}

  {componentFlags values for sequence grabber panel components}
  channelFlagDontOpenResFile  = 2;   {do not open resource file}
  channelFlagHasDependency    = 4;   {channel has special hardware}

  {sequence grabber panel component request codes}
  kSGCPanelGetDitlSelect          = $200;   {SGCPanelGetDitl}
  kSGCPanelCanRunSelect           = $202;   {SGCPanelCanRun}
  kSGCPanelInstallSelect          = $203;   {SGCPanelInstall}
  kSGCPanelEventSelect            = $204;   {SGCPanelEvent}
  kSGCPanelItemSelect             = $205;   {SGCPanelItem}
  kSGCPanelRemoveSelect           = $206;   {SGCPanelRemove}
  kSGCPanelSetGrabberSelect       = $207;   {SGCPanelSetGrabber}
  kSGCPanelSetResFileSelect       = $208;   {SGCPanelSetResFile}
  kSGCPanelGetSettingsSelect      = $209;   {SGCPanelGetSettings}
  kSGCPanelSetSettingsSelect      = $20A;   {SGCPanelSetSettings}
  kSGCPanelValidateInputSelect    = $20B;   {SGCPanelValidateInput}
```

Routines

Managing Your Panel Component

```
FUNCTION SGPanelSetGrabber    (s: SeqGrabComponent; sg: SeqGrabComponent):
                               ComponentResult;
FUNCTION SGPanelCanRun        (s: SeqGrabComponent; c: SGChannel):
                               ComponentResult;
FUNCTION SGPanelSetResFile    (s: SeqGrabComponent; resRef: Integer):
                               ComponentResult;
FUNCTION SGPanelGetDITL       (s: SeqGrabComponent; VAR ditl: Handle):
                               ComponentResult;
```

```
FUNCTION SGPanelInstall         (s: SeqGrabComponent; c: SGChannel;
                                 d: DialogPtr; itemOffset: Integer):
                                 ComponentResult;
FUNCTION SGPanelRemove          (s: SeqGrabComponent; c: SGChannel;
                                 d: DialogPtr; itemOffset: Integer):
                                 ComponentResult;
```

Processing Your Panel's Events

```
FUNCTION SGPanelItem            (s: SeqGrabComponent; c: SGChannel;
                                 d: DialogPtr; itemOffset: Integer;
                                 itemNum: Integer): ComponentResult;
FUNCTION SGPanelEvent           (s: SeqGrabComponent; c: SGChannel;
                                 d: DialogPtr; itemOffset: Integer;
                                 VAR theEvent: EventRecord;
                                 VAR itemHit: Integer;
                                 VAR handled: Boolean): ComponentResult;
FUNCTION SGPanelValidateInput
                                (s: SeqGrabComponent; VAR ok: Boolean):
                                 ComponentResult;
```

Managing Your Panel's Settings

```
FUNCTION SGPanelGetSettings     (s: SeqGrabComponent; c: SGChannel;
                                 VAR ud: UserData; flags: LongInt):
                                 ComponentResult;
FUNCTION SGPanelSetSettings     (s: SeqGrabComponent; c: SGChannel;
                                 ud: UserData; flags: LongInt): ComponentResult;
```

Result Codes

noDeviceForChannel	−9408	Cannot work with specified channel
badComponentSelector	0x80008002	Function not supported

CHAPTER 8

Video Digitizer Components

Contents

About Video Digitizer Components   8-3
   Types of Video Digitizer Components   8-5
   Source Coordinate Systems   8-6
Using Video Digitizer Components   8-7
   Specifying Destinations   8-7
   Starting and Stopping the Digitizer   8-7
   Multiple Buffering   8-8
   Obtaining an Accurate Time of Frame Capture   8-8
Creating Video Digitizer Components   8-8
   Component Type and Subtype Values   8-11
   Required Functions   8-11
   Optional Functions   8-12
      Frame Grabbers Without Playthrough   8-12
      Frame Grabbers With Hardware Playthrough   8-12
      Key Color and Alpha Channel Devices   8-13
      Compressed Source Devices   8-13
Video Digitizer Components Reference   8-14
   Constants   8-14
      Capability Flags   8-14
      Current Flags   8-19
   Data Types   8-20
      The Digitizer Information Structure   8-20
      The Buffer List Structure   8-22
      The Buffer Structure   8-23
   Video Digitizer Component Functions   8-23
      Getting Information About Video Digitizer Components   8-24
      Setting Source Characteristics   8-26
      Selecting an Input Source   8-30
      Setting Video Destinations   8-34
      Controlling Compressed Source Devices   8-42

Controlling Digitization 8-52
Controlling Color 8-60
Controlling Analog Video 8-65
Selectively Displaying Video 8-81
Clipping 8-89
Utility Functions 8-92
Application-Defined Function 8-98
Summary of Video Digitizer Components 8-99
  C Summary 8-99
    Constants 8-99
    Data Types 8-104
    Video Digitizer Component Functions 8-105
    Application-Defined Function 8-111
  Pascal Summary 8-111
    Constants 8-111
    Data Types 8-116
    Video Digitizer Component Routines 8-117
    Application-Defined Routine 8-123
  Result Codes 8-124

CHAPTER 8

Video Digitizer Components

This chapter discusses video digitizer components. **Video digitizer components** provide an interface for obtaining digitized video from an analog video source. In QuickTime, the typical client of a video digitizer component is a sequence grabber component (sequence grabber components are described in the chapter "Sequence Grabber Components" in this book). Sequence grabber components use the services of video digitizer components and image compressor components to create a simple interface for making and previewing movies. However, video digitizer components can also operate independently, placing video into a window.

IMPORTANT
Most applications never need to communicate directly with a video digitizer component. It is strongly advised that your application use the sequence grabber component instead; it isolates you from the myriad of details associated with video digitization. ▲

This chapter has been divided into the following major sections:

- "About Video Digitizer Components" presents some general information about video digitizer components.

- "Using Video Digitizer Components" gives details on how you tell the digitizer where to put the data and how to control digitization. It describes a technique for improving performance.

- "Creating Video Digitizer Components" discusses how to create a video digitizer component.

- "Video Digitizer Components Reference" describes the constants, data structures, and functions associated with video digitizer components.

- "Summary of Video Digitizer Components" supplies a summary of the constants, data types, and functions associated with video digitizer components in C and in Pascal.

About Video Digitizer Components

Video digitizer components convert video input into a digitized color image that is compatible with the graphics system of a computer. For example, a video digitizer may convert input analog video into a specified digital format. The input may be any video format and type, whereas the output must be intelligible to the Macintosh computer's display system. Once the digitizer has converted the input signal to an appropriate digital format, it then prepares the image for display by resizing the image, performing necessary color conversions, and clipping to the output window. At the end of this process, the digitizer component places the converted image into a buffer you specify—if that buffer is the current frame buffer, the image appears on the user's computer screen.

Video Digitizer Components

Figure 8-1 shows the steps involved in converting the analog video signal to digital format and preparing the digital data for display. Some video digitizer components perform all these steps in hardware. Others perform some or all of these steps in software. Others may perform only a few of these steps—in which case, it is up to the program that is using the video digitizer to perform these tasks.

Figure 8-1 Basic tasks of a video digitizer

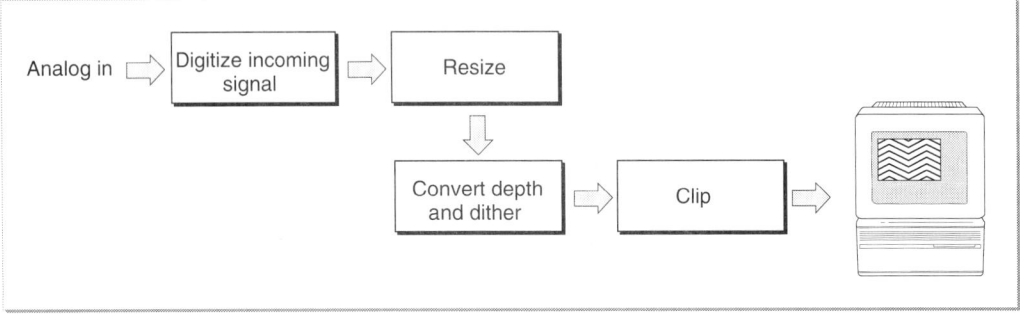

Video digitizer components resize the image by applying a transformation matrix to the digitized image. Your application specifies the matrix that is applied to the image. Matrix operations can enlarge or shrink an image, distort the image, or move the location of an image. The Movie Toolbox provides a set of functions that make it easy for you to work with transformation matrices. See the chapter "Movie Toolbox" in *Inside Macintosh: QuickTime* for more information about matrix operations.

Before the digitized image can be displayed on your computer, the video digitizer component must convert the image into an appropriate color representation. This conversion may involve dithering or pixel depth conversion. The digitizer component handles this conversion based on the destination characteristics you specify.

Video digitizer components may support clipping. Digitizers that do support clipping can display the resulting image in regions of arbitrary shapes. See the next section for a complete discussion of the techniques that digitizer components can use to perform clipping.

Video Digitizer Components

Types of Video Digitizer Components

Video digitizer components fall into four categories, distinguished by their support for clipping a digitized video image:

- basic digitizers, which do not support clipping
- alpha channel digitizers, which clip by means of an alpha channel
- mask plane digitizers, which clip by means of a mask plane
- key color digitizers, which clip by means of key colors

Basic video digitizer components are capable of placing the digitized video into memory, but they do not support any graphics overlay or video blending. If you want to perform these operations, you must do so in your application. For example, you can stop the digitizer after each frame and do the work necessary to blend the digitized video with a graphics image that is already being displayed. Unfortunately, this may cause jerkiness or discontinuity in the video stream. Other types of digitizers that support clipping make this operation much easier for your application.

Alpha channel digitizer components use a portion of each display pixel to represent the blending of video and graphical image data. This part of each pixel is referred to as an **alpha channel.** The size of the alpha channel differs depending upon the number of bits used to represent each pixel. For 32 bits per pixel modes, the alpha channel is represented in the 8 high-order bits of each 32-bit pixel. These 8 bits can define up to 256 levels of blend. For 16 bits per pixel modes, the alpha channel is represented in the high-order bit of the pixel and defines one level of blend (on or off).

Mask plane digitizer components use a pixel map to define blending. Values in this mask correspond to pixels on the screen, and they define the level of blend between video and graphical image data.

Key color digitizer components determine where to display video data based upon the color currently being displayed on the output device. These digitizers reserve one or more colors in the color table; these colors define where to display video. For example, if blue is reserved as the key color, the digitizer replaces all blue pixels in the display rectangle with the corresponding pixels of video from the input video source.

Video Digitizer Components

Source Coordinate Systems

Your application can control what part of the source video image is extracted. The digitizer then converts the specified portion of the source video signal into a digital format for your use. Video digitizer components define four areas you may need to manipulate when you define the source image for a given operation. These areas are

- the maximum source rectangle
- the active source rectangle
- the vertical blanking rectangle
- the digitizer rectangle

Figure 8-2 shows the relationships between these rectangles.

Figure 8-2   Video digitizer rectangles

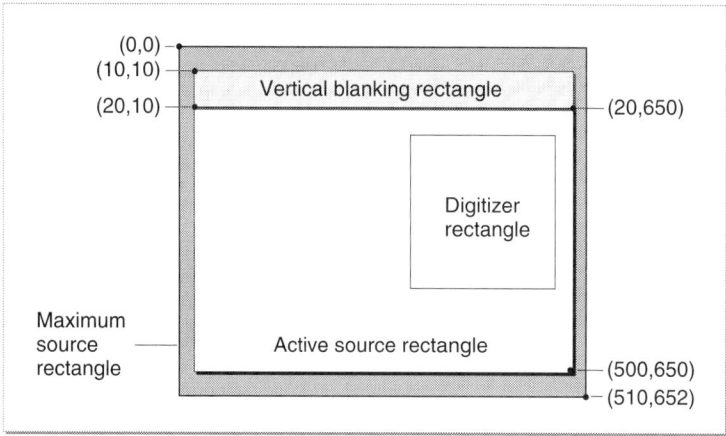

The **maximum source rectangle** defines the maximum source area that the digitizer component can grab. This rectangle usually encompasses both the vertical and horizontal blanking areas. The **active source rectangle** defines that portion of the maximum source rectangle that contains active video. The **vertical blanking rectangle** defines that portion of the input video signal that is devoted to vertical blanking. This rectangle occupies lines 10 through 19 of the input signal. Broadcast video sources may use this portion of the input signal for closed captioning, teletext, and other nonvideo information. Note that the blanking rectangle might not be contained in the maximum source rectangle.

You specify the **digitizer rectangle,** which defines that portion of the active source rectangle that you want to capture and convert.

Using Video Digitizer Components

This section describes how you can control a video digitizer component. It has been divided into the following topics:

- "Specifying Destinations" discusses how you tell the digitizer where to put the converted video data.
- "Starting and Stopping the Digitizer" discusses how you control digitization.
- "Multiple Buffering" describes a technique for improving performance.
- "Obtaining an Accurate Time of Frame Capture" tells how the sequence grabber usually supplies video digitizers with a time base. This time base lets your application get an accurate time for the capture of any specified frame.

Specifying Destinations

Video digitizer components provide several functions that allow applications to specify the destination for the digitized video stream produced by the digitizer component. You have two options for specifying the destination for the video data stream in your application.

The first option requires that the video be digitized as RGB pixels and placed into a destination pixel map. This option allows the video to be placed either onscreen or offscreen, depending upon the placement of the pixel map. Your application can use the VDSetPlayThruDestination function (described on page 8-35) to set the characteristics for this option. Your application can use the VDPreflightDestination function (described on page 8-36) to determine the capabilities of the digitizer. All video digitizer components must support this option.

The second option uses a global boundary rectangle to define the destination for the video. This option always results in onscreen images and is useful with digitizers that support hardware direct memory access (DMA) across multiple screens. The digitizer component is responsible for any required color depth conversions, image clipping and resizing, and so on. Your application can use the VDSetPlayThruGlobalRect function (described on page 8-39) to set the characteristics for this option. Your application can use the VDPreflightGlobalRect function (described on page 8-40) to determine the capabilities of the digitizer. Not all video digitizer components support this option.

Starting and Stopping the Digitizer

You can control digitization on a frame-by-frame basis in your application. The VDGrabOneFrame function (described on page 8-54) digitizes a single video frame. All video digitizer components support this function.

Alternatively, you can use the `VDSetPlayThruOnOff` function (described on page 8-53) to enable or disable digitization. When digitization is enabled, the video digitizer component places video into the specified destination continuously. The application stops the digitizer by disabling digitization. This function can be used with both destination options. However, not all video digitizer components support this function.

Multiple Buffering

You can improve the performance of frame-by-frame digitization by using multiple destination buffers for the digitized video. Your application defines a number of destination buffers to the video digitizer component and specifies the order in which those buffers are to be used. The digitizer component then fills the buffers, allowing you to switch between the buffers more quickly than your application otherwise could. In this manner, you can grab a video sequence at a higher rate with less chance of data loss. This technique can be used with both destination options.

You define the buffers to the digitizer by calling the `VDSetupBuffers` function (described on page 8-54). The `VDGrabOneFrameAsync` function (described on page 8-56) starts the process of grabbing a single video frame. The `VDDone` function (described on page 8-58) allows you to determine when the digitizer component has finished a given frame.

Obtaining an Accurate Time of Frame Capture

The sequence grabber typically gives video digitizers a time base so your application can obtain an accurate time for the capture of any given frame. Applications can set the digitizer's time base by calling the `VDSetTimeBase` function, which is described on page 8-51.

Creating Video Digitizer Components

Video digitizer components are the most convenient mechanism for presenting new sources of video data to QuickTime. For example, if you are developing special-purpose video hardware that digitizes video images from a previously unsupported source device, you should create a video digitizer component so that applications or sequence grabber components can obtain data from your device.

Refer to the chapter "Component Manager" in *Inside Macintosh: More Macintosh Toolbox* for a general discussion of how to create a component.

The remaining topics in this section discuss issues you should consider when creating a video digitizer component.

Apple has defined a functional interface for video digitizer components. For information about the functions your digitizer component must support, see "Video Digitizer Component Functions" beginning on page 8-23.

Video Digitizer Components

You can use the following enumerators to refer to the request codes for each of the functions that your component must support.

```
enum {
    /* video digitizer interface */
    kSelectVDGetMaxSrcRect              = 0x1,/* VDGetMaxSrcRect (required) */
    kSelectVDGetActiveSrcRect           = 0x2,/* VDGetActiveSrcRect
                                                        (required) */
    kSelectVDSetDigitizerRect           = 0x3,/* VDSetDigitizerRect
                                                        (required) */
    kSelectVDGetDigitizerRect           = 0x4,/* VDGetDigitizerRect
                                                        (required) */
    kSelectVDGetVBlankRect              = 0x5,/* VDGetVBlankRect (required) */
    kSelectVDGetMaskPixMap              = 0x6,/* VDGetMaskPixMap */
    kSelectVDGetPlayThruDestination     = 0x8,/* VDGetPlayThruDestination
                                                        (required) */
    kSelectVDUseThisCLUT                = 0x9,/* VDUseThisCLUT */
    kSelectVDSetInputGammaValue         = 0xA,/* VDSetInputGammaValue */
    kSelectVDGetInputGammaValue         = 0xB,/* VDGetInputGammaValue */
    kSelectVDSetBrightness              = 0xC,/* VDSetBrightness */
    kSelectVDGetBrightness              = 0xD,/* VDGetBrightness */
    kSelectVDSetContrast                = 0xE,/* VDSetContrast */
    kSelectVDSetHue                     = 0xF,/* VDSetHue */
    kSelectVDSetSharpness               = 0x10,/* VDSetSharpness */
    kSelectVDSetSaturation              = 0x11,/* VDSetSaturation */
    kSelectVDGetContrast                = 0x12,/* VDGetContrast */
    kSelectVDGetHue                     = 0x13,/* VDGetHue */
    kSelectVDGetSharpness               = 0x14,/* VDGetSharpness */
    kSelectVDGetSaturation              = 0x15,/* VDGetSaturation */
    kSelectVDGrabOneFrame               = 0x16,/* VDGrabOneFrame
                                                        (required) */
    kSelectVDGetMaxAuxBuffer            = 0x17,/* VDGetMaxAuxBuffer */
    kSelectVDGetDigitizerInfo           = 0x19,/* VDGetDigitizerInfo
                                                        (required) */
    kSelectVDGetCurrentFlags            = 0x1A,/* VDGetCurrentFlags
                                                        (required) */
    kSelectVDSetKeyColor                = 0x1B,/* VDSetKeyColor */
    kSelectVDGetKeyColor                = 0x1C,/* VDGetKeyColor */
    kSelectVDAddKeyColor                = 0x1D,/* VDAddKeyColor */
    kSelectVDGetNextKeyColor            = 0x1E,/* VDGetNextKeyColor */
    kSelectVDSetKeyColorRange           = 0x1F,/* VDSetKeyColorRange */
    kSelectVDGetKeyColorRange           = 0x20,/* VDGetKeyColorRange */
    kSelectVDSetDigitizerUserInterrupt  = 0x21,
                                               /* VDSetDigitizerUserInterrupt */
```

CHAPTER 8

Video Digitizer Components

```
kSelectVDSetInputColorSpaceMode      = 0x22,/* VDSetInputColorSpaceMode */
kSelectVDGetInputColorSpaceMode      = 0x23,/* VDGetInputColorSpaceMode */
kSelectVDSetClipState                = 0x24,/* VDSetClipState */
kSelectVDSetClipState                = 0x25,/* VDGetClipState */
kSelectVDSetClipRgn                  = 0x26,/* VDSetClipRgn */
kSelectVDClearClipRgn                = 0x27,/* VDClearClipRgn */
kSelectVDGetCLUTInUse                = 0x28,/* VDGetCLUTInUse */
kSelectVDSetPLLFilterType            = 0x29,/* VDSetPLLFilterType */
kSelectVDGetPLLFilterType            = 0x2A,/* VDGetPLLFilterType */
kSelectVDGetMaskandValue             = 0x2B,/* VDGetMaskandValue */
kSelectVDSetMasterBlendLevel         = 0x2C,/* VDSetMasterBlendLevel */
kSelectVDSetPlayThruDestination      = 0x2D,/* VDSetPlayThruDestination */
kSelectVDSetPlayThruOnOff            = 0x2E,/* VDSetPlayThruOnOff */
kSelectVDSetFieldPreference          = 0x2F,/* VDSetFieldPreference
                                                 (required) */
kSelectVDGetFieldPreference          = 0x30,/* VDGetFieldPreference
                                                 (required) */
kSelectVDPreflightDestination        = 0x32,/* VDPreflightDestination
                                                 (required) */
kSelectVDPreflightGlobalRect         = 0x33,/* VDPreflightGlobalRect */
kSelectVDSetPlayThruGlobalRect       = 0x34,/* VDSetPlayThruGlobalRect */
kSelectVDSetInputGammaRecord         = 0x35,/* VDSetInputGammaRecord */
kSelectVDGetInputGammaRecord         = 0x36,/* VDGetInputGammaRecord */
kSelectVDSetBlackLevelValue          = 0x37,/* VDSetBlackLevelValue */
kSelectVDGetBlackLevelValue          = 0x38,/* VDGetBlackLevelValue */
kSelectVDSetWhiteLevelValue          = 0x39,/* VDSetWhiteLevelValue */
kSelectVDGetWhiteLevelValue          = 0x3A,/* VDGetWhiteLevelValue */
kSelectVDGetVideoDefaults            = 0x3B,/* VDGetVideoDefaults */
kSelectVDGetNumberOfInputs           = 0x3C,/* VDGetNumberOfInputs */
kSelectVDGetInputFormat              = 0x3D,/* VDGetInputFormat */
kSelectVDSetInput                    = 0x3E,/* VDSetInput */
kSelectVDGetInput                    = 0x3F,/* VDGetInput */
kSelectVDSetInputStandard            = 0x40,/* VDSetInputStandard */
kSelectVDSetupBuffers                = 0x41,/* VDSetupBuffers */
kSelectVDGrabOneFrameAsync           = 0x42,/* VDGrabOneFrameAsync */
kSelectVDDone                        = 0x43,/* VDDone */
kSelectVDSetCompression              = 0x44,/* VDSetCompression */
kSelectVDCompressOneFrameAsync       = 0x45,/* VDCompressOneFrameAsync */
kSelectVDCompressDone                = 0x46,/* VDCompressDone */
kSelectVDReleaseCompressBuffer       = 0x47,/* VDReleaseCompressBuffer */
kSelectVDGetImageDescription         = 0x48,/* VDGetImageDescription */
kSelectVDResetCompressSequence       = 0x49,/* VDResetCompressSequence */
kSelectVDSetCompressionOnOff         = 0x4A,/* VDSetCompressionOnOff */
```

```
kSelectVDGetCompressionTypes        = 0x4B,/* VDGetCompressionTypes */
kSelectVDSetTimeBase                = 0x4C,/* VDSetTimeBase */
kSelectVDSetFrameRate               = 0x4D,/* VDSetFrameRate */
kSelectVDGetDataRate                = 0x4E,/* VDGetDataRate */
kSelectVDGetSoundInputDriver        = 0x4F,/* VDGetSoundInputDriver */
kSelectVDGetDMADepths               = 0x50,/* VDGetDMADepths */
kSelectVDGetPreferredTimeScale      = 0x51,/* VDGetPreferredTimeScale */
kSelectVDReleaseAsyncBuffers        = 0x52,/* VDReleaseAsyncBuffers */
};
```

Component Type and Subtype Values

Apple has defined a type value for video digitizer components. All video digitizer components have a component type value of 'vdig'. You can use the following constant to specify the component type value.

```
#define videoDigitizerComponentType = 'vdig'
```

There are no special conventions applied to the subtype value of video digitizer components.

Required Functions

Video digitizer components support a rich functional interface that can accommodate devices with quite varied capabilities. To relieve you from having to support irrelevant functions, Apple has made several video digitizer functions optional.

At a minimum, your video digitizer component must support the following functions:

VDGetActiveSrcRect	VDGetCurrentFlags
VDGetDigitizerInfo	VDGetDigitizerRect
VDGetFieldPreference	VDGetInput
VDGetInputFormat	VDGetMaxSrcRect
VDGetNumberOfInputs	VDGetPlayThruDestination
VDGetVBlankRect	VDGetVideoDefaults
VDGrabOneFrame	VDPreflightDestination
VDSetDigitizerRect	VDSetFieldPreference
VDSetInput	VDSetInputStandard
VDSetPlayThruDestination	

All of these functions are required for all video digitizer components.

Optional Functions

Based on the type of device your component supports, you may have to implement functions other than those listed in "Required Functions," and you may have to set some of your component's capability flags. Read this section to learn which additional functions your component needs to support and how to set your capability flags properly.

If your component does not support a particular function, be sure to return a result code value of `digiUnimpErr`.

Note
Hardware support for the simultaneous capture and display of frames on the screen is called *playthrough* in these sections. ◆

Frame Grabbers Without Playthrough

Suppose your video digitization hardware grabs frames but cannot simultaneously display the frames on the screen. Suppose also that your hardware supplies the grabbed frames in QuickDraw pixel maps at specific pixel depths (say, 16 and 32 bits per pixel). For details on QuickDraw pixel maps, see the chapter "Basic QuickDraw" in *Inside Macintosh: Imaging*.

In this case, you should set the following component capability flags:

`digiOutDoes16`   Set this flag to 1.
`digiOutDoes32`   Set this flag to 1.
                    Set other depth flags to 0.
`digiOutDoesHWPlayThru`
                    Set this flag to 0.
`digiOutDoesDMA`
                    Set this flag to 0.

If your component can operate asynchronously, you should also set the following flag:

`digiOutDoesAsyncGrabs`
                    Set this flag to 1 if your component can operate asynchronously.

Frame grabbers that support asynchronous operation must support the following optional functions:

VDDone   VDGrabOneFrameAsync
VDReleaseAsyncBuffers   VDSetupBuffers

Frame Grabbers With Hardware Playthrough

If your frame grabber hardware provides support for playing the captured images directly, you need to support one additional function beyond those discussed in "Frame Grabbers Without Playthrough." The `VDSetPlayThruOnOff` function (described on page 8-53) allows the application to turn playthrough on and off.

CHAPTER 8

Video Digitizer Components

You should also set the `digiOutDoesHWPlayThru` capability flag (described on page 8-18) to 1. In addition, be sure to use the `gdh` field in the digitizer information structure to identify your component's display device. For details on the video digitizer information structure, see page 8-20.

Key Color and Alpha Channel Devices

As a further elaboration on a basic frame grabber, your device could support the display or mixing of output data via an alpha channel or through the use of key colors (see "Types of Video Digitizer Components" on page 8-5 for more information about alpha channels and key colors). In either case, image data cannot be read directly from the screen. Therefore, you must set the `digiOutDoesUnreadableScreenBits` capability flag to 1. For more on the video digitizer capability flags, see "Capability Flags" beginning on page 8-14.

Your component must load its alpha channel or fill in the key color whenever playthrough is enabled or when the destination changes.

Compressed Source Devices

You may create a video digitizer component that supports a device that delivers compressed image data. In this case, your component is not capable of displaying the data directly.

Your component should set the following capability flags:

`digiOutDoesCompress`
: Set this flag to 1.

`digiOutDoesCompressOnly`
: Set this flag to 1 if your component cannot display the images directly.

`digiOutDoesPlayThruDuringCompress`
: Set this flag to 1 if your component cannot display the images directly.

In addition, frame grabbers that support compressed source devices must support the following optional functions:

`VDCompressDone`	`VDCompressOneFrameAsync`
`VDGetCompressionTypes`	`VDGetDataRate`
`VDGetImageDescription`	`VDResetCompressSequence`
`VDSetCompression`	`VDSetCompressionOnOff`
`VDSetFrameRate`	`VDSetTimeBase`

If your hardware generates compressed data that cannot be decompressed by any standard QuickTime image decompressor components, be sure to provide an appropriate decompressor component so that the data you provide can be displayed.

Video Digitizer Components Reference

The following sections describe the constants, data structures, and functions that are specific to video digitizer components.

Constants

This section provides details on the video digitizer component's capability and current flags.

Capability Flags

Video digitizer components report their capabilities to your application by means of capability flags. These flags are formatted as part of the digitizer information structure you obtain by calling the `VDGetDigitizerInfo` function, which is described on page 8-24. There are two sets of flags: one set describes the input capabilities of the video digitizer component; the other describes its output capabilities.

Video digitizer components support the following input capability flags:

`digiInDoesNTSC`
: Indicates that the video digitizer supports **National Television System Committee (NTSC)** format input video signals. This flag is set to 1 if the digitizer component supports NTSC video.

`digiInDoesPAL`
: Indicates that the video digitizer component supports **Phase Alternation Line (PAL)** format input video signals. This flag is set to 1 if the digitizer component supports PAL video.

`digiInDoesSECAM`
: Indicates that the video digitizer component supports **Systeme Electronique Couleur avec Memoire (SECAM)** format input video signals. This flag is set to 1 if the digitizer component supports SECAM video.

`digiInDoesGenLock`
: Indicates that the video digitizer component supports **genlock;** that is, the digitizer can derive its timing from an external time base. This flag is set to 1 if the digitizer component supports genlock.

`digiInDoesComposite`
: Indicates that the video digitizer component supports composite input video. This flag is set to 1 if the digitizer component supports composite input.

Video Digitizer Components

digitInDoesSVideo
: Indicates that the video digitizer component supports **s-video** input video. This flag is set to 1 if the digitizer component supports s-video input.

digiInDoesComponent
: Indicates that the video digitizer component supports RGB input video. This flag is set to 1 if the digitizer component supports RGB input.

digiInVTR_Broadcast
: Indicates that the video digitizer component can distinguish between an input signal that emanates from a videotape player and a broadcast signal. This flag is set to 1 if the digitizer component can differentiate between the two different signal types.

digiInDoesColor
: Indicates that the video digitizer component supports color input. This flag is set to 1 if the digitizer component can accept color input.

digiInDoesBW
: Indicates that the video digitizer component supports grayscale input. This flag is set to 1 if the digitizer component can accept grayscale input.

Video digitizer components support the following output capability flags:

digiOutDoes1
: Indicates that the video digitizer component can work with pixel maps that contain 1-bit pixels. If this flag is set to 1, then the digitizer component can write images that contain 1-bit pixels. If this flag is set to 0, then the digitizer component cannot handle such images.

digiOutDoes2
: Indicates that the video digitizer component can work with pixel maps that contain 2-bit pixels. If this flag is set to 1, then the digitizer component can write images that contain 2-bit pixels. If this flag is set to 0, then the digitizer component cannot handle such images.

digiOutDoes4
: Indicates that the video digitizer component can work with pixel maps that contain 4-bit pixels. If this flag is set to 1, then the digitizer component can write images that contain 4-bit pixels. If this flag is set to 0, then the digitizer component cannot handle such images.

digiOutDoes8
: Indicates that the video digitizer component can work with pixel maps that contain 8-bit pixels. If this flag is set to 1, then the digitizer component can write images that contain 8-bit pixels. If this flag is set to 0, then the digitizer component cannot handle such images.

digiOutDoes16
: Indicates that the video digitizer component can work with pixel maps that contain 16-bit pixels. If this flag is set to 1, then the digitizer component can write images that contain 16-bit pixels. If this flag is set to 0, then the digitizer component cannot handle such images.

`digiOutDoes32`
: Indicates that the video digitizer component can work with pixel maps that contain 32-bit pixels. If this flag is set to 1, then the digitizer component can write images that contain 32-bit pixels. If this flag is set to 0, then the digitizer component cannot handle such images.

`digiOutDoesDither`
: Indicates that the video digitizer component supports dithering. If this flag is set to 1, the component supports dithering of colors. If this flag is set to 0, the digitizer component does not support dithering.

`digiOutDoesStretch`
: Indicates that the video digitizer component can stretch images to arbitrary sizes. If this flag is set to 1, the digitizer component can stretch images. If this flag is set to 0, the digitizer component does not support stretching.

`digiOutDoesShrink`
: Indicates that the video digitizer component can shrink images to arbitrary sizes. If this flag is set to 1, the digitizer component can shrink images. If this flag is set to 0, the digitizer component does not support shrinking.

`digiOutDoesMask`
: Indicates that the video digitizer component can handle clipping regions. If this flag is set to 1, the digitizer component can mask to an arbitrary clipping region. If this flag is set to 0, the digitizer component does not support clipping regions.

`digiOutDoesDouble`
: Indicates that the video digitizer component supports stretching to quadruple size when displaying the output video. The parameters for the stretch operation are specified in the matrix structure for the request—the component modifies the scaling attributes of the matrix (see the chapter "Movie Toolbox" in *Inside Macintosh: QuickTime* for information about transformation matrices). If this flag is set to 1, the digitizer component can stretch an image to exactly four times its original size, up to the maximum size specified by the `maxDestHeight` and `maxDestWidth` fields in the digitizer information structure. If this flag is set to 0, the digitizer component does not support stretching to quadruple size.

`digiOutDoesQuad`
: Indicates that the video digitizer component supports stretching an image to 16 times its original size when displaying the output video. The parameters for the stretch operation are specified in the matrix structure for the request—the component modifies the scaling attributes of the matrix (see the chapter "Movie Toolbox" in *Inside Macintosh: QuickTime* for information about transformation matrices). If this flag is set to 1, the digitizer component can stretch an image to exactly 16 times its original size, up to the maximum size specified by the `maxDestHeight` and `maxDestWidth` fields in the digitizer information structure. If this flag is set to 0, the digitizer component does not support this capability.

Video Digitizer Components

`digiOutDoesQuarter`
: Indicates that the video digitizer component can shrink an image to one-quarter of its original size when displaying the output video. The parameters for the shrink operation are specified in the matrix structure for the request—the component modifies the scaling attributes of the matrix (see the chapter "Movie Toolbox" in *Inside Macintosh: QuickTime* for information about transformation matrices). If this flag is set to 1, the digitizer component can shrink an image to exactly one-quarter of its original size, down to the minimum size specified by the `minDestHeight` and `minDestWidth` fields in the digitizer information structure. If this flag is set to 0, the digitizer component does not support this capability.

`digiOutDoesSixteenth`
: Indicates that the video digitizer component can shrink an image to 1/16 of its original size when displaying the output video. The parameters for the shrink operation are specified in the matrix structure for the request—the digitizer component modifies the scaling attributes of the matrix (see the chapter "Movie Toolbox" in *Inside Macintosh: QuickTime* for information about transformation matrices). If this flag is set to 1, the digitizer component can shrink an image to exactly 1/16 of its original size, down to the minimum size specified by the `minDestHeight` and `minDestWidth` fields in the digitizer information structure. If this flag is set to 0, the digitizer component does not support this capability.

`digiOutDoesRotate`
: Indicates that the video digitizer component can rotate an image when displaying the output video. The parameters for the rotation are specified in the matrix structure for an operation. If this flag is set to 1, the digitizer component can rotate the image. If this flag is set to 0, the digitizer component cannot rotate the resulting image.

`digiOutDoesHorizFlip`
: Indicates that the video digitizer component can flip an image horizontally when displaying the output video. The parameters for the horizontal flip are specified in the matrix structure for an operation. If this flag is set to 1, the digitizer component can flip the image. If this flag is set to 0, the digitizer component cannot flip the resulting image.

`digiOutDoesVertFlip`
: Indicates that the video digitizer component can flip an image vertically when displaying the output video. The parameters for the vertical flip are specified in the matrix structure for an operation. If this flag is set to 1, the digitizer component can flip the image. If this flag is set to 0, the digitizer component cannot flip the resulting image.

`digiOutDoesSkew`
: Indicates that the video digitizer component can skew an image when displaying the output video. Skewing an image distorts it linearly along only a single axis—for example, drawing a rectangular image into a parallelogram-shaped region. The parameters for the skew operation are specified in the matrix structure for the request. If this flag is set to 1, the digitizer component can skew an image. If this flag is set to 0, the digitizer component does not support this capability.

CHAPTER 8

Video Digitizer Components

`digiOutDoesBlend`
: Indicates that the video digitizer component can blend the resulting image with a matte when displaying the output video. The matte is provided by the application by defining either an alpha channel or a mask plane. If this flag is set to 1, the digitizer component can blend. If this flag is set to 0, the digitizer component does not support this capability.

`digiOutDoesWarp`
: Indicates that the video digitizer component can warp an image when displaying the output video. Warping an image distorts it along one or more axes, perhaps nonlinearly, in effect "bending" the result region. The parameters for the warp operation are specified in the matrix structure for the request. If this flag is set to 1, the digitizer component can warp an image. If this flag is set to 0, the digitizer component does not support this capability.

`digiOutDoesDMA`
: Indicates that the video digitizer component can write to any screen or to offscreen memory. If this flag is set to 1, the digitizer component can use DMA to write to any screen or memory location.

`digiOutDoesHWPlayThru`
: Indicates that the video digitizer component does not need idle time in order to display its video. If this flag is set to 1, your application does not need to grant processor time to the digitizer component at normal display speeds.

`digiOutDoesILUT`
: Indicates that the video digitizer component supports inverse lookup tables for indexed color modes. If this flag is set to 1, the digitizer component uses inverse lookup tables when appropriate.

`digiOutDoesKeyColor`
: Indicates that the video digitizer component supports clipping by means of key colors. If this flag is set to 1, the digitizer component can clip to a region defined by a key color.

`digiOutDoesAsyncGrabs`
: Indicates that the video digitizer component can operate asynchronously. If this flag is set to 1, your application can use the `VDSetupBuffers` and `VDGrabOneFrameAsync` functions (described on page 8-54 and page 8-56, respectively).

`digiOutDoesUnreadableScreenBits`
: Indicates that the video digitizer may place pixels on the screen that cannot be used when compressing images.

`digiOutDoesCompress`
: Indicates that the video digitizer component supports compressed source devices. These devices provide compressed data directly, without having to use the Image Compression Manager. See "Controlling Compressed Source Devices" beginning on page 8-42 for more information about the functions that applications can use to work with compressed source devices.

CHAPTER 8

Video Digitizer Components

`digiOutDoesCompressOnly`
: Indicates that the video digitizer component only provides compressed image data; the component cannot provide displayable data. This flag only applies to digitizers that support compressed source devices.

`digiOutDoesPlayThruDuringCompress`
: Indicates that the video digitizer component can draw images on the screen at the same time that it is delivering compressed image data. This flag only applies to digitizers that support compressed source devices.

Current Flags

Video digitizer components report their current status to your application by means of flags. These flags are formatted as part of the digitizer information structure that you obtain by calling the `VDGetDigitizerInfo` function (described on page 8-24). Alternatively, you can obtain these flags by calling the `VDGetCurrentFlags` function (described on page 8-25). There are two sets of flags: one set describes the status of the digitizer with respect to its input signal; the other describes its status with respect to its output.

Video digitizer components report their current status by returning a flags field that contains 1 bit for each of the capability flags (discussed in "Capability Flags" beginning on page 8-14) plus additional flags as appropriate. The digitizer component sets these flags to reflect its current status. When reporting input status, for example, a video digitizer component sets the `digiInDoesGenLock` flag to 1 whenever the digitizer component is deriving its time signal from the input video. When reporting its input capabilities, the digitizer component sets this flag to 1 to indicate that it can derive its timing from the input video.

Video digitizer components report their current input status by returning a flags field that contains a bit for each of the input capability flags (discussed in "Capability Flags" beginning on page 8-14) plus one additional flag.

The additional flag is as follows:

`digiInSignalLock`
: Indicates that the video digitizer component is locked onto the input signal. If this flag is set to 1, the digitizer component detects either vertical or horizontal signal lock.

Video digitizer components report their current output status by returning a flags field that contains a bit for each of the output capability flags discussed in "Capability Flags" beginning on page 8-14. The digitizer component sets these flags to reflect its current output status.

Data Types

This section discusses the data structures that are used by video digitizer components and by applications that use video digitizer components.

The Digitizer Information Structure

Your application can retrieve information about the capabilities and current status of a video digitizer component. You call the `VDGetDigitizerInfo` function, described on page 8-24, to retrieve all this information from a video digitizer component. In response, the component formats a digitizer information structure. The contents of this structure fully define the capabilities and current status of the video digitizer component.

Note

If you are interested only in the current status information, you can call the `VDGetCurrentFlags` function, which is described on page 8-25. This function returns the input and output current flags of the video digitizer component. ◆

The `DigitizerInfo` data type defines the layout of the digitizer information structure.

```
struct DigitizerInfo {
    short    vdigType;              /* type of digitizer component */
    long     inputCapabilityFlags;  /* input video signal features */
    long     outputCapabilityFlags; /* output digitized video data
                                       features of digitizer component */
    long     inputCurrentFlags;     /* status of input video signal */
    long     outputCurrentFlags;    /* status of output digitized
                                       video information */
    short    slot;                  /* for connection purposes */
    GDHandle gdh;                   /* for digitizers with preferred
                                       screen */
    GDHandle maskgdh;               /* for digitizers with mask planes */
    short    minDestHeight;         /* smallest resizable height */
    short    minDestWidth;          /* smallest resizable width */
    short    maxDestHeight;         /* largest resizable height */
    short    maxDestWidth;          /* largest resizable width */
    short    blendLevels;           /* number of blend levels supported
                                       (2 if 1-bit mask) */
    long     private;               /* reserved--set to 0 */
};
typedef struct DigitizerInfo DigitizerInfo;
```

CHAPTER 8

Video Digitizer Components

Field descriptions

`vdigType`   Specifies the type of video digitizer component. Valid values are

  `vdTypeBasic`
  Basic video digitizer—does not support any clipping

  `vdTypeAlpha`
  Supports clipping by means of an alpha channel

  `vdTypeMask`
  Supports clipping by means of a mask plane

  `vdTypeKey`
  Supports clipping by means of key colors

`inputCapabilityFlags`
  Specifies the capabilities of the video digitizer component with respect to the input video signal. These flags are discussed in "Capability Flags" beginning on page 8-14.

`outputCapabilityFlags`
  Specifies the capabilities of the video digitizer component with respect to the output digitized video information. These flags are discussed in "Capability Flags" beginning on page 8-14.

`inputCurrentFlags`
  Specifies the current status of the video digitizer with respect to the input video signal. These flags are discussed in "Current Flags" on page 8-19.

`outputCurrentFlags`
  Specifies the current status of the video digitizer with respect to the output digitized video information. These flags are discussed in "Current Flags" on page 8-19.

`slot`   Identifies the slot that contains the video digitizer interface card.

`gdh`   Contains a handle to the graphics device that defines the screen to which the digitized data is to be written. Set this field to `nil` if your application is not constrained to a particular graphics device.

`maskgdh`   Contains a handle to the graphics device that contains the mask plane. This field is used only by digitizers that clip by means of mask planes.

`minDestHeight`
  Indicates the smallest height value the digitizer component can accommodate in its destination.

`minDestWidth`
  Indicates the smallest width value the digitizer component can accommodate in its destination.

`maxDestHeight`
  Indicates the largest height value the digitizer component can accommodate in its destination.

`maxDestWidth`
  Indicates the largest width value the digitizer component can accommodate in its destination.

CHAPTER 8

Video Digitizer Components

blendLevels
: Specifies the number of blend levels the video digitizer component supports.

private
: Reserved. Set this field to 0.

The Buffer List Structure

If you are using more than one asynchronous output buffer, you must define the output buffers to the video digitizer component. You define these output buffers by calling the `VDSetupBuffers` function (described on page 8-54). You specify the buffers to that function in a buffer list structure. Note that all the output buffers must be the same size and must accommodate output rectangles of the same dimensions.

The `VdigBufferRecList` data type defines a buffer list structure.

```
struct VdigBufferRecList {
    short           count;    /* number of buffers defined by
                                 this structure */
    MatrixRecordPtr matrix;   /* tranformation matrix applied to
                                 destination rectangles before
                                 video image is displayed */
    RgnHandle       mask;     /* clipping region applied to
                                 destination rectangle before
                                 video image is displayed */
    VdigBufferRec   list[1];  /* array of output buffer
                                 specifications */
};
```

Field descriptions

count
: Specifies the number of buffers defined by this structure. The value of this field must correspond to the number of entries in the `list` array.

matrix
: Specifies the transformation matrix that is applied to all of the destination rectangles before the video image is displayed. You must specify a matrix. If you do not want to perform any transformations, use the identity matrix.

mask
: Specifies a clipping region that is applied to the destination rectangle before the video image is displayed. Note that this region applies to only the first destination buffer. If you want the region to apply to all of your destination buffers, you must do this yourself. For example, you can use QuickDraw's `OffsetRgn` function, which is described in the chapter "Basic QuickDraw" in *Inside Macintosh: Imaging*. If you do not want to specify a clipping region, set this field to `nil`.

list
: Contains an array of output buffer specifications. Each buffer is represented by a buffer structure. The format and content of this structure are described in the next section.

The Buffer Structure

The `VdigBufferRec` data type defines a buffer structure.

```
typedef struct {
   PixMapHandle    dest;        /* handle to pixel map for
                                   destination buffer */
   Point           location;    /* location of video destination
                                   in pixel map */
   long            reserved;    /* reserved--set to 0 */
} VdigBufferRec;
```

Field descriptions

dest
: Contains a handle to the pixel map that defines the destination buffer.

location
: Specifies the location of the video destination in the pixel map specified by the `dest` field. This point identifies the upper-left corner of the destination rectangle. The size and scaling of the destination rectangle are governed by the `matrix` and `mask` fields of the buffer list structure that contains this structure.

reserved
: Reserved for use by Apple. Set this field to 0.

Video Digitizer Component Functions

This section describes the functions that are provided by video digitizer components. These functions are described from the perspective of an application that uses video digitizer components. If you are developing a video digitizer component, your digitizer component must behave as described here.

This section has been divided into the following topics:

- "Getting Information About Video Digitizer Components" describes the functions that allow applications to obtain information about the capabilities of video digitizer components.

- "Setting Source Characteristics" discusses the video digitizer functions that allow applications to establish the source video environment.

- "Selecting an Input Source" describes how applications select the input video source.

- "Setting Video Destinations" describes the functions that allow applications to establish the destination display environment.

- "Controlling Compressed Source Devices" describes the functions that allow applications to work with devices that return compressed image data.

- "Controlling Digitization" describes functions that allow applications to start and stop digitization.

- "Controlling Color" discusses the functions that allow applications to control color mapping in the video digitizer component.

- "Controlling Analog Video" describes several functions that allow applications to control the characteristics of the input analog video signal.
- "Selectively Displaying Video" discusses functions that allow applications to work with the key colors that are used to control video display.
- "Clipping" discusses functions that allow applications to control the clipping region used by video digitizer components.
- "Utility Functions" describes a few utility functions that are supported by video digitizer components.

Note

If you are developing an application that uses video digitizer components, you should read the sections that are appropriate to your application. If you are developing a video digitizer component, you should read all the sections. ◆

These functions specify the video digitizer components for their requests with a reference obtained from the Component Manager's `OpenComponent` function. See the chapter "Component Manager" in *Inside Macintosh: More Macintosh Toolbox* for details.

Getting Information About Video Digitizer Components

This section discusses functions that allow applications to obtain information about the capabilities and current state of video digitizer components.

You can use the `VDGetDigitizerInfo` function in your application to retrieve information about the capabilities of a video digitizer component. You can use the `VDGetCurrentFlags` function to obtain current status information from a video digitizer component.

VDGetDigitizerInfo

The `VDGetDigitizerInfo` function returns capability and status information about a specified video digitizer component.

All video digitizer components must support this function.

```
pascal VideoDigitizerError VDGetDigitizerInfo
                            (VideoDigitizerComponent ci,
                             DigitizerInfo *info);
```

ci   Specifies the video digitizer component for the request. Applications obtain this reference from the Component Manager's `OpenComponent` function.

Video Digitizer Components

info
Contains a pointer to a digitizer information structure. The `VDGetDigitizerInfo` function returns information describing the capabilities of the specified video digitizer into this structure. See "The Digitizer Information Structure" on page 8-20 for a complete description.

DESCRIPTION

The `VDGetDigitizerInfo` function returns the capability and status information in a digitizer information structure (defined by the `DigitizerInfo` data type).

RESULT CODE

noErr   0   No error

SEE ALSO

Your application may also use the `VDGetCurrentFlags` function (described in the next section) to retrieve just the current status information about a video digitizer component.

VDGetCurrentFlags

The `VDGetCurrentFlags` function returns status information about a specified video digitizer component.

All video digitizer components must support this function.

```
pascal VideoDigitizerError VDGetCurrentFlags
                                (VideoDigitizerComponent ci,
                                long *inputCurrentFlag,
                                long *outputCurrentFlag);
```

ci
Specifies the video digitizer component for the request. Applications obtain this reference from the Component Manager's `OpenComponent` function.

inputCurrentFlag
Contains a pointer to a long integer that is to receive the current input state flags for the video digitizer component. The `VDGetCurrentFlags` function returns the current input state flags into this location. See "Current Flags" on page 8-19 for a complete description of these flags.

outputCurrentFlag
Contains a pointer to a long integer that is to receive the current output state flags for the video digitizer component. The `VDGetCurrentFlags` function returns the current output state flags into this location. See "Current Flags" on page 8-19 for a complete description of these flags.

DESCRIPTION

The `VDGetCurrentFlags` function returns the status information into two fields that contain flags specifying the current input and output status of the digitizer component.

You can also use the `VDGetDigitizerInfo` function (described in the previous section) in your application to retrieve capability and current status information about a video digitizer component.

The `VDGetCurrentFlags` function is often more convenient than the `VDGetDigitizerInfo` function. For example, this function provides a simple mechanism for determining whether a video digitizer is receiving a valid input signal. An application can retrieve the current input state flags and test the high-order bit by examining the sign of the returned value. If the value is negative (that is, the high-order bit, `digiInSignalLock`, is set to 1), the digitizer component is receiving a valid input signal.

RESULT CODE

noErr   0   No error

Setting Source Characteristics

This section discusses the video digitizer component functions that allow applications to set the spatial characteristics of the source video signal. You can use these functions in your application to set and retrieve information about the maximum source rectangle, the active source rectangle, the vertical blanking rectangle, and the digitizer rectangle. For a complete discussion of the relationship between these rectangles, see "About Video Digitizer Components," which begins on page 8-3.

You can use the `VDGetMaxSrcRect` function in your application to get the size and location of the maximum source rectangle. Similarly, the `VDGetActiveSrcRect` function allows you to get this information about the active source rectangle, and the `VDGetVBlankRect` function enables you to obtain information about the vertical blanking rectangle.

You can use the `VDSetDigitizerRect` function to set the size and location of the digitizer rectangle. The `VDGetDigitizerRect` function lets you retrieve the size and location of this rectangle.

VDGetMaxSrcRect

The `VDGetMaxSrcRect` function returns the maximum source rectangle.

```
pascal VideoDigitizerError VDGetMaxSrcRect
                        (VideoDigitizerComponent ci,
                         short inputStd,
                         Rect *maxSrcRect);
```

Video Digitizer Components

`ci` Specifies the video digitizer component for the request. Applications obtain this reference from the Component Manager's `OpenComponent` function.

`inputStd` A short integer that specifies the input video signal associated with this maximum source rectangle.

`maxSrcRect` Contains a pointer to a rectangle that is to receive the size and location information for the maximum source rectangle.

DESCRIPTION

The maximum source rectangle defines the spatial boundaries of the input video signal. All other rectangles—active source rectangle, digitizer rectangle, and vertical blanking rectangle—are defined relative to the maximum source rectangle. For a complete discussion of the relationship between these rectangles, see "About Video Digitizer Components," which begins on page 8-3.

All video digitizer components must support this function.

RESULT CODES

```
noErr            0      No error
qtParamErr      –2202   Invalid parameter value
```

VDGetActiveSrcRect

The `VDGetActiveSrcRect` function allows applications to obtain the size and location information for the active source rectangle used by a video digitizer component.

```
pascal VideoDigitizerError VDGetActiveSrcRect
                            (VideoDigitizerComponent ci,
                             short inputStd,
                             Rect *activeSrcRect);
```

`ci` Specifies the video digitizer component for the request. Applications obtain this reference from the Component Manager's `OpenComponent` function.

`inputStd` A short integer that specifies the input video signal associated with this maximum source rectangle.

`activeSrcRect` Contains a pointer to a rectangle that is to receive the size and location information for the active source rectangle.

DESCRIPTION

The source rectangle is that area in the source video image that contains active video. The video digitizer component returns spatial information that is relative to the maximum source rectangle. For a complete discussion of the relationship between these rectangles, see "About Video Digitizer Components," which begins on page 8-3.

All video digitizer components must support this function.

RESULT CODES

```
noErr          0      No error
qtParamErr    –2202   Invalid parameter value
```

VDGetVBlankRect

The `VDGetVBlankRect` function returns the vertical blanking rectangle.

```
pascal VideoDigitizerError VDGetVBlankRect
                            (VideoDigitizerComponent ci,
                                short inputStd,
                                Rect *vBlankRect);
```

ci
: Specifies the video digitizer component for the request. Applications obtain this reference from the Component Manager's `OpenComponent` function.

inputStd
: Specifies a short integer for the signaling standard used in the source video signal. Valid values are

    ntscIn   Input video signal to digitize is in NTSC format
    palIn   Input video signal to digitize is in PAL format
    secamIn Input video signal to digitize is in SECAM format

vBlankRect
: Contains a pointer to a rectangle that is to receive the size and location information for the vertical blanking rectangle.

DESCRIPTION

The vertical blanking rectangle defines the vertical blanking area in the input video signal, and it corresponds to lines 10 through 19 of the incoming video signal. The video digitizer component returns spatial information that is relative to the maximum source

CHAPTER 8

Video Digitizer Components

rectangle. For a complete discussion of the relationship between these rectangles, see "About Video Digitizer Components," which begins on page 8-3.

All video digitizer components must support this function.

RESULT CODES

noErr	0	No error
qtParamErr	–2202	Invalid parameter value

VDSetDigitizerRect

The `VDSetDigitizerRect` function allows applications to set the current digitizer rectangle.

```
pascal VideoDigitizerError VDSetDigitizerRect
                              (VideoDigitizerComponent ci,
                                Rect *digitizerRect);
```

ci
: Specifies the video digitizer component for the request. Applications obtain this reference from the Component Manager's `OpenComponent` function.

digitizerRect
: Contains a pointer to a rectangle that contains the size and location information for the digitizer rectangle. The coordinates of this rectangle must be relative to the maximum source rectangle. In addition, the digitizer rectangle must be within the maximum source rectangle.

DESCRIPTION

The current digitizer rectangle defines the area that the digitizer component reads from the input video signal. Applications can crop the input video signal by manipulating this rectangle. The digitizer rectangle coordinates must be specified relative to the maximum source rectangle. Furthermore, the digitizer rectangle must be completely within the maximum source rectangle. For a complete discussion of the relationship between these rectangles, see "About Video Digitizer Components," which begins on page 8-3.

All video digitizer components must support this function.

RESULT CODES

noErr	0	No error
qtParamErr	–2202	Invalid parameter value

CHAPTER 8

Video Digitizer Components

VDGetDigitizerRect

The `VDGetDigitizerRect` function returns the current digitizer rectangle.

```
pascal VideoDigitizerError VDGetDigitizerRect
                            (VideoDigitizerComponent ci,
                             Rect *digitizerRect);
```

ci
: Specifies the video digitizer component for the request. Applications obtain this reference from the Component Manager's `OpenComponent` function.

digitizerRect
: Contains a pointer to a rectangle that is to receive the size and location information for the current digitizer rectangle.

DESCRIPTION

The current digitizer rectangle defines the area that the digitizer component reads from the input video signal. The video digitizer component returns spatial information that is relative to the maximum source rectangle. For a complete discussion of the relationship between these rectangles, see "About Video Digitizer Components," which begins on page 8-3.

All video digitizer components must support this function.

RESULT CODE

noErr   0   No error

Selecting an Input Source

This section discusses the video digitizer component functions that allow applications to select an input video source.

Some of these functions provide information about the available video inputs. Applications can use the `VDGetNumberOfInputs` function to determine the number of video inputs supported by the digitizer component. The `VDGetInputFormat` function allows applications to find out the video format (composite, s-video, or component) employed by a specified input.

You can use the `VDSetInput` function in your application to specify the input to be used by the digitizer component. The `VDGetInput` function returns the currently selected input.

The `VDSetInputStandard` function allows you to specify the video signaling standard to be used by the video digitizer component.

CHAPTER 8

Video Digitizer Components

VDGetNumberOfInputs

The `VDGetNumberOfInputs` function returns the number of input video sources that a video digitizer component supports.

All video digitizer components must support this function.

```
pascal VideoDigitizerError VDGetNumberOfInputs
                            (VideoDigitizerComponent ci,
                             short *inputs);
```

ci   Specifies the video digitizer component for the request. Applications obtain this reference from the Component Manager's `OpenComponent` function.

inputs   Contains a pointer to an integer that is to receive the number of input video sources supported by the specified component. Video digitizer components number video sources sequentially, starting at 0. So, if a digitizer component supports two inputs, this function sets the field referred to by the `inputs` parameter to 1.

RESULT CODE

noErr   0   No error

VDSetInput

The `VDSetInput` function allows applications to select the input video source for a video digitizer component.

All video digitizer components must support this function.

```
pascal VideoDigitizerError VDSetInput (VideoDigitizerComponent ci,
                                       short input);
```

ci   Specifies the video digitizer component for the request. Applications obtain this reference from the Component Manager's `OpenComponent` function.

input   Specifies the input video source for this request. Video digitizer components number video sources sequentially, starting at 0. So, to request the first video source, an application sets this parameter to 0.

CHAPTER 8

Video Digitizer Components

RESULT CODES

noErr	0	No error
qtParamErr	–2202	Invalid parameter value

SEE ALSO

Applications can get the number of video sources supported by a video digitizer component by calling the `VDGetNumberOfInputs` function (described in the previous section). Applications can get more information about a video source by calling the `VDGetInputFormat` function (described on page 8-32).

VDGetInput

The `VDGetInput` function returns data that identifies the currently active input video source.

All video digitizer components must support this function.

```
pascal VideoDigitizerError VDGetInput (VideoDigitizerComponent ci,
                                        short *input);
```

ci
: Specifies the video digitizer component for the request. Applications obtain this reference from the Component Manager's `OpenComponent` function.

input
: Contains a pointer to a short integer that is to receive the identifier for the currently active input video source. Video digitizer components number video sources sequentially, starting at 0. So, if the first source is active, this function sets the field referred to by the `input` parameter to 0.

RESULT CODES

noErr	0	No error
qtParamErr	–2202	Invalid parameter value

VDGetInputFormat

The `VDGetInputFormat` function allows applications to determine the format of the video signal provided by a specified video input source.

```
pascal VideoDigitizerError VDGetInputFormat
                                        (VideoDigitizerComponent ci,
                                         short input, short *format);
```

ci
: Specifies the video digitizer component for the request. Applications obtain this reference from the Component Manager's `OpenComponent` function.

input
: Specifies the input video source for this request. Video digitizer components number video sources sequentially, starting at 0. So, to request information about the first video source, an application sets this parameter to 0. Applications can get the number of video sources supported by a video digitizer component by calling the `VDGetNumberOfInputs` function, discussed on page 8-31.

format
: Contains a pointer to a short integer that is to receive the specification of the video format of the specified input source. This function updates the field referred to by the `format` parameter. Valid values are

    compositeIn
    : The input video signal is in composite format

    sVideoIn
    : The input video signal is in s-video format

    rgbComponentIn
    : The input video signal is in RGB component format

DESCRIPTION

Video digitizer components support three video formats: composite video, s-video, and component video (RGB signal).

All video digitizer components must support this function.

RESULT CODES

```
noErr              0     No error
qtParamErr     –2202    Invalid parameter value
```

VDSetInputStandard

The `VDSetInputStandard` function allows applications to specify the input signaling standard to digitize. Video digitizer components support three input signaling standards: NTSC, PAL, and SECAM.

```
pascal VideoDigitizerError VDSetInputStandard
                            (VideoDigitizerComponent ci,
                                short inputStandard);
```

ci
: Specifies the video digitizer component for the request. Applications obtain this reference from the Component Manager's `OpenComponent` function.

CHAPTER 8

Video Digitizer Components

`inputStandard`
: A short integer that specifies the signaling standard used in the source video signal. Valid values are

  `ntscIn`   Input video signal to digitize is in NTSC format
  `palIn`   Input video signal to digitize is in PAL format
  `secamIn` Input video signal to digitize is in SECAM format

DESCRIPTION

Applications can use the `VDGetDigitizerInfo` function (described on page 8-24) to determine the capabilities of a specified video digitizer component. Applications can use the `VDGetCurrentFlags` function (described on page 8-25) to determine the current input state of a digitizer component.

All video digitizer components must support this function.

SPECIAL CONSIDERATIONS

Your digitizer component should ensure that spatial characteristics that were set for one standard are not interpreted within another standard.

RESULT CODES

`noErr`	0	No error
`qtParamErr`	–2202	Invalid parameter value

Setting Video Destinations

Video digitizer components provide several functions that allow applications to specify the destination for the digitized video stream produced by the digitizer component. Applications have two options for specifying the destination for the video data stream.

The first option requires that the video be digitized as RGB pixels and placed into a destination pixel map. This option allows the video to be placed either onscreen or offscreen, depending upon the placement of the pixel map. You can use the `VDSetPlayThruDestination` function in your application to set the characteristics for this option. The `VDPreflightDestination` function lets you determine the capabilities of the digitizer in your application. All video digitizer components must support this option. The `VDGetPlayThruDestination` function lets you get data about the current video destination.

The second option uses a global boundary rectangle to define the destination for the video. This option is useful only with digitizers that support hardware DMA. You can use the `VDSetPlayThruGlobalRect` function in your application to set the characteristics for this option. You can use the `VDPreflightGlobalRect` function in your application to determine the capabilities of the digitizer. Not all video digitizer components support this option.

CHAPTER 8

Video Digitizer Components

The `VDGetMaxAuxBuffer` function returns information about a buffer that may be located on some special hardware.

VDSetPlayThruDestination

You can use the `VDSetPlayThruDestination` function in your application to establish the destination settings for a video digitizer component.

All video digitizer components must support this function.

```
pascal VideoDigitizerError VDSetPlayThruDestination
                        (VideoDigitizerComponent ci,
                         PixMapHandle dest,
                         Rect *destRect,
                         MatrixRecord *m, RgnHandle mask);
```

ci   Specifies the video digitizer component for the request. Applications obtain this reference from the Component Manager's `OpenComponent` function.

dest   Contains a handle to the destination pixel map. This pixel map may be in the video frame buffer of the Macintosh computer, or it may specify an offscreen buffer.

          The video digitizer component examines this pixel map to determine the display characteristics of the video destination, including the base address, row bytes, and pixel depth. If the digitizer component does not support these characteristics, it sets the return value to `badDepth`. If the digitizer component cannot accommodate the location of the destination pixel map, it sets the return value to `noDMA`.

          If you are going to use multiple output buffers, be sure to include this buffer in the buffer list that you define with the `VDSetupBuffers` function, which is described on page 8-54. You may call the `VDSetupBuffers` function before calling `VDSetPlayThruDestination`.

destRect Contains a pointer to a rectangle that specifies the size and location of the video destination. This rectangle must be in the coordinate system of the destination pixel map specified by the `dest` parameter.

          This is an optional parameter. Applications may specify a transformation matrix to control the placement and scaling of the video image in the destination pixel map. In this case, the `destRect` parameter is set to `nil` and the m parameter specifies the matrix.

          If the `destRect` parameter is `nil`, you can determine the destination rectangle for simple matrices by calling the `TransformRect` function using the current digitizer rectangle and this matrix. For more information on `TransformRect`, see the chapter "Movie Toolbox" in *Inside Macintosh: QuickTime*.

Video Digitizer Components

m
Contains a pointer to a matrix structure containing the transformation matrix for the destination video image. To determine the capabilities of a video digitizer component, you can call the `VDGetDigitizerInfo` function, described on page 8-24, in your application.

This is an optional parameter. Applications may specify a destination rectangle to control the placement and scaling of the video image in the destination pixel map. In this case, the m parameter is set to nil and the destRect parameter specifies the destination rectangle.

mask
Contains a region handle that defines a mask. Applications can use masks to control clipping of the video into the destination rectangle. This mask region is defined in the destination coordinate space.

This is an optional parameter. Applications may use alpha channels or key colors to control video blending. If there is no mask, applications should set the mask parameter to nil.

DESCRIPTION

The application provides the desired settings as parameters to this function. Applications should verify that the video digitizer component can accommodate the settings by calling the `VDPreflightDestination` function, described in the next section.

Applications set the source digitizer rectangle by calling the `VDSetDigitizerRect` function, described on page 8-29.

RESULT CODES

noErr	0	No error
badDepth	–2207	Digitizer cannot accommodate pixel depth
noDMA	–2208	Digitizer cannot use DMA to this destination

VDPreflightDestination

You can use the `VDPreflightDestination` function in your application to verify that a video digitizer component can support a set of destination settings intended for use with the `VDSetPlayThruDestination` function, which is described in the previous section.

```
pascal VideoDigitizerError VDPreflightDestination
                            (VideoDigitizerComponent ci,
                             Rect *digitizerRect,
                             PixMapHandle dest,
                             Rect *destRect,
                             MatrixRecord *m);
```

ci
: Specifies the video digitizer component for the request. Applications obtain this reference from the Component Manager's OpenComponent function.

digitizerRect
: Contains a pointer to a rectangle that contains the size and location information for the digitizer rectangle. The coordinates of this rectangle must be relative to the maximum source rectangle. In addition, the digitizer rectangle must be within the maximum source rectangle. For a complete discussion of the relationship between these rectangles, see "About Video Digitizer Components," which begins on page 8-3.

    If the video digitizer component cannot accommodate the specified rectangle, it changes the coordinates in this structure to specify a rectangle that it can support and sets the result to qtParamErr.

dest
: Contains a handle to the destination pixel map.

destRect
: Contains a pointer to a rectangle that specifies the size and location of the video destination. This rectangle must be in the coordinate system of the destination pixel map specified by the dest parameter. If the video digitizer component cannot accommodate this rectangle, it changes the coordinates in the structure to specify a rectangle that it can support and sets the result to qtParamErr.

    This is an optional parameter. Applications may specify a transformation matrix to control the placement and scaling of the video image in the destination pixel map. In this case, the destRect parameter is set to nil and the m parameter specifies the matrix.

m
: Contains a pointer to a matrix structure containing the transformation matrix for the destination video image. If the video digitizer component cannot accommodate this matrix, it changes the values in the structure to define a matrix that it can support and sets the result to qtParamErr. Applications can determine the capabilities of a video digitizer component by calling the VDGetDigitizerInfo function, described on page 8-24.

    This is an optional parameter. Applications may specify a destination rectangle to control the placement and scaling of the video image in the destination pixel map. In this case, the m parameter is set to nil and the destRect parameter specifies the destination rectangle.

    If the destRect parameter is nil, you can determine the destination rectangle for simple matrices by calling the TransformRect function using the current digitizer rectangle and this matrix. For more information on TransformRect, see the chapter "Movie Toolbox" in *Inside Macintosh: QuickTime*.

CHAPTER 8

Video Digitizer Components

DESCRIPTION

The application provides the desired settings as parameters to this function. The video digitizer component then examines those settings. If the digitizer component can support the specified settings, it sets the result code to noErr. If the digitizer component cannot support the settings, it alters the input settings to reflect values that it can support and returns a result code of qtParamErr. The application can then use the settings with the VDSetPlayThruDestination function (described in the previous section).

All video digitizer components must support this function.

Applications should use the VDPreflightDestination function to test destination settings whenever the video digitizer component cannot support arbitrary scaling.

RESULT CODES

noErr	0	No error
qtParamErr	–2202	Invalid parameter value

SEE ALSO

Applications can determine the capabilities of a video digitizer component by examining the output capability flags (see the discussion of the VDGetCurrentFlags function, which begins on page 8-25, for more information about retrieving these flags). Specifically, if the digiOutDoesStretch and digiOutDoesShrink flags are set to 1 in the output capability flag, the digitizer component supports arbitrary scaling.

VDGetPlayThruDestination

The VDGetPlayThruDestination function allows applications to obtain information about the current video destination.

All video digitizer components must support this function.

```
pascal VideoDigitizerError VDGetPlayThruDestination
                        (VideoDigitizerComponent ci,
                         PixMapHandle *dest, Rect *destRect,
                         MatrixRecord *m, RgnHandle *mask);
```

ci   Specifies the video digitizer component for the request. Applications obtain this reference from the Component Manager's OpenComponent function.

dest   Contains a pointer to a pixel map handle. The video digitizer component returns a handle to the destination pixel map in the field referred to by this parameter. It is the caller's responsibility to dispose of the pixel map.

CHAPTER 8

Video Digitizer Components

destRect   Contains a pointer to a rectangle structure. The video digitizer component places the coordinates of the output rectangle into the structure referred to by this parameter. If there is no output rectangle defined, the component returns an empty rectangle.

m   Contains a pointer to a matrix structure. The video digitizer component places the transformation matrix into the structure referred to by this parameter.

mask   Contains a pointer to a region handle. The video digitizer component places a handle to the mask region into the field referred to by this parameter. Applications can use masks to control the video into the destination rectangle. For more information about masks, see "About Video Digitizer Components," which begins on page 8-3. If there is no mask region defined, the digitizer component sets this returned handle to nil. The caller is responsible for disposing of this region.

DESCRIPTION

Applications can set the video destination by calling either the VDSetPlayThruDestination function (described on page 8-35) or the VDSetPlayThruGlobalRect function (described in the next section). Applications should call the VDGetPlayThruDestination function only after having set the destination with the VDSetPlayThruDestination function.

RESULT CODE

noErr   0   No error

VDSetPlayThruGlobalRect

You can use the VDSetPlayThruGlobalRect function in your application to establish the destination settings for a video digitizer component that is to digitize into a global rectangle. The application provides the desired settings as parameters to this function. Not all video digitizer components support global rectangles.

```
pascal VideoDigitizerError VDSetPlayThruGlobalRect
                            (VideoDigitizerComponent ci,
                             GrafPtr theWindow,
                             Rect *globalRect);
```

ci   Specifies the video digitizer component for the request. Applications obtain this reference from the Component Manager's OpenComponent function.

theWindow   Contains a pointer to the destination window.

Video Digitizer Components

globalRect
Contains a pointer to a rectangle that specifies the size and location of the video destination. This rectangle must be in the coordinate system of the destination window specified by the `theWindow` parameter.

DESCRIPTION

Applications should verify that the digitizer component can accommodate the settings by calling the `VDPreflightGlobalRect` function, described in the next section.

RESULT CODES

```
noErr           0      No error
digiUnimpErr   -2201   Function not supported
```

SEE ALSO

Applications set the source digitizer rectangle by calling the `VDSetDigitizerRect` function, described on page 8-29.

VDPreflightGlobalRect

You can use the `VDPreflightGlobalRect` function in your application to verify that a video digitizer component can support a set of destination settings intended for use with the `VDSetPlayThruGlobalRect` function (described in the previous section).

```
pascal VideoDigitizerError VDPreflightGlobalRect
                            (VideoDigitizerComponent ci,
                             GrafPtr theWindow,
                             Rect *globalRect);
```

ci
Specifies the video digitizer component for the request. Applications obtain this reference from the Component Manager's `OpenComponent` function.

theWindow
Contains a pointer to the destination window.

globalRect
Contains a pointer to a rectangle that specifies the size and location of the video destination. This rectangle must be in the coordinate system of the destination window specified by the `theWindow` parameter. If the video digitizer component cannot accommodate this rectangle, it changes the coordinates in the structure to specify a rectangle that it can support and sets the result to `qtParamErr`.

CHAPTER 8

Video Digitizer Components

DESCRIPTION

The application provides the desired settings as parameters to this function. The video digitizer component then examines those settings. If the digitizer component can support the specified settings, it sets the result code to `noErr`. If the digitizer component cannot support the settings, it alters the input settings to reflect values that it can support and returns a result code of `qtParamErr`.

Applications should use this function to determine whether a video digitizer supports placing destination video into a rectangle that crosses screens. Digitizers that do not support this capability return a result of `digiUnimpErr`.

RESULT CODES

```
noErr            0      No error
digiUnimpErr    -2201   Function not supported
qtParamErr      -2202   Invalid parameter value
```

VDGetMaxAuxBuffer

The `VDGetMaxAuxBuffer` function allows applications to obtain access to buffers that are located on special hardware. Digitizer components that are constrained to a single output device can provide an auxiliary buffer to support multiple buffering.

```
pascal VideoDigitizerError VDGetMaxAuxBuffer
                        (VideoDigitizerComponent ci,
                         PixMapHandle *pm, Rect *r);
```

ci
: Specifies the video digitizer component for the request. Applications obtain this reference from the Component Manager's `OpenComponent` function.

pm
: Contains a pointer to a pixel map handle. The video digitizer component returns a handle to the destination pixel map in the field referred to by this parameter. Do not dispose of this pixel map. If the digitizer component cannot allocate a buffer, this handle is set to `nil`.

r
: Contains a pointer to a rectangle structure. The video digitizer component places the coordinates of the largest output rectangle it can support into the structure referred to by this parameter.

DESCRIPTION

You can use the `VDGetMaxAuxBuffer` function in your application to determine whether a video digitizer component supports an auxiliary buffer. If the digitizer component provides an auxiliary buffer, it is to your advantage to use it. By using the buffer, you may achieve better performance under some circumstances, such as when the digitizer component does not support DMA.

RESULT CODES

noErr	0	No error
digiUnimpErr	−2201	Function not supported

Controlling Compressed Source Devices

Some video digitizer components may provide functions that allow applications to work with digitizing devices that can provide compressed image data directly. Such devices allow applications to retrieve compressed image data without using the Image Compression Manager. However, in order to display images from the compressed data stream, there must be an appropriate decompressor component available to decompress the image data.

Video digitizers that can support compressed source devices set the `digiOutDoesCompress` flag to 1 in their capability flags (see "Capability Flags" beginning on page 8-14 for more information about these flags).

Applications can use the `VDGetCompressionTypes` function to determine the image-compression capabilities of a video digitizer. The `VDSetCompression` function allows applications to set some parameters that govern image compression.

Applications control digitization by calling the `VDCompressOneFrameAsync` function, which instructs the video digitizer to create one frame of compressed image data. The `VDCompressDone` function returns that frame. When an application is done with a frame, it calls the `VDReleaseCompressBuffer` function to free the buffer. An application can force the digitizer to place a key frame into the sequence by calling the `VDResetCompressSequence` function. Applications can turn compression on and off by calling `VDSetCompressionOnOff`.

Applications can obtain the digitizer's image description structure by calling the `VDGetImageDescription` function. Applications can set the digitizer's time base by calling the `VDSetTimeBase` function.

All of the digitizing functions described in this section support only asynchronous digitization. That is, the video digitizer works independently to digitize each frame. Applications are free to perform other work while the digitizer works on each frame.

The video digitizer component manages its own buffer pool for use with these functions. In this respect, these functions differ from the other video digitizer functions that support asynchronous digitization (see "Controlling Digitization" beginning on page 8-52 for more information about these functions).

CHAPTER 8

Video Digitizer Components

VDGetCompressionTypes

The `VDGetCompressionTypes` function allows an application to determine the image-compression capabilities of the video digitizer.

```
pascal VideoDigitizerError VDGetCompressionTypes
                        (VideoDigitizerComponent ci,
                         VDCompressionListHandle h);
```

ci   Identifies an application's connection to the video digitizer component. An application obtains this value from the Component Manager's `OpenComponent` function.

h   Identifies a handle to receive the compression information. The video digitizer returns information about its capabilities by formatting one or more compression list structures in this handle (the format and content of the compression list structure are discussed later). If the digitizer supports more than one compression type, it creates an array of structures in this handle.

The video digitizer sizes this handle appropriately. It is the application's responsibility to dispose of this handle when it is done with it.

DESCRIPTION

The video digitizer places its preferred, or default, compression options in the first compression list structure in the returned array.

Note that there must be a decompressor component of the appropriate type available in the system if an application is to display images from a compressed image sequence.

The `VDCompressionList` data type defines the format and content of the compression list structure:

```
typedef struct VDCompressionList {
    CodecComponent   codec;          /* component ID */
    CodecType        cType;          /* compressor type */
    Str63            typeName;       /* compression algorithm */
    Str63            name;           /* compressor name string */
    long             formatFlags;    /* data format flags */
    long             compressFlags;  /* capabilities flags */
    long             reserved;       /* set to 0 */
} VDCompressionList, *VDCompressionListPtr,
**VDCompressionListHandle;
```

Field descriptions

codec
Contains the component identifier for the video digitizer's compressor component. Some video digitizers may also implement their image-compression capabilities in an Image Compression Manager compressor component. In this case, the digitizer may allow the application to connect to and use the compressor. If so, the digitizer provides the compressor component's identifier here. If not, the digitizer sets this field to `nil`.

cType
Identifies the compression algorithm supported by the video digitizer. See the chapter "Image Compression Manager" in *Inside Macintosh: QuickTime* for a list of values supported by Apple.

typeName
Contains a text string that identifies the compression algorithm. An application may display this string to the user to identify the type of image compression being performed. See the chapter "Image Compression Manager" in *Inside Macintosh: QuickTime* for a list of values supported by Apple.

name
Specifies the name of the compressor. The developer of the video digitizer assigns this name. An application may display this string to the user.

formatFlags
Contains flags that describe the data formats supported by the video digitizer. Typically, these flags are of interest only to developers of video digitizers and image compressors. See the chapter "Image Compressor Components" in this book for more information.

compressFlags
Contains flags that describe the compression capabilities of the video digitizer. Typically, these flags are of interest only to developers of video digitizers and image compressors. See the chapter "Image Compressor Components" in this book for more information.

reserved
Reserved for Apple. Always set to 0.

RESULT CODES

noErr	0	No error
digiUnimpErr	−2201	Function not supported

CHAPTER 8

Video Digitizer Components

VDSetCompression

The `VDSetCompression` function allows applications to specify some compression parameters.

```
pascal VideoDigitizerError VDSetCompression
                    (VideoDigitizerComponent ci,
                     OSType compressType, short depth,
                     Rect *bounds, CodecQ spatialQuality,
                     CodecQ temporalQuality,
                     long keyFrameRate);
```

`ci`
Identifies the application's connection to the video digitizer component. An application obtains this value from the Component Manager's `OpenComponent` function.

`compressType`
Specifies a compressor type. This value corresponds to the component subtype of the compressor component. See the chapter "Image Compression Manager" in *Inside Macintosh: QuickTime* for more information about compressor types and for valid values for this parameter.

`depth`
Specifies the depth at which the image is likely to be viewed. Compressors may use this as an indication of the color or grayscale resolution of the image. Values of 1, 2, 4, 8, 16, 24, and 32 indicate the number of bits per pixel for color images. Values of 33, 34, 36, and 40 correspond to 1-bit, 2-bit, 4-bit, and 8-bit grayscale images.

`bounds`
Contains a pointer to a rectangle that defines the desired boundaries of the compressed image.

`spatialQuality`
Indicates the desired image quality for each frame in the sequence. See the chapter "Image Compression Manager" in *Inside Macintosh: QuickTime* for valid compression quality values.

`temporalQuality`
Indicates the desired temporal quality for the sequence as a whole. See the chapter "Image Compression Manager" in *Inside Macintosh: QuickTime* for valid compression quality values.

`keyFrameRate`
Specifies the maximum number of frames to allow between key frames. This value defines the minimum rate at which key frames are to appear in the compressed sequence; however, the video digitizer may insert key frames more often than an application specifies. If the application requests no temporal compression (that is, the application set the `temporalQuality` parameter to 0), the video digitizer ignores this parameter.

For more information about key frames, see the chapter "Image Compression Manager" in *Inside Macintosh: QuickTime*.

Video Digitizer Components Reference

CHAPTER 8

Video Digitizer Components

DESCRIPTION

An application may use the `VDSetCompression` function to control the parameters that govern image compression. An application may change the compressor type, image depth, and boundary rectangle parameters only when the digitizer is stopped. However, if an application sets these three parameters (that is, the `compressType`, `depth`, and `bounds` parameters) to 0, it may work with the other parameters while digitization is active. This allows an application to vary the data rate during digitization.

RESULT CODES

noErr	0	No error
digiUnimpErr	–2201	Function not supported
qtParamErr	–2202	Invalid parameter value

VDSetCompressionOnOff

The `VDSetCompressionOnOff` function allows an application to start and stop compression by digitizers that can deliver either compressed or uncompressed image data.

```
pascal VideoDigitizerError VDSetCompressionOnOff
                    (VideoDigitizerComponent ci,
                    Boolean state);
```

ci
: Identifies the application's connection to the video digitizer component. An application obtains this value from the Component Manager's `OpenComponent` function.

state
: Contains a Boolean value that indicates whether to enable or disable compression. Applications set this parameter to `true` to enable compression. Setting it to `false` disables compression.

DESCRIPTION

This is a required function for digitizers that are going to perform compression. These digitizers have their `digiOutDoesCompress` capability flag set to 1 and their `digiOutDoesCompressOnly` flag set to 0. Digitizers that support this capability typically deliver uncompressed image data in addition to the compressed data stream; the uncompressed data is ready for display.

Digitizers that only provide compressed data have their `digiOutDoesCompressOnly` flag set to 1, rather than 0. These digitizers may either ignore this function or return a nonzero result code.

Applications must call this function before they call either `VDSetCompression` or `VDCompressOneFrameAsync`. This allows the video digitizer to prepare for the operation.

RESULT CODES

`noErr`	0	No error
`digiUnimpErr`	–2201	Function not supported

VDCompressOneFrameAsync

The `VDCompressOneFrameAsync` function instructs the video digitizer to digitize and compress a single frame of image data. Because the component performs this action asynchronously, the application is free to do other things while the digitizer works on the image.

```
pascal VideoDigitizerError VDCompressOneFrameAsync
                    (VideoDigitizerComponent ci);
```

`ci` Identifies the application's connection to the video digitizer component. An application obtains this value from the Component Manager's `OpenComponent` function.

DESCRIPTION

An application can determine when the digitizer is done with the frame by calling the `VDCompressDone` function, which is discussed next.

Unlike the `VDGrabOneFrameAsync` function (discussed on page 8-56), the video digitizer handles all details of managing data buffers.

RESULT CODES

`noErr`	0	No error
`digiUnimpErr`	–2201	Function not supported

VDCompressDone

The `VDCompressDone` function allows an application to determine whether the video digitizer has finished digitizing and compressing a frame of image data. An application starts the digitizing process by calling the `VDCompressOneFrameAsync` function, which was just discussed.

```
pascal VideoDigitizerError VDCompressDone
                    (VideoDigitizerComponent ci,
                     Boolean *done, Ptr *theData,
                     long *dataSize,
                     unsigned char *similarity,
                     TimeRecord *t);
```

ci
: Identifies the application's connection to the video digitizer component. An application obtains this value from the Component Manager's `OpenComponent` function.

done
: Contains a pointer to a Boolean value. Applications set this value to `true` when they are done, and set it to `false` if the operation is incomplete.

theData
: Contains a pointer to a field that is to receive a pointer to the compressed image data. The digitizer returns a pointer that is valid in the application's current memory mode.

    The digitizer allocates the memory into which it places the digitized data. An application must call the `VDReleaseCompressBuffer` function to dispose of this memory; this function is discussed next.

dataSize
: Contains a pointer to a field to receive a value indicating the number of bytes of compressed image data.

similarity
: Contains a pointer to a field to receive an indication of the relative similarity of this image to the previous image in a sequence. A value of 0 indicates that the current frame is a key frame in the sequence. A value of 255 indicates that the current frame is identical to the previous frame. Values from 1 through 254 indicate relative similarity, ranging from very different (1) to very similar (254). This field is only filled in if the temporal quality passed in with the `VDSetCompression` function (described on page 8-45) is not 0—that is, if it is not frame-differenced.

t
: Contains a pointer to a time record. When the operation is complete, the digitizer fills in this structure with information indicating when the frame was grabbed. The time value stored in this structure is in the time base that the application sets with the `VDSetTimeBase` function (see page 8-51 for more information about this function). The format and content of this structure are discussed in the chapter "Movie Toolbox" in *Inside Macintosh: QuickTime*.

DESCRIPTION

An application can determine when the digitizer is done with the frame by calling the `VDCompressDone` function. When the digitizer is done, it sets the Boolean value referred to by the done parameter to `true`, and then returns information about the digitized and compressed frames via the `theData`, `dataSize`, `similarity`, and `t` parameters.

If the digitizer is not yet done, it sets the Boolean value to `false`. In this case, the digitizer does not return any other information.

Note that the digitizer is careful to return the frames in temporal order, and to avoid returning two frames with the same time value (unless the rate is set to 0).

RESULT CODES

`noErr`	0	No error
`digiUnimpErr`	–2201	Function not supported

SEE ALSO

Applications must use the `VDReleaseCompressBuffer` function to free the memory that contains the compressed image data. This function is described in the next section.

VDReleaseCompressBuffer

The `VDReleaseCompressBuffer` function allows an application to free a buffer received from the `VDCompressDone` function.

```
pascal VideoDigitizerError VDReleaseCompressBuffer
                    (VideoDigitizerComponent ci,
                    Ptr bufferAddr);
```

ci
: Identifies the application's connection to the video digitizer component. An application obtains this value from the Component Manager's `OpenComponent` function.

bufferAddr
: Points to the location of the buffer to be released. This address must correspond to a buffer address that the application obtained from the `VDCompressDone` function (discussed in the previous section).

CHAPTER 8

Video Digitizer Components

DESCRIPTION

Once an application frees the buffer, the video digitizer is able to use the buffer for other images. Applications should try to free these buffers as quickly as possible, so that the video digitizer can make optimum use of its buffer, and thereby support higher frame rates.

RESULT CODES

noErr	0	No error
digiUnimpErr	−2201	Function not supported

VDGetImageDescription

The `VDGetImageDescription` function allows an application to retrieve an image description structure from a video digitizer.

```
pascal VideoDigitizerError VDGetImageDescription
                    (VideoDigitizerComponent ci,
                    ImageDescriptionHandle desc);
```

ci Identifies the application's connection to the video digitizer component. An application obtains this value from the Component Manager's `OpenComponent` function.

desc Specifies a handle. The video digitizer fills this handle with an Image Compression Manager image description structure containing information about the digitizer's current compression settings. The digitizer resizes the handle appropriately. It is the application's responsibility to dispose of this handle.

RESULT CODES

noErr	0	No error
digiUnimpErr	−2201	Function not supported

SEE ALSO

See the chapter "Image Compression Manager" in *Inside Macintosh: QuickTime* for a complete description of the image description structure.

CHAPTER 8

Video Digitizer Components

VDResetCompressSequence

The `VDResetCompressSequence` function allows an application to force the video digitizer to insert a key frame into a temporally compressed image sequence.

```
pascal VideoDigitizerError VDResetCompressSequence
                        (VideoDigitizerComponent ci);
```

ci Identifies the application's connection to the video digitizer component. An application obtains this value from the Component Manager's `OpenComponent` function.

DESCRIPTION

After an application calls this function, the digitizer ensures that the next frame returned to the application is a key frame.

RESULT CODES

noErr   0 No error
digiUnimpErr –2201 Function not supported

SEE ALSO

An application can control the rate at which the digitizer inserts key frames by calling the `VDSetCompression` function, which is discussed beginning on page 8-45.

VDSetTimeBase

The `VDSetTimeBase` function allows an application to establish the video digitizer's time coordinate system.

```
pascal VideoDigitizerError VDSetTimeBase
                        (VideoDigitizerComponent ci,
                         TimeBase t);
```

ci Identifies the application's connection to the video digitizer component. An application obtains this value from the Component Manager's `OpenComponent` function.

t Specifies the video digitizer's new time base.

Video Digitizer Components

DESCRIPTION

Video digitizers return all time information in relation to the specified time base. For example, whenever a digitizer returns a compressed frame from its `VDCompressDone` function, it returns time information relating to the time when the frame was digitized and compressed. This time information is expressed in the time base that the application specifies with this function.

RESULT CODES

`noErr`	0	No error
`digiUnimpErr`	–2201	Function not supported

Controlling Digitization

This section describes the video digitizer component functions that allow applications to control video digitization. Video digitizer components allow applications to start and stop the digitizing process. Your application can request continuous digitization or single-frame digitization. When a digitizer component is operating continuously, it automatically places successive frames of digitized video into the specified destination. When a digitizer component works with a single frame at a time, the application and other software, such as an image compressor component, control the speed at which the digitized video is processed.

You can use the `VDSetPlayThruOnOff` function in your application to enable or disable digitization. When digitization is enabled, the video digitizer component places digitized video frame into the specified destination continuously. The application stops the digitizer by disabling digitization. This function can be used with both destination options.

Alternatively, your application can control digitization on a frame-by-frame basis. The `VDGrabOneFrame` and `VDGrabOneFrameAsync` functions digitize a single video frame; `VDGrabOneFrame` works synchronously, returning control to your application when it has obtained a complete frame, while `VDGrabOneFrameAsync` works asynchronously. The `VDDone` function helps you to determine when the `VDGrabOneFrameAsync` function is finished with a video frame. Your application can define the buffers for use with asynchronous digitization by calling the `VDSetupBuffers` function. Free the buffers by calling the `VDReleaseAsyncBuffers` function.

The `VDSetFrameRate` function allows applications to control the digitizer's frame rate. The `VDGetDataRate` function returns the digitizer's current data rate.

CHAPTER 8

Video Digitizer Components

VDSetPlayThruOnOff

The `VDSetPlayThruOnOff` function allows applications to control continuous digitization.

```
pascal VideoDigitizerError VDSetPlayThruOnOff
                         (VideoDigitizerComponent ci,
                         short state);
```

ci
: Specifies the video digitizer component for the request. Applications obtain this reference from the Component Manager's `OpenComponent` function.

state
: A short integer that specifies whether to use continuous digitization. The following values are valid:

    digitizerOff
    : Turns off continuous digitization

    digitizerOn
    : Turns on continuous digitization

    When an application stops continuous digitization, the video digitizer component must restore its alpha channel, blending mask, or key color settings to graphics mode.

DESCRIPTION

When opened, video digitizer components are always set to off, so that no digitization is taking place. Your application can use the `VDSetPlayThruOnOff` function to turn continuous digitization on and off.

RESULT CODES

noErr	0	No error
digiUnimpErr	–2201	Function not supported
qtParamErr	–2202	Invalid parameter value

SEE ALSO

Applications can also use single-frame digitization by calling the `VDGrabOneFrame` or `VDGrabOneFrameAsync` function, described in the next section and on page 8-56, respectively.

VDGrabOneFrame

The `VDGrabOneFrame` function instructs the video digitizer component to digitize a single frame of source video.

All video digitizer components must support this function.

```
pascal VideoDigitizerError VDGrabOneFrame
                    (VideoDigitizerComponent ci);
```

ci   Specifies the video digitizer component for the request. Applications obtain this reference from the Component Manager's `OpenComponent` function.

DESCRIPTION

The application specifies the destination for the digitized frame by calling either the `VDSetPlayThruDestination` function (described on page 8-35) or the `VDSetPlayThruGlobalRect` function (described on page 8-39).

If the specified digitizer component is already digitizing continuously when the application calls `VDGrabOneFrame`, the digitizer component returns the next digitized frame and then stops. If the digitizer component is stopped, the component digitizes a single frame and then stops. To resume continuous digitization, applications should call the `VDSetPlayThruOnOff` function, which is described in the previous section.

The `VDGrabOneFrame` function supports synchronous single-frame video digitization—that is, the digitizer component does not return control to your application until it has successfully processed the next video frame. Some video digitizer components may also support asynchronous single-frame digitization. Applications can use asynchronous digitization by calling the `VDGrabOneFrameAsync` function, described on page 8-56.

RESULT CODE

noErr   0   No error

VDSetupBuffers

The `VDSetupBuffers` function allows applications to define output buffers for use with asynchronous grabs. Video digitizer components extract information about the spatial characteristics of the video destinations from these buffers.

```
pascal VideoDigitizerError VDSetupBuffers
                    (VideoDigitizerComponent ci,
                     VdigBufferRecListHandle bufferList);
```

Video Digitizer Components

ci
: Specifies the video digitizer component for the request. Applications obtain this reference from the Component Manager's `OpenComponent` function.

bufferList
: Contains a handle to a list of output buffers. This buffer list is contained in a buffer list structure. This structure is described in "The Buffer List Structure" on page 8-22. Note that the video digitizer component makes a copy of the buffer list—you may dispose of this handle when the function returns to your application.

▲ **WARNING**
If you are developing a video digitizer component, note that the `matrix` field in the buffer list structure contains a pointer to the matrix structure. It is your responsibility to copy that matrix structure. ▲

SPECIAL CONSIDERATIONS

Applications must define the output buffers before starting an asynchronous grab.

RESULT CODES

noErr	0	No error
digiUnimpErr	–2201	Function not supported
qtParamErr	–2202	Invalid parameter value
badDepth	–2207	Digitizer cannot accommodate specified depth
noDMA	–2208	Digitizer cannot use DMA to this destination

SEE ALSO

Applications instruct digitizer components to grab a single frame by calling the `VDGrabOneFrameAsync` function, which is described on page 8-56.

Applications free these buffers by calling the `VDReleaseAsyncBuffers` function, which is described next.

VDReleaseAsyncBuffers

The `VDReleaseAsyncBuffers` function allows an application to release the buffers that it allocates with the `VDSetupBuffers` function.

```
pascal VideoDigitizerError VDReleaseAsyncBuffers
                                (VideoDigitizerComponent ci);
```

ci
: Specifies the video digitizer component for the request. Applications obtain this reference from the Component Manager's `OpenComponent` function.

CHAPTER 8

Video Digitizer Components

DESCRIPTION

Applications release the buffers used in an asynchronous grab by calling the `VDReleaseAsyncBuffers` function.

RESULT CODES

noErr	0	No error
digiUnimpErr	–2201	Function not supported

SEE ALSO

Applications allocate buffers for asynchronous grabs by calling the `VDSetupBuffers` function, which is discussed in the previous section.

VDGrabOneFrameAsync

The `VDGrabOneFrameAsync` function instructs the video digitizer component to start to digitize asynchronously a single frame of source video. Because the component digitizes the video asynchronously, the application is free to do other things while the digitization is performed.

```
pascal VideoDigitizerError VDGrabOneFrameAsync
                    (VideoDigitizerComponent ci,
                     short buffer);
```

ci   Specifies the video digitizer component for the request. Applications obtain this reference from the Component Manager's `OpenComponent` function.

buffer   Identifies the next output buffer. The value of this parameter must correspond to a valid index into the list of buffers that you supply when your application calls the `VDSetupBuffers` function (which is described on page 8-54). Note that this value is zero-based (that is, you must set this parameter to 0 to refer to the first buffer in the buffer list).

The video digitizer component uses this buffer for the *next* video frame (that is, the frame that will be digitized the next time the application calls the `VDGrabOneFrameAsync` function). In this manner, video digitizer components can quickly and efficiently prepare for the next video frame.

Some digitizer components may not allow your application to queue more than one asynchronous frame grab at a time. These components may not return control to your application until a previously requested grab has been completed.

DESCRIPTION

Applications determine when the digitizer component is finished with a frame by calling the `VDDone` function, which is described in the next section.

When calling the `VDGrabOneFrameAsync` function, the application specifies the next destination video buffer, allowing the digitizer component to quickly switch from the current buffer to the next buffer. In this manner, your application's ability to grab video at high frame rates is enhanced. See "Multiple Buffering" on page 8-8 for a discussion of multiple-buffered video digitization.

Applications can determine whether a video digitizer component supports asynchronous frame grabbing by examining the output capability flags of the digitizer component. Specifically, if the `digiOutDoesAsyncGrabs` flag is set to 1, the digitizer component supports the `VDGrabOneFrameAsync` function and the `VDDone` function, which is described in the next section.

Applications can use the `VDGetCurrentFlags` function (described on page 8-25) to retrieve the digitizer component's output capability flags. If a video digitizer component does not support asynchronous digitization, applications must use the `VDGrabOneFrame` function (described on page 8-54) to perform single-frame digitization.

If the specified digitizer component is already digitizing continuously when the application calls `VDGrabOneFrameAsync`, the digitizer component returns the next digitized frame and then stops. If the digitizer component is stopped, the component digitizes a single frame and then stops. To resume continuous digitization, applications should call the `VDSetPlayThruOnOff` function, which is described on page 8-53.

The `VDGrabOneFrameAsync` function also allows applications to use more than one destination buffer for the digitized video. The application defines these buffers by calling the `VDSetupBuffers` function (described on page 8-54). The application specifies one of these destination buffers for the digitized frame when it calls the `VDSetPlayThruDestination` function (described on page 8-35) or the `VDSetPlayThruGlobalRect` function (described on page 8-39).

RESULT CODES

noErr	0	No error
digiUnimpErr	–2201	Function not supported

VDDone

You can use the `VDDone` function in your application to determine if the `VDGrabOneFrameAsync` function is finished with a specific output buffer (`VDGrabOneFrameAsync` is described in the previous section). Applications that use the `VDGrabOneFrameAsync` function to digitize video frames should call `VDDone` before working with a digitized image.

```
pascal long VDDone (VideoDigitizerComponent ci, short buffer);
```

ci
: Specifies the video digitizer component for the request. Applications obtain this reference from the Component Manager's `OpenComponent` function.

buffer
: Identifies the buffer for the operation. The value of this parameter must correspond to a valid index into the list of buffers you supply when your application calls the `VDSetupBuffers` function (which is described on page 8-54). Note that this value is zero-based (that is, you must set this parameter to 0 to refer to the first buffer in the buffer list).

DESCRIPTION

If the `VDDone` function returns a 0 result, the video digitizer component has not finished the specified asynchronous frame grab. If the result is nonzero, the frame has been processed and the application can proceed to use the contents of the specified buffer.

Applications can determine whether a video digitizer component supports asynchronous frame grabbing by examining the output capability flags of the digitizer component. Specifically, if the `digiOutDoesAsyncGrabs` flag is set to 1, the digitizer component supports the `VDGrabOneFrameAsync` and `VDDone` functions. Applications can use the `VDGetCurrentFlags` function to retrieve the component's output capability flags. See page 8-25 for a description of the `VDGetCurrentFlags` function.

The `VDDone` function returns a long integer indicating whether the specified asynchronous frame grab is complete. If the returned value is 0, the video digitizer component is still working on the frame. If the returned value is nonzero, the digitizer component is finished with the frame and the application can perform its processing.

CHAPTER 8

Video Digitizer Components

VDSetFrameRate

The `VDSetFrameRate` function allows an application to indicate its desired frame rate to the video digitizer. Note that some digitizers may not be able to support high frame rates.

```
pascal VideoDigitizerError VDSetFrameRate
                                (VideoDigitizerComponent ci,
                                Fixed framesPerSecond);
```

ci Identifies the application's connection to the video digitizer component. An application obtains this value from the Component Manager's `OpenComponent` function.

framesPerSecond
Specifies the application's desired frame rate. Applications may set this parameter to 0 to return the digitizer to its default frame rate (typically 29.97 frames per second).

DESCRIPTION

In some cases, the digitizer component may not be able to control its frame rate. These digitizers can run at only a single rate of speed. In this case, the digitizer returns a result code of `digiUnimpErr`.

RESULT CODES

noErr   0   No error
digiUnimpErr   –2201   Function not supported

VDGetDataRate

The `VDGetDataRate` function allows an application to retrieve information that describes the performance capabilities of a video digitizer.

```
pascal VideoDigitizerError VDGetDataRate
                                (VideoDigitizerComponent ci,
                                long *milliSecPerFrame,
                                Fixed *framesPerSecond,
                                long *bytesPerSecond);
```

Video Digitizer Components Reference

CHAPTER 8

Video Digitizer Components

ci
: Identifies the application's connection to the video digitizer component. An application obtains this value from the Component Manager's `OpenComponent` function.

milliSecPerFrame
: Contains a pointer to a long integer. The video digitizer returns a value that indicates the number of milliseconds of synchronous overhead involved in digitizing a single frame. This value includes the average delay incurred between the time when the digitizer requests a frame from its associated device, and the time at which the device delivers the frame.

framesPerSecond
: Contains a pointer to a fixed value. The video digitizer supplies the maximum rate at which it can capture video. Note that this value may differ from the rate that the application set with the `VDSetFrameRate` function, described in the previous section.

bytesPerSecond
: Contains a pointer to a long integer. Video digitizers that can return compressed image data return a value that indicates the approximate number of bytes per second that the digitizer is generating compressed data, given the current compression settings and frame rate settings.

RESULT CODES

noErr	0	No error
digiUnimpErr	–2201	Function not supported

Controlling Color

Video digitizer components support color digitization. Therefore, these components provide several functions that allow applications to control the color digitization process.

You can use `VDSetInputColorSpaceMode` in your application to enable and disable color digitization; you can use the `VDGetInputColorSpaceMode` function to determine whether color digitization is enabled. The `VDUseThisCLUT` function allows you to specify a color lookup table to be used by the video digitizer component. In cases where the component cannot accommodate a particular lookup table, your application can use the `VDGetCLUTInUse` function to retrieve the color lookup table used by the digitizer component.

Your application can determine whether a digitizer component supports color digitization by examining the input capability flags of the component. Specifically, if the `digiInDoesColor` flag is set to 1, the component supports color digitization. Applications can use the `VDGetCurrentFlags` function to obtain the input capability flags of a component (see "Getting Information About Video Digitizer Components" on page 8-24 for more information).

Your application can determine a digitizer's supported pixel depths by calling the `VDGetDMADepths` function.

CHAPTER 8

Video Digitizer Components

VDUseThisCLUT

Some video digitizer components allow applications to specify the lookup table for color digitization. Your application can set the color lookup table by calling the `VDUseThisCLUT` function.

```
pascal VideoDigitizerError VDUseThisCLUT
                            (VideoDigitizerComponent ci,
                                CTabHandle colorTableHandle);
```

ci Specifies the video digitizer component for the request. Applications obtain this reference from the Component Manager's `OpenComponent` function.

colorTableHandle
    Contains a color table handle. The video digitizer component uses the color table referred to by this parameter.

DESCRIPTION

Applications can determine whether a digitizer component supports specified lookup tables by examining the digitizer component's output capability flags. Specifically, if the `digiOutDoesILUT` flag is set to 1, the digitizer component allows applications to specify color lookup tables. Applications can use the `VDGetCurrentFlags` function (described on page 8-25) to obtain the input capability flags of a component.

This feature is only useful for capturing 8-bit color video.

RESULT CODES

noErr	0	No error
digiUnimpErr	–2201	Function not supported

VDGetCLUTInUse

The `VDGetCLUTInUse` function allows an application to obtain the color lookup table used by a video digitizer component. By using the Palette Manager, the application can then set the destination so that it uses the same lookup table.

```
pascal VideoDigitizerError VDGetCLUTInUse
                            (VideoDigitizerComponent ci,
                                CTabHandle *colorTableHandle);
```

ci Specifies the video digitizer component for the request. Applications obtain this reference from the Component Manager's `OpenComponent` function.

Video Digitizer Components Reference

CHAPTER 8

Video Digitizer Components

`colorTableHandle`
: Contains a pointer to a field that is to receive a color table handle. The video digitizer component returns a handle to its color lookup table. Applications can then set the destination to use this returned color table. Your application is responsible for disposing of this handle.

DESCRIPTION

In general, applications use this function only when a video digitizer component does not allow applications to specify lookup tables with the `VDUseThisCLUT` function. Applications can determine whether a digitizer component supports specified lookup tables by examining the component's output capability flags. Specifically, if the `digiOutDoesILUT` flag is set to 1, the digitizer component allows applications to specify color lookup tables. Applications can use the `VDGetCurrentFlags` function (described on page 8-25) to obtain the input capability flags of a component.

RESULT CODES

`noErr`	0	No error
`memFullErr`	–108	Not enough room in heap zone
`digiUnimpErr`	–2201	Function not supported

VDSetInputColorSpaceMode

The `VDSetInputColorSpaceMode` function allows applications to choose between color and grayscale digitized video.

```
pascal VideoDigitizerError VDSetInputColorSpaceMode
                    (VideoDigitizerComponent ci,
                     short colorSpaceMode);
```

`ci`
: Specifies the video digitizer component for the request. Applications obtain this reference from the Component Manager's `OpenComponent` function.

`colorSpaceMode`
: Controls color digitization. The following values are valid:

    0   Grayscale digitization
    1   Color digitization

CHAPTER 8

Video Digitizer Components

DESCRIPTION

Applications can determine whether a digitizer component supports grayscale or color digitization by examining the digitizer component's input capability flags. Specifically, if the `digiInDoesColor` flag is set to 1, the digitizer component supports color digitization. Similarly, if the `digiInDoesBW` flag is set to 1, the digitizer component supports grayscale digitization. Applications can use the `VDGetCurrentFlags` function (described on page 8-25) to obtain the input capability flags of a digitizer component.

RESULT CODES

`noErr`	0	No error
`digiUnimpErr`	–2201	Function not supported
`qtParamErr`	–2202	Invalid parameter value

VDGetInputColorSpaceMode

The `VDGetInputColorSpaceMode` function allows applications to determine whether a digitizer is operating in color or grayscale mode.

```
pascal VideoDigitizerError VDGetInputColorSpaceMode
                    (VideoDigitizerComponent ci,
                     short *colorSpaceMode);
```

ci
: Specifies the video digitizer component for the request. Applications obtain this reference from the Component Manager's `OpenComponent` function.

colorSpaceMode
: Contains a pointer to a value that indicates whether the digitizer is operating in color or grayscale mode. The following values are valid:

0	Grayscale digitization
1	Color digitization

DESCRIPTION

Applications can determine whether a digitizer component supports grayscale or color digitization by examining the digitizer component's input capability flags. Specifically, if the `digiInDoesColor` flag is set to 1, the digitizer component supports color digitization. Similarly, if the `digiInDoesBW` flag is set to 1, the digitizer component supports grayscale digitization. Applications can use the `VDGetCurrentFlags` function (described on page 8-25) to obtain the input capability flags of a digitizer component.

CHAPTER 8

Video Digitizer Components

RESULT CODES

noErr	0	No error
digiUnimpErr	–2201	Function not supported
qtParamErr	–2202	Invalid parameter value

SEE ALSO

Applications can choose between color and grayscale digitization by calling the `VDSetInputColorSpaceMode` function, which is described in the previous section.

VDGetDMADepths

The `VDGetDMADepths` function allows an application to determine which pixel depths a digitizer supports. This function is supported only by digitizers that support DMA (that is, their `digiOutDoesDMA` output capability flag is set to 1).

```
pascal VideoDigitizerError VDGetDMADepths
                        (VideoDigitizerComponent ci,
                         long *depthArray,
                         long *preferredDepth);
```

ci
: Identifies the application's connection to the video digitizer component. An application obtains this value from the Component Manager's `OpenComponent` function.

depthArray
: Contains a pointer to a long integer. The video digitizer returns a value that indicates the depths it can support. Each depth is represented by a single bit in this field. More than one bit may be set to 1.

preferredDepth
: Contains a pointer to a long integer. Video digitizers that have a preferred depth value return that value in this field, using one of the possible values of the `depthArray` parameter. Digitizers that do not prefer any given value set this field to 0.

DESCRIPTION

The flags returned by this function augment the information that an application can obtain from the digitizer's output capability flags in the digitizer information structure (see "Capability Flags" beginning on page 8-14 for more information). If a digitizer does not support this function but does support DMA, an application may assume that the digitizer can handle offscreen buffers at all of the depths indicated in its output capabilities flags.

Before a program that uses a video digitizer creates an offscreen buffer, it should call the `VDGetDMADepths` function to determine the pixel depths supported by the digitizer. If possible, the program should use the preferred depth, in order to obtain the best possible display performance.

Applications may use the following enumerators to set bits in the field referred to by the `depthArray` parameter.

```
enum {
    dmaDepth1     = 1,   /* supports black and white */
    dmaDepth2     = 2,   /* supports 2-bit color */
    dmaDepth4     = 4,   /* supports 4-bit color */
    dmaDepth8     = 8,   /* supports 8-bit color */
    dmaDepth16    = 16,  /* supports 16-bit color */
    dmaDepth32    = 32,  /* supports 32-bit color */
    dmaDepth2Gray = 64,  /* supports 2-bit grayscale */
    dmaDepth4Gray = 128, /* supports 4-bit grayscale */
    dmaDepth8Gray = 256  /* supports 8-bit grayscale */
};
```

RESULT CODES

`noErr`	0	No error
`digiUnimpErr`	–2201	Function not supported

Controlling Analog Video

Some video digitizer components may provide functions that allow applications to control the characteristics of the input analog video signal. This section describes these analog video functions.

The `VDGetVideoDefaults` function returns the suggested default values for the analog video parameters that can be affected by functions described in this section.

A number of functions affect gamma correction. The `VDSetInputGammaRecord` and `VDGetInputGammaRecord` functions work with gamma structures (see *Designing Cards and Drivers for the Macintosh Family*, third edition, for more information about gamma structures). You can use the `VDSetInputGammaValue` and `VDGetInputGammaValue` functions to allow your application to set particular gamma values.

The `VDSetBlackLevelValue`, `VDGetBlackLevelValue`, `VDSetWhiteLevelValue`, and `VDGetWhiteLevelValue` functions allow applications to work with black levels and white levels in the source video. **Black level** refers to the degree of blackness in an image. This is a common setting on a video digitizer. The highest setting produces an all-black image; on the other hand, the lowest setting yields little, if any, black even with black objects in the scene. Black level is a significant setting because it can be adjusted so that there is little or no noise in an image. **White level** refers to the degree of whiteness in an image. It is also a common video digitizer setting.

CHAPTER 8

Video Digitizer Components

The `VDSetContrast`, `VDGetContrast`, `VDSetSharpness`, and `VDGetSharpness` functions allow applications to work with contrast and sharpness values in the source video. The `VDGetBrightness` and `VDSetBrightness` functions allow applications to work with the image brightness setting.

The `VDSetHue`, `VDGetHue`, `VDSetSaturation`, and `VDGetSaturation` functions allow applications to work with hue and saturation settings in the source video.

VDGetVideoDefaults

The `VDGetVideoDefaults` function returns the recommended values for many of the analog video parameters that may be set by applications.

All video digitizer components must support this function.

```
pascal VideoDigitizerError VDGetVideoDefaults
                          (VideoDigitizerComponent ci,
                           unsigned short *blackLevel,
                           unsigned short *whiteLevel,
                           unsigned short *brightness,
                           unsigned short *hue,
                           unsigned short *saturation,
                           unsigned short *contrast,
                           unsigned short *sharpness);
```

ci
: Specifies the video digitizer component for the request. Applications obtain this reference from the Component Manager's `OpenComponent` function.

blackLevel
: Contains a pointer to an integer that is to receive the default black level value. The video digitizer component places the default black level value into the field referred to by this parameter. Refer to the discussion of the `VDSetBlackLevelValue` function in the next section for more information about black level values.

whiteLevel
: Contains a pointer to an integer that is to receive the default white level value. The video digitizer component places the default white level value into the field referred to by this parameter. Refer to the discussion of the `VDSetWhiteLevelValue` function on page 8-69 for more information about white level values.

brightness
: Contains a pointer to an integer that is to receive the default brightness value. The video digitizer component places the default brightness value into the field referred to by this parameter. Refer to the discussion of the `VDSetBrightness` function on page 8-73 for more information about brightness values.

CHAPTER 8

Video Digitizer Components

hue Contains a pointer to an integer that is to receive the default hue value. The video digitizer component places the default hue value into the field referred to by this parameter. Refer to the discussion of the `VDSetHue` function on page 8-70 for more information about hue values.

saturation
Contains a pointer to an integer that is to receive the default saturation value. The video digitizer component places the default saturation value into the field referred to by this parameter. Refer to the discussion of the `VDSetSaturation` function on page 8-72 for more information about saturation values.

contrast Contains a pointer to an integer that is to receive the default contrast value. The video digitizer component places the default contrast value into the field referred to by this parameter. Refer to the discussion of the `VDSetContrast` function on page 8-75 for more information about contrast values.

sharpness Contains a pointer to an integer that is to receive the default sharpness value. The video digitizer component places the default sharpness value into the field referred to by this parameter. Refer to the discussion of the `VDSetSharpness` function on page 8-76 for more information about sharpness values.

RESULT CODE

noErr   0   No error

VDSetBlackLevelValue

The `VDSetBlackLevelValue` function sets the current black level value. Black level values range from 0 to 65,535, where 0 represents the maximum black value and 65,535 represents the minimum black value.

```
pascal VideoDigitizerError VDSetBlackLevelValue
                    (VideoDigitizerComponent ci,
                        unsigned short *blackLevel);
```

ci Specifies the video digitizer component for the request. Applications obtain this reference from the Component Manager's `OpenComponent` function.

blackLevel
Contains a pointer to an integer that contains the new black level value. The video digitizer component attempts to set the black level value to the value specified by this parameter. The digitizer component returns the new value, so that the application can avoid using unsupported values in future requests.

CHAPTER 8

Video Digitizer Components

RESULT CODES

noErr	0	No error
digiUnimpErr	−2201	Function not supported
qtParamErr	−2202	Invalid parameter value

SEE ALSO

Applications can get the current black level value by calling the `VDGetBlackLevelValue` function (described in the next section). Applications can obtain the recommended black level value by calling the `VDGetVideoDefaults` function (described in the previous section).

VDGetBlackLevelValue

The `VDGetBlackLevelValue` function returns the current black level value. Black level values range from 0 to 65,535, where 0 represents the maximum black value and 65,535 represents the minimum black value.

```
pascal VideoDigitizerError VDGetBlackLevelValue
                    (VideoDigitizerComponent ci,
                     unsigned short *blackLevel);
```

ci Specifies the video digitizer component for the request. Applications obtain this reference from the Component Manager's `OpenComponent` function.

blackLevel
Contains a pointer to an integer that is to receive the current black level value. The video digitizer component places the black level value into the field referred to by this parameter.

DESCRIPTION

Applications can set the black level value by calling the `VDSetBlackLevelValue` function (described in the previous section). Applications can obtain the recommended black level value by calling the `VDGetVideoDefaults` function (described on page 8-66).

RESULT CODES

noErr	0	No error
digiUnimpErr	−2201	Function not supported

CHAPTER 8

Video Digitizer Components

VDSetWhiteLevelValue

The `VDSetWhiteLevelValue` function sets the white level value. White level values range from 0 to 65,535, where 0 represents the minimum white value and 65,535 represents the maximum white value.

```
pascal VideoDigitizerError VDSetWhiteLevelValue
                            (VideoDigitizerComponent ci,
                                unsigned short *whiteLevel);
```

ci
Specifies the video digitizer component for the request. Applications obtain this reference from the Component Manager's `OpenComponent` function.

whiteLevel
Contains a pointer to an integer that contains the new white level value. The video digitizer component attempts to set the white level value to the value specified by this parameter. The digitizer component returns the new value, so that the application can avoid using unsupported values in future requests.

RESULT CODES

noErr	0	No error
digiUnimpErr	−2201	Function not supported
qtParamErr	−2202	Invalid parameter value

SEE ALSO

Applications can get the current white level value by calling the `VDGetWhiteLevelValue` function (described in the next section). Applications can obtain the recommended white level value by calling the `VDGetVideoDefaults` function (described on page 8-66).

VDGetWhiteLevelValue

The `VDGetWhiteLevelValue` function returns the current white level value. White level values range from 0 to 65,535, where 0 represents the minimum white value and 65,535 represents the maximum white value.

```
pascal VideoDigitizerError VDGetWhiteLevelValue
                            (VideoDigitizerComponent ci,
                                unsigned short *whiteLevel);
```

Video Digitizer Components Reference

CHAPTER 8

Video Digitizer Components

ci
: Specifies the video digitizer component for the request. Applications obtain this reference from the Component Manager's `OpenComponent` function.

whiteLevel
: Contains a pointer to an integer that is to receive the current white level value. The video digitizer component places the white level value into the field referred to by this parameter.

RESULT CODES

noErr	0	No error
digiUnimpErr	–2201	Function not supported

SEE ALSO

Your application can set the white level value by calling the `VDSetWhiteLevelValue` function (described in the previous section). Your application can obtain the recommended white level value by calling the `VDGetVideoDefaults` function (described on page 8-66).

VDSetHue

The `VDSetHue` function sets the current **hue value.** Hue is similar to the tint control on a television, and it is specified in degrees with complementary colors set 180 degrees apart (red is 0°, green is +120°, and blue is –120°). Video digitizer components support hue values that range from 0 (–180° shift in hue) to 65,535 (+179° shift in hue), where 32,767 represents a 0° shift in hue.

```
pascal VideoDigitizerError VDSetHue (VideoDigitizerComponent ci,
                                     unsigned short *hue);
```

ci
: Specifies the video digitizer component for the request. Applications obtain this reference from the Component Manager's `OpenComponent` function.

hue
: Contains a pointer to an integer that contains the new hue value. The video digitizer component attempts to set the hue value to the value specified by this parameter. The digitizer component returns the new value, so that the application can avoid using unsupported values in future requests.

CHAPTER 8

Video Digitizer Components

RESULT CODES

noErr	0	No error
digiUnimpErr	–2201	Function not supported
qtParamErr	–2202	Invalid parameter value

SEE ALSO

Your application can obtain the current hue value by calling the `VDGetHue` function (described in the next section). To retrieve the recommended hue value, your application can call the `VDGetVideoDefaults` function (described on page 8-66).

VDGetHue

The `VDGetHue` function returns the current hue value. Hue is similar to the tint control on a television, and it is specified in degrees with complementary colors set 180 degrees apart (red is 0°, green is +120°, and blue is –120°). Video digitizer components support hue values that range from 0 (–180° shift in hue) to 65,535 (+179° shift in hue), where 32,767 represents a 0° shift in hue.

```
pascal VideoDigitizerError VDGetHue (VideoDigitizerComponent ci,
                                      unsigned short *hue);
```

ci Specifies the video digitizer component for the request. Applications obtain this reference from the Component Manager's `OpenComponent` function.

hue Contains a pointer to an integer that is to receive the current hue value. The video digitizer component places the hue value into the field referred to by this parameter.

RESULT CODES

noErr	0	No error
digiUnimpErr	–2201	Function not supported

SEE ALSO

Your application can set the hue value by calling the `VDSetHue` function (described in the previous section). To obtain the recommended hue value, your application can call the `VDGetVideoDefaults` function (described on page 8-66).

VDSetSaturation

The `VDSetSaturation` function sets the **saturation value,** which controls color intensity. For example, at high saturation levels, red appears to be red; at low saturation, red appears pink. Valid saturation values range from 0 to 65,535, where 0 is the minimum saturation value and 65,535 specifies maximum saturation.

```
pascal VideoDigitizerError VDSetSaturation
                    (VideoDigitizerComponent ci,
                      unsigned short *saturation);
```

ci
: Specifies the video digitizer component for the request. Applications obtain this reference from the Component Manager's `OpenComponent` function.

saturation
: Contains a pointer to an integer that contains the new saturation value. The video digitizer component attempts to set the saturation value to the value specified by this parameter. The digitizer component returns the new value, so that the application can avoid using unsupported values in future requests.

RESULT CODES

noErr	0	No error
digiUnimpErr	−2201	Function not supported
qtParamErr	−2202	Invalid parameter value

SEE ALSO

Applications can get the current saturation value by calling the `VDGetSaturation` function (described in the next section). Applications can obtain the recommended saturation value by calling the `VDGetVideoDefaults` function (described on page 8-66).

VDGetSaturation

The `VDGetSaturation` function returns the current saturation value, which controls color intensity. For example, at high saturation levels red appears to be red, while at low saturation red appears pink. Valid saturation values range from 0 to 65,535, where 0 is the minimum saturation value and 65,535 specifies maximum saturation.

```
pascal VideoDigitizerError VDGetSaturation
                    (VideoDigitizerComponent ci,
                      unsigned short *saturation);
```

Video Digitizer Components

ci
: Specifies the video digitizer component for the request. Applications obtain this reference from the Component Manager's `OpenComponent` function.

saturation
: Contains a pointer to an integer that is to receive the current saturation value. The video digitizer component places the saturation value into the field referred to by this parameter.

DESCRIPTION

The `VDGetSaturation` function returns the current saturation value.

RESULT CODES

noErr	0	No error
digiUnimpErr	–2201	Function not supported

SEE ALSO

Your application can set the saturation value by calling the `VDSetSaturation` function (described in the previous section). To obtain the recommended saturation value, your application can call the `VDGetVideoDefaults` function (described on page 8-66).

VDSetBrightness

The `VDSetBrightness` function sets the current brightness value, which controls the overall brightness of the digitized video image. Brightness values range from 0 to 65,535, where 0 is the darkest possible setting and 65,535 is the lightest possible setting.

```
pascal VideoDigitizerError VDSetBrightness
                    (VideoDigitizerComponent ci,
                     unsigned short *brightness);
```

ci
: Specifies the video digitizer component for the request. Applications obtain this reference from the Component Manager's `OpenComponent` function.

brightness
: Contains a pointer to an integer that contains the new brightness value. The video digitizer component attempts to set the brightness value to the value specified by this parameter. The digitizer component returns the new value, so that the application can avoid using unsupported values in future requests.

CHAPTER 8

Video Digitizer Components

RESULT CODES

```
noErr            0     No error
digiUnimpErr  –2201    Function not supported
```

SEE ALSO

Your application can get the current brightness value by calling the `VDGetBrightness` function (described in the next section). To obtain the recommended brightness value, your application can call the `VDGetVideoDefaults` function (described on page 8-66).

VDGetBrightness

The `VDGetBrightness` function returns the current brightness value, which reflects the overall brightness of the digitized video image. Brightness values range from 0 to 65,535, where 0 is the darkest possible setting and 65,535 is the lightest possible setting.

```
pascal VideoDigitizerError VDGetBrightness
                            (VideoDigitizerComponent ci,
                             unsigned short *brightness);
```

ci
: Specifies the video digitizer component for the request. Applications obtain this reference from the Component Manager's `OpenComponent` function.

brightness
: Contains a pointer to an integer that is to receive the current brightness value. The video digitizer component places the brightness value into the field referred to by this parameter.

RESULT CODES

```
noErr            0     No error
digiUnimpErr  –2201    Function not supported
```

SEE ALSO

Your application can set the brightness value by calling the `VDSetBrightness` function (described in the previous section). To obtain the recommended brightness value, your application can call the `VDGetVideoDefaults` function (described on page 8-66).

CHAPTER 8

Video Digitizer Components

VDSetContrast

The `VDSetContrast` function sets the current contrast value. The contrast value ranges from 0 to 65,535, where 0 represents no change to the basic image and larger values increase the contrast of the video image (that is, increase the slope of the transform).

```
pascal VideoDigitizerError VDSetContrast
                        (VideoDigitizerComponent ci,
                            unsigned short *contrast);
```

ci Specifies the video digitizer component for the request. Applications obtain this reference from the Component Manager's `OpenComponent` function.

contrast Contains a pointer to an integer that contains the new contrast value. The video digitizer component attempts to set the contrast value to the value specified by this parameter. The digitizer component returns the new value, so that the application can avoid using unsupported values in future requests.

RESULT CODES

noErr	0	No error
digiUnimpErr	–2201	Function not supported
qtParamErr	–2202	Invalid parameter value

SEE ALSO

Your application can obtain the current contrast value by calling the `VDGetContrast` function (described in the next section). To retrieve the recommended contrast value, your application can call the `VDGetVideoDefaults` function (described on page 8-66).

VDGetContrast

The `VDGetContrast` function returns the current contrast value. The contrast value ranges from 0 to 65,535, where 0 represents no change to the basic image and larger values increase the contrast of the video image (that is, increase the slope of the transform).

```
pascal VideoDigitizerError VDGetContrast
                        (VideoDigitizerComponent ci,
                            unsigned short *contrast);
```

ci Specifies the video digitizer component for the request. Applications obtain this reference from the Component Manager's `OpenComponent` function.

Video Digitizer Components

contrast   Contains a pointer to an integer that is to receive the current contrast value. The video digitizer component places the contrast value into the field referred to by this parameter.

RESULT CODES

noErr	0	No error
digiUnimpErr	–2201	Function not supported

SEE ALSO

Your application can set the contrast value by calling the `VDSetContrast` function (described in the previous section). To obtain the recommended contrast value, your application can call the `VDGetVideoDefaults` function (described on page 8-66).

VDSetSharpness

The `VDSetSharpness` function sets the sharpness value. The sharpness value ranges from 0 to 65,535, where 0 represents no sharpness filtering and 65,535 represents full sharpness filtering. Higher values result in a visual impression of increased picture sharpness.

```
pascal VideoDigitizerError VDSetSharpness
                    (VideoDigitizerComponent ci,
                    unsigned short *sharpness);
```

ci   Specifies the video digitizer component for the request. Applications obtain this reference from the Component Manager's `OpenComponent` function.

sharpness   Contains a pointer to an integer that contains the new sharpness value. The video digitizer component attempts to set the sharpness value to the value specified by this parameter. The digitizer component returns the new value, so that the application can avoid using unsupported values in future requests.

RESULT CODES

noErr	0	No error
digiUnimpErr	–2201	Function not supported
qtParamErr	–2202	Invalid parameter value

CHAPTER 8

Video Digitizer Components

SEE ALSO

Your application can obtain the current sharpness value by calling the `VDGetSharpness` function (described in the next section). To retrieve the recommended sharpness value, your application can call the `VDGetVideoDefaults` function (described on page 8-66).

VDGetSharpness

The `VDGetSharpness` function returns the current sharpness value. The sharpness value ranges from 0 to 65,535, where 0 represents no sharpness filtering and 65,535 represents full sharpness filtering. Higher values result in a visual impression of increased picture sharpness.

```
pascal VideoDigitizerError VDGetSharpness
                            (VideoDigitizerComponent ci,
                            unsigned short *sharpness);
```

ci   Specifies the video digitizer component for the request. Applications obtain this reference from the Component Manager's `OpenComponent` function.

sharpness   Contains a pointer to an integer that is to receive the current sharpness value. The video digitizer component places the sharpness value into the field referred to by this parameter.

RESULT CODES

noErr	0	No error
digiUnimpErr	–2201	Function not supported

SEE ALSO

Your application can set the sharpness value by calling the `VDSetSharpness` function (described in the previous section). To obtain the recommended sharpness value, your application can call the `VDGetVideoDefaults` function (described on page 8-66).

Video Digitizer Components Reference

CHAPTER 8

Video Digitizer Components

VDSetInputGammaRecord

The `VDSetInputGammaRecord` function allows an application to change the active input gamma data structure. Gamma structures give applications complete control over color filtering transforms.

```
pascal VideoDigitizerError VDSetInputGammaRecord
                        (VideoDigitizerComponent ci,
                         VDGamRecPtr inputGammaPtr);
```

ci
: Specifies the video digitizer component for the request. Applications obtain this reference from the Component Manager's `OpenComponent` function.

inputGammaPtr
: Contains a pointer to an input gamma structure. The input gamma structure is defined by the `gammaTbl` data type. For more information about gamma structures, see *Designing Cards and Drivers for the Macintosh Family*, third edition. The video digitizer component uses the input gamma structure specified by this parameter.

SPECIAL CONIDERATIONS

Note that the `VDSetInputGammaRecord` function may override the current gamma value and contrast settings if the video digitizer component uses a lookup table to implement brightness and contrast.

RESULT CODES

noErr	0	No error
digiUnimpErr	–2201	Function not supported

SEE ALSO

Your application can get a pointer to the current input gamma structure by calling the `VDGetInputGammaRecord` function, which is described in the next section.

VDGetInputGammaRecord

The `VDGetInputGammaRecord` function allows your application to retrieve a pointer to the active input gamma structure. Gamma structures give applications complete control over color filtering transforms and are therefore more precise than the gamma values that can be set by calling the `VDSetInputGammaValue` function (described in the next section).

```
pascal VideoDigitizerError VDGetInputGammaRecord
                        (VideoDigitizerComponent ci,
                         VDGamRecPtr *inputGammaPtr);
```

ci
: Specifies the video digitizer component for the request. Applications obtain this reference from the Component Manager's `OpenComponent` function.

inputGammaPtr
: Contains a pointer to a field that is to receive a pointer to an input gamma structure. The input gamma structure is defined by the `gammaTbl` data type. For more information about gamma structures, see *Designing Cards and Drivers for the Macintosh Family*, third edition. The video digitizer component places a pointer to its input gamma structure into the field referred to by this parameter.

RESULT CODES

noErr	0	No error
digiUnimpErr	–2201	Function not supported

SEE ALSO

Your application can set the input gamma structure by calling the `VDSetInputGammaRecord` function, which is described in the previous section.

VDSetInputGammaValue

The `VDSetInputGammaValue` function sets the gamma values. These gamma values control the brightness of the input video signal. Your application can implement special color effects, such as turning off specific color channels, by calling this function.

```
pascal VideoDigitizerError VDSetInputGammaValue
                            (VideoDigitizerComponent ci,
                                Fixed channel1,
                                Fixed channel2,
                                Fixed channel3);
```

ci
: Specifies the video digitizer component for the request. Applications obtain this reference from the Component Manager's `OpenComponent` function.

channel1
: Specifies the gamma value for the red component of the input video signal.

channel2
: Specifies the gamma value for the green component of the input video signal.

channel3
: Specifies the gamma value for the blue component of the input video signal.

RESULT CODES

noErr	0	No error
digiUnimpErr	–2201	Function not supported

SEE ALSO

Your application can retrieve the current gamma values by calling the `VDGetInputGammaValue` function (described in the next section). To obtain the recommended gamma values, your application can call the `VDGetVideoDefaults` function (described on page 8-66).

VDGetInputGammaValue

The `VDGetInputGammaValue` function returns the current gamma values. These gamma values control the brightness of the input video signal.

```
pascal VideoDigitizerError VDGetInputGammaValue
                            (VideoDigitizerComponent ci,
                                Fixed *channel1, Fixed *channel2,
                                Fixed *channel3);
```

ci
: Specifies the video digitizer component for the request. Applications obtain this reference from the Component Manager's `OpenComponent` function.

channel1
: Contains a pointer to a fixed field that is to receive the gamma value for the red component of the input video signal. The video digitizer component places the appropriate gamma value into the field referred to by this parameter.

channel2
: Contains a pointer to a fixed field that is to receive the gamma value for the green component of the input video signal. The video digitizer component places the appropriate gamma value into the field referred to by this parameter.

channel3
: Contains a pointer to a fixed field that is to receive the gamma value for the blue component of the input video signal. The video digitizer component places the appropriate gamma value into the field referred to by this parameter.

RESULT CODES

noErr	0	No error
digiUnimpErr	–2201	Function not supported

SEE ALSO

Your application can set the gamma values by calling the `VDSetInputGammaValue` function (described in the previous section). To obtain the recommended gamma values, you can call the `VDGetVideoDefaults` function (described on page 8-66).

Selectively Displaying Video

Video digitizer components may support one of three methods of selectively displaying video on the screen of a Macintosh computer. The three methods are key colors, alpha channels, and blend masks. For a complete description of these techniques for selectively displaying video, see "About Video Digitizer Components," which begins on page 8-3.

Your application can determine whether a video digitizer component supports selective video display by examining the component's digitizer information structure (described on page 8-20). Specifically, the `vdigType` field indicates the type of blending supported by the digitizer. Applications can use the `VDGetDigitizerInfo` function (described on page 8-24) to retrieve a component's digitizer information structure.

Some video digitizer components support the use of key colors as a mechanism for selectively displaying video on the screen of a Macintosh computer. When a key color is active, the digitizer component replaces all screen occurrences of that color with the appropriate portion of the source video. Video digitizer components that support key colors provide a number of functions to applications. Those functions are described in this section.

Your applications can use the `VDSetKeyColor`, `VDAddKeyColor`, and `VDSetKeyColorRange` functions to set one or more key colors for a video digitizer component. The `VDGetKeyColor`, `VDGetNextKeyColor`, and `VDGetKeyColorRange` functions allow your application to retrieve information about the currently active key colors.

Alpha channels and blend masks work similarly to one another. Digitizer components that support alpha channels use a portion of each pixel value to indicate the degree of video display for that pixel. Digitizer components that support blend masks use the mask to indicate the degree of video display for corresponding pixels.

Your applications can use the `VDGetMaskandValue` function to determine the appropriate mask value for a desired blend level. The `VDSetMasterBlendLevel` function allows applications to set a blend level that applies to the entire source video image. The `VDGetMaskPixMap` function allows applications to retrieve the pixel map that defines the blend mask.

VDSetKeyColor

The `VDSetKeyColor` function allows applications to set the key color.

All video digitizer components that support key colors must support this function.

```
pascal VideoDigitizerError VDSetKeyColor
                            (VideoDigitizerComponent ci,
                             long index);
```

ci
: Specifies the video digitizer component for the request. Applications obtain this reference from the Component Manager's `OpenComponent` function.

index
: Specifies the new key color. The value of the `index` field corresponds to a color in the current color lookup table.

DESCRIPTION

Some video digitizer components support multiple key colors. The `VDSetKeyColor` function instructs such digitizer components to clear the key color list and insert a single entry for the specified color. Applications can then use the `VDAddKeyColor` function, described on page 8-84, to place additional colors into the key color list.

RESULT CODES

```
noErr              0      No error
digiUnimpErr      –2201   Function not supported
qtParamErr        –2202   Invalid parameter value
```

VDGetKeyColor

The `VDGetKeyColor` function allows your application to obtain the index value of the active key color.

All video digitizer components that support key colors must support this function.

```
pascal VideoDigitizerError VDGetKeyColor
                            (VideoDigitizerComponent ci,
                                long *index);
```

ci
: Specifies the video digitizer component for the request. Applications obtain this reference from the Component Manager's `OpenComponent` function.

index
: Contains a pointer to a field that is to receive the index of the key color. This index value identifies the key color within the currently active color lookup table. If there are several active key colors, the video digitizer returns the first color from the key color list. Subsequently, applications use the `VDGetNextKeyColor` function (described on page 8-86) to obtain other colors from the list. If there is no active key color, the `VDGetKeyColor` function sets the field to –1.

DESCRIPTION

In cases where there are several key colors, the `VDGetKeyColor` function always returns the index of the first color in the list. Applications should then use the `VDGetNextKeyColor` function (described on page 8-86) to retrieve the remaining colors in the list.

RESULT CODES

noErr	0	No error
digiUnimpErr	–2201	Function not supported

VDSetKeyColorRange

Some video digitizer components that support key colors may allow applications to set a range of key color values. The key color range is expressed as a range of RGB color values. The `VDSetKeyColorRange` function allows your application to define a key color range.

```
pascal VideoDigitizerError VDSetKeyColorRange
                            (VideoDigitizerComponent ci,
                                RGBColor *minRGB,
                                RGBColor *maxRGB);
```

ci
: Specifies the video digitizer component for the request. Applications obtain this reference from the Component Manager's `OpenComponent` function.

minRGB
: Contains a pointer to a field that contains the lower bound of the key color range. All colors in the color table between the color specified by the `minRGB` parameter and the color specified by the `maxRGB` parameter are considered key colors.

maxRGB
: Contains a pointer to a field that contains the upper bound of the key color range. All colors in the color table between the color specified by the `minRGB` parameter and the color specified by the `maxRGB` parameter are considered key colors.

DESCRIPTION

If the digitizer component cannot accommodate all the colors that are defined in the specified range, it returns a result value of `noMoreKeyColors`.

RESULT CODES

```
noErr              0      No error
digiUnimpErr      -2201   Function not supported
noMoreKeyColors   -2205   Key color list is full
```

SEE ALSO

Your application can obtain the current key color range by calling the `VDGetKeyColorRange` function, which is described on page 8-85.

VDAddKeyColor

Some video digitizer components can support more than one active key color. The `VDAddKeyColor` function allows applications to add a key color to a component's list of active key colors.

```
pascal VideoDigitizerError VDAddKeyColor
                                (VideoDigitizerComponent ci,
                                 long *index);
```

ci
: Specifies the video digitizer component for the request. Applications obtain this reference from the Component Manager's `OpenComponent` function.

index
: Contains a pointer to the color to add to the key color list. The value of the `index` field corresponds to a color in the current color lookup table.

CHAPTER 8

Video Digitizer Components

DESCRIPTION

If the digitizer component cannot accommodate any more key colors, it returns a result code of `noMoreKeyColors`.

RESULT CODES

```
noErr              0      No error
digiUnimpErr      –2201   Function not supported
qtParamErr        –2202   Invalid parameter value
noMoreKeyColors   –2205   Key color list is full
```

SEE ALSO

To ensure that the key color list contains only the desired colors, your application should use the `VDSetKeyColor` function (described on page 8-82) to set the first key color.

VDGetKeyColorRange

Some video digitizer components that support key colors may allow applications to set a range of key color values. The key color range is expressed as a range of RGB color values. The `VDGetKeyColorRange` function allows applications to obtain the currently defined key color range.

```
pascal VideoDigitizerError VDGetKeyColorRange
                    (VideoDigitizerComponent ci,
                     RGBColor *minRGB,
                     RGBColor *maxRGB);
```

ci
: Specifies the video digitizer component for the request. Applications obtain this reference from the Component Manager's `OpenComponent` function.

minRGB
: Contains a pointer to a field that is to receive the lower bound of the key color range. The video digitizer component places the RGB color that corresponds to the lower end of the range in the field referred to by this parameter.

maxRGB
: Contains a pointer to a field that is to receive the upper bound of the key color range. The video digitizer component places the RGB color that corresponds to the upper end of the range in the field referred to by this parameter.

RESULT CODES

```
noErr           0      No error
digiUnimpErr   –2201   Function not supported
badCallOrder   –2209   Digitizer component not ready for this function
```

Video Digitizer Components

SEE ALSO

Your application can set the color range by calling the `VDSetKeyColorRange` function, which is described on page 8-83.

VDGetNextKeyColor

The `VDGetNextKeyColor` function allows your application to obtain the index value of the active key colors in cases where the digitizer component supports multiple key colors. Your application can use the `VDGetKeyColor` function (described on page 8-83) to retrieve the first key color in the list. Subsequently, your application can call the `VDGetNextKeyColor` function to retrieve the other colors in the key color list.

All video digitizer components that support multiple key colors must support this function.

```
pascal VideoDigitizerError VDGetNextKeyColor
                    (VideoDigitizerComponent ci,
                    long index);
```

ci
: Specifies the video digitizer component for the request. Applications obtain this reference from the Component Manager's `OpenComponent` function.

index
: Specifies a field that is to receive the index of the next key color. This index value identifies the key color within the currently active color lookup table. If there are no more colors left in the list, the digitizer component sets the field referred to by the `index` parameter to –1.

DESCRIPTION

The `VDGetNextKeyColor` function returns an index value of –1 when there are no more colors in the list.

RESULT CODES

noErr	0	No error
digiUnimpErr	–2201	Function not supported

VDSetMasterBlendLevel

The `VDSetMasterBlendLevel` function allows your application to set the blend level value for the input video signal. This value applies to the entire source video image.

```
pascal VideoDigitizerError VDSetMasterBlendLevel
                            (VideoDigitizerComponent ci,
                             unsigned short *blendLevel);
```

ci
: Specifies the video digitizer component for the request. Applications obtain this reference from the Component Manager's `OpenComponent` function.

blendLevel
: Contains a pointer to a field that specifies the new master blend level. Valid values range from 0 to 65,535, where 0 corresponds to no video and 65,535 corresponds to all video. The digitizer component returns the new value in this field, so your application can avoid using unsupported values in future requests.

RESULT CODES

noErr	0	No error
digiUnimpErr	–2201	Function not supported

VDGetMaskandValue

The `VDGetMaskandValue` function allows your application to obtain the appropriate alpha channel or blend mask value for a desired level of video blending. Your application specifies a desired level of video blend.

```
pascal VideoDigitizerError VDGetMaskandValue
                            (VideoDigitizerComponent ci,
                             unsigned short blendLevel,
                             long *mask, long *value);
```

ci
: Specifies the video digitizer component for the request. Applications obtain this reference from the Component Manager's `OpenComponent` function.

blendLevel
: Specifies the desired blend level. Valid values range from 0 to 65,535, where 0 corresponds to no video and 65,535 corresponds to all video.

Video Digitizer Components

mask   Contains a pointer to a field that is to receive a value indicating which bits are meaningful in the data returned for the `value` parameter. The video digitizer component sets to 1 the bits that correspond to meaningful bits in the data returned for the `value` parameter.

value   Contains a pointer to a field that is to receive data that can be used to obtain the desired blend level. The data returned for the `mask` parameter indicates which bits are valid in the data returned for this parameter.

DESCRIPTION

The video digitizer returns the corresponding mask value. The application can then use this value to set the alpha channel or blend mask.

The information returned by the digitizer component differs based on the type of blending supported by the component. In all cases, however, the returned value of the `value` parameter contains the value for the desired blend level, and the returned value of the `mask` parameter indicates which bits in the `value` parameter are meaningful. Bits in the returned `mask` parameter value that are set to 1 correspond to meaningful bits in the returned `value` parameter value.

For example, if an application requests a 50 percent video blend level from a digitizer that supports 8-bit alpha channels, the digitizer component might return the following values:

mask	0xFF000000	Identifies full upper byte as the alpha channel
value	0x80000000	Value for 50 percent blend level

RESULT CODES

noErr	0	No error
digiUnimpErr	–2201	Function not supported

VDGetMaskPixMap

The `VDGetMaskPixMap` function allows applications to retrieve the pixel map data for a component's blend mask. This function is supported only by digitizer components that support blend masks.

```
pascal VideoDigitizerError VDGetMaskPixMap
                            (VideoDigitizerComponent ci,
                             PixMapHandle maskPixMap);
```

CHAPTER 8

Video Digitizer Components

ci
: Specifies the video digitizer component for the request. Applications obtain this reference from the Component Manager's `OpenComponent` function.

maskPixMap
: Contains a handle to a pixel map. The video digitizer component returns the pixel map data for its blend mask into the pixel map specified by this parameter. The video digitizer component resizes the handle as appropriate. Your application is responsible for disposing of this handle.

RESULT CODES

`noErr`	0	No error
`digiUnimpErr`	–2201	Function not supported

Clipping

Some video digitizer components can clip the output video image based on an arbitrary clipping region. Your application can determine whether a video digitizer component supports clipping by examining the digitizer information structure of the component. Specifically, if the `digiOutDoesMask` flag is set to 1 in the `outputCapabilityFlags` field of the appropriate digitizer information structure, the component supports clipping. See "The Digitizer Information Structure" beginning on page 8-20 for details. Your application can obtain a component's digitizer information structure by calling the `VDGetDigitizerInfo` function, which is described on page 8-24. This section describes the functions provided to applications by components that support clipping.

Applications can use the `VDSetClipState` and `VDGetClipState` functions to enable and disable clipping, and to determine whether clipping is enabled. Applications can use the `VDSetClipRgn` and `VDClearClipRgn` functions to manipulate the clipping region. Applications can use these functions only during an active grab sequence. Applications set the initial clipping settings by calling either `VDSetPlayThruDestination` or `VDSetPlayThruGlobalRect` (described on page 8-35 and page 8-39, respectively).

Note
The functions that manipulate clipping and clipping state operate on a clipping region in addition to the one specified by the mask passed by the `VDSetPlayThruDestination` and `VDSetUpBuffers` functions (described on page 8-35 and page 8-54, respectively). To determine the final clipping regions, intersect these two clippings. ◆

CHAPTER 8

Video Digitizer Components

VDSetClipRgn

The `VDSetClipRgn` function allows your application to define a clipping region.

```
pascal VideoDigitizerError VDSetClipRgn
                            (VideoDigitizerComponent ci,
                            RgnHandle clipRegion);
```

ci
: Specifies the video digitizer component for the request. Applications obtain this reference from the Component Manager's `OpenComponent` function.

clipRegion
: Specifies the clipping region.

DESCRIPTION

When clipping is enabled, the video digitizer component performs clipping in the region specified with this function.

RESULT CODES

| noErr | 0 | No error |
| digiUnimpErr | –2201 | Function not supported |

SEE ALSO

Applications can disable all or part of a clipping region by calling the `VDClearClipRgn` function, described in the next section.

VDClearClipRgn

The `VDClearClipRgn` function allows your application to disable all or part of a clipping region that was previously set with the `VDSetClipRgn` function, which is described in the previous section.

```
pascal VideoDigitizerError VDClearClipRgn
                            (VideoDigitizerComponent ci,
                            RgnHandle clipRegion);
```

CHAPTER 8

Video Digitizer Components

ci
Specifies the video digitizer component for the request. Applications obtain this reference from the Component Manager's `OpenComponent` function.

clipRegion
Specifies the clipping region to clear. This region must correspond to all or part of the clipping region established previously with the `VDSetClipRgn` function.

RESULT CODES

noErr	0	No error
digiUnimpErr	–2201	Function not supported

VDSetClipState

The `VDSetClipState` function allows applications to control whether clipping is enabled.

```
pascal VideoDigitizerError VDSetClipState
                            (VideoDigitizerComponent ci,
                             short clipEnable);
```

ci
Specifies the video digitizer component for the request. Applications obtain this reference from the Component Manager's `OpenComponent` function.

clipEnable
Controls whether clipping is enabled. Valid values are

0	Disable clipping
1	Enable clipping

RESULT CODES

noErr	0	No error
digiUnimpErr	–2201	Function not supported

SEE ALSO

Applications can determine whether clipping is enabled by calling the `VDGetClipState` function, which is described in the next section.

VDGetClipState

The `VDGetClipState` function allows applications to determine whether clipping is enabled.

```
pascal VideoDigitizerError VDGetClipState
                            (VideoDigitizerComponent ci,
                             short *clipEnable);
```

ci
: Specifies the video digitizer component for the request. Applications obtain this reference from the Component Manager's `OpenComponent` function.

clipEnable
: Contains a pointer to a field that is to receive a value indicating whether clipping is enabled. The video digitizer component places one of the following values into the field referred to by the `clipEnable` parameter:

  | 0 | Clipping disabled |
  | 1 | Clipping enabled |

RESULT CODES

| noErr | 0 | No error |
| digiUnimpErr | –2201 | Function not supported |

SEE ALSO

Applications can enable and disable clipping by calling the `VDSetClipState` function, described in the previous section.

Utility Functions

This section describes a number of utility functions that may be supported by some video digitizer components.

The `VDSetPLLFilterType` and `VDGetPLLFilterType` functions allow applications to control which **phase-locked loop (PLL)** is used by a video digitizer component that supports multiple PLLs.

The `VDSetFieldPreference` and `VDGetFieldPreference` functions allow applications to control which field is used for some vertical scaling operations.

The `VDSetDigitizerUserInterrupt` function allows applications to install custom interrupt functions that are called by the video digitizer component.

The `VDGetSoundInputDriver` function allows an application to retrieve information about a digitizer's sound input driver.

The `VDGetPreferredTimeScale` function allows an application to determine a digitizer's preferred time scale.

Video Digitizer Components

VDSetPLLFilterType

The `VDSetPLLFilterType` function allows applications to specify which PLL is to be active.

```
pascal VideoDigitizerError VDSetPLLFilterType
                            (VideoDigitizerComponent ci,
                                short pllType);
```

ci Specifies the video digitizer component for the request. Applications obtain this reference from the Component Manager's `OpenComponent` function.

pllType Indicates which PLL is to be active. Available values are

   0   Broadcast mode
   1   VTR mode (stands for video tape recorder—equivalent to VCR, which stands for video cassette recorder)

RESULT CODES

noErr	0	No error
digiUnimpErr	−2201	Function not supported
qtParamErr	−2202	Invalid parameter value

SEE ALSO

Applications can get the active PLL type by calling the `VDGetPLLFilterType` function, which is described in the next section.

VDGetPLLFilterType

The `VDGetPLLFilterType` function allows applications to determine which PLL is currently active.

```
pascal VideoDigitizerError VDGetPLLFilterType
                            (VideoDigitizerComponent ci,
                                short *pllType);
```

ci Specifies the video digitizer component for the request. Applications obtain this reference from the Component Manager's `OpenComponent` function.

pllType Points to a field that is to receive a value indicating which PLL is active. Available values are

   0   Broadcast mode
   1   VTR mode

Video Digitizer Components Reference

CHAPTER 8

Video Digitizer Components

RESULT CODES

noErr	0	No error
digiUnimpErr	−2201	Function not supported
qtParamErr	−2202	Invalid parameter value

SEE ALSO

Applications can set the PLL type by calling the `VDSetPLLFilterType` function, which is described in the previous section.

VDSetFieldPreference

The `VDSetFieldPreference` function allows applications to specify which field to use in cases where the vertical scaling is less than half size.

All video digitizer components must support this function.

```
pascal VideoDigitizerError VDSetFieldPreference
                    (VideoDigitizerComponent ci,
                    short fieldFlag);
```

ci   Specifies the video digitizer component for the request. Applications obtain this reference from the Component Manager's `OpenComponent` function.

fieldFlag Indicates which field to use. Valid values are

   vdUseAnyField
              Digitizer component decides which field to use
   vdUseOddField
              Digitizer uses odd field
   vdUseEvenField
              Digitizer uses even field

DESCRIPTION

Applications can specify that the digitizer use either the odd-line field or the even-line field; alternatively, applications can let the component decide which field to use.

RESULT CODES

noErr	0	No error
qtParamErr	−2202	Invalid parameter value

CHAPTER 8

Video Digitizer Components

VDGetFieldPreference

The `VDGetFieldPreference` function allows applications to determine which field is being used in cases where the image is vertically scaled to half its original size.

```
pascal VideoDigitizerError VDGetFieldPreference
                                (VideoDigitizerComponent ci,
                                    short *fieldFlag);
```

ci   Specifies the video digitizer component for the request. Applications obtain this reference from the Component Manager's `OpenComponent` function.

fieldFlag Points to a field that is to receive a value indicating which field is being used. Valid values are

   vdUseAnyField
             Digitizer component decides which field to use
   vdUseOddField
             Digitizer component uses odd field
   vdUseEvenField
             Digitizer component uses even field

DESCRIPTION

Video digitizer components can use either the odd-line field or the even-line field. All video digitizer components must support this function.

RESULT CODES

    noErr   0   No error
    qtParamErr   –2202   Invalid parameter value

VDSetDigitizerUserInterrupt

The `VDSetDigitizerUserInterrupt` function allows applications to set custom interrupt functions.

```
pascal VideoDigitizerError VDSetDigitizerUserInterrupt
                                (VideoDigitizerComponent ci,
                                    long flags,
                                    VdigIntProc userInterruptProc,
                                    long refcon);
```

Video Digitizer Components Reference   8-95

CHAPTER 8

Video Digitizer Components

ci
: Specifies the video digitizer component for the request. Applications obtain this reference from the Component Manager's `OpenComponent` function.

flags
: Indicates when the interrupt function is to be called. Applications may set more than one flag to 1. The following flags are defined:

    Bit 0
    : Calls the interrupt function on even-line fields. If this flag is set to 1, the video digitizer component calls the custom interrupt procedure each time it starts to display an even-line field.

    Bit 1
    : Calls the interrupt function on odd-line fields. If this flag is set to 1, the video digitizer component calls the custom interrupt procedure each time it starts to display an odd-line field.

userInterruptProc
: Contains a pointer to the custom interrupt function. Applications set this parameter to `nil` to remove a custom interrupt function.

    Every custom interrupt function must support the following interface:

    ```
    pascal void MyInterruptProc (long flags, long refcon);
    ```

    See page 8-98 for details on the parameters of the `MyInterruptProc` function.

refcon
: Contains parameter data that is appropriate for the interrupt procedure.

DESCRIPTION

The video digitizer component calls these custom interrupt functions during field or frame interrupt processing. The application function can then perform special processing.

RESULT CODES

noErr   0   No error
digiUnimpErr   –2201   Function not supported

VDGetSoundInputDriver

The `VDGetSoundInputDriver` function allows an application to retrieve information about a digitizer's sound input driver.

```
pascal VideoDigitizerError VDGetSoundInputDriver
                            (VideoDigitizerComponent ci,
                             Str255 soundDriverName);
```

CHAPTER 8

Video Digitizer Components

ci	Identifies the application's connection to the video digitizer component. An application obtains this value from the Component Manager's `OpenComponent` function.

soundDriverName
	Specifies a pointer to a string. The video digitizer returns the name of its sound input driver. If the digitizer does not have an associated driver, it returns a result code of `digiUnimpErr`.

DESCRIPTION

An application can use the driver name returned by this function to choose an appropriate sound input device to use with this digitizer.

RESULT CODES

```
noErr        0      No error
qtParamErr  –2202   Invalid parameter value
```

VDGetPreferredTimeScale

The `VDGetPreferredTimeScale` function allows an application to determine a digitizer's preferred time scale.

```
pascal VideoDigitizerError VDGetPreferredTimeScale
                        (VideoDigitizerComponent ci,
                         TimeScale *preferred);
```

ci	Identifies the application's connection to the video digitizer component. An application obtains this value from the Component Manager's `OpenComponent` function.

preferred	Contains a pointer to a time scale structure. The video digitizer returns information about its preferred time scale.

DESCRIPTION

Apple's sequence grabber component uses this function to establish the time scale of the media that it creates from the digitizer's output. This is especially beneficial for digitizers that return compressed data, because it allows these digitizers to timestamp the frames very accurately.

If the digitizer does not have a preferred time scale, it returns a result code of `digiUnimpErr`.

CHAPTER 8

Video Digitizer Components

RESULT CODES

```
noErr           0      No error
qtParamErr   –2202     Invalid parameter value
```

Application-Defined Function

Applications can provide a custom interrupt function in the `userInterruptProc` parameter of the `VDSetDigitizerUserInterrupt` function. Every custom interrupt function must support the following interface:

```
pascal void MyInterruptProc (long flags, long refcon);
```

flags
: Indicates when the interrupt function has been called. The video digitizer component sets these flags to indicate the circumstances in which the function has been called. The following flags are defined:

    Bit 0
    : Even-line field interrupt. If this flag is set to 1, the video digitizer component is about to display an even-line field.

    Bit 1
    : Odd-line field interrupt. If this flag is set to 1, the video digitizer component is about to display an odd-line field.

refcon
: Contains parameter data that is appropriate for the interrupt function. The application assigns the value of the reference constant when it sets the interrupt function.

CHAPTER 8

Video Digitizer Components

Summary of Video Digitizer Components

C Summary

Constants

```
enum {
    videoDigitizerComponentType = 'vdig',/* standard type for video
                                             digitizer components */

    /* input format standards */
    ntscIn              = 0,    /* National Television System Committee */
    palIn               = 1,    /* Phase Alternation Line */
    secamIn             = 2,    /* Sequential Color with Memory */

    /* input formats */
    compositeIn         = 0,    /* no color separation of channels */
    sVideoIn            = 1,    /* s-video (super VHS) */
    rgbComponentIn      = 2,    /* separate channels for red, green, & blue */

    /* video digitizer component PlayThru states */
    vdPlayThruOff       = 0,    /* playthrough off */
    vdPlayThruOn        = 1,    /* playthrough on */

    /* field preference options in VDGetFieldPreference function */
    vdUseAnyField  = 0,  /* digitizer component decides which field to use */
    vdUseOddField  = 1,  /* digitizer component uses odd field */
    vdUseEvenField = 2,  /* digitizer component uses even field */

    /* input color space modes */
    vdDigitizerBW  = 0,  /* digitizer component uses black and white */
    vdDigitizerRGB = 1,  /* digitizer component uses red, green, & blue */

    /* phase lock loop modes */
    vdBroadcastMode     = 0,   /* broadcast (laser disk) video mode */
    vdVTRMode           = 1,   /* VCR (magnetic media) mode */
```

```c
/* video digitizer component types */
vdTypeBasic = 0,/* basic component does not support clipping */
vdTypeAlpha = 1,/* component supports clipping with alpha channel */
vdTypeMask  = 2,/* component supports clipping with mask plane */
vdTypeKey   = 3, /* component supports clipping with one or more key
                    colors */

/* digitizer input capability/current flags */
digiInDoesNTSC      = (1L<<0),  /* NTSC input */
digiInDoesPAL       = (1L<<1),  /* PAL input */
digiInDoesSECAM     = (1L<<2),  /* SECAM format */
digiInDoesGenLock   = (1L<<7),  /* digitizer performs genlock */
digiInDoesComposite = (1L<<8),  /* composite input */
digiInDoesSVideo    = (1L<<9),  /* s-video input type */
digiInDoesComponent = (1L<<10), /* component (RGB) input type */
digiInVTR_Broadcast =  (1L<<11),/* differentiates between magnetic
                                   media and broadcast input */
digiInDoesColor     = (1L<<12),/* digitizer supports color */
digiInDoesBW        = (1L<<13),/* digitizer supports black & white */

/* digitizer input current flags (these are valid only during active
   operating conditions) */
digiInSignalLock    = (1L<<31), /* digitizer detects locked input signal
                                   - this bit =
                                   horiz lock || vertical lock */

/* digitizer output capability/current flags */
digiOutDoes1     = (1L<<0), /* digitizer supports 1-bit pixels */
digiOutDoes2     = (1L<<1), /* digitizer supports 2-bit pixels */
digiOutDoes4     = (1L<<2), /* digitizer supports 4-bit pixels */
digiOutDoes8     = (1L<<3), /* digitizer supports 8-bit pixels */
digiOutDoes16    = (1L<<4), /* digitizer supports 16-bit pixels */
digiOutDoes32    = (1L<<5), /* digitizer supports 32-bit pixels */
digiOutDoesDither = (1L<<6), /* digitizer dithers in indexed modes */
digiOutDoesStretch= (1L<<7), /* digitizer can arbitrarily stretch */
digiOutDoesShrink = (1L<<8), /* digitizer can arbitrarily shrink */

digiOutDoesMask      = (1L<<9), /* masks to clipping regions */
digiOutDoesDouble    = (1L<<11),/* stretches to exactly double size */
digiOutDoesQuad      = (1L<<12),/* stretches to exactly quadruple size */
digiOutDoesQuarter   = (1L<<13),/* shrinks to exactly one-quarter size */
digiOutDoesSixteenth = (1L<<14),/* shrinks to exactly one-sixteenth */
digiOutDoesRotate    = (1L<<15),/* supports rotation transformations */
digiOutDoesHorizFlip = (1L<<16),/* supports horizontal flips Sx < 0 */
```

CHAPTER 8

Video Digitizer Components

```
    digiOutDoesVertFlip     =   (1L<<17),/* supports vertical flips Sy < 0 */
    digiOutDoesSkew         =   (1L<<18),/* supports skew (shear,twist) */
    digiOutDoesBlend        =   (1L<<19),/* supports blend operations */
    digiOutDoesWarp         =   (1L<<20),/* supports warp operations */
    digiOutDoesHW_DMA       =   (1L<<21),/* not constrained to local device */
    digiOutDoesHWPlayThru=      (1L<<22),/* doesn't need time to play */
    digiOutDoesILUT         =   (1L<<23),/* does lookup table for index modes */
    digiOutDoesKeyColor     =   (1L<<24),/* performs key color functions too */
    digiOutDoesAsyncGrabs=      (1L<<25),/* supports asynchronous grabs */
    digiOutDoesUnreadableScreenBits
                            =   (1L<<26),/* playthru doesn't generate readable
                                            bits on screen */
    digiOutDoesCompress     =   (1L<<27),/* supports compressed source devices */
    digiOutDoesCompressOnly
                            =   (1L<<28),/* can't draw images */
    digiOutDoesPlayThruDuringCompress
                            =   (1L<<29) /* can play while providing compressed
                                            data */
};

enum {
    /* video digitizer interface */
    kSelectVDGetMaxSrcRect              = 0x1,/* VDGetMaxSrcRect (required) */
    kSelectVDGetActiveSrcRect           = 0x2,/* VDGetActiveSrcRect
                                                    (required) */
    kSelectVDSetDigitizerRect           = 0x3,/* VDSetDigitizerRect
                                                    (required) */
    kSelectVDGetDigitizerRect           = 0x4,/* VDGetDigitizerRect
                                                    (required) */
    kSelectVDGetVBlankRect              = 0x5,/* VDGetVBlankRect (required) */
    kSelectVDGetMaskPixMap              = 0x6,/* VDGetMaskPixMap */

    /* 1 available selector here */
    kSelectVDGetPlayThruDestination     = 0x8,/* VDGetPlayThruDestination
                                                    (required) */
    kSelectVDUseThisCLUT                = 0x9,/* VDUseThisCLUT */
    kSelectVDSetInputGammaValue         = 0xA,/* VDSetInputGammaValue */
    kSelectVDGetInputGammaValue         = 0xB,/* VDGetInputGammaValue */
    kSelectVDSetBrightness              = 0xC,/* VDSetBrightness */
    kSelectVDGetBrightness              = 0xD,/* VDGetBrightness */
    kSelectVDSetContrast                = 0xE,/* VDSetContrast */
    kSelectVDSetHue                     = 0xF,/* VDSetHue */
    kSelectVDSetSharpness               = 0x10,/* VDSetSharpness */
    kSelectVDSetSaturation              = 0x11,/* VDSetSaturation */
```

CHAPTER 8

Video Digitizer Components

```
kSelectVDGetContrast              = 0x12,/* VDGetContrast */
kSelectVDGetHue                   = 0x13,/* VDGetHue */
kSelectVDGetSharpness             = 0x14,/* VDGetSharpness */
kSelectVDGetSaturation            = 0x15,/* VDGetSaturation */
kSelectVDGrabOneFrame             = 0x16,/* VDGrabOneFrame
                                            (required) */
kSelectVDGetMaxAuxBuffer          = 0x17,/* VDGetMaxAuxBuffer */
kSelectVDGetDigitizerInfo         = 0x19,/* VDGetDigitizerInfo
                                            (required) */
kSelectVDGetCurrentFlags          = 0x1A,/* VDGetCurrentFlags
                                            (required) */
kSelectVDSetKeyColor              = 0x1B,/* VDSetKeyColor */
kSelectVDGetKeyColor              = 0x1C,/* VDGetKeyColor */
kSelectVDAddKeyColor              = 0x1D,/* VDAddKeyColor */
kSelectVDGetNextKeyColor          = 0x1E,/* VDGetNextKeyColor */
kSelectVDSetKeyColorRange         = 0x1F,/* VDSetKeyColorRange */
kSelectVDGetKeyColorRange         = 0x20,/* VDGetKeyColorRange */
kSelectVDSetDigitizerUserInterrupt = 0x21,
                                    /* VDSetDigitizerUserInterrupt */
kSelectVDSetInputColorSpaceMode   = 0x22,/* VDSetInputColorSpaceMode */
kSelectVDGetInputColorSpaceMode   = 0x23,/* VDGetInputColorSpaceMode */
kSelectVDSetClipState             = 0x24,/* VDSetClipState */
kSelectVDGetClipState             = 0x25,/* VDGetClipState */
kSelectVDSetClipRgn               = 0x26,/* VDSetClipRgn */
kSelectVDClearClipRgn             = 0x27,/* VDClearClipRgn */
kSelectVDGetCLUTInUse             = 0x28,/* VDGetCLUTInUse */
kSelectVDSetPLLFilterType         = 0x29,/* VDSetPLLFilterType */
kSelectVDGetPLLFilterType         = 0x2A,/* VDGetPLLFilterType */
kSelectVDGetMaskandValue          = 0x2B,/* VDGetMaskandValue */
kSelectVDSetMasterBlendLevel      = 0x2C,/* VDSetMasterBlendLevel */
kSelectVDSetPlayThruDestination   = 0x2D,/* VDSetPlayThruDestination */
kSelectVDSetPlayThruOnOff         = 0x2E,/* VDSetPlayThruOnOff */
kSelectVDSetFieldPreference       = 0x2F,/* VDSetFieldPreference
                                            (required) */
kSelectVDGetFieldPreference       = 0x30,/* VDGetFieldPreference
                                            (required) */
kSelectVDPreflightDestination     = 0x32,/* VDPreflightDestination
                                            (required) */
kSelectVDPreflightGlobalRect      = 0x33,/* VDPreflightGlobalRect */
kSelectVDSetPlayThruGlobalRect    = 0x34,/* VDSetPlayThruGlobalRect */
kSelectVDSetInputGammaRecord      = 0x35,/* VDSetInputGammaRecord */
kSelectVDGetInputGammaRecord      = 0x36,/* VDGetInputGammaRecord */
kSelectVDSetBlackLevelValue       = 0x37,/* VDSetBlackLevelValue */
```

```
    kSelectVDGetBlackLevelValue         = 0x38,/* VDGetBlackLevelValue */
    kSelectVDSetWhiteLevelValue         = 0x39,/* VDSetWhiteLevelValue */
    kSelectVDGetWhiteLevelValue         = 0x3A,/* VDGetWhiteLevelValue */
    kSelectVDGetVideoDefaults           = 0x3B,/* VDGetVideoDefaults */
    kSelectVDGetNumberOfInputs          = 0x3C,/* VDGetNumberOfInputs */
    kSelectVDGetInputFormat             = 0x3D,/* VDGetInputFormat */
    kSelectVDSetInput                   = 0x3E,/* VDSetInput */
    kSelectVDGetInput                   = 0x3F,/* VDGetInput */
    kSelectVDSetInputStandard           = 0x40,/* VDSetInputStandard */
    kSelectVDSetupBuffers               = 0x41,/* VDSetupBuffers */
    kSelectVDGrabOneFrameAsync          = 0x42,/* VDGrabOneFrameAsync */
    kSelectVDDone                       = 0x43,/* VDDone */
    kSelectVDSetCompression             = 0x44,/* VDSetCompression */
    kSelectVDCompressOneFrameAsync      = 0x45,/* VDCompressOneFrameAsync */
    kSelectVDCompressDone               = 0x46,/* VDCompressDone */
    kSelectVDReleaseCompressBuffer      = 0x47,/* VDReleaseCompressBuffer */
    kSelectVDGetImageDescription        = 0x48,/* VDGetImageDescription */
    kSelectVDResetCompressSequence      = 0x49,/* VDResetCompressSequence */
    kSelectVDSetCompressionOnOff        = 0x4A,/* VDSetCompressionOnOff */
    kSelectVDGetCompressionTypes        = 0x4B,/* VDGetCompressionTypes */
    kSelectVDSetTimeBase                = 0x4C,/* VDSetTimeBase */
    kSelectVDSetFrameRate               = 0x4D,/* VDSetFrameRate */
    kSelectVDGetDataRate                = 0x4E,/* VDGetDataRate */
    kSelectVDGetSoundInputDriver        = 0x4F,/* VDGetSoundInputDriver */
    kSelectVDGetDMADepths               = 0x50,/* VDGetDMADepths */
    kSelectVDGetPreferredTimeScale      = 0x51,/* VDGetPreferredTimeScale */
    kSelectVDReleaseAsyncBuffers        = 0x52,/* VDReleaseAsyncBuffers */
};

/* flags for VDGetDMADepths depthArray parameter */
enum {
    dmaDepth1       = 1,      /* supports black and white */
    dmaDepth2       = 2,      /* supports 2-bit color */
    dmaDepth4       = 4,      /* supports 4-bit color */
    dmaDepth8       = 8,      /* supports 8-bit color */
    dmaDepth16      = 16,     /* supports 16-bit color */
    dmaDepth32      = 32,     /* supports 32-bit color */
    dmaDepth2Gray   = 64,     /* supports 2-bit grayscale */
    dmaDepth4Gray   = 128,    /* supports 4-bit grayscale */
    dmaDepth8Gray   = 256     /* supports 8-bit grayscale */
};
```

CHAPTER 8

Video Digitizer Components

Data Types

```c
typedef ComponentInstance VideoDigitizerComponent;/* video digitizer
                                                     component */

typedef ComponentResult VideoDigitizerError;    /* video digitizer error */
struct DigitizerInfo {
    short     vdigType;             /* type of digitizer component */
    long      inputCapabilityFlags;/* input video signal features */
    long      outputCapabilityFlags;/* output digitized video data features
                                       of digitizer component */
    long      inputCurrentFlags;    /* status of input video signal */
    long      outputCurrentFlags;   /* status of output digitized video data */
    short     slot;                 /* temporary for connection purposes */
    GDHandle  gdh;                  /* temporary for digitizers with
                                       preferred screen */
    GDHandle  maskgdh;              /* temporary for digitizers with
                                       mask planes */
    short     minDestHeight;        /* smallest resizable height */
    short     minDestWidth;         /* smallest resizable width */
    short     maxDestHeight;        /* largest resizable height */
    short     maxDestWidth;         /* largest resizable width */
    short     blendLevels;          /* number of blend levels supported
                                       (2 if 1 bit mask) */
    long      Private;              /* reserved--set to 0 */
};
typedef struct DigitizerInfo DigitizerInfo;

struct VdigBufferRecList {
    short            count;    /* # of buffers defined by this structure */
    MatrixRecordPtr  matrix;   /* tranformation matrix applied to dest rects
                                  before video image is displayed */
    RgnHandle        mask;     /* clip region applied to dest rect before
                                  video image is displayed */
    VdigBufferRec    list[1];  /* array of output buffer specifications */
};

typedef struct {
    PixMapHandle  dest;      /* handle to pixel map for destination buffer */
    Point         location;/* location of video destination in pixel map */
    long          reserved;/* reserved--set to 0 */
} VdigBufferRec;
```

```
typedef struct VDCompressionList {
    CodecComponent    codec;          /* component ID */
    CodecType         cType;          /* compressor type */
    Str63             typeName;       /* compression algorithm */
    Str63             name;           /* compressor name string */
    long              formatFlags;    /* data format flags */
    long              compressFlags;  /* capabilities flags */
    long              reserved;       /* set to 0 */
} VDCompressionList, *VDCompressionListPtr, **VDCompressionListHandle;
```

Video Digitizer Component Functions

Getting Information About Video Digitizer Components

```
pascal VideoDigitizerError VDGetDigitizerInfo
                    (VideoDigitizerComponent ci,
                     DigitizerInfo *info);
pascal VideoDigitizerError VDGetCurrentFlags
                    (VideoDigitizerComponent ci,
                     long *inputCurrentFlag,
                     long *outputCurrentFlag);
```

Setting Source Characteristics

```
pascal VideoDigitizerError VDGetMaxSrcRect
                    (VideoDigitizerComponent ci, short inputStd,
                     Rect *maxSrcRect);
pascal VideoDigitizerError VDGetActiveSrcRect
                    (VideoDigitizerComponent ci,
                     short inputStd, Rect *activeSrcRect);
pascal VideoDigitizerError VDGetVBlankRect
                    (VideoDigitizerComponent ci,
                     short inputStd, Rect *vBlankRect);
pascal VideoDigitizerError VDSetDigitizerRect
                    (VideoDigitizerComponent ci,
                     Rect *digitizerRect);
pascal VideoDigitizerError VDGetDigitizerRect
                    (VideoDigitizerComponent ci,
                     Rect *digitizerRect);
```

Selecting an Input Source

```
pascal VideoDigitizerError VDGetNumberOfInputs
                    (VideoDigitizerComponent ci, short *inputs);
pascal VideoDigitizerError VDSetInput
                    (VideoDigitizerComponent ci, short input);
pascal VideoDigitizerError VDGetInput
                    (VideoDigitizerComponent ci, short *input);
pascal VideoDigitizerError VDGetInputFormat
                    (VideoDigitizerComponent ci, short input,
                        short *format);
pascal VideoDigitizerError VDSetInputStandard
                    (VideoDigitizerComponent ci,
                        short inputStandard);
```

Setting Video Destinations

```
pascal VideoDigitizerError VDSetPlayThruDestination
                    (VideoDigitizerComponent ci,
                        PixMapHandle dest, Rect *destRect,
                        MatrixRecord *m, RgnHandle mask);
pascal VideoDigitizerError VDPreflightDestination
                    (VideoDigitizerComponent ci,
                        Rect *digitizerRect, PixMapHandle dest,
                        Rect *destRect, MatrixRecord *m);
pascal VideoDigitizerError VDGetPlayThruDestination
                    (VideoDigitizerComponent ci,
                        PixMapHandle *dest, Rect *destRect,
                        MatrixRecord *m, RgnHandle *mask);
pascal VideoDigitizerError VDSetPlayThruGlobalRect
                    (VideoDigitizerComponent ci,
                        GrafPtr theWindow, Rect *globalRect);
pascal VideoDigitizerError VDPreflightGlobalRect
                    (VideoDigitizerComponent ci,
                        GrafPtr theWindow, Rect *globalRect);
pascal VideoDigitizerError VDGetMaxAuxBuffer
                    (VideoDigitizerComponent ci,
                        PixMapHandle *pm, Rect *r);
```

Controlling Compressed Source Devices

```
pascal VideoDigitizerError VDGetCompressionTypes
                    (VideoDigitizerComponent ci,
                        VDCompressionListHandle h);
```

```
pascal VideoDigitizerError VDSetCompression
                                (VideoDigitizerComponent ci,
                                 OSType compressType, short depth,
                                 Rect *bounds, CodecQ spatialQuality,
                                 CodecQ temporalQuality, long keyFrameRate);
pascal VideoDigitizerError VDSetCompressionOnOff
                                (VideoDigitizerComponent ci, Boolean state);
pascal VideoDigitizerError VDCompressOneFrameAsync
                                (VideoDigitizerComponent ci);
pascal VideoDigitizerError VDCompressDone
                                (VideoDigitizerComponent ci, Boolean *done,
                                 Ptr *theData, long *dataSize,
                                 unsigned char *similarity, TimeRecord *t);
pascal VideoDigitizerError VDReleaseCompressBuffer
                                (VideoDigitizerComponent ci, Ptr bufferAddr);
pascal VideoDigitizerError VDGetImageDescription
                                (VideoDigitizerComponent ci,
                                 ImageDescriptionHandle desc);
pascal VideoDigitizerError VDResetCompressSequence
                                (VideoDigitizerComponent ci);
pascal VideoDigitizerError VDSetTimeBase
                                (VideoDigitizerComponent ci, TimeBase t);
```

Controlling Digitization

```
pascal VideoDigitizerError VDSetPlayThruOnOff
                                (VideoDigitizerComponent ci, short state);
pascal VideoDigitizerError VDGrabOneFrame
                                (VideoDigitizerComponent ci);
pascal VideoDigitizerError VDSetupBuffers
                                (VideoDigitizerComponent ci,
                                 VdigBufferRecListHandle bufferList);
pascal VideoDigitizerError VDReleaseAsyncBuffers
                                (VideoDigitizerComponent ci);
pascal VideoDigitizerError VDGrabOneFrameAsync
                                (VideoDigitizerComponent ci, short buffer);
pascal long VDDone         (VideoDigitizerComponent ci, short buffer);
pascal VideoDigitizerError VDSetFrameRate
                                (VideoDigitizerComponent ci,
                                 Fixed framesPerSecond);
pascal VideoDigitizerError VDGetDataRate
                                (VideoDigitizerComponent ci,
                                 long *milliSecPerFrame,
                                 Fixed *framesPerSecond, long *bytesPerSecond);
```

Controlling Color

```
pascal VideoDigitizerError VDUseThisCLUT
                                (VideoDigitizerComponent ci,
                                 CTabHandle colorTableHandle);
pascal VideoDigitizerError VDGetCLUTInUse
                                (VideoDigitizerComponent ci,
                                 CTabHandle *colorTableHandle);
pascal VideoDigitizerError VDSetInputColorSpaceMode
                                (VideoDigitizerComponent ci,
                                 short colorSpaceMode);
pascal VideoDigitizerError VDGetInputColorSpaceMode
                                (VideoDigitizerComponent ci,
                                 short *colorSpaceMode);
pascal VideoDigitizerError VDGetDMADepths
                                (VideoDigitizerComponent ci,
                                 long *depthArray, long *preferredDepth);
```

Controlling Analog Video

```
pascal VideoDigitizerError VDGetVideoDefaults
                                (VideoDigitizerComponent ci,
                                 unsigned short *blackLevel,
                                 unsigned short *whiteLevel,
                                 unsigned short *brightness,
                                 unsigned short *hue,
                                 unsigned short *saturation,
                                 unsigned short *contrast,
                                 unsigned short *sharpness);
pascal VideoDigitizerError VDSetBlackLevelValue
                                (VideoDigitizerComponent ci,
                                 unsigned short *blackLevel);
pascal VideoDigitizerError VDGetBlackLevelValue
                                (VideoDigitizerComponent ci,
                                 unsigned short *blackLevel);
pascal VideoDigitizerError VDSetWhiteLevelValue
                                (VideoDigitizerComponent ci,
                                 unsigned short *whiteLevel);
pascal VideoDigitizerError VDGetWhiteLevelValue
                                (VideoDigitizerComponent ci,
                                 unsigned short *whiteLevel);
pascal VideoDigitizerError VDSetHue
                                (VideoDigitizerComponent ci,
                                 unsigned short *hue);
```

Video Digitizer Components

```
pascal VideoDigitizerError VDGetHue
                        (VideoDigitizerComponent ci,
                         unsigned short *hue);
pascal VideoDigitizerError VDSetSaturation
                        (VideoDigitizerComponent ci,
                         unsigned short *saturation);
pascal VideoDigitizerError VDGetSaturation
                        (VideoDigitizerComponent ci,
                         unsigned short *saturation);
pascal VideoDigitizerError VDSetBrightness
                        (VideoDigitizerComponent ci,
                         unsigned short *brightness);
pascal VideoDigitizerError VDGetBrightness
                        (VideoDigitizerComponent ci,
                         unsigned short *brightness);
pascal VideoDigitizerError VDSetContrast
                        (VideoDigitizerComponent ci,
                         unsigned short *contrast);
pascal VideoDigitizerError VDGetContrast
                        (VideoDigitizerComponent ci,
                         unsigned short *contrast);
pascal VideoDigitizerError VDSetSharpness
                        (VideoDigitizerComponent ci,
                         unsigned short *sharpness);
pascal VideoDigitizerError VDGetSharpness
                        (VideoDigitizerComponent ci,
                         unsigned short *sharpness);
pascal VideoDigitizerError VDSetInputGammaRecord
                        (VideoDigitizerComponent ci,
                         VDGamRecPtr inputGammaPtr);
pascal VideoDigitizerError VDGetInputGammaRecord
                        (VideoDigitizerComponent ci,
                         VDGamRecPtr *inputGammaPtr);
pascal VideoDigitizerError VDSetInputGammaValue
                        (VideoDigitizerComponent ci,
                         Fixed channel1, Fixed channel2,
                         Fixed channel3);
pascal VideoDigitizerError VDGetInputGammaValue
                        (VideoDigitizerComponent ci,
                         Fixed *channel1, Fixed *channel2,
                         Fixed *channel3);
```

Selectively Displaying Video

```
pascal VideoDigitizerError VDSetKeyColor
                            (VideoDigitizerComponent ci,long index);
pascal VideoDigitizerError VDGetKeyColor
                            (VideoDigitizerComponent ci, long *index);
pascal VideoDigitizerError VDSetKeyColorRange
                            (VideoDigitizerComponent ci,
                             RGBColor *minRGB, RGBColor *maxRGB);
pascal VideoDigitizerError VDAddKeyColor
                            (VideoDigitizerComponent ci, long *index);
pascal VideoDigitizerError VDGetKeyColorRange
                            (VideoDigitizerComponent ci,
                             RGBColor *minRGB, RGBColor *maxRGB);
pascal VideoDigitizerError VDGetNextKeyColor
                            (VideoDigitizerComponent ci, long index);
pascal VideoDigitizerError VDSetMasterBlendLevel
                            (VideoDigitizerComponent ci,
                             unsigned short *blendLevel);
pascal VideoDigitizerError VDGetMaskandValue
                            (VideoDigitizerComponent ci,
                             unsigned short blendLevel, long *mask,
                             long *value);
pascal VideoDigitizerError VDGetMaskPixMap
                            (VideoDigitizerComponent ci,
                             PixMapHandle maskPixMap);
```

Clipping

```
pascal VideoDigitizerError VDSetClipRgn
                            (VideoDigitizerComponent ci,
                             RgnHandle clipRegion);
pascal VideoDigitizerError VDClearClipRgn
                            (VideoDigitizerComponent ci,
                             RgnHandle clipRegion);
pascal VideoDigitizerError VDSetClipState
                            (VideoDigitizerComponent ci, short clipEnable);
pascal VideoDigitizerError VDGetClipState
                            (VideoDigitizerComponent ci, short *clipEnable);
```

CHAPTER 8

Video Digitizer Components

Utility Functions

```
pascal VideoDigitizerError VDSetPLLFilterType
                    (VideoDigitizerComponent ci, short pllType);
pascal VideoDigitizerError VDGetPLLFilterType
                    (VideoDigitizerComponent ci, short *pllType);
pascal VideoDigitizerError VDSetFieldPreference
                    (VideoDigitizerComponent ci, short fieldFlag);
pascal VideoDigitizerError VDGetFieldPreference
                    (VideoDigitizerComponent ci, short *fieldFlag);
pascal VideoDigitizerError VDSetDigitizerUserInterrupt
                    (VideoDigitizerComponent ci, long flags,
                     VdigIntProc userInterruptProc, long refcon);
pascal VideoDigitizerError VDGetSoundInputDriver
                    (VideoDigitizerComponent ci,
                     Str255 soundDriverName);
pascal VideoDigitizerError VDGetPreferredTimeScale
                    (VideoDigitizerComponent ci,
                     TimeScale *preferred);
```

Application-Defined Function

```
pascal void MyInterruptProc (long flags, long refcon);
```

Pascal Summary

Constants

```
CONST
   videoDigitizerComponentType = 'vdig';   {standard type for video }
                                           { digitizer components}

   {input format standards}
   ntscIn            = 0;   {National Television System Committee}
   palIn             = 1;   {Phase Alternation Line}
   secamIn           = 2;   {Sequential Color with Memory}

   {input formats}
   compositeIn       = 0;   {no color separation of channels}
   sVideoIn          = 1;   {s-video (Super VHS)}
   rgbComponentIn    = 2;   {separate channels for red, green, & blue}
```

```
{video digitizer PlayThru states}
vdPlayThruOff       = 0;    {playthrough off}
vdPlayThruOn        = 1;    {playthrough on}

{field preference options in VDGetFieldPreference function}
vdUseAnyField       = 0;    {digitizer component decides which field to use}
vdUseOddField       = 1;    {digitizer component uses odd field}
vdUseEvenField      = 2;    {digitizer component uses even field}

{input color space modes}
vdDigitizerBW       = 0;    {digitizer component uses black and white}
vdDigitizerRGB      = 1;    {digitizer component uses red, green, and blue}

{phase lock loop modes}
vdBroadcastMode     = 0;    {broadcast or laser disk video mode}
vdVTRMode           = 1;    {video cassette recorder or magnetic media mode}

{video digitizer component types}
vdTypeBasic         = 0;    {basic component does not support clipping}
vdTypeAlpha         = 1;    {component supports clipping with alpha channel}
vdTypeMask          = 2;    {component supports clipping with mask plane}
vdTypeKey           = 3;    {supports clipping with one or more key colors}

{digitizer input capability/current flags}
digiInDoesNTSC      = $1;       {digitizer supports NTSC input}
digiInDoesPAL       = $2;       {digitizer supports PAL input}
digiInDoesSECAM     = $4;       {digitizer supports SECAM input}
digiInDoesGenLock   = $80;      {digitizer supports genlock}
digiInDoesComposite = $100;     {digitizer supports composite input type}
digiInDoesSVideo    = $200;     {digitizer supports s-video input type}
digiInDoesComponent = $400;     {digitizer supports component input type}
digiInVTR_Broadcast = $800;     {digitizer can differentiate between }
                                { magnetic media & broadcast}
digiInDoesColor     = $1000;    {digitizer supports color}
digiInDoesBW        = $2000;    {digitizer supports black and white}

{digitizer input current flag (valid only during active operating }
{ conditions)}
digiInSignalLock    = $80000000;{digitizer detects input signal is }
                                { locked--this bit equals }
                                { horiz lock || vertical lock}
```

```
{digitizer output capability/current flags}
digiOutDoes1            = $1;        {digitizer supports 1-bit pixels}
digiOutDoes2            = $2;        {digitizer supports 2-bit pixels}
digiOutDoes4            = $4;        {digitizer supports 4-bit pixels}
digiOutDoes8            = $8;        {digitizer supports 8-bit pixels}
digiOutDoes16           = $10;       {digitizer supports 16-bit pixels}
digiOutDoes32           = $20;       {digitizer supports 32-bit pixels}
digiOutDoesDither       = $40;       {digitizer dithers in indexed modes}
digiOutDoesStretch      = $80;       {digitizer can arbitrarily stretch}
digiOutDoesShrink       = $100;      {digitizer can arbitrarily shrink}
digiOutDoesMask         = $200;      {digitizer can mask to clipping }
                                     { regions}
digiOutDoesDouble       = $800;      {can stretch to exactly double size}
digiOutDoesQuad         = $1000;     {can stretch to exactly quadruple }
                                     { size}
digiOutDoesQuarter      = $2000;     {can shrink to exactly 1/4 size}
digiOutDoesSixteenth    = $4000;     {can shrink to exactly 1/16 size}
digiOutDoesRotate       = $8000;     {supports rotation transformations}
digiOutDoesHorizFlip    = $10000;    {supports horizontal flips Sx < 0}
digiOutDoesVertFlip     = $20000;    {supports vertical flips Sy < 0}
digiOutDoesSkew         = $40000;    {supports skew (shear, twist)}
digiOutDoesBlend        = $80000;    {digitizer performs blend operations}
digiOutDoesWarp         = $100000;   {digitizer performs warp operations}
digiOutDoesHW_DMA       = $200000;   {not constrained to logical device}
digiOutDoesHWPlayThru   = $400000;   {doesn't need time to play through}
digiOutDoesILUT         = $800000;   {does lookup for index modes}
digiOutDoesKeyColor     = $1000000;  {performs key color functions too}
digiOutDoesAsyncGrabs   = $2000000;  {performs asynchronous grabs}
digiOutDoesUnreadableScreenBits
                        = $4000000;  {playthru doesn't generate readable }
                                     { bits on screen}
digiOutDoesCompress     = $8000000;  {supports compressed source devices}
digiOutDoesCompressOnly
                        = $10000000; {can't draw images}
digiOutDoesPlayThruDuringCompress
                        = $2000000;  {can play while providing compressed }
                                     { data}

{video digitizer interface}
kSelectVDGetMaxSrcRect        = $1; {VDGetMaxSrcRect (required)}
kSelectVDGetActiveSrcRect     = $2; {VDGetActiveSrcRect (required)}
kSelectVDSetDigitizerRect     = $3; {VDSetDigitizerRect (required)}
kSelectVDGetDigitizerRect     = $4; {VDGetDigitizerRect (required)}
kSelectVDGetVBlankRect        = $5; {VDGetVBlankRect (required)}
```

CHAPTER 8

Video Digitizer Components

```
kSelectVDGetMaskPixMap              = $6; {VDGetMaskPixMap}
kSelectVDGetPlayThruDestination     = $8; {VDGetPlayThruDestination }
                                          { (required)}
kSelectVDUseThisCLUT                = $9; {VDUseThisCLUT}
kSelectVDSetInputGammaValue         = $A; {VDSetInputGammaValue}
kSelectVDGetInputGammaValue         = $B; {VDGetInputGammaValue}
kSelectVDSetBrightness              = $C; {VDSetBrightness}
kSelectVDGetBrightness              = $D; {VDGetBrightness}
kSelectVDSetContrast                = $E; {VDSetContrast}
kSelectVDSetHue                     = $F; {VDSetHue}
kSelectVDSetSharpness               = $10;{VDSetSharpness}
kSelectVDSetSaturation              = $11;{VDSetSaturation}
kSelectVDGetContrast                = $12;{VDGetContrast}
kSelectVDGetHue                     = $13;{VDGetHue}
kSelectVDGetSharpness               = $14;{VDGetSharpness}
kSelectVDGetSaturation              = $15;{VDGetSaturation}
kSelectVDGrabOneFrame               = $16;{VDGrabOneFrame (required)}
kSelectVDGetMaxAuxBuffer            = $17;{VDGetMaxAuxBuffer}
kSelectVDGetDigitizerInfo           = $19;{VDGetDigitizerInfo}
kSelectVDGetCurrentFlags            = $1A;{VDGetCurrentFlags}
kSelectVDSetKeyColor                = $1B;{VDSetKeyColor}
kSelectVDGetKeyColor                = $1C;{VDGetKeyColor}
kSelectVDAddKeyColor                = $1D;{VDAddKeyColor}
kSelectVDGetNextKeyColor            = $1E;{VDGetNextKeyColor}
kSelectVDSetKeyColorRange           = $1F;{VDSetKeyColorRange}
kSelectVDGetKeyColorRange           = $20;{VDGetKeyColorRange}
kSelectVDSetDigitizerUserInterrupt
                                    = $21;{VDSetDigitizerUserInterrupt}
kSelectVDSetInputColorSpaceMode     = $22;{VDSetInputColorSpaceMode}
kSelectVDGetInputColorSpaceMode     = $23;{VDGetInputColorSpaceMode}
kSelectVDSetClipState               = $24;{VDSetClipState}
kSelectVDGetClipState               = $25;{VDGetClipState}
kSelectVDSetClipRgn                 = $26;{VDSetClipRgn}
kSelectVDClearClipRgn               = $27;{VDClearClipRgn}
kSelectVDGetCLUTInUse               = $28;{VDGetCLUTInUse}
kSelectVDSetPLLFilterType           = $29;{VDSetPLLFilterType}
kSelectVDGetPLLFilterType           = $2A;{VDGetPLLFilterType}
kSelectVDGetMaskandValue            = $2B;{VDGetMaskandValue}
kSelectVDSetMasterBlendLevel        = $2C;{VDSetMasterBlendLevel}
kSelectVDSetPlayThruDestination     = $2D;{VDSetPlayThruDestination}
kSelectVDSetPlayThruOnOff           = $2E;{VDSetPlayThruOnOff}
kSelectVDSetFieldPreference         = $2F;{VDSetFieldPreference }
                                          { (required)}
```

Video Digitizer Components

```
kSelectVDGetFieldPreference        = $30;{VDGetFieldPreference }
                                        { (required)}
kSelectVDPreflightDestination      = $32;{VDPreflightDestination }
                                        { (required)}
kSelectVDPreflightGlobalRect       = $33;{VDPreflightGlobalRect}
kSelectVDSetPlayThruGlobalRect     = $34;{VDSetPlayThruGlobalRect}
kSelectVDSetInputGammaRecord       = $35;{VDSetInputGammaRecord}
kSelectVDGetInputGammaRecord       = $36;{VDGetInputGammaRecord}
kSelectVDSetBlackLevelValue        = $37;{VDSetBlackLevelValue}
kSelectVDGetBlackLevelValue        = $38;{VDGetBlackLevelValue}
kSelectVDSetWhiteLevelValue        = $39;{VDSetWhiteLevelValue}
kSelectVDGetWhiteLevelValue        = $3A;{VDGetWhiteLevelValue}
kSelectVDGetVideoDefaults          = $3B;{VDGetVideoDefaults}
kSelectVDGetNumberOfInputs         = $3C;{VDGetNumberOfInputs}
kSelectVDGetInputFormat            = $3D;{VDGetInputFormat}
kSelectVDSetInput                  = $3E;{VDSetInput}
kSelectVDGetInput                  = $3F;{VDGetInput}
kSelectVDSetInputStandard          = $40;{VDSetInputStandard}
kSelectVDSetupBuffers              = $41;{VDSetupBuffers}
kSelectVDGrabOneFrameAsync         = $42;{VDGrabOneFrameAsync}
kSelectVDDone                      = $43;{VDDone}
kSelectVDSetCompression            = $44;{VDSetCompression}
kSelectVDCompressOneFrameAsync     = $45;{VDCompressOneFrameAsync}
kSelectVDCompressDone              = $46;{VDCompressDone}
kSelectVDReleaseCompressBuffer     = $47;{VDReleaseCompressBuffer}
kSelectVDGetImageDescription       = $48;{VDGetImageDescription}
kSelectVDResetCompressSequence     = $49;{VDResetCompressSequence}
kSelectVDSetCompressionOnOff       = $4A;{VDSetCompressionOnOff}
kSelectVDGetCompressionTypes       = $4B;{VDGetCompressionTypes}
kSelectVDSetTimeBase               = $4C;{VDSetTimeBase}
kSelectVDSetFrameRate              = $4D;{VDSetFrameRate}
kSelectVDGetDataRate               = $4E;{VDGetDataRate}
kSelectVDGetSoundInputDriver       = $4F;{VDGetSoundInputDriver}
kSelectVDGetDMADepths              = $50;{VDGetDMADepths}
kSelectVDGetPreferredTimeScale     = $51;{VDGetPreferredTimeScale}
kSelectVDReleaseAsyncBuffers       = $52;{VDReleaseAsyncBuffers}
```

Data Types

```
TYPE
  VideoDigitizerComponent          = ComponentInstance;  {video digitizer }
                                                         { component}
  VideoDigitizerError              = ComponentResult;    {video digitizer }
                                                         { error}
  VdigIntProc                      = ComponentResult;

  DigitizerInfo =
  RECORD
    vdigType:             Integer;   {type of digitizer component}
    inputCapabilityFlags: LongInt;   {input video signal features}
    outputCapabilityFlags:LongInt;   {output digitized video data features}
    inputCurrentFlags:    LongInt;   {status of input video signal}
    outputCurrentFlags:   LongInt;   {status of output digitized data}
    slot:                 Integer;   {temporary for connection purposes}
    gdh:                  GDHandle;  {temporary for digitizers with }
                                     { preferred screen}
    maskgdh:              GDHandle;  {temporary for digitizers }
                                     { with mask planes}
    minDestHeight:        Integer;   {smallest resizable height}
    minDestWidth:         Integer;   {smallest resizable width}
    maxDestHeight:        Integer;   {largest resizable height}
    maxDestWidth:         Integer;   {largest resizable width}
    blendLevels:          Integer;   {number of blend levels supported (2 }
                                     { if 1 bit mask)}
    Private:              LongInt;   {reserved--set to 0}
  END;

  VdigBufferRec =
  RECORD
    dest:      PixMapHandle;  {handle to pixel map for destination buffer}
    location:  Point;         {location of video destination in pixel map}
    reserved:  LongInt;       {reserved--set to 0}
  END;

  VdigBufferRecListPtr     = ^VdigBufferRecList;
  VdigBufferRecListHandle  = ^VdigBufferRecListPtr;
  VdigBufferRecList =
  RECORD
    count:   Integer;         {buffers defined by this record}
    matrix:  MatrixRecordPtr ;{transformation matrix applied to }
                              { dest rect before image displayed}
```

```
      mask:            RgnHandle;          {clip rgn applied to dest rect }
                                           { before image displayed}
      list:            ARRAY[0..0] OF VdigBufferRec;
                                           {array of output buffer specs}
   END;

VDCompressionListHandle = ^VDCompressionListPtr;
VDCompressionList =
   RECORD
      codec:           CodecComponent;     {component ID}
      cType:           CodecType;          {compressor type}
      typeName:        Str63;              {compression algorithm}
      name:            Str63;              {compressor name string}
      formatFlags:     LongInt;            {data format flags}
      compressFlags:   LongInt;            {capabilities flags}
      reserved:        LongInt;            {set to 0}
   END;
```

Video Digitizer Component Routines

Getting Information About Video Digitizer Components

```
FUNCTION VDGetDigitizerInfo
                             (ci: VideoDigitizerComponent;
                              VAR info: DigitizerInfo): VideoDigitizerError;
FUNCTION VDGetCurrentFlags   (ci: VideoDigitizerComponent;
                              VAR inputCurrentFlag: LongInt;
                              VAR outputCurrentFlag: LongInt):
                              VideoDigitizerError;
```

Setting Source Characteristics

```
FUNCTION VDGetMaxSrcRect     (ci: VideoDigitizerComponent;
                              VAR maxSrcRect: Rect): VideoDigitizerError;
FUNCTION VDGetActiveSrcRect
                             (ci: VideoDigitizerComponent; inputStd: Integer;
                              VAR activeSrcRect: Rect): VideoDigitizerError;
FUNCTION VDGetVBlankRect     (ci: VideoDigitizerComponent;
                              VAR vBlankRect: Rect): VideoDigitizerError;
FUNCTION VDSetDigitizerRect
                             (ci: VideoDigitizerComponent;
                              VAR digitizerRect: Rect): VideoDigitizerError;
```

```
FUNCTION VDGetDigitizerRect
                           (ci: VideoDigitizerComponent;
                            VAR digitizerRect: Rect): VideoDigitizerError;
```

Selecting an Input Source

```
FUNCTION VDGetNumberOfInputs
                           (ci: VideoDigitizerComponent;
                            VAR inputs: Integer): VideoDigitizerError;
FUNCTION VDSetInput        (ci: VideoDigitizerComponent;
                            input: Integer): VideoDigitizerError;
FUNCTION VDGetInput        (ci: VideoDigitizerComponent;
                            VAR input: Integer): VideoDigitizerError;
FUNCTION VDGetInputFormat  (ci: VideoDigitizerComponent; input: Integer;
                            VAR format: Integer): VideoDigitizerError;
FUNCTION VDSetInputStandard
                           (ci: VideoDigitizerComponent;
                            inputStandard: Integer): VideoDigitizerError;
```

Setting Video Destinations

```
FUNCTION VDSetPlayThruDestination
                           (ci: VideoDigitizerComponent;
                            dest: PixMapHandle; VAR destRect: Rect;
                            VAR m: MatrixRecord;
                            mask: RgnHandle): VideoDigitizerError;
FUNCTION VDPreflightDestination
                           (ci: VideoDigitizerComponent;
                            VAR digitizerRect: Rect; dest: PixMapHandle;
                            VAR destRect: Rect;
                            VAR m: MatrixRecord): VideoDigitizerError;
FUNCTION VDGetPlayThruDestination
                           (ci: VideoDigitizerComponent;
                            VAR dest: PixMapHandle; VAR destRect: Rect;
                            VAR m: MatrixRecord;
                            VAR mask: RgnHandle): VideoDigitizerError;
FUNCTION VDSetPlayThruGlobalRect
                           (ci: VideoDigitizerComponent;
                            theWindow: GrafPtr; VAR globalRect: Rect):
                            VideoDigitizerError;
FUNCTION VDPreflightGlobalRect
                           (ci: VideoDigitizerComponent;
                            theWindow: GrafPtr; VAR globalRect: Rect):
                            VideoDigitizerError;
```

```
FUNCTION VDGetMaxAuxBuffer    (ci: VideoDigitizerComponent;
                               VAR pm: PixMapHandle; VAR r: Rect):
                               VideoDigitizerError;
```

Controlling Compressed Source Devices

```
FUNCTION VDGetCompressionTypes
                              (ci: VideoDigitizerComponent;
                               h: VDCompressionListHandle):
                               VideoDigitizerError;
FUNCTION VDSetCompression     (ci: VideoDigitizerComponent;
                               compressType: OSType; depth: Integer;
                               VAR bounds: Rect; spatialQuality: CodecQ;
                               temporalQuality: CodecQ;
                               keyFrameRate: LongInt): VideoDigitizerError;
FUNCTION VDSetCompressionOnOff
                              (ci: VideoDigitizerComponent; state: Boolean):
                               VideoDigitizerError;
FUNCTION VDGrabOneFrameAsync
                              (ci: VideoDigitizerComponent; buffer: Integer):
                               VideoDigitizerError;
FUNCTION VDCompressDone       (ci: VideoDigitizerComponent;
                               VAR done: Boolean; VAR theData: Ptr;
                               VAR dataSize: LongInt; VAR similarity: Byte;
                               VAR t: TimeRecord): VideoDigitizerError;
FUNCTION VDReleaseCompressBuffer
                              (ci: VideoDigitizerComponent;
                               bufferAddr: Ptr): VideoDigitizerError;
FUNCTION VDGetImageDescription
                              (ci: VideoDigitizerComponent;
                               desc: ImageDescriptionHandle):
                               VideoDigitizerError;
FUNCTION VDResetCompressSequence
                              (ci: VideoDigitizerComponent):
                               VideoDigitizerError;
FUNCTION VDSetTimeBase        (ci: VideoDigitizerComponent; t: TimeBase):
                               VideoDigitizerError;
```

Controlling Digitization

```
FUNCTION VDSetPlayThruOnOff   (ci: VideoDigitizerComponent;
                               state: Integer): VideoDigitizerError;
FUNCTION VDGrabOneFrame       (ci: VideoDigitizerComponent):
                               VideoDigitizerError;
```

```
FUNCTION VDSetupBuffers        (ci: VideoDigitizerComponent;
                                bufferList: VdigBufferRecListHandle):
                                VideoDigitizerError;
FUNCTION VDReleaseAsyncBuffers
                               (ci: VideoDigitizerComponent):
                                VideoDigitizerError;
FUNCTION VDGrabOneFrameAsync
                               (ci: VideoDigitizerComponent;
                                nextBuffer: Integer): VideoDigitizerError;
FUNCTION VDDone                (ci: VideoDigitizerComponent,
                                buffer: Integer): LongInt;
FUNCTION VDSetFrameRate        (ci: VideoDigitizerComponent;
                                framesPerSecond: Fixed): VideoDigitizerError;
FUNCTION VDGetDataRate         (ci: VideoDigitizerComponent;
                                VAR milliSecPerFrame: LongInt;
                                VAR framesPerSecond: Fixed;
                                VAR bytesPerSecond: LongInt):
                                VideoDigitizerError;
```

Controlling Color

```
FUNCTION VDUseThisCLUT         (ci: VideoDigitizerComponent;
                                colorTableHandle: CTabHandle):
                                VideoDigitizerError;
FUNCTION VDGetCLUTInUse        (ci: VideoDigitizerComponent;
                                VAR colorTableHandle: CTabHandle):
                                VideoDigitizerError;
FUNCTION VDSetInputColorSpaceMode
                               (ci: VideoDigitizerComponent;
                                colorSpaceMode: Integer): VideoDigitizerError;
FUNCTION VDGetInputColorSpaceMode
                               (ci: VideoDigitizerComponent;
                                VAR colorSpaceMode: Integer):
                                VideoDigitizerError;
FUNCTION VDGetDMADepths        (ci: VideoDigitizerComponent;
                                VAR depthArray: LongInt; VAR preferredDepth:
                                LongInt): VideoDigitizerError;
```

Controlling Analog Video

```
FUNCTION VDGetVideoDefaults  (ci: VideoDigitizerComponent;
                              VAR blackLevel: Integer;
                              VAR whiteLevel: Integer;
                              VAR brightness: Integer; VAR hue: Integer;
                              VAR saturation: Integer; VAR contrast: Integer;
                              VAR sharpness: Integer): VideoDigitizerError;
FUNCTION VDSetBlackLevelValue
                             (ci: VideoDigitizerComponent;
                              VAR blackLevel: Integer): VideoDigitizerError;
FUNCTION VDGetBlackLevelValue
                             (ci: VideoDigitizerComponent;
                              VAR blackLevel: Integer): VideoDigitizerError;
FUNCTION VDSetWhiteLevelValue
                             (ci: VideoDigitizerComponent;
                              VAR whiteLevel: Integer): VideoDigitizerError;
FUNCTION VDGetWhiteLevelValue
                             (ci: VideoDigitizerComponent;
                              VAR whiteLevel: Integer): VideoDigitizerError;
FUNCTION VDSetHue            (ci: VideoDigitizerComponent;
                              VAR hue: Integer): VideoDigitizerError;
FUNCTION VDGetHue            (ci: VideoDigitizerComponent;
                              VAR hue: Integer): VideoDigitizerError;
FUNCTION VDSetSaturation     (ci: VideoDigitizerComponent;
                              VAR saturation: Integer): VideoDigitizerError;
FUNCTION VDGetSaturation     (ci: VideoDigitizerComponent;
                              VAR saturation: Integer): VideoDigitizerError;
FUNCTION VDSetBrightness     (ci: VideoDigitizerComponent;
                              VAR brightness: Integer): VideoDigitizerError;
FUNCTION VDGetBrightness     (ci: VideoDigitizerComponent;
                              VAR brightness: Integer): VideoDigitizerError;
FUNCTION VDSetContrast       (ci: VideoDigitizerComponent;
                              VAR contrast: Integer): VideoDigitizerError;
FUNCTION VDGetContrast       (ci: VideoDigitizerComponent;
                              VAR contrast: Integer): VideoDigitizerError;
FUNCTION VDSetSharpness      (ci: VideoDigitizerComponent;
                              VAR sharpness: Integer): VideoDigitizerError;
FUNCTION VDGetSharpness      (ci: VideoDigitizerComponent;
                              VAR sharpness: Integer): VideoDigitizerError;
FUNCTION VDSetInputGammaRecord
                             (ci: VideoDigitizerComponent;
                              inputGammaPtr: VDGamRecPtr):
                              VideoDigitizerError;
```

```
FUNCTION VDGetInputGammaRecord
                            (ci: VideoDigitizerComponent;
                             VAR inputGammaPtr: VDGamRecPtr):
                             VideoDigitizerError;
FUNCTION VDSetInputGammaValue
                            (ci: VideoDigitizerComponent; channel1: Fixed;
                             channel2: Fixed; channel3: Fixed):
                             VideoDigitizerError;
FUNCTION VDGetInputGammaValue
                            (ci: VideoDigitizerComponent;
                             VAR channel1: Fixed; VAR channel2: Fixed;
                             VAR channel3: Fixed): VideoDigitizerError;
```

Selectively Displaying Video

```
FUNCTION VDSetKeyColor      (ci: VideoDigitizerComponent;
                             index: LongInt): VideoDigitizerError;
FUNCTION VDGetKeyColor      (ci: VideoDigitizerComponent;
                             VAR index: LongInt): VideoDigitizerError;
FUNCTION VDSetKeyColorRange
                            (ci: VideoDigitizerComponent;
                             VAR minRGB: RGBColor; VAR maxRGB: RGBColor):
                             VideoDigitizerError;
FUNCTION VDAddKeyColor      (ci: VideoDigitizerComponent;
                             VAR index: LongInt): VideoDigitizerError;
FUNCTION VDGetKeyColorRange
                            (ci: VideoDigitizerComponent;
                             VAR minRGB: RGBColor; VAR maxRGB: RGBColor):
                             VideoDigitizerError;
FUNCTION VDGetNextKeyColor  (ci: VideoDigitizerComponent;
                             index: LongInt): VideoDigitizerError;
FUNCTION VDSetMasterBlendLevel
                            (ci: VideoDigitizerComponent;
                             VAR blendLevel: Integer): VideoDigitizerError;
FUNCTION VDGetMaskandValue  (ci: VideoDigitizerComponent;
                             blendLevel: Integer; VAR mask: LongInt;
                             VAR value: LongInt): VideoDigitizerError;
FUNCTION VDGetMaskPixMap    (ci: VideoDigitizerComponent;
                             maskPixMap: PixMapHandle): VideoDigitizerError;
```

Clipping

```
FUNCTION VDSetClipRgn       (ci: VideoDigitizerComponent;
                             clipRegion: RgnHandle): VideoDigitizerError;
FUNCTION VDClearClipRgn     (ci: VideoDigitizerComponent;
                             clipRegion: RgnHandle): VideoDigitizerError;
FUNCTION VDSetClipState     (ci: VideoDigitizerComponent;
                             clipEnable: Integer): VideoDigitizerError;
FUNCTION VDGetClipState     (ci: VideoDigitizerComponent;
                             VAR clipEnable: Integer): VideoDigitizerError;
```

Utility Functions

```
FUNCTION VDSetPLLFilterType
                            (ci: VideoDigitizerComponent;
                             pllType: Integer): VideoDigitizerError;
FUNCTION VDGetPLLFilterType
                            (ci: VideoDigitizerComponent;
                             VAR pllType: Integer): VideoDigitizerError;
FUNCTION VDSetFieldPreference
                            (ci: VideoDigitizerComponent;
                             fieldFlag: Integer): VideoDigitizerError;
FUNCTION VDGetFieldPreference
                            (ci: VideoDigitizerComponent;
                             VAR fieldFlag: Integer): VideoDigitizerError;
FUNCTION VDSetDigitizerUserInterrupt
                            (ci: VideoDigitizerComponent;
                             flags: LongInt; userInterruptProc: ProcPtr;
                             refcon: LongInt): VideoDigitizerError;
FUNCTION VDGetSoundInputDriver
                            (ci: VideoDigitizerComponent;
                             soundDriverName: Str255): VideoDigitizerError;
FUNCTION VDGetPreferredTimeScale
                            (ci: VideoDigitizerComponent;
                             preferred: TimeScale): VideoDigitizerError;
```

Application-Defined Routine

```
PROCEDURE MyInterruptProc   (flags: LongInt; refcon: LongInt);
```

Result Codes

`noErr`	0	No error
`digiUnimpErr`	−2201	Function not supported
`qtParamErr`	−2202	Invalid parameter value
`noMoreKeyColors`	−2205	Key color list is full
`badDepth`	−2207	Digitizer cannot accommodate pixel depth
`noDMA`	−2208	Digitizer cannot use DMA to this destination
`badCallOrder`	−2209	Invalid call order (usually due to status call that was made prior to initial setup)

CHAPTER 9

Movie Data Exchange Components

Contents

About Movie Data Exchange Components 9-3
Using Movie Data Exchange Components 9-5
    Importing and Exporting Movie Data 9-6
    Configuring a Movie Data Exchange Component 9-6
    Finding a Specific Movie Data Exchange Component 9-6
Creating a Movie Data Exchange Component 9-8
    A Sample Movie Import Component 9-9
        Implementing the Required Import Component Functions 9-10
        Importing a Scrapbook File 9-12
    A Sample Movie Export Component 9-15
        Implementing the Required Export Component Functions 9-16
        Exporting Data to a PICS File 9-18
Movie Data Exchange Components Reference 9-20
    Importing Movie Data 9-20
    Configuring Movie Data Import Components 9-26
    Exporting Movie Data 9-34
    Configuring Movie Data Export Components 9-37
Summary of Movie Data Exchange Components 9-41
    C Summary 9-41
        Constants 9-41
        Data Type 9-42
        Functions 9-42
    Pascal Summary 9-44
        Constants 9-44
        Data Type 9-45
        Routines 9-45
    Result Codes 9-47

Movie Data Exchange Components

This chapter discusses movie data exchange components. **Movie data exchange components** allow applications to move various types of data into and out of a QuickTime movie. These components provide data conversion services to and from standard QuickTime movie data formats. **Movie data import components** convert other data formats into QuickTime's movie data format; **movie data export components** convert QuickTime movie data into other formats.

This chapter is divided into the following sections:

- "About Movie Data Exchange Components" provides a general introduction to components of this type.
- "Using Movie Data Exchange Components" discusses how applications use these components.
- "Creating a Movie Data Exchange Component" describes how to create movie import and export components with sample programs for their implementation.
- "Movie Data Exchange Components Reference" presents detailed information about the functions that are supported by these components.
- "Summary of Movie Data Exchange Components" contains a condensed listing of the constants, data structures, and functions supported by these components.

This chapter addresses developers of movie data exchange components. If you plan to create either a movie data import component or a movie data export component (or both), you should read the entire chapter. If you are writing an application that uses components of this type, you should read the first two sections ("About Movie Data Exchange Components" and "Using Movie Data Exchange Components"), and consult "Movie Data Exchange Components Reference" as appropriate.

As components, movie data exchange components rely on the facilities of the Component Manager. In order to use any component, your application must also use the Component Manager. If you are not familiar with this manager, see the chapter "Component Manager" in *Inside Macintosh: More Macintosh Toolbox*. In addition, you should be familiar with the Movie Toolbox. See "Movie Toolbox" in *Inside Macintosh: QuickTime* for more information.

About Movie Data Exchange Components

This section provides background information about movie data exchange components. After reading this section, you should understand why these components exist and whether you need to create or use one.

Movie data exchange components allow applications to place various types of data into a QuickTime movie or extract data from a movie in a specified format. Movie data import components translate foreign (that is, nonmovie) data formats into QuickTime movie data format. For example, a movie data import component might convert images from a paint application into frames in a QuickTime movie.

Movie Data Exchange Components

Conversely, movie data export components convert movie data into other formats, so that the data can be used by other applications. As an example, a movie data export component might allow an application to extract the sound track from a QuickTime movie in AIFF format. The extracted sound track may then be manipulated by applications that are not QuickTime-aware.

Applications use the services of movie data exchange components by calling the Movie Toolbox. Figure 9-1 shows the relationship between the Movie Toolbox and movie data import components; Figure 9-2 shows how movie data export components fit into the picture.

Figure 9-1 The Movie Toolbox, movie data import components, and your application

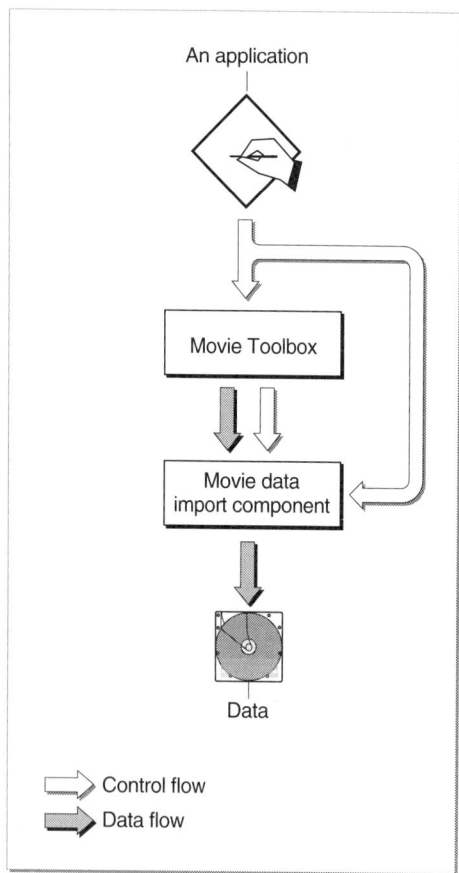

CHAPTER 9

Movie Data Exchange Components

Figure 9-2 The Movie Toolbox, movie data export components, and your application

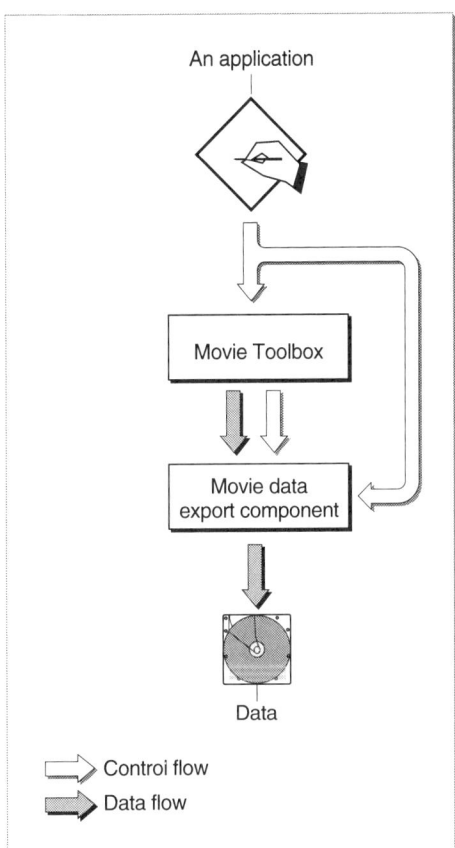

The next section describes in detail how to use each of these components.

If you are writing a media handler that works with a new type of data, you will probably need to use one or more data exchange components to facilitate the importing and exporting of data to QuickTime movies.

Using Movie Data Exchange Components

This section discusses how applications use movie data exchange components. You should read this section if you are writing an application that uses these components or if you are creating one of these components.

Importing and Exporting Movie Data

Your application starts a data import or export operation by calling the Movie Toolbox. There are several Movie Toolbox functions that allow you to specify a data import or data export component. For example, the `PasteHandleIntoMovie` and `ConvertFileToMovieFile` functions allow you to specify a movie data import component. The `PutMovieIntoTypedHandle` and `ConvertMovieToFile` functions allow you to specify a movie data export component. All of these functions select a component for you if you do not specify one yourself. For more information about these functions, see the chapter "Movie Toolbox" in *Inside Macintosh: QuickTime*.

When you import data into a QuickTime movie, you can specify that the data be placed into a specific existing track in the movie, into a new track that is created by the movie data import component, or into one or more existing tracks (in this case, the component may create additional tracks, if necessary).

When you export data from a QuickTime movie, you can request data from a specific track or from the entire movie. In addition, you can specify a segment of the track or movie to be exported.

Configuring a Movie Data Exchange Component

You do not need to configure a movie data exchange component before you use it to convert data into or out of a QuickTime movie. These components are implemented in such a way that they can operate successfully using their own default configuration information. In fact, some data exchange components do not allow you to configure them. However, most data exchange components do support some or all of the configuration functions that are defined for components of this type.

If you are going to configure a data exchange component, you must do so before you start the data exchange operation. You must call the component directly in order to set the configuration—the Movie Toolbox does not do this for you. Use the functions described in "Configuring Movie Data Import Components" and "Configuring Movie Data Export Components," as appropriate. Note that all of these functions are optional; that is, it is up to the developer of the component to decide whether or not to support a given configuration function. If the component does not support a function you have called, the component returns an error code of `badComponentSelector`.

Finding a Specific Movie Data Exchange Component

If you are going to specify a particular data exchange component to the Movie Toolbox, you must first open a connection to that component. Use the Component Manager's `OpenDefaultComponent` or `OpenComponent` function to open a connection to a movie data exchange component (see the chapter "Component Manager" in *Inside Macintosh: More Macintosh Toolbox* for more information about these functions). Before you can open that connection, however, you must find an appropriate movie data exchange component.

To find an appropriate data exchange component, you may need to use the Component Manager's `FindNextComponent` function. You specify the characteristics of the component you are seeking in a component description record—in particular, in the `componentType`, `componentSubtype`, `componentManufacturer`, and `componentFlags` fields.

Movie data import components have a component type value of `'eat '`, which is defined by the `MovieImportType` constant. Movie data export components have a type value of `'spit'`, which is defined by the `MovieExportType` constant.

Movie data exchange components use their component subtype and manufacturer values to indicate the type of data that they support. The subtype value indicates the type of data that these components can import or export. For example, movie data import components that convert text into QuickTime movie data have a component subtype value of `'TEXT'`. A single data exchange component may support only one data type.

The manufacturer field indicates the QuickTime media type that is supported by the component. For example, movie data export components that can read data from a sound media have a manufacturer value of `'soun'` (this value is defined by the `SoundMediaType` constant). If a data exchange component can work with more than one media type, it specifies a manufacturer value of 0.

In addition, these components use the `componentFlags` field to indicate more specific information about their capabilities. The following flags are currently defined:

```
enum {
    canMovieImportHandles       = 1,   /* can import from
                                          handles */
    canMovieImportFiles         = 2,   /* can import from files */
    hasMovieImportUserInterface = 4,   /* import has user
                                          interface */
    canMovieExportHandles       = 8,   /* can export to handles */
    canMovieExportFiles         = 16,  /* can export to files */
    hasMovieExportUserInterface = 32,  /* export has user
                                          interface */
    dontAutoFileMovieImport     = 64   /* turn off automatic file
                                          conversion */
};
```

Movie data import components use the first three flags to specify their capabilities. If a component can convert data from a handle, its `canMovieImportHandles` flag is set to 1. If it can work with files, its `canMovieImportFiles` flag is set to 1. Note that both of these flags may be set to 1 if a single component can work with both files and handles.

Movie Data Exchange Components

If a component provides a dialog box that allows the user to specify configuration information, the `hasMovieImportUserInterface` flag is set to 1. If a component does not support the automatic conversion of standard files to movies in an import component, set the `dontAutoFileMovieImport` flag to 1 (the default setting is 0).

Movie data export components use the other three flags in the same way.

Creating a Movie Data Exchange Component

This section discusses the details of creating a movie data exchange component. This section includes source code for two simple movie data exchange components.

You should consider creating a movie data import component if you have data that you would like to place in a QuickTime movie and there are not currently facilities for placing that type of data into a movie. Similarly, if you want to work with data from a QuickTime movie without using QuickTime, you might consider creating a movie data export component that can convert the data into a format your program can understand.

After reading this section, you should understand all of the special requirements of these components. The functional interface that your component must support is described in "Movie Data Exchange Components Reference" beginning on page 9-20. Note that a single component may support only import or export functions, not both.

Before reading this section, you should be familiar with how to create components. See the chapter "Component Manager" in *Inside Macintosh: More Macintosh Toolbox* for a complete discussion of components, how to use them, and how to create them.

Apple has defined component type values for movie data exchange components. You can use the following constants to specify this component type:

```
#define MovieImportType  'eat '    /* movie data import */
#define MovieExportType  'spit'    /* movie data export */
```

Apple has defined a functional interface for movie data exchange components. For information about the functions that your component must support, see "Movie Data Exchange Components Reference" beginning on page 9-20. You can use the following constants to refer to the request codes for each of the functions that your component must support:

```
enum {
   /* movie data import components */
   kMovieImportHandleSelect            = 1,   /* import from handle */
   kMovieImportFileSelect              = 2,   /* import from file */
   kMovieImportSetSampleDurationSelect = 3,   /* set sample duration */
   kMovieImportSetSampleDescriptionSelect
                                       = 4,   /* set sample description */
   kMovieImportSetMediaFileSelect      = 5,   /* set media file */
   kMovieImportSetDimensionsSelect     = 6,   /* set track dimensions */
```

CHAPTER 9

Movie Data Exchange Components

```
kMovieImportSetChunkSizeSelect        = 7,   /* set chunk size */
kMovieImportSetProgressProcSelect     = 8,   /* set progress function */
kMovieImportSetAuxiliaryDataSelect    = 9,   /* set additional data */
kMovieImportSetFromScrapSelect        = 10,  /* data from scrap */
kMovieImportDoUserDialogSelect        = 11,  /* invoke user dialog box */
kMovieImportSetDurationSelect         = 12   /* set paste duration */

/* movie data export components */
kMovieExportToHandleSelect            = 128,/* export to handle */
kMovieExportToFileSelect              = 129,/* export to file */
kMovieExportDoUserDialogSelect        = 130,/* invoke user dialog box */
kMovieExportGetAuxiliaryDataSelect    = 131,/* get additional data */
kMovieExportSetProgressProcSelect     = 132 /* set progress function */
};
```

A Sample Movie Import Component

This section describes how to create a movie import component. First you implement the required functions. Then you instruct your component to obtain the movie data from a handle or a file. This section then supplies a sample program that implements a movie data exchange component that imports a Scrapbook file containing QuickDraw PICT images. (For details on QuickDraw PICT images, see the chapter "Basic QuickDraw" in *Inside Macintosh: Imaging*.)

Your movie data import component may provide a user dialog box. You may use this dialog box in any way that is appropriate for your component—for example, to obtain certain parameter information governing the import operation, such as the image-compression method.

In addition, the requesting application may use one or more of the configuration functions to establish parameters for the import operation.

You should not rely on any outside configuration information. Your component should work properly knowing only the source data and the target movie. The Movie Toolbox supplies this information to your component when it calls your `MovieImportHandle` function (described on page 9-21) or `MovieImportFile` function (described on page 9-24).

Your movie data import component may implement either one or both of these functions, which allow the Movie Toolbox to request that data be converted into a format for use in a QuickTime movie.

- If the data is to be imported from a handle, the `MovieImportHandle` function is used.

- If data is to be imported from a file, the `MovieImportFile` function is used.

Set the appropriate flags in your component's `componentFlags` field to indicate which of these functions your component supports. Note that your component may support both functions.

Creating a Movie Data Exchange Component

Chapter 9

Movie Data Exchange Components

Implementing the Required Import Component Functions

Listing 9-1 supplies a sample program that implements a movie data exchange component that imports a Scrapbook file containing QuickDraw PICT images. (For details on QuickDraw PICT images, see the chapter "Basic QuickDraw" in *Inside Macintosh: Imaging*.) The sample program also provides the dispatchers for the movie import component together with the required functions.

Listing 9-1 Implementing the required import functions

```
#define kMediaTimeScale 600

typedef struct {
    ComponentInstance self
    TimeValue         frameDuration;
} ImportScrapbookGlobalsRecord, **ImportScrapbookGlobals;

/* entry point for all Component Manager requests */
pascal ComponentResult ImportScrapbookDispatcher
                            (ComponentParameters *params,
                             Handle storage)
{
    OSErr err = badComponentSelector;
    ComponentFunction componentProc = 0;

    switch (params->what) {
        case kComponentOpenSelect:
            componentProc = ImportScrapbookOpen; break;

        case kComponentCloseSelect:
            componentProc = ImportScrapbookClose; break;

        case kComponentCanDoSelect:
            componentProc = ImportScrapbookCanDo; break;

        case kComponentVersionSelect:
            componentProc = ImportScrapbookVersion; break;

        case kMovieImportFileSelect:
            componentProc = ImportScrapbookFile; break;

        case kMovieImportSetSampleDurationSelect:
            componentProc = ImportScrapbookSetSampleDuration; break;

    }
```

CHAPTER 9

Movie Data Exchange Components

```c
      if (componentProc)
         err = CallComponentFunctionWithStorage (storage, params,
                                             componentProc);

      return err;
}

pascal ComponentResult ImportScrapbookCanDo
                              (ImportScrapbookGlobals storage,
                                 short ftnNumber)
{
   switch (ftnNumber) {
      case kComponentOpenSelect:
      case kComponentCloseSelect:
      case kComponentCanDoSelect:
      case kComponentVersionSelect:
      case kMovieImportFileSelect:
      case kMovieImportSetSampleDurationSelect:
         return true;
      default:
         return false;
   }
}

pascal ComponentResult ImportScrapbookVersion
                              (ImportScrapbookGlobals storage)
{
   return 0x00010001;
}

pascal ComponentResult ImportScrapbookOpen
                              (ImportScrapbookGlobals storage,
                                 ComponentInstance self)
{
   storage = (ImportScrapbookGlobals) NewHandleClear
                     (sizeof (ImportScrapbookGlobalsRecord));
   if (!storage) return MemError();
   (**storage).self = self;
   SetComponentInstanceStorage (self, (Handle)storage);
   return noErr;
}

pascal ComponentResult ImportScrapbookClose
                              (ImportScrapbookGlobals storage,
                                 ComponentInstance self)
```

Creating a Movie Data Exchange Component

Movie Data Exchange Components

```
{
    if (storage) DisposeHandle((Handle)storage);
    return noErr;
}
```

Importing a Scrapbook File

Before the import operation begins, the client may set the duration of samples to be added by the movie data import component by calling the `MovieImportSetDuration` function (described on page 9-27).

The `MovieImportFile` function (described on page 9-24) performs the import operation. The tasks involved in importing the data include

- opening the source file
- retrieving the first sample in order to determine the track dimension
- creating a new track and media
- determining the frame duration
- setting up a sample description structure
- cycling through all the frames in the Scrapbook and adding them to the new media
- adding the new media to the track
- closing the source file

Listing 9-2 supplies an example in which a Scrapbook file is imported.

Listing 9-2   Importing a Scrapbook file

```
/* if this function is called, it provides a hint from the caller
as to the desired sample (frame) duration in the new media */

pascal ComponentResult ImportScrapbookSetSampleDuration
                                (ImportScrapbookGlobals storage,
                                    TimeValue duration,
                                    TimeScale scale)
{
    TimeRecord tr;
    tr.value.lo = duration;
    tr.value.hi = 0;
    tr.scale = 0;
    tr.base = nil;
    ConvertTimeScale (&tr, kMediaTimeScale);
            /* your new media will have a time scale of 600 */
    (**storage).frameDuration = tr.value.lo;
```

Movie Data Exchange Components

```
      return noErr;
}
pascal ComponentResult ImportScrapbookFile
                            (ImportScrapbookGlobals storage,
                             FSSpec *theFile, Movie theMovie,
                             Track targetTrack, Track *usedTrack,
                             TimeValue atTime,
                             TimeValue *addedTime,
                             long inFlags, long *outFlags)
{
   OSErr err;
   short resRef = 0, saveRes = CurResFile();
   PicHandle thePict;
   Rect trackRect;
   short pageIndex = 0;
   Track newTrack = 0;
   Media newMedia;
   Boolean endMediaEdits = false;
   TimeValue frameDuration;
   SampleDescriptionHandle sampleDesc = 0;

   *outFlags = 0;
   if (inFlags & movieImportMustUseTrack)
      return invalidTrack;

   /* open source file */
   resRef = FSpOpenResFile (theFile, fsRdPerm);
   if (err = ResError()) goto bail;
   UseResFile(resRef);

   /* get the first PICT to determine the track size */
   thePict = (PicHandle)Get1IndResource ('PICT', 1);
   if (!thePict) {
      err = ResError();
      goto bail;

   }
   trackRect = (**thePict).picFrame;
   OffsetRect(&trackRect, -trackRect.left, -trackRect.top);
```

Creating a Movie Data Exchange Component

```c
/* create a track and PICT media */
newTrack = NewMovieTrack (theMovie, trackRect.right << 16,
                         trackRect.bottom << 16, kNoVolume);
if (err = GetMoviesError()) goto bail;
newMedia = NewTrackMedia (newTrack, 'PICT', kMediaTimeScale,
                          nil, 0);
if (err = GetMoviesError()) goto bail;
if (err = BeginMediaEdits (newMedia)) goto bail;
endMediaEdits = true;

/* determine the frame duration (check the hint you may
   have been called with) */
frameDuration = (**storage).frameDuration;
if (!frameDuration) frameDuration = kMediaTimeScale/5;
                              /* default is 1/5th second */

/* set up a simple sample description */
sampleDesc = (SampleDescriptionHandle) NewHandleClear
                            (sizeof (SampleDescription));
(**sampleDesc).descSize = sizeof(SampleDescription);
(**sampleDesc).dataFormat = 'PICT';

/* cycle through all source frames and add them to the media */
do {
   Handle thePict;
   short resID = pageToMapIndex (++pageIndex,
                            *GetResource ('SMAP', 0));

   if (resID == 0) break;
   thePict = Get1Resource ('PICT', resID);
   if (thePict == nil) continue; /* some pages may not
                                    contain a 'PICT' */

   err = AddMediaSample(newMedia, thePict, 0,
                     GetHandleSize (thePict),
                     frameDuration, sampleDesc, 1, 0, nil);

   ReleaseResource (thePict);
   DisposeHandle (thePict);
} while (!err);
if (err) goto bail;
```

Movie Data Exchange Components

```
    /* add the new media to the track */
    err = InsertMediaIntoTrack (newTrack, 0, 0,
                                GetMediaDuration (newMedia), kFix1);

bail:
    if (resRef) CloseResFile (resRef);
    if (endMediaEdits) EndMediaEdits (newMedia);
    if (err && newTrack) {
        DisposeMovieTrack (newTrack);
        newTrack = 0;
    }
    UseResFile (saveRes);
    if (sampleDesc) DisposeHandle ((Handle)sampleDesc);
    *usedTrack = newTrack;

    return err;
}

/* map from a Scrapbook page number to a resource ID */
short pageToMapIndex (short page, Ptr map)
{
    short mapIndex;
    for (mapIndex = 0; mapIndex < 256; mapIndex++)
        if (*map++ == page)
            return mapIndex | 0x8000;
    return 0;
}
```

A Sample Movie Export Component

As with movie data import components, the movie data export component should not rely on any configuration information beyond that which is supplied by the Movie Toolbox when it calls the `MovieExportToHandle` or `MovieExportToFile` function (described on page 9-35 and page 9-36, respectively).

This section provides an implementation of a movie data exchange component that exports a movie or movie's track to a PICS animation file.

Movie Data Exchange Components

Implementing the Required Export Component Functions

Listing 9-3 provides the component dispatchers for the movie export component together with the required functions.

Listing 9-3 Implementing the required export functions

```c
typedef struct {
   ComponentInstance self;
} ExportPICSGlobalsRecord, *ExportPICSGlobals;

/* entry point for all Component Manager requests */
pascal ComponentResult ExportPICSDispatcher
                              (ComponentParameters *params,
                               Handle storage)
{
   OSErr err = badComponentSelector;
   ComponentFunction componentProc = 0;

   switch (params->what) {
      case kComponentOpenSelect:
         componentProc = ExportPICSOpen; break;
      case kComponentCloseSelect:
         componentProc = ExportPICSClose; break;
      case kComponentCanDoSelect:
         componentProc = ExportPICSCanDo; break;
      case kComponentVersionSelect:
         componentProc = ExportPICSVersion; break;
      case kMovieExportToFileSelect:
         componentProc = ExportPICSToFile; break;
   }
   if (componentProc)
      err = CallComponentFunctionWithStorage (storage, params,
                                              componentProc);

   return err;
}
```

Movie Data Exchange Components

```c
pascal ComponentResult ExportPICSCanDo (ExportPICSGlobals store,
                                        short ftnNumber)
{
   switch (ftnNumber) {
      case kComponentOpenSelect:
      case kComponentCloseSelect:
      case kComponentCanDoSelect:
      case kComponentVersionSelect:
      case kMovieExportToFileSelect:
         return true;
         break;
      default:
         return false;
         break;
   }
}

pascal ComponentResult ExportPICSVersion (ExportPICSGlobals store)
{
   return 0x00010001;
}

pascal ComponentResult ExportPICSOpen (ExportPICSGlobals store,
                                       ComponentInstance self)
{
   OSErr err;

   store = (ExportPICSGlobals) NewPtrClear
            (sizeof(ExportPICSGlobalsRecord));
   if (err = MemError()) goto bail;
   store->self = self;

   SetComponentInstanceStorage(self, (Handle)store);

bail:
   return err;
}

pascal ComponentResult ExportPICSClose (ExportPICSGlobals store,
                                        ComponentInstance self)
{
   if (store) DisposPtr((Ptr)store);

   return noErr;
}
```

Creating a Movie Data Exchange Component

Exporting Data to a PICS File

To export data to a PICS file, your component must

- allow the Movie Toolbox to call the `MovieExportToFile` function in order to export movie data into a file
- read the data from the track or movie
- perform appropriate conversions on that data
- place the data into the specified file (the file's type corresponds to the component subtype of your movie data export component)

Listing 9-4 provides an implementation of these tasks in a movie export component. The `ExportPICSToFile` function performs the export operation by opening the resource fork of the PICS file and cycling through the movie time segment, adding a frame to the PICS file.

Listing 9-4   Exporting a frame of movie data to a PICS file

```
pascal ComponentResult ExportPICSToFile (ExportPICSGlobals store,
                                         const FSSpec *theFile,
                                         Movie m,
                                         Track onlyThisTrack,
                                         TimeValue startTime,
                                         TimeValue duration)
{
   OSErr err = noErr;
   short resRef = 0;
   short saveResFile = CurResFile();
   short resID = 128;
   PicHandle thePict = nil;

   /* open the resource fork of the PICS file
      (the caller is responsible for creating the file) */
   resRef = FSpOpenResFile (theFile, fsRdWrPerm);
   if (err = ResError()) goto bail;

   UseResFile(resRef);

   /* cycle through the movie time segment you were given */
   while (startTime < duration) {
      Byte c = 0;
```

Movie Data Exchange Components

```c
        if (onlyThisTrack)
            thePict = GetTrackPict (onlyThisTrack, startTime);
        else
            thePict = GetMoviePict(m, startTime);
        if (!thePict) continue;

        /* add a frame to the PICS file */
        AddResource ((Handle)thePict, 'PICT', resID++, &c);
        err = ResError();
        WriteResource ((Handle)thePict);
        DetachResource ((Handle)thePict);
        KillPicture (thePict);
        thePict = nil;
        if (err) break;

        /* find the time of the next frame */
        do {
            TimeValue nextTime;
            if (onlyThisTrack)
                GetTrackNextInterestingTime (onlyThisTrack,
                                    nextTimeMediaSample, startTime,
                                    kFix1, &nextTime, nil);
            else {
                OSType mediaType = VisualMediaCharacteristic;

                GetMovieNextInterestingTime (m, nextTimeMediaSample,
                                    1, &mediaType,
                                    startTime, kFix1,
                                    &nextTime, nil);
            }

            if (GetMoviesError ()) goto bail;
            if (nextTime != startTime) {
                startTime = nextTime;
                break;
            }
        } while (++startTime < duration);
    }
bail:
    if (thePict) KillPicture (thePict);
    if (resRef) CloseResFile (resRef);
    UseResFile (saveResRef);
    return err;
}
```

Movie Data Exchange Components Reference

This section describes the functions that your movie data exchange component may support. Many of these functions are optional—your component should support only those functions that are appropriate to it.

This section is divided into the following topics:

- "Importing Movie Data" discusses the functions that allow the Movie Toolbox to import movie data using the services of a movie data import component.
- "Configuring Movie Data Import Components" describes the functions that allow applications to configure a movie data import component prior to importing movie data.
- "Exporting Movie Data" tells you about the functions that allow the Movie Toolbox to export movie data using the services of a movie data export component.
- "Configuring Movie Data Export Components" provides information about the functions that allow applications to configure a movie data export component prior to exporting movie data.

Note
All of the functions described in "Configuring Movie Data Import Components" and "Configuring Movie Data Export Components" are optional. Your import or export component must be able to work properly if none of these functions is called. ◆

Importing Movie Data

Movie data import components may provide one or two functions that allow the Movie Toolbox to request a data conversion operation. The `MovieImportHandle` function instructs your component to retrieve the data that is to be imported from a specified handle. The `MovieImportFile` function instructs you to retrieve the data from a file. You should set the appropriate flags in your component's `componentFlags` field to indicate which of these functions your component supports. Note that your component may support both functions.

Before the Movie Toolbox calls one of these functions, a requesting application may call one or more of your component's configuration functions (see "Configuring Movie Data Import Components" beginning on page 9-26 for more information about these functions). However, your component should work properly even if none of these configuration functions is called.

MovieImportHandle

The `MovieImportHandle` function allows the Movie Toolbox to import data from a handle, using your movie data import component.

```
pascal ComponentResult MovieImportHandle (ComponentInstance ci,
                                          Handle dataH,
                                          Movie theMovie,
                                          Track targetTrack,
                                          Track *usedTrack,
                                          TimeValue atTime,
                                          TimeValue *addedDuration,
                                          long inFlags,
                                          long *outFlags);
```

`ci`
: Identifies the Movie Toolbox's connection to your movie data import component.

`dataH`
: Contains a handle to the data that is to be imported into the movie identified by the parameter `theMovie`. The data contained in this handle has a data type value that corresponds to your component's subtype value.

  Your component is not responsible for disposing of this handle.

`theMovie`
: Identifies the movie for this operation. This movie identifier is supplied by the Movie Toolbox. Your component may use this identifier to add sample data to the target movie, or to obtain information about the movie.

`targetTrack`
: Identifies the track that is to receive the imported data. This track identifier is supplied by the Movie Toolbox and is valid only if the `movieImportMustUseTrack` flag in the `inFlags` parameter is set to 1.

`usedTrack`
: Contains a pointer to the track that received the imported data. Your component returns this track identifier to the Movie Toolbox. Your component needs to set this parameter only if you operate on a single track or if you create a new track. If you modify more than one track, leave the field referred to by this parameter unchanged.

`atTime`
: Specifies the time corresponding to the location where your component is to place the imported data. This time value is expressed in the movie's time coordinate system.

`addedDuration`
: Contains a pointer to the duration of the data that your component added to the movie. Your component must specify this value in the movie's time coordinate system.

CHAPTER 9

Movie Data Exchange Components

inFlags
: Specifies control information governing the import operation. The following flags are defined:

  movieImportCreateTrack
  : Indicates that your component should create a new track to receive the imported data. You must create a track whose type value corresponds to the media type that you have specified in your component's manufacturer code. You should return the track identifier of this new track in the field referred to by the usedTrack parameter, unless you create more than one track. If you create more than one track, be sure to set the movieImportResultUsedMultipleTracks flag (in the field referred to by the outFlags parameter) to 1.

    If the movieImportCreateTrack flag is set to 1, then the movieImportMustUseTrack flag is set to 0.

  movieImportMustUseTrack
  : Indicates that your component must use an existing track. That track is identified by the targetTrack parameter. If you create more than one track, be sure to set the movieImportResultUsedMultipleTracks flag (in the field referred to by the outFlags parameter) to 1.

    If the movieImportMustUseTrack flag is set to 1, then the movieImportCreateTrack flag is set to 0.

    If both the movieImportCreateTrack and movieImportMustUseTrack flags are set to 0, then you are free to use any existing tracks in the movie or to create a new track (or tracks) as needed.

  movieImportInParallel
  : Indicates whether you are to perform an insert operation or a paste operation. If this flag is set to 0, then you should insert the imported data into the target track. If this flag is set to 1, then you should add the imported data to the track, overwriting preexisting open space currently in the track. Note that an application may use the MovieImportSetDuration function (described on page 9-27) to control the amount of data you paste into a movie.

    If the movieImportMustUseTrack flag is set to 1, then you should use the track specified by the targetTrack parameter. If this is not possible, return an appropriate Movie Toolbox result code.

Movie Data Exchange Components

<dl>
<dt><code>outFlags</code></dt>
<dd>Contains a pointer to a field that is to receive status information about the import operation. Your component sets the appropriate flags in this field when the operation is complete. The following flags are defined:

<dl>
<dt><code>movieImportResultUsedMultipleTracks</code></dt>
<dd>Indicates that your component modified more than one track in the movie. Set this flag to 1 if your component places imported data into more than one track. In this case, you do not need to update the field referred to by the <code>usedTrack</code> parameter.</dd>

<dt><code>movieImportInParallel</code></dt>
<dd>Indicates whether you performed an insert operation or a paste operation. Set this flag to 0 if you inserted the imported data into the target track. Set this flag to 1 if you added the imported data to the track, overwriting preexisting open space currently in the track.</dd>
</dl>
</dd>
</dl>

DESCRIPTION

The Movie Toolbox calls the `MovieImportHandle` function in order to import movie data from a handle. The data stored in the handle has a data type that corresponds to the component subtype of your movie data import component. Your component must read the data from the supplied handle, perform appropriate conversions on that data, and place the data into the movie.

If your component can accept data from a handle, be sure to set the `canMovieImportHandles` flag in your component's `componentFlags` field.

Your component must be prepared to perform this function at any time. You should not expect that any of your component's configuration functions will be called first.

RESULT CODES

`invalidTrack`   –2009   Specified track cannot receive imported data

Other appropriate Movie Toolbox result codes

SEE ALSO

The Movie Toolbox uses the `MovieImportFile` function to import data from a file; this function is described next.

CHAPTER 9

Movie Data Exchange Components

MovieImportFile

The `MovieImportFile` function allows the Movie Toolbox to import data from a file, using your movie data import component.

```
pascal ComponentResult MovieImportFile (ComponentInstance ci,
                                        const FSSpec *theFile,
                                        Movie theMovie,
                                        Track targetTrack,
                                        Track *usedTrack,
                                        TimeValue atTime,
                                        TimeValue *addedDuration,
                                        long inFlags,
                                        long *outFlags);
```

ci
: Identifies the Movie Toolbox's connection to your movie data import component.

theFile
: Contains a pointer to the file that contains the data that is to be imported into the movie. This file's type value corresponds to your component's subtype value.

theMovie
: Identifies the movie for this operation. This movie identifier is supplied by the Movie Toolbox. Your component may use this identifier to add sample data to the target movie or to obtain information about the movie.

targetTrack
: Identifies the track that is to receive the imported data. This track identifier is supplied by the Movie Toolbox and is valid only if the `movieImportMustUseTrack` flag in the `inFlags` parameter is set to 1.

usedTrack
: Contains a pointer to the track that received the imported data. Your component returns this track identifier to the Movie Toolbox. Your component needs to set this parameter only if you operate on a single track or if you create a new track. If you modify more than one track, leave the field referred to by this parameter unchanged.

atTime
: Specifies the time corresponding to the location where your component is to place the imported data. This time value is expressed in the movie's time coordinate system.

addedDuration
: Contains a pointer to the duration of the data that your component added to the movie. Your component must specify this value in the movie's time coordinate system.

inFlags
: Specifies control information governing the import operation. The following flags are defined:

    movieImportCreateTrack
    : Indicates that your component should create a new track to receive the imported data. You must create a track whose type value corresponds to the media type you have specified in your component's manufacturer code. You

Movie Data Exchange Components

should return the track identifier of this new track in the field referred to by the `usedTrack` parameter, unless you create more than one track. If you create more than one track, be sure to set the `movieImportResultUsedMultipleTracks` flag (in the field referred to by the `outFlags` parameter) to 1.

If the `MovieImportCreateTrack` flag is set to 1, then the `movieImportMustUseTrack` flag is set to 0.

`movieImportMustUseTrack`
  Indicates that your component must use an existing track. That track is identified by the `targetTrack` parameter. If you create more than one track, be sure to set the `movieImportResultUsedMultipleTracks` flag (in the field referred to by the `outFlags` parameter) to 1.

  If the `movieImportMustUseTrack` flag is set to 1, then the `movieImportCreateTrack` flag is set to 0.

  If both the `movieImportCreateTrack` and `movieImportMustUseTrack` flags are set to 0, then you are free to use any existing tracks in the movie, or to create a new track (or tracks) as needed.

`movieImportInParallel`
  Indicates whether you are to perform an insert operation or a paste operation. If this flag is set to 0, then you should insert the imported data into the target track. If this flag is set to 1, then you should add the imported data to the track, overwriting the preexisting open space currently in the track. Note that an application may use the `MovieImportSetDuration` function to control the amount of data you paste into a movie.

  If the `movieImportMustUseTrack` flag is set to 1, then you should use the track specified by the `targetTrack` parameter. If this is not possible, return an appropriate Movie Toolbox result code.

outFlags Identifies a field that is to receive status information about the import operation. Your component sets the appropriate flags in this field when the operation is complete. The following flags are defined:

  `movieImportResultUsedMultipleTracks`
    Indicates that your component modified more than one track in the movie. Set this flag to 1 if your component places imported data into more than one track. In this case, you do not need to update the field referred to by the `usedTrack` parameter.

  `movieImportInParallel`
    Indicates whether you performed an insert operation or a paste operation. Set this flag to 0 if you inserted the imported data into the target track. Set this flag to 1 if you added the imported data to the track, overwriting preexisting open space currently in the track.

CHAPTER 9

Movie Data Exchange Components

DESCRIPTION

The Movie Toolbox calls the `MovieImportFile` function in order to import movie data from a file. The file's type corresponds to the component subtype of your movie data import component. Your component must read the data from the supplied file, perform appropriate conversions on that data, and place the data into the movie.

If your component can accept data from a file, be sure to set the `canMovieImportFiles` flag in your component's `componentFlags` field.

Your component must be prepared to perform this function at any time. You should not expect that any of your component's configuration functions will be called first.

RESULT CODES

`invalidTrack`   –2009   Specified track cannot receive imported data

Other appropriate Movie Toolbox result codes

SEE ALSO

The Movie Toolbox uses the `MovieImportHandle` function to import data from a handle; this function is described on page 9-21.

Configuring Movie Data Import Components

Your component may provide one or more configuration functions. These functions allow applications to configure your component before the Movie Toolbox calls your component to start the import process. Note that applications may call these functions directly.

All of these functions are optional. If your component receives a request that it does not support, you should return the `badComponentSelector` error code. In addition, your component should work properly even if none of these functions is called.

These functions address a variety of configuration issues. The `MovieImportSetSampleDuration` function allows an application to set your component's sample duration. Use the `MovieImportSetDuration` function to control the duration of the imported data. Applications can use the `MovieImportSetDimensions` function to specify the spatial dimensions of a new track. Use the `MovieImportSetSampleDescription` function to supply a sample description structure to your movie data import component.

The `MovieImportSetMediaFile` function allows applications to direct your component's output to a specific media file. Applications can provide additional data to your component by calling the `MovieImportSetAuxiliaryData` function. The `MovieImportSetChunkSize` function allows applications to control the chunk size in the new media. Applications can inform you that the source data came from the scrap by calling your `MovieImportSetFromScrap` function.

CHAPTER 9

Movie Data Exchange Components

Applications can specify a progress function for use by your component by calling the `MovieImportSetProgressProc` function.

Applications can instruct your component to display its user dialog box by calling the `MovieImportDoUserDialog` function.

MovieImportSetDuration

The `MovieImportSetDuration` function allows an application to control the duration of the data that your component pastes into the target movie.

```
pascal ComponentResult MovieImportSetDuration
                                    (ComponentInstance ci,
                                     TimeValue duration);
```

ci   Identifies the application's connection to your movie data import component.

duration   Specifies the duration in the movie's time scale. If this parameter is set to 0, then you may paste any amount of movie data that is appropriate for the data to be imported.

DESCRIPTION

Applications may use the `MovieImportSetDuration` function to set the duration of the data to be pasted by your movie data import component. This duration is expressed in the movie's time scale.

If your component supports paste operations (that is, your component allows the application to set the `movieImportInParallel` flag to 1 with the `MovieImportHandle` or `MovieImportFile` function), then you must support this function. If an application calls this function and sets a duration limit, you must abide by that limit. This function is not valid for insert operations (where the `movieImportInParallel` flag is set to 0).

RESULT CODE

badComponentSelector   0x80008002   Function not supported

MovieImportSetSampleDuration

The `MovieImportSetSampleDuration` function allows an application to set the sample duration for new samples to be created with your component.

```
pascal ComponentResult MovieImportSetSampleDuration
                            (ComponentInstance ci,
                                TimeValue duration,
                                TimeScale scale);
```

ci
: Identifies the application's connection to your movie data import component.

duration
: Specifies the sample duration in units specified by the `scale` parameter.

scale
: Specifies the time scale for the duration value. This may be any arbitrary time scale; that is, it may not correspond to the movie's time scale. You should convert this time scale to the movie's time scale before using the `duration` value, using the Movie Toolbox's `ConvertTimeScale` function.

DESCRIPTION

Applications may use the `MovieImportSetSampleDuration` function to set the duration of samples to be added by your movie data import component. This duration is expressed in an arbitrary time scale.

RESULT CODE

badComponentSelector   0x80008002   Function not supported

MovieImportSetSampleDescription

The `MovieImportSetSampleDescription` function allows an application to provide a sample description to your movie data import component.

```
pascal ComponentResult MovieImportSetSampleDescription
                            (ComponentInstance ci,
                                SampleDescriptionHandle desc,
                                OSType mediaType);
```

ci
: Identifies the application's connection to your movie data import component.

Movie Data Exchange Components

desc   Contains a handle to a sample description. Your component must not dispose of this handle. If you want to save any data from the sample description, be sure to copy it at this time.

mediaType   Specifies the type of sample description referred to by the `desc` parameter. If the `desc` parameter refers to an image description structure, this parameter is set to `VideoMediaType` (`'vide'`); for sound description structures, this parameter is set to `SoundMediaType` (`'soun'`).

DESCRIPTION

Applications may use the `MovieImportSetSampleDescription` function to supply a sample description to your movie data import component. This can be useful in cases where your component must transform the data before adding it to the movie's media. For example, your component may be responsible for adding image data to a movie. In this case, you may allow applications to specify image-compression parameters by supplying a formatted image description structure.

RESULT CODE

badComponentSelector   0x80008002   Function not supported

MovieImportSetMediaFile

The `MovieImportSetMediaFile` function allows an application to specify a media file that is to receive the imported movie data.

```
pascal ComponentResult MovieImportSetMediaFile
                                (ComponentInstance ci,
                                 AliasHandle alias);
```

ci   Identifies the application's connection to your movie data import component.

alias   Identifies the media file that is to receive the imported movie data. Your component must make a copy of this parameter. You should not dispose of it.

DESCRIPTION

Applications may use the `MovieImportSetMediaFile` function to specify a destination media file for imported movie data. By default, your movie data import component should add new data to an existing media file that is associated with the movie. However, you may choose to allow applications to specify an alternative destination file. This can be useful when your component is importing data into a new

Movie Data Exchange Components

track. In this case, the application can use this function to tell your component where the media's data should reside.

RESULT CODE

badComponentSelector   0x80008002   Function not supported

MovieImportSetDimensions

The `MovieImportSetDimensions` function allows an application to specify a new track's spatial dimensions.

```
pascal ComponentResult MovieImportSetDimensions
                        (ComponentInstance ci, Fixed width,
                        Fixed height);
```

ci
: Identifies the application's connection to your movie data import component.

width
: Indicates the width, in pixels, of the track rectangle. This parameter, along with the `height` parameter, specifies a rectangle that surrounds the image that is to be displayed when the current media is played. This value corresponds to the x coordinate of the lower-right corner of the rectangle, and it is expressed as a fixed-point number.

height
: Indicates the height, in pixels, of the track rectangle. This value corresponds to the y coordinate of the lower-right corner of the rectangle, and it is expressed as a fixed-point number.

DESCRIPTION

Applications may use this function to specify the spatial dimensions of a new track. Although your movie data import component may not change the spatial characteristics of an existing track, if you are importing image data into a new track, you may choose to allow applications to specify the spatial characteristics of the new track.

If you want to change the track's matrix, use the Movie Toolbox's `SetTrackMatrix` function after performing the import operation.

RESULT CODE

badComponentSelector   0x80008002   Function not supported

MovieImportSetChunkSize

The `MovieImportSetChunkSize` function allows an application to specify the amount of data your component works with at a time.

```
pascal ComponentResult MovieImportSetChunkSize
                              (ComponentInstance ci,
                               long chunkSize);
```

ci
: Identifies the application's connection to your movie data import component.

chunkSize
: Specifies the number of seconds of data your movie data import component places into each chunk of movie data. This parameter may not be set to a value less than 1.

DESCRIPTION

The chunk size controls the amount of data in each of a media's data chunks (for more information about data chunks in a media, see the chapter "QuickTime Movie Format" in *Inside Macintosh: QuickTime*). Generally, your component should determine a reasonable default chunk size, based on the type of data you are importing. However, you may choose to allow applications to override your default value—this can be especially useful for sound data, where the chunk size affects the quality of sound playback.

RESULT CODE

badComponentSelector	0x80008002	Function not supported

MovieImportSetProgressProc

The `MovieImportSetProgressProc` function allows an application to assign a movie progress function.

```
pascal ComponentResult MovieImportSetProgressProc
                              (ComponentInstance ci,
                               MovieProgressProcPtr proc,
                               long refcon);
```

ci
: Identifies the application's connection to your movie data import component.

CHAPTER 9

Movie Data Exchange Components

proc Contains a pointer to the application's movie progress function. See the chapter "Movie Toolbox" in *Inside Macintosh: QuickTime* for a complete description of the interface supported by movie progress functions. If this parameter is set to `nil`, the application is removing its progress function. In this case, your component should stop calling the progress function.

refcon Specifies a reference constant. Your component should pass this constant back to the application's progress function whenever you call that function.

DESCRIPTION

Some data import operations may be time consuming, and application developers may therefore choose to display progress information to the user. Your component provides this information to an application's progress function. As your component processes an import request, you should call the progress function occasionally in order to report on the progress of the operation. Use an operation code value of `progressOpImportMovie`. The application can then present this information to the user.

These progress functions must support the same interface as Movie Toolbox progress functions. That interface is discussed in the chapter "Movie Toolbox" in *Inside Macintosh: QuickTime*. Note that this interface not only allows you to report progress to the application, but also allows the application to cancel the request.

RESULT CODE

badComponentSelector   0x80008002   Function not supported

MovieImportSetAuxiliaryData

The `MovieImportSetAuxiliaryData` function allows an application to provide additional data to your component. Your component can then use this data during the data import process.

```
pascal ComponentResult MovieImportSetAuxiliaryData
                            (ComponentInstance ci,
                            Handle data,
                            OSType handleType);
```

ci Identifies the application's connection to your movie data import component.

data Contains a handle to the additional data. Your component should not dispose of this handle. Be sure to copy any data you need to keep.

handleType
   Identifies the type of data in the specified handle.

Movie Data Exchange Components

DESCRIPTION

The `MovieImportSetAuxiliaryData` function allows your component to accept additional data for use during the data import process. Your component may use this data in any way that is appropriate for a given import operation. For example, if your component imports data stored in `'TEXT'` handles, you might choose to accept style information for that text. An application could provide that style information in a `'styl'` handle supplied to your component by calling this function.

Your component should expect the application to call this function before the import process begins.

RESULT CODES

`unsupportedAuxiliaryImportData`	−2057	Cannot work with specified handle type
`badComponentSelector`	0x80008002	Function not supported

MovieImportSetFromScrap

The `MovieImportSetFromScrap` function allows an application to indicate that the source data resides on the scrap.

```
pascal ComponentResult MovieImportSetFromScrap
                        (ComponentInstance ci,
                         Boolean fromScrap);
```

ci   Identifies the application's connection to your movie data import component.

fromScrap   Indicates whether or not the source data resides on the scrap. This parameter is set to `true` if the data originated on the scrap; otherwise, the parameter is set to `false`.

DESCRIPTION

The `MovieImportSetFromScrap` function allows an application to indicate that the data to be imported originated on the scrap. In some cases, your component may be able to use this information during the import process. For example, you may establish the convention that additional data that is pertinent to an import operation should be stored on the scrap along with the data to be imported. Your component can then look in the scrap for the additional data.

RESULT CODE

`badComponentSelector`	0x80008002	Function not supported

CHAPTER 9

Movie Data Exchange Components

MovieImportDoUserDialog

The `MovieImportDoUserDialog` function allows an application to request that your component display its user dialog box.

```
pascal ComponentResult MovieImportDoUserDialog
                            (ComponentInstance ci,
                             const FSSpec *theFile,
                             Handle theData, Boolean *canceled);
```

ci
    Identifies the application's connection to your movie data import component.

theFile
    Contains a pointer to a valid file specification. If the import request pertains to a file, the application must specify the source file with this parameter and set the parameter `theData` to `nil`. If the request is for a handle, this parameter is set to `nil`.

theData
    Contains a handle to the data to be imported. If the import request pertains to a handle, the application must specify the source of the data with this parameter, and set the parameter `theFile` to `nil`. If the request is for a file, this parameter is set to `nil`.

canceled
    Contains a pointer to a Boolean value. Your component should set this Boolean value to reflect whether the user cancels the dialog box. If the user cancels the dialog box, set the Boolean value to `true`. Otherwise, set it to `false`.

DESCRIPTION

Your movie data import component may support a user dialog box that allows the user to configure an import operation. For components that support such a dialog box, the `MovieImportDoUserDialog` function allows an application to tell you when to display the dialog box to the user.

If your component supports a user dialog box, be sure to set the `hasMovieImportUserInterface` flag in your component's `componentFlags` field.

RESULT CODE

badComponentSelector   0x80008002   Function not supported

Exporting Movie Data

Movie data export components may provide one or two functions that allow the Movie Toolbox to request a data conversion operation. The `MovieExportToHandle` function instructs your component to place the converted data into a specified handle. The `MovieExportToFile` function instructs you to put the data into a file. You should set the appropriate flags in your component's `componentFlags` field to indicate which of

CHAPTER 9

Movie Data Exchange Components

these functions your component supports. Note that your component may support both functions.

Before the Movie Toolbox calls one of these functions, a requesting application may call one or more of your component's configuration functions (see "Configuring Movie Data Export Components" beginning on page 9-37 for more information about these functions). However, your component should work properly even if none of these configuration functions is called.

MovieExportToHandle

The `MovieExportToHandle` function allows the Movie Toolbox to export data from a movie, using your movie data export component.

```
pascal ComponentResult MovieExportToHandle
                        (ComponentInstance ci,
                        Handle dataH, Movie theMovie,
                        Track onlyThisTrack,
                        TimeValue startTime,
                        TimeValue duration);
```

ci
: Identifies the Movie Toolbox's connection to your movie data export component.

dataH
: Handle to be filled with the converted movie data. Your component must write data into this handle that corresponds to your component's subtype value.

    Your component should resize this handle as appropriate.

theMovie
: Identifies the movie for this operation. This movie identifier is supplied by the Movie Toolbox. Your component may use this identifier to obtain sample data from the movie or to obtain information about the movie.

onlyThisTrack
: Identifies a track that is to be converted. This track identifier is supplied by the Movie Toolbox. If this parameter contains a track identifier, your component must convert only the specified track.

startTime
: Specifies the starting point of the track or movie segment to be converted. This time value is expressed in the movie's time coordinate system.

duration
: Specifies the duration of the track or movie segment to be converted. This duration value is expressed in the movie's time coordinate system.

DESCRIPTION

The Movie Toolbox calls the `MovieExportToHandle` function in order to export movie data into a handle. Your component must read the data from the specified movie or track, perform appropriate conversions on that data, and place the data into the handle.

CHAPTER 9

Movie Data Exchange Components

The data stored in the handle must have a data type that corresponds to the component subtype of your movie data export component.

If your component can write data to a handle, be sure to set the `canMovieExportHandles` flag in your component's `componentFlags` field.

Your component must be prepared to perform this function at any time. You should not expect that any of your component's configuration functions will be called first.

RESULT CODES

`invalidTrack` –2009 Specified track cannot be converted

Other appropriate Movie Toolbox result codes

SEE ALSO

The Movie Toolbox uses the `MovieExportToFile` function to export data to a file; this function is described next.

MovieExportToFile

The `MovieExportToFile` function allows the Movie Toolbox to export data to a file, using your movie data export component.

```
pascal ComponentResult MovieExportToFile (ComponentInstance ci,
                                         const FSSpec *theFile,
                                         Movie theMovie,
                                         Track onlyThisTrack,
                                         TimeValue startTime,
                                         TimeValue duration);
```

`ci` Identifies the Movie Toolbox's connection to your movie data import component.

`theFile` Contains a pointer to the file that is to receive the converted movie data. This file's type value corresponds to your component's subtype value.

`theMovie` Identifies the movie for this operation. This movie identifier is supplied by the Movie Toolbox. Your component may use this identifier to obtain sample data from the movie or to obtain information about the movie.

`onlyThisTrack`
Identifies a track that is to be converted. This track identifier is supplied by the Movie Toolbox. If this parameter contains a track identifier, your component must convert only the specified track.

`startTime` Specifies the starting point of the track or movie segment to be converted. This time value is expressed in the movie's time coordinate system.

CHAPTER 9

Movie Data Exchange Components

duration   Specifies the duration of the track or movie segment to be converted. This duration value is expressed in the movie's time coordinate system.

DESCRIPTION

The Movie Toolbox calls the `MovieExportToFile` function in order to export movie data into a file. Your component must read the data from the track or movie, perform appropriate conversions on that data, and place the data into the specified file. The file's type corresponds to the component subtype of your movie data export component.

Note that the requesting program or toolbox must create the destination file before calling this function. Furthermore, your component may not destroy any data in the destination file. If you cannot add data to the specified file, return an appropriate error.

If your component can write data to a file, be sure to set the `canMovieExportFiles` flag in your component's `componentFlags` field.

Your component must be prepared to perform this function at any time. You should not expect that any of your component's configuration functions will be called first.

RESULT CODES

invalidTrack   –2009   Specified track cannot be converted

Other appropriate Movie Toolbox result codes

SEE ALSO

The Movie Toolbox uses the `MovieExportToHandle` function to export data to a file; this function is described in the previous section.

Configuring Movie Data Export Components

Your component may provide one or more configuration functions. These functions allow applications to configure your component before the Movie Toolbox calls your component to start the export process. Note that applications may call these functions directly.

All of these functions are optional. If your component receives a request that it does not support, you should return the `badComponentSelector` error code. In addition, your component should work properly even if none of these functions is called.

These functions address a variety of configuration issues. Applications can retrieve additional data from your component by calling the `MovieExportGetAuxiliaryData` function.

Applications can specify a progress function for use by your component by calling the `MovieExportSetProgressProc` function.

Applications can instruct your component to display its user dialog box by calling the `MovieExportDoUserDialog` function.

CHAPTER 9

Movie Data Exchange Components

MovieExportSetProgressProc

The `MovieExportSetProgressProc` function allows an application to assign a movie progress function.

```
pascal ComponentResult MovieExportSetProgressProc
                            (ComponentInstance ci,
                             MovieProgressProcPtr proc,
                             long refcon);
```

ci   Identifies the application's connection to your movie data export component.

proc   Contains a pointer to the application's movie progress function. See the chapter "Movie Toolbox" in *Inside Macintosh: QuickTime* for a complete description of the interface supported by movie progress functions. If this parameter is set to `nil`, the application is removing its progress function. In this case, your component should stop calling the progress function.

refcon   Specifies a reference constant. Your component should pass this constant back to the application's progress function whenever you call that function.

DESCRIPTION

Some data export operations may be time-consuming, and application developers may therefore choose to display progress information to the user. Your component provides this information to an application's progress function. As your component processes an export request, you should call the progress function occasionally in order to report on the progress of the operation. Use a progress code of `progressOpExportMovie`. The application can then present this information to the user.

These progress functions must support the same interface as Movie Toolbox progress functions. That interface is discussed in the chapter "Movie Toolbox" in *Inside Macintosh: QuickTime*. Note that this interface not only allows you to report progress to the application, but also allows the application to cancel the request.

RESULT CODE

badComponentSelector   0x80008002   Function not supported

CHAPTER 9

Movie Data Exchange Components

MovieExportGetAuxiliaryData

The `MovieExportGetAuxiliaryData` function allows an application to retrieve additional data from your component. This additional data may be created during the data export process.

```
pascal ComponentResult MovieExportGetAuxiliaryData
                                    (ComponentInstance ci,
                                     Handle dataH,
                                     OSType *handleType);
```

ci
: Identifies the application's connection to your movie data export component.

data
: Contains a handle that is to be filled with the additional data. Your component should resize this handle as appropriate. Your component is not responsible for disposing of this handle.

handleType
: Contains a pointer to the type of data you place in the handle specified by the `data` parameter.

DESCRIPTION

The `MovieExportGetAuxiliaryData` function allows an application to retrieve additional data that is generated during the data export process. The application may then use the data as appropriate. Your component may create this data in cases where the target data type cannot accommodate all of the converted data. For example, if your component exports data into `'TEXT'` handles or files, you might choose to preserve associated style information for that text. However, `'TEXT'` resources cannot store that style information. You could save that style information in a `'styl'` handle and allow an application to retrieve it after the conversion.

Your component should expect the application to call this function after the export process ends.

RESULT CODE

badComponentSelector   0x80008002   Function not supported

CHAPTER 9

Movie Data Exchange Components

MovieExportDoUserDialog

The `MovieExportDoUserDialog` function allows an application to request that your component display its user dialog box.

```
pascal ComponentResult MovieExportDoUserDialog
                                (ComponentInstance ci,
                                 const FSSpec *theFile,
                                 Handle theData,
                                 Boolean *canceled);
```

ci
: Identifies the application's connection to your movie data export component.

theFile
: Contains a pointer to a valid file specification. If the export request pertains to a file, the application must specify the destination file with this parameter and set the parameter `theData` to `nil`. If the request is for a handle, this parameter is set to `nil`.

theData
: Contains a handle to receive the converted data. If the export request pertains to a handle, the application must specify the destination handle with this parameter, and set the parameter `theFile` to `nil`. If the request is for a file, this parameter is set to `nil`.

canceled
: Contains a pointer to a Boolean value. Your component should set this Boolean value to reflect whether the user cancels the dialog box. If the user cancels the dialog box, set the Boolean value to `true`. Otherwise, set it to `false`.

DESCRIPTION

Your movie data export component may support a user dialog box that allows the user to configure an export operation. For components that support such a dialog box, the `MovieExportDoUserDialog` function allows an application to tell you when to display the dialog box to the user.

If your component supports a user dialog box, be sure to set the `hasMovieExportUserInterface` flag in your component's `componentFlags` field.

RESULT CODE

badComponentSelector   0x80008002   Function not supported

Summary of Movie Data Exchange Components

C Summary

Constants

```c
/* component type values */
#define MovieImportType 'eat '     /* movie data import */
#define MovieExportType 'spit'     /* movie data export */

/* componentFlags values for movie import and movie export components */
enum {
    canMovieImportHandles       = 1,  /* can import from handles */
    canMovieImportFiles         = 2,  /* can import from files */
    hasMovieImportUserInterface = 4,  /* import has user interface */
    canMovieExportHandles       = 8,  /* can export to handles */
    canMovieExportFiles         = 16, /* can export to files */
    hasMovieExportUserInterface = 32, /* export has user interface */
    dontAutoFileMovieImport     = 64  /* do not automatically import
                                         movie files */
};

/* flags for MovieImportHandle and MovieImportFile */
enum {
    movieImportCreateTrack      = 1,  /* create a new track */
    movieImportInParallel       = 2,  /* paste imported data */
    movieImportMustUseTrack     = 4   /* use specified track */
};

enum {
    movieImportResultUsedMultipleTracks = 8,  /* component used several
                                                 tracks */
};

enum {
    /* movie data import components */
    kMovieImportHandleSelect            = 1,  /* import from handle */
    kMovieImportFileSelect              = 2,  /* import from file */
    kMovieImportSetSampleDurationSelect = 3,  /* set sample duration */
```

```
kMovieImportSetSampleDescriptionSelect = 4,   /* set sample description */
kMovieImportSetMediaFileSelect         = 5,   /* set media file */
kMovieImportSetDimensionsSelect        = 6,   /* set track dimensions */
kMovieImportSetChunkSizeSelect         = 7,   /* set chunk size */
kMovieImportSetProgressProcSelect      = 8,   /* set progress func */
kMovieImportSetAuxiliaryDataSelect     = 9,   /* set additional data */
kMovieImportSetFromScrapSelect         = 10,  /* data from scrap */
kMovieImportDoUserDialogSelect         = 11,  /* invoke user dialog */
kMovieImportSetDurationSelect          = 12   /* set paste duration */

/* movie data export components */
kMovieExportToHandleSelect             = 128,/* export to handle */
kMovieExportToFileSelect               = 129,/* export to file */
kMovieExportDoUserDialogSelect         = 130,/* invoke user dialog */
kMovieExportGetAuxiliaryDataSelect     = 131,/* get additional data */
kMovieExportSetProgressProcSelect      = 132 /* set progress function */
};
```

Data Type

```
typedef ComponentInstance MovieImportComponent, MovieExportComponent;
```

Functions

Importing Movie Data

```
pascal ComponentResult MovieImportHandle
                        (ComponentInstance ci,
                         Handle dataH, Movie theMovie,
                         Track targetTrack, Track *usedTrack,
                         TimeValue atTime, TimeValue *addedDuration,
                         long inFlags, long *outFlags);
pascal ComponentResult MovieImportFile
                        (ComponentInstance ci,
                         const FSSpec *theFile, Movie theMovie,
                         Track targetTrack, Track *usedTrack,
                         TimeValue atTime, TimeValue *addedDuration,
                         long inFlags, long *outFlags);
```

Configuring Movie Data Import Components

```
pascal ComponentResult MovieImportSetDuration
                        (ComponentInstance ci, TimeValue duration);
pascal ComponentResult MovieImportSetSampleDuration
                        (ComponentInstance ci, TimeValue duration,
                         TimeScale scale);
pascal ComponentResult MovieImportSetSampleDescription
                        (ComponentInstance ci,
                         SampleDescriptionHandle desc,
                         OSType mediaType);
pascal ComponentResult MovieImportSetMediaFile
                        (ComponentInstance ci, AliasHandle alias);
pascal ComponentResult MovieImportSetDimensions
                        (ComponentInstance ci,
                         Fixed width, Fixed height);
pascal ComponentResult MovieImportSetChunkSize
                        (ComponentInstance ci, long chunkSize);
pascal ComponentResult MovieImportSetProgressProc
                        (ComponentInstance ci,
                         MovieProgressProcPtr proc, long refcon);
pascal ComponentResult MovieImportSetAuxiliaryData
                        (ComponentInstance ci,
                         Handle data, OSType handleType);
pascal ComponentResult MovieImportSetFromScrap
                        (ComponentInstance ci, Boolean fromScrap);
pascal ComponentResult MovieImportDoUserDialog
                        (ComponentInstance ci, const FSSpec *theFile,
                         Handle theData, Boolean *canceled);
```

Exporting Movie Data

```
pascal ComponentResult MovieExportToHandle
                        (ComponentInstance ci, Handle dataH,
                         Movie theMovie, Track onlyThisTrack,
                         TimeValue startTime, TimeValue duration);
pascal ComponentResult MovieExportToFile
                        (ComponentInstance ci,
                         const FSSpec *theFile, Movie theMovie,
                         Track onlyThisTrack, TimeValue startTime,
                         TimeValue duration);
```

Configuring Movie Data Export Components

```
pascal ComponentResult MovieExportSetProgressProc
                        (ComponentInstance ci,
                         MovieProgressProcPtr proc, long refcon);
pascal ComponentResult MovieExportGetAuxiliaryData
                        (ComponentInstance ci, Handle dataH,
                         OSType *handleType);
pascal ComponentResult MovieExportDoUserDialog
                        (ComponentInstance ci, const FSSpec *theFile,
                         Handle theData, Boolean *canceled);
```

Pascal Summary

Constants

```
CONST
{component type values}
   MovieImportType = 'eat '          {movie data import}
   MovieExportType = 'spit'          {movie data export}

{componentFlags values for movie import and movie export components}
   canMovieImportHandles           = 1;   {can import from handles}
   canMovieImportFiles             = 2;   {can import from files}
   hasMovieImportUserInterface     = 4;   {import has user interface}
   canMovieExportHandles           = 8;   {can export to handles}
   canMovieExportFiles             = $10; {can export to files}
   hasMovieExportUserInterface     = $20; {export has user interface}
   dontAutoFileMovieImport         = $40; {do not automatically import movie }
                                          { files}

{flags for MovieImportHandle and MovieImportFile functions}
   movieImportCreateTrack               = 1;   {create a new track}
   movieImportInParallel                = 2;   {paste imported data}
   movieImportMustUseTrack              = 4;   {use specified track}
   movieImportResultUsedMultipleTracks  = 8;   {component used several }
                                               { tracks}

{movie data import components}
   kMovieImportHandleSelect            = 1;   {import from handle}
   kMovieImportFileSelect              = 2;   {import from file}
   kMovieImportSetSampleDurationSelect  = 3;   {set sample duration}
```

CHAPTER 9

Movie Data Exchange Components

```
kMovieImportSetSampleDescriptionSelect = 4;   {set sample description}
kMovieImportSetMediaFileSelect         = 5;   {set media file}
kMovieImportSetDimensionsSelect        = 6;   {set track dimensions}
kMovieImportSetChunkSizeSelect         = 7;   {set chunk size}
kMovieImportSetProgressProcSelect      = 8;   {set progress function}
kMovieImportSetAuxiliaryDataSelect     = 9;   {set additional data}
kMovieImportSetFromScrapSelect         = $A;  {data from scrap}
kMovieImportDoUserDialogSelect         = $B;  {invoke user dialog box}
kMovieImportSetDurationSelect          = $C;  {set paste duration}

{movie data export components}
kMovieExportToHandleSelect             = $80; {export to handle}
kMovieExportToFileSelect               = $81; {export to file}
kMovieExportDoUserDialogSelect         = $82; {invoke user dialog box}
kMovieExportGetAuxiliaryDataSelect     = $83; {get additional data}
kMovieExportSetProgressProcSelect      = $84; {set progress function}
```

Data Type

```
TYPE

  MovieImportComponent = ComponentInstance;
  MovieExportComponent = ComponentInstance;
```

Routines

Importing Movie Data

```
FUNCTION MovieImportHandle    (ci: MovieImportComponent; dataH: Handle;
                               theMovie: Movie; targetTrack: Track;
                               VAR usedTrack: Track; atTime: TimeValue;
                               VAR addedDuration: TimeValue;
                               inFlags: LongInt; VAR outFlags: LongInt):
                               ComponentResult;

FUNCTION MovieImportFile      (ci: MovieImportComponent; theFile: FSSpec;
                               theMovie: Movie; targetTrack: Track;
                               VAR usedTrack: Track; atTime: TimeValue;
                               VAR addedDuration: TimeValue;
                               inFlags: LongInt; VAR outFlags: LongInt):
                               ComponentResult;
```

Configuring Movie Data Import Components

```
FUNCTION MovieImportSetDuration
                    (ci: MovieImportComponent;
                     duration: TimeValue): ComponentResult;
FUNCTION MovieImportSetSampleDuration
                    (ci: MovieImportComponent; duration: TimeValue;
                     scale: TimeScale): ComponentResult;
FUNCTION MovieImportSetSampleDescription
                    (ci: MovieImportComponent;
                     desc: SampleDescriptionHandle;
                     mediaType: OSType): ComponentResult;
FUNCTION MovieImportSetMediaFile
                    (ci: MovieImportComponent; alias: AliasHandle):
                     ComponentResult;
FUNCTION MovieImportSetDimensions
                    (ci: MovieImportComponent;
                     width, height: Fixed): ComponentResult;
FUNCTION MovieImportSetChunkSize
                    (ci: MovieImportComponent; chunkSize: LongInt):
                     ComponentResult;
FUNCTION MovieImportSetProgressProc
                    (ci: MovieImportComponent; proc: ProcPtr;
                     refCon: LongInt): ComponentResult;
FUNCTION MovieImportSetAuxiliaryData
                    (ci: MovieImportComponent; data: Handle;
                     handleType: OSType): ComponentResult;
FUNCTION MovieImportSetFromScrap
                    (ci: MovieImportComponent; fromScrap: Boolean):
                     ComponentResult;
FUNCTION MovieImportDoUserDialog
                    (ci: MovieImportComponent; srcFile: FSSpec;
                     data: Handle; VAR canceled: Boolean):
                     ComponentResult;
```

Exporting Movie Data

```
FUNCTION MovieExportToHandle
                            (ci: MovieExportComponent; data: Handle;
                             theMovie: Movie; onlyThisTrack: Track;
                             startTime: TimeValue; duration: TimeValue):
                             ComponentResult;
FUNCTION MovieExportToFile  (ci: MovieExportComponent; dstFile: FSSpec;
                             theMovie: Movie; onlyThisTrack: Track;
                             startTime: TimeValue; duration: TimeValue):
                             ComponentResult;
```

Configuring Movie Data Export Components

```
FUNCTION MovieExportSetProgressProc
                            (ci: MovieExportComponent; proc: ProcPtr;
                             refCon: LongInt): ComponentResult;
FUNCTION MovieExportGetAuxiliaryData
                            (ci: MovieExportComponent; dstFile: Handle;
                             VAR handleType: OSType): ComponentResult;
FUNCTION MovieExportDoUserDialog
                            (ci: MovieExportComponent; dstFile: FSSpec;
                             data: Handle; VAR canceled: Boolean):
                             ComponentResult;
```

Result Codes

`invalidTrack`	−2009	Specified track cannot receive imported data
`unsupportedAuxiliaryImportData`	−2057	Cannot work with specified handle type
`badComponentSelector`	0x80008002	Function not supported

CHAPTER 10

Derived Media Handler Components

Contents

About Derived Media Handler Components   10-4
   Media Handler Components   10-4
   Derived Media Handler Components   10-6
Creating a Derived Media Handler Component   10-7
   Component Flags for Derived Media Handlers   10-8
   Request Processing   10-8
   A Sample Derived Media Handler Component   10-9
      Implementing the Required Component Functions   10-9
      Initializing a Derived Media Handler Component   10-12
      Drawing the Media Sample   10-13
Derived Media Handler Components Reference   10-15
   Data Type   10-15
   Functions   10-18
      Managing Your Media Handler Component   10-18
      General Data Management   10-23
      Graphics Data Management   10-31
      Sound Data Management   10-37
      Base Media Handler Utility Function   10-38
Summary of Derived Media Handler Components   10-41
   C Summary   10-41
      Constants   10-41
      Data Type   10-43
      Functions   10-43
   Pascal Summary   10-45
      Constants   10-45
      Data Type   10-46
      Routines   10-47

Derived Media Handler Components

This chapter discusses derived media handler components. **Derived media handler components** allow the Movie Toolbox to play the data in a media. These components isolate the Movie Toolbox from the details of how or where a particular media is stored. This not only frees the Movie Toolbox from reading and writing media data, but also makes QuickTime extensible to new data formats.

These components are referred to as *derived* components because they rely on the services of a common base media handler component, which is supplied by Apple. The **base media handler component** handles most of the duties that must be performed by all media handlers. Your derived media handler component extends the services provided by the base media handler.

This chapter is divided into the following sections:

- "About Derived Media Handler Components" provides a general introduction to components of this type.
- "Creating a Derived Media Handler Component" provides a sample program for the implementation of such a component for PICT files.
- "Derived Media Handler Components Reference" presents detailed information about the functions that are supported by these components.
- "Summary of Derived Media Handler Components" contains a condensed listing of the constants, data structures, and functions supported by these components.

This chapter addresses developers of derived media handler components. You should never need to use the facilities of a derived media handler directly—only the Movie Toolbox calls derived media handler components. The functions described in this chapter define the functional interface that your component must support.

As components, derived media handlers rely on the facilities of the Component Manager. To use any component, your application must also use the Component Manager. If you are not familiar with this manager, see the chapter "Component Manager" in *Inside Macintosh: More Macintosh Toolbox*. In addition, you should be familiar with the Movie Toolbox in general and the concept of media structures in particular. See the chapter "Movie Toolbox" in *Inside Macintosh: QuickTime* for more information.

Note
Throughout this chapter, the terms *media handler* and *handler* refer to media handler components. Apple's sound and video handlers are not derived media handlers, so you cannot override them using the functions described in this chapter. Apple's text media handler, on the other hand, is built on the base media handler. ◆

About Derived Media Handler Components

This section provides background information about media handler components in general and derived media handler components in particular. After reading this section, you should understand why media handler components exist and whether you need to create a derived media handler component.

Media Handler Components

Media handler components allow the Movie Toolbox to play a movie's data. The Movie Toolbox, by itself, cannot read or write movie data. Rather, media handlers perform input and output services on behalf of the Movie Toolbox. The Movie Toolbox gains access to the appropriate media handler for a particular movie track by examining the track's media. That data structure identifies the media handler that created and maintains the media (see the chapter "Movie Toolbox" in *Inside Macintosh: QuickTime* for more information about the relationship between a movie, its tracks, and each track's media).

Each media handler is primarily responsible for understanding the format and content of the media type it supports. The media handler is intimately familiar with the sample structure used in its media, the compression techniques used to store the media's sample data, and the performance characteristics of the device that stores the media.

During movie playback, the media handler draws its media's data on the screen and plays the media's sounds. The media handler may use the services of other managers such as the Image Compression Manager for compressed image data and the Sound Manager for sound data. When an application creates a movie, media handlers store the movie's data. The actual reading and writing of media data are performed by another component, the **data handler.** For details on the Image Compression Manager, see *Inside Macintosh: QuickTime*. For more on the Sound Manager, see *Inside Macintosh: More Macintosh Toolbox*.

Applications never directly use the services of media handlers. The Movie Toolbox controls all movie data storage and retrieval on behalf of QuickTime applications.

Derived Media Handler Components

Figure 10-1 shows the logical relationships between applications, the Movie Toolbox, media handlers, and data handlers.

Figure 10-1 Logical relationships between the Movie Toolbox and media handlers

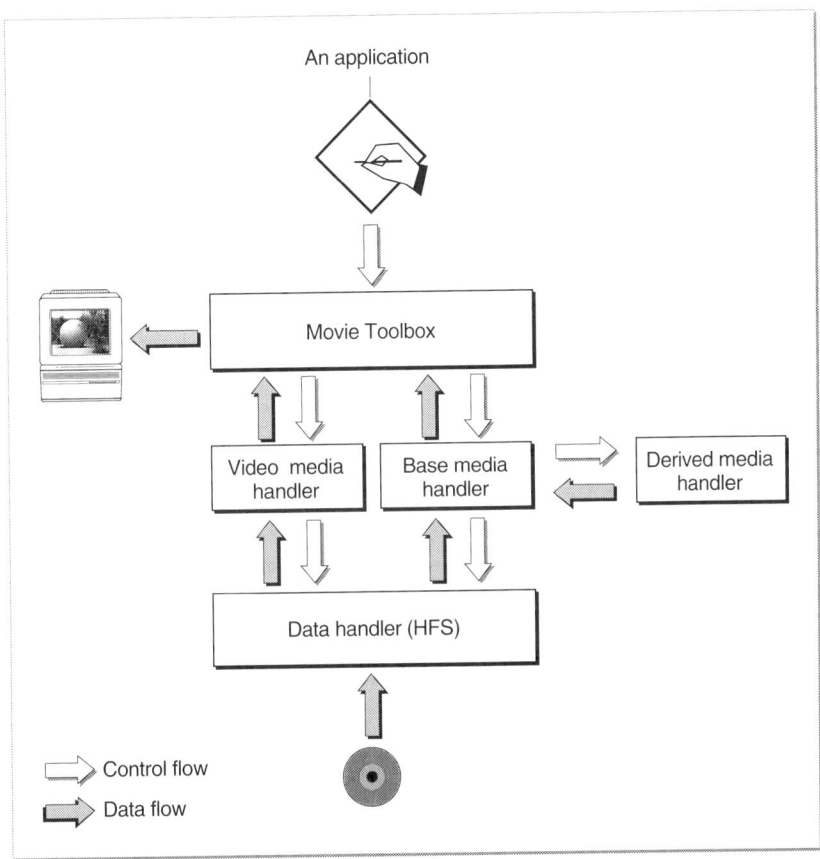

Apple had three primary goals for isolating the Movie Toolbox and QuickTime applications from the details of media data access. First, the isolation allows programmers who develop the Movie Toolbox and QuickTime applications to focus on the specifics of the problems they are addressing, freed from concerns about data access. Second, this architecture allows QuickTime to be easily extended to accommodate new storage devices and technologies. Third, by documenting the media handler interface, developers can create their own, special-purpose media handlers that work with QuickTime.

Derived Media Handler Components

Derived Media Handler Components

Much of what a media handler component must do is common to all media handlers. Managing a connection with the appropriate data handler, retrieving movie data from media samples, and storing movie data into new samples account for a substantial part of every media handler's responsibilities. To make it easier for developers to create media handler components, Apple provides a base media handler component that performs most of the common duties of a media handler.

Apple's base media handler component eliminates much of the work you would have to do to create your own media handler component. The base media handler interacts with both the Movie Toolbox and the appropriate data handler, so that your media handler only has to deal with service requests, and you can ignore many of the housekeeping functions. It understands the format of Apple's media samples and sample descriptions, so that your media handler only has to worry about the actual media data. Finally, it provides basic services that your media handler can use to accommodate unusual display environments.

When you build your media handler component on top of the base media handler, your media handler is known as a *derived media handler component*. This terminology is borrowed from object-oriented development and refers to the fact that your media handler is based on, or derived from, the services provided by Apple's base media handler. Figure 10-2 shows the relationship between the base media handler, derived media handlers, the Movie Toolbox, and data handler components.

Figure 10-2 Relationship between the base media handler component and derived media handlers

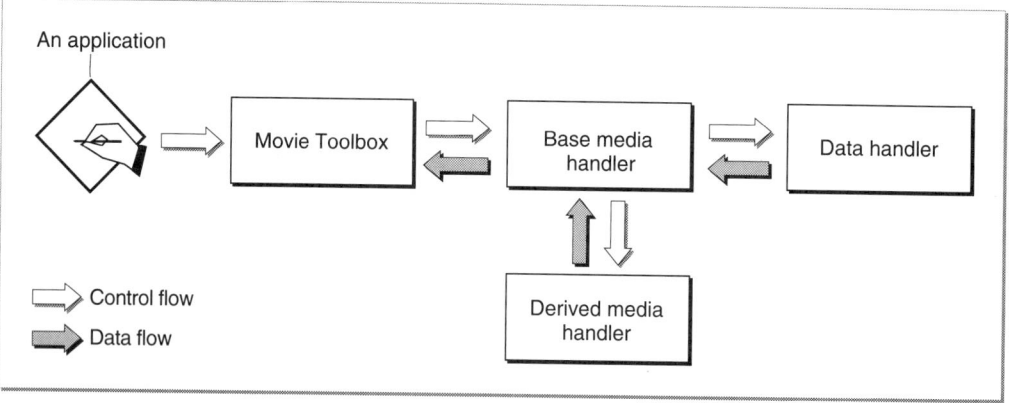

You should consider deriving your media handler from Apple's base media handler component if your media requires low to moderate data throughput. Apple's base media handler can support data rates up to 32 kilobits per second. This rate is adequate for such data types as text, sound effects, animation, annotations, or MIDI (Musical

Instrument Digital Interface) sound data. However, Apple's base media handler is not appropriate for CD-quality sound, which may require data rates of up to 176 kilobits per second.

Creating a Derived Media Handler Component

This section provides an example of creating a derived media handler component. The functional interface that your derived media handler component must support is described in "Derived Media Handler Components Reference" beginning on page 10-15.

Before reading this section, you should be familiar with how to create components. See the chapter "Component Manager" in *Inside Macintosh: More Macintosh Toolbox* for a complete discussion of components—how to use them and how to create them.

Apple has defined a component type value for media handler components. All components of this type have the same type value. You can use the following constant to specify this component type:

```
#define  MediaHandlerType   'mhlr'      /* media handler */
```

Apple has defined a functional interface for derived media handler components. For information about the functions that your component must support, see "Derived Media Handler Components Reference" beginning on page 10-15. You can use the following constants to refer to the request codes for each of the functions that your component must support:

```
enum {
    kMediaInitializeSelect              = 0x501, /* MediaInitialize */
    kMediaSetHandlerCapabilitiesSelect  = 0x502,
                                        /* MediaSetHandlerCapabilities */
    kMediaIdleSelect                    = 0x503, /* MediaIdle */
    kMediaGetMediaInfoSelect            = 0x504, /* MediaGetMediaInfo */
    kMediaPutMediaInfoSelect            = 0x505, /* MediaPutMediaInfo */
    kMediaSetActiveSelect               = 0x506, /* MediaSetActive */
    kMediaSetRateSelect                 = 0x507, /* MediaSetRate */
    kMediaGGetStatusSelect              = 0x508, /* MediaGGetStatus */
    kMediaTrackEditedSelect             = 0x509, /* MediaTrackEdited */
    kMediaSetMediaTimeScaleSelect       = 0x50A, /* MediaSetMediaTimeScale */
    kMediaSetMovieTimeScaleSelect       = 0x50B, /* MediaSetMovieTimeScale */
    kMediaSetGWorldSelect               = 0x50C, /* MediaSetGWorld */
    kMediaSetDimensionsSelect           = 0x50D, /* MediaSetDimensions */
    kMediaSetClipSelect                 = 0x50E, /* MediaSetClip */
    kMediaSetMatrixSelect               = 0x50F, /* MediaSetMatrix */
    kMediaGetTrackOpaqueSelect          = 0x510, /* MediaGetTrackOpaque */
    kMediaSetGraphicsModeSelect         = 0x511, /* MediaSetGraphicsMode */
```

```
kMediaGetGraphicsModeSelect            = 0x512, /* MediaGetGraphicsMode */
kMediaGSetVolumeSelect                 = 0x513, /* MediaGSetVolume */
kMediaSetSoundBalanceSelect            = 0x514, /* MediaSetSoundBalance */
kMediaGetSoundBalanceSelect            = 0x515, /* MediaGetSoundBalance */
kMediaGetNextBoundsChangeSelect        = 0x516,
                                                /* MediaGetNextBoundsChange */
kMediaGetSrcRgnSelect                  = 0x517, /* MediaGetSrcRgn */
kMediaPrerollSelect                    = 0x518, /* MediaPreroll */
kMediaSampleDescriptionChangedSelect   = 0x519,
                                                /* MediaSampleDescriptionChanged */
kMediaHasCharacteristicSelect          = 0x51A  /* MediaHasCharacteristic */
};
```

Component Flags for Derived Media Handlers

The Component Manager allows you to specify information about your component's capabilities in the `componentFlags` field of the component description record. You must set this component flag to 1 in the component description that is associated with your derived media handler:

`mediaHandlerFlagBaseClient`
> Indicates that your component is derived from another component. Setting this flag to 1 tells the Component Manager that your component is a client of the base media handler.

Request Processing

Because your derived media handler is based on the base media handler component, you avoid many of the details involved in creating a media handler. However, your derived media handler must observe a few rules when processing service requests. These rules are as follows:

- When you receive an open request from the Component Manager, in addition to the other processing you perform on your own behalf, you must also open a connection to the base media handler component. You should save the component instance that is returned by the Component Manager so that your media handler can use the services of the base media handler.

- The base media handler has a component type of `MediaHandlerType` (which is set to `'mhlr'`) and a component subtype of `BaseMediaType` (which is set to `'gnrc'`). You can use these values with the Component Manager's `OpenDefaultComponent` function to open a connection to the base media handler.

Derived Media Handler Components

- At this time, you must also tell the base media handler that your handler is derived from it. Use the Component Manager's `OpenComponent` function to create a component instance of your media handler as a descendant of the base media handler. After calling that function, you should send the `kComponentSetTargetSelect` request to the base media handler, so that it knows your media handler is derived from it. Use the Component Manager's `ComponentSetTarget` function to send a target request.

- When you receive a close request from the Component Manager, be sure to close your handler's connection to the base media handler component. Use the Component Manager's `CloseComponent` function.

- Your derived media handler must support the target request, so that your component can be used by other media handlers.

- Be sure to pass all unsupported service requests to the base media handler component. Use the Component Manager's `DelegateComponentCall` function to pass these requests to the base media handler.

- If your media handler component competes for potentially scarce system resources, your component should release those resources when you aren't using them. For example, if you are creating a media handler that uses sound, you might use sound channels. Because there are a limited number of sound channels available, your component should free its channels whenever your media is not playing or has been stopped. You can reallocate the channels when you start playing or your component's `MediaPreroll` function is called.

A Sample Derived Media Handler Component

This section supplies a sample program that implements a derived media handler component for PICT images.

Implementing the Required Component Functions

Listing 10-1 supplies the component dispatchers for the media handler component for PICT images together with the required functions.

Listing 10-1 Implementing the required functions

```
typedef struct {
   ComponentInstance self;
   ComponentInstance parent;
   ComponentInstance delegateComponent;
   Fixed             width;
   Fixed             height;
   MatrixRecord      matrix;
   Media             media;
   Track             track;
} PictGlobalsRecord, *PictGlobals;
```

Derived Media Handler Components

```
pascal ComponentResult PictMediaDispatch
                                (ComponentParameters *params,
                                 Handle storage)
{
   OSErr err = badComponentSelector;
   ComponentFunction componentProc = 0;

   switch (params->what) {
      case kComponentOpenSelect:
         componentProc = PictOpen; break;
      case kComponentCloseSelect:
         componentProc = PictClose; break;
      case kComponentCanDoSelect:
         componentProc = PictCanDo; break;
      case kComponentVersionSelect:
         componentProc = PictVersion; break;
      case kComponentTargetSelect:
         componentProc = PictVersion; break;
      case kMediaInitializeSelect:
         componentProc = PictInitialize; break;
      case kMediaIdleSelect:
         componentProc = PictIdle; break;
      case kMediaSetDimensionsSelect:
         componentProc = PictSetDimensions; break;
      case kMediaSetMatrixSelect:
         componentProc = PictSetMatrix; break;
   }
   if (componentProc)
      err = CallComponentFunctionWithStorage (storage, params,
                                              componentProc);
   else
      err = DelegateComponentCall (params, ((PictGlobals)
                                   storage)->delegateComponent);

   return err;
}

pascal ComponentResult PictCanDo (PictGlobals globals,
                                  short ftnNumber)
{
   switch (ftnNumber) {
      case kComponentOpenSelect:
      case kComponentCloseSelect:
```

Derived Media Handler Components

```
      case kComponentCanDoSelect:
      case kComponentVersionSelect:
      case kComponentTargetSelect:

      case kMediaInitializeSelect:
      case kMediaIdleSelect:
      case kMediaSetDimensionsSelect:
      case kMediaSetMatrixSelect:
         return true;
      default:
         return ComponentFunctionImplemented
                     (globals->delegateComponent, ftnNumber);
   }
}

pascal ComponentResult PictVersion (PictGlobals globals)
{
   return 0x00020001;
}

pascal ComponentResult PictOpen(PictGlobals globals,
                                ComponentInstance self)
{
   OSErr err;

   /* allocate storage */
   globals = (PictGlobals)NewPtrClear(sizeof(PictGlobalsRecord));
   if (err = MemError()) return err;
   SetComponentInstanceStorage(self, (Handle)globals);
   globals->self = self;
   globals->parent = self;

   /* find a base media handler to serve as a delegate */
   globals->delegateComponent =
            OpenDefaultComponent (MediaHandlerType,
                                  BaseMediaType);
   if (globals->delegateComponent)
      PictTarget(globals, self); /* set up the calling chain */
   else {
      DisposePtr((Ptr)globals);
      err = cantOpenHandler;
   }
   return err;
}
```

Creating a Derived Media Handler Component

Derived Media Handler Components

```
pascal ComponentResult PictClose (PictGlobals globals,
                                  ComponentInstance self)
{
   if (globals) {
      if (globals->delegateComponent)
         CloseComponent(globals->delegateComponent);

      DisposePtr((Ptr)globals);
   }

   return noErr;
}

pascal ComponentResult PictTarget(PictGlobals store,
                                  ComponentInstance parentComponent)
{
   /* remember who is at the top of your calling chain */
   store->parent = parentComponent;

   /* and inform your delegate component of the change */
   ComponentSetTarget(store->delegateComponent, parentComponent);

   return noErr;
}
```

Initializing a Derived Media Handler Component

The derived media handler component is initialized by the Movie Toolbox's calling of the `MediaInitialize` function (described on page 10-18). You should then report the derived media handler capabilities to the base media handler before the Movie Toolbox starts working with your media by calling the `MediaSetHandlerCapabilities` function (described on page 10-38) from your `MediaInitialize` function.

Listing 10-2 is the initialization function for a derived media handler. The `PictInitialize` function stores the initial height, width, track movie matrix, media, and track of the derived media handler component. From `PictInitialize`, the `MediaSetHandlerCapabilities` function is called to inform the base media handler of its existence and features.

Derived Media Handler Components

Listing 10-2 Initializing a derived media handler

```
pascal ComponentResult PictInitialize (PictGlobals store,
                                       GetMovieCompleteParams *gmc)
{
   /* remember some useful parameters */
   store->width = gmc->width;
   store->height = gmc->height;
   store->matrix = gmc->trackMovieMatrix;
   store->media = gmc->theMedia;
   store->track = gmc->theTrack;

   /* tell the base media handler about your derived
      media handler */
   MediaSetHandlerCapabilities(store->delegateComponent,
   handlerHasSpatial, handlerHasSpatial);

   return noErr;
}
```

Drawing the Media Sample

The Movie Toolbox provides processing time to your derived media handler to display samples by calling the `MediaIdle` function (described on page 10-20). Your media handler may use this time to play its media sample. The code in Listing 10-3 allows the derived media handler component to draw the current media sample (in this case, a PICT image).

Listing 10-3 Drawing the media sample

```
pascal ComponentResult PictIdle (PictGlobals store,
                                 TimeValue atMediaTime,
                                 long flagsIn, long *flagsOut,
                                 const TimeValue *tr)
{
   OSErr err;
   Rect r;
   Handle sample = NewHandle (0);

   if (err = MemError()) goto bail;
```

Derived Media Handler Components

```
    /* get the current sample */
    err = GetMediaSample (store->media, sample, 0, nil,
                        atMediaTime, nil, 0, 0, 0, 0, 0, 0);
    if (err) goto bail;

    /* draw it using the current matrix */
    SetRect (&r, 0, 0, FixRound (store->width),
            FixRound (store->height));
    TransformRect (&store->matrix, &r, nil);
    EraseRect (&r);
    DrawPicture ((PicHandle)sample, &r);
bail:
    DisposeHandle (sample);
    *flagsOut |= mDidDraw;   /* let Movie Toolbox know you drew
                                something */

    return err;
}

pascal ComponentResult PictSetDimensions (PictGlobals store,
                                            Fixed width,
                                            Fixed height)
{
    /* remember the new track */
    store->width = width;
    store->height = height;
    return noErr;
}

pascal ComponentResult PictSetMatrix (PictGlobals store,
                                        MatrixRecord *trackMovieMatrix)
{
    /* remember the new display matrix */
    store->matrix = *trackMovieMatrix;
    return noErr;
}
```

Derived Media Handler Components Reference

This section describes the functions that your derived media handler may support and the data structure that your component may use to interact with the base media handler.

Data Type

The `GetMovieCompleteParams` data type defines the layout of the complete movie parameter structure used by the `MediaInitialize` function (described on page 10-18):

```
typedef struct {
    short            version;           /* version; always 0 */
    Movie            theMovie;          /* movie identifier */
    Track            theTrack;          /* track identifier */
    Media            theMedia;          /* media identifier */
    TimeScale        movieScale;        /* movie's time scale */
    TimeScale        mediaScale;        /* media's time scale */
    TimeValue        movieDuration;     /* movie's duration */
    TimeValue        trackDuration;     /* track's duration */
    TimeValue        mediaDuration;     /* media's duration */
    Fixed            effectiveRate;     /* media's effective rate */
    TimeBase         timeBase;          /* media's time base */
    short            volume;            /* media's volume */
    Fixed            width;             /* width of display area */
    Fixed            height;            /* height of display area */
    MatrixRecord     trackMovieMatrix;  /* transformation matrix */
    CGrafPtr         moviePort;         /* movie's graphics port */
    GDHandle         movieGD;           /* movie's graphics device */
    PixMapHandle     trackMatte;        /* track's matte */
} GetMovieCompleteParams;
```

Field descriptions

version Specifies the version of this structure. This field is always set to 0.

theMovie Identifies the movie that contains the current media's track. This movie identifier is supplied by the Movie Toolbox. Your component may use this identifier to obtain information about the movie that is using your media.

Derived Media Handler Components

theTrack
: Identifies the track that contains the current media. This track identifier is supplied by the Movie Toolbox. Your component may use this identifier to obtain information about the track that contains your media. For example, you might call the Movie Toolbox's `GetTrackNextInterestingTime` function in order to examine the track's edit list.

theMedia
: Identifies the current media. This media identifier is supplied by the Movie Toolbox. Your derived media handler can use this identifier to read samples or sample descriptions from the current media, using the Movie Toolbox's `GetMediaSample` and `GetMediaSampleDescription` functions (see *Inside Macintosh: QuickTime* for information about the Movie Toolbox).

movieScale
: Specifies the time scale of the movie that contains the current media's track. If the Movie Toolbox changes the movie's time scale, the toolbox calls your derived media handler's `MediaSetMovieTimeScale` function, which is described on page 10-30.

mediaScale
: Specifies the time scale of the current media. If the Movie Toolbox changes your media's time scale, the toolbox calls your derived media handler's `MediaSetMediaTimeScale` function, which is described on page 10-30.

movieDuration
: Contains the movie's duration. This value is expressed in the movie's time scale.

trackDuration
: Contains the track's duration. This value is expressed in the movie's time scale.

mediaDuration
: Contains the media's duration. This value is expressed in the media's time scale.

effectiveRate
: Contains the media's effective rate. This rate ties the media's time scale to the passage of absolute time, and does not necessarily correspond to the movie's rate. This value takes into account any master time bases that may be serving the media's time base. The value of this field indicates the number of time units (in the media's time scale) that pass each second.

    This rate is represented as a 32-bit, fixed-point number. The high-order 16 bits contain the integer portion, and the low-order 16 bits contain the fractional portion. The rate is negative when time is moving backward for the media.

    Whenever the Movie Toolbox changes your media's effective rate, it calls your derived media handler's `MediaSetRate` function, which is discussed on page 10-26.

timeBase
: Identifies the media's time base.

volume
: Contains the media's current volume setting. This value is represented as a 16-bit, fixed-point number. The high-order 8 bits contain the integer portion; the low-order 8 bits contain the

Derived Media Handler Components

fractional part. Volume values range from –1.0 to 1.0. Negative values play no sound but preserve the absolute value of the volume setting.

If the Movie Toolbox changes your media's volume, it calls your derived media handler's `MediaGSetVolume` function, which is discussed on page 10-38.

`width`   Indicates the width, in pixels, of the track rectangle. This field, along with the `height` field, specifies a rectangle that surrounds the image that is displayed when the current media is played. This value corresponds to the x coordinate of the lower-right corner of the rectangle and is expressed as a fixed-point number.

If the Movie Toolbox modifies this rectangle, the toolbox calls your derived media handler's `MediaSetDimensions` function, which is discussed on page 10-32.

Note that your media need not present only a rectangular image. The Movie Toolbox can use a clipping region to cause your media's image to be displayed in a region of arbitrary shape, and it can use a matte to control the image's transparency. The toolbox calls your derived media handler's `MediaSetClip` function whenever it changes your media's clipping region (see page 10-34 for more information about this function). The `trackMatte` field in this structure specifies a matte region.

`height`   Indicates the height, in pixels, of the track rectangle. This value corresponds to the y coordinate of the lower-right corner of the rectangle and is expressed as a fixed-point number.

`trackMovieMatrix`
Specifies the matrix that transforms your media's pixels into the movie's coordinate system. The Movie Toolbox obtains this matrix by concatenating the track matrix and the movie matrix. You should use this matrix whenever you are displaying graphical data from your media.

Whenever the Movie Toolbox modifies this matrix, it calls your derived media handler's `MediaSetMatrix` function, which is discussed on page 10-33.

`moviePort`   Indicates the movie's graphics port. Whenever the Movie Toolbox changes the movie's graphics world, it calls your derived media handler's `MediaSetGWorld` function, which is discussed on page 10-31.

`movieGD`   Specifies the movie's graphics device. Whenever the Movie Toolbox changes the movie's graphics world, it calls your derived media handler's `MediaSetGWorld` function, which is discussed on page 10-31.

`trackMatte`   Identifies the matte region assigned to the track that uses your media. This field contains a handle to a pixel map that contains a blend matte. Your component is not responsible for disposing of this matte. If there is no matte, this field is set to `nil`.

CHAPTER 10

Derived Media Handler Components

Functions

This section describes the functions that may be supported by derived media handler components. It is divided into the following topics:

- "Managing Your Media Handler Component" discusses the functions that allow the Movie Toolbox to manage its connection to your component.

- "General Data Management" describes the functions that allow the Movie Toolbox to manage the general characteristics of the control path through your component.

- "Graphics Data Management" tells you about the functions that allow the Movie Toolbox to manage the graphical characteristics of the control path through your component.

- "Sound Data Management" provides information about the function that allows the Movie Toolbox to manage the sound characteristics of the control path through your component.

- "Base Media Handler Utility Function" discusses a function that allows your derived media handler to report its capabilities to the base media handler.

Note
Many of the functions described in this chapter are optional—that is, your derived media handler may not need to support them. The description of each function discusses the issues you should consider when deciding whether or not to support a specific function. ◆

Managing Your Media Handler Component

Derived media handlers provide three functions that allow the Movie Toolbox to manage its relationship with the media handler. The Movie Toolbox calls your `MediaInitialize` function in order to give you an opportunity to prepare to provide access to your media. The Movie Toolbox grants processing time to your handler by calling your `MediaIdle` function. Your `MediaGGetStatus` function allows the Movie Toolbox to retrieve status information after calling `MediaIdle`.

MediaInitialize

The `MediaInitialize` function allows your derived media handler component to prepare itself for providing access to its media.

```
pascal ComponentResult MediaInitialize (ComponentInstance ci,
                                        GetMovieCompleteParams *gmc);
```

ci   Identifies the Movie Toolbox's connection to your derived media handler.

CHAPTER 10

Derived Media Handler Components

gmc Contains a pointer to a complete movie parameter structure, which is described in "Data Type" beginning on page 10-15. You can obtain information about the current media from this structure. You should copy any values you need to save into your derived media handler's local data area.

Because this data structure is owned by the Movie Toolbox, you do not need to worry about disposing of any of the data in it.

DESCRIPTION

Once the Movie Toolbox has loaded a movie's data from its file, the toolbox calls your derived media handler's `MediaInitialize` function. If the user is creating a new movie, the Movie Toolbox calls your media handler anyway, even though there may be no media data.

This function gives your media handler an opportunity to get ready to support the Movie Toolbox. As part of these preparations, your derived media handler should report its capabilities to the base media handler by calling the `MediaSetHandlerCapabilities` function (see page 10-38 for more information about this function).

You may choose to examine the data in the movie parameter structure; you may also save values from this structure. If you save references to structures (such as the matte pixel map), do not dispose of the memory associated with these structures. The Movie Toolbox owns these structures.

All derived media handlers should support this function. In addition, if your media handler saves values from the movie parameter structure that may change, be sure to support the corresponding functions that allow the Movie Toolbox to report changes to your media handler. For example, if your handler saves the movie time scale from the `movieScale` field, you should also support the `MediaSetMovieTimeScale` function.

If you return an error, the Movie Toolbox disables the track that uses your media. In cases where your media has just been created, the Movie Toolbox immediately disposes of your media.

Note that the Movie Toolbox may call other functions supported by your media handler before it calls your `MediaInitialize` function. In particular, it may call your `MediaGetMediaInfo` and `MediaPutMediaInfo` functions. However, before the Movie Toolbox tries to do anything with the data in your media, it will call your `MediaInitialize` function. The Movie Toolbox loads the movie's data using functions that are supported by the base media handler—your media handler does not have to support those functions.

RESULT CODES

Any Component Manager result code

MediaIdle

The `MediaIdle` function allows the Movie Toolbox to provide processing time to your derived media handler during movie playback. Your media handler may use this time to play its media.

```
pascal ComponentResult MediaIdle (ComponentInstance ci,
                                  TimeValue atMediaTime,
                                  long flagsIn, long *flagsOut,
                                  const TimeRecord *movieTime);
```

`ci`
: Identifies the Movie Toolbox's connection to your derived media handler.

`atMediaTime`
: Specifies the current time, in your media's time base. You can use this time to determine the appropriate media data to work with.

`flagsIn`
: Contains flags that indicate what the Movie Toolbox wants your media handler to do. These flags are applicable only to media handlers that perform their own scheduling.

  The following flags are defined—the Movie Toolbox may use none, or it may set one or more flag to 1:

  `mMustDraw`
  : Indicates that your media handler must play its media at this time. For graphical media, this means that your handler must draw the appropriate media data on the screen. For sound-based media, your handler must play the media's sounds. If this flag is set to 1, the Movie Toolbox has encountered a new sample in your media.

  `mAtEnd`
  : Indicates that the current time corresponds to the end of the movie.

  `mPreflightDraw`
  : Indicates that your media handler must not play its media at this time. Your handler may examine the media data and prepare to play it, but you should not draw any graphical data or play any sounds. If this flag is set to 1, your handler must not play its data.

  If these flags are set to 0, then your media handler is free to decide whether to play the media data or not.

`flagsOut`
: Contains a pointer to a long integer that your media handler uses to indicate to the Movie Toolbox what the handler did. You must always set the values of these flags appropriately.

  The following flags are defined:

  `mDidDraw`
  : Indicates that your media handler played its media's data with the `handlerHasSpatial` flag set, then it drew the data. Any time your media handler plays its media's data, you should set this flag to 1 when you return from your `MediaIdle` function. The Movie Toolbox uses this

CHAPTER 10

Derived Media Handler Components

information when it is displaying a composited movie—that is, a movie whose image is derived by blending several tracks together. If your media's track is obscured by other, semitransparent tracks, the Movie Toolbox must redraw those other tracks whenever your media's image changes.

`mNeedsToDraw`
Indicates that your media handler needs to play its data. Typically, you use this flag when the Movie Toolbox calls your `MediaIdle` function with the `mPreflightDraw` flag in the `flagsIn` field set to 1, and you discover that you have data that must be played at the current time. Set this flag to 1 if your handler needs to play its media's data.

`movieTime`   Contains a pointer to the movie time value corresponding to the `atMediaTime` parameter. Note that this may differ from the current value returned by the Movie Toolbox's `GetMovieTime` function.

DESCRIPTION

The Movie Toolbox uses your `MediaIdle` function to provide processing time to your derived media handler during movie playback. Your media handler is free to use this time in any appropriate manner. For example, if your media handler supports a sound data type, you might prepare to play your media's sounds or actually play them, depending upon the options asserted by the Movie Toolbox. Your media handler is responsible for limiting the amount of processing time it uses.

The Movie Toolbox provides the current time, in your media's time base, in the `atMediaTime` parameter. You can use this value to obtain the appropriate samples and sample descriptions from your media (using the Movie Toolbox's `GetMediaSample` function). Your media handler may then work with the sample data and descriptions as appropriate.

If you encounter an error, save the result code. The Movie Toolbox polls you for status information using the `MediaGGetStatus` function, which is described next.

Your handler should examine the `flagsIn` parameter each time the Movie Toolbox calls its `MediaIdle` function. The flags in this parameter indicate the actions that your handler may perform. In addition, when you return from your `MediaIdle` function, you should report what you did using the `flagsOut` parameter. You tell the base media handler that you perform your own scheduling by setting the `handlerNoScheduler` flag to 1 in the `flags` parameter of the `MediaSetHandlerCapabilities` function (see page 10-38 for more information about this function).

If your media handler changes any of the settings of the movie's graphics port or graphics world, be sure to restore the original settings before you exit. In addition, note that you may be drawing into a black-and-white graphics port. Finally, be aware that the Movie Toolbox also uses this function to obtain data for QuickDraw pictures. Therefore, if your media handler does not use QuickDraw when drawing to the screen, be sure to examine the `picSave` field in the graphics port so that you can detect when the toolbox wants to save an image. Your media handler is then responsible for performing the appropriate display processing. (For details on QuickDraw pictures, see the chapter "Basic QuickDraw" in *Inside Macintosh: Imaging*.)

Your derived media handler should support this function if you need to do work during movie playback. If you set the `handlerNoIdle` flag to 1 in the `flags` parameter of the `MediaSetHandlerCapabilities` function, the Movie Toolbox does not call your `MediaIdle` function.

RESULT CODES

Any Component Manager result code

MediaGGetStatus

The `MediaGGetStatus` function allows your derived media handler to report error conditions to the Movie Toolbox.

```
pascal ComponentResult MediaGGetStatus (ComponentInstance ci,
                                        ComponentResult *statusErr);
```

ci
: Identifies the Movie Toolbox's connection to your derived media handler.

statusErr
: Contains a pointer to a component result field. If you have error information that you would like to report to the Movie Toolbox, place an appropriate result code into the field referred to by this pointer.

DESCRIPTION

The Movie Toolbox calls your `MediaGGetStatus` function whenever an application calls the toolbox's `GetMovieStatus` or `GetTrackStatus` function. This provides your media handler an opportunity to report any difficulties it may be having in playing your media. You should use this mechanism to report any errors you encounter in your `MediaIdle` function (described in the previous section). You may use any appropriate result code.

Your derived media handler should support this function if you anticipate that you may encounter an error when playing your media. Because these errors may include such conditions as low memory or missing hardware, you should only rarely create a derived media handler that does not support this function. If your media handler does not support this function, the base media handler always sets the returned result code to `noErr`.

RESULT CODES

Any Component Manager result code

General Data Management

While the base media handler isolates your component from the details of media data access, your derived media handler still needs to keep track of certain information in order to support movie playback and creation. This section discusses functions that help your media handler manage its information.

Your media handler may store proprietary information in its media. The Movie Toolbox calls two media handler functions in order to give you an opportunity to retrieve or store this information. The `MediaPutMediaInfo` function allows you to store your special information in your media. The `MediaGetMediaInfo` function delivers that data to your media handler.

The Movie Toolbox tells your media handler when its track has been enabled or disabled by calling your `MediaSetActive` function. The Movie Toolbox prepares your handler for playback by calling your `MediaPreroll` function. Whenever your media's playback rate changes, the Movie Toolbox calls your `MediaSetRate` function. Whenever the track that uses your media is edited, the Movie Toolbox calls your `MediaTrackEdited` function.

If the Movie Toolbox has called its `SetMediaSampleDescription` function on a sample description, it uses the `MediaSampleDescriptionChanged` function to notify your media handler of the change.

The Movie Toolbox allows tracks to be identified by various characteristics. For instance, it is possible to request that all tracks containing audio information be searched. To determine whether a track has a given characteristic, the Movie Toolbox queries the media handler for each track. The Movie Toolbox calls the `MediaHasCharacteristic` function with the specified characteristic.

The Movie Toolbox uses two functions to inform you about changes to your media's time environment. The `MediaSetMediaTimeScale` function allows the Movie Toolbox to change your media's time scale. The `MediaSetMovieTimeScale` function allows the Movie Toolbox to tell you when the movie's time scale has changed.

MediaPutMediaInfo

The `MediaPutMediaInfo` function allows your derived media handler to store proprietary information in its media.

```
pascal ComponentResult MediaPutMediaInfo (ComponentInstance ci,
                                          Handle h);
```

ci   Identifies the Movie Toolbox's connection to your derived media handler.

CHAPTER 10

Derived Media Handler Components

h   Contains a handle to storage into which your media handler may place its proprietary information. You determine the format and content of the data that you store in this handle. Your media handler must resize the handle as appropriate before you exit this function. Do not dispose of this handle—it is owned by the Movie Toolbox. The Movie Toolbox uses the base media handler to write this data to your media.

DESCRIPTION

The Movie Toolbox uses the `MediaPutMediaInfo` function to provide you an opportunity to store private data in your media. You determine the format and content of this data. The base media handler stores some information for you, including the media's transfer mode, opcolor, and sound balance. However, you may need to store additional information. For example, you may want to place a version number in each media you create.

Whenever the Movie Toolbox opens your media, it provides this private data to your media handler by calling your `MediaGetMediaInfo` function, which is described next.

Note that the Movie Toolbox may call this function before it calls your `MediaInitialize` function.

Your derived media handler should support this function if you need to store private data in your media.

RESULT CODES

Any Component Manager result code

MediaGetMediaInfo

The `MediaGetMediaInfo` function allows your derived media handler to obtain the private data you have stored in your media.

```
pascal ComponentResult MediaGetMediaInfo (ComponentInstance ci,
                                          Handle h);
```

ci   Identifies the Movie Toolbox's connection to your derived media handler.

h   Contains a handle to storage containing your media handler's proprietary information. Your media handler creates this private data when the Movie Toolbox calls your `MediaPutMediaInfo` function. Do not dispose of this handle—it is owned by the Movie Toolbox.

DESCRIPTION

If you placed private data into your media, the Movie Toolbox calls your media handler's `MediaPutMediaInfo` function whenever it opens your media. Your

Derived Media Handler Components

media handler determines the format and content of this private data. Note that the Movie Toolbox may call this function before it calls your `MediaInitialize` function.

Your derived media handler should support this function if you store private data in your media.

RESULT CODES

Any Component Manager result code

MediaSetActive

The `MediaSetActive` function allows the Movie Toolbox to enable and disable your media.

```
pascal ComponentResult MediaSetActive (ComponentInstance ci,
                                        Boolean enableMedia);
```

ci
: Identifies the Movie Toolbox's connection to your derived media handler.

enableMedia
: Contains a Boolean value that indicates whether your media is enabled or disabled. If this parameter is set to `true`, your media is enabled; if the parameter is `false`, your media is disabled.

DESCRIPTION

The Movie Toolbox calls your derived media handler's `MediaSetActive` function whenever your media is either enabled or disabled. Initially, your media is disabled. Subsequently, the enabled state of your media is controlled by the state of the track that is using your media. When that track is enabled, your media is enabled; when that track is disabled, your media is disabled. Applications can control the enabled state of a track by using the Movie Toolbox's `SetTrackEnabled` function.

Your derived media handler should support this function if you perform your own scheduling or if your media handler uses significant amounts of temporary storage. If you are doing your own scheduling (that is, you have set the `handlerNoScheduler` flag to 1 in the `flags` parameter of the `MediaSetHandlerCapabilities` function—see page 10-38 for more information about this function), your media handler needs to keep account of the media's active state so that you can properly respond to Movie Toolbox requests. When your media is disabled, you may choose to dispose of temporary storage you have allocated, so that the storage is available to other programs.

RESULT CODES

Any Component Manager result code

MediaPreroll

The `MediaPreroll` function allows the Movie Toolbox to prepare your media handler for playback.

```
pascal ComponentResult MediaPreroll (ComponentInstance ci,
                                     TimeValue time, Fixed rate);
```

ci   Identifies the Movie Toolbox's connection to your derived media handler.

time   Contains the starting time of the media segment to play. This time value is expressed in your media's time scale.

rate   Specifies the rate at which the Movie Toolbox expects to play the media. This is a 32-bit, fixed-point number. Positive values indicate forward rates; negative values correspond to reverse rates.

DESCRIPTION

Use this as an opportunity to load data from your media, so that when the Movie Toolbox starts to play, your media can play smoothly from the start.

RESULT CODES

Any Component Manager result code

MediaSetRate

The `MediaSetRate` function allows the Movie Toolbox to set your media's playback rate.

```
pascal ComponentResult MediaSetRate (ComponentInstance ci,
                                     Fixed rate);
```

ci   Identifies the Movie Toolbox's connection to your derived media handler.

rate   Contains a 32-bit, fixed-point number that indicates your media's new effective playback rate. This effective rate accounts for any master time bases that may be in use with the current movie. Positive values represent forward rates and negative values indicate reverse rates.

DESCRIPTION

The Movie Toolbox calls your derived media handler's `MediaSetRate` function whenever the movie's playback rate changes. The Movie Toolbox provides you with a new effective rate for your media. This effective rate accounts for any master time bases

Derived Media Handler Components

that may be in use with the current movie. Consequently, you may use this rate without having to further transform it.

You obtain the initial rate information from the `effectiveRate` field of the movie parameter structure that the Movie Toolbox provides to your `MediaInitialize` function.

Your derived media handler should support this function if you perform your own scheduling. If you are doing your own scheduling (that is, you have set the `handlerNoScheduler` flag to 1 in the `flags` parameter of the `MediaSetHandlerCapabilities` function—see page 10-38 for more information about this function), your media handler can use this function to determine when your media is playing, and the direction and rate of playback. This information can help you prepare for playback more efficiently.

RESULT CODES

Any Component Manager result code

MediaTrackEdited

The `MediaTrackEdited` function allows the Movie Toolbox to inform your derived media handler about edits to its track.

```
pascal ComponentResult MediaTrackEdited (ComponentInstance ci);
```

ci   Identifies the Movie Toolbox's connection to your derived media handler.

DESCRIPTION

The Movie Toolbox calls your derived media handler's `MediaTrackEdited` function whenever the track that is using your media is edited. While these edits do not directly affect the data in your media, they can change the way in which the movie uses your media's data.

Your derived media handler should support this function if you are caching location information about track edits, or if you are using any time values in the movie's time base. Whenever the Movie Toolbox calls this function, your media handler should recalculate this type of information.

RESULT CODES

Any Component Manager result code

Derived Media Handler Components Reference

MediaSampleDescriptionChanged

The `MediaSampleDescriptionChanged` function allows the Movie Toolbox to inform your media handler that its `SetMediaSampleDescription` function has been called for a specified sample description.

```
pascal ComponentResult MediaSampleDescriptionChanged
                                  (ComponentInstance ci,
                                   long index);
```

ci Identifies the Movie Toolbox's connection to your derived media handler.

index Specifies the index of the sample description that has been changed.

DESCRIPTION

If your media handler caches sample description structures for any reason, it should support the `MediaSampleDescriptionChanged` function so that it will know when to update or invalidate the contents of that cache.

RESULT CODES

Any Component Manager result code

MediaHasCharacteristic

The Movie Toolbox calls the `MediaHasCharacteristic` function with a specified characteristic to allow tracks to be identified by various attributes.

```
pascal ComponentResult MediaHasCharacteristic
                                  (ComponentInstance ci,
                                   OSType characteristic,
                                   Boolean *hasIt);
```

ci Identifies the Movie Toolbox's connection to your derived media handler.

characteristic
  Contains a constant that specifies the attribute of a track. Examples of characteristics that are currently defined are the Movie Toolbox constants `VisualMediaCharacteristic` and `AudioMediaCharacteristic`.

CHAPTER 10

Derived Media Handler Components

hasIt   Contains a pointer to a Boolean value that specifies whether the track has the attribute specified in the characteristic parameter. Set this value to `true` if the attribute applies to your media handler; otherwise, set this value to `false`.

DESCRIPTION

The Movie Toolbox might request the search of all tracks with audio data. For example, to find out if a track has a given attribute, the Movie Toolbox queries the media handler for each track by calling `MediaHasCharacteristic` with a particular constant specified in the `characteristic` parameter. If your media handler does not recognize a characteristic, return a value of `false`.

You should implement this function for any media handler that has characteristics in addition to spatial ones. If you have set the `handlerHasSpatial` capabilities flag, the base media handler automatically handles the `VisualMediaCharacteristic` constant for you.

RESULT CODES

Any Component Manager result code

MediaSetMediaTimeScale

The `MediaSetMediaTimeScale` function allows the Movie Toolbox to inform your media handler that your media's time scale has been changed.

```
pascal ComponentResult MediaSetMediaTimeScale
                                (ComponentInstance ci,
                                 TimeScale newTimeScale);
```

ci   Identifies the Movie Toolbox's connection to your derived media handler.

newTimeScale
                 Specifies your media's new time scale.

DESCRIPTION

The Movie Toolbox calls your derived media handler's `MediaSetMediaTimeScale` function whenever your media's time scale is changed. Applications can change your media's time scale by using the Movie Toolbox's `SetMediaTimeScale` function. When the Movie Toolbox calls this function, your media handler should recalculate any time values you have stored that are expressed in your media's time coordinate system. Changing your media's time scale may also affect media playback.

Derived Media Handler Components

You obtain the initial media time scale information from the `mediaScale` field of the movie parameter structure that the Movie Toolbox provides to your `MediaInitialize` function.

Your derived media handler should support this function if your media handler stores time information that pertains to its media.

RESULT CODES

Any Component Manager result code

MediaSetMovieTimeScale

The `MediaSetMovieTimeScale` function allows the Movie Toolbox to inform your media handler that the movie's time scale has been changed.

```
pascal ComponentResult MediaSetMovieTimeScale
                                (ComponentInstance ci,
                                 TimeScale newTimeScale);
```

`ci` Identifies the Movie Toolbox's connection to your derived media handler.

`newTimeScale`
    Specifies the movie's new time scale.

DESCRIPTION

The Movie Toolbox calls your derived media handler's `MediaSetMovieTimeScale` function whenever the movie's time scale is changed. Applications can change the movie's time scale by using the Movie Toolbox's `SetMovieTimeScale` function. When the Movie Toolbox calls this function, your media handler should recalculate any time values you have stored that are expressed in the movie's time coordinate system. Changing the movie's time scale may also affect playback of your media.

You obtain the initial movie time scale information from the `movieScale` field of the movie parameter structure that the Movie Toolbox provides to your `MediaInitialize` function.

Your derived media handler should support this function if your media handler stores time information in the movie's time coordinate system.

RESULT CODES

Any Component Manager result code

Graphics Data Management

If your media handler draws media data on the screen, you need to manage your media's graphics environment. The Movie Toolbox uses a number of functions to inform you about changes to the graphics environment. The Movie Toolbox only calls these functions if you have set the `handlerHasSpatial` flag to 1 in the `flags` parameter of the `MediaSetHandlerCapabilities` function.

The Movie Toolbox calls your handler's `MediaSetGWorld` function whenever your media's graphics port or graphics device has changed. The `MediaSetDimensions` function allows the Movie Toolbox to inform your handler about changes to its spatial dimensions. Whenever either the movie or track matrix changes, the Movie Toolbox calls your `MediaSetMatrix` function. Similarly, if your media's clipping region changes, the Movie Toolbox calls your `MediaSetClip` function.

When it is building up a movie's image from its component tracks, the Movie Toolbox must be able to determine which tracks are transparent. The Movie Toolbox calls your `MediaGetTrackOpaque` function to retrieve this information about your media.

The Movie Toolbox calls your `MediaGetNextBoundsChange` function so that it can learn when your media will next change its display shape. When the Movie Toolbox wants to find out the shape of the region into which you draw your media, it calls your `MediaGetSrcRgn` function.

MediaSetGWorld

The `MediaSetGWorld` function allows your derived media handler to learn about changes to your media's graphic environment.

```
pascal ComponentResult MediaSetGWorld (ComponentInstance ci,
                                       CGrafPtr aPort,
                                       GDHandle aGD);
```

ci
: Identifies the Movie Toolbox's connection to your derived media handler.

aPort
: Contains a pointer to the new graphics port. Note that this may be either a color or a black-and-white port.

aGD
: Contains a handle to the new graphics device.

DESCRIPTION

The Movie Toolbox calls your derived media handler's `MediaSetGWorld` function whenever your media's graphics world changes. The toolbox provides you with the new graphics port and graphics device. You should then use this information for subsequent graphics operations.

Derived Media Handler Components

Your derived media handler should support this function if you perform specialized graphics processing or if you are using the Image Compression Manager to decompress your media. Note that when the Movie Toolbox calls your `MediaIdle` function, it supplies you with information about the current graphics environment. Consequently, you do not need to support the `MediaSetGWorld` function in order to draw during playback. However, if your media data is compressed and you are using the Image Compression Manager to decompress sequences, you may need to provide updated graphics environment information before playback.

You obtain the initial graphics environment information from the `moviePort` and `movieGD` fields of the movie parameter structure that the Movie Toolbox provides to your `MediaInitialize` function.

The Movie Toolbox calls this function only if you have set the `handlerHasSpatial` flag to 1 in the `flags` parameter of the `MediaSetHandlerCapabilities` function.

RESULT CODES

Any Component Manager result code

MediaSetDimensions

The `MediaSetDimensions` function allows the Movie Toolbox to inform your media handler when its media's spatial dimensions change.

```
pascal ComponentResult MediaSetDimensions (ComponentInstance ci,
                                           Fixed width,
                                           Fixed height);
```

`ci` Identifies the Movie Toolbox's connection to your derived media handler.

`width` Indicates the width, in pixels, of the track rectangle. This field, along with the `height` field, specifies a rectangle that surrounds the image that is displayed when the current media is played. This value corresponds to the x coordinate of the lower-right corner of the rectangle and is expressed as a fixed-point number.

`height` Indicates the height, in pixels, of the track rectangle. This value corresponds to the y coordinate of the lower-right corner of the rectangle and is expressed as a fixed-point number.

DESCRIPTION

The Movie Toolbox calls your derived media handler's `MediaSetDimensions` function whenever the spatial dimensions of your media's track change. The toolbox provides you with the dimensions of the rectangle that encloses your media's graphical image. Changes to this rectangle may affect the way in which you display your media's data.

Derived Media Handler Components

You obtain the initial dimension information from the `width` and `height` fields of the movie parameter structure that the Movie Toolbox provides to your `MediaInitialize` function (described on page 10-18).

Your derived media handler should support this function if you draw during playback.

The Movie Toolbox calls this function only if you have set the `handlerHasSpatial` flag to 1 in the `flags` parameter of the `MediaSetHandlerCapabilities` function (described on page 10-38).

RESULT CODES

Any Component Manager result code

SEE ALSO

The Movie Toolbox uses the `MediaSetMatrix` function (described in the next section) to tell your media handler about changes to either the movie matrix or the track matrix. In addition, your media handler's `MediaSetClip` function allows you to learn about changes to your media's clipping region. This function is discussed on page 10-34.

MediaSetMatrix

The `MediaSetMatrix` function allows the Movie Toolbox to tell your media handler about changes to either the movie matrix or the track matrix.

```
pascal ComponentResult MediaSetMatrix (ComponentInstance ci,
                        const MatrixRecord *trackMovieMatrix);
```

`ci` Identifies the Movie Toolbox's connection to your derived media handler.

`trackMovieMatrix`
Contains a pointer to the matrix that transforms your media's pixels into the movie's coordinate system. The Movie Toolbox obtains this matrix by concatenating the track matrix and the movie matrix. You should use this matrix whenever you are displaying graphical data from your media.

DESCRIPTION

The Movie Toolbox calls your derived media handler's `MediaSetMatrix` function whenever either the movie matrix or track matrix changes. The toolbox provides you with a matrix that concatenates the transformations defined by both the movie and track matrices. You can use this matrix to map your media's display representation into the movie's coordinate system. For example, by applying this matrix to the track rectangle, you can determine the display boundaries of your media (the track rectangle is defined by the `width` and `height` fields in the movie parameter structure that you obtain when the toolbox calls your `MediaInitialize` function).

CHAPTER 10

Derived Media Handler Components

You obtain the initial matrix from the `trackMovieMatrix` field of the movie parameter structure that the Movie Toolbox provides to your `MediaInitialize` function.

Your derived media handler should support this function if you draw during playback.

The Movie Toolbox calls this function only if you have set the `handlerHasSpatial` flag to 1 in the `flags` parameter of the `MediaSetHandlerCapabilities` function (described on page 10-38).

SPECIAL CONSIDERATIONS

Before you try to use this matrix, you should make sure that your media handler can accommodate its transformations. You can use the Movie Toolbox's `GetMatrixType` function to learn about the matrix. If the matrix includes transformations that are beyond the capabilities of your media handler, you can direct the base media handler to do display processing on your behalf. Call the `MediaSetHandlerCapabilities` function and set the `handlerNeedsBuffer` flag to 1 in the `flags` parameter. This forces the base media handler to draw your media into an offscreen buffer.

RESULT CODES

Any Component Manager result code

SEE ALSO

The Movie Toolbox uses the `MediaSetDimensions` function to tell your media handler about changes to the rectangle that surrounds the graphical representation of your media; this function is described in the previous section. In addition, your media handler's `MediaSetClip` function allows you to learn about changes to your media's clipping region. This function is discussed next.

MediaSetClip

The `MediaSetClip` function allows your derived media handler to learn about changes to its clipping region.

```
pascal ComponentResult MediaSetClip (ComponentInstance ci,
                                     RgnHandle theClip);
```

ci   Identifies the Movie Toolbox's connection to your derived media handler.

Derived Media Handler Components

theClip Contains a handle to your media's clipping region. Your media handler is responsible for disposing of this region when you are done with it. Note that this region lies in the movie's coordinate system.

DESCRIPTION

The Movie Toolbox calls your derived media handler's `MediaSetClip` function whenever the track's clipping region changes. The toolbox provides you with a handle to a clipping region that supersedes any other clipping region you may be using.

Your derived media handler should support this function if you draw during playback.

The Movie Toolbox calls this function only if you have set the `handlerHasSpatial` and `handlerCanClip` flags to 1 in the `flags` parameter of the `MediaSetHandlerCapabilities` function (described on page 10-38).

RESULT CODES

Any Component Manager result code

MediaGetTrackOpaque

The `MediaGetTrackOpaque` function allows the Movie Toolbox to determine whether your media is transparent or opaque when displayed.

```
pascal ComponentResult MediaGetTrackOpaque (ComponentInstance ci,
                                            Boolean *trackIsOpaque);
```

ci Identifies the Movie Toolbox's connection to your derived media handler.

trackIsOpaque
    Contains a pointer to a Boolean value. Your media handler must set this Boolean value to indicate whether your media is transparent or opaque when displayed. Set the Boolean value to `true` if your media is semitransparent (that is, you draw in blend mode); otherwise, leave the flag unchanged.

DESCRIPTION

The Movie Toolbox uses this function when it is building a movie from composited images. Your media handler returns information that tells the toolbox whether your media's displayed image is to be combined with other images that are already on the screen. If you draw your media in blend mode, for example, your media is semitransparent, and its display relies upon other images on the screen. The Movie Toolbox needs to know this in order to correctly display the movie to the user.

Derived Media Handler Components

Your derived media handler should support this function if your media is semitransparent when displayed or if you handle display transfer modes.

The Movie Toolbox calls this function only if you have set the `handlerHasSpatial` or `handlerCanTransferMode` flag to 1 in the `flags` parameter of the `MediaSetHandlerCapabilities` function.

RESULT CODES

Any Component Manager result code

MediaGetNextBoundsChange

The `MediaGetNextBoundsChange` function allows the Movie Toolbox to determine when your media causes a spatial change to the movie.

```
pascal ComponentResult MediaGetNextBoundsChange
                                    (ComponentInstance ci,
                                    TimeValue *when);
```

ci Identifies the Movie Toolbox's connection to your derived media handler.

when Contains a pointer to a movie time value. Your media handler must set this time value. Be sure to return a time value in the movie's time base. Use the current effective rate to determine the direction your media is playing. Set this value to –1 if there are no more changes in the specified direction.

DESCRIPTION

The Movie Toolbox uses this function to determine when the next spatial change will occur in the current movie. Your media handler returns a time value. Your media handler must examine the edit list of the track that contains your media in order to derive this duration. You can use the Movie Toolbox's `GetTrackNextInterestingTime` function to retrieve time values in the movie's time coordinate system. For details on this function and on movie time values, see the chapter "Movie Toolbox" in *Inside Macintosh: QuickTime*.

Your derived media handler should support this function if you change the shape of your media's spatial representation during playback.

The Movie Toolbox calls this function only if you have set the `handlerHasSpatial` flag to 1 in the `flags` parameter of the `MediaSetHandlerCapabilities` function.

RESULT CODES

Any Component Manager result code

MediaGetSrcRgn

The `MediaGetSrcRgn` function allows your derived media handler to specify an irregular destination display region to the Movie Toolbox.

```
pascal ComponentResult MediaGetSrcRgn (ComponentInstance ci,
                                       RgnHandle rgn,
                                       TimeValue atMediaTime);
```

ci
: Identifies the Movie Toolbox's connection to your derived media handler.

rgn
: Contains a handle to a region. When the Movie Toolbox calls your function, this region is initialized to the track's boundary rectangle (which is defined by the `width` and `height` fields in the movie parameter structure that you obtain when the toolbox calls your `MediaInitialize` function, which is described on page 10-18). Your media handler may then alter this region as appropriate, so that it corresponds to the boundaries of your media's display image. Note that this region is in the track's coordinate system, not the movie's.

  Do not dispose of this region—it is owned by the Movie Toolbox.

atMediaTime
: Specifies the time value at which the Movie Toolbox wants to know what the source region is.

DESCRIPTION

The Movie Toolbox uses this function to determine whether your media has an irregularly shaped display area. If your media is displayed in a nonrectangular area, or if your media uses only a portion of the track rectangle, you can use this function to report that fact to the toolbox.

Your derived media handler should support this function if your media does not completely fill the track rectangle during playback.

The Movie Toolbox calls this function only if you have set the `handlerHasSpatial` flag to 1 in the `flags` parameter of the `MediaSetHandlerCapabilities` function.

RESULT CODES

Any Component Manager result code

Sound Data Management

The Movie Toolbox uses your `MediaGSetVolume` function to tell your media handler when its sound volume has changed.

CHAPTER 10

Derived Media Handler Components

MediaGSetVolume

The `MediaGSetVolume` function allows your derived media handler to learn about changes to its sound volume setting.

```
pascal ComponentResult MediaGSetVolume (ComponentInstance ci,
                                        short volume);
```

ci
: Identifies the Movie Toolbox's connection to your derived media handler.

volume
: Contains the media's current volume setting. This value is represented as a 16-bit, fixed-point number. The high-order 8 bits contain the integer portion; the low-order 8 bits contain the fractional part. Volume values range from –1.0 to 1.0. Negative values play no sound but preserve the absolute value of the volume setting.

  The Movie Toolbox scales your media's volume in light of the track's and movie's volume settings, but it does not take into account the system speaker volume setting. This value is appropriate for use with the Sound Manager.

DESCRIPTION

The Movie Toolbox uses this function to tell your derived media handler about changes to your media's sound volume.

Your derived media handler should support this function if it can play sounds.

RESULT CODES

Any Component Manager result code

Base Media Handler Utility Function

Apple's base media handler component provides a utility function, `MediaSetHandlerCapabilities`, which allows you to tell the base handler what your derived handler can do.

MediaSetHandlerCapabilities

The `MediaSetHandlerCapabilities` function allows your derived media handler to report its capabilities to the base media handler.

```
pascal ComponentResult MediaSetHandlerCapabilities
                                       (ComponentInstance ci,
                                        long flags,
                                        long flagsMask);
```

10-38   Derived Media Handler Components Reference

Derived Media Handler Components

`ci`
: Identifies your derived media handler's connection to the base media handler.

`flags`
: Specifies the capabilities of your derived media handler. This parameter contains a number of flags, each of which corresponds to a particular feature. You may work with more than one flag at a time. The following flags are defined (be sure to set unused flags to 0):

   `handlerHasSpatial`
   : Indicates that your handler does spatial processing. If you set this flag to 1, the Movie Toolbox informs your derived media handler about changes to the graphics environment or spatial representation of your media.

   `handlerCanClip`
   : Indicates that your media handler can perform clipping. If you set this flag to 1, the Movie Toolbox calls your `MediaSetClip` function (described on page 10-34) whenever the clipping region changes.

   `handlerCanMatte`
   : Reserved for Apple. Do not set this flag to 1.

   `handlerCanTransferMode`
   : Indicates that you can work with transfer modes other than source copy or dither copy. If you set this flag to 1, the Movie Toolbox calls your `MediaGetTrackOpaque` function to determine whether your track is transparent.

   `handlerNeedsBuffer`
   : Indicates that your media handler needs help during playback. If you set this flag to 1, the base media handler allocates an offscreen buffer and handles all display transformations for you.

   `handlerNoIdle`
   : Indicates that your derived media handler does not need any processing time during playback. If you set this flag to 1, the Movie Toolbox never calls your `MediaIdle` function. This is useful for media handlers that store data in a media, but do not play that data.

   `handlerNoScheduler`
   : Indicates that your media handler performs special processing during playback. Normally, the Movie Toolbox calls your `MediaIdle` function only when it is time for your handler to draw data from a new media sample. If you set this flag to 1, the Movie Toolbox calls that function other times as well, so that your media handler can prepare for playback or perform other necessary processing.

   `handlerWantsTime`
   : Indicates that your media handler needs additional processing time. If you set this flag to 1, the Movie Toolbox calls your `MediaIdle` function as often as possible.

CHAPTER 10

Derived Media Handler Components

> handlerCGrafPortOnly
> : Indicates that your media handler can only draw into color graphics ports. If you set this flag to 1, the base media handler performs the necessary processing to display your color media on a black-and-white graphics port (this involves drawing to an offscreen buffer and then transferring the image to the screen).
>
> flagsMask
> : Indicates which flags in the `flags` parameter are to be considered in this operation. For each bit in the `flags` parameter that you want the base media handler to consider, you must set the corresponding bit in the `flagsMask` parameter to 1. Set unused flags to 0. This allows you to work with a single flag without altering the settings of other flags.

DESCRIPTION

Use the `MediaSetHandlerCapabilities` function to tell the base media handler what your derived media handler can do. By default, all of the flags are set to 0—in this case, your media handler is only responsible for storing and retrieving data. You can specify further capabilities by setting various flags to 1. For example, if your handler draws data on the screen, be sure to set the `handlerHasSpatial` flag to 1. Other flags govern more detailed aspects of handler operation.

This function uses both a `flags` parameter and a `flagsMask` parameter. You specify which flags are to be changed in a given operation by setting the `flagsMask` parameter. You then specify the new values for those affected flags with the `flags` parameter. In this manner, you can work with a single flag without affecting the settings of any other flags.

Your media handler may call this function at any time. In general, you should call it from your `MediaInitialize` function (described on page 10-18), so that you report your capabilities to the base media handler before the Movie Toolbox starts working with your media. You may call this function again later, in response to changing conditions. For example, if your media handler receives a matrix that it cannot accommodate from the `MediaSetMatrix` function, you can allow the base media handler to handle your drawing by calling this function and setting the `handlerNeedsBuffer` flag in both the `flags` and `flagsMask` parameters to 1.

Note that this function is provided by the base media handler—your media handler does not support this function.

RESULT CODES

Any Component Manager result code

Summary of Derived Media Handler Components

C Summary

Constants

```
/* flags in flags parameter of MediaSetHandlerCapabilities function */
enum {
    handlerHasSpatial       = 1<<0,     /* draws */
    handlerCanClip          = 1<<1,     /* clips */
    handlerCanMatte         = 1<<2,     /* reserved */
    handlerCanTransferMode  = 1<<3,     /* does transfer modes */
    handlerNeedsBuffer      = 1<<4,     /* use offscreen buffer */
    handlerNoIdle           = 1<<5,     /* never draws */
    handlerNoScheduler      = 1<<6,     /* schedules self */
    handlerWantsTime        = 1<<7,     /* needs more time */
    handlerCGrafPortOnly    = 1<<8      /* color only */
};

/* values for inFlags parameter of MediaIdle function */
enum {
    mMustDraw       = 1<<3,     /* must draw now */
    mAtEnd          = 1<<4,     /* current time corresponds to
                                   end of movie */
    mPreflightDraw  = 1<<5      /* must not draw */
};

/* values for outFlags parameter of MediaIdle function */
enum {
    mDidDraw        = 1<<0,     /* did draw */
    mNeedsToDraw    = 1<<2      /* needs to draw */
};

/* component type and subtype values */
#define MediaHandlerType    'mhlr'      /* derived media handler */
#define BaseMediaType       'gnrc'      /* base media handler */
```

CHAPTER 10

Derived Media Handler Components

```c
/* constants used in the characteristic parameter of the
   MediaHasCharacteristic function */
#define VisualMediaCharacteristic 'eyes'   /* visual media characteristic */
#define AudioMediaCharacteristic  'ears'   /* audio media characteristic */

/* selectors for derived media handler components */
enum {
    enum {
    kMediaInitializeSelect                = 0x501, /* MediaInitialize */
    kMediaSetHandlerCapabilitiesSelect    = 0x502,
                                                   /* MediaSetHandlerCapabilities */
    kMediaIdleSelect                      = 0x503, /* MediaIdle */
    kMediaGetMediaInfoSelect              = 0x504, /* MediaGetMediaInfo */
    kMediaPutMediaInfoSelect              = 0x505, /* MediaPutMediaInfo */
    kMediaSetActiveSelect                 = 0x506, /* MediaSetActive */
    kMediaSetRateSelect                   = 0x507, /* MediaSetRate */
    kMediaGGetStatusSelect                = 0x508, /* MediaGGetStatus */
    kMediaTrackEditedSelect               = 0x509, /* MediaTrackEdited */
    kMediaSetMediaTimeScaleSelect         = 0x50A, /* MediaSetMediaTimeScale */
    kMediaSetMovieTimeScaleSelect         = 0x50B, /* MediaSetMovieTimeScale */
    kMediaSetGWorldSelect                 = 0x50C, /* MediaSetGWorld */
    kMediaSetDimensionsSelect             = 0x50D, /* MediaSetDimensions */
    kMediaSetClipSelect                   = 0x50E, /* MediaSetClip */
    kMediaSetMatrixSelect                 = 0x50F, /* MediaSetMatrix */
    kMediaGetTrackOpaqueSelect            = 0x510, /* MediaGetTrackOpaque */
    kMediaSetGraphicsModeSelect           = 0x511, /* MediaSetGraphicsMode */
    kMediaGetGraphicsModeSelect           = 0x512, /* MediaGetGraphicsMode */
    kMediaGSetVolumeSelect                = 0x513, /* MediaGSetVolume */
    kMediaSetSoundBalanceSelect           = 0x514, /* MediaSetSoundBalance */
    kMediaGetSoundBalanceSelect           = 0x515, /* MediaGetSoundBalance */
    kMediaGetNextBoundsChangeSelect       = 0x516,
                                                   /* MediaGetNextBoundsChange */
    kMediaGetSrcRgnSelect                 = 0x517, /* MediaGetSrcRgn */
    kMediaPrerollSelect                   = 0x518, /* MediaPreroll */
    kMediaSampleDescriptionChangedSelect  = 0x519,
                                                   /* MediaSampleDescriptionChanged */
    kMediaHasCharacteristicSelect         = 0x51A  /* MediaHasCharacteristic */
};
```

Data Type

```
typedef struct {
    short           version;          /* version--always 0 */
    Movie           theMovie;         /* movie identifier */
    Track           theTrack;         /* track identifier */
    Media           theMedia;         /* media identifier */
    TimeScale       movieScale;       /* movie's time scale */
    TimeScale       mediaScale;       /* media's time scale */
    TimeValue       movieDuration;    /* movie's duration */
    TimeValue       trackDuration;    /* track's duration */
    TimeValue       mediaDuration;    /* media's duration */
    Fixed           effectiveRate;    /* media's effective rate */
    TimeBase        timeBase;         /* media's time base */
    short           volume;           /* media's volume */
    Fixed           width;            /* width of display area */
    Fixed           height;           /* height of display area */
    MatrixRecord    trackMovieMatrix; /* transformation matrix */
    CGrafPtr        moviePort;        /* movie's graphics port */
    GDHandle        movieGD;          /* movie's graphics device */
    PixMapHandle    trackMatte;       /* track's matte */
} GetMovieCompleteParams;
```

Functions

Managing Your Media Handler Component

```
pascal ComponentResult MediaInitialize
                    (ComponentInstance ci,
                     GetMovieCompleteParams *gmc);
pascal ComponentResult MediaIdle
                    (ComponentInstance ci,
                     TimeValue atMediaTime, long flagsIn,
                     long *flagsOut, const TimeRecord *movieTime);
pascal ComponentResult MediaGGetStatus
                    (ComponentInstance ci,
                     ComponentResult *statusErr);
```

General Data Management

```
pascal ComponentResult MediaPutMediaInfo
                    (ComponentInstance ci, Handle h);
pascal ComponentResult MediaGetMediaInfo
                    (ComponentInstance ci, Handle h);
```

CHAPTER 10

Derived Media Handler Components

```
pascal ComponentResult MediaSetActive
                    (ComponentInstance ci, Boolean enableMedia);
pascal ComponentResult MediaPreroll
                    (ComponentInstance ci, TimeValue time,
                     Fixed rate);
pascal ComponentResult MediaSetRate
                    (ComponentInstance ci, Fixed rate);
pascal ComponentResult MediaTrackEdited
                    (ComponentInstance ci);
pascal ComponentResult MediaSampleDescriptionChanged
                    (ComponentInstance ci, long index);
pascal ComponentResult MediaHasCharacteristic
                    (ComponentInstance ci,
                     OSType characteristic, Boolean *hasIt);
pascal ComponentResult MediaSetMediaTimeScale
                    (ComponentInstance ci, TimeScale newTimeScale);
pascal ComponentResult MediaSetMovieTimeScale
                    (ComponentInstance ci, TimeScale newTimeScale);
```

Graphics Data Management

```
pascal ComponentResult MediaSetGWorld
                    (ComponentInstance ci, CGrafPtr aPort,
                     GDHandle aGD);
pascal ComponentResult MediaSetDimensions
                    (ComponentInstance ci, Fixed width,
                     Fixed height);
pascal ComponentResult MediaSetMatrix
                    (ComponentInstance ci,
                     const MatrixRecord *trackMovieMatrix);
pascal ComponentResult MediaSetClip
                    (ComponentInstance ci, RgnHandle theClip);
pascal ComponentResult MediaGetTrackOpaque
                    (ComponentInstance ci, Boolean *trackIsOpaque);
pascal ComponentResult MediaGetNextBoundsChange
                    (ComponentInstance ci, TimeValue *when);
pascal ComponentResult MediaGetSrcRgn
                    (ComponentInstance ci, RgnHandle rgn,
                     TimeValue atMediaTime);
```

Sound Data Management

```
pascal ComponentResult MediaGSetVolume
                    (ComponentInstance ci, short volume);
```

Derived Media Handler Components

Base Media Handler Utility Function

```
pascal ComponentResult MediaSetHandlerCapabilities
                            (ComponentInstance ci, long flags,
                             long flagsMask);
```

Pascal Summary

Constants

```
CONST
{flags in flags parameter of MediaSetHandlerCapabilities function}
    handlerHasSpatial        =  $1;       {draws}
    handlerCanClip           =  $2;       {clips}
    handlerCanMatte          =  $4;       {reserved}
    handlerCanTransferMode   =  $8;       {does transfer modes}
    handlerNeedsBuffer       =  $10;      {use offscreen buffer}
    handlerNoIdle            =  $20;      {never draws}
    handlerNoScheduler       =  $40;      {schedules self}
    handlerWantsTime         =  $80;      {needs more time}
    handlerCGrafPortOnly     =  $100;     {color only}

{values for inFlags parameter of MediaIdle function}
    mMustDraw                =  $8;       {must draw now}
    mAtEnd                   =  $10;      {current time corresponds to }
                                          { end of movie}
    mPreflightDraw           =  $20;      {must not draw}

{values for outFlags parameter of MediaIdle function}
    mDidDraw                 =  $1;       {did draw}
    mNeedsToDraw             =  $4;       {needs to draw}

{component type and subtype values}
    MediaHandlerType            'mhlr'    {derived media handler}
    BaseMediaType               'gnrc'    {base media handler}

{constants used in the characteristic parameter of the }
{ MediaHasCharacteristic function}
    VisualMediaCharacteristic   'eyes'    {visual media characteristic}
    AudioMediaCharacteristic    'ears'    {audio media characteristic}
```

CHAPTER 10

Derived Media Handler Components

```
{selectors for derived media handler components}
   kMediaInitializeSelect                    = $501;   {MediaInitialize}
   kMediaSetHandlerCapabilitiesSelect        = $502;   {MediaSetHandlerCapabilities}
   kMediaIdleSelect                          = $503;   {MediaIdle}
   kMediaGetMediaInfoSelect                  = $504;   {MediaGetMediaInfo}
   kMediaPutMediaInfoSelect                  = $505;   {MediaPutMediaInfo}
   kMediaSetActiveSelect                     = $506;   {MediaSetActive}
   kMediaSetRateSelect                       = $507;   {MediaSetRate}
   kMediaGGetStatusSelect                    = $508;   {MediaGGetStatus}
   kMediaTrackEditedSelect                   = $509;   {MediaTrackEdited}
   kMediaSetMediaTimeScaleSelect             = $50A;   {MediaSetMediaTimeScale}
   kMediaSetMovieTimeScaleSelect             = $50B;   {MediaSetMovieTimeScale}
   kMediaSetGWorldSelect                     = $50C;   {MediaSetGWorld}
   kMediaSetDimensionsSelect                 = $50D;   {MediaSetDimensions}
   kMediaSetClipSelect                       = $50E;   {MediaSetClip}
   kMediaSetMatrixSelect                     = $50F;   {MediaSetMatrix}
   kMediaGetTrackOpaqueSelect                = $510;   {MediaGetTrackOpaque}
   kMediaSetGraphicsModeSelect               = $511;   {MediaSetGraphicsMode}
   kMediaGetGraphicsModeSelect               = $512;   {MediaGetGraphicsMode}
   kMediaGSetVolumeSelect                    = $513;   {MediaGSetVolume}
   kMediaSetSoundBalanceSelect               = $514;   {MediaSetSoundBalance}
   kMediaGetSoundBalanceSelect               = $515;   {MediaGetSoundBalance}
   kMediaGetNextBoundsChangeSelect           = $516;   {MediaGetNextBoundsChange}
   kMediaGetSrcRgnSelect                     = $517;   {MediaGetSrcRgn}
   kMediaPrerollSelect                       = $518;   {MediaPreroll}
   kMediaSampleDescriptionChangedSelect      = $519;
                                                       {MediaSampleDescriptionChanged}
   kMediaHasCharacteristicSelect             = $51A;   {MediaHasCharacteristic}
```

Data Type

```
TYPE
   GetMovieCompleteParams =
   RECORD
      version:          Integer;        {version; always 0}
      theMovie:         Movie;          {movie identifier}
      theTrack:         Track;          {track identifier}
      theMedia:         Media;          {media identifier}
      movieScale:       TimeScale;      {movie's time scale}
      mediaScale:       TimeScale;      {media's time scale}
      movieDuration:    TimeValue;      {movie's duration}
      trackDuration:    TimeValue;      {track's duration}
      mediaDuration:    TimeValue;      {media's duration}
```

Derived Media Handler Components

```
        effectiveRate:      Fixed;              {media's effective rate}
        timeBase:           TimeBase;           {media's time base}
        volume:             Integer;            {media's volume}
        width:              Fixed;              {width of display area}
        height:             Fixed;              {height of display area}
        trackMovieMatrix:   MatrixRecord;       {transformation matrix}
        moviePort:          CGrafPtr;           {movie's graphics port}
        movieGD:            GDHandle;           {movie's graphics device}
        trackMatte:         PixMapHandle;       {track's matte}
    END;
```

Routines

Managing Your Media Handler Component

```
FUNCTION MediaInitialize        (ci: ComponentInstance;
                                 VAR gmc: GetMovieCompleteParams):
                                 ComponentResult;

FUNCTION MediaIdle              (ci: ComponentInstance; atMediaTime: TimeValue;
                                 flagsIn: LongInt; VAR flagsOut: LongInt;
                                 VAR movieTime: TimeRecord): ComponentResult;

FUNCTION MediaGGetStatus        (ci: ComponentInstance;
                                 VAR statusErr: ComponentResult):
                                 ComponentResult;
```

General Data Management

```
FUNCTION MediaPutMediaInfo      (ci: ComponentInstance; h: Handle):
                                 ComponentResult;

FUNCTION MediaGetMediaInfo      (ci: ComponentInstance; h: Handle):
                                 ComponentResult;

FUNCTION MediaSetActive         (ci: ComponentInstance; enableMedia: Boolean):
                                 ComponentResult;

FUNCTION MediaPreroll           (ci: ComponentInstance; time: TimeValue;
                                 rate: Fixed): ComponentResult;

FUNCTION MediaSetRate           (ci: ComponentInstance; rate: Fixed):
                                 ComponentResult;

FUNCTION MediaTrackEdited       (ci: ComponentInstance): ComponentResult;

FUNCTION MediaSampleDescriptionChanged
                                (ci: ComponentInstance; index: LongInt):
                                 ComponentResult;
```

CHAPTER 10

Derived Media Handler Components

```
FUNCTION MediaHasCharacteristic
                            (ci: ComponentInstance; characteristic: OSType;
                             VAR hasIt: Boolean): ComponentResult;
FUNCTION MediaSetMediaTimeScale
                            (ci: ComponentInstance;
                             newTimeScale: TimeScale): ComponentResult;
FUNCTION MediaSetMovieTimeScale
                            (ci: ComponentInstance;
                             newTimeScale: TimeScale): ComponentResult;
```

Graphics Data Management

```
FUNCTION MediaSetGWorld       (ci: ComponentInstance; aPort: CGrafPtr;
                               aGD: GDHandle): ComponentResult;
FUNCTION MediaSetDimensions   (ci: ComponentInstance; width: Fixed;
                               height: Fixed): ComponentResult;
FUNCTION MediaSetMatrix       (ci: ComponentInstance;
                               VAR trackMovieMatrix: MatrixRecord):
                               ComponentResult;
FUNCTION MediaSetClip         (ci: ComponentInstance; theClip: RgnHandle):
                               ComponentResult;
FUNCTION MediaGetTrackOpaque
                              (ci: ComponentInstance;
                               VAR trackIsOpaque: Boolean): ComponentResult;
FUNCTION MediaGetNextBoundsChange
                              (ci: ComponentInstance; VAR when: TimeValue):
                               ComponentResult;
FUNCTION MediaGetSrcRgn       (ci: ComponentInstance; rgn: RgnHandle;
                               atMediaTime: TimeValue): ComponentResult;
```

Sound Data Management

```
FUNCTION MediaGSetVolume      (ci: ComponentInstance; volume: Integer):
                               ComponentResult;
```

Base Media Handler Utility Routine

```
FUNCTION MediaSetHandlerCapabilities
                            (ci: ComponentInstance; flags: LongInt;
                             flagsMask: LongInt): ComponentResult;
```

CHAPTER 11

Clock Components

Contents

About Clock Components   11-3
Clock Components Reference   11-5
   Component Capability Flags for Clocks   11-5
   Component Types for Clocks   11-6
   Data Type   11-6
   Clock Component Functions   11-7
     Getting the Current Time   11-9
     Using the Callback Functions   11-9
     Managing the Time   11-15
   Movie Toolbox Clock Support Functions   11-18
Summary of Clock Components   11-22
   C Summary   11-22
     Constants   11-22
     Data Type   11-24
     Clock Component Functions   11-24
     Movie Toolbox Clock Support Functions   11-25
   Pascal Summary   11-25
     Constants   11-25
     Data Type   11-27
     Clock Component Routines   11-27
     Movie Toolbox Clock Support Routines   11-28

CHAPTER 11

Clock Components

This chapter discusses clock components. **Clock components** provide timing information. In QuickTime, the Movie Toolbox is the primary client of clock components. Applications seldom call clock components directly. However, you may want to develop your own clock component for use by the Movie Toolbox. Therefore, this chapter focuses on what you must do to create a clock component.

- "About Clock Components" presents some general information about clock components.
- "Clock Components Reference" describes the constants, data structures, and functions that are specific to clock components.
- "Summary of Clock Components" provides summaries of the clock component constants, data structures, and functions in C and in Pascal.

Before learning about clock components, you must be familiar with QuickTime time bases. See the chapter "Movie Toolbox" in *Inside Macintosh: QuickTime* for a complete description of time bases and of the Movie Toolbox functions that support time bases.

About Clock Components

Clock components provide two basic services: they generate time information and schedule time-based callback events. In QuickTime, the Movie Toolbox is the primary user of clock components. Specifically, the Movie Toolbox uses clock components to provide basic timing to time bases. In general, clock components derive their timing information from some external source. For example, a clock component could use the Macintosh tick count to provide its basic timing. Alternatively, a clock component could use some special hardware installed in the Macintosh computer to provide its basic timing. Figure 11-1 shows the relationships between an application, the movie controller component, the Movie Toolbox, and a clock component.

Figure 11-1 Relationships of an application, the movie controller component, the Movie Toolbox, and a clock component

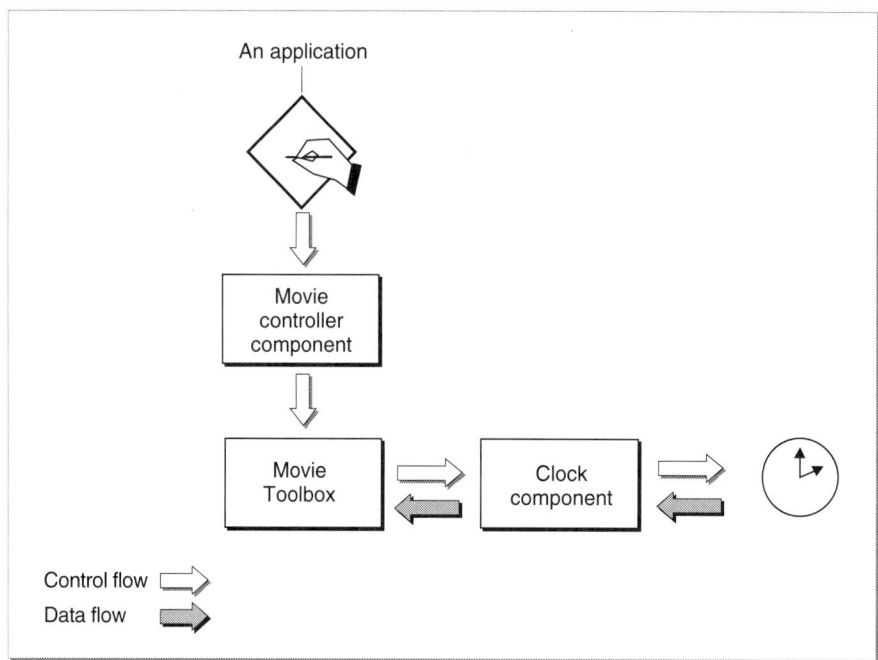

Clock components may also support time-based callback events. The Movie Toolbox's time base functions allow applications and other programs to schedule functions to be called in specified circumstances. Since time bases derive their time information from clock components, ultimate responsibility for servicing these callback functions also falls to clock components. The Movie Toolbox provides a set of support functions that your clock component can use to manage its callback events—these functions are described later in this chapter.

Your clock component is not required to support callback functions. You can delegate this responsibility to another clock component. "Component Capability Flags for Clocks" on page 11-5 describes how you can tell the Component Manager that your clock component does not support callback functions.

CHAPTER 11

Clock Components

Clock Components Reference

This section describes the constants, data type, and functions that are specific to clock components.

Component Capability Flags for Clocks

The Component Manager allows you to specify information about your component's capabilities in the `componentFlags` field of the component description structure. Apple has defined two component flags for clock components. These flags specify information about the capabilities of the clock component. You set these flags in the `componentFlags` field of your component's component description structure. You can use the following constants to manipulate these flags. You should set them appropriately for your clock. For more on the component description structure, see the chapter "Component Manager" in *Inside Macintosh: More Macintosh Toolbox*.

```
enum {
   kClockRateIsLinear = 1,         /* clock keeps constant
                                      rate */
   kClockImplementsCallBacks = 2   /* clock supports callback
                                      events */
};
```

kClockRateIsLinear
: Indicates that your clock maintains a constant rate. Most clocks that you deal with in the everyday world fall into this category. An example of a clock with an irregular rate is a clock that is dependent on the position of the Macintosh computer's mouse—the clock's rate might change depending upon where the user moves the mouse. Set this flag to 1 if your clock has a constant rate.

kClockImplementsCallBacks
: Indicates that your clock supports callback events. Set this flag to 1 if your clock supports callback events.

You should set the `componentFlags` field appropriately in the component description structure that is associated with your clock component.

Clock Components

Component Types for Clocks

Apple has defined a type value and a number of subtype values for clock components. All clock components have a component type value of 'clok'. The component subtype value indicates the type of clock. You can use the following constants to specify these type and subtype values.

```
#define clockComponentType        'clok'  /* clock component type */
#define systemTickClock           'tick'  /* system tick clock */
#define systemSecondClock         'seco'  /* system seconds clock */
#define systemMillisecondClock    'mill'  /* system millisecond clock */
#define systemMicrosecondClock    'micr'  /* system microsecond clock */
```

Data Type

The clock component data structure is a private data structure. Programs that use your clock component never change the contents of this data structure directly. Your clock component provides functions that allow programs to use this data structure.

The callback header structure specifies the callback function for an operation. Your application can obtain callback function identifiers by calling its clock component's `ClockNewCallBack` function (described on page 11-10).

The `QTCallBackHeader` data type defines the callback header structure.

```
struct QTCallBackHeader {
      long    callBackFlags;   /* flags used by clock
                                  component to communicate
                                  scheduling data about
                                  callback to Movie Toolbox */
      long    reserved1;       /* reserved for use by Apple */
      char    qtPrivate[40];   /* reserved for use by Apple */
};
```

Field descriptions

callBackFlags
> Contains flags that your component can use to communicate scheduling information about the callback event to the Movie Toolbox. This scheduling information tells the Movie Toolbox what time base events your clock component needs to know about in order to support the callback event. The following flags are defined (all other flags must be set to 0):
>
> ```
> enum {
>     qtcbNeedsRateChanges = 1,  /* clock needs to
>                                   know about rate
>                                   changes */
> ```

CHAPTER 11

Clock Components

```
                    qtcbNeedsTimeChanges = 2    /* clock needs to
                                                    know about time
                                                    changes */
                    qtcbNeedsStartStopChanges
                                         = 4    /* clock needs to
                                                    know about time
                                                    base changes */
    };
```

qtcbNeedsRateChanges
: Indicates that your clock component needs to know about rate changes. If you set this flag to 1, the Movie Toolbox calls your `ClockRateChanged` function (described on page 11-16) whenever the rate of the callback event's time base changes.

qtcbNeedsTimeChanges
: Indicates that your clock component needs to know about time changes. If you set this flag to 1, the Movie Toolbox calls your `ClockTimeChanged` function (described on page 11-15) whenever a program changes the time value of the time base, or when the time value changes by an amount that is different from the time base's rate.

qtcbNeedsStartStopChanges
: Indicates that your clock component needs to know about the time base's start and stop changes. If you set this flag to 1, the Movie Toolbox calls your `ClockStartStopChanged` function (described on page 11-16) whenever a program changes the start or stop time of the time base.

`reserved1`   Reserved for use by Apple.

`qtPrivate`   Reserved for use by Apple.

Clock Component Functions

This section describes the functions that are provided by clock components. These functions are described from the perspective of the Movie Toolbox, the entity that is most likely to call clock components. If you are developing a clock component, your component must behave as described here.

Clock Components

This section has been divided into the following topics:

- "Getting the Current Time" describes the function that allows the Movie Toolbox to obtain the current time from a clock component.
- "Using the Callback Functions" discusses the functions that allow clock components to help applications define and schedule time base callback functions.
- "Managing the Time" describes functions that help clock components manage their time correctly.

If you are developing an application that uses clock components, you should read the next section, "Getting the Current Time."

If you are developing a clock component, you need to be familiar with all the functions described in this section.

Note
Your application can call any clock component function at interrupt time, except for the `ClockNewCallBack` and `ClockDisposeCallBack` functions (described on page 11-10 and page 11-14, respectively). In addition, your application should not call the Component Manager's `OpenComponent` and `CloseComponent` functions at interrupt time. ◆

You can use the following constants to refer to the request codes for each of the functions that your clock component must support:

```
/* constants to refer to request codes for supported functions */
enum {
    kClockGetTimeSelect              = 0x1,/* ClockGetTime */
    kClockNewCallBackSelect          = 0x2,/* ClockNewCallBack */
    kClockDisposeCallBackSelect      = 0x3,/* ClockDisposeCallBack */
    kClockCallMeWhenSelect           = 0x4,/* ClockCallMeWhen */
    kClockCancelCallBackSelect       = 0x5,/* ClockCancelCallBack */
    kClockRateChangedSelect          = 0x6,/* ClockRateChanged */
    kClockTimeChangedSelect          = 0x7,/* ClockTimeChanged */
    kClockSetTimeBaseSelect          = 0x8,/* ClockSetTimeBase */
    kClockStartStopChangedSelect     = 0x9,/* ClockStartStopChanged */
    kClockGetRateSelect              = 0xA /* ClockGetRate */
};
```

CHAPTER 11

Clock Components

Getting the Current Time

Clock components provide a single function that allows the Movie Toolbox to obtain the current time.

ClockGetTime

The `ClockGetTime` function allows the Movie Toolbox to obtain the current time according to the specified clock.

```
pascal ComponentResult ClockGetTime (ComponentInstance aClock,
                                     TimeRecord *out);
```

aClock   Specifies the clock for the operation. You obtain this identifier from the Component Manager's `OpenComponent` function. See the chapter "Component Manager" in *Inside Macintosh: More Macintosh Toolbox* for details.

out   Contains a pointer to a time structure. (For details on the time structure, see the chapter "Movie Toolbox" in *Inside Macintosh: QuickTime*.) The clock component updates this structure with the current time information. Specifically, the clock component sets the `value` and `scale` fields in the time structure. Your clock component should always return values in its native time scale—this time scale does not change during the life of the component connection.

DESCRIPTION

The `ClockGetTime` function is the most important function for most clock components. The Movie Toolbox calls this function very often, so it should be fast.

Using the Callback Functions

Applications that use QuickTime time bases may define callback functions that are associated with a specific time base. Applications can then use these callback functions to perform activities that are triggered by temporal events, such as a certain time being reached or a specified rate being achieved. The time base functions of the Movie Toolbox interact with clock components to schedule the invocation of these callback functions—your clock component is responsible for calling the callback function at its scheduled time.

CHAPTER 11

Clock Components

The functions described in this section are called by the Movie Toolbox to support applications that define time base callback functions. For more information about time base callback functions, see the chapter "Movie Toolbox" in *Inside Macintosh: QuickTime*. Note that your clock component can delegate its callback events to another component by calling the Component Manager's `DelegateComponent` function, which is described in the chapter "Component Manager" in *Inside Macintosh: More Macintosh Toolbox*.

The `ClockNewCallBack` function allows your clock component to allocate the memory to support a new callback event. When an application discards a callback event, the Movie Toolbox calls your clock component's `ClockDisposeCallBack` function.

The Movie Toolbox calls your clock component's `ClockCallMeWhen` function when an application wants to schedule a callback event. When the callback function is to be invoked to service the event, the Movie Toolbox calls your component's `ClockCancelCallBack` function so that you can remove the callback event from the list of scheduled events.

ClockNewCallBack

Your component's `ClockNewCallBack` function allocates the memory for a new callback event. The Movie Toolbox calls this function when an application defines a time base callback event with the Movie Toolbox's `NewCallBack` function. The callback event created at this time is not active until it has been scheduled. An application schedules a callback event by calling the Movie Toolbox's `CallMeWhen` function.

Your component allocates the memory required to support the callback event. The memory must be in a locked block and must begin with a callback header structure. This structure is described in "Data Type," which begins on page 11-6.

You should not call this function at interrupt time.

```
pascal QTCallBack ClockNewCallBack (ComponentInstance aClock,
                                    TimeBase tb,
                                    short callBackType);
```

aClock   Specifies the clock for the operation. Applications obtain this identifier from the Component Manager's `OpenComponent` function.

tb   Specifies the callback event's time base. Typically, your component does not need to save this specification. You can use the Movie Toolbox's `GetCallBackTimeBase` function to determine the callback event's time base when it is invoked (see the discussion of time bases in the chapter "Movie Toolbox" in *Inside Macintosh: QuickTime* for more information about this function).

Clock Components

`callBackType`

Specifies when the callback event is to be invoked. The value of this field governs how your component interprets the data supplied in the `param1`, `param2`, and `param3` parameters to the `ClockCallMeWhen` function, which is described in the next section. The following three values are valid for this parameter:

`callBackAtTime`

Indicates that the callback event is to be invoked at a specified time. The Movie Toolbox supplies this time to your component in the parameter data of the `ClockCallMeWhen` function (described in the next section).

`callBackAtRate`

Indicates that the callback event is to be invoked when the rate for the time base reaches a specified value. The Movie Toolbox supplies this value to your component in the parameter data of the `ClockCallMeWhen` function.

`callBackAtTimeJump`

Indicates that the callback event is to be invoked when a program changes the time value for the time base.

In addition, if the high-order bit of the `callBackType` parameter is set to 1 (this bit is defined by the `callBackAtInterrupt` flag), the callback event may be invoked at interrupt time.

DESCRIPTION

Your clock component allocates the memory for the event and returns a pointer to that memory. If your clock component cannot satisfy the request or detects invalid or unsupported parameter values, you should set the `QTCallBack` result to `nil`.

Your component can allocate an arbitrarily large piece of memory for the callback event. That memory must begin with a callback header structure, which must be initialized to 0.

ClockCallMeWhen

Your clock component's `ClockCallMeWhen` function schedules a callback event for invocation. The Movie Toolbox calls this function when an application schedules a callback event using the `CallMeWhen` function of the Movie Toolbox (described in the chapter "Movie Toolbox" in *Inside Macintosh: QuickTime*).

CHAPTER 11

Clock Components

The Movie Toolbox passes the parameter data from its `CallMeWhen` function to your component in the `param1`, `param2`, and `param3` parameters to this function. Your clock component interprets these parameters based on the value of the `callBackType` parameter to the `ClockNewCallBack` function (see page 11-10).

```
pascal ComponentResult ClockCallMeWhen (ComponentInstance aClock,
                                        QTCallBack cb,
                                        long param1,
                                        long param2,
                                        long param3);
```

aClock Specifies the clock for the operation. Applications obtain this identifier from the Component Manager's `OpenComponent` function.

cb Specifies the callback event for the operation. The Movie Toolbox obtains this value from your component's `ClockNewCallBack` function.

param1 Contains data supplied to the Movie Toolbox in the `param1` parameter to the `CallMeWhen` function. Your component interprets this parameter based on the value of the `callBackType` parameter to the `ClockNewCallBack` function.

If `callBackType` is set to `callBackAtTime`, `param1` contains QuickTime callback flags indicating when to invoke the callback function. The following values are defined:

triggerTimeFwd
: Indicates that the callback function should be called at the time specified by `param2` only when time is moving forward (positive rate). The value of this flag is 0x0001.

triggerTimeBwd
: Indicates that the callback function should be called at the time specified by `param2` only when time is moving backward (negative rate). The value of this flag is 0x0002.

triggerTimeEither
: Indicates that the callback function should be called at the time specified by `param2` without regard to direction. The value of this flag is 0x0003.

If `callBackType` is set to `callBackAtRate`, `param1` contains flags indicating when to invoke the callback function.

The following values are defined:

triggerRateChange
: Indicates that the callback function should be called whenever the rate changes. The value of this flag is 0.

triggerRateLT
: Indicates that the callback function should be called when the rate changes to a value less than that specified by `param2`. The value of this flag is 0x0004.

Clock Components

> **triggerRateGT**
> Indicates that the callback function should be called when the rate changes to a value greater than that specified by `param2`. The value of this flag is 0x0008.
>
> **triggerRateEqual**
> Indicates that the callback function should be called when the rate changes to a value equal to that specified by `param2`. The value of this flag is 0x0010.
>
> **triggerRateLTE**
> Indicates that the callback function should be called when the rate changes to a value that is less than or equal to that specified by `param2`. The value of this flag is 0x0014.
>
> **triggerRateGTE**
> Indicates that the callback function should be called when the rate changes to a value that is less than or equal to that specified by `param2`. The value of this flag is 0x0018.
>
> **triggerRateNotEqual**
> Indicates that the callback function should be called when the rate changes to a value that is not equal to that specified by `param2`. The value of this flag is 0x001C.

`param2`   Contains data supplied to the Movie Toolbox in the `param2` parameter to the `CallMeWhen` function (see page 11-11). Your component interprets this parameter based on the value of the `callBackType` parameter to the `ClockNewCallBack` function, described on page 11-10.

If `callBackType` is set to `callBackAtTime`, `param2` contains the time value at which your component should invoke the callback function for this event. The `param1` parameter contains flags affecting when you should call the function.

If `callBackType` is set to `callBackAtRate`, `param2` contains the rate value at which your component should invoke the callback function for this event. The `param1` parameter contains flags affecting when you should call the function.

`param3`   Contains data supplied to the Movie Toolbox in the `param3` parameter to the `CallMeWhen` function. If `qtType` is set to `callBackAtTime`, `param3` contains the time scale in which to interpret the time value that is stored in `param2`.

DESCRIPTION

The Movie Toolbox maintains control information about the callback event. Your clock component only needs to maintain the invocation schedule. For example, the Movie Toolbox saves the address of the callback event, its reference constant, and the value of the A5 register. In addition, the Movie Toolbox prevents applications from scheduling a single callback event more than once.

Clock Components

If your clock component successfully schedules the callback event, you should call the `AddCallBackToTimeBase` function (described on page 11-18) to add it to the list of callback events for the corresponding time base. If your component cannot schedule the callback event, it should return an appropriate error.

ClockCancelCallBack

Your clock component's `ClockCancelCallBack` function removes the specified callback event from the list of scheduled callback events for a time base.

```
pascal ComponentResult ClockCancelCallBack
                        (ComponentInstance aClock,
                         QTCallBack cb)
```

aClock
: Specifies the clock for the operation. Your application obtains this identifier from the Component Manager's `OpenComponent` function.

cb
: Specifies the callback event for the operation. The Movie Toolbox obtains this value from your component's `ClockNewCallBack` function (described on page 11-10).

DESCRIPTION

The Movie Toolbox calls this function when an application cancels its callback event by calling `CancelCallBack`. The Movie Toolbox also calls this function whenever it executes the callback event, thus removing it from the list of scheduled callback events. The application is then responsible for rescheduling the event, if appropriate.

If your clock component successfully cancels the callback event, you should call the `RemoveCallBackFromTimeBase` function, described on page 11-19, so that the Movie Toolbox can remove the callback event from its list of scheduled events.

ClockDisposeCallBack

Your clock component's `ClockDisposeCallBack` function disposes of the memory associated with the specified callback event.

```
pascal ComponentResult ClockDisposeCallBack
                        (ComponentInstance aClock,
                         QTCallBack cb);
```

aClock
: Specifies the clock for the operation. Applications obtain this identifier from the Component Manager's `OpenComponent` function.

CHAPTER 11

Clock Components

cb Specifies the callback event for the operation. The Movie Toolbox obtains this value from your component's `ClockNewCallBack` function (described on page 11-10).

DESCRIPTION

The Movie Toolbox calls this function when an application discards its callback event by calling the `DisposeCallBack` function. Your clock component should cancel the callback event before you dispose of it.

You should not call this function at interrupt time.

Managing the Time

Clock components provide several functions that allow the Movie Toolbox to alert your component to changes in its environment. Three of these functions, `ClockTimeChanged`, `ClockRateChanged`, and `ClockStartStopChanged`, are associated with application callback functions and help your component determine whether to invoke the callback function. The fourth, the `ClockSetTimeBase` function, tells your clock component about the time base it is supporting.

ClockTimeChanged

The Movie Toolbox calls your component's `ClockTimeChanged` function whenever the callback's time base time value is set. The Movie Toolbox calls this function only if the `qtcbNeedsTimeChanges` flag is set to 1 in the `callBackFlags` field of the QuickTime callback header structure allocated by your clock component (see "Data Type" beginning on page 11-6 for more information).

```
pascal ComponentResult ClockTimeChanged
                                (ComponentInstance aClock,
                                QTCallBack cb);
```

aClock Specifies the clock for the operation. Applications obtain this identifier from the Component Manager's `OpenComponent` function.

cb Specifies the callback for the operation. The Movie Toolbox obtains this value from your component's `ClockNewCallBack` function.

DESCRIPTION

The Movie Toolbox calls this function once for each qualified callback function associated with the time base. Note that the Movie Toolbox calls this function only for callback events that are currently scheduled.

CHAPTER 11

Clock Components

ClockRateChanged

The Movie Toolbox calls your component's `ClockRateChanged` function whenever the callback's time base rate changes. The Movie Toolbox calls this function only if the `qtcbNeedsRateChanges` flag is set to 1 in the `callBackFlags` field of the callback header structure in the `QTCallBackHeader` structure allocated by your clock component (see "Data Type" beginning on page 11-6 for more information about the callback header structure).

```
pascal ComponentResult ClockRateChanged (ComponentInstance aClock,
                                          QTCallBack cb);
```

aClock Specifies the clock for the operation. Applications obtain this identifier from the Component Manager's `OpenComponent` function.

cb Specifies the callback for the operation. The Movie Toolbox obtains this value from your component's `ClockNewCallBack` function (described on page 11-10).

DESCRIPTION

The Movie Toolbox calls this function once for each qualified callback function associated with the time base. Note that the Movie Toolbox calls this function only for callback events that are currently scheduled.

ClockStartStopChanged

The Movie Toolbox calls your component's `ClockStartStopChanged` function whenever the start or stop time of the callback's time base changes. The Movie Toolbox calls this function only if the `qtcbNeedsStartStop` flag is set to 1 in the `callBackFlags` field of the callback header structure in the `QTCallBackHeader` structure allocated by your clock component (see "Data Type" beginning on page 11-6 for more information about the callback header structure).

```
pascal ComponentResult ClockStartStopChanged
                (ComponentInstance aClock, QTCallBack cb,
                 Boolean startChanged,
                 Boolean stopChanged);
```

aClock Specifies the clock for the operation. Applications obtain this identifier from the Component Manager's `OpenComponent` function.

Clock Components

cb
: Specifies the callback for the operation. The Movie Toolbox obtains this value from your component's `ClockNewCallBack` function (described on page 11-10).

startChanged
: Indicates that the start time of the time base associated with the clock component instance has changed.

stopChanged
: Indicates that the stop time of the time base associated with the clock component instance has changed.

DESCRIPTION

The Movie Toolbox calls this function once for each qualified callback function associated with the time base. Note that the Movie Toolbox calls this function only for callback events that are currently scheduled.

ClockSetTimeBase

The Movie Toolbox calls your component's `ClockSetTimeBase` function when an application creates a time base that uses your clock component. The `tb` parameter indicates the time base that is associated with your clock.

```
pascal ComponentResult ClockSetTimeBase (ComponentInstance aClock,
                                         TimeBase tb);
```

aClock
: Specifies the clock for the operation. Applications obtain this identifier from the Component Manager's `OpenComponent` function.

tb
: Specifies the time base that is associated with the clock.

DESCRIPTION

Your clock component may need to know its time base if the rate or time value of the time base can be changed without using Movie Toolbox functions. This could be the case if your clock supports an external clock. Under these circumstances, the Movie Toolbox cannot use the `ClockRateChanged` and `ClockTimeChanged` functions (described on page 11-16 and page 11-15, respectively) to alert your component to changes in its environment. Instead, your component can use the time base provided here to seed the `GetFirstCallBack` function, described on page 11-20, and then scan all its associated callback functions.

CHAPTER 11

Clock Components

Movie Toolbox Clock Support Functions

The Movie Toolbox provides a number of support functions for clock components. All of these functions help your component manage its associated callback functions. Your clock component may call any of these functions at interrupt time. These functions should only be called by clock components.

Use the `AddCallBackToTimeBase` function to add a callback event to the list of scheduled callback events maintained by the Movie Toolbox. You should use the `RemoveCallBackFromTimeBase` function to remove a callback event from the list.

When your clock component determines that it is time to invoke a callback function, you should use the `ExecuteCallBack` function to cause the Movie Toolbox to call the function.

If your clock component needs to scan all its associated callback events, you can use the `GetFirstCallBack` and `GetNextCallBack` functions.

AddCallBackToTimeBase

Your clock component uses the `AddCallBackToTimeBase` function to place a callback event into the list of scheduled callback events. The Movie Toolbox maintains this list.

```
pascal OSErr AddCallBackToTimeBase (QTCallBack cb);
```

cb　　　　Specifies the callback event for the operation. Your clock component obtains this value from the parameters passed to your `ClockCallMeWhen` function (described on page 11-11).

DESCRIPTION

Your component should call the `AddCallBackToTimeBase` function when your `ClockCallMeWhen` function determines that your component can support the callback event (see "Using the Callback Functions," which begins on page 11-9, for more information about the `ClockCallMeWhen` function).

If your component does not call this function, the Movie Toolbox does not notify your component of time, rate, or stop and start changes (via the `ClockRateChanged` and `ClockTimeChanged` functions, described on page 11-16 and page 11-15, respectively).

ExecuteCallBack

When your clock component determines that it is time to execute a callback function, your component should call the `ExecuteCallBack` function.

```
pascal void ExecuteCallBack (QTCallBack cb);
```

cb Specifies the callback event for the operation. Your clock component obtains this value from the parameters passed to your `ClockCallMeWhen` function (described on page 11-11).

DESCRIPTION

This function handles all the details of invoking the callback function properly. For example, the `ExecuteCallBack` function queues the callback function correctly, according to the function's ability to execute at interrupt time (specified in the `callBackType` parameter to your `ClockNewCallBack` function, described on page 11-10).

Before calling the application's function, the `ExecuteCallBack` function cancels the callback event. In this manner, the callback event is prevented from executing twice in succession. It is up to the application, or the callback function itself, to reschedule the callback event.

SPECIAL CONSIDERATIONS

This function sets the A5 register to the value it contained at the time the callback event was scheduled when calling the callback function.

Your clock component should not release the memory associated with the callback event at this time. You should do so only in your `ClockDisposeCallBack` function (described on page 11-14). This is particularly important when a callback function cannot execute at interrupt time, since the Movie Toolbox schedules such functions for invocation at a later time.

RemoveCallBackFromTimeBase

Your clock component uses the `RemoveCallBackFromTimeBase` function to remove a callback event from the list of scheduled callback events. The Movie Toolbox maintains this list.

```
pascal OSErr RemoveCallBackFromTimeBase (QTCallBack cb);
```

cb Specifies the callback event for the operation. Your clock component obtains this value from the parameters passed to your `ClockCallMeWhen` function (described on page 11-11).

Clock Components

DESCRIPTION

Your component should call the `RemoveCallBackToTimeBase` function when your `ClockCancelCallBack` function determines that your component can cancel the callback event (see "Using the Callback Functions" beginning on page 11-9 for more information about the `ClockCancelCallBack` function).

SPECIAL CONSIDERATIONS

Your component should call the `RemoveCallbackFromTimeBase` function only for callback events that were successfully added to the schedule with the `AddCallBackToTimeBase` function (described on page 11-18).

GetFirstCallBack

The `GetFirstCallBack` function returns the first callback event associated with a specified time base. Your component can use this function, along with the `GetNextCallBack` function (described in the next section), to scan all callback events associated with a time base.

```
pascal QTCallBack GetFirstCallBack (TimeBase tb);
```

tb   Specifies the time base for the operation. Your component can obtain the time base reference from your `ClockSetTimeBase` function (described on page 11-17) or from the Movie Toolbox's `GetCallBackTimeBase` function.

DESCRIPTION

The `GetFirstCallBack` function returns the first callback event in the list managed for the specified time base. If there are no callback events associated with the time base, the `QTCallBack` result is set to `nil`. Your component cannot assume that the Movie Toolbox maintains the callback list in any particular order.

GetNextCallBack

The `GetNextCallBack` function returns the next callback event associated with a specified time base. Your component can use this function, along with the `GetFirstCallBack` function (described in the previous section), to scan all callback events associated with a time base.

```
pascal QTCallBack GetNextCallBack (QTCallBack cb);
```

cb Specifies the starting callback event for the operation. Your clock component obtains this value from the `GetFirstCallBack` function or from previous calls to the `GetNextCallBack` function.

DESCRIPTION

The `GetNextCallBack` function returns the next callback event in the list managed for the specified time base. If there are no more callback events associated with the time base, the returned QuickTime callback header structure is set to `nil`. Your component cannot assume that the Movie Toolbox maintains the callback list in any particular order.

Summary of Clock Components

C Summary

Constants

```
/* type value */
#define clockComponentType      'clok'      /* clock component */

/* subtype values */
#define systemTickClock         'tick'      /* system tick clock */
#define systemMicrosecondClock  'micr'      /* system microsecond clock */
#define systemSecondClock       'seco'      /* system second clock */
#define systemMillisecondClock  'mill'      /* system millisecond clock */

/* constants for manipulating clock component capability flags */
enum{
    kClockRateIsLinear = 1,             /* clock keeps constant rate */
    kClockImplementsCallBacks = 2       /* clock supports callback events */
};

#define ClockGetTime GetClockTime

/* constants to refer to request codes for supported functions */
enum {
    kClockGetTimeSelect             = 0x1,  /* ClockGetTime */
    kClockNewCallBackSelect         = 0x2,  /* ClockNewCallBack */
    kClockDisposeCallBackSelect     = 0x3,  /* ClockDisposeCallBack */
    kClockCallMeWhenSelect          = 0x4,  /* ClockCallMeWhen */
    kClockCancelCallBackSelect      = 0x5,  /* ClockCancelCallBack */
    kClockRateChangedSelect         = 0x6,  /* ClockRateChanged */
    kClockTimeChangedSelect         = 0x7,  /* ClockTimeChanged */
    kClockSetTimeBaseSelect         = 0x8,  /* ClockSetTimeBase */
    kClockStartStopChangedSelect    = 0x9,  /* ClockStartStopChanged */
    kClockGetRateSelect             = 0xA   /* ClockGetRate */
};
```

Clock Components

```
enum {
    qtcbNeedsRateChanges      = 1,/* wants to know about rate changes */
    qtcbNeedsTimeChanges      = 2,/* wants to know about time changes */
    qtcbNeedsStartStopChanges = 4 /* wants to know when time base start
                                     or stop has changed */
};

/* values for callBackType parameter of ClockNewCallBack function that
   indicate when a callback event is to be invoked */

enum
    {
    callBackAtTime      = 1,    /* at specific time */
    callBackAtRate      = 2,    /* when the rate for the time base
                                   reaches a specific value */
    callBackAtTimeJump  = 3,    /* when a program changes the time value
                                   for a time base */
    };
typedef unsigned short QTCallBackType;

/* callback equates--values for the parameter param1 of the
   ClockCallMeWhen function that indicate when the callback function should
   be called */

enum
    {
    triggerTimeFwd      = 0x0001,/* when current time exceeds trigger time
                                    going forward */
    triggerTimeBwd      = 0x0002,/* when current time exceeds trigger time
                                    going backward */
    triggerTimeEither   = 0x0003,/* when curTime exceeds triggerTime going
                                    either direction */
    triggerRateLT       = 0x0004,/* when rate changes to less than trigger
                                    value */
    triggerRateGT       = 0x0008,/* when rate changes to greater than trigger
                                    value */
    triggerRateEqual    = 0x0010,/* when rate changes to equal trigger
                                    value */
    triggerRateLTE      = triggerRateLT | triggerRateEqual,
                                 /* when rate changes to a value less than
                                    or equal to param2 rate */
    triggerRateGTE      = triggerRateGT | triggerRateEqual,
                                 /* when rate changes to value greater than
                                    or equal to param2 rate */
```

```
    triggerRateNotEqual = triggerRateGT | triggerRateEqual | triggerRateLT,
                            /* when rate changes to value not equal to
                                param2 rate */
    triggerRateChange   = 0,    /* whenever rate changes */
};
typedef unsigned short QTCallBackFlags;
```

Data Type

```
struct QTCallBackHeader {
    long    callBackFlags;  /* flags used by clock component to
                                communicate scheduling data about
                                callback to Movie Toolbox */
    long    reserved1;      /* reserved for use by Apple */
    char    qtPrivate[40];  /* reserved for use by Apple */
};
```

Clock Component Functions

Getting the Current Time

```
pascal ComponentResult ClockGetTime
                    (ComponentInstance aClock, TimeRecord *out);
```

Using the Callback Functions

```
pascal QTCallBack ClockNewCallBack
                    (ComponentInstance aClock, TimeBase tb,
                     short callBackType);
pascal ComponentResult ClockCallMeWhen
                    (ComponentInstance aClock, QTCallBack cb,
                     long param1, long param2, long param3);
pascal ComponentResult ClockCancelCallBack
                    (ComponentInstance aClock, QTCallBack cb);
pascal ComponentResult ClockDisposeCallBack
                    (ComponentInstance aClock, QTCallBack cb);
```

Managing the Time

```
pascal ComponentResult ClockTimeChanged
                    (ComponentInstance aClock, QTCallBack cb);
pascal ComponentResult ClockRateChanged
                    (ComponentInstance aClock, QTCallBack cb);
```

Clock Components

```
pascal ComponentResult ClockStartStopChanged
                        (ComponentInstance aClock, QTCallBack cb,
                         Boolean startChanged, Boolean stopChanged);
pascal ComponentResult ClockSetTimeBase
                        (ComponentInstance clock, TimeBase tb);
```

Movie Toolbox Clock Support Functions

```
pascal OSErr AddCallBackToTimeBase
                        (QTCallBack cb);
pascal void ExecuteCallBack
                        (QTCallBack cb);
pascal OSErr RemoveCallBackFromTimeBase
                        (QTCallBack cb);
pascal QTCallBack GetFirstCallBack
                        (TimeBase tb);
pascal QTCallBack GetNextCallBack
                        (QTCallBack cb);
```

Pascal Summary

Constants

```
CONST
   {type value}
   clockComponentType            = 'clok';   {clock component}

   {subtype values}
   systemTickClock               = 'tick';   {system tick clock}
   systemMicrosecondClock        = 'micr';   {system microsecond clock}
   systemSecondClock             = 'seco';   {system second clock}
   systemMillisecondClock        = 'mill';   {system microsecond clock}

   {constants for manipulating clock component capability flags}
   kClockRateIsLinear            = 1;        {linear clock rate}
   kClockImplementsCallBacks     = 2;        {clock to implement callback }
                                             { routines}

   {constants to refer to request codes for supported routines}
   kClockGetClockTimeSelect      = $1;       {ClockGetTime}
   kClockNewCallBackSelect       = $2;       {ClockNewCallBack}
```

CHAPTER 11

Clock Components

```
kClockDisposeCallBackSelect    = $3;     {ClockDisposeCallBack}
kClockCallMeWhenSelect         = $4;     {ClockCallMeWhen}
kClockCancelCallBackSelect     = $5;     {ClockCancelCallBack}
kClockRateChangedSelect        = $6;     {ClockRateChanged}
kClockTimeChangedSelect        = $7;     {ClockTimeChanged}
kClockSetTimeBaseSelect        = $8;     {ClockSetTimeBase}
kClockStartStopChangedSelect   = $9;     {ClockStartStopChanged}
kClockGetRateSelect            = $A;     {ClockGetRate}

qtcbNeedsRateChanges       = 1;  {wants to know about rate changes}
qtcbNeedsTimeChanges       = 2;  {wants to know about time changes}
qtcbNeedsStartStopChanges  = 4;  {wants to know when time base start }
                                 { or stop has changed}

{values for callBackType parameter of ClockNewCallBack function that }
{ indicate when a callback event is to be invoked}
    callBackAtTime      = 1;    {at specific time}
    callBackAtRate      = 2;    {when the rate for the time base }
                                { reaches a specific value}
    callBackAtTimeJump  = 3;    {when a program changes the time value }
                                { for a time base}

{values for the parameter param1 of ClockCallMeWhen function that indicate }
{ when callback function should be called}
triggerTimeFwd      = $0001; {when current time exceeds trigger time going }
                             { forward}
triggerTimeBwd      = $0002; {when current time exceeds trigger time going }
                             { backward}
triggerTimeEither   = $0003; {when current time exceeds trigger time going }
                             { either direction}
triggerRateLT       = $0004; {when rate changes to less than trigger value}
triggerRateGT       = $0008; {when rate changes to greater than trigger }
                             { value}
triggerRateEqual    = $0010; {when rate changes to equal trigger value}
triggerRateLTE      = $0014; {when rate changes to less than or equal }
                             { trigger value}
triggerRateGTE      = $0018; {when rate changes to greater than or equal }
                             { to trigger value}
triggerRateNotEqual = $001C; {when rate is not equal to trigger value}
triggerRateChange   = 0;     {whenever rate changes}
```

Data Type

```
TYPE
   QTCallBack                    = ^CallBackRecord;

   QTCallBackHeader =
      RECORD
         callBackFlags:     LongInt;    {component flags about callback }
                                        { events}
         reserved1:         LongInt;    {reserved}
         qtPrivate:         ARRAY[0..39] OF Byte;
                                        {reserved}
      END;

   QTCallBackFlags   = Byte;

   QTCallBackType    = Byte;

   QTCallBackProc    = ProcPtr;
```

Clock Component Routines

Getting the Current Time

```
FUNCTION ClockGetTime         (aClock: ComponentInstance;
                               VAR out: TimeRecord): ComponentResult;
```

Using the Callback Functions

```
FUNCTION ClockNewCallBack     (aClock: ComponentInstance; tb: TimeBase;
                               callBackType: Integer): QTCallBack;
FUNCTION ClockCallMeWhen      (aClock: ComponentInstance; cb: QTCallBack;
                               param1: LongInt; param2: LongInt;
                               param3: LongInt): ComponentResult;
FUNCTION ClockCancelCallBack
                              (aClock: ComponentInstance;
                               cb: QTCallBack): ComponentResult;
FUNCTION ClockDisposeCallBack
                              (aClock: ComponentInstance;
                               cb: QTCallBack): ComponentResult;
```

Managing the Time

```
FUNCTION ClockTimeChanged     (aClock: ComponentInstance;
                               cb: QTCallBack): ComponentResult;
FUNCTION ClockRateChanged     (aClock: ComponentInstance;
                               cb: QTCallBack): ComponentResult;
FUNCTION ClockStartStopChanged
                              (clock: ComponentInstance; cb: QTCallBack;
                               startChanged: Boolean; stopChanged: Boolean):
                               ComponentResult;
FUNCTION ClockSetTimeBase     (aClock: ComponentInstance;
                               tb: TimeBase): ComponentResult;
```

Movie Toolbox Clock Support Routines

```
FUNCTION AddCallBackToTimeBase
                              (cb: QTCallBack): OSErr;
PROCEDURE ExecuteCallBack     (cb: QTCallBack);
FUNCTION RemoveCallBackFromTimeBase
                              (cb: QTCallBack): OSErr;
FUNCTION GetFirstCallBack     (tb: TimeBase): QTCallBack;
FUNCTION GetNextCallBack      (cb: QTCallBack): QTCallBack;
```

CHAPTER 12

Preview Components

Contents

About Preview Components   12-3
   Obtaining Preview Data   12-3
   Storing Preview Data in Files   12-5
   Using the Preview Data   12-5
Creating Preview Components   12-6
   Implementing Required Component Functions   12-7
   Displaying Image Data as a Preview   12-8
Preview Components Reference   12-10
   Functions   12-10
      Displaying Previews   12-10
      Handling Events   12-11
      Creating Previews   12-11
   Resources   12-13
      The Preview Resource   12-14
      The Preview Resource Item Structure   12-15
Summary of Preview Components   12-16
   C Summary   12-16
      Constants   12-16
      Data Types   12-16
      Functions   12-17
   Pascal Summary   12-17
      Constants   12-17
      Data Types   12-18
      Routines   12-19

Preview Components

This chapter discusses preview components. **Preview components** are used by the Image Compression Manager's standard file preview functions to display and create visual previews for files. Previews usually consist of a single image, but they may contain many kinds of data, including sound. In QuickTime, the Image Compression Manager is the primary client of preview components. Rarely, if ever, do applications call preview components directly. However, you may want to develop your own preview component for use by the Image Compression Manager. Therefore, this chapter focuses on what you must do to create a preview component.

- "About Preview Components" presents some general information about how preview components obtain, store, and use preview data.
- "Creating Preview Components" presents a sample program for the implementation of a preview component that displays PICT images.
- "Preview Components Reference" describes the functions and resources that are specific to preview components.
- "Summary of Preview Components" provides summaries of the preview component constants, data structures, and functions in C and in Pascal.

Before learning about preview components, you must be familiar with QuickTime movie previews. See the chapter "Movie Toolbox" in *Inside Macintosh: QuickTime* for a complete description of movie previews and of the Image Compression Manager functions that support standard file previews.

About Preview Components

Preview components provide two basic services: they draw and create previews. This section describes how preview components obtain preview data, what kind of information is stored with the file, and what they do with the preview data.

Obtaining Preview Data

Preview components obtain data from

- a small data cache
- a reference they create to another resource in the file
- the file for which they are invoked

The preview component can create a small data cache containing the preview. Although creation of the preview cache may be time-consuming, the cache can then be stored in the file and used to display the preview for the file rapidly on subsequent occasions. The picture file preview component, which creates a thumbnail picture for the file and stores it in the file's resource fork, is one way of getting information from a data cache.

The preview component can create a reference to another resource in the file. For example, some file types already contain a picture preview in them. The preview component can then create a pointer to that existing data, rather than making another copy of it. The movie preview component works in this way when the preview for the movie is actually the movie's preview, rather than only its poster picture.

If the preview component can display the preview for the file quickly enough in every case, there is no need for a cache. Such a preview component reinterprets the data in the file each time it is invoked, rather than creating a preview cache once. This method of getting the information allows the file to remain untouched, requires no disk space, and does not demand that the user or the application make any special effort to create the preview. Unfortunately, in most cases, it is not possible to interpret the data quickly enough to use this approach. Preview components that handle this type of preview should set the `pnotComponentNeedsNoCache` flag in their component flags field.

```
enum {
    pnotComponentNeedsNoCache = 2
};
```

If a preview component relies on other system software services, it must make sure they are present. For example, if your preview component uses the Movie Toolbox, it is responsible for calling the Movie Toolbox's `EnterMovies` and `ExitMovies` functions.

When previewing is complete, the component receives a normal Component Manager close request. If you add any controls to the window, you should dispose of them while you are calling the Component Manager's `CloseComponent` function.

A preview component should never write back to the file directly. The caller of the preview component is responsible for actually modifying the file. You should open all access paths to the file with read permission only.

Figure 12-1 illustrates the relationships of a preview component, the Image Compression Manager, and an application.

Figure 12-1 Relationships of a preview component, the Image Compression Manager, and an application

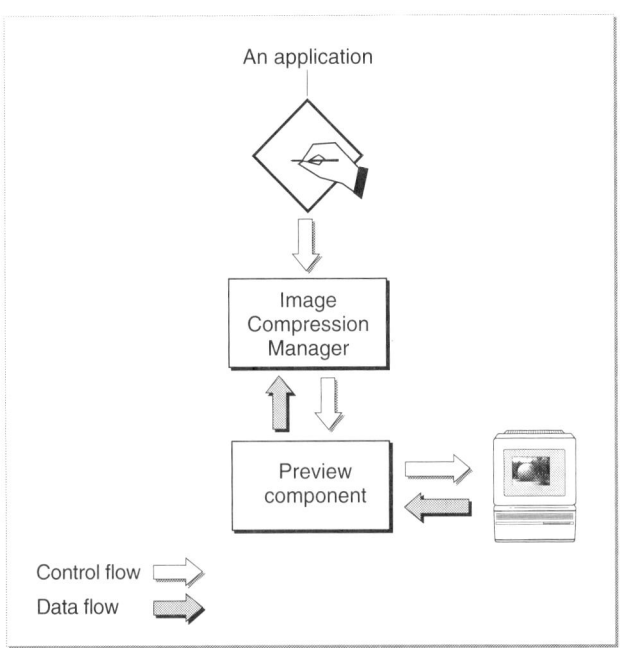

Storing Preview Data in Files

A preview may or may not contain sound or text data or other types of information. In addition to the visual preview, QuickTime provides the preview resource, described on page 12-14, which also allows you to store

- a brief description of the file
- a list of keywords
- an associated language code to allow use of a single file in more than one region
- a modification date to help applications determine when the data has been changed

Using the Preview Data

Preview components may

- create a preview
- draw a preview
- create and draw a preview

Preview Components

Some preview components only create a preview and rely on another component to display it. For example, by default, the movie preview component creates a picture preview for the file. This is displayed by the picture preview component.

Most preview components simply draw the preview. These are the simplest type of display components. They do not require any other event processing—including the scheduling of idle time—for example, to play a movie. The picture preview component is an example of this type of component.

Preview components that do not require a cache should have a subtype that matches the type of file for which they can display previews.

A preview component for sound would require event processing, since it would need time to play the sound. If your preview component requires event processing, you must have the `pnotComponentWantsEvents` flag set in its component flags field.

```
enum {
    pnotComponentWantsEvents = 1,
};
```

Creating Preview Components

This section describes how to create your own preview component.

Preview components that create previews have a type of `'pmak'` and a subtype that matches the type of the file for which they create previews.

Preview components that display previews have a type of `'pnot'` and a subtype that matches the type of the resource that they display.

You can use the following constants to refer to the request codes for each of the functions that your preview component must support.

```
enum {
    kPreviewShowDataSelector            = 1, /* PreviewShowData */
    kPreviewMakePreviewSelector         = 2, /* PreviewMakePreview */
    kPreviewMakePreviewReferenceSelector = 3,/* PreviewMakePreviewReference */
    kPreviewEventSelector               = 4  /* PreviewEvent */
};
```

This section presents a sample program that displays a preview component for the display of PICS animation files. First it implements the required Component Manager functions. Then it converts the PICT image data into a format for display as a preview.

Preview Components

Implementing Required Component Functions

Listing 12-1 supplies the component dispatchers for the preview component together with the can do, version, open, and close functions.

Listing 12-1   Implementing the required Component Manager functions

```
typedef struct {
   ComponentInstance self;
} PICSPreviewRecord, **PICSPreviewGlobals;

/* entry point for all Component Manager requests */
pascal ComponentResult PICSPreviewDispatch
                  (ComponentParameters *params, Handle store)
{
   OSErr err = badComponentSelector;
   ComponentFunction componentProc = 0;

   switch (params->what) {
      case kComponentOpenSelect:
         componentProc = PICSPreviewOpen; break;
      case kComponentCloseSelect:
         componentProc = PICSPreviewClose; break;
      case kComponentCanDoSelect:
         componentProc = PICSPreviewCanDo; break;
      case kComponentVersionSelect:
         componentProc = PICSPreviewVersion; break;
      case kPreviewShowDataSelector:
         componentProc = PICSPreviewShowData; break;
   }

   if (componentProc)
      err = CallComponentFunctionWithStorage (store, params,
                                              componentProc);

   return err;
}

pascal ComponentResult PICSPreviewCanDo
                  (PICSPreviewGlobals store, short ftnNumber)
{
   switch (ftnNumber) {
      case kComponentOpenSelect:
      case kComponentCloseSelect:
      case kComponentCanDoSelect:
```

Creating Preview Components

Preview Components

```
      case kComponentVersionSelect:
      case kPreviewShowDataSelector:
         return true;
      default:
         return false;
   }
}

pascal ComponentResult PICSPreviewVersion
                                 (PICSPreviewGlobals store)
{
   return 0x00010001;
}

pascal ComponentResult PICSPreviewOpen (PICSPreviewGlobals store,
                                 ComponentInstance self)
{
   store = (PICSPreviewGlobals)NewHandle
                                 (sizeof (PICSPreviewRecord));
   if (!store) return MemError();
   SetComponentInstanceStorage (self, (Handle)store);
   (**store).self = self;

   return noErr;
}

pascal ComponentResult PICSPreviewClose
                                 (PICSPreviewGlobals store,
                                 ComponentInstance self)
{
   if (store) DisposeHandle ((Handle)store);
   return noErr;
}
```

Displaying Image Data as a Preview

To display a file's image preview, your `PreviewShowData` function is called. Listing 12-2 includes the `PICSPreviewShowData` function, which previews a PICS file. The function loads the first PICT image from the PICS file and uses the PICT file preview component to display it.

Listing 12-2 Converting data into a form that can be displayed as a preview

```
pascal ComponentResult PICSPreviewShowData
                                (PICSPreviewGlobals store,
                                 OSType dataType, Handle data,
                                 const Rect *inHere)
{
   OSErr err = noErr;
   short resRef = 0, saveRes = CurResFile();
   FSSpec theFile;
   Boolean whoCares;
   Handle thePict = nil;
   ComponentInstance ci;

   /* because your component has the pnotComponentNeedsNoCache
      flag set, it should only be called to display files */
   if (dataType != rAliasType)
      return paramErr;

   /* open up the file to preview */
   if (err = ResolveAlias (nil, (AliasHandle)data, &theFile,
                       &whoCares)) goto bail;
   resRef = FSpOpenResFile (&theFile, fsRdPerm);
   if (err = ResError()) goto bail;

   /* get the first 'PICT' */
   UseResFile (resRef);
   thePict = Get1IndResource ('PICT', 1);
   if (!thePict) goto bail;

   /* use the PICT preview component to display the preview */
   if (ci = OpenDefaultComponent (ShowFilePreviewComponentType,
                                  'PICT')) {
      PreviewShowData (ci, 'PICT', thePict, inHere);
      CloseComponent (ci);
   }
bail:
   if (resRef) CloseResFile (resRef);
   if (thePict) DisposeHandle (thePict);
   UseResFile (saveRes);
   return err;
}
```

CHAPTER 12

Preview Components

Preview Components Reference

This section describes the functions and resources that are specific to preview components.

Functions

This section describes the functions for displaying previews, handling events in previews, and creating previews that are provided by preview components. These functions are described from the perspective of the Image Compression Manager, which is most likely to call preview components. If you are developing a preview component, your component must behave as described here.

Displaying Previews

The preview component supplies a single function for displaying movie previews. If your preview component does not handle events (that is, does not contain time-based data), you should use this function.

PreviewShowData

The `PreviewShowData` function allows you to display a preview if your preview component does not handle events.

```
pascal ComponentResult PreviewShowData (pnotComponent p,
                                        OSType dataType,
                                        Handle data,
                                        const Rect *inHere);
```

p
: Specifies your preview component. You obtain this identifier from the Component Manager's `OpenComponent` function. See the chapter "Component Manager" in *Inside Macintosh: More Macintosh Toolbox* for details.

dataType
: Contains the type of handle pointing to the data to be displayed in the preview.

data
: Contains a handle to the data, which is typically the same as the subtype of your preview component.

inHere
: Contains a pointer to a rectangle that defines the area into which you draw the preview. The current port is set to the correct graphics port for drawing. You must not draw outside the given rectangle.

DESCRIPTION

If your preview component can display the data for the preview quickly enough that it does not need a cache (that is, you have set the `pnotComponentNeedsNoCache` flag), you should consider the `PreviewShowData` function an initialization function. Therefore, you should remember the location of the preview rectangle and set up any necessary data structures. An update event is generated after this function for your initial drawing. In this case, the type of the handle in the `data` parameter is an alias (that is, it is the `rAliasType` resource type), and the handle contains an alias to the file to be previewed.

Handling Events

The `PreviewEvent` function is provided so that your preview component can do standard event filtering. See *Inside Macintosh: Files* for details on the standard dialog event filter function.

PreviewEvent

If your preview component handles events, the `PreviewEvent` function is called as appropriate.

```
pascal ComponentResult PreviewEvent (pnotComponent p,
                                     EventRecord *e,
                                     Boolean *handledEvent);
```

p   Specifies your preview component. You obtain this identifier from the Component Manager's `OpenComponent` function. See the chapter "Component Manager" in *Inside Macintosh: More Macintosh Toolbox* for details.

e   Contains a pointer to the event structure for this operation.

handledEvent
           Contains a pointer to a Boolean value. If you completely handle an event such as a mouse-down event or keystroke, you should set the `handledEvent` parameter to `true`. Otherwise, set it to `false`.

Creating Previews

Two functions are available for use in creating previews. The `PreviewMakePreview` function creates previews by allocating a handle to data to be added to the file. On the other hand, the `PreviewMakePreviewReference` function makes previews by returning the type and identification number of a resource within the file to be used as the preview for the file.

CHAPTER 12

Preview Components

PreviewMakePreview

The `PreviewMakePreview` function creates previews by allocating a handle to data that is to be added to the file.

```
pascal ComponentResult PreviewMakePreview (pnotComponent p,
                                OSType *previewType,
                                Handle *previewResult,
                                const FSSpec *sourceFile,
                                ProgressProcRecordPtr progress);
```

p
: Specifies your preview component. You obtain this identifier from the Component Manager's `OpenComponent` function. See the chapter "Component Manager" in *Inside Macintosh: More Macintosh Toolbox* for details.

previewType
: Contains a pointer to the type of preview component that should be used to display the preview.

previewResult
: Contains a pointer to a handle of cached preview data created by this function.

sourceFile
: Contains a pointer to a reference to the file for which the preview is created.

progress
: Points to a progress function. For details on progress functions, see the chapter "Image Compression Manager" in *Inside Macintosh: QuickTime*. If the process of creating a preview takes more than a few seconds, you should call the progress function that is provided.

DESCRIPTION

Your preview component should not actually write the preview to the given file. It should simply return the handle. The data is added to the file by the caller.

CHAPTER 12

Preview Components

PreviewMakePreviewReference

Instead of creating a handle to data that is to be added to the file, the `PreviewMakePreviewReference` function returns the type and identification number of a resource within the file to be used as the preview for the file.

```
pascal ComponentResult PreviewMakePreviewReference
                    (pnotComponent p, OSType *previewType,
                     short *resID, const FSSpec *sourceFile);
```

p
: Specifies your preview component. You obtain this identifier from the Component Manager's `OpenComponent` function. See the chapter "Component Manager" in *Inside Macintosh: More Macintosh Toolbox* for details.

previewType
: Contains a pointer to the type of preview component that should be used to display the preview.

resID
: Contains a pointer to the identification number of a resource within the file to be used as the preview for the file.

sourceFile
: Contains a pointer to a reference to the file for which the preview is created.

DESCRIPTION

If your preview component creates previews by reference, you must also implement the `PreviewMakePreview` function, described in the previous section. However, you should return an error from it. `PreviewMakePreview` is always called first. If it fails, `PreviewMakePreviewReference` is tried next.

Resources

This section describes the preview resource and the preview resource item structures. The preview component uses the preview resource to store visual preview information. The preview resource item structure stores an unlimited number of additional pieces of file data.

The Preview Resource

QuickTime uses the preview resource (defined by the `pnotResource` data type) with a resource ID of 0 to store the visual preview information. The structure of the preview resource is shown in Listing 12-3.

▲ **WARNING**
If you parse this resource directly, please do extensive error checking in your code so as not to hinder future expansion of the data structure. In particular, if you encounter unknown version bits, exercise caution. Unexpected results may occur. ▲

Listing 12-3 The preview resource

```
typedef struct pnotResource {
    unsigned long   modDate;      /* modification date */
    short           version;      /* version number of preview
                                     resource */
    OSType          resType;      /* type of resource used as preview
                                     cache */
    short           resID;        /* resource identification number
                                     of resource used as preview
                                     cache */
    short           numResItems;  /* number of additional file
                                     descriptions */
    pnotResItem     resItem[ ];   /* array of file descriptions */
} pnotResource;
```

Field descriptions

modDate
: Contains the modification time (in standard Macintosh seconds since midnight, January 1, 1904) of the file for which the preview was created. This parameter allows you to find out if the preview is out of date with the contents of the file.

version
: Contains the version number of the preview resource. The low bit of the version is a flag for preview components that only reference their data. If the bit is set, it indicates that the resource identified in the preview resource is not owned by the preview component, but is part of the file. It is not removed when the preview is updated or removed (using the Image Compression Manager's `MakeFilePreview` or `AddFilePreview` function), as it would be if the version number were 0.

resType
: Contains the type of a resource used as a preview cache for the given file. The type of the resource determines the subtype of the preview component that should be used to display the preview.

resID
: Contains the identification number of a resource used as a preview cache for the specified file.

numResItems Specifies the number of additional file descriptions stored with this preview.

resItem Contains the preview resource item structure (defined by the pnotResItem data type), which is described next.

The Preview Resource Item Structure

The preview resource item structure is an array that allows you to store an unlimited number of additional pieces of file information. Each piece of data contains a reference to its information using the structure defined by the pnotResItem data type, which is shown in Listing 12-4.

Listing 12-4 The preview resource item structure

```
typedef struct pnotResItem {
   unsigned long  modDate; /* last modification date of item */
   OSType         useType; /* what type of data */
   OSType         resType; /* resource type containing item */
   short          resID;   /* resource ID containing this item */
   short          rgnCode; /* region code */
   long           reserved;/* set to 0 */
} pnotResItem; *pnotResItemPtr;
```

Field descriptions

modDate Contains the modification time (in standard Macintosh seconds since midnight, January 1, 1904) of this item. This parameter allows you to find out if the item is out of date with the rest of the items in the array.

useType Indicates the meaning of the data pointed to by this item. Two values are currently defined for this field.

- KeyW Indicates that this item points to a list of keywords, typically stored in an 'STR#' resource.
- Desc Indicates that the item points to a brief text description of the file, typically stored in a 'TEXT' resource.

Developers are encouraged to expand the list of types to include additional relevant kinds of information.

resType Contains the type of a resource used as a preview cache for the file associated with the given item. The type of the resource determines which preview component should be used to display the preview.

resID Contains the identification number of a resource used as a preview cache for the specified file.

rgnCode Contains the region code for this item.

reserved Reserved for use by Apple. Set this field to 0.

Summary of Preview Components

C Summary

Constants

```
enum {
   pnotComponentWantsEvents    = 1,  /* component requires events */
   pnotComponentNeedsNoCache   = 2   /* component does not require cache */
};

enum {
   kPreviewShowDataSelector              = 1,  /* PreviewShowData */
   kPreviewMakePreviewSelector           = 2,  /* PreviewMakePreview */
   kPreviewMakePreviewReferenceSelector  = 3,
                                               /* PreviewMakePreviewReference */
   kPreviewEventSelector                 = 4   /* PreviewEvent */
};

#define ShowFilePreviewComponentType   'pnot'   /* creates previews */
#define CreateFilePreviewComponentType 'pmak'   /* displays previews */
```

Data Types

```
typedef ComponentInstance pnotComponent;

typedef struct pnotResource {
   unsigned long  modDate;      /* modification date */
   short          version;      /* version number of preview resource */
   OSType         resType;      /* type of resource used as preview cache */
   short          resID;        /* resource identification number
                                   of resource used as preview cache */
   short          numResItems;  /* number of additional file descriptions */
   pnotResItem    resItem[ ];   /* array of file descriptions */
} pnotResource;
```

```
typedef struct pnotResItem {
   unsigned long   modDate; /* last modification date of item */
   OSType          useType; /* what type of data */
   OSType          resType; /* resource type containing item */
   short           resID;   /* resource ID containing this item */
   short           rgnCode; /* region code */
   long            reserved;/* set to 0 */
} pnotResItem; *pnotResItemPtr;
```

Functions

Displaying Previews

```
pascal ComponentResult PreviewShowData
                        (pnotComponent p, OSType dataType,
                         Handle data, const Rect *inHere);
```

Handling Events

```
pascal ComponentResult PreviewEvent
                        (pnotComponent p, EventRecord *e,
                         Boolean *handledEvent);
```

Creating Previews

```
pascal ComponentResult PreviewMakePreview
                        (pnotComponent p, OSType *previewType,
                         Handle *previewResult,
                         const FSSpec *sourceFile,
                         ProgressProcRecordPtr progress);
pascal ComponentResult PreviewMakePreviewReference
                        (pnotComponent p, OSType *previewType,
                         short *resID, const FSSpec *sourceFile);
```

Pascal Summary

Constants

```
CONST
   {flags for component flags field for your preview component}
   pnotComponentWantsEvents   = 1;  {component requires events}
   pnotComponentNeedsNoCache  = 2;  {component does not require cache}
```

CHAPTER 12

Preview Components

```
{selectors for preview components}
kPreviewShowDataSelector              = 1;   {PreviewShowData}
kPreviewMakePreviewSelector           = 2;   {PreviewMakePreview}
kPreviewMakePreviewReferenceSelector  = 3;   {PreviewMakePreviewReference}
kPreviewEventSelector                 = 4;   {PreviewEvent}

{component types and subtypes}
ShowFilePreviewComponentType      'pnot'    {creates previews}
CreateFilePreviewComponentType    'pmak'    {displays previews}
```

Data Types

```
TYPE
    pnotComponent = ComponentInstance;{preview component type}

    pnotResource =
    RECORD
        modDate:         LongInt;      {modification date}
        version:         Integer;      {version number of preview }
                                       { resource}
        resType:         OSType;       {type of resource used as preview }
                                       { cache}
        resID:           Integer;      {resource identification number }
                                       { of resource used as preview }
                                       { cache}
        numResItems:     Integer;      {number of additional file }
                                       { descriptions}
        ARRAY OF resItem[ ]: pnotResItem;
                                       {array of file descriptions}
    END;

    pnotResItem =
    RECORD
        modDate:    LongInt;     {last modification date of item}
        useType:    OSType;      {what type of data}
        resType:    OSType;      {resource type containing item}
        resID:      Integer;     {resource ID containing this item}
        rgnCode:    Integer;     {region code}
        reserved:   LongInt;     {set to 0}
    END;
```

Routines

Displaying Previews

```
FUNCTION PreviewShowData      (p: pnotComponent; dataType: OSType;
                               data: Handle; VAR inHere: Rect):
                               ComponentResult;
```

Handling Events

```
FUNCTION PreviewEvent         (p: pnotComponent; VAR e: EventRecord;
                               VAR handledEvent: Boolean): ComponentResult;
```

Creating Previews

```
FUNCTION PreviewMakePreview
                              (p: pnotComponent; VAR previewType: OSType;
                               VAR previewResult: Handle;
                               VAR sourceFile: FSSpec;
                               progress: ProgressProcRecordPtr):
                               ComponentResult;
FUNCTION PreviewMakePreviewReference
                              (p: pnotComponent; VAR previewType: OSType;
                               VAR resID: Integer; VAR sourceFile: FSSpec):
                               ComponentResult;
```

Glossary

action One of many integer constants used by QuickTime movie controller components in the `MCDoAction` function. Applications that include action filters may receive any of these actions.

active movie segment A portion of a QuickTime movie that is to be used for playback. By default, the active segment is set to the entire movie. You can change the active segment of a movie by using the Movie Toolbox.

active source rectangle The portion of the **maximum source rectangle** that contains active video that can be digitized by a video digitizer component.

aliasing The result of sampling a signal at less than twice its natural frequency. Aliasing causes data to be lost in the conversion that occurs when resampling an existing signal at more than twice its natural frequency.

alpha channel The portion of each display pixel that represents the blending of video and graphical image data for a video digitizer component.

alternate group A collection of movie **tracks** that contain alternate data for one another. The Movie Toolbox chooses one track from the group to be used when the movie is played. The choice may be based on such considerations as quality or language.

anti-aliasing The process of sampling a signal at more than twice its natural frequency to ensure that **aliasing** artifacts do not occur.

area of interest The portion of a test image that is to be displayed in the standard image-compression dialog box.

atom The basic unit of data in a movie resource. There are a number of different atom types, including movie atoms, track atoms, and media atoms. There are two varieties of atoms: container atoms, which contain other atoms, and leaf atoms, which do not contain any other atoms.

attached controller A movie controller with an attached movie.

automatic key frame A key frame that is inserted automatically by the Image Compression Manager when it detects a scene change. When performing temporal compression, the Image Compression Manager looks for frames that have changed more than 90 percent since the previous frame. If such a change occurs, the Image Compression Manager assumes a scene change and inserts a key frame. A **key frame** allows fast random access and reverse play in addition to efficient compression and picture quality of the frame.

badge A visual element in a movie's display that distinguishes a movie from a static image. The movie controller component supplied by Apple supports badges.

band A horizontal strip from an image. The Image Compression Manager may break an image into bands if a compressor or decompressor component cannot handle an entire image at once.

base media handler component A component that handles most of the duties that must be performed by all **media handlers**. See also **derived media handler component**.

black level The degree of blackness in an image. This is a common setting on a video digitizer. The highest setting will produce an all-black image, whereas the lowest setting will yield very little, if any, black even with black objects in the scene. Black level is an important digitization setting since it can be adjusted so that there is little or no noise in an image.

blend matte A pixel map that defines the blending of video and digital data for a video digitizer component. The value of each pixel in the pixel map governs the relative intensity of the video data for the corresponding pixel in the result image.

callback event A scheduled invocation of a Movie Toolbox **callback function.** Applications establish the criteria that determine when the callback function is to be invoked. When those criteria are met, the Movie Toolbox invokes the callback function.

callback function An application-defined function that is invoked at a specified time or based on specified criteria. These callback functions are data-loading functions, data-unloading functions, completion functions, and progress functions. See also **callback event.**

chunk In the movie resource formats, a collection of sample data in a media. Chunks allow optimized data access. A chunk may contain one or more samples. Chunks in a media may have different sizes, and the samples within a chunk may have different sizes. In the Sound Manager, a chunk may refer to a collection of sampled sound and definitions of the characteristics of sampled sound and other relevant details about the sound.

clipped movie boundary region The region that is clipped by the Movie Toolbox. This region combines the union of all track movie boundary regions for a movie, which is the movie's **movie boundary region,** with the movie's **movie clipping region,** which defines the portion of the movie boundary region that is to be used.

clock component A **component** that supplies basic time information to its clients. Clock components have a **component type** value of `'clok'`.

color ramps Images in which the shading goes from light to dark in smooth increments.

component A software entity, managed by the Component Manager, that provides a defined set of services to its clients. Examples include clock components, movie controller components, and image compressor components.

component instance A channel of communication between a **component** and its client.

component subtype An element in the classification hierarchy used by the Component Manager to define the services provided by a **component.** Within a **component type,** the component subtype provides additional information about the component. For example, image compressor components all have the same component type value; the component subtype value indicates the compression algorithm implemented by the component.

component type An element in the classification hierarchy used by the Component Manager to define the services provided by a **component.** The component type value indicates the type of services provided by the component. For example, all image compressor components have a component type value of `'imco'`. See also **component subtype.**

compressor component A general term used to refer to both **image compressor components** and **image decompressor components.**

connection A channel of communication between a **component** and its client. A **component instance** is used to identify the connection.

container atom A QuickTime atom that contains other atoms, possibly including other container atoms. Examples of container atoms are track atoms and edit atoms. Compare **leaf atom.**

controller boundary rectangle The rectangle that completely encloses a movie controller. If the controller is attached to its movie, the rectangle also encloses the movie image.

controller boundary region The region occupied by a movie controller. If the controller is attached to its movie, the region also includes the movie image.

controller clipping region The clipping region of a movie controller. Only the portion of the controller and its movie that lies within the clipping region is visible to the user.

controller window region The portion of a movie controller and its movie that is visible to the user.

cover function An application-defined function that is called by the Movie Toolbox whenever a movie covers a portion of the screen or reveals a portion of the screen that was previously hidden by the movie.

current error   One of two error values maintained by the Movie Toolbox. The current error value is updated by every Movie Toolbox function. The other error value, the **sticky error,** is updated only when an application directs the Movie Toolbox to do so.

current selection   A portion of a QuickTime movie that has been selected for a cut, copy, or paste operation.

current time   The time value that represents the point of a QuickTime movie that is currently playing or would be playing if the movie had a nonzero rate value.

data dependency   An aspect of image compression in which compression ratios are highly dependent on the image content. Using an algorithm with a high degree of data dependency, an image of a crowd at a football game (which contains a lot of detail) may produce a very small compression ratio, whereas an image of a blue sky (which consists mostly of constant colors and intensities) may produce a very high compression ratio.

data handler   A piece of software that is responsible for reading and writing a media's data. The data handler provides data input and output services to the media's **media handler.**

data reference   A reference to a media's data.

derived media handler component   A component that allows the Movie Toolbox to access the data in a media. Derived media handler components isolate the Movie Toolbox from the details of how or where a particular media is stored. This not only frees the Movie Toolbox from reading and writing media data, but also makes QuickTime extensible to new data formats and storage devices. These components are referred to as *derived* components because they rely on the services of a common base media handler component, which is supplied by Apple. See also **base media handler component.**

detached controller   A movie controller component that is separate from its associated movie.

digitizer rectangle   The portion of the **active source rectangle** that you want to capture and convert with a video digitizer component.

display coordinate system   The QuickDraw graphics world, which can be used to display QuickTime movies, as opposed to the movie's **time coordinate system,** which defines the basic time unit for each of the movie's tracks.

dithering   A technique used to improve picture quality when you are attempting to display an image that exists at a higher bit-depth representation on a lower bit-depth device. For example, you might want to dither a 24 bits per pixel image for display on an 8-bit screen.

duration   A time interval. Durations are time values that are interpreted as spans of time, rather than as points in time.

edit state   Information defining the current state of a movie or track with respect to an edit session. The Movie Toolbox uses edit states to support its undo facilities.

fixed point   A point that uses fixed-point numbers to represent its coordinates. The Movie Toolbox uses fixed points to provide greater display precision for graphical and image data.

fixed rectangle   A rectangle that uses **fixed points** to represent its vertices. The Movie Toolbox uses fixed rectangles to provide greater display precision.

flattening   The process of copying all of the original data referred to by reference in QuickTime tracks into a QuickTime movie file. This can also be called *resolving references*. Flattening is used to bring in all of the data that may be referred to from multiple files after QuickTime editing is complete. It makes a QuickTime movie stand-alone—that is, it can be played on any system without requiring any additional QuickTime movie files or tracks, even if the original file referenced hundreds of files. The flattening operation is essential if QuickTime movies are to be used with CD-ROM discs.

frame   A single image in a **sequence** of images.

frame differencing   A form of temporal compression that involves examining redundancies between adjacent frames in a moving image sequence. Frame differencing can improve compression ratios considerably for a video sequence.

frame rate   The rate at which a movie is displayed—that is, the number of frames per second that are actually being displayed. In QuickTime the frame rate at which a movie was recorded may be different from the frame rate at which it is displayed. On very fast machines, the playback frame rate may be faster than the record frame rate; on slow machines, the playback frame rate may be slower than the record frame rate. Frame rates may be fractional.

genlock   A circuit that locks the frequency of an internal clock to an external timing source. This term is used to refer to the ability of a video digitizer to rely on external clocking.

hue value   A setting that is similar to the tint control on a television. Hue value can be specified in degrees with complementary colors set 180° apart (red is 0°, green is +120°, and blue is –120°). Video digitizer components support hue values that range from 0 (–180° shift in hue) to 65,535 (+179° shift in hue), where 32,767 represents a 0° shift in hue. Hue value is set with the video digitizer component's `VDSetHue` function.

identity matrix   A **transformation matrix** that specifies no change in the coordinates of the source image. The resulting image corresponds exactly to the source image.

image compressor component   A **component** that provides image-compression services. Image compressor components have a **component type** of `'imco'`.

image decompressor component   A **component** that provides image-decompression services. Image decompressor components have a **component type** value of `'imdc'`.

image sequence   A series of visual representations usually represented by video over time. Image sequences may also be generated synthetically, such as from an animation sequence.

interesting time   A time value in a movie, track, or media that meets certain search criteria. You specify the search criteria in the Movie Toolbox. The Movie Toolbox then scans the movie, track, or media and locates time values that meet those search criteria.

interlacing   A video mode that updates half the scan lines on one pass and goes through the second half during the next pass.

interleaving   A technique in which sound and video data are alternated in small pieces, so the data can be read off disk as it is needed. Interleaving allows for movies of almost any length with little delay on startup.

intraframe coding   A process that compresses only a single frame. It does not require looking at adjacent frames in time to achieve compression, but allows fast random access and reverse play.

Joint Photographic Experts Group (JPEG)   Refers to an international standard for compressing still images. This standard supplies the algorithm for image compression. The version of JPEG supplied with QuickTime complies with the baseline International Standards Organization (ISO) standard bitstream, version 9R9. This algorithm is best suited for use with natural images.

JPEG   See **Joint Photographic Experts Group**.

key color   A color in a destination image that is replaced with video data by a video digitizer component. Key colors represent one technique for selectively displaying video on a computer display. Other techniques include the use of **alpha channels** and **blend mattes**.

key frame   A sample in a sequence of temporally compressed samples that does not rely on other samples in the sequence for any of its information. Key frames are placed into temporally compressed sequences at a frequency that is determined by the **key frame rate**. Typically, the term *key frame* is used with respect to temporally compressed sequences of image data. See also **sync sample**.

key frame rate   The frequency with which **key frames** are placed into temporally compressed data sequences.

layer   A mechanism for prioritizing the tracks in a movie. When it plays a movie, the Movie Toolbox displays the movie's tracks according to their layer—tracks with lower layer numbers are displayed first; tracks with higher layer numbers are displayed over those tracks.

leaf atom   A QuickTime atom that contains no other atoms. A leaf atom, however, may contain a table. An example of a leaf atom is an edit list atom. The edit list atom contains the edit list table. Compare **container atom.**

lossless compression   A compression scheme that preserves all of the original data.

lossy compression   A compression scheme that does not preserve the data precisely; some data is lost, and it cannot be recovered after compression. Most lossy schemes try to compress the data as much as possible, without decreasing the image quality in a noticeable way.

mask region   A 1-bit-deep region that defines how an image is to be displayed in the destination coordinate system. For example, during decompression the Image Compression Manager displays only those pixels in the source image that correspond to bits in the mask region that are set to 1. Mask regions must be defined in the destination coordinate system.

master clock component   A movie's clock component.

matrix   See **transformation matrix.**

matte   See **blend matte, track matte.**

maximum source rectangle   A rectangle representing the maximum source area that a video digitizer component can grab. This rectangle usually encompasses both the vertical and horizontal blanking areas.

media   A Movie Toolbox data structure that contains information that describes the data for a track in a movie. Note that a media does not contain its data; rather, a media contains a reference to its data, which may be stored on disk, CD-ROM disc, or any other mass storage device.

media handler   A piece of software that is responsible for mapping from the movie's time coordinate system to the media's time coordinate system. The media handler also interprets the media's data. The **data handler** for the media is responsible for reading and writing the media's data. See also **base media handler component, derived media handler component.**

media information   Control information about a media's data that is stored in the media structure by the appropriate **media handler.**

movie   A set of time-based data that is managed by the Movie Toolbox. A QuickTime movie may contain sound, video, animation, laboratory results, financial data, or a combination of any of these types of time-based data. A QuickTime movie contains one or more **tracks;** each track represents a single data stream in the movie.

movie boundary region   A region that describes the area occupied by a movie in the movie coordinate system, before the movie has been clipped by the **movie clipping region.** A movie's boundary region is built up from the **track movie boundary regions** for each of the movie's **tracks.**

movie box   A rectangle that completely encloses the **movie display boundary region.** The movie box is defined in the display coordinate system.

movie clipping region   The clipping region of a movie in the movie's coordinate system. The Movie Toolbox applies the movie's clipping region to the **movie boundary region** to obtain a clipped movie boundary region. Only that portion of the movie that lies in the clipped movie boundary region is then transformed into an image in the display coordinate system.

movie controller component   A component that manages movie controllers, which present a user interface for playing and editing movies.

movie data exchange component   A component that allows applications to move various types of data into and out of a QuickTime movie. The two types of data exchange components, which provide data conversion services to and from standard QuickTime movie data formats, are the movie import component and the movie export component.

movie data export component   A component that converts QuickTime movie data into other formats.

movie data import component   A component that converts other data formats into QuickTime movie data format.

movie display boundary region   A region that describes the display area occupied by a movie in the display coordinate system, before the movie has been clipped by the **movie display clipping region.**

movie display clipping region   The clipping region of a movie in the display coordinate system. Only that portion of the movie that lies in the clipping region is visible to the user. The Movie Toolbox applies the movie's display clipping region to the **movie display boundary region** to obtain the visible image.

movie file   A QuickTime file that stores all information about the movie in a Macintosh resource, and stores all the associated data for the movie separately. The resource is stored in the resource fork, and the data in the data fork. Most QuickTime movies are stored in files with double forks. Compare **single-fork movie file.**

movie poster   A single visual image representing a QuickTime movie. You specify a poster as a point in time in the movie and specify the tracks that are to be used to constitute the poster image.

movie preview   A short dynamic representation of a QuickTime movie. Movie previews typically last no more than 3 to 5 seconds, and they should give the user some idea of what the movie contains. You define a movie preview by specifying its start time, its duration, and its tracks.

movie resource   One of several data structures that provide the medium of exchange for movie data between applications on a Macintosh computer and between computers, even computers of different types.

National Television System Committee (NTSC)   Refers to the color-encoding method adopted by the committee in 1953. This standard was the first monochrome-compatible, simultaneous color transmission system used for public broadcasting. This method is used widely in the United States.

NTSC   See **National Television System Committee.**

offset-binary encoding   A method of digitally encoding sound that represents the range of amplitude values as an unsigned number, with the midpoint of the range representing silence. For example, an 8-bit sound sample stored in offset-binary format would contain sample values ranging from 0 to 255, with a value of 128 specifying silence (no amplitude). Samples in Macintosh sound resources are stored in offset-binary form. Compare **twos-complement encoding.**

PAL   See **Phase Alternation Line.**

palindrome looping   Running a movie in a circular fashion from beginning to end and end to beginning, alternating forward and backward. Looping must also be enabled in order for palindrome looping to take effect.

Phase Alternation Line (PAL)   A color-encoding system used widely in Europe, in which one of the subcarrier phases derived from the color burst is inverted in phase from one line to the next. This technique minimizes hue errors that may result during color video transmission. Sometimes called *Phase Alternating Line.*

phase-locked loop (PLL)   A piece of hardware that synchronizes itself to an input signal—for example, a video digitizer card that synchronizes to an incoming video source. The video digitizer component's `VDSetPLLFilterType` function allows applications to specify which phase-locked loop is to be active.

playback quality   A relative measure of the fidelity of a track in a QuickTime movie. You can control the playback (or language) quality of a movie during movie playback. The Movie Toolbox chooses tracks from **alternate groups** that most closely correspond to the display quality you desire. In this manner you can create a single movie that can take advantage of the hardware configurations of different computer systems during playback.

PLL   See **phase-locked loop.**

preferred rate   The default playback rate for a QuickTime movie.

preferred volume   The default sound volume for a QuickTime movie.

preroll   A technique for improving movie playback performance. When prerolling a movie, the Movie Toolbox informs the movie's **media handlers** that the movie is about to be played. The media handlers can then load the appropriate movie data. In this manner, the movie can play smoothly from the start.

preview   A short, potentially dynamic, visual representation of the contents of a file. The Standard File Package can use file previews in file dialog boxes to give the user a visual cue about a file's contents.

preview component   A component used by the Movie Toolbox's standard file preview functions to display and create visual previews for files. Previews usually consist of a single image, but they may contain many kinds of data, including sound. In QuickTime, the Movie Toolbox is the primary client of preview components. Rarely, if ever, do applications call preview components directly.

progress function   An application-defined function that is invoked by the Movie Toolbox or the Image Compression Manager. You can use these functions to track the progress of time-consuming activities, and thereby keep the user informed about that progress.

rate   A value that specifies the pace at which time passes for a **time base**. A time base's rate is multiplied by the time scale to obtain the number of **time units** that pass per second. For example, consider a time base that operates in a time coordinate system that has a time scale of 60. If that time base has a rate of 1, 60 time units are processed per second. If the rate is set to 1/2, 30 time units pass per second. If the rate is 2, 120 time units pass per second.

sample   A single element of a sequence of time-ordered data.

sample number   A number that identifies the sample with data for a specified time.

saturation value   A setting that controls color intensity. For example, at high saturation levels, red appears to be red; at low saturation, red appears pink. Valid saturation values range from 0 to 65,535, where 0 is the minimum saturation value and 65,535 specifies maximum saturation. Saturation value is set with the video digitizer component's `VDSetSaturation` function.

SECAM   See **Systeme Electronique Couleur avec Memoire.**

selection duration   A time value that specifies the duration of the **current selection** of a movie.

selection time   A time value that specifies the starting point of the **current selection** of a movie.

sequence   A series of images that may be compressed as a sequence. To do this, the images must share an image description structure. In other words, each image or **frame** in the sequence must have the same compressor type, pixel depth, color lookup table, and boundary dimensions.

sequence grabber channel component   A component that manipulates captured data for **sequence grabber components.**

sequence grabber component   A component that allows applications to obtain digitized data from sources that are external to a Macintosh computer. For example, you can use a sequence grabber component to record video data from a **video digitizer component.** Your application can then request that the sequence grabber store the captured video data in a QuickTime movie. In this manner you can acquire movie data from various sources that can augment the movie data you create by other means, such as computer animation. You can also use sequence grabber components to obtain and display data from external sources, without saving the captured data in a movie.

sequence grabber panel component   A component that allows sequence grabber components to obtain configuration information from the user for a particular **sequence grabber channel component.** An application never calls a sequence grabber panel component directly; application developers use panel components only by calling the **sequence grabber component.**

shadow sync sample A self-contained sample that is an alternate for an already existing frame difference sample. During certain random-access operations, a shadow sync sample is used instead of a normal key frame, which may be very far away from the desired frame. See also **frame differencing.**

single-fork movie file A QuickTime movie file that stores both the movie data and the movie resource in the data fork of the movie file. You can use single-fork movie files to ease the exchange of QuickTime movie data between Macintosh computers and other computer systems. Compare **movie file.**

spatial compression Image compression that is performed within the context of a single **frame.** This compression technique takes advantage of redundancy in the image to reduce the amount of data required to accurately represent the image. Compare **temporal compression.**

standard image-compression dialog component A component that provides a consistent user interface for selecting parameters that govern compression of an image or image sequence and then manages the compression operation.

sticky error One of two error values maintained by the Movie Toolbox. The **sticky error** is updated only when an application directs the Movie Toolbox to do so. The other error value, the **current error,** is updated by every Movie Toolbox function.

s-video A video format in which color and brightness information are encoded as separate signals. The s-video format is component video, as opposed to composite video, which is the NTSC standard.

sync sample A sample that does not rely on preceding frames for content. See also **key frame.**

Systeme Electronique Couleur avec Memoire (SECAM) Sequential Color With Memory; refers to a color-encoding system in which the red and blue color-difference information is transmitted on alternate lines, requiring a one-line memory in order to decode green information.

tearing The effect you obtain if you redraw the screen from the buffer while the buffer is only half updated, so that you get one-half of one image and one-half of another on a single raster scan.

temporal compression Image compression that is performed between **frames** in a sequence. This compression technique takes advantage of redundancy between adjacent frames in a sequence to reduce the amount of data that is required to accurately represent each frame in the sequence. Sequences that have been temporally compressed typically contain **key frames** at regular intervals. Compare **spatial compression.**

thumbnail picture A picture that can be created from an existing image that is stored as a pixel map, a picture, or a picture file. A thumbnail picture is useful for creating small representative images of a source image and in previews for files that contain image data.

time base A set of values that define the time basis for an entity, such as a QuickTime movie. A time base consists of a **time coordinate system** (that is, a **time scale** and a **duration**) along with a rate value. The rate value specifies the speed with which time passes for the time base.

time coordinate system A set of values that defines the context for a **time base.** A time coordinate system consists of a **time scale** and a **duration.** Together, these values define the coordinate system in which a **time value** or a time base has meaning.

time scale The number of **time units** that pass per second in a **time coordinate system.** A time coordinate system that measures time in sixtieths of a second, for example, has a time scale of 60.

time unit The basic unit of measure for time in a time coordinate system. The value of the time unit for a time coordinate system is represented by the formula (1/time scale) seconds. A time coordinate system that has a time scale of 60 measures time in terms of sixtieths of a second.

time value A value that specifies a number of time units in a **time coordinate system.** A time value may contain information about a point in time or about a **duration.**

track   A Movie Toolbox data structure that represents a single data stream in a QuickTime **movie.** A movie may contain one or more tracks. Each track is independent of other tracks in the movie and represents its own data stream. Each track has a corresponding **media.** The media describes the data for the track.

track boundary region   A region that describes the area occupied by a track in the track's coordinate system. The Movie Toolbox obtains this region by applying the **track clipping region** and the **track matte** to the visual image contained in the **track rectangle.**

track clipping region   The clipping region of a track in the track's coordinate system. The Movie Toolbox applies the track's clipping region and the **track matte** to the image contained in the **track rectangle** to obtain the **track boundary region.** Only that portion of the track that lies in the track boundary region is then transformed into an image in the movie coordinate system.

track height   The height, in pixels, of the **track rectangle.**

track matte   A pixel map that defines the blending of track visual data. The value of each pixel in the pixel map governs the relative intensity of the track data for the corresponding pixel in the result image. The Movie Toolbox applies the track matte, along with the **track clipping region,** to the image contained in the **track rectangle** to obtain the **track boundary region.**

track movie boundary region   A region that describes the area occupied by a track in the movie coordinate system, before the movie has been clipped by the **movie clipping region.** The **movie boundary region** is built up from the track movie boundary regions for each of the movie's **tracks.**

track offset   The blank space that represents the intervening time between the beginning of a movie and the beginning of a track's data. In an audio track, the blank space translates to silence; in a video track, the blank space generates no visual image. All of the tracks in a movie use the movie's time coordinate system. That is, the movie's time scale defines the basic time unit for each of the movie's tracks. Each track begins at the beginning of the movie, but the track's data might not begin until some time value other than 0.

track rectangle   A rectangle that completely encloses the visual representation of a track in a QuickTime movie. The width of this rectangle in pixels is referred to as the **track width;** the height, as the **track height.**

track width   The width, in pixels, of the track rectangle.

transformation matrix   A 3-by-3 matrix that defines how to map points from one coordinate space into another coordinate space.

twos-complement encoding   A system for digitally encoding sound that stores the amplitude values as a signed number—silence is represented by a sample with a value of 0. For example, with 8-bit sound samples, twos-complement values would range from –128 to 127, with 0 meaning silence. The Audio Interchange File Format (AIFF) used by the Sound Manager stores samples in twos-complement form. Compare **offset-binary encoding.**

user data   Auxiliary data that your application can store in a QuickTime movie, track, or media structure. The user data is stored in a **user data list;** items in the list are referred to as **user data items.** Examples of user data include a copyright, date of creation, name of a movie's director, and special hardware and software requirements.

user data item   A single element in a **user data list.**

user data list   The collection of **user data** for a QuickTime movie, track, or media. Each element in the user data list is referred to as a **user data item.**

vertical blanking rectangle   A rectangle that defines a portion of the input video signal that is devoted to vertical blanking. This rectangle occupies lines 10 through 19 of the input signal. Broadcast video sources may use this portion of the input signal for closed captioning, teletext, and other nonvideo information. Note that the blanking rectangle cannot be contained in the **maximum source rectangle.**

video digitizer component A component that provides an interface for obtaining digitized video from an analog video source. The typical client of a video digitizer component is a sequence grabber component, which uses the services of video digitizer components to create a very simple interface for making and previewing movies. Video digitizer components can also operate independently, placing live video into a window.

white level The degree of whiteness in an image. It is a common video digitizer setting.

Index

A

accuracy for image decompression
 changes for a sequence 4-49
 dithering and 4-18
 specifying for an image 4-52
action filter functions
 establishing the form of 2-61
 specifying to movie controller components 2-47
 using 2-13
actions
 defined 2-13
 movie controller 2-15 to 2-27
 performing with movie controller components 2-47
activate events, handling with movie controller components 2-58
active source rectangles 8-6
`AddCallBackToTimeBase` function 11-18
add-frame functions 5-107, 5-116
alpha channels 8-5
 blending and 8-18
 blend masks and 8-82
 clipping and 8-21
 continuous digitization and 8-53
 masks and 8-36
analog video digitizers, recommended values for 8-66
Animation Compressor, compressor type value for 5-80, 6-66
areas of interest
 defined 3-9
 specifying in test images 3-37, 3-39, 3-41
associating a movie with a movie controller 2-31
asynchronous compression, reporting 4-61
asynchronous compression and decompression of images 4-8 to 4-9, 4-50, 4-61

B

badges, movie
 controlling use of 2-20
 determining use of 2-20
 drawing 2-38
 support for 2-6
Balloon Help, controlling with movie controller components 2-27
bands of images 4-4 to 4-5
 compressing horizontal 4-13 to 4-16
 decompressing horizontal 4-21 to 4-25
 defined 4-4
`'barg'` component type value 5-5
base media handler components
 client status of component 10-8
 defined 10-3
 derived media handler capabilities, notifying of 10-12, 10-38 to 10-40
 opening a connection to 10-8
 relationship to derived media handler components 10-6
 saving component instance for 10-8
 utility function provided by 10-38 to 10-40
`BeginUpdate` function 5-14
black-and-white input video 8-15
black levels
 default value for video digitizer 8-66
 defined 8-65
 returning current video digitizer 8-68
 setting current 8-67
blend masks 8-82
brightness of digitized video image
 controlling overall 8-73
 receiving default value for 8-66
 returning current value of 8-74
brightness of input video signal, controlling 8-80
broadcast input video 8-15
buffer list structures 8-22
buffer structures 8-23

C

callback events 11-9 to 11-15
 assigning to time base by a clock component 11-18
 callback header structures 11-6 to 11-11
 canceling by a clock component 11-14
 changes in start or stop time 11-16
 control flags for a clock component 11-6
 creating for a clock component 11-10
 detecting rate changes by a clock component 11-7
 detecting time changes by a clock component 11-7
 disposing by a clock component 11-15
 finding by a clock component 11-20 to 11-21
 removing from a clock component 11-15
 removing from time base by a clock component 11-20
 rescheduling by a clock component 11-14

INDEX

callback events (*continued*)
  scheduling by a clock component 11-11
  time base rate, changing 11-16
callback functions
  assigning to a video channel 5-101, 5-102
  for clock components 11-9 to 11-15
  clock component support for time bases 11-4
  completion functions for image compressors and decompressors 4-4
  data-loading functions for image decompressors 4-4
  data-unloading functions for image compressors 4-4
  executing by clock components 11-19
  identifiers 11-6
  progress functions for image compressors and decompressors 4-4
  reference constants for, setting value of 6-53
  sequence grabber channel components and 6-35 to 6-37
  sequence grabber components and 5-102 to 5-111
  setting value of reference constant for 5-67
  supported by image compressor components 4-4
callback header structures 11-6 to 11-7
caller flags. *See* control flags
capability flags
  for image compressor components 4-26 to 4-31
  input video signal 8-21
  optional video digitizer component functions and 8-12 to 8-13
  output video signal 8-21
  and video digitizer component current flags 8-19
  for video digitizer components 8-14 to 8-19
capturing image data 5-103, 5-112 to 5-113
capturing sound and video data 5-18
`CDBandCompress` function 4-13, 4-63
`CDBandDecompress` function 4-17, 4-21, 4-64
`CDCodecBusy` function 4-61 to 4-62
`CDGetCodecInfo` function 4-54
`CDGetCompressedImageSize` function 4-58 to 4-59
`CDGetCompressionTime` function 4-56 to 4-57
`CDGetMaxCompressionSize` function 4-55
`CDGetSimilarity` function 4-57 to 4-58
`CDPreCompress` function 4-10, 4-62
`CDPreDecompress` function 4-16, 4-20 to 4-21, 4-63 to 4-64
`CDTrimImage` function 4-59 to 4-61
`'cflg'` request type 3-15
channel components. *See* sequence grabber channel components
chunks of sound samples 6-80
clear operations, and movie controller components 2-54
clipping
  image decompressor components and 4-19, 4-38
  movie controller components and 2-42
  sequence grabber channel components and 6-17

sequence grabber components and
  display-compress functions 5-110, 5-119
  display functions 5-105, 5-113
  transfer-frame functions 5-108, 5-117
video digitizer components and 8-5, 8-21
clipping regions
  image decompressor components and 4-29
  movie controller components and 2-9, 2-43
  sequence grabber channel components and 6-56
  sequence grabber components and 5-47, 5-69
  video digitizer components and 8-16
`ClockCallMeWhen` function 11-11 to 11-14
`ClockCancelCallBack` function 11-14
clock components 11-3 to 11-28
  assigning a time base to 11-17
  callback events 11-6 to 11-21
  callback functions 11-9 to 11-15
  callback header structures 11-6 to 11-11
  component flags, defined 11-5
  component subtype values 11-6
  component type value 11-6
  constant rate for 11-5
  current time and 11-9
  data structures in 11-6 to 11-7
  defined 1-3
  functions in 11-7 to 11-21
    getting the current time 11-9
    managing the time 11-15 to 11-17
    Movie Toolbox clock support functions 11-18 to 11-21
    using the callback functions 11-9 to 11-15
  rate changes in 11-7
  request code values 11-8
  support functions, Movie Toolbox 11-18 to 11-21
  time base, creating 11-17
  time changes 11-15
  variable rate for 11-5
`ClockDisposeCallBack` function 11-14 to 11-15
`ClockGetTime` function 11-9
`ClockNewCallBack` function 11-10 to 11-11
`ClockRateChanged` function 11-7, 11-16
`ClockSetTimeBase` function 11-17
`ClockStartStopChanged` function 11-16 to 11-17
`ClockTimeChanged` function 11-15
`'clok'` component type 11-6
`CloseComponent` function 5-14, 10-9
`CloseDefaultComponent` function 3-8
`'clut'` request type 3-15
`'cmpr'` manufacturer value 7-8
`CodecCapabilities` data type 4-35 to 4-39
`CodecCompressParams` data type 4-40 to 4-45
`CodecDecompressParams` data type 4-46 to 4-53
`CodecType` data type 6-66, 8-44
color input video 8-15
color lookup tables for video digitizer components 8-61

INDEX

color remapping, image decompressor components and 4-18
Compact Video Compressor
  component type value for 5-80, 6-66
complete movie parameter structures 10-15 to 10-17
completion functions 4-4, 4-44, 4-51
completion function structures 4-51
`CompletionProcRecord` data type 4-51
Component Manager
  image compressor components and 4-4
  standard image-compression dialog components and 3-6
components
  component flags for
    image compressor components 4-26 to 4-31
    movie data exchange components 9-7
    preview components 12-6
  defined xvii
  manufacturer field, movie data exchange values for 9-7
  manufacturer values for sequence grabber panel components 7-8
  request codes for functions
    image compressor components 4-53
    movie controller components 2-14
    standard image-compression dialog components 3-14
  subtypes
    base media handler components value for 10-8
    clock components values for 11-6
    defined 4-4
    image compressor values for 5-80
    movie data exchange values for 9-7
    preview components values for 12-6
    sequence grabber channel components value for 6-6
    sequence grabber panel components value for 7-7
    standard image-compression dialog value for 3-8
    video digitizer components values for 8-11
  types
    base media handler components value for 10-8
    clock components value for 11-6
    decompressor components values for 4-4
    derived media handler components value for 10-7
    image compressor components values for 4-4
    movie controller component value for 2-4
    movie data exchange components values for 9-8
    preview components values for 12-6
    sequence grabber channel components value for 6-6
    sequence grabber channel values for 6-66
    sequence grabber components value for 5-5
    sequence grabber panel components value for 7-7
    standard image-compression value for 3-8
    video digitizer components values for 8-11

`ComponentSetTarget` function 10-9
compress buffers 5-87 to 5-89
compress-complete functions 5-115, 6-36
compressed source devices, video digitizer components and 8-13
compress functions 5-114
compressing images 5-105, 5-114
compressing still images 1-8 to 1-10
compression. See image compression
compression dialog, standard image. See standard image-compression dialog components
compression information structures 5-22 to 5-23
compression list structures 8-43 to 8-44
compression parameters structures 4-40 to 4-45
compressor capabilities structures 4-35 to 4-39
compressor information structures
  format flags 4-32
  image compressor component capability flags in 4-26
compressor names 5-80, 6-66
compressor types 5-81. See also components, types
compressor type values. See components, types
continuous digitization 8-53
contrast in video digitizer components 8-67
control flags
  determining for image compression components 4-49
  determining for image compressor components 4-42 to 4-43
  determining for movie controller components 2-20, 2-26
  determining for sequence grabber channel components 6-51
  determining for sequence grabber components 5-63
  modifying for standard image-compression dialog components 3-36
  request type for standard image-compression dialog components 3-25
  returning for standard image-compression dialog components 3-35
  setting for movie controller components 2-20, 2-26
  setting for sequence grabber channel components 6-51
  setting for sequence grabber components 5-57
controlled grab 5-57
controller boundary rectangles 2-8
controller boundary regions 2-8
controller clipping regions 2-9
controller window regions 2-9
`ConvertFileToMovieFile` function 9-6
`ConvertMovieToFile` function 9-6
copy operations, and movie controller components 2-52
`CountImageDescriptionExtension` function 4-67 to 4-68

IN-3

INDEX

creating
  attached movie controllers 2-29
  sound and video channels for sequence grabber channel components 5-12
current flags, video digitizer component 8-19
current time, determining with clock components 11-9
cut operations, and movie controller components 2-52
`'cvid'` compressor type value 5-80

D

data exchange components. *See* movie data exchange components
data-loading functions
  indicating use by image compressor components 4-31
  introduced 4-4
  specifying to image decompressor components 4-51
  spooling data to decompressor with 4-23
  use by decompressor components 4-6 to 4-7
  use in compressing a horizontal band of an image 4-15
data-loading function structures 4-51
`dataProcRecord` data type 4-51
data-rate settings structure 3-19 to 3-20
data-unloading functions
  data buffers and 4-7 to 4-8
  Image Compression Manager and 4-4
  specifying to image compressor components 4-44
data-unloading function structures 4-44
deactivate events, handling with movie controller components 2-58
deactivating movie controllers 2-17
decompressing still images 1-8 to 1-10
decompression parameters structures 4-46 to 4-53
decompression. *See* image decompression
decompressors. *See* image decompressor components
`DelegateComponent` function 10-9
depth conversion, during image decompression operations 4-18
derived media handler components 10-3 to 10-48
  activating a media 10-25
  base media handlers and 10-6, 10-38 to 10-40
  black-and-white screen support, indicating 10-40
  boundary changes, determining 10-36
  capabilities, reporting to base media handler 10-38
  clipping capability, indicating 10-39
  clipping region, setting 10-34
  complete movie parameter structures 10-15 to 10-17
  component flags 10-8
  component type value 10-7
  creating 10-7 to 10-14
  data structure in 10-15 to 10-17
  defined 10-3
  destination region, setting 10-37
  displaying samples 10-13
  drawing a media sample 10-13 to 10-14
  duration of media 10-16
  effective rate of media 10-16
  function selector values 10-7
  functions in 10-18 to 10-40
    base media handler utility function 10-38 to 10-40
    general data management 10-23 to 10-30
    graphics data management 10-31 to 10-37
    media handler management 10-18 to 10-22
    sound data management 10-37 to 10-38
  graphics world, changing 10-31
  identifier of current media 10-16
  identifier of movie containing current track 10-15
  idle processor time, getting more 10-39
  image dimensions, setting 10-32
  initializing 10-12 to 10-13, 10-18
  irregular destination region, setting 10-37
  matrices 10-17, 10-33
  media characteristics of tracks 10-28
  movie time scale, changed 10-30
  Movie Toolbox and 10-13
  offscreen buffer, using 10-39
  opaqueness, determining 10-35
  prerolling a media 10-26
  rate, setting 10-26
  receiving idle processor time 10-20
  reporting errors to Movie Toolbox 10-22
  required component functions for, implementing 10-9 to 10-12
  retrieving auxiliary data 10-24
  sound volume 10-17, 10-38
  spatial dimensions, changing 10-32
  spatial processing capability, indicating 10-39
  storing auxiliary data 10-23
  suppressing idle events 10-39
  time base for media 10-16
  time scales 10-16, 10-29
  track edits, finding out about 10-27
  transfer mode support, indicating 10-39
  transparency, determining 10-35
device list structures 6-58 to 6-59
device name structures 5-72 to 5-73
`DigitizerInfo` data type 8-20 to 8-22
digitizer information structures 8-20 to 8-22
  retrieving 8-24
digitizer rectangles
  determining for video digitizer component 8-30
  setting for video digitizer component 8-29
display boundary rectangles 6-17
display functions 5-114, 6-36
displaying data 5-113 to 5-114, 6-36
displaying image data as a preview 12-8 to 12-9

INDEX

displaying movie controllers 2-7
display transformation matrices 6-17
`DisposeMovieController` function 2-12, 2-32
`DisposeWindow` function 5-14, 5-18
dithering
   during image-decompression operations 4-18
   image compressor components and 4-28, 4-39
   video digitizer component support for 8-16
`'drat'` request type 3-15
duration of movie controller components 2-57

E

`'eat '` component type value 9-8
editing movies
   clear operations and movie controller components 2-54
   copy operations and movie controller components 2-52
   cut operations and movie controller components 2-52
   enabling editing 2-50
   with a movie controller component 2-4
   movie controller component functions 2-50 to 2-56
   paste operations and movie controller components and 2-53
   undo operations and movie controller components 2-54
Edit menu 2-55 to 2-56
`EndUpdate` function 5-14
exchanging movie data. *See* movie data exchange components
`ExecuteCallBack` function 11-19
exporting data to a PICS file 9-18 to 9-19
exporting movie data. *See* movie data exchange components
extended data, setting for an image 4-66
extended functions structure 3-21 to 3-22
extension of images 4-4 to 4-5

F

filter buffers. *See* compress buffers
filtering source image data 5-117, 6-37
`FlushProcRecord` data type 4-44
frame compression, determining completion of 5-115
frame differencing in image compression
   reference constant for 5-23
   retrieving desired temporal quality of a sequence 5-84, 6-70

specifying desired temporal quality of a sequence 6-68
frame grabbers with hardware playthrough, video digitizer components and 8-12
frame grabbers without playthrough, video digitizer components and 8-12
frame information structures 5-23, 6-84
frames
   adding to a movie 5-116
   adding with sequence grabber components 5-107
   compressing with sequence grabber components 5-105
   controlling in movies 2-20, 2-26
   determining if displayed by movie controller components 2-20, 2-26
   displaying with sequence grabber components 5-105
   transferring 5-108

G

genlock 8-14
`GetBestDeviceRect` function 5-14
`GetFirstCallBack` function 11-20
`GetImageDescriptionExtension` function 4-66
`GetMovieCompleteParams` data type 10-15 to 10-17
`GetNextCallBack` function 11-21
`GetNextImageDescriptionExtensionType` function 4-68
`'gnrc'` component subtype 10-8
grab-complete functions
   application-defined 5-112 to 5-113
   default behavior for 5-104
   using 5-20 to 5-21
grab functions 5-112
   application-defined 5-112
   default behavior for 5-103
   identifying 5-100
Graphics Compressor, component type value for 6-66
graphics device for current movie 10-17
graphics port for current movie 10-17
grayscale input 8-15

H

hue values 8-70
   receiving default 8-67
   returning current 8-71
   setting current 8-70
human interface guidelines
   for badges 2-6
   for movie controllers 2-4 to 2-5

INDEX

I

icons for channel devices 5-73, 6-59
idle events
   handling with movie controller components 2-60
   sending to movie controller components 2-17
`'imag'` component subtype 3-8
image compression 4-3
   applying to captured video images 6-28
   controlling temporal compression with sequence grabbers 5-82
   depth conversion during 4-11
   extended data 4-65, 4-66
   extension during 4-11
   image description structures and 4-65
   pixel shifting during 4-11
   preparing for simple 4-12
   responsibilities of image compressors 4-10. *See also* image compressor components
   temporal compression with sequence grabbers 5-84
   type for channel to apply to captured image 6-66
   updating previous pixel maps during 4-11
Image Compression Manager
   compression information structure format flags 4-32 to 4-34
   compressor capabilities, determining 4-26 to 4-31
   compressor components, functions for 4-65 to 4-68
   compressor data formats, determining 4-32 to 4-34
   extended data 4-65, 4-66
   preview components and 12-5
   standard image-compression dialog components and 3-6
image compressor components 4-3 to 4-84
   asynchronous compression, reporting 4-61
   asynchronous compression and decompression of images 4-39, 4-44
   capabilities 4-26 to 4-31
      data structure for 4-35 to 4-39
      format of data and files 4-32 to 4-34
      reporting 4-54
   choosing 4-10 to 4-12
   clipping images, support for 4-29
   color tables and 4-39
   completion, reporting 4-61
   completion functions and 4-44
   component type value 4-4
   compressing an image 4-10
      horizontal band of 4-13 to 4-16
      request for 4-63
   compression parameters structures 4-40 to 4-45
   compressor capabilities structures 4-35 to 4-39
   condition flag values 4-48 to 4-49
   custom color tables and 4-34
   data structures in 4-35 to 4-53
   data unloading and 4-7
   data-unloading functions
      determining component use 4-31
      providing 4-44
      using 4-15
   defined 1-4
   dithering and 4-28, 4-39
   extended image data 4-66
   extracting part of an image 4-39
   first band in frame 4-42, 4-48
   frame number in sequence and 4-41
   functions in 4-53 to 4-65
      direct 4-54 to 4-62
      Image Compression Manager utility 4-65 to 4-68
      indirect 4-62 to 4-64
   grayscale depth of 4-33
   Image Compression Manager functions for 4-65 to 4-68
   Image Compressor Manager and 4-3
   image description structures and 4-41
   interframe compression 4-29
   last band in frame and 4-42, 4-48
   live video and 4-43, 4-50
   nonaligned pixels and 4-39
   operations performed during compression 4-11
   output location and 4-41
   pixel depth for an image 4-36
   pixel map images, support for 4-28
   preparing to compress an image 4-62
   previously compressed images and 4-43, 4-49
   progress functions and 4-13, 4-43
   recompressing without loss 4-31
   reporting returned data to application 4-41
   request code values 4-53
   sequence compression, specifying 4-41
   shrinking images, support for 4-28
   similarity, reporting 4-45
   size of image 4-55, 4-58
   spatial quality and 4-45
   specifying images to be compressed 4-44
   stretching images, support for 4-28
   temporal compression and 4-29
   temporal quality and 4-45
   time to compress image 4-36, 4-57
   updating previous image buffer
      during compression 4-49
      during sequence compression 4-39
      with temporally compressed sequences 4-42
image decompression 4-3
   clipping during 4-19
   color remapping during 4-18
   depth conversion during 4-18
   dithering during 4-18
   extending during 4-19
   matting during 4-19
   operations performed during 4-18

partial extraction during 4-19
pixel shifting during 4-19
preparing for 4-20 to 4-21. *See also* image decompressor components

image decompressor components
   accuracy, specifying 4-52
   application use by calling Image Compression Manager 4-3
   asynchronous decompression, reporting 4-61
   asynchronous operation of 4-51
   blending images 4-31
   capabilities 4-28 to 4-31
   choosing a decompressor 4-17
   clipping 4-39
   color depth of 4-33
   completion functions and 4-51
   component type value 4-4
   compressed image data for 4-47
   data formats 4-32 to 4-34
   data loading and 4-6
   data-loading functions, determining component use 4-38
   data-loading functions and 4-23, 4-51
      determining use by decompressor 4-31
   decompressing an image 4-16 to 4-25
      request for 4-64
   decompression parameters structures 4-46 to 4-53
   destination pixel map, specifying 4-52
   flipping images 4-30
   frame number in sequence 4-47
   graphics port and 4-52
   halving image size 4-30
   image bands and 4-47, 4-48
   image description structures for 4-47
   image source rectangle, specifying 4-52
   input buffer size and 4-47
   masking images 4-38
   matrices, specifying 4-52
   mattes
      for blending during decompression 4-31, 4-38
      change in pixel map for 4-49
      defining pixel depth for 4-52
   modification masks
      changes in mask bits 4-42, 4-49
      creating during decompression 4-39
      updating result data 4-52
   preparing to decompress an image 4-63
   previous buffer updating and 4-38
   progress functions and 4-25, 4-50
   quartering image size 4-30
   recompressing images without loss 4-31
   reporting completion of asynchronous operation 4-61
   resizing a compressed image 4-59
   responsibilities 4-16 to 4-17
   rotating images 4-30
   scaling images 4-38
   sequence decompression, specifying 4-47
   similarity between frames, reporting 4-57
   skewing images 4-31
   transfer modes and 4-38, 4-53
   transforming images 4-38
   trimming a compressed image 4-59
   warping images 4-31

image description extensions 4-67, 4-68
'imco' component type value 4-4
'imdc' component type value 4-4
importing a Scrapbook file 9-12
importing movie data. *See* movie data exchange components
initializing
   derived media handler components 10-12 to 10-13, 10-18 to 10-19
   sequence grabber channel components 6-15, 6-38
   sequence grabber components 5-11, 5-25
interframe compression 6-70
   controlling with sequence grabber 6-68
   sequence grabbers and 5-82, 5-84

J

'jpeg' compressor type value 5-80, 6-66, 6-67

K

keyboard events
   handling with movie controller components 2-61
   sending to movie controller components 2-17
key color digitizer components 8-5
key colors 8-82 to 8-86
   adding to list in video digitizer component 8-85
   determining for video digitizer component 8-83
   setting for video digitizer components 8-82
   used by video digitizer components 8-5, 8-13
   video digitizer component support for 8-18
key frames
   determining rate 5-85
   inserting into compressed sequences 8-51
   setting rate 5-83, 6-69
keystrokes 2-19

L

looping 2-18. *See also* palindrome looping

M

'MAC3' sound data format value 5-98
'MAC6' sound data format value 5-98
mask planes 8-5
matrices
    channel, adjusting 6-17
    display transformation for video channels 6-17
    doubling operations and 8-16
    image decompressor components and 4-38, 4-52
    one-quarter reduction operations and 8-17
    quadrupling operations and 8-16
    vertical flip operations and 8-17
    video digitizer component uses of 8-4
mattes 8-18
    blending images with 4-31, 4-38
    location of pixel map containing 4-52
    media handler components and 10-17
    preparing for simple decompression 4-19
maximum source rectangles 8-27
mcAction data type 2-15
MCActivate function 2-58
MCClear function 2-54
MCClick function 2-59
MCCopy function 2-52 to 2-53
MCCut function 2-52
MCDoAction function 2-12, 2-47
MCDrawBadge function 2-38
MCDraw function 2-59 to 2-60
MCEnableEditing function 2-50 to 2-51
MCGetClip function 2-43
MCGetControllerBoundsRect function 2-12, 2-39 to 2-40
MCGetControllerBoundsRgn function 2-40 to 2-41
MCGetControllerInfo function 2-48 to 2-49
MCGetControllerPort function 2-44
MCGetCurrentTime function 2-57
MCGetMenuString function 2-55 to 2-56
MCGetMovie function 2-32
MCGetVisible function 2-37
MCGetWindowRgn function 2-41 to 2-42
MCIdle function 2-60
MCIsControllerAttached function 2-35
MCIsEditingEnabled function 2-51
MCIsPlayerEvent function 2-45
MCKey function 2-61
MCMovieChanged function 2-49
MCNewAttachedController function 2-30
MCPaste function 2-53
MCPositionController function 2-33 to 2-34
MCSetActionFilterWithRefCon function 2-13, 2-47 to 2-48
MCSetClip function 2-42 to 2-43
MCSetControllerAttached function 2-35
MCSetControllerBoundsRect function 2-38 to 2-39
MCSetControllerPort function 2-44
MCSetDuration function 2-57
MCSetMovie function 2-31
MCSetUpEditMenu function 2-55
MCSetVisible function 2-36 to 2-37
MCUndo function 2-54
media characteristics 10-28
MediaGetMediaInfo function 10-24
MediaGetNextBoundsChange function 10-36
MediaGetSrcRgn function 10-37
MediaGetTrackOpaque function 10-35 to 10-36
MediaGGetStatus function 10-22
MediaGSetVolume function 10-38
media handlers, defined 1-4. *See also* base media handler components; derived media handler components
MediaHasCharacteristic function 10-28 to 10-29
MediaIdle function 10-13, 10-20 to 10-22
MediaInitialize function 10-12, 10-18 to 10-19
MediaPreroll function 10-26
MediaPutMediaInfo function 10-23
MediaSampleDescriptionChanged function 10-28
MediaSetActive function 10-25
MediaSetClip function 10-34
MediaSetDimensions function 10-32 to 10-33
MediaSetGWorld function 10-31 to 10-32
MediaSetHandlerCapabilities function 10-12, 10-38
MediaSetMatrix function 10-33 to 10-34
MediaSetMediaTimeScale function 10-29 to 10-30
MediaSetMovieTimeScale function 10-30
MediaSetRate function 10-26
MediaTrackEdited function 10-27
'mhlr' component subtype 10-8
'micr' component subtype 11-6
'mill' component subtype value 11-6
mouse events
    handling with movie controller components 2-59
    sending to movie controller components 2-17
movable modal dialog boxes, saving last window position for 3-25
movie controller components 2-3 to 2-75
    action filter functions 2-13, 2-61
    actions, specifying to 2-47
    activating a controller 2-17
    advantages of using 2-4
    Apple-supplied component 2-4
    application-defined functions in 2-61 to 2-62
    assigning a movie to a controller 2-30, 2-31
    assigning attached controller to a movie 2-29
    attached controllers 2-35
    badges 2-6, 2-20, 2-38
    Balloon Help, controlling 2-27

beginning of current selection, setting 2-19
boundary rectangles 2-38, 2-39
boundary regions 2-40
clear operations and 2-54
clipping regions 2-42, 2-43
closing connection for 2-32
component type value 2-4
control flags 2-20, 2-26
controlling the play of every frame 2-21
controls for 2-5
copy operations and 2-52
current time, getting 2-57
customizing 2-15 to 2-27
cut operations and 2-52
deactivating a controller 2-17
defined 1-3
detached controllers 2-35
display size for, determining 2-41
disposing of 2-32
duration of current selection 2-19
duration of movie controller components 2-57
editing 2-50, 2-51
establishing a component instance for 2-29
establishing a connection for a movie 2-29
event handling
 activate events 2-58
 click events 2-59
 deactivate events 2-58
 idle events 2-17, 2-22, 2-60
 keyboard events 2-17, 2-61
 mouse events 2-58, 2-59
 movie events 2-44
 resume events 2-58
 suspend events 2-58
 update events 2-17, 2-22, 2-59
frame-by-frame playback 2-18, 2-24
frame display 2-20, 2-26
frames around 2-30
functions in 2-28 to 2-61
 associating movies with controllers 2-28 to 2-32
 editing movies 2-50 to 2-56
 event handling 2-58 to 2-61
 handling movie events 2-44 to 2-50
 managing display attributes 2-33 to 2-44
 working with time 2-56 to 2-58
graphics port for 2-44
looping 2-18
movie rate 2-17, 2-22, 2-23
palindrome looping 2-18
paste operations and 2-53
play in current selections 2-19
playing a movie 2-17, 2-21, 2-23
positioning movie and controller 2-31, 2-33
 for attached controllers 2-30
 boundary rectangles and 2-38 to 2-40

computer display and 2-34
creation of controllers and 2-29
removing a movie from a controller 2-31
request code values 2-14 to 2-15
resizing controller 2-24
resizing the movie 2-27
scaling movies 2-29, 2-34
single-step playback 2-18, 2-24
size of controller 2-38 to 2-40
sound volume 2-18
spatial properties of 2-6
speaker buttons 2-20, 2-26
status, retrieving 2-48
step buttons 2-20
stopping a movie from playing 2-17, 2-23
undo operations and 2-54
update events 2-17
visibility of 2-30, 2-37
window for display, identifying 2-30
window region in use 2-41
movie data exchange components 9-3 to 9-47
 auxiliary data 9-32, 9-39
 chunk size, setting 9-31
 component flags 9-7
 component subtype values 9-7
 component type values 9-7, 9-8
 configuring 9-6
 creating 9-8 to 9-19
 creating tracks for imported data 9-22, 9-25
 defined 1-11
 duration of data, setting 9-27
 exporting data
  to a file 9-36 to 9-37
  to a handle 9-35 to 9-36
  to a PICS file 9-18 to 9-19
 function selector values 9-8
 functions in 9-20 to 9-40
  configuring movie export components 9-37 to 9-40
  configuring movie import components 9-26 to 9-34
  exporting movie data 9-34 to 9-37
  importing movie data 9-20 to 9-26
 importing
  data 9-21, 9-24
  data to paste or insert 9-22, 9-25
  into existing tracks 9-22, 9-25
  from scrap 9-33
  a Scrapbook file 9-12 to 9-15
 invoking via Movie Toolbox functions 9-6
 manufacturer values 9-7
 media files and 9-29
 output file, setting 9-29
 progress functions, setting 9-31, 9-38
 required component functions for export, implementing 9-16 to 9-17

movie data exchange components (*continued*)
  required component functions for import, implementing 9-10 to 9-12
  sample descriptions and 9-28
  sample duration, setting 9-28
  spatial dimensions of new track, setting 9-30
  tracks and 9-22, 9-24, 9-30
  user dialog boxes 9-34, 9-40
`MovieExportComponent` data type 9-42
`MovieExportDoUserDialog` function 9-40
`MovieExportGetAuxiliaryData` function 9-39
`MovieExportSetProgressProc` function 9-38
`MovieExportToFile` function 9-18, 9-36 to 9-37
`MovieExportToHandle` function 9-35 to 9-36
`MovieImportComponent` data type 9-42
`MovieImportDoUserDialog` function 9-34
`MovieImportFile` function 9-12, 9-24 to 9-26
`MovieImportHandle` function 9-21 to 9-23
`MovieImportSetAuxiliaryData` function 9-32 to 9-33
`MovieImportSetChunkSize` function 9-31
`MovieImportSetDimensions` function 9-30
`MovieImportSetDuration` function 9-27
`MovieImportSetFromScrap` function 9-33
`MovieImportSetMediaFile` function 9-29 to 9-30
`MovieImportSetProgressProc` function 9-31 to 9-32
`MovieImportSetSampleDescription` function 9-28, 9-28 to 9-29
`MovieImportSetSampleDuration` function 9-12, 9-28
movie parameter structures, saving values from 10-19
movies 9-3
  adding data to 6-85, 6-86
  adding frames to 5-107, 5-116, 6-36
  adding recorded data to 6-43
  badges 2-6, 2-20, 2-38
  beginning of current selection, setting 2-19
  changing characteristics of 2-49
  creating 6-41
  current time, setting 2-18
  duration of 10-16
  exporting data to a PICS file 9-18 to 9-19
  getting 5-45
  graphics device for 10-17
  graphics port for 10-17
  identifier of movie containing current media's track 10-15
  importing a Scrapbook file 9-12 to 9-15
  obtaining last resource ID for 5-45
  opening 2-10
  playback, providing 1-3 to 1-4
  playing with movie controller components 2-10 to 2-13
  previews for, displaying 12-10
  references for, obtaining 2-32. *See also* movie controller components; Movie Toolbox
  selection duration, setting 2-19
  sound volume 2-18
  time scale for 10-16
Movie Toolbox
  clock components and 11-4
  clock component support functions 11-18 to 11-21
  data conversion operations and 9-20, 9-34
  derived media handler components and 10-13
  function for assigning movie to a controller 2-29
  movie controller components and 2-3
  movie data export components and 9-5
  movie data import components and 9-4
  user data items for sequence grabber configuration settings 7-25
  user data lists for sequence grabber settings 6-31
MultiFinder events, and movie controller components 2-46
`MyAddFrameFunction` function 5-116
`MyCompressCompleteFunction` function 5-115
`MyCompressFunction` function 5-114
`MyDataFunction` function 5-120 to 5-121
`MyDisplayCompressFunction` function 5-119 to 5-120
`MyDisplayFunction` function 5-113 to 5-114
`MyGrabCompleteFunction` function 5-112 to 5-113
`MyGrabCompressCompleteFunction` function 5-118 to 5-119
`MyGrabFunction` function 5-112
`MyHook` function 3-46
`MyInterruptProc` function 8-96, 8-98
`MyModalFilter` function 5-122
`MyPlayerFilterWithRefCon` function 2-61 to 2-62
`MyTransferFrameFunction` function 5-117 to 5-118

N

National Television System Committee (NTSC) 8-14
`NewMovieController` function 2-11, 2-29 to 2-30
NTSC input video 8-14

O

`OpenComponent` function
  creating a component instance of a media handler 10-8
  identifying application's connection to digitizer components 8-24

INDEX

identifying a preview component with 12-10
opening connection to channel component 6-33
sequence grabber components and 5-9
specifying a clock component for an operation 11-9
specifying a data exchange component to the Movie Toolbox 9-6
specifying movie controller components with 2-30
`OpenDefaultComponent` function 11-8
   creating a sequence grabber component 5-11
   creating preview component with 12-9
   establishing a connection to a standard image-compression dialog component 3-8
   finding a specific data exchange component 9-6
   opening a connection to a base media handler 10-8
   specifying movie controller for operation 2-30
opening a connection
   to a base media handler component 10-8
   to a channel component 6-33
   to a movie data exchange component 9-6
   to a sequence grabber channel component 6-33
   to the sequence grabber component 5-9
   to a sequence grabber panel component 7-15
   to a standard image-compression dialog component 3-6 to 3-8
opening a movie 2-10
opening an image file 3-9
opening a sequence grabber panel component resource file 7-16, 7-18

P

palindrome looping
   controller currently set to 2-49
   defined 2-18
   turning on or off 2-24
PAL input video 8-14
panel components. *See* sequence grabber panel components
`PasteHandleIntoMovie` function 9-6
paste operations, movie controller components and 2-53
Phase Alternation Line (PAL) 8-14
phase-locked loops (PLL) 8-92
photo compressor, component type for 5-80, 6-66
picture files 3-11
pictures
   compared to compressed images 4-57
   compressing 3-30
   compression settings for 3-27
   getting from sequence grabber components 5-46 to 5-47

obtaining data for QuickDraw 10-21
test images
   for standard image-compression dialog box 3-9
   stored in files 3-8
   stored in handles 3-8
   stored in picture files 3-9
playback control flags. *See* control flags
play buttons 2-5
`'play'` component type value 2-4
playing movies
   action-filter functions and 2-23
   with movie controller components 2-4
   starting or stopping with movie controller components 2-17
PLL (phase-locked loops) 8-93
`'pmak'` component type 12-6
`'pnot'` component type 12-6
`pnotResItem` data type 12-15
`pnotResource` data type 12-14 to 12-15
positioning a movie in a movie controller 2-34
`'pref'` request type 3-15
preview components 12-3 to 12-19
   caches and 12-4
   converting data for display as preview 12-8
   defined 1-11, 12-3
   displaying movie previews 12-10 to 12-11
   event handling and 12-6, 12-11
   functions in 12-10 to 12-13
      creating previews 12-11 to 12-13
      displaying previews 12-10 to 12-11
      handling events 12-11
   obtaining data for 12-3
   required component functions, implementing 12-7 to 12-8
   resources for 12-13 to 12-15
   storing preview data in files 12-5
   using preview data 12-5
`PreviewEvent` function 12-11
previewing a PICS file 12-8 to 12-9
previewing image data 6-20
previewing sound and video sequences in a window 5-14
`PreviewMakePreview` function 12-12
`PreviewMakePreviewReference` function 12-13
preview resource item structures 12-15
preview resources 12-14 to 12-15
`PreviewShowData` function 12-8, 12-10 to 12-11
`'prog'` request type 3-15
progress functions 4-4, 4-9
   specifying to image compressor components 4-43
   specifying to image decompressor components 4-50
`PutMovieIntoTypedHandle` function 9-6

Q

`QTCallBackHeader` data type 11-6 to 11-7
quality of image
    spatial 4-45, 4-56
    temporal 4-45, 4-56
QuickDraw, standard image-compression dialog
    components and 3-6

R

rate, movie
    determining 2-22
    setting 2-17, 2-23
Raw Compressor, compressor type value 5-80
`'raw '` compressor type value 5-80, 6-66
`'raw '` sound data format value 5-98
recording image data 6-20, 6-24 to 6-28
`RemoveCallBackToTimeBase` function 11-19 to 11-20
`RemoveImageDescriptionExtension` function 4-67
request codes, component
    clock component values 11-8
    derived media handler component values 10-7 to 10-8
    image compressor component values 4-53
    movie controller component values 2-14 to 2-15
    movie data exchange component values 9-8 to 9-9
    preview component values 12-6
    sequence grabber channel component values 6-7 to 6-9
    sequence grabber component values 5-6 to 5-8
    sequence grabber panel component values 7-8
    standard image-compression dialog component values 3-14
    video digitizer component values 8-9 to 8-20
request processing, derived media handler components and 10-8 to 10-9
resume events, handling with movie controller components 2-58
RGB input 8-15
`'rle '` compressor type value 5-80, 6-66
`'rpza'` compressor type value 5-80, 6-66

S

saturation in video digitizer components 8-67
saturation value 8-72
saving changes to sequence grabber settings dialog box 7-20
saving compressed pictures 3-13
saving movie data 6-43
saving sample description data 9-29
scaling movies 2-29, 2-34
`SCCompressImage` function 3-30
`SCCompressPictureFile` function 3-31
`SCCompressPicture` function 3-30
`SCCompressSequenceBegin` function 3-32
`SCDataRateSettings` data type 3-19
`SCDefaultPictFileSettings` function 3-27
`SCDefaultPictHandleSettings` function 3-27
`SCDefaultPixMapSettings` function 3-26
`'scdi'` component type value 3-8
`SCExtendedProcs` data type 3-21
`scExtendedProcsType` data type 3-12
`SCGetBestDeviceRect` function 3-44
`SCGetInfo` function 3-34 to 3-35, 3-36 to 3-37
`SCNewGWorld` function 3-45
`SCParams` data type 3-50
`SCPositionDialog` function 3-13, 3-43
`SCPositionRect` function 3-13, 3-42 to 3-43
`SCRequestImageSettings` function 3-10, 3-28
`SCRequestSequenceSettings` function 3-10, 3-29
`SCSequenceCompressFrame` function 3-33
`SCSequenceCompressSequenceEnd` function 3-34
`SCSetInfo` function 3-12
`SCSetTestImagePictFile` function 3-39 to 3-40
`SCSetTestImagePictHandle` function 3-37 to 3-38
`SCSetTestImagePixMap` function 3-40 to 3-41
`SCSpatialSettings` data type 3-16
`SCTemporalSettings` data type 3-18
SECAM input video 8-14
`'seco'` component subtype value 11-6
`SeqGrabDataOutputEnum` data type 5-26
`SeqGrabFrameInfo` data type 5-23, 6-84
`SeqGrabUsageEnum` data type 5-59, 6-48
sequence grabber channel components 6-3 to 6-107
    adding data to a movie 6-85
    adding frames to a movie 6-36
    aligning captured images 6-76
    audio representation of channel 6-50
    boundary rectangles, size of 6-64
    callback functions
        using utility functions for 6-36 to 6-37
        working with 6-35
    captured data, playing all 6-51
    capturing movie data 6-34 to 6-35
    channel devices
        managing 6-24
        working with 6-58 to 6-61
    channel information flags 6-50
    channel state, setting and retrieving 6-16
    chunk size of sound samples 6-80, 6-81

clipping regions 5-69
   disposing of 6-17
   retrieving 6-56
   setting 6-56
component type value 6-6
compress buffers
   creating 6-72
   retrieving information 6-73
compression parameters for 6-66, 6-69
compressors for 6-69
compressor type for 6-66, 6-67
control flags for playback 5-63
controlling 6-39 to 6-46
creating 6-5 to 6-33
data rate and 6-54
defined 1-6
depth of images 6-68, 6-69
destination graphics world for captured image 6-17
device list
   assigning 6-61
   retrieving 6-60
   sorting 6-89
discrete frames and 6-50
display boundary rectangles 6-17, 6-63
   determining 6-63
   specifying 6-63
display destinations, setting 6-39
displaying image data 6-36
display quality of 6-50, 6-51
display status 6-49
filtering source image data
   filter buffers for 6-72, 6-73
   transfer-frame functions and 6-37
frame rate 6-74
frames and 6-53, 6-88
functions in 6-37 to 6-90
   channel devices, working with 6-58 to 6-61
   configuration functions for all channels 6-46 to 6-58
   configuring 6-38 to 6-39
   configuring sound channels 6-77 to 6-84
   configuring video channels 6-61 to 6-77
   controlling 6-39 to 6-46
   utility 6-84 to 6-90
graphics device for display of captured image 6-17
image-compression parameters for 6-68
image compressors for 6-67, 6-69
image quality 6-68
initializing 6-15, 6-38
initializing control values for 7-19
key frame rates for 6-68, 6-69
matrices 6-57, 6-58
media-specific functions, providing 6-28
offscreen buffer, using 6-75, 6-76

panel components, working with 7-17
parameters for image compression 6-66
pausing 6-44
playback control flags 6-50, 6-51
playing data 6-33 to 6-34
previewing data 6-20, 6-33 to 6-34
preview operations
   display quality of 6-50, 6-51
   pausing 6-44
   preparing for 6-45
   processing time for 6-42
   restarting 6-44
   starting 6-40
   stopping 6-43
   use during 6-48, 6-49
quality of images 6-68, 6-69
recording 6-20, 6-34 to 6-35
recording time left 6-54
record operations
   display quality of 6-50, 6-51
   limiting number of frames for 6-52
   pausing 6-44
   playing captured data during 6-49
   preparing for 6-45
   processing time for 6-42
   restarting 6-44
   starting 6-41
   stopping 6-43
   use during 6-48, 6-49
required component functions 6-6
   implementing 6-10 to 6-15
resources, releasing 6-46
sample description, retrieving 6-55
sample rate for sound data 6-81
sample references 6-87, 6-89
samples, saving 6-44
saving captured data 6-34 to 6-35, 6-44
settings dialog box 6-5
   displaying channel information in 6-31 to 6-33
   managing 6-29 to 6-31
sound chunk size 6-80, 6-81
sound input devices 6-78, 6-79
sound parameters 6-82, 6-83
sound sample compression format 6-83
sound sample rate 6-81, 6-82
sound volume 6-77, 6-78
source devices, changing 6-90
source rectangles
   determining portion for capture 6-65
   determining size of 6-64
   specifying portion for capture 6-65
spatial properties of 6-17
stopping 6-43
target requests, support for 6-7

sequence grabber channel components (*continued*)
  tick counts
    checkbox in dialog box 6-29 to 6-31
    showing 6-28
  time scale, retrieving 6-55
  update events, handling 6-42
  usage data, getting 6-16
  usage parameters, determining 6-16
  use by sequence grabber 6-4
  use by sequence grabber channel components 5-4
  video digitizers for 6-70, 6-71, 6-72
  visual representation of channel 6-50
  writing movie data to a channel 6-86
sequence grabber components 5-3 to 5-149
  add-frame functions 5-101, 5-116
    default behavior for 5-107
    identifying 5-101
  adding frames to a movie 5-107, 5-116
  allocating channels 5-31
  alpha channels, loading 8-13
  appending to a movie file 5-26
  application-defined functions 5-111 to 5-122
  boundary rectangles and 5-65, 5-66
  buffer information and callback functions 5-102
  callback functions 5-102
  capturing image data 5-18 to 5-19
    default behavior for 5-103
    drawing information over frames during 5-20
    start of 5-112
  capturing movie files 5-26
  channel data organization 5-61
  channel device lists 5-73, 5-75
  channel devices 5-72 to 5-77
  channels
    assigning from component 5-32
    chunk size 5-95, 5-96
    configuring 5-58 to 5-77
    configuring video 5-77 to 5-92
    creating 5-12 to 5-13
    device lists for 5-73
    display boundary rectangle 5-66
    display of 5-60
    and key frames 5-83
    parameters for image compression 5-82, 5-83
    for preview operations 5-60
    for record operations 5-60
    sound 5-92 to 5-99
    and source data 5-87, 5-89
    source video boundary rectangle for 5-78
    time scale 5-68
    video 5-99 to 5-102, 5-102 to 5-111, 5-112
    and video digitizers 5-85, 5-86
  channel type 5-31, 5-61
  clipping regions 5-70

component type value 5-5
compress-complete functions 5-115
  default behavior for 5-106
  identifying 5-100
compress functions 5-114
  default behavior for 5-105
  identifying 5-100
compressing images 5-105, 5-114
compression information structures 5-22 to 5-23
compressor types and 5-80, 5-81
control flags and 5-57
controlled grab 5-57
controlled record operations 5-58
creating sound and video channels 5-12 to 5-13
data functions 5-120
  assigning 5-35
data structures in 5-22 to 5-23
defined 1-6
depth of images 5-83
display boundary rectangles 5-65
display-compress functions 5-119 to 5-120
  default behavior for 5-110 to 5-111
  identifying 5-101
display destinations 5-29, 5-30
display functions 5-113 to 5-114
  default behavior for 5-105
  identifying 5-100
displaying image data 5-105, 5-114
display quality 5-63
disposing of a channel 5-34
filtering source image data
  filter buffers for 5-87, 5-89
  transfer-frame functions and 5-117
format of sound data 5-97
frame addition 5-107, 5-116
frame information structures 5-23
frame rate
  retrieving 5-90
  setting 5-89
frames and 5-63, 5-64
functions in 5-24 to 5-122
  channel devices 5-72 to 5-77
  configuring 5-24 to 5-36
  configuring channels 5-58 to 5-71
  controlling 5-36 to 5-47
  managing characteristics 5-53 to 5-58
  settings 5-47 to 5-53
  sound channels, working with 5-92 to 5-99
  utility for video channel callback 5-102 to 5-111
  video callback 5-99 to 5-102
  video channels, working with 5-77 to 5-92
getting movies 5-45
grab-complete functions
  application defined 5-112

calling default 5-20
default behavior for 5-104
identifying 5-100
using 5-20
grab-compress–complete functions 5-118 to 5-119
default behavior for 5-109 to 5-110
identifying 5-101
grab functions 5-103, 5-112
image compression type of channel data 5-81
initializing 5-11, 5-25
input devices and 5-93
key frame rate and 5-82, 5-83
matrices and 5-70, 5-71
modal-dialog filter functions 5-48, 5-122
movie creation and 5-38
movie files and 5-26
offscreen buffer for 5-91
panel components, identifying to 7-16
parameters for image compression
   determining 5-83
   specifying 5-82
   specifying type of compression 5-80
pausing 5-41, 5-42
pictures, getting from captured data 5-46
playing data 5-9
preparing for operation 5-43
previewing data 5-9
previewing sound and video sequences in a window 5-14 to 5-17
preview operations
   pausing 5-41
   preparing for 5-43
   starting 5-37
   stopping 5-40
rate for sound channel 5-96, 5-97
record, preparing for 5-43
recording 5-10 to 5-11
record operations
   counting frames to be captured 5-64
   limiting frames for capture during 5-63
   pausing 5-41
   space remaining for storage during 5-55
   starting 5-38
   stopping 5-40
   time limits for 5-54
   time remaining for 5-56
reference constants 5-67
releasing resources 5-44
request code values 5-6
sample description, retrieving 5-68
sample rates for sound channels 5-97
saving captured data 5-10 to 5-11
screen position, determining optimum 5-36
sequence grabber channel components and 5-4

settings 5-47 to 5-53
   modifying 5-50, 5-52
   retrieving 5-49, 5-51
settings dialog box 5-5, 7-18
   displaying 5-48
sound channels 5-61, 5-92 to 5-99
sound input devices 5-94
sound parameters 5-97, 5-98
sound volume 5-66 to 5-67
source boundary rectangles 5-78, 5-79
storing data outside of movie 5-35
time bases, determining 5-56
time of record operations 5-53 to 5-56
time scale, retrieving 5-68
transfer-frame functions
   application-defined 5-117
   default behavior for 5-108
   identifying 5-101
update events, handling 5-39
video channels 5-77 to 5-92
   callback functions and 5-101
   determining 5-61
   filter buffers for 5-87, 5-89
   frame rate for 5-89, 5-90
video digitizers and 5-86
windows, previewing sequences in 5-14
sequence grabber panel components 7-3 to 7-30
   component flags 7-15
   component subtype values 6-6, 7-7
   component type value 7-7
   creating 7-8 to 7-15
   defined 1-6
   dependency upon device 7-15
   dialog items, installing 7-18
   digitizing hardware required 7-15
   event processing 7-22
   functions in 7-15 to 7-26
      managing panel components 7-15 to 7-20
      managing panel settings 7-24 to 7-26
      processing panel events 7-21 to 7-23
   hardware dependency 7-15
   identifying sequence grabber components to 7-17
   installing 7-19
   manufacturer values 7-8
   mouse clicks, processing 7-21
   panel settings, managing 7-13 to 7-14
   processing mouse clicks 7-21
   removing 7-20
   request code values 7-8
   required component functions for, implementing 7-9 to 7-11
   resource files
      accessing 7-18
      preventing sequence grabber from opening 7-15

sequence grabber panel components (*continued*)
 sequence grabber, connecting to 7-16
 sequence grabbers and 7-5
 settings
  modifying 7-25
  retrieving 7-24
 settings dialog box
  creating 7-6
  managing 7-11 to 7-13
  mouse clicks, processing 7-21
  removing from panel 7-20
  validating user input 7-23
sequences of images, capturing 1-6 to 1-7
'sequ' request type 3-15
SetIdentityMatrix function 6-15
SetImageDescriptionExtension function 4-65 to 4-66
SetRect function 6-15
SGAddFrame function 5-107 to 5-108, 6-36
SGAddFrameReference function 6-87
SGAddMovieData function 6-85 to 6-86
SGAlignChannelRect function 6-76
SGAppendDeviceListToMenu function 5-75
SGChangedSource function 6-90
'sgch' component type value 6-6
SGCompressFrameComplete function 5-106 to 5-107, 6-36
SGCompressFrame function 5-105, 6-36
SGCompressInfo data type 5-22 to 5-23
SGDeviceListRecord data type 5-72
SGDeviceName data type 5-72 to 5-73
SGDisplayCompress function 5-110 to 5-111
SGDisplayFrame function 5-105, 6-36
SGDisposeChannel function 5-12, 5-34 to 5-35
SGDisposeDeviceList function 5-75
SGGetAlignmentProc function 5-36
SGGetBufferInfo function 5-102 to 5-103
SGGetChannelBounds function 5-66, 6-63
SGGetChannelClip function 5-70, 6-17, 6-56
SGGetChannelDeviceList function 5-73 to 5-74, 6-24, 6-60 to 6-61
SGGetChannelInfo function 5-61, 6-49 to 6-50
SGGetChannelMatrix function 5-71, 6-58
SGGetChannelMaxFrames function 5-64 to 5-65, 6-53
SGGetChannelPlayFlags function 5-63, 6-51 to 6-52
SGGetChannelSampleDescription function 5-68, 6-24, 6-55
SGGetChannelSettings function 5-51 to 5-52
SGGetChannelTimeScale function 5-68, 6-24, 6-55
SGGetChannelUsage function 5-60 to 5-61, 6-49
SGGetChannelVolume function 5-67, 6-78
SGGetCompressBuffer function 5-89, 6-73
SGGetDataOutput function 5-28 to 5-29
SGGetDataRate function 6-25, 6-54
SGGetFlags function 5-57 to 5-58

SGGetFrameRate function 5-90, 6-74
SGGetGWorld function 5-30 to 5-31
SGGetIndChannel function 5-33 to 5-34
SGGetLastMovieResID function 5-45 to 5-46
SGGetMaximumRecordTime function 5-54
SGGetMovie function 5-45
SGGetNextFrameReference function 6-25, 6-88 to 6-89
SGGetPause function 5-42
SGGetSettings function 5-49 to 5-50, 6-31
SGGetSoundInputDriver function 5-93, 6-79
SGGetSoundInputParameters function 5-98, 6-83
SGGetSoundInputRate function 5-97, 6-82
SGGetSoundRecordChunkSize function 5-96, 6-81
SGGetSrcVideoBounds function 5-78, 6-64
SGGetStorageSpaceRemaining function 5-55
SGGetTimeBase function 5-56 to 5-57
SGGetTimeRemaining function 5-56
SGGetUseScreenBuffer function 5-91, 6-76
SGGetVideoBottlenecks function 5-102
SGGetVideoCompressor function 5-83 to 5-85, 6-69 to 6-70
SGGetVideoCompressorType function 5-81, 6-28, 6-67
SGGetVideoDigitizerComponent function 5-86, 6-71
SGGetVideoRect function 5-79, 6-65
SGGrabCompressComplete function 5-109 to 5-110
SGGrabFrameComplete function 5-104, 6-36
SGGrabFrame function 5-103 to 5-104
SGGrabPict function 5-46 to 5-47
SGIdle function 5-14, 5-18, 5-39, 6-20, 6-42
SGInitChannel function 6-38
SGInitialize function 5-11, 5-25
SGNewChannelFromComponent function 5-32 to 5-33
SGNewChannel function 5-12, 5-31 to 5-32
SGPanelCanRun function 7-17
SGPanelEvent function 6-29, 7-11, 7-22
SGPanelGetDITL function 6-29, 7-11, 7-18 to 7-19
SGPanelGetSettings function 7-24 to 7-25
SGPanelInstall function 6-29, 7-11, 7-19
SGPanelItem function 7-11, 7-21
SGPanelRemove function 6-29, 7-11, 7-20
SGPanelSetGrabber function 7-16
SGPanelSetResFile function 7-18
SGPanelSetSettings function 7-25 to 7-26
SGPanelValidateInput function 7-23
SGPause function 5-41, 6-20, 6-44 to 6-45
'sgpn' component type 7-7
SGPrepare function 5-43 to 5-44, 6-20, 6-45 to 6-46
SGRelease function 5-44, 6-20, 6-46
SGSetChannelBounds function 5-12, 5-65, 6-17, 6-63
SGSetChannelClip function 5-69, 6-17, 6-56
SGSetChannelDevice function 5-76, 6-24, 6-61
SGSetChannelMatrix function 5-70, 6-17, 6-57

INDEX

`SGSetChannelMaxFrames` function 5-63 to 5-64, 6-52
`SGSetChannelPlayFlags` function 5-61 to 5-62, 6-50 to 6-51
`SGSetChannelRefCon` function 5-67, 6-53 to 6-54
`SGSetChannelSettings` function 5-52 to 5-53
`SGSetChannelUsage` function 5-12, 5-59 to 5-60, 6-48
`SGSetChannelVolume` function 5-66, 6-77
`SGSetCompressBuffer` function 5-87 to 5-88, 6-72 to 6-73
`SGSetDataOutput` function 5-26 to 5-27, 5-35
`SGSetDataProc` function 5-35
`SGSetFlags` function 5-57
`SGSetFrameRate` function 5-89 to 5-90, 6-74
`SGSetGWorld` function 5-11, 5-29 to 5-30, 6-17, 6-39
`SGSetMaximumRecordTime` function 5-18, 5-53 to 5-54
`SGSetSettings` function 5-50
`SGSetSoundInputDriverChanged` function 6-80
`SGSetSoundInputDriver` function 5-93, 6-78
`SGSetSoundInputParameters` function 5-97, 6-82 to 6-83
`SGSetSoundInputRate` function 5-96 to 5-97, 6-81
`SGSetSoundRecordChunkSize` function 5-95, 6-80
`SGSettingsDialog` function 5-5, 5-18, 5-48 to 5-49, 6-5, 6-31
`SGSetUseScreenBuffer` function 5-91, 6-75
`SGSetVideoBottlenecks` function 5-101
`SGSetVideoCompressor` function 5-82 to 5-83, 6-68 to 6-69
`SGSetVideoCompressorType` function 5-80 to 5-81, 6-28, 6-66
`SGSetVideoDigitizerComponent` function 5-85, 6-70 to 6-71
`SGSetVideoRect` function 5-78 to 5-79, 6-64 to 6-65
`SGSortDeviceList` function 6-89
`SGSoundInputDriverChanged` function 5-94 to 5-95, 6-80
`SGStartPreview` function 5-37, 6-20, 6-40
   using 5-14
`SGStartRecord` function 5-38, 6-41
   using 5-18, 6-20
`SGStop` function 5-18, 5-40, 6-43
   using 5-14, 6-20
`SGTransferFrameForCompress` function 5-108 to 5-109, 6-37
`SGUpdate` function 5-14, 5-39 to 5-40, 6-42
`SGVideoDigitizerChanged` function 5-86 to 5-87, 6-72
`SGWriteMovieData` function 6-86
`SGWriteSamples` function 6-24, 6-43 to 6-44
sharpness in video digitizer components 8-67
sliders 2-5
`'smc '` compressor type value 5-80, 6-66
sound channel components. *See* sequence grabber channel components

`SoundMediaType` component subtype 5-31, 5-34
sound volume
   for media 10-17
   for movie 2-18
`'soun'` media type 9-29
source coordinate systems, video digitizer components 8-6
`'sour'` manufacturer value 7-8
spatial settings structures 3-16 to 3-17
speaker buttons 2-20, 2-26
`'spit'` component type value 9-8
spooling data. *See* data-loading function structures; data-unloading function structures
spooling images 4-38. *See also* data-loading function structures; data-unloading function structures
spooling of compressed data 4-6
`'sptl'` request type 3-15
`'ssta'` request type 3-15
standard compression parameter block structures 3-50
standard image-compression dialog. *See* standard image-compression dialog components
standard image-compression dialog components 3-3 to 3-57
   application-defined function in 3-45
   closing a connection 3-8
   color tables 3-20, 3-35
   compressing still images 3-29 to 3-31
   compression data rate 3-35
   compressor components, selecting 3-16
   compressor flags 3-25
   compressor list, controlling content of 3-23
   compressor type value 3-16
   configuration information
      modifying 3-36 to 3-37
      retrieving 3-34 to 3-35
   control flags 3-25, 3-35
   custom button name 3-22
   data rate parameters 3-19
   data-rate settings request type 3-19
   data rate value 3-19
   data structures in 3-15 to 3-25
   default settings 3-8, 3-26, 3-27
   depth, allowing the user to select best 3-24
   dialog boxes 3-4 to 3-5
      defining custom buttons in 3-12
      displaying 3-8 to 3-11
      extending 3-11 to 3-13, 3-35
      image-sequence compression 3-5
      parts of 3-7
      position of 3-13, 3-25, 3-35, 3-43
      single-frame compression 3-4
   display device, determining best 3-44
   extended functions request type 3-21
   filter functions 3-11, 3-21
   frame duration value 3-19

standard image-compression dialog components
(*continued*)
  frame rate value 3-18
  functions in 3-25 to 3-45
    compressing image sequences 3-31 to 3-34
    compressing still images 3-29 to 3-31
    creating a graphics world for compression settings 3-44 to 3-45
    displaying the standard dialog box 3-28 to 3-29
    getting default settings for an image or sequence 3-26 to 3-28
    image or sequence settings 3-34 to 3-37
    positioning dialog boxes and rectangles 3-42 to 3-44
    specifying a test image 3-37 to 3-41
  graphics world, creating 3-45
  hook functions 3-12, 3-22, 3-46
  key frame rate and 3-19, 3-23
  modal-dialog filter functions 3-11
  movable dialog boxes, specifying 3-24
  opening a connection 3-8
  parameters, retrieving default 3-10 to 3-11
  pixel depth value 3-17
  preference flags 3-22, 3-35
  preference flags request type 3-22
  progress function request type 3-20
  progress functions 3-20, 3-35
  rate, allowing user to select best 3-23
  rectangles, positions of 3-42
  request types used by 3-15 to 3-25
  sequence-compression parameters 3-17
  sequence identifier 3-35
  sequence ID request type 3-24
  settings 3-15 to 3-25, 3-34 to 3-37
  settings information box 3-15, 3-34, 3-36
  settings state request type 3-24
  spatial compression parameters 3-15, 3-35
  spatial quality value 3-17, 3-20
  spatial settings request type 3-15
  subtype value 3-8
  temporal compression parameters 3-35
  temporal quality value 3-18, 3-20
  temporal settings request type 3-17
  test images 3-9 to 3-10, 3-37
    area of interest 3-9
    from picture file 3-39
    from pixel map 3-40
  type value 3-8
  window position request type 3-25
status flags, video digitizer component 8-19
step buttons 2-5, 2-20, 2-26
still images, compressing and decompressing 1-8 to 1-10

stopping movies from playing with movie controller components 2-17, 2-23
suspend events, handling with movie controller components 2-58
s-video input 8-15
system clocks, component types for 11-6
Systeme Electronique Couleur avec Memoire (SECAM) 8-14

T

target requests, sending 10-9
temporal compression 6-70
  controlling with sequence grabber 6-68
  sequence grabber channels and 6-68
  sequence grabbers and 5-82, 5-84
temporal settings structure 3-18 to 3-19
test images. *See* standard image-compression dialog components
'TEXT' component subtype value 9-7
'tick' component subtype value 11-6
time
  callback functions for clock components 11-9 to 11-15
  current, getting for movie controller component 2-57
  providing to sequence grabber channel component 6-42
  required to compress image 4-57
time bases
  assigning callback events 11-18
  assigning to a clock component 11-17
  callback events, finding by clock component 11-20 to 11-21
  clock components and 11-3
  clock component support for callback functions 11-4
  executing a callback function 11-19
  removing callback events 11-20
  sequence grabber components, determining 5-56
  video digitizer components, setting for 8-8
'tprl' request type 3-15
tracks
  duration of 10-16
  identifier for track containing current media 10-16
  identifying by media characteristics 10-28
  image height of track rectangle 10-17
  image width of track rectangle 10-17
  matte region for 10-17
transfer-frame functions 6-37
transfer modes, specifying in image decompressor components 4-53

INDEX

U

undo operations, and movie controller components 2-54
update events
  handling with movie controller component 2-59
  sending to movie controller components 2-17
user data items 7-7
user data lists 7-14

V

`VDAddKeyColor` function 8-84 to 8-85
`VDClearClipRegion` function 8-90
`VDCompressDone` function 8-48 to 8-49
`VDCompressionList` data type 8-43 to 8-44
`VDCompressOneFrameAsync` function 8-47
`VDDone` function 8-58
`VDGetActiveSrcRect` function 8-27 to 8-28
`VDGetBlackLevelValue` function 8-68
`VDGetBrightness` function 8-74
`VDGetClipState` function 8-92
`VDGetCLUTInUse` function 8-61 to 8-62
`VDGetCompressionTypes` function 8-43 to 8-44
`VDGetContrast` function 8-75 to 8-76
`VDGetCurrentFlags` function 8-19, 8-20, 8-25 to 8-26
`VDGetDataRate` function 8-59 to 8-60
`VDGetDigitizerInfo` function 8-14, 8-19, 8-20, 8-24 to 8-25
`VDGetDigitizerRect` function 8-30
`VDGetDMADepths` function 8-64 to 8-65
`VDGetFieldPreference` function 8-95
`VDGetHue` function 8-71
`VDGetImageDescription` function 8-50
`VDGetInputColorSpaceMode` function 8-63 to 8-64
`VDGetInputFormat` function 8-33
`VDGetInput` function 8-32
`VDGetInputGammaRecord` function 8-79
`VDGetInputGammaValue` function 8-80 to 8-81
`VDGetKeyColor` function 8-83
`VDGetKeyColorRange` function 8-85
`VDGetMaskandValue` function 8-87 to 8-88
`VDGetMaskPixMap` function 8-88 to 8-89
`VDGetMaxAuxBuffer` function 8-41 to 8-42
`VDGetMaxSrcRect` function 8-26 to 8-27
`VDGetNextKeyColor` function 8-86
`VDGetNumberOfInputs` function 8-31
`VDGetPlayThruDestination` function 8-38 to 8-39
`VDGetPLLFilterType` function 8-93
`VDGetPreferredTimeScale` function 8-97 to 8-98
`VDGetSaturation` function 8-72 to 8-73
`VDGetSharpness` function 8-77
`VDGetSoundInputDriver` function 8-96
`VDGetVBlankRect` function 8-28 to 8-29
`VDGetVideoDefaults` function 8-66 to 8-67
`VDGetWhiteLevelValue` function 8-69 to 8-70
`VDGrabOneFrameAsync` function 8-56 to 8-57
`VDGrabOneFrame` function 8-54
`VdigBufferRec` data type 8-23
`VdigBufferRecList` data type 8-22 to 8-23
`'vdig'` component type value 8-11
`VDPreflightDestination` function 8-36 to 8-38
`VDPreflightPlayThruGlobalRect` function 8-40 to 8-41
`VDReleaseAsyncBuffers` function 8-55
`VDReleaseCompressBuffer` function 8-49
`VDResetCompressSequence` function 8-51
`VDSetBlackLevelValue` function 8-67 to 8-68
`VDSetBrightness` function 8-73
`VDSetClipRegion` function 8-90
`VDSetClipState` function 8-91
`VDSetCompression` function 8-45 to 8-46
`VDSetCompressionOnOff` function 8-46 to 8-47
`VDSetContrast` function 8-75
`VDSetDigitizerRect` function 8-29
`VDSetDigitizerUserInterrupt` function 8-95 to 8-96
`VDSetFieldPreference` function 8-94
`VDSetFrameRate` function 8-59
`VDSetHue` function 8-70
`VDSetInputColorSpaceMode` function 8-62 to 8-63
`VDSetInput` function 8-31
`VDSetInputGammaRecord` function 8-78
`VDSetInputGammaValue` function 8-80
`VDSetInputStandard` function 8-33
`VDSetKeyColor` function 8-82
`VDSetKeyColorRange` function 8-83 to 8-84
`VDSetMasterBlendLevel` function 8-87
`VDSetPlayThruDestination` function 8-35 to 8-36
`VDSetPlayThruGlobalRect` function 8-39
`VDSetPlayThruOnOff` function 8-53
`VDSetPLLFilterType` function 8-93
`VDSetSaturation` function 8-72
`VDSetSharpness` function 8-76 to 8-77
`VDSetTimeBase` function 8-51
`VDSetupBuffers` function 8-54 to 8-55
`VDSetWhiteLevelValue` function 8-69
`VDUseThisCLUT` function 8-61
vertical blanking rectangles
  defined 8-6
  and video digitizer component 8-29
`'vide'` component subtype value 6-6
`'vide'` media type 9-29
video bottleneck functions, setting up 5-19
video bottlenecks structures 5-100 to 5-101
`VideoBottles` data type 5-100 to 5-101
video channel components. *See* sequence grabber channel components

IN-19

Video Compressor, component type value for 5-80, 6-66
video digitizer components 8-3 to 8-124
   accessing from sequence grabbers 5-86
   active source rectangles 8-28
   alpha channel devices and 8-13
   alpha channels 8-87
   application-defined function in 8-98
   assigning to a video channel 5-85
   asynchronous digitization 8-47, 8-54, 8-57, 8-58
   auxiliary buffers for non-DMA components 8-41
   black-and-white digitization 8-62, 8-63
   blend levels
      channel, determining 8-87
      master 8-87
      supported by 8-22
   blend masks
      clipping region for 8-22
      defining 8-36, 8-39
      pixel map data for 8-88
   buffer count 8-22
   buffers for asynchronous digitization
      releasing 8-55
      setting up 8-54
      specifying 8-57
   capabilities of 8-24
   capability flags 8-14 to 8-19
   clipping 8-89 to 8-92
      alpha channels and 8-5, 8-21
      clearing regions 8-90
      disabling 8-91
      disabling region 8-90
      enabling 8-91
      key colors and 8-21
      mask planes and 8-21
      no support for 8-21
      output images 8-16
      region for destination rectangle 8-22
      state of 8-92
   color digitization 8-62
   color effects and 8-80
   color filtering transforms and 8-78
   color lookup tables for 8-61
   component type values 8-11
   compressed source devices and 8-13
   compressed sources 8-42 to 8-52
   compression parameters, setting 8-45
   continuous digitization 8-53
   contrast in analog video 8-67, 8-75
   counting number of inputs to 8-31
   creating 8-8 to 8-13
      minimum support required 8-11
   current flags 8-19, 8-25
   data rate, determining 8-59 to 8-60
   data structures in 8-20 to 8-23
   defined 1-6
   destination buffers 8-23
   destination characteristics of 8-34 to 8-42
   destination graphics device for 8-21
   destination height for 8-21
   destinations, specifying 8-7, 8-34 to 8-42
   destination width for 8-21
   digitizer rectangles 8-6, 8-37
   digitizing and compressing frame 8-47
   DMA 8-18
   even-field preference 8-94, 8-95
   frame rate, setting 8-59
   functions in 8-23 to 8-98
      analog video, controlling 8-65 to 8-81
      clipping 8-89 to 8-92
      color, controlling 8-60 to 8-65
      compressed source devices, controlling 8-42 to 8-52
      digitization, controlling 8-52 to 8-60
      getting information about 8-24 to 8-26
      input sources, selecting 8-30 to 8-34
      selectively displaying video 8-81 to 8-89
      source characteristics, setting 8-26 to 8-30
      utility functions 8-92 to 8-98
   gamma structures for 8-78 to 8-79
   gamma values for 8-80
   idle time needed for display 8-18
   image description structures, getting 8-50
   input capabilities 8-21
      black-and-white input 8-15
      broadcast input 8-15
      color input 8-15
      composite input 8-14
      genlock support 8-14
      NTSC input 8-14, 8-33
      PAL input 8-14, 8-33
      RGB input 8-15
      SECAM input 8-14, 8-33
      signal lock input report 8-19
      s-video input 8-15
      VTR input 8-15
   input sources to 8-31 to 8-32
   input video format, determining 8-33
   interface card, slot for 8-21
   interrupt functions 8-95, 8-98
   inverse color lookup tables 8-18
   key color devices and 8-13
   key colors
      adding to list 8-85
      determining 8-83
      digitizer components 8-5
      getting from list 8-86

range, determining 8-86
settings 8-82
support 8-18
values, setting range of 8-83
key frames, inserting into compressed
    sequences 8-51
mask plane devices 8-5, 8-21
matrices and 8-4, 8-22, 8-36, 8-39
maximum source rectangles 8-6, 8-27
multiple buffering 8-8, 8-41
notifying sequence grabber of changes to 5-86
odd-field preference 8-94, 8-95
offscreen digitizing 8-7
onscreen digitizing 8-7
optional functions for 8-12 to 8-13
output capabilities 8-21
    asynchronous grabs 8-18
    blending 8-18
    compressed image data only 8-19
    compressed-source devices 8-18
    dithering of output images 8-16
    drawing images during compression 8-19
    flipping output images 8-17
    increasing size 8-16
    quadrupling size 8-16
    quartering size 8-17
    rotating 8-17
    screen bits, unreadable 8-18
    shrinking 8-16
    skewing 8-17
    stretching 8-16
    warping 8-18
phase-locked loops 8-93
pixel depth 8-15 to 8-16
request code values 8-9 to 8-20
required functions for 8-11
saturation 8-67, 8-72
selectively displaying video 8-81 to 8-89
sharpness in analog video 8-67, 8-76, 8-77
single-frame digitization 8-7, 8-54, 8-57
sound input driver, getting 8-96
source coordinate systems 8-6
source video, selecting 8-30 to 8-34
source video signal
    characteristics of 8-26 to 8-30
    standard used 8-28
status flags 8-19
status of 8-24
time base, setting 8-51
time scale, getting preferred 8-97
transformation matrix support 8-37
types of 8-5, 8-21
video destination buffers 8-23

`VideoMediaType` component subtype 5-31, 5-34
visibility of movie controllers 2-36
volume, sound
    determining with movie controller component 2-18
    setting with movie controller component 2-18
volume controls 2-5
VTR input video 8-15

W

white level values
    defined 8-65
    returning current 8-69
    returning default 8-66
    setting for video digitizer components 8-69
`'wndw'` request type 3-15

X, Y, Z

`'xprc'` request type 3-15

This Apple manual was written, edited, and composed on a desktop publishing system using Apple Macintosh computers and FrameMaker software. Proof pages were created on an Apple LaserWriter IINTX printer. Final page negatives were output directly from text files on an AGFA ProSet 9800 imagesetter. Line art was created using Adobe™ Illustrator. PostScript™, the page-description language for the LaserWriter, was developed by Adobe Systems Incorporated.

Text type is Palatino® and display type is Helvetica®. Bullets are ITC Zapf Dingbats®. Some elements, such as program listings, are set in Apple Courier.

WRITERS
Doug Engfer and Patria Brown

DEVELOPMENTAL EDITOR
Sue Factor

ILLUSTRATOR
Ruth Anderson

PRODUCTION EDITORS
Pat Christenson and Alan Morgenegg

PROJECT MANAGER
Patricia Eastman

COVER DESIGNER
Barbara Smyth

Special thanks to Jim Batson, Sean Callahan, Ken Doyle, Peter Hoddie, Mark Krueger, Bruce Leak, and Kip Olson.

Acknowledgments to Eric Chan, Mike Dodd, Bill Guschwan, Eric Hoffert, Miki Lee, Guillermo Ortiz, Martha Steffen, John Wang, Gary Woodcock, Bill Wright, and the entire *Inside Macintosh* team.

Please keep me informed about future volumes in *New Inside Macintosh.*

Name
Company
Address

City
State
Zip

Please tear out card, put in an envelope, and mail to:
Chris Platt
Addison-Wesley Publishing Company
One Jacob Way
Reading, MA 01867

APDA

Your main source for Apple development products

Get easy access to *New Inside Macintosh* and over 300 other programming products through APDA, Apple's worldwide source for Apple and third-party development products. Ordering is easy. APDA offers convenient payment and shipping options.

Call today for your FREE APDA Tools Catalog

1-800-282-2732	U.S.
1-800-637-0029	Canada
(716) 871-6555	International

Site licensing is available for many of the development tools. For information, contact Apple Software Licensing at (408) 974-4667.

© 1992 Apple Computer, Inc. Apple, the Apple logo, APDA, and Macintosh are registered trademarks of Apple Computer, Inc.

*762-5-SB
5-01
CC
5